AF716557

Trilingual Swiss Law Dictionary

French-German-English
German-French-English

THOMAS L. WEST III, J.D.

Author of *Spanish-English Dictionary of Law and Business*

NOTE: The content of this book should not be relied upon for legal or accounting advice. If you require legal advice or othe professional assistance, you should engage a competent professional. Suggestions and corrections can be sent to dictionary@intermarkls.com.

Intermark Language Publications. Chattanooga, TN USA.
www.intermarkls.com

Copyright © 2017 Thomas L. West III

All rights reserved.

ISBN: 1929570031
ISBN-13: 9781929570034

INTRODUCTION

Swiss legal terminology has long been a difficult challenge for legal translators into English because the standard monolingual law dictionaries for French (Cornu) and German (Creifelds) do not include any Swiss terms whatsoever. And the *Schweizerisches juristisches Wörterbuch*[1] published in 1996 by Dr. Peter Metzer turned out to be a disappointment because it fails to include so many important terms and often does not provide a clear definition of the terms that it does include. In fact, Markus Nussbaumer, a translator in the language services department at the Swiss Federal Chancellery, goes so far as to call it "unbrauchbar" (unusable) because it is "ohne lexikographischen Verstand geschrieben, vereint Rechtswortschatz mit ganz anderem Wortschatz, lässt keinerlei Auswahlkriterien erkennen, nennt keine Fundstellen, markiert nicht Helvetismen vs. Gemeindeutsches".[2]

Unfortunately, the bilingual legal dictionaries on the market are not much more useful than the monolingual ones. For example, although the back cover of the latest edition (2002) of the *Wörterbuch der Rechts- und Wirtschaftssprache*[3] by Romain/Byrd/Thielecke promises that it contains "Austrian and Swiss legal terminology," those entries are few and far between; indeed, I have never found a Swiss term in that dictionary at all. And while the very useful Council of Europe French-English Legal Dictionary[4] does contain a handful of Swiss terms, its primary focus is clearly French law. In addition, it was compiled in the late 1980s and is now showing its age.

The advent of the Internet brought some relief to translators asked to

[1] Metzger, Peter. *Schweizerisches juristisches Wörterbuch.* Verlag Paul Haupt, 1996. ISBN 3-258-05191-7.

[2] "Die deutsche Gesetzessprache in der Schweiz" by Markus Nussbaumer, in Brambilla, Marina, Gerdes Joachim and Messina, Chiara, ed. *Diatopische Variation in der deutschen Rechtssprache*, Frank & Timme, p. 136. ISBN 978-3-86596-447-2.

[3] Romain/Byrd/Thielecke, *Wörterbuch der Rechts- und Wirtschaftssprache, Deutsch-Englisch.* 4th edition, C.H. Beck, 2002. ISBN 3-406-48068-3.

[4] Bridge, F.H.S. *The Council of Europe French-English Legal Dictionary.* Strasbourg: Council of Europe, 1994. ISBN 92-871-2496-5.

translate Swiss legal documents from French or German into English. For example, in 2009 the Swiss Federal Chancellery officially released the online public version of their terminology database TERMDAT *(www.termdat.ch).* Unfortunately, however, the vast majority of terms found there give "no equivalent" in English, so translators into English "werden nicht fündig" (as they say in German) and "restent sur leur faim" (as they say in French). Much of the terminology in TERMDAT appears to be taken from the French-to-German legal dictionary published by Piccard/Thilo/Steiner in 1950, which was undoubtedly complied in the 1940s and is hopelessly outdated, especially in view of the new uniform codes of civil and criminal procedure that took effect in 2011.

The Swiss government has also published English translations of the major Swiss codes (https://www.admin.ch/gov/en/start/federal-law/classified-compilation.html), and in this dictionary, as much as possible I have indicated where a term can be found in the codes so that the translator can consult the article in question and gain a fuller understanding of the context. Because I have translated the terms into American rather than British English, I have not always translated the terms in the same way as in the unofficial translations found on that website. I have used American terms instead of British ones, e.g. court of appeals (not court of appeal); railroad (not railway); plaintiff (not claimant); disability (not invalidity); elementary education (not primary education). I have also consistently used American spelling (e.g., check, offense, defense, indorsement, labor).

Although this dictionary is strictly a legal one, I have nonetheless included certain non-legal terms that are likely to appear in Swiss contracts (especially leases) and differ from the way they are said in Germany and France. Examples of these terms include attic, hot water heater, radiator, sink and wall-to-wall carpet.

Finally, it is important to note that not until now has the time been ripe for a trilingual Swiss law dictionary, because until 2011 there was not a single code of civil procedure or criminal procedure for the entire country. Instead, each canton had its own code, and terminology varied widely. On January 1, 2011, a new federal (nationwide) Code of Civil Procedure and Code of Criminal Procedure entered into force in Switzerland. Some of the terminology is new, e.g., what was known as an "appel incident" in the former Loi de procédure civile in Geneva is now called an "appel joint" in the federal code, while the term "transport sur place" in Geneva law is now referred to as "inspection." I have not included the old terminology in this dictionary because it would have been an overwhelming task to compile the civil procedure terms of 26 cantonal laws that have now been repealed anyway.

Two terms included in this book may be confusing because they are sometimes translated using the same word in English even though their meanings are different. One of these pairs is séquestre/Arrest and saisie/Pfändung, both of which are sometimes translated as attachment. But the first term (séquestre/Arrest) is really the one that refers to "attachment" in the sense of "freezing" an asset, while the second refers to actually seizing and levying execution on an asset. The second pair, appel/Berufung and recours/Beschwerde, are both translated as "appeal" but the first pair refers to an appeal to the highest court in a canton, while the second refers to an appeal to the Swiss Federal Supreme Court. The online translation of the Swiss Code of Civil Procedure translates recours/Beschwerde as "objection," but that term is needed to translate opposition/Einsprache under the Debt Collection and Bankruptcy Act.

Where possible, I have indicated the different word used in Germany (D) and France (F).

The author would be happy to receive comments and corrections. These can be sent to dictionary@intermarkls.com.

à bien plaire (F : à titre précaire)	auf Widerruf	revocable
à demande	auf Gesuch hin	upon request
à l'extérieur des localités	ausserorts	out of town
à l'intérieur des localités	innerorts	in an urban area
à ses risques et périls	auf eigene Gefahr	at one's own risk
à titre volontaire	freiwillig	voluntarily
à vie	auf Lebenszeit	for life
abandon de la chose (art. 194 CO)	Herausgabe	relinquishment
absence	Absenz, Abwesenheit	absence
absence injustifiée	unerlaubte Entfernung	unjustified absence
abus d'autorité (art. 312 CP)	Amtsmissbrauch	abuse of public office
abus de cartes-chèques (art. 148 CP)	Checkkartenmissbrauch	misuse of a check card
abus de confiance (art. 138 CP)	Veruntreuung	misappropriation
abus de droit (art. 2 al. 2 CC)	Rechtsmissbrauch	abuse of a right
abus de la détresse (art. 193 CP)	Ausnützung der Notlage	exploitation of a person in a position of need or dependency
abus de pouvoir	Gewaltmissbrauch	abuse of power
abus de prix	Preismissbrauch	unfair pricing
abus de stupéfiants	Betäubungsmittelmissbrauch	abuse of narcotics
abus du pouvoir d'appréciation	Missbrauch des Ermessens	abuse of discretionary powers
acceptation de l'offre	Annahme des Antrags	acceptance of the offer
acceptation d'héritage	Erbschaftsannahme	acceptance of an inheritance
acceptation d'un avantage (art. 322sexties CP)	Vorteilsannahme	acceptance of an advantage
acceptation tacite (art. 6 CO)	stillschweigende Annahme	implied acceptance (of an offer)
acceptation tacite de compétence (art. 18 CPC)	Einlassung	acceptance by appearance
accès à la route	Zufahrt	access (road)
accès à un tribunal	Zugang zu einem Gericht	access to a court
accès indu à un système informatique (art. 143bis CP)	unbefugtes Eindringen in ein Datenverarbeitungssystem	unauthorized access to a data processing system
accessoriété	Akzessorietät	accessoriness
accident	Unfall	accident
accident anodin	Bagatellunfall	minor accident
accident de la circulation	Verkehrsunfall	traffic accident

accident non professionnel	Nichtberufsunfall	accident that is not work-related
accident professionnel	Berufsunfall	occupational accident
accord	Vereinbarung	agreement
accord de double imposition (ADI)	Doppelbesteuerungsabkomme n (DBA)	double taxation treaty
accord de droit	rechtlicher Konsens	legal consensus
accord de fait	tatsächlicher Konsens	actual consensus
accord de soumission	Submissionsabsprache	collusive bidding
accord de volontés	Konsens	meeting of the minds
accord en matière de concurrence (art. 4 LCart)	Wettbewerbsabrede	agreement affecting competition
Accord sur la libre circulation des personnes (ALCP)	Freizügigkeitsabkommen (FZA)	Agreement on the Free Movement of Persons
Accord sur le transfert des corps des personnes décédées	Übereinkommen über die Leichenbeförderung	Agreement on the Transfer of Corpses
Accord sur les marchés publics (AMP)	Übereinkommen über das öffentliche Beschaffungswesen (ÜoeB)	Government Procurement Agreement
accréditation	Akkreditierung	accreditation
accréditation des médias	Akkreditierung von Medienschaffenden	journalist accreditation
accréditif	Akkreditiv	letter of credit (L/C)
accumuler	äufnen	to accumulate
accusation (1)	Anklage	indictment
accusation (2) (tribunal militaire)	Auditor (Militärgericht)	prosecutor
accuser	anklagen	to indict
achat de couverture	Deckungskauf	hedge buying
acheteur	Käufer	buyer, purchaser
acompte	Anzahlung	payment on account, down payment
acomptes (art. 123 al. 3, 326 et 348 al. 1 lit. 1 LP)	Abschlagszahlungen	down payments, installment payments
acquêt (art. 197 CC)	Errungenschaft	property acquired during marriage
acquiescement (art. 241 CPC)	Klageanerkennung	acceptance of the plaintiff's claim (by the defendant)
acquisition de la possession	Besitzerwerb	acquisition of possession
acquisition de la propriété	Eigentumserwerb	acquisition of ownership
acquisition dérivée	derivativer Erwerb	derivative acquisition

acquit de douane	Zollausweis	customs clearance document
acquittement	Freispruch	acquittal
acte administratif	Verfügung	administrative act
acte commis en état d'irresponsabilité fautive (art. 263 CP)	Rauschtat	offense committed while intoxicated
acte concluant	konkludentes Verhalten	implicit, implicitly, implied contract
acte constitutif (art. 629 CO)	Errichtungsakt	charter
acte d'accusation (art. 360 CPP)	Anklageschrift	indictment
acte de cautionnement	Bürgschaftserklärung	guarantee commitment
acte de défaut de biens (art. 149 ss LP)	Verlustschein	certificate of unpaid debt (if the liquidation proceeds do not cover the debts in question and the costs of the proceedings, the creditors will receive a certificate of unpaid debt allowing them to recommence debt collection proceedings later)
acte de défaut de biens après faillite	Konkursverlustschein	certificate of unpaid debt established after bankruptcy
acte de disposition	Verfügungsgeschäft	act of disposal
acte de légitime défense	Abwehrhandlung	self-defense
acte de l'état civil	Zivilstandsurkunde	vital record
acte de naissance	Geburtsschein (D: Geburtsurkunde)	birth certificate
acte de nomination	Brevet	appointment
acte de non-conciliation	Leitschein	certificate from justice of the peace that the case was not able to be settled
acte de partage successoral	Erbteilungsvertrag	contract between heirs regarding the distribution of the estate
acte de portée générale	Allgemeinverfügung	general ruling
acte de poursuite (art. 56 LP)	Betreibungshandlung	debt collection proceeding
acte de procédure	Verfahrenshandlung	procedural act

acte d'ordre sexuel	sexuelle Handlung	sexual act
acte d'ordre sexuel avec des mineurs contre rémunération (art. 196 CP)	sexuelle Handlung mit Minderjährigen gegen Entgelt	sexual act with minors against payment
acte d'ordre sexuel avec un enfant (art. 187 CP)	sexuelle Handlung mit einem Kind	sexual act with a child
acte d'ordre sexuel avec une personne dépendante (art. 188 CP)	sexuelle Handlung mit einem Abhängigen	sexual act with a dependent person
acte d'ordre sexuel avec une personne détenue (art. 192 CP)	sexuelle Handlung mit einem Gefangenen	sexual act with a prisoner
acte d'ordre sexuel sur un incapable de discernement (art. 191 CP)	Schändung	sexual acts with persons incapable of judgment or resistance
acte d'origine	Heimatschein	certificate of family origin
acte entre vifs	Rechtsgeschäft unter Lebenden	inter vivos transaction
acte illicite (F : délit civil)	unerlaubte Handlung	tort
acte juridique	Rechtsgeschäft	legal transaction
acte juridique bilatéral	zweiseitiges Rechtsgeschäft	bilateral legal transaction
acte législatif	Erlass	legislation, an enactment
acte matériel	Realakt	physical act
acte ordinaire de la vie	alltägliche Lebensverrichtung	daily chores
acte pour cause de mort	Rechtsgeschäft von Todes wegen	transaction causa mortis
acte préparatoire punissable (art. 260bis CP)	strafbare Vorbereitungshandlung	acts preparatory to the commission of an offense
acte unilatéral	einseitiges Rechtsgeschäft	unilateral transaction (such as making a last will and testament)
actes à notifier (art. 136 CPC)	zuzustellende Urkunden	documents to be served
actes abusifs (art. 132 CPC)	rechtsmissbräuchliche Eingaben	abusive pleadings, abusive submissions
actes commis à l'étranger (art. 264m CP)	Auslandstaten	acts carried out abroad
actes commis en état d'irresponsabilité fautive (art. 263 CP)	Verübung einer Tat in selbstverschuldeter Unzurechnungsfähigkeit	committing an offense while in a state of voluntarily induced mental incapacity
actes de disposition (art. 204 al. 1 LP)	Rechtshandlungen	disposals

actes de parties (art. 130 CPC)	Eingaben der Parteien	pleadings, submissions of the parties
actes d'hostilité contre un belligérant ou des troupes étrangères (art. 300 CP)	Feindseligkeiten gegen einen Kriegführenden oder fremde Truppen	hostility towards a country at war or foreign troops
actes édictés par l'Assemblée fédérale	Erlasse der Bundesversammlung	enactments of the Federal Assembly
actes exécutés sans droit pour un état étranger (art. 271 CP)	verbotene Handlungen für einen fremden Staat	unlawful activities on behalf of a foreign state
actes introduits de manière procédurière (art. 132 CPC)	querulatorische Eingaben	querulous pleadings, querulous submissions
actes révocables	anfechtbare Rechtshandlungen	revocable transactions
actes se rattachant à l'exercice d'une industrie	gewerbliche Verrichtungen	commercial duties
actif circulant	Umlaufvermögen	current assets
actif immobilisé	Anlagevermögen	fixed assets
actifs transitoires	transitorische Aktiven	accrued assets, prepaid expenses
action	Aktie	share, share of stock
action à droit de vote privilégié (art. 693 CO)	Stimmrechtsaktie	preferred stock
action au porteur (art. 683 CO)	Inhaberaktie	bearer share
action civile (art. 122 ss CPP)	Zivilklage	civil action (in a criminal case)
action collective (art. 89 CPC)	Verbandsklage	group action (not the same thing as a "class action" in the USA)
action condamnatoire (art. 84 CPC)	Leistungsklage	action for performance
action de droit administratif	verwaltungsrechtliche Klage	administrative lawsuit
action découlant d'un contrat (art. 31 CPC)	Klage aus Vertrag	action in contract, action sounding in contract
action défensive	Abwehrklage	action to quiet title
action du légataire (art. 601 CC)	Vermächtnisklage	action by a legatee
action en bornage	Grenzscheidungsklage	action for demarcation
action en cessation de trouble (art. 28a al. 1 CC)	Beseitigungsklage	action to have violence, threats or harassment cease
action en cession de la demande de brevet	Klage auf Abtretung des Patentgesuchs	action for assignment of a patent
action en cession du droit à la marque (art. 53 LPM)	Klage auf Übertragung der Marke	action for assignment of the trademark

action en constatation de droit (art. 84 CPC)	Feststellungsklage	action for a declaratory judgment
action en constatation de la créance	Klage auf Anerkennung der Forderung	action for recognition of the claim
action en constatation du droit de gage (art. 153a al. 1 LP)	Klage auf Feststellung des Pfandrechts	action for recognition of a pledge
action en constatation du non-retour à la meilleure fortune (art. 265a al. 4 LP)	Klage auf Bestreitung des neuen Vermögens	action for recognition of a lack of improvement in the debtor's fortune
action en constatation du retour à la meilleure fortune (art. 265a al. 4 LP)	Klage auf Feststellung des neuen Vermögens	action for recognition of an improvement in the debtor's fortune
action en contestation	Anfechtungsklage, Deliktspauliana	avoidance action (action by creditors to void a fraudulent conveyance)
action en contestation de l'état de collocation (art. 148 et 250 LP)	Kollokationsklage	action to challenge the schedule of claims
action en contestation du cas de séquestre (art. 279 LP)	Arrestaufhebungsklage	action challenging the attachment of assets
action en déguerpissement	Räumungsklage	action to evict a holdover tenant
action en désaveu	Anfechtung der Vermutung der Vaterschaft	contesting the presumption of paternity
action en dommages-intérêts	Schadenersatzklage	action for damages
action en enrichissement illégitime	Bereicherungsklage	action based on unjust enrichment
action en entretien (art. 26 CPC)	Unterhaltsklage	action for maintenance
action en exécution d'une prestation	Leistungsklage	action for performance
action en expulsion	Räumungsklage	action to evict a holdover tenant
action en interdiction	Unterlassungsklage	action for an injunction
action en justice	Klage	lawsuit, court action
action en libération de dette (art. 83 LP)	Aberkennungsklage	action for a declaratory judgment that a debt does not exist
action en nullité	Ungültigkeitsklage	action for annulment
action en paiement	Klage auf Zahlung	action for payment

action en paiement (dette alimentaire (art. 26 CPC)	Unterstützungsklage	action for assistance
action en paiement non chiffrée (art. 85 CPC)	unbezifferte Forderungsklage	action for an unquantified debt
action en partage	Teilungsklage	action for distribution of an estate
action en partage successoral	Erbteilungsklage	action for distribution of an estate
action en participation (art. 111 LP)	Anschlussklage	action for participation
action en paternité (art. 261 CC) (F : action en recherche de paternité)	Vaterschaftsklage	paternity suit
action en pétition d'hérédité	Erbschaftsklage	action for recovery of an inheritance
action en raison du trouble de la possession (art. 928 CC)	Klage aus Besitzesstörung	action for trespass
action en reconnaissance de dette (art. 79 LP)	Schuldanerkennungsklage	action for the recognition of a claim
action en rectification	Berichtigungsklage	action to have an employment record corrected
action en rectification du registre foncier	Grundbuchberichtigungsklage	action to correct the land register
action en réduction (art. 522 CC)	Herabsetzungsklage	action in abatement
action en réduction du prix (art. 205 CO)	Minderungsklage	claim to a reduction in the purchase price
action en réintégration des biens soumis au droit de rétention (art. 284 LP)	Klage auf Rückschaffung von Retentionsgegenständen	action to recover items subject to a right of retention
action en remise de gain (art. 423 CO)	Gewinnherausgabe	restitution
action en réparation du tort moral	Genugtuungsklage	action for pain and suffering
action en répétition de l'indu	Rückforderungsklage	action to recover an amount paid in error
action en responsabilité (art. 325 LP)	Verantwortlichkeitsklage	liability action
action en revendication (1)	Eigentumsklage, Eigentumsherausgabeklage	action to establish ownership

action en revendication (2) (art. 106-109 LP)	Widerspruchsklage	third party objection action (action filed by a creditor against a third party when the item to be seized is not in the debtor's possession, but in the possession of the third party, who claims to own it or hold a lien on it)
action en revendication de tiers (art. 242 LP)	Aussonderungsklage	third party action
action en révocation d'actes dolosifs (art. 288 LP)	Absichtsanfechtung, Absichtspauliana	challenge of a debtor's fraudulent conveyance of assets
action en séparation de corps	Trennungsklage	action for legal separation (as opposed to divorce)
action en validation de séquestre	Arrestprosequierungsklage	action for ratification of the attachment of assets
action fondée sur le droit du mariage (art. 23 CPC)	eherechtliche Klage	action based on marital law
action fondée sur un acte illicite (art. 36 CPC)	Klage aus unerlaubter Handlung	action in tort, action sounding in tort
action formatrice (art. 87 CPC)	Gestaltungsklage	action to modify a legal relationship
action gratuite	Gratisaktie	bonus share
action négatoire	Eigentumsfreiheitsklage	action to establish the nonexistence of an easement
action nominative (art. 684 CO)	Namenaktie (D: Namensaktie)	registered share
action nominative liée	vinkulierte Namenaktie	registered shares with restricted transferability
action non chiffrée (art. 85 CPC)	unbezifferte Forderungsklage	action for an unquantified debt
action partielle (art.86 CPC)	Teilklage	partial action (action for part of a divisible claim)
action paulienne	Anfechtungsklage, paulianische Anfechtung	avoidance action (action by creditors to void a fraudulent conveyance)
action populaire	Popularbeschwerde	popular complaint
action privilégiée	Vorzugsaktie	preferred shares

action récursoire	Regressklage (D: Rückgriffsklage)	recourse against those who are secondarily liable
action rédhibitoire (art. 205 CO)	Wandelungsklage	action for rescission of a sale
action réelle (art. 29 CO)	dingliche Klage	action in rem
action remise au salarié	Arbeitnehmeraktie	employee share, employee stock
action révocatoire	paulianische Anfechtung	avoidance action (action by creditors to void a fraudulent conveyance)
actionnaire	Aktionär	shareholder
actionnaire majoritaire	Mehrheitsaktionär	majority shareholder
actionnaire minoritaire	Minderheitsaktionär	minority shareholder
actionnaire unique	Alleinaktionär	sole shareholder, single shareholder
actionnariat	Aktionariat	shareholders
actions liées (F : actions à cessibilité restreinte)	vinkulierte Aktien	restricted shares, shares with restricted transferability
activation	Aktivierung	capitalization
activité	Tätigkeit	activity
activité accessoire	Nebenbeschäftigung	secondary employment
activité au service de plusieurs employeurs	Mehrfachbeschäftigung	working for several employers at the same time
activité lucrative	Erwerbstätigkeit	gainful employment
activité lucrative indépendante	selbständige Erwerbstätigkeit	self-employment
activité relevant de la puissance publique	hoheitliche Tätigkeit	sovereign activity
activités à l'étranger	Auslandgeschäft	international business
activités de jeunesse extra-scolaires	ausserschulische Jugendarbeit	extracurricular youth activities
adjudicataire	Ersteigerer	successful bidder
adjudicateur	Auftraggeber	contracting authority
adjudication	Zuschlag	award
adjuger	zuschlagen	to award
admettre	gutheissen	to admit
administrateur de la faillite	Konkursverwalter	administrator in bankruptcy or liquidation
administrateur officiel de la succession	Erbschaftsverwalter	administrator of the estate
administration	Verwaltung	administration

administration de justice civile	Zivilrechtspflege	administration of civil justice
administration de la faillite (art. 240 LP)	Konkursverwaltung	bankruptcy administration
administration des preuves (art. 231 CPC)	Beweisabnahme	taking evidence, taking of evidence
administration d'office de la succession	Erbschaftsverwaltung	administration of an estate
administration du tribunal	Gerichtsverwaltung	court administration
Administration fédérale (Adm. féd.)	Bundesverwaltung (BVerw)	Federal Administration
Administration fédérale des contributions (AFC)	Eidgenössische Steuerverwaltung (ESTV)	Swiss Federal Tax Administration
Administration fédérale des douanes (AFD)	Eidgenössische Zollverwaltung (EZV)	Federal Customs Administration
Administration fédérale des finances (AFF)	Eidgenössische Finanzverwaltung (EFV)	Federal Finance Administration
administration paritaire (LPP)	paritätische Verwaltung (BVG)	equal representation management
admission au négoce	Zulassung zum Handel	admission to trading
admission de la demande	Gutheissung	admission of the complaint
admission du recours	Gutheissung der Beschwerde	granting the appeal
adoption	Adoption, Kindesannahme	adoption
adoption de mineurs	Adoption Unmündiger	adoption of minors
adoption d'interdits	Adoption Entmündigter	adoption of incapacitated persons
adoption par une personne seule	Einzeladoption	adoption by a single person
affaire civile	Zivilsache	civil case
affaire pénale	Strafsache	criminal case
affaires administratives	Verwaltungssachen	administrative matters
affaires étrangères (art. 54 CF)	auswärtige Angelegenheiten	foreign affairs
affiliation	Mitgliedschaftsrecht	membership right (the rights of the shareholder, as embodied in the share, to participate in shareholders' meetings and in votes and elections, and to receive information, as well as rights of inspection)
affiliation à une bande	Bandenmässigkeit	membership in a gang

affirmation fallacieuse	Vorspiegelung	misrepresentation, false pretenses
affirmer	behaupten	to claim, to allege
affranchissement postal	Frankatur	postage
affréteur	Charterer	charterer
âge de la retraite	Pensionierungsalter	retirement age
âge d'entrée	Eintrittsalter	age at entry
âge terme	Schlussalter	final age
agence de presse	Presseagentur	press agency
agence de travail temporaire	Temporärfirma	"temp agency"
Agence internationale de l'énergie	Internationale Energieagentur	International Energy Agency
agent	Agent	agent
agent d'affaires	Kleinanwalt	professional who represents parties in cases such as bankruptcy, employment disputes and landlord-tenant disputes
agent de probation	Betreuer, Bewährungshelfer, Fürsorger	probation officer
agent en brevets	Patentanwalt	patent agent
agent immobilier	Immobilienhändler	real estate agent, realtor
agent payeur	Zahlstelle	paying agent
agent provocateur	V-Mann	informer
agent solitaire	Alleintäter	lone offender
aggravation de la peine	Strafschärfung	aggravation of the sentence
agio	Agio, Aufgeld	premium (difference between the nominal value of a security and its issue or market price)
agir dans un dessein de lucre	Gewinnsucht: aus Gewinnsucht handeln	to act with motives of financial gain

agrément d'un ambassadeur	Agrément eines Botschafters	agrément of an ambassador (Diplomatic courtesy requires that before a state appoints a new chief of diplomatic mission to represent it in another state, it must be first ascertained whether the proposed appointee is acceptable to the receiving state. The acquiescence of the receiving state is signified by its granting its agrément to the appointment.)
agression (art. 134 CP)	Angriff	attack
aide à la formation (art. 66 CF)	Ausbildungsbeitrag	educational grant
aide au développement	Entwicklungshilfe	foreign aid
aide au retour	Rückkehrhilfe	aiding immigrants to return to their home country
aide aux réfugiés	Flüchtlingshilfe	aid to refugees
aide aux victimes	Opferhilfe	victim support
aide d'autrui	Dritthilfe	assistance by a third party
aide en capital	Kapitalhilfe	capital injection
aide financière	Finanzhilfe	financial aid
aide immédiate	Soforthilfe	immediate aid
aide-mémoire	Behelf (D: Anleitung)	instructions, guide
aide transitoire	Überbrückungshilfe	transitional assistance
aire d'exploitation	Betriebsstandort	company site
ajournement de la décision	Aufschub des Entscheides	postponement of the decision
ajournement de la faillite (art. 173 al. 1 et 331 al. 2 LP)	Konkursaufschub	stay of insolvency proceedings, stay of bankruptcy proceedings
ajournement du paiement d'intérêts	Stundung von Zinsen	moratorium on interest
alibi	Alibi	alibi
aliénateur	Veräusserer (D: Veräußerer)	seller
aliénation	Veräusserung (D: Veräußerung)	sale
aliéner	veräussern (D: veräußern)	to sell

alignement	Baulinie	building line
alimentation	Ernährung	food, nutrition
allégation défendable	vertretbare Behauptung	defensible allegation
allègement du fardeau de la preuve	Beweislasterleichterung	reduced burden of proof
alléguer	behaupten	to claim, to allege
aller aux urnes	Urnengang	going to the polls, voter turnout
alliance	Schwägerschaft	kinship by marriage
allocation d'ancienneté	Alterszulage	superannuation allowance
allocation d'assistance	Assistenzentschädigung	personal assistance benefits for disabled persons
allocation de formation	Ausbildungszuschuss	training allowance
allocation de maternité	Mutterschaftsentschädigung	maternity allowance
allocation de ménage	Haushaltungszulage	household allowance
allocation de séjour à l'étranger	Auslandszulage	foreign assignment allowance
allocation familiale	Familienzulage	family allowance
allocation pour enfant	Kinderzulage	child allowance
allocation pour impotent (API) (art. 26-27 LAA)	Hilflosenentschädigung (HE)	incapacitation compensation
allocation pour perte de gain	Erwerbsersatz	unemployment benefits
altération de fourrages (art. 235 CP)	Herstellen von gesundheitsschädlichem Futter	production of harmful animal feed
aménagement du territoire	Raumplanung	spatial planning
amende	Busse (D: Buße)	fine
amende avec sursis	bedingte Busse	suspended fine
amende de stationnement	Parkbusse	parking fine
amende disciplinaire (art. 128 CPC)	Ordnungsbusse	disciplinary fine
amende d'ordre	Ordnungsbusse	disciplinary fine
amnistie	Amnestie	amnesty
amnistie fiscale	Steueramnestie	tax amnesty
amortissement	Abschreibung	depreciation (of tangible assets); amortization (of intangible assets)
analyse des risques	Risikoanalyse	risk analysis
analyste financier	Finanzanalytiker	financial analyst
ancienneté de service	Dienstalter	seniority
animaux échappés (art. 719 CC)	herrenlos werdende Tiere	escaped animals
animaux vivant en milieu domestique (art. 651a CC)	Tiere des häuslichen Bereichs	animals kept as pets

année de construction	Baujahr	year built
annexe (1)	Beilage (D: Anlage)	exhibit (to a document)
annexe (2) (aux comptes annuels)	Anhang (zur Jahresrechnung)	notes (to the financial statements)
annexe au bilan	Anhang zur Bilanz	notes to the balance sheet
annexe du défendeur	beklagtische Beilage (BB)	defendant's exhibit
annotation au registre foncier (art. 101 LP)	Vormerkung im Grundbuch	priority notice in the land register
annuité	Annuität	annuity
annulabilité	Anfechtbarkeit	voidability
annulation (papier-valeur)	Kraftloserklärung	cancellation
annulation de la poursuite (art. 85 LP)	Aufhebung der Betreibung	annulment of the insolvency proceeding
annulation du contrat de reprise de dette (art. 180 LP)	Dahinfallen des Schuldübernahmevertrages	failure of debt assumption contract
annulation du mariage (art. 104-110 CC)	Eheungültigkeit	annulment of marriage
antécédent	Vorleben	backstory
antidater	zurückdatieren	to backdate
apostille	Apostille	apostille
appareil automatique servant au jeu	Spielautomat	slot machine
appareils de falsification et emploi illicite d'appareils (art. 247 CP)	Fälschungsgeräte; unrechtmässiger Gebrauch von Geräten	counterfeiting equipment and unlawful use of equipment
apparence de droit	Rechtsschein	color of law
apparentement de listes	Listenverbindung	list combination
appariement des paiements	Abstimmung der Zahlungen	reconciliation of payments
appartement de vacances	Ferienwohnung	vacation apartment
appauvrissement	Entreicherung	impoverishment
appel (art. 308-318 CPC) L'appel est ouvert	Berufung, Appellation Die Berufung steht offen	appeal The appeal lies
appel aux créanciers (art. 232 al. 2 et 300 art. 1 LP)	Schuldenruf	call to creditors
appel dévolutif	devolutives Rechtsmittel	appeal to a higher court (rather than to the court that handed down the ruling)
appel d'offres (marchés publics)	Ausschreibung, Offertanfrage	request for proposals (RFP)
appel en cause (art. 81 CPC)	Streitverkündungsklage	third party action

appel joint (art. 313 CPC)	Anschlussberufung	cross appeal
appel suspensif	suspensives Rechtsmittel	appeal with a stay of execution (of the lower court's judgment pending appeal)
appelant	Berufungskläger, Rekurrent	appellant
appellatoire	appellatorisch	unsubstantiated
Appenzell Rhodes-Extérieures	Appenzell Ausserrhoden	Appenzell Outer Rhodes (canton)
Appenzell Rhodes-Intérieures	Appenzell Innerrhoden	Appenzell Inner Rhodes (canton)
applicabilité	Anwendbarkeit	applicability
application de la peine	Zumessung der Strafe	sentencing
application de la règle de droit	Subsumtion	applying the law to the facts of the case
application du droit	Rechtsanwendung	application of the law
application du droit d'office	Rechtsanwendung von Amts wegen	sua sponte application of the law
apport	Einlage	contribution
apport en espèces (art. 631 CO)	Geldeinlage	cash contribution
apport en nature (art. 628 CO)	Sacheinlage	contribution in kind
apport minimum (art. 632 CO)	Mindesteinlage	minimum contribution (to capital)
appréciation anticipée des preuves	antizipierte Beweiswürdigung	anticipated assessment of the evidence (the court can refuse evidence when it feels that it is sufficiently informed and anticipates that the evidence offered would not change its opinion)
appréciation des preuves	Beweiswürdigung	evaluation of the evidence
appréhender	anhalten	to stop
appréhension (art. 215 CPP)	polizeiliche Anhaltung	police power to stop
apprenti	Lehrling	apprentice
apprentissage	Berufslehre	apprenticeship
apprentissage de coiffeur	Coiffeurlehre (D: Friseurlehre)	hairdresser apprenticeship

approbation des comptes annuels	Abnahme der Jahresrechnung (D: Billigung des Jahresabschlusses)	approval of the annual financial statements
appropriation illégitime (art. 137 CP)	unrechtmässige Aneignung	unlawful appropriation
approvisionnement	Versorgung	supply, provision
approvisionnement du pays (art. 102 CF)	Landesversorgung	national economic supply
approvisionnement économique du pays	wirtschaftliche Landesversorgung	economic supply
aptitude au placement	Vermittlungsfähigkeit	ability to be hired
aptitude au service	Diensttauglichkeit	fitness for duty
arbitrabilité (art. 177 LDIP)	Schiedsfähigkeit	arbitrability
arbitrage (1)	Schiedsverfahren	arbitration
arbitrage (2)	Arbitrage	arbitrage
Archives fédérales suisses (AFS)	Schweizerisches Bundesarchiv (BAR)	Swiss Federal Archives
Argovie	Aargau	Aargau (canton)
armée (art. 58 CF)	Armee	armed forces
Armée suisse	Schweizer Armee	Swiss Armed Forces
arrestation (art. 217 CPP)	Festnahme	arrest
arrêt	Entscheid (D: Entscheidung)	decision
arrêté fédéral (AF)	Bundesbeschluss (BB)	federal decree
arrêté fédéral urgent	dringlicher Bundesbeschluss	urgent federal decree
Arrêts du Tribunal fédéral (ATF)	Bundesgerichtsentscheide (BGE)	Supreme Court Reports
arrhes (art. 158 CO)	Haftgeld	earnest money
arrhes et dédit (art. 158 CO)	Haft- und Reugeld	earnest money and forfeit money
arrière-caution (art. 498 CO)	Rückbürgschaft	counter-surety
arrondissement de poursuite (art. 1 ss LP)	Betreibungskreis	district
arrondissement du registre foncier	Grundbuchkreis	land register district
article	Artikel	section
article de marque	Markenartikel	brand item
ascendant	Vorfahre	ancestor, ascendant
asile	Pfrundanstalt (D: Pfründhaus)	retirement home, old-age home
assainissement (1)	Sanierung (1)	reorganization
assainissement (2)	Sanierung (2)	remediation
assassinat (art. 112 CP)	Mord	murder
assemblée bourgeoisiale	Bürgergemeindeversammlung	citizens' assembly
assemblée communale	Gemeindeversammlung	municipal assembly
assemblée constituante	Verfassungsrat	constitutional assembly

assemblée consultative	Konsultativversammlung	organizational meeting
assemblée des copropriétaires d'étages	Stockwerkeigentümerversammlung	meeting of condominium owners
assemblée des créanciers (art. 232 al. 2, 252 ss LP)	Gläubigerversammlung	creditors meeting
assemblée des délégués	Delegiertenversammlung	meeting of delegates
Assemblée fédérale (Ass. féd.)	Bundesversammlung (BVers)	Federal Assembly (the Swiss legislature, made up of two houses: the National Council and the Council of States)
Assemblée fédérale (Chambres réunies)	Vereinigte Bundesversammlung	United Federal Assembly
assemblée générale	Generalversammlung	shareholders' meeting
assemblée générale constitutive	konstitutive Generalversammlung	organizational meeting
assemblée générale extraordinaire	ausserordentliche Generalversammlung	special meeting of shareholders
assemblée générale ordinaire	ordentliche Generalversammlung	annual shareholders' meeting
assemblée universelle (art. 701 CO)	Universalversammlung	meeting of all shareholders
assentiment	Einwilligung	consent
assermentation	Vereidigung	swearing in
assermenter	vereidigen	to swear someone in, to administer an oath to someone
assesseur de la justice de paix	Beisitzer des Friedengerichts	assessor to the justice of the peace
assesseur suppléant de la justice de paix	Ersatzbeisitzer des Friedensgerichts	Deputy Assessor to the Justice of the Peace
assignant (art. 467 CO)	Anweisender	principal
assignataire (art. 467 CO)	Anweisungsempfänger	payee
assignation (art. 466-471 CO)	Anweisung	payment instruction, authorization to pay a third party
assigner	zitieren	to summon
assistance	Hilfeleistung	assistance
assistance à l'évasion (art. 319 CP)	Entweichenlassen von Gefangenen	assistance by a public official in the escape of prisoners
assistance au suicide (art. 115 CP)	Beihilfe zum Selbstmord	assisted suicide
assistance aux personnes libérées	Entlassenenhilfe	aftercare

assistance gratuite d'un défenseur (art. 29 al. 3 CF)	unentgeltlicher Rechtsbeistand, unentgeltliche Verbeiständung	free legal representation in court
assistance judiciaire gratuite (art. 29 al. 3 CF, art. 117 CPC)	unentgeltliche Rechtspflege	right to proceed in forma pauperis
assistance publique	Sozialhilfe	welfare
assistance social	Betreuung	social assistance
assistant social	Sozialarbeiter	social worker
association (art. 60-79 CC)	Verband, Verein	association
association de bailleurs	Vermieterverband	landlord association
association de locataires	Mieterverband	tenant association
association d'employeurs	Arbeitgeberverband	employers association
Association des Intérêts (F : syndicat d'initiative)	Tourismusbüro	tourist office
association faîtière	Dachverband	umbrella association
association professionnelle	Berufsverband	trade association
associé	Gesellschafter	partner, shareholder
associé gérant	geschäftsführender Gesellschafter	managing partner, managing shareholder
associe indéfiniment responsable	unbeschränkt haftender Gesellschafter (UG)	unlimited partner
associé indéfiniment responsable	Komplementär	general partner
assujettissement	Steuerpflicht	taxation
assujettissement au contrôle douanier	Zollmeldepflicht	duty to declare to customs officials
assurance	Versicherung	insurance
assurance-accidents	Unfallversicherung	accident insurance (similar to workers' compensation)
assurance aérienne	Luftfahrtversicherung	aviation insurance
assurance-chômage (AC)	Arbeitslosenversicherung (ALV)	unemployment insurance (mandatory for all employees and withheld from monthly paycheck)
assurance collective	Kollektivversicherung	group insurance
assurance contre la grêle	Hagelversicherung	hail insurance
assurance contre le bris de glaces	Glasversicherung	glass insurance, plate glass insurance
assurance contre les accidents non professionnels	Nicht-Betriebs-Unfall-Versicherung	insurance covering accidents that are not work-related
assurance-crédit	Kreditversicherung	credit insurance
assurance de la valeur à neuf	Neuwertversicherung	replacement value insurance

assurance de protection juridique	Rechtsschutzversicherung	legal expenses insurance (LEI), legal protection insurance (LPI)
assurance de responsabilité civile	Haftpflichtversicherung	liability insurance
assurance de responsabilité civile d'entreprise	Betriebs-Haftpflichtversicherung	business third-party insurance
assurance de responsabilité civile professionnelle	Berufs-Haftpflichtversicherung	professional liability insurance
assurance des hypothèques	Hypothekenversicherung	mortgage insurance
assurance des risques de la construction	Bauwesenversicherung	builders' risk insurance
assurance d'indemnités journalières en cas de maladie	Krankentaggeldversicherung	daily benefit health insurance
assurance d'interruption d'exploitation	Betriebsunterbrechungs-Versicherung	business interruption insurance
assurance directe	Direktversicherung	direct insurance
assurance donnée	Zusicherung	representation (and warranty)
assurance du patrimoine	Vermögensversicherung	property insurance
assurance en cas de décès	Todesfallversicherung	death risk insurance
assurance-invalidité (AI)	Invalidenversicherung (IV)	disability insurance
assurance-maladie	Krankenversicherung	health insurance
assurance-maladie et accidents (art. 117 CF)	Kranken- und Unfallversicherung (KUV)	health and accident insurance
assurance maritime	Seeversicherung	maritime insurance
assurance-maternité	Mutterschaftsversicherung	maternity insurance
assurance obligatoire	obligatorische Versicherung	mandatory insurance
assurance par convention	Abredeversicherung	interim accident insurance
assurance pour cadres	Kaderversicherung	executive management insurance
assurance pour patient privé	Privatpatientenversicherung	private patient insurance
assurance pour soins dentaires	Zahnpflegeversicherung	dental insurance
assurance privée	Privatversicherung	private insurance
assurance salaire	Salärausfallversicherung	salary continuation insurance (disability insurance)
assurance sociale	Sozialversicherung	social insurance

assurance-vie	Lebensversicherung	life insurance
Assurance-vieillesse et survivants (AVS)	Alters- und Hinterlassenenversicherung (AHV)	Old Age and Survivors Insurance
assurance-vol	Diebstahlversicherung	theft insurance
assuré	Versicherter	the insured
assureur	Versicherer	insurer
assureur-accidents	Unfallversicherer	accident insurer (similar to workers' compensation insurer)
assureur-maladie	Krankenversicherer	health insurer
assureur privé	Privatversicherer	private insurer
assureur responsabilité civile	Haftpflichtversicherer	liability insurer
astreinte	Zwangsgeld	fine, penalty
astreinte au travail	Verpflichtung zu einer Arbeitsleistung	order to perform work
astuce	Arglist	malice, fraud
attaquer	anfechten	to challenge, to contest, to object to
atteinte à la liberté de croyance et des cultes (art. 261 CP)	Störung der Glaubens- und Kultusfreiheit	attack on the freedom of faith and the freedom to worship
atteinte à la liberté et l'honneur sexuels (art. 129 CP)	Angriffe auf die sexuelle Freiheit und Ehre	offenses against sexual liberty and honor
atteinte à la paix des morts (art. 262 CP)	Störung des Totfriedens	disturbing the peace of the dead
atteinte à la sécurité militaire (art. 276 CP)	Störung der militärischen Sicherheit	disruption of military security
atteinte à l'honneur (art. 173-178 CP)	Ehrverletzung	crime against personal honor
atteinte à l'indépendance de la Confédération (art. 266 CP)	Angriffe auf die Unabhängigkeit der Eidgenossenschaft	attacks on the independence of the Confederation
atteinte à l'intégrité	Integritätsschaden	impairment
atteinte à un droit constitutionnel	Grundrechtseingriff	constitutional right violation
atteinte astucieuse aux intérêts pécuniaires (art. 151 CP)	arglistige Vermögensschädigung	maliciously causing financial loss to another
atteinte au droit de vote (art. 280 CP)	Eingriffe in das Stimm- und Wahlrecht	attacks on the right to vote
atteinte aux emblèmes nationaux étrangers (art. 298 CP)	tätliche Angriffe auf fremde Hoheitszeichen	attacks on the national emblems of a foreign state

atteinte aux emblèmes suisses (art. 270 CP)	tätliche Angriffe auf Schweizerische Hoheitszeichen	attacks on Swiss national emblems
atteinte nuisible (art. 4 LEaux)	nachteilige Einwirkung	detrimental effect
atteintes à l'ordre constitutionnel (art. 275 CP)	Angriffe auf die verfassungsmässige Ordnung	attacks on the constitutional order
attentat	Attentat	attack
atténuation de la peine (art. 48, 308 CP)	Strafmilderung	mitigation of the sentence
attestation	Bescheinigung	certificate
attestation authentique	Beglaubigung	certification
attestation de l'employeur	Arbeitgeberbescheinigung	employer's certificate
attestation de non-recours	Bestätigung, dass keine Beschwerde eingegangen ist	certificate that no appeal has been filed
attestation de salaire	Lohnausweis	annual salary statement
attestation de vérification (art. 635a CO)	Prüfungsbestätigung	audit confirmation
attestation solennelle	Handgelübde	affirmation (taken without swearing an oath)
attraction de compétence	Kompetenzattraktion	ancillary jurisdiction (power of a court to take jurisdiction over matters that are normally outside its jurisdiction, in order to settle all claims in one court)
attribution	Zuweisung	allocation
attroupement	Zusammenrottung	mob
audience	Verhandlung	hearing
audience de conciliation	Vermittlungsvorstand	mediation hearing
audience de faillite (art. 168 LP)	Konkursverhandlung	bankruptcy hearing
audience d'homologation (art. 304 LP)	Verhandlung vor dem Nachlassgericht	ratification hearing
audition (1)	Einvernahme	examination, interrogation
audition (2)	Anhörung	hearing
audition de l'enfant	Anhörung des Kindes	hearing of the child
audition des témoins	Zeugeneinvernahme, Zeugenvernehmung	examination of witnesses
audition d'un parent	Anhörung eines Elternteils	hearing of a parent
audition menée par la police (art. 159 CPP)	polizeiliche Einvernahme	police examination

augmentation	Erhöhung	increase
augmentation conditionnelle (art. 653 CO)	bedingte Kapitalerhöhung	contingent capital increase
augmentation des possibilités d'utilisation du sol	Aufzonung	increasing the permissible uses of land
augmentation du capital-actions (art. 650-656 CO)	Erhöhung des Aktienkapitals	share capital increase
auteur (1) (droit d'auteur)	Urheber	author
auteur (2) (droit pénal)	Täter	perpetrator
auteur de l'offre (art. 7 CO)	Antragsteller, Offerent	offeror
auteur médiat	mittelbarer Täter	indirect offender (a person who commits an offense by using another person to unwillingly perform the criminal act)
auteur/promoteur d'une initiative	Initiant	initiator
authentifier	visieren, beglaubigen	to authenticate, certify
autonomie des cantons (art. 47 CF)	Eigenständigkeit der Kantone	autonomy of the cantons
autonomie privée	Privatautonomie	freedom of contract
autoréglementation	Selbstregulierung	self-regulation
autorisation	Bewilligung	authorization
autorisation de commencer les travaux	Baufreigabe	authorization to commence construction work
autorisation de déposer	Deponiebewilligung	authorization to dump
autorisation de frontalier	Grenzgängerbewilligung	cross-border commuter permit
autorisation de la poursuite pénale	Ermächtigung zur Strafverfolgung	authorization to prosecute
autorisation de procéder (art. 209 CPC)	Klagebewilligung	conciliation authority's authorization to proceed
autorisation de séjour (F : carte de séjour)	Aufenthaltsbewilligung	residence permit
autorisation de séquestre (art. 272 LP)	Arrestbewilligung	authorization to attach assets
autorisation de travail	Arbeitsbewilligung	work permit
autorisation d'établissement	Niederlassungsbewilligung	residence permit (for foreign nationals to live in Switzerland)
autorisation d'exercer	Berufsausübungsbewilligung	license to practice a profession

autorisation générale	Rahmenbewilligung	general authorization
autorisation partielle	Teilbewilligung	partial authorization
autorisation subséquente	nachträgliche Bewilligung	subsequent authorization
autorité	Behörde	authority
autorité administrative	Verwaltungsbehörde	administrative authority
autorité cantonale	kantonale Amtsstelle, kantonale Behörde	cantonal authority
autorité concordataire	Nachlassbehörde	debt restructuring authority
autorité de conciliation	Schlichtungsbehörde	conciliation authority
autorité de poursuite pénale	Strafverfolgungsbehörde	prosecuting authorities (includes the police, the investigator, the prosecutor, and the indicting authority)
Autorité de protection de l'enfant et de l'adulte (APEA)	Kinder- und Erwachsenenschutzbehörde (KESB)	Child and Adult Protection Authority
autorité de recours	Beschwerdeinstanz	appellate authorities
autorité de séquestre	Arrestbehörde	attachment authority
autorité de surveillance	Aufsichtsbehörde	supervisory authority
Autorité de surveillance du registre foncier	Inspektorat der Bezirksschreibereien, Inspektorat für die Notariate, Grundbuch- und Konkursämter	Land Register Inspectorate
autorité de tutelle	vormundschaftliche Behörde (D: Vormundschaftsgericht)	guardianship authority
autorité d'incarcération	einweisende Behörde	authority responsible for incarceration
autorité disciplinaire	Disziplinarbehörde	disciplinary authority
autorité douanière	Zollbehörde	customs official
autorité électorale	Wahlbehörde	election official
autorité exécutive	Exekutive	executive authority
autorité fédérale	Bundesbehörde	federal authority
Autorité fédérale de surveillance des marchés financiers (FINMA)	Eidgenössische Finanzmarktaufsicht (FINMA)	Swiss Financial Market Supervisory Authority (FINMA)
autorité fiscale	Steuerbehörde	tax authority
Autorité indépendante d'examen des plaintes en matière de radio-télévision (AIEP)	Unabhängige Beschwerdeinstanz für Radio und Television (UBI)	Independent Complaints Authority for Radio and Television
autorité intercantonale	interkantonale Behörde	intercantonal authority

autorité judiciaire	richterliche Behörde	judicial authority
autorité parentale (art. 296-297 CC)	elterliche Sorge (früher "elterliche Gewalt" genannt)	parental authority (the authority of the father and mother over their children)
autorité précédente	Vorinstanz	the lower court, the court below
autorité tutélaire	Vormundschaftsbehörde	guardianship authority
autres produits d'exploitation	betrieblicher Nebenerfolg	other operating income
aval	Wechselbürgschaft, Checkbürgschaft	guaranty (on a bill or check)
avance de fonds	Vorschussgewährung	advance
avance de frais (art. 98 CPC)	Kostenvorschuss	advance payment of court costs
avance ferme	Festvorschuss	fixed advance (a short-term loan)
avancement d'hoirie	Erbvorbezug	advance on an inheritance
avant bourse	vorbörslich	pre-market trading
avantage accordé à un créancier (art. 167 CP)	Bevorzugung eines Gläubigers	undue preference of a creditor
aveu	Geständnis	confession
avis (1)	Anzeige	notice, notification
avis (2)	Meinung	opinion
avis au débiteur (art. 120 LP)	Anzeige an den Schuldner	notice to the debtor
avis aux créanciers (art. 233 LP)	Anzeige an die Gläubiger	notice to creditors
avis aux intéressés (art. 139 LP)	Anzeige an die Beteiligten	notice to the interested parties
avis aux locataires et aux fermiers (art. 152 LP)	Anzeige an Mieter und Pächter	notice to lessees
avis de la partie adverse (art. 330 CPC)	Stellungnahme der Gegenpartei	response by the opposing party
avis de saisie	Pfändungsankündigung	notice of seizure
avis formel	Abmahnung	formal notice
avis obligatoire	Anzeigepflicht	duty of disclosure, duty to give notice, duty to notify
avocat	Advokat, Rechtsanwalt	lawyer, attorney
avocat de la partie adverse	Gegenanwalt	opposing counsel
avocat d'office	Offizialanwalt	court-appointed attorney
avocat et notaire	Fürsprecher	lawyer and notary
avoir de vieillesse	Altersguthaben	retirement savings
avoir en déshérence	nachrichtenloses Vermögen	dormant asset

avoir surobligatoire	vorobligatorische Guthaben	pre-compulsory credit balance
avoir un accident	verunfallen, verunglücken	to have an accident
avoirs à vue	Sichtguthaben	demand deposit
avoirs bancaires	Bankguthaben	bank balance
avoirs en banque à terme	Bankendebitoren auf Zeit	term deposits with banks
avoirs en banque à vue	Bankendebitoren auf Sicht	sight deposits with banks
avoirs en comptes courants auprès de banques	Kontokorrentguthaben bei der Bank	cash in bank, checking account balance
avoirs sans nouvelles	nachrichtenlose Vermögenswerte	dormant assets
AVS (assurance vieillesse et survivants)	AHV (Alters- und Hinterlassenenversicherung)	old age and survivors insurance
ayant-cause	Rechtsnachfolger	legal successor
ayant droit économique	wirtschaftlich Berechtigter	beneficial owner
ayant force de chose jugée	rechtskräftig	res judicata
ayant force obligatoire	verbindlich	binding
bail à ferme (art. 275 ss CO)	Pacht	usufructuary lease
bail à loyer (art. 253-304 CO)	Mietvertrag	lease agreement, rental agreement
bail agricole (art. 276a CC)	landwirtschaftliche Pacht	agricultural lease
bailleur	Vermieter	landlord, lessor
bailleur à ferme	Verpächter	usufructuary lessor
balance des paiements	Zahlungsbilanz	balance of payments
Bâle-Campagne	Basel-Landschaft	Basel-Landschaft (canton)
Bâle-Ville	Basel-Stadt	Basel-Stadt (canton)
bancassurance	Allfinanz	one-stop financial service center
bancomat (F : distributeur automatique de billets)	Bankomat (D: Geldautomat)	ATM
bande	Bande	gang
banque cantonale	Kantonalbank	cantonal bank
banque confirmatrice	bestätigende Bank	confirming bank
banque correspondante	Korrespondenzbank	correspondent bank
banque d'émission	Notenbank	issuing bank, bank of issue
banque d'émission de lettres de gage	Pfandbriefbank	mortgage bond bank
banque dépositaire	Depotbank	custodian bank
banque émettrice	Emissionsbank	issuing bank
banque hypothécaire	Hypothekenbank	mortgage bank
banque locale	Lokalbank	local bank
banque nationale	Nationalbank	national bank

Banque nationale suisse	Schweizerische Nationalbank (SNB)	Swiss National Bank (Switzerland's central bank)
banque notificatrice	avisierende Bank, Avis-Bank	advising bank (in documentary credit business, the bank that informs the beneficiary of the credit that the credit has been opened)
banque privée	Privatbank	private bank
banque restante	banklagernd	held-mail service at banks
banqueroute frauduleuse (art. 163 CP)	betrügerischer Konkurs	fraudulent bankruptcy
banquier	Bankier	banker
barrage	Stauwehr	dam
barreau	Rechtsanwaltschaft	bar
base de calcul	Berechnungsgrundlage	basis for calculation
bâtiment ouvert au public	der Öffentlichkeit zugängliche Baute	building open to the public
bâtonnier	Vorsitzender des Anwaltsverbands	president of the Bar Association
bénéfice comptable	Buchgewinn	book profit
bénéfice de l'exercice	Jahresgewinn	profit for the year
bénéfice de l'union conjugale (art. 210 CC)	Vorschlag	net gain (assets acquired during marriage by one spouse after debts are paid)
bénéfice de réévaluation	Aufwertungsgewinn	revaluation gain
bénéfice du concordat	Rechtswohltat des Nachlassvertrags	benefit of a debt restructuring agreement
bénéfice net	Reingewinn	net profit
bénéfices des entreprises	Unternehmensgewinne	business profits
bénéficiaire	Begünstigter	beneficiary
Berne	Bern	Bern (canton and city)
besoin	Bedürfnis	need
besoin de rester à libre disposition	Freihaltebedürfnis	public interest (against exclusive use)
besoin de soins	Pflegebedürftigkeit	need of nursing care
besoin d'une formation scolaire spéciale	Sonderschulbedürftigkeit	need for a special school
bien à affectation déterminée	zweckgebundenes Vermögen	earmarked asset

bien à protéger	Schutzgut	subject of protection, protected entity
bien acquis en remploi	Ersatzanschaffung	replacement acquisition
bien appartenant à autrui	fremde Sache	object belonging to someone else
bien culturel (art. 196a CO)	Kulturgut	cultural property, cultural heritage site
bien de stricte nécessité (art. 224 LP)	Kompetenzstück	bare necessity good
bien du pupille	Mündelvermögen	ward's asset
bien-fonds	Liegenschaft	property
bien immatériel	Immaterialgut	intangible asset
bien juridique protégé	geschütztes Rechtsgut	object of legal protection
bien meuble	Fahrhabe (D: Fahrnis)	chattel
bien que	obschon (D: obwohl)	although
Bienne	Biel	Biel/Bienne
biens	Vermögenswerte	assets
biens de famille	Familienvermögen	family assets
biens propres (art. 198 CC)	Eigengut	personal property
biens remis en gage (art. 262 al. 2 LP)	Pfandgegenstände	pledged assets
bifurcation de la voie de droit	Rechtswegsgabelung, Gabelung des Rechtsweges	bifurcation of appeals
bilan	Bilanz	balance sheet
bilan de clôture	Abschlussbilanz	closing balance sheet
bilan intermédiaire	Zwischenbilanz	interim balance sheet
billet à ordre (art. 1096-1099 CO)	Eigenwechsel	promissory note
billet de banque	Banknote	banknote
blanchiment d'argent	Geldwäscherei (D: Geldwäsche)	money laundering
blanc-seing	Blankett	blank form, blank document
blankettnorm	Blankettnorm	blanket provision of the law
blesser	lädieren, beschädigen, verletzen	to damage, to injure
blocage du registre foncier	Grundbuchsperre	prohibition on recording in the land register
boiler (F : chauffe-eau)	Boiler	hot water heater
bon de jouissance (art. 657 CO)	Genussschein	dividend rights certificate
bon de participation (art. 656a-656g CO)	Partizipationsschein	participation certificate

bon de participation au porteur	Inhaberpartizipationsschein	bearer participation certificate
bon de participation nominatif	Namenpartizipationsschein	registered participation certificate
bon de récupération	Besserungsschein	debtor warrant (written promise from a debtor to make periodic payments to a creditor, with the payments being contingent on the profits generated by the debtor's company, thus compensating the creditor for not enforcing his right to have a restructuring program imposed on the debtor)
bonification de vieillesse	Altersgutschrift	retirement pension credit
bonification du salaire	Lohngutschrift	wife's compensation (for working in her husband's business)
bonification pour tâches éducatives	Erziehungsgutschrift	parenting credit
bonne foi (art. 3 CC)	guter Glaube	good faith
bonnes raisons de soupçonner	begründeter Verdacht	justified suspicion
bons offices	gute Dienste	good offices (a dispute settlement procedure in which a respected third party or a neutral State acting on request or at its own discretion seeks through diplomatic means to persuade the disputing parties to meet and resume direct negotiation)
bouclement individuel statutaire avec présentation fiable	statutarischer Einzelabschluss mit zuverlässiger Darstellung	reliable assessment statutory single-entity financial statements
bouquet de chantier	Richtfest	topping-out ceremony (in a construction project)

bourse	Börse	stock market, stock exchange
bourse de l'électricité (art. 47 LIMF)	Strombörse	power exchange
bourse d'études	Stipendium	scholarship
bourse électronique	elektronische Börse	automated exchange
boycott	Boykott	boycott
branche de l'économie	Wirtschaftszweig	branch of the economy
brevet d'avocat	Anwaltspatent	admission to the bar, license to practice law
brevet d'invention	Erfindungspatent	patent
brevetabilité	Patentfähigkeit	patentability
brigand	Räuber	robber
brigandage (art. 140 CP)	Raub	robbery
brigandage simple	einfacher Raub	common robbery
bris de scellés (art. 290 CP)	Siegelbruch	breaking seals
bruit (art. 684 CC)	Lärm	noise
budget	Budget, Haushalt	budget
bulldozer	Trax (D: Bagger, Schaufellader)	bulldozer, excavator
bulletin blanc	leerer Wahlzettel, leerer Stimmzettel	blank ballot
bulletin de commande	Bestelltalon	order form
bulletin de souscription (art. 652 CO)	Zeichnungsschein	subscription form
bulletin de versement (F : mandat-poste)	Einzahlungsschein (D: Zahlkarte)	giro transfer form
bulletin de vote	Stimmzettel	ballot
bulletin électoral	Wahlzettel	ballot
Bulletin officiel de l'Assemblée fédérale (BO)	Amtliches Bulletin der Bundesversammlung (Amtl. Bull.; AB)	Official Bulletin of the Federal Assembly
bulletin scolaire	Schulzeugnis	report card
bureau	Sekretariat	presiding officers (at a meeting)
Bureau de communication en matière de blanchiment d'argent (MROS)	Meldestelle für Geldwäscherei (MROS)	Money Laundering Reporting Office Switzerland (MROS)
Bureau de l'Assemblée fédérale	Büro der Vereinigten Bundesversammlung	Office of the United Federal Assembly
Bureau de l'égalité entre femmes et hommes	Fachstelle für die Gleichstellung von Frauen und Männern	Office for Gender Equality
bureau des impôts	Steueramt	tax office
Bureau du Conseil des États	Büro des Ständerates	Office of the Council of States
Bureau du Conseil national	Büro des Nationalrates	Office of the National Council

bureau électoral	Stimmbüro	polling station
Bureau fédéral de l'égalité entre femmes et hommes (BFEG)	Eidgenössisches Büro für die Gleichstellung von Frau und Mann (EBG)	Federal Office for Gender Equality
Bureau fédéral de l'égalité pour les personnes handicapées (BFEG)	Eidgenössisches Büro für die Gleichstellung von Menschen mit Behinderungen (EBGB)	Federal Office for the Equality of People with Disabilities
Bureau National Suisse d'Assurance (BNA)	Nationales Versicherungsbüro Schweiz (NVB)	Swiss National Bureau of Insurance
but	Zweck (D: Gegenstand)	purpose (of a company or partnership)
but de bienfaisance	wohltätiger Zweck	charitable purpose
cabinet d'avocats	Advokaturbüro (D: Anwaltskanzlei)	law firm
cadastre	Kataster	cadaster
cadastre de bruit	Lärmbelastungskataster	register of noise pollution
cadastre des sites pollués	Kataster der belasteten Standorte	register of polluted sites
cadre	Kadermitarbeiter	management employee
caducité du séquestre (art. 280 LP)	Dahinfallen des Arrests	lapsing of the attachment
cahier des charges	Pflichtenheft	performance specifications
caisse de chômage	Arbeitslosenkasse	unemployment office
caisse de compensation	Ausgleichskasse	pension fund
caisse de compensation AVS	AHV-Ausgleichskasse	old age and survivors insurance compensation fund
Caisse de compensation fédérale (CFC)	Eidgenössische Ausgleichskasse (EAK)	Federal Compensation Office
caisse d'épargne	Sparkasse	savings bank
caisse des dépôts et consignations (art. 9, 24, 264 al. 3 et 329 al. 1 LP)	Depositenanstalt	deposit and consignment office
caisse du tribunal	Gerichtskasse	court cashier's office
caisse du tribunal de district	Bezirksgerichtskasse	office of the district court cashier
Caisse fédérale de pensions (PUBLICA)	Pensionskasse des Bundes (PUBLICA)	Federal Pension Fund
caisse maladie	Krankenkasse	health insurance
Caisse suisse de compensation	Schweizerische Ausgleichskasse	Swiss Compensation Office
caissier	Kassier (D: Kassierer)	treasurer; cashier
calamité publique (art. 62 LP)	Landesunglück	public calamity

calcul	Berechnung	calculation
calcul de la contribution causale	Bemessung der Kausalabgabe	calculation of tax for services rendered
calcul de l'impôt	Steuermass	calculation of the tax
calcul des dommages-intérêts	Schadenberechnung	calculation of damages
calcul du délai	Fristberechnung	calculation of the deadline, calculation of the time limit
calculer	berechnen	to calculate
calomnie (art. 174 CP)	Verleumdung	intentional defamation
campagne	Abstimmungskampf	campaign
campagne électorale	Wahlkampf	electoral campaign
cancellation	Entkräftung	cancellation
candidature multiple	Mehrfachkandidatur	multiple candidacy
canton	Stand, Kanton	canton
capacité civique active (droit de vote)	aktives Wahlrecht	right to vote
capacité civique passive (éligibilité)	passives Wahlrecht	right to be elected
capacité de conduire	Fahrfähigkeit	driving ability, ability to drive
capacité de crédit	Kreditfähigkeit	creditworthiness
capacité de discernement (art. 16 CC)	Urteilsfähigkeit	discernment, capacity to make rational decisions
capacité de disposer (art. 457 CC)	Verfügungsfähigkeit	testamentary capacity
capacité de prendre part aux débats (art. 114 CPP)	Verhandlungsfähigkeit	fitness to plead
capacité de risque	Risikofähigkeit	risk capability
capacité de s'obliger par effet de change	Wechselfähigkeit	ability to draw or accept bills of exchange
capacité de témoigner (art. 163 CPP)	Zeugnisfähigkeit	capacity to testify
capacité de travail partielle	Teilarbeitsfähigkeit	partial disability
capacité délictuelle	Deliktsfähigkeit	capacity to commit a tort
capacité d'ester en justice (art. 67 CPC, art. 106 CPP)	Prozessfähigkeit	capacity to act, capacity to take legal action
capacité d'être partie (art. 66 CPC)	Parteifähigkeit	capacity to be a party
capacité matrimoniale (art. 94 CC)	Ehefähigkeit	capacity to marry

capital-actions (F : capital social)	Aktienkapital (D: Grundkapital)	share capital, capital stock
capital en cas de décès	Todesfallkapital	capital sum payable upon death
capital-participation (art. 656b CO)	Partizipationskapital	participation certificate capital
capital risque	Risikokapital	venture capital
capital social	Gesellschaftskapital	share capital
capital-vieillesse	Alterskapital	endowment sum for old age
capitale fédérale	Bundesstadt (D: Bundeshauptstadt)	federal capital
capitalisation de marché	Marktkapitalisierung	market capitalization
capitaux étrangers à court terme	kurzfristiges Fremdkapital	short-term liabilities
captation de suffrages (art. CP 282bis)	Stimmenfang	vote catching
caractère extraordinaire	Ausserordentlichkeit	exceptionality
caractère odieux	Verwerflichkeit	reprehensibility
caractère onéreux	Entgeltlichkeit	compensation, consideration
cartable	Schulsack (D: Ranzen)	school bag
carte civique	Stimmrechtsausweis	voter registration card
carte de crédit	Kreditkarte	credit card
carte d'étudiant	Legitimationskarte (D: Studentenausweis)	student ID
carte d'identité	Identitätskarte (D: Personalausweis)	identity card
carte grise	Immatrikulation	vehicle registration
cartel	Kartell	cartel
cas d'assurance	Versicherungsfall	insured event
cas de décès	Todesfall	event of death
cas de maladie	Krankheitsfall	case of illness
cas de préemption (art. 216c CO)	Vorkaufsfall	right of first refusal event
cas de protection juridique	Rechtsschutzfall	insured event
cas de rigueur	Härtefall	hardship case
cas de séquestre (art. 271 LP)	Arrestgrund	ground for attaching assets
cas par cas	Einzelfallweise	on a case-by-case basis
case postale (F : boîte postale)	Postfach	post office box
casier judiciaire (art. 365-371a CP)	Strafregister	criminal record
catalogue de prestations	Leistungskatalog	list of insurance benefits
causalité	Kausalität	causation

causalité adéquate	adäquate Kausalität	proximate cause
causalité naturelle	natürliche Kausalität	necessary causation
cause de divorce	Scheidungsgrund	ground for divorce
caution	Bürge	guarantor
cautionnement (art. 492-512 CO)	Bürgschaft	surety
cautionnement bancaire	Bankbürgschaft	bank guaranty
cautionnement conjoint (art. 497 CO)	Mitbürgschaft	co-surety
cautionnement de soumission	Offertgarantie	bid bond
cautionnement indépendant (art. 497 CO)	Nebenbürgschaft	independent surety
cautionnement pour le découvert	Schadlosbürgschaft	conditional surety
cautionnement préventif (art. 66 CP)	Friedensbürgschaft	good behavior bond
cautionnement simple (art. 495 CO)	einfache Bürgschaft	simple surety
cautionnement solidaire (art. 496 CO)	Solidarbürgschaft	joint and several surety
cédant	Zedent	transferor, assignor
cédule hypothécaire (art. 842 ss CC)	Schuldbrief	mortgage note (a written promise to repay a mortgage loan plus interest)
célation de biens	Vermögensverheimlichung	concealment of assets
célébration du mariage	Trauung	wedding ceremony
censure	Zensur	censorship
centime	Rappen	cent
centrale de compensation	zentrale Ausgleichsstelle	clearing house
Centrale des voyages de la Confédération (CVC)	Bundesreisezentrale (BRZ)	Swiss Government Travel Centre
Centrale nationale d'alarme (CCENAL)	Nationale Alarmzentrale (NAZ)	National Emergency Operations Center
centre de distribution	Verteilerzentrum	distribution center
centre de réadaptation	Eingliederungsstätte	rehabilitation center
centre d'enregistrement et de procédure (art. 26 LAsi)	Empfangs- und Verfahrenszentrum	reception and processing center
Centre fédéral de situation (CFS)	Bundeslagezentrum (BLZ)	National Intelligence Centre
certificat d'actions	Aktienzertifikat (D: Aktienurkunde)	share certificate, stock certificate
certificat d'assurance	Versicherungsausweis, Versicherungsschein	certificate of insurance
certificat de bonne vie et mœurs	Leumundszeugnis	character reference

certificat de capacité	Fähigkeitsausweis (D: Gesellenbrief)	certificate of qualification (for passing final examination in apprenticeship)
certificat de décès	Todesbescheinigung	death certificate
certificat de dépôt	Lagerschein	warehouse receipt
certificat de domicile	Niederlassungsausweis	certificate of residence
certificat de famille	Familienausweis (D: Familienstammbuch)	family certificate
certificat de mariage	Eheschein (D: Heiratsurkunde)	marriage certificate
certificat de maturité	Maturitätsausweis, Maturitätszeugnis	certificate of passing the high school graduation exam
certificat de prévoyance	Vorsorgeausweis	pension statement
certificat de travail	Arbeitszeugnis	certificate of employment
certificat d'héritier	Erbbescheinigung	certificate of inheritance
certificat d'importation	Einfuhrzertifikat	import certificate
certificat d'insuffisance de gage	Pfandausfallschein	insufficient pledge certificate
certificat global (art. 973b CC)	Globalurkunde	global certificate
certificat intérimaire	Interimsschein	interim certificate
certificateur de caution (art. 498 CO)	Nachbürge, Nachbürgschaft	collateral surety
cessation de l'activité lucrative	Aufgabe der Erwerbstätigkeit	stopping work
cessation de l'exploitation	Ausserbetriebnahme	decommissioning
cessation de paiements	Zahlungseinstellung	insolvency
cessibilité (créance)	Abtretbarkeit	assignability
cession (art. 164 ss CO)	Zession	transfer, assignment
cession contractuelle	Abtretung durch Vertrag	assignment by contract
cession de contrat	Vertragsübernahme	assignment of contract
cession de créance (art. 164 CO)	Abtretung einer Forderung	assignment of a claim
cession des droits de la masse	Abtretung von Rechtsansprüchen der Masse	assignment of the rights of creditors
cession d'un patrimoine ou d'une entreprise (art. 181-183 CO)	Übernahme eines Vermögens oder eines Geschäftes	assignment of assets or a business with assets and liabilities
cession globale	Globalzession	assignment of all outstanding receivables as security for a loan

cession légale	Legalzession, Übergang kraft Gesetzes	transfer by operation of law
cessionnaire	Zessionar	transferee, assignee
chambre	Kammer	chamber (of a court)
chambre de commerce	Handelskammer	chamber of commerce
Chambre de commerce internationale (CCI)	Internationale Handelskammer (IHK)	International Chamber of Commerce (ICC)
chambre de compensation	Abrechnungsstelle	clearing house
chambre des avocats	Anwaltskammer	bar association
Chambre des mineurs	Jugendgerichtskammer	Juvenile Court of Appeals
champ d'application	Geltungsbereich	scope
chancelier d'État	Staatschreiber	official recorder (publicly elected head of cantonal government chancery)
Chancelier fédéral	Bundeskanzler	Federal Chancellor
chancellerie	Kanzlei	office of the court clerk
chancellerie d'État	Staatskanzlei	cantonal government offices
Chancellerie du Tribunal fédéral	Bundesgerichtskanzlei	Chancellery of the Federal Supreme Court
Chancellerie fédérale (ChF)	Bundeskanzlei (BK)	Federal Chancellery
chancellerie municipale	Gemeindekanzlei	municipal chancellery
changement de créancier (art. 77 LP)	Gläubigerwechsel	change of creditor
changement de débiteur	Schuldnerwechsel	change of debtor
changement de domicile	Wohnsitzwechsel	change of domicile
changement de profession	Berufswechsel	change of profession
chantage (art. 156 CP)	Erpressung	extortion, blackmail
charge (obligation)	Auflage (Verpflichtung)	condition
charge de la preuve	Beweislast	burden of proof, onus probandi
charge du sol en polluants	Bodenbelastung	soil pollution
charge fiscale	Steuerbelastung	tax burden
charge foncière (art. 782-792 CC)	Grundlast	real estate charge
charge neutre	neutraler Aufwand	non-operating expense
charge publique	öffentliches Amt	public office
chargement de marchandises	Güterumschlag	handling of goods, cargo handling
charges commerciales	geschäftlicher Aufwand	business expenses
charges d'exploitation	Betriebsaufwand	operating expenses
charges financières	Finanzaufwand	finance expenses

charges hors exploitation	betriebsfremder Aufwand	nonoperating expenses
charges sociales	Sozialabgaben	social security contributions
chauffage à distance	Fernheizung	district heating
chef de chantier	Bauführer	construction site manager
chef de famille	Familienhaupt	head of the family
chef des finances	Finanzchef	chief financial officer (CFO)
chef d'état	Staatsoberhaupt	head of state
Chemins de fer suisses (CSS)	Schweizerische Eisenbahnen (SBB)	Swiss Railroads
chèque (art. 1100 ss CO, art. 177 LP)	Check (D: Scheck)	check
chèque à barrement général (art. 1124 CO)	allgemein gekreuzter Check	generally crossed check
chèque à barrement spécial (art. 1124 CO)	besonders gekreuzter Check	specially crossed check
chèque à porter en compte (art. 1123 CO)	Verrechnungscheck	account-payee-only check
chèque bancaire	Bankcheck	bank check
chèque barré (art. 1123 CO)	gekreuzter Check	crossed check
chèque domicilié (art. 1107 CO)	Domizilcheck	domiciled check
chèque falsifié (art. 1132 CO)	gefälschter Check	forged check
chèque postal	Postcheck	postal check
chiffre d'affaires	Umsatz	revenue, sales
chiffre marginal	Randziffer	margin number
chirographaire	nicht gesichert	unsecured
chômage	Arbeitslosigkeit	unemployment
chômage complet	Ganzarbeitslosigkeit	full unemployment
chômage partiel	Teilarbeitslosigkeit	partial unemployment
chose	Sache	thing, item
chose accessoire (art. 644 CC)	Zugehör	accessory
chose assurée	versicherte Sache	insured item
chose confiée	anvertraute Sache	entrusted item of property
chose consomptible	verbrauchbare Sache	consumables
chose de genre	Gattungssache	type of thing
chose de peu de valeur (art. 138 et 142 CP)	Sache von geringem Wert (D: geringwertige Sache)	low-value item
chose divisible	teilbare Sache	divisible thing
chose fongible	vertretbare Sache	fungible thing

chose hors commerce	nichtverkehrsfähige Sache	thing not subject to contract or exchange (such as the human body)
chose jugée	Rechtskraft	res judicata
chose louée	Mietsache	rented premises, demised premises
chose mobilière	bewegliche Sache	chattel, movable property
chose perdue ou volée	abhanden gekommene Sache	lost or stolen item
chose sans maître (art. 664 CC)	herrenlose Sache	res nullius
chose trouvée	Fund	find
chose vendue	Kaufsache (D: Kaufgegenstand)	item sold
choses formant l'objet du contrat de commission (art. 426 CO)	Kommissionsgut	goods for sale on commission
circonscription électorale	Wahlbezirk, Wahlkreis	voting district
circonstance aggravante (art. 184 CP)	Straferhöhungsgrund, Strafschärfungsgrund	aggravating circumstance (justifying the imposing of a harsher sentence)
circonstance atténuante	Strafmilderungsgrund	mitigating circumstance (justifying the imposing of a lesser sentence)
circonstances locales	örtliche Verhältnisse	local circumstances
circonstances personnelles (art. 27 CP)	persönliche Verhältnisse	personal circumstances
circulaire	Kreisschreiben	circular
circulation en file	Kolonnenverkehr	line of traffic
circulation routière	Strassenverkehr (D: Straßenverkehr)	road traffic
circulation sans permis de circulation	Fahren ohne Fahrzeugausweis	driving without a vehicle title
circulation sans permis de conduire	Fahren ohne Führerausweis	driving without a license
citation (art. 170 CPC)	Vorladung	summons
citoyen actif	Aktivbürger	citizen who is eligible to vote
classement (zone)	Einzonung	zoning
classement de la procédure (art. 319 CPP)	Einstellung des Verfahrens	abandonment of the proceedings
classement d'un projet d'acte	Abschreibung eines Entlassentwurfes	abandoning a bill

classement d'une intervention	Abschreibung eines Vorstosses	abandoning a procedural request
classeur à levier	Bundesordner (D: Leitz-Ordner)	ring binder
clause à ordre	Ordreklausel	order clause
clause contractuelle	Vertragsklausel	contract clause
clause de la nation la plus favorisée	Meistbegünstigungsklausel	MFN clause, most favored nation clause
clause de retrait	Rückzugsklausel	withdrawal clause
clause de valeur réelle	Sachwertklausel	material value clause
clause d'élection de for (F : clause attributive de compétence)	Gerichtsstandsklausel	forum selection clause
clause d'exclusion des héritiers	Erbenausschlussklause	heir exclusion clause
clause exclusive de responsabilité	Wegbedingung der Haftung	disclaimer of liability
clause non à ordre	Rektaklausel	not-to-order clause
clause obligationnelle	schuldrechtliche Bestimmung	obligation clause
clause pénale (art. 160 CO)	Konventionalstrafe (D: Vertragsstrafe)	liquidated damages
clé de signature (art. 59a CO)	Signaturschlüssel	signature key
clés en main	schlussfertig (D: schlüsselfertig)	turnkey
clientèle	Kundschaft	clientele
clôture	Einfriedung	fence, enclosure
clôture de la procédure d'entraide	Abschluss des Rechtshilfeverfahrens	completion of the mutual assistance procedure
coauteur (1)	Mittäter	co-offender
coauteur (2)	Miturheber	coauthor
cobailleur	Mitvermieter	colandlord
Code civil	Zivilgesetzbuch (ZGB) (D: Bürgerliches Gesetzbuch)	Civil Code
Code de procédure administrative cantonal	Kantonales Verwaltungsrechtspflegegesetz	Cantonal Code of Administrative Procedure
Code de procédure civile (CPC)	Zivilprozessordnung (ZPO)	Code of Civil Procedure
Code de procédure pénale suisse (CPP)	Schweizerische Strafprozessordnung (StPO)	Swiss Criminal Procedure Code
Code des frais de construction (CFC)	Baukostenplan (BKP)	construction cost budget
Code des obligations (CO) PG = partie générale PS = partie spéciale	Obligationenrecht (OR) AT = allgemeiner Teil BT = besonderer Teil	Code of Obligations general part special part
Code pénal (CP)	Strafgesetzbuch (StGB)	Criminal Code
Code pénal militaire (CPM)	Militärstrafgesetz (MStG)	Military Criminal Code

codébiteurs	Mitschuldner	joint debtors
codicille	Nachtrag	codicil (to a will)
coexistence pacifique	friedliche Koexistenz	peaceful coexistence
coffre-fort	Tresor	safe
collaborateur	Mitarbeiter	employee
collaborateur libre	freier Mitarbeiter	independent contractor
collaboration	Zusammenarbeit	cooperation
collectivité publique	Gemeinwesen	public authority
collège de cinq juges	Fünferbesetzung der Kammer	presence of five judges on the bench
collège présidentiel (art. 34 LParl)	Präsidium	presiding college
collocation (art. 247 ss LP)	Kollokation, Kollozierung	schedule of admission of the accepted claims
colocataire	Mitmieter	cotenant
colportage	Hausieren	peddling, door-to-door selling
combles	Dachgeschoss	top floor, attic floor
comité	Ausschuss, Komitee	committee
comité de contrôle	Prüfungsausschuss	audit committee
comité de nomination	Nominationsausschuss	nominating committee
comité de rémunération	Vergütungsausschuss	compensation committee
commande	Bestellung	order
commandement de payer (art. 69 ss LP)	Zahlungsbefehl	order to pay (beginning of debt collection)
commanditaire (art. 600 CO)	Kommanditär (D: Kommanditist)	limited partner
commandite (art. 609 CO)	Kommanditsumme	limited partner's contribution
commencement de preuve	Glaubhaftmachung	presentation of prima facie evidence
commencer à faire la preuve	glaubhaft machen	to present prima facie evidence (in order to obtain preliminary injunctive relief)
commentaire (1) (ouvrage)	Kommentar (Werk)	commentary
commentaire (2) (remarque)	Kommentar (Bemerkung)	comment
commerçant	Kaufmann	merchant
commerce d'armes	Waffenhandel	arms trade
commerce de détail	Detailhandel, Kleinhandel (D: Einzelhandel)	retail trade
commerce de stupéfiants	Handel mit Betäubungsmitteln	narcotics trade

commerce du bétail (art. 198 CO)	Viehhandel (Art. 198 OR)	livestock trading
commerce extérieur	Aussenhandel (D: Außenhandel)	foreign trade
commercial	geschäftlich	commercial, business-related
commettant (art. 425 CO)	Kommittent	principal
commination de faillite	Konkursandrohung	threat of bankruptcy, threat of insolvency, bankruptcy warning, insolvency warning
commis avec dol éventuel	eventualvorsätzlich	recklessly
commissaire (art. 239 ss et 334 ss LP)	Sachwalter	administrator
commission (art. 425-439 CO)	Kommission	commission contract
Commission administrative	Verwaltungskommission	Administrative Commission (of the Swiss Federal Supreme Court)
Commission de la concurrence	Wettbewerbskommission	Competition Commission
Commission de l'AVS/AI	AHV/IV-Kommission	Old Age and Survivors Insurance Commission
commission de prévoyance	Vorsorgekommission	pension committee
commission de recours	Rekurskommission	appeals commission
Commission de recours en matière de douane (CRD)	Zollrekurskommission (ZRK)	Customs Appeals Commission
commission de surveillance (art. 237 al. 3 LP)	Gläubigerausschuss	supervisory commission
commission d'émission	Ausgabekommission	issuing commission
Commission d'enquête parlementaire (CEP)	parlamentarische Untersuchungskommission (PUK)	parliamentary investigation committee
Commission des OPA (COPA)	Übernahmekommission (UEK)	Swiss Takeover Board
Commission des professions médicales (MEBEKO)	Medizinalberufekommission (MEBEKO)	Commission for Medical Professions
commission d'estimation	Schätzungskommission	valuation committee
Commission d'estimation en matière d'expropriation	Schätzungskommission für die Enteignung	Compulsory Purchase Tribunal
commission d'éthique	Ethikkommission	ethics commission
Commission d'examen des avocats	Advokatenprüfungsbehörde	Lawyers Examination Board
commission disciplinaire	Disziplinarkommission	disciplinary commission

Commission du Tribunal des mineurs	Jugendgerichtskommission	Juvenile Court Commission
commission extraparlementaire	ausserparlamentarische Kommission	extraparliamentary committee
Commission fédérale de la formation professionnelle (CFFP)	Eidgenössische Berufsbildungskommission (EBBK)	Federal Commission for Vocational and Professional Education and Training
Commission fédérale de la maturité professionnelle (CFMP)	Eidgenössische Berufsmaturitätskommission (EBMK)	Federal Vocational Baccalaureate Commission
Commission fédérale des médicaments (CFM)	Eidgenössische Arzneimittelkommission (EAK)	Federal Medicines Commission
Commission fédérale du design (CFD)	Eidgenössische Designkommission (EDnK)	Federal Design Commission
Commission fédérale pour les problèmes liés à l'alcool (CFAL)	Eidgenössische Kommission für Alkoholfragen (EKAL)	Federal Commission for Alcohol-Related Issues
Commission fédérale pour les problèmes liés aux drogues (CFPD)	Eidgenössiche Kommission für Drogenfragen (EKDF)	Federal Commission for Drug-Related Issues
commission forfaitaire de gestion	pauschale Verwaltungskommission	all-in fee
commission rogatoire	Rechtshilfeersuchen	letters rogatory
commission scolaire	Schulpflege	school board
commission thématique	Sachbereichskommission	specialized committee
commissionnaire	Kommissionär	commission agent
commissionnaire en matière de vente (art. 425 CO)	Verkaufskommissionär	selling commission agent
commissionnaire-expéditeur	Spediteur	forwarding agent
communauté de biens (art. 221-246 CC)	Gütergemeinschaft	community property
communauté des copropriétaires	Miteigentümergemeinschaft	community of co-owners
communauté des créanciers	Gläubigergemeinschaft	community of creditors
communauté des propriétaires par étages (art. 712a ss CC, art. 46 al. 4 LP)	Gemeinschaft der Stockwerkeigentümer, Stockwerkeigentümergemeinschaft	community of condominium owners
communauté héréditaire	Erbengemeinschaft	community of heirs
communauté universelle	allgemeine Gütergemeinschaft	general community of property
commune (art. 50 CF)	Gemeinde	municipality
commune bourgeoise	Bürgergemeinde	citizens' community

commune d'origine	Heimatgemeinde	municipality of origin
communiqué de presse	Pressemitteilung	press release
communiste (art. 653 CC)	Gesamteigentümer	collective owner
comparaison des coûts	Kostenvergleich	cost comparison
comparaison des prix	Preisvergleich	price comparison
compartiment	Subfonds	subfund, compartment
compartiment de coffre-fort	Schrankfach	safe deposit box
comparution personnelle	persönliches Erscheinen	personal appearance
compensation	Abrechnung	clearing
compensation de créances (art. 120-126 CO)	Verrechnung	offset
compensation de la différence	Differenzausgleich	offset of the difference
compensation des dépens	Wettschlagen der Parteikosten (D: Kostenaufhebung)	each party paying his own costs
compensation du renchérissement	Teuerungsausgleich	adjustment (of wages and pensions) for inflation
compensation d'une amende	Abverdienen einer Busse (D: Buße)	working off of a fine
compensation écologique	ökologischer Ausgleich	ecological compensation
compenser les dépens	wettschlagen: Die Parteikosten werden wettgeschlagen. (D: Die Parteikosten werden gegeneinander aufgerechnet).	Each party pays his own costs.
compétence	Zuständigkeit	jurisdiction
compétence à raison de la fonction (art. 4 CPC)	funktionelle Zuständigkeit	functional jurisdiction
compétence à raison de la matière (art. 4 CPC)	sachliche Zuständigkeit	subject matter jurisdiction
compétence à raison du lieu (art. 9 ss CPC)	örtliche Zuständigkeit	territorial jurisdiction
compétence d'autoriser les dépenses	Ausgabenbewilligungs-kompetenz	authority to authorize expenses
compétence de la compétence	Kompetenz-Kompetenz	power of a court or tribunal to decide questions concerning its own jurisdiction
compétence directe	direkte Zuständigkeit	direct jurisdiction
compétence exclusive	ausschliessliche Zuständigkeit	exclusive jurisdiction
compétence impérative	zwingende Zuständigkeit	mandatory jurisdiction
compétence matérielle (art. 4 CPC, art. 22 ss CPP)	sachliche Zuständigkeit	subject matter jurisdiction
compétence ratione loci (art. 9 ss CPC)	örtliche Zuständigkeit	territorial jurisdiction

compétence ratione materiae	sachliche Zuständigkeit	subject matter jurisdiction
compétence spéciale	besondere Zuständigkeit	special jurisdiction
complicité (art. 25 CP)	Gehilfenschaft	complicity
comportement dilatoire	trölerisches Verhalten	dilatory conduct
comportement irrespectueux	ungebührliches Benehmen	disorderly conduct
comportement sur le marché	Marktverhalten	market conduct
composition du tribunal	Zusammensetzung des Gerichts	composition of the court
comptabilisation erronée	Buchungsfehler	accounting error
comptabilité	Buchhaltung	accounting, bookkeeping
comptabilité commerciale (art. 957 CO)	kaufmännische Buchführung	commercial accounting
comptabilité financière (COFI)	Finanzbuchhaltung (FIBU)	financial accounting
comptable	Buchhalter, Rechnungsführer	accountant, bookkeeper
compte bancaire	Bankkonto	bank account
compte bloqué	Sperrkonto	blocked account
compte courant	Kontokorrent	checking account
compte de libre passage	Freizügigkeitskonto	vested benefits account
compte de profits et pertes	Erfolgsrechnung (D: G.u.V.-Rechnung)	income statement
compte d'épargne	Sparkonto	savings account
compte final	Schlussrechnung	final account
compte individuel	individuelles Konto	individual account
compte numéroté	Nummernkonto	numbered account
comptes annuels	Jahresrechnung (D: Jahresabschluss)	annual financial statements
comptes de groupe	Konzernrechnung (D: Konzernabschluss)	consolidated financial statements
concentration d'entreprises (art. 4 LCart)	Unternehmenszusammen-schluss	combination of enterprises
conception juridique	Rechtsauffassung	legal opinion
concession	Konzession	concession
concessionnaire	Konzessionär	concessionaire
concessionnaire exclusif	Alleinvertreter	sole agent, sole representative
concierge	Abwart (D: Hausmeister)	janitor, caretaker
conciliation	Sühne	conciliation
conclure	abschliessen	to enter into (a contract)

conclusion du contrat	Vertragsabschluss, Abschluss des Vertrages	entry into the contract
conclusion du mariage	Eheschliessung	marriage
conclusions	Rechtsbegehren	prayer for relief, demand for relief
concordat (1) (traité avec le siège apostolique)	Konkordat (Vertrag mit dem Apostolischen Stuhl)	concordat (convention with the Holy See)
concordat (2) (traité entre cantons)	Konkordat (Vertrag zwischen Kantonen)	treaty between cantons
concordat (3) (art. 293 ss LP)	Nachlassvertrag (D: Zwangsvergleich)	debt restructuring agreement
concordat dans la procédure de faillite (art. 332 LP)	Nachlassvertrag im Konkurs	debt restructuring agreement in bankruptcy
concordat judiciaire (art. 171 CP)	gerichtlicher Nachlassvertrag	judicial debt restructuring agreement
concordat ordinaire (art. 314 LP)	ordentlicher Nachlassvertrag	ordinary debt restructuring agreement
concordat par abandon d'actif (art. 317 ss LP)	Nachlassvertrag mit Vermögensabtretung	debt restructuring agreement with assignment of assets
concordat-dividendes	Dividendenvergleich	debt restructuring agreement on dividends
concordat-sursis	Stundungsvergleich	remission debt restructuring agreement
concourir avec	konkurrenzieren (D: mit jemandem oder etwas konkurrieren)	to compete with
concours de requêtes d'extradition	gleichzeitige Auslieferungsgesuche	concurrent extradition requests
concours de responsabilités	Haftungskonkurrenz	joint liability
concours idéal	Idealkonkurrenz	commission of a single act that results in several criminal offenses (multiple offenses committed by one act)
concours réel	Realkonkurrenz	series of offenses prosecuted jointly (one person commits two or more crimes)
concubinage, union libre	Konkubinat	cohabitation
concurrence	Wettbewerb	competition

concurrence déloyale	unlauterer Wettbewerb	unfair competition
concurrent	Konkurrent	competitor
concussion (art. 313 CP)	Gebührenüberforderung	overcharging of taxes
condamnation	Verurteilung	conviction
condamnation avec sursis	bedingte Verurteilung	conviction with suspended sentence
condamné	Verurteilter	convict
condition	Bedingung, Voraussetzung	condition, prerequisite
condition du droit à la prestation d'assurance	Anspruchsvoraussetzung	prerequisite to the right to insurance benefits
condition en suspens	schwebende Bedingung	condition that has not yet occurred
condition potestative	Potestativbedingung (D: Willensbedingung)	discretionary condition
condition résolutoire	Resolutivbedingung (D: auflösende Bedingung)	condition subsequent
condition suspensive	Suspensivbedingung (D: aufschiebende Bedingung)	condition precedent
conditions à l'ouverture de l'action	Prozessvoraussetzungen	procedural requirements
conditions de paiement	Zahlungsbedingungen	payment terms
conditions de travail	Arbeitsbedingungen	working conditions
conditions des enchères	Steigerungsbedingungen	auction terms and conditions
conditions générales du contrat	allgemeine Vertragsbedingungen	general terms and conditions
conducteur	Fahrzeugführer	driver
conducteur de bateau	Schiffsführer	skipper
conduite du procès	Prozessleitung	judicial control of the proceedings
conduite en état d'ivresse	Fahren in angetrunkenem Zustand (FiaZ)	drunk driving
confédération	Eidgenossenschaft, Bund	confederation
Conférence des présidents	Präsidentenkonferenz	Presidents' Conference (of the Swiss Federal Supreme Court)
confinement	Sicherung	containment
confiscation (art. 69, 249 CP)	Einziehung	forfeiture
confisquer	einziehen	to confiscate
conflit armé	bewaffneter Konflikt	armed conflict
conflit collectif du travail	Kollektivarbeitsstreitigkeit	collective bargaining dispute
conflit de compétences	Kompetenzkonflikt	jurisdictional conflict
conflit de lois	Rechtskollision	conflict of laws
conflit d'intérêts	Interessenkonflikt	conflict of interest

conflit mobile	Statutenwechsel	mobile conflict of laws
conformité	Gemässigkeit	compliance, conformity
conformité à la zone	Zonenkonformität	compliance with zoning requirements
confrontation (art. 174 CPC)	Konfrontation	confrontation (of witnesses)
confrontation à un acte d'ordre sexuel (art. 198 CP)	sexuelle Belästigungen	sexual harassment
confronter	gegenüberstellen	to compare
confusion (art. 118 CO)	Vereinigung	merger (of obligations)
congé de maternité	Mutterschaftsurlaub	maternity leave
congé de représailles	Vergeltungskündigung	retaliatory termination (of a lease)
congé-pression	Änderungskündigung	notice of termination pending a change of contract
congé-vente	Congé-Vente-Kündigung	termination of a lease to force the tenant to purchase the premises
conjoint (art. 105 CC)	Ehegatte	spouse
conjoint innocent	schuldloser Ehegatte	innocent spouse
conjoint survivant	überlebender Ehegatte	surviving spouse
conjoncture	Konjunktur	the economy, economic climate, economic conditions, the overall economic picture
connaissances juridiques	Rechtskunde	legal fundamentals (name of a course)
connaissement	Konnossement	bill of lading
connaissement maritime	Seekonnossement	maritime bill of lading
conscience de l'illicéité	Unrechtsbewusstsein	awareness of wrongdoing
conseil bourgeoisial	Bürgergemeinderat	citizens' council
conseil consultatif	Beirat	board of advisors
conseil d'administration (art. 707 CO)	Verwaltungsrat	board of directors
conseil de paroisse	Kirchenpflege	parish council
Conseil des États	Ständerat	Council of States (upper house of the Federal Assembly)
conseil des ministres	Ministerrat	Council of Ministers

Conseil d'État	Regierungsrat	Council of State (government of one of the French-speaking cantons, except for the République et Canton du Jura, whose government is called le Gouvernement)
conseil en placement	Anlageberatung	portfolio management
conseil exécutif	Gemeinderat	municipal council
Conseil fédéral (CF)	Bundesrat (BR) (D: Bundesregierung)	Federal Council
conseil juridique (art. 127 CPP)	Rechtsbeistand	legal advisor (appointed by the accused or the private claimant to safeguard their interests)
Conseil national	Nationalrat	National Council (lower house of the Federal Assembly)
conseiller juridique	Rechtsberater	legal counsel, legal adviser
Conseils fédéraux	Eidgenössische Räte	Federal Councils (the two houses of Parliament, i.e., the National Council and the Council of States)
consentement du lésé	Einwilligung des Verletzten	consent of the injured party
conséquence juridique	Rechtsfolge	legal result
conservateur du registre foncier	Grundbuchführer, Grundbuchverwalter	land registrar
conservation	Aufbewahrung	safekeeping
conservation de la preuve	Beweissicherung	preservation of evidence
conservation des documents	Aktenaufbewahrung	archiving
conservation des données	Datenaufbewahrung	data retention
considérants	Entscheidgründe	grounds for the decisions
considérations	Erwägungen	court's findings (set forth in the decision)
consignataire	Trödler	consignee
consignateur	Vertrödler	consignor
consignation à titre de sûreté	Sicherheitshinterlegung, Hinterlegung sicherheitshalber	escrow, placing in escrow

consignation de loyer	Hinterlegung der Miete	deposit of rent (by tenant when landlord fails to repair defects in the lease premises)
consignation en justice	gerichtliche Hinterlegung	deposit into court
consigne	Depot (D: Flaschenpfand)	deposit
consigne de vote	Abstimmungsparole	voting recommendation
consommateur	Konsument, Verbraucher	consumer
consommation	Konsum	consumption
consommation de stupéfiants	Betäubungsmittelkonsum	consumption of narcotics
consommer	verbrauchen	to consume
consorité (art. 70 CPC)	Streitgenossenschaft	joinder of parties
consorité nécessaire (art. 70 CPC)	notwendige Streitgenossenschaft	necessary joinder
consorité simple (art. 71 CPC)	einfache Streitgenossenschaft	voluntary joinder
consort	Streitgenosse	colitigant
consortium	Konsortium	consortium
constatation des faits	Feststellung des Sachverhaltes, Sachverhaltsfeststellung	establishing the facts of the case
constatation du retour à meilleure fortune (art. 265a LP)	Feststellung des neuen Vermögens	recognition of an improvement in the debtor's fortune
constituer : Le conseil se constitue lui-même.	konstituieren: Der Verwaltungsrat konstituiert sich selbst.	The board shall organize itself internally [i.e., the directors decide who does what].
constitut possessoire (art. 717 CC)	Erwerb ohne Besitz	acquisition without possession
constitution	Verfassung	constitution
constitution cantonale (art. 51 CF)	Kantonsverfassung (KV)	cantonal constitution
constitution de la société	Gründung der Gesellschaft	organization of a company
constitution de partie civile	Adhäsionsklage	filing a civil action for damages as part of a criminal action
constitution d'un capital	Vermögensbildung	wealth creation
constitution d'un droit réel	Errichtung eines dinglichen Rechts	creation of a right in rem
Constitution fédérale (CF)	Bundesverfassung (BV) (D: Grundgesetz)	Swiss Federal Constitution
constitutionnalité	Verfassungsmässigkeit	constitutionality
construction	Baute (D: Bauwerk)	building

construction à la limite	Grenzanbau	zero lot line building (construction of a building directly on a property line)
construction annexe	Nebenbaute	outbuilding, annex
construction de logements	Wohnungsbau	residential construction
construction en ruines	abbruchreife Baute	condemned building
construction existante	bestehende Baute	existing construction
construction massive	Massivbaute (D: Massivbau)	massive construction
construction mobilière (art. 266b CO)	Fahrnisbaute	movable construction
constructions empiétant sur le fonds d'autrui (art. 674 CC)	überragende Bauten	encroaching buildings, buildings that cross the property line
consultation du dossier	Akteneinsicht	inspection of the record
contamination d'eau potable (art. 234 CP)	Verunreinigung von Trinkwasser	contamination of drinking water
contestation	Bestreitung	challenge
contestation civile (F : litige de droit commun)	Zivilrechtsstreitigkeit	civil dispute
contestation de droit public	öffentlich-rechtliche Streitigkeit	public law dispute
contestation de la compensation (art. 214 LP)	Bestreitung der Verrechnung	challenge to the setoff
contestation de la légitimation	Anfechtung der Ehelicherklärung	contesting a declaration of legitimacy
contestation de la réalisation (art. 132a LP)	Bestreitung der Verwertung	challenge to the realization
contestation de la reconnaissance de l'enfant	Anfechtung der Anerkennung des Kindes	contesting the acknowledgment of the child (born out of wedlock)
contestation de l'état de collocation (art. 148 et 250 LP)	Bestreitung des Kollokationsplans	challenge to the schedule of claims
contestation de l'état des charges	Bestreitung des Lastenverzeichnisses	challenge to the schedule of charges
contestation d'un testament	Anfechtung eines Testaments	challenge of a will, contest of a will
contester	bestreiten	to challenge
continuation de la poursuite (art. 88 LP)	Fortsetzung der Betreibung	continuation of debt collection proceedings

continuation du commerce ou de l'industrie (art. 237 al. 3 LP)	Fortsetzung des Handels oder Gewerbes	continuation of business
contrainte (art. 181 CP)	Nötigung	coercion
contrainte par corps	Schuldhaft	debtor's prison (abolished by Constitution of 1874)
contrainte sexuelle (art. 189 CP)	sexuelle Nötigung	indecent assault
contraire aux pièces	aktenwidrig	contrary to the record, error apparent on the face of the record
contrat	Vertrag	contract, agreement
contrat à terme de marchandises	Warenterminkontrakt	commodity futures
contrat à terme d'instruments financiers	Finanz-Termingeschäft	financial future
contrat à terme sur taux d'intérêt	Zinsterminkontrakt	interest rate future
contrat avec effet de protection envers les tiers	Vertrag mit Schutzwirkung zugunsten Dritter	third-party beneficiary contract
contrat avec soi-même (art. 436 CO)	Selbsteintritt	self-dealing
contrat bilatéral	zweiseitiger Vertrag	bilateral contract
contrat-cadre	Rahmenvertrag	framework agreement
contrat conclu avec des consommateurs	Vertrag mit Konsumenten	consumer contract
contrat d'affacturage	Factoringvertrag	factoring agreement
contrat d'affrètement	Chartervertrag	charter agreement
contrat d'agence (art. 418a ss CO)	Agenturvertrag	agency agreement
contrat d'apprentissage (art. 344a CO)	Lehrvertrag (D: Berufsausbildungsvertrag)	apprenticeship contract
contrat d'assurance	Versicherungsvertrag	insurance policy
contrat de bail	Mietverhältnis	landlord-tenant relationship, tenancy
contrat de cautionnement (art. 492 ss CO)	Bürgschaftsvertrag	contract of surety
contrat de commission	Kommissionsverhältnis	commission agency relationship
contrat de consignation à titre de sûreté	Vertrag auf Hinterlegung Sicherheitshalber	escrow agreement
contrat de constitution de gage	Pfandvertrag	pledge agreement
contrat de construction	Bauwerkvertrag	construction agreement
contrat de consultant	Beratungsvertrag	consultant agreement

contrat de crédit à la consommation	Konsumkreditvertrag	consumer credit agreement
contrat de crédit à la consommation (art. 1 LCC)	Konsumkreditvertrag	consumer credit contract
contrat de dépôt (art. 472-491 CO)	Hinterlegungsvertrag	contract of bailment; deposit agreement
contrat de dépôt bancaire	Depotvertrag	deposit agreement
contrat de droit d'auteur	Urheberrechtsvertrag	copyright agreement
contrat de durée déterminée (F : contrat à durée déterminée	befristeter Vertrag	fixed-term employment agreement
contrat de durée indéterminée (F : contrat à durée indéterminée)	unbefristeter Vertrag	open-ended contract, permanent contract
contrat de franchisage	Franchisevertrag	franchise agreement
contrat de génie civil	Tiefbauvertrag	civil engineering agreement
contrat de gérance d'immeubles	Liegenschaftverwaltungsvertrag	property management agreement
contrat de leasing	Leasingvertrag	leasing agreement
contrat de licence	Lizenzvertrag	license agreement
contrat de mariage	Ehevertrag	prenuptial agreement
contrat de placement collectif	Kollektivanlagevertrag	collective investment agreement
contrat de prestation de services	Dienstleistungsvertrag	contract to provide services
contrat de rente viagère (art. 516-520 CO)	Leibrentenvertrag	life annuity agreement
contrat de représentation exclusive	Alleinvertriebsvertrag	exclusive distribution agreement
contrat de servitude	Dienstbarkeitsvertrag	easement agreement
contrat de soins	Behandlungsvertrag	treatment contract
contrat de sous-traitance	Subunternehmervertrag	subcontracting agreement
contrat de swap	Swapvertrag	swap agreement
contrat de transport de marchandises (art. 440-457 CO)	Frachtvertrag	contract of carriage
contrat de travail (art. 319-362 CO)	Arbeitsvertrag	employment agreement
contrat de travail à domicile (art. 351 CO)	Heimarbeitsvertrag	work-at-home agreement
contrat de vente (art. 184-221 CO)	Kaufvertrag	sales agreement
contrat de vente par acomptes	Abzahlungsvertrag	installment sales agreement

contrat de vente par livraisons successives	Sukzessivlieferungsvertrag	multiple delivery contract
contrat d'échange	Tauschvertrag	barter agreement
contrat d'édition (art. 380-393 CO)	Verlagsvertrag	publishing agreement
contrat d'engagement des voyageurs de commerce	Handelsreisendervertrag	traveling salesman agreement
contrat d'enseignement à distance	Fernunterrichtsvertrag	distance learning agreement
contrat d'entrepôt (art. 482 CO)	Lagergeschäft	warehousing
contrat d'entreprise (art. 363-379 CO)	Werkvertrag	contract for work and services
contrat d'entreprise générale	Generalunternehmervertrag	general contractor agreement
contrat d'entreprise totale (F : contrat clés en main)	Totalunternehmervertrag	turnkey contract
contrat d'entretien	Wartungsvertrag	maintenance agreement
contrat d'entretien viager (art. 516-529 CO)	Verpfründungsvertrag	lifelong support agreement
contrat d'épargne-logement	Bausparvertrag	building loan agreement
contrat d'expédition (art. 439 CO)	Speditionsvertrag	forwarding contract
contrat d'institution d'héritier (art. 494 CC)	Erbeinsetzungsvertrag	contract appointing heirs
contrat estimatoire	Trödelvertrag	agreement to sell on commission
contrat fiduciaire	Treuhandvertrag	fiduciary agreement, trust agreement, escrow agreement
contrat individuel de travail	Einzelarbeitsvertrag	(individual) employment agreement (as opposed to a collective bargaining agreement)
contrat innommé	Innominatvertrag (D: atypischer Vertrag)	innominate contract (one not provided for by the code)
contrat nommé	Nominatvertrag (D: typischer Vertrag)	nominate contract (one provided for by the code)
contrat possessoire	Besitzvertrag	possessory contract
contrat réel	dinglicher Vertrag	contract related to real property rights

contrat-type de travail (CTT)	Normalarbeitsvertrag (NAV)	standard form employment agreement
contrat unilatéral	einseitiger Vertrag	unilateral contract
contravention (art. 103, 106 CP)	Übertretung	infraction (The punishment for an infraction is an *amende*, generally in the amount of 10,000 francs).
contre-épreuve	Gegenmehr	votes against something
contre-offre	Gegenangebot, Gegenofferte	counteroffer
contre-prestation	Entgelt, Gegenleistung	consideration, good and valuable consideration
contre-projet direct	direkter Gegenentwurf	direct counterproposal
contre remboursement	per Nachnahme	cash on delivery (COD)
contrepartie centrale (art. 48 LIMF)	zentrale Gegenpartei	central counterparty
contribuable	Steuerpflichtiger, Abgabepflichtiger	taxpayer
contribution aux frais de déplacement	Pendlerkostenbeitrag	commuting costs contribution
contribution aux frais de soins	Pflegebeitrag	contribution to the costs of care
contribution causale	Kausalabgabe	tax for services rendered
contribution de remplacement	Ersatzabgabe	exemption tax (e.g. tax payable by people who are exempted from military or fire brigade service)
contribution d'estivage	Sömmerungsbeitrag	summer grazing contribution
contribution ecclésiastique	Kirchensteuer	church tax
contribution écologique	öko-Beitrag	ecological contribution
contributions publiques	öffentliche Abgaben	public levies
contrôle	Revision	audit
contrôle antidopage	Dopingkontrolle	anti-doping control
contrôle des marchandises	Warenprüfung	inspection of goods, inspection of merchandise
contrôle des normes	Normenkontrolle	judicial review
contrôle des prix	Preiskontrolle	price control
Contrôle fédéral des finances (CDF)	Eidgenössische Finanzkontrolle (EFK)	Swiss Federal Audit Office

contrôle ordinaire (art. 728 CO)	ordentliche Revision	ordinary audit
Contrôle parlementaire de l'administration (CPA)	parlamentarische Verwaltungskontrolle (PVK)	parliamentary control of the administration
contrôle restreint (art. 727a CO)	eingeschränkte Revision	limited audit
contrôleur	Kondukteur (D: Schaffner)	ticket collector
convention	Vereinbarung	agreement
Convention alpine	Alpenkonvention	Alpine Convention (international treaty between the Alpine countries (Austria, France, Germany, Italy, Liechtenstein, Monaco, Slovenia and Switzerland) and the EU, aimed at promoting sustainable development in the Alpine area and at protecting the interests of its inhabitants)
convention collective de travail	Gesamtarbeitsvertrag (GAV) (D: Tarifvertrag)	collective bargaining agreement
Convention concernant la compétence judiciaire, la reconnaissance et l'exécution des décisions en matière civile et commerciale (Convention de Lugano, CL)	Übereinkommen über die gerichtliche Zuständigkeit und die Anerkennung und Vollstreckung von Entscheidungen in Zivil- und Handelssachen (Lugano-Übereinkommen, LugÜ)	Convention on jurisdiction and the recognition and enforcement of judgments in civil and commercial matters (Lugano Convention)
Convention concernant la distribution des signaux porteurs de programmes	Übereinkommen über die Verbreitung der Programmtragenden	Convention relating to the Distribution of Programme-Carrying Signals Transmitted by Satellite
Convention concernant les congés payés dans l'agriculture	Übereinkommen über den bezahlten Urlaub in der Landwirtschaft	Holidays with Pay (Agriculture) Convention
Convention concernant l'interdiction des pires formes de travail des enfants	Übereinkommen über das Verbot der schlimmsten Formen der Kinderarbeit	Worst Forms of Child Labor Convention
Convention contre la criminalité transnationale organisée	Übereinkommen gegen die grenzüberschreitende organisierte Kriminalität	UN Convention against Transnational Organized Crime

convention d'actionnaires	Aktionärbindungsvertrag (ABV)	shareholders' agreement
convention d'arbitrage	Schiedsvereinbarung	arbitration agreement, agreement to arbitrate
Convention d'entraide judiciaire en matière pénale	Übereinkommen über die Rechtshilfe in Strafsachen	European Convention on Mutual Assistance in Criminal Matters
convention intercantonale (art. 48 CF)	Vertrag zwischen Kantonen	intercantonal agreement
conversion (de devises)	Umrechnung	translation of foreign currency
conversion de l'amende	Bussenumwandlung (D: Bußenumwandlung)	conversion of the fine
convocation	Einberufung	convening meeting
convocation de l'assemblée des créanciers (art. 301 LP)	Einberufung der Gläubigerversammlung	notice of the creditor's meeting
convoquer	einberufen	to convene
coobligé (art. 217 al. 1 et 303 al. 1 LP)	Mitverpflichteter	co-obligor
coopération du failli (art. 229 LP)	Mitwirkung des Schuldners	cooperation by the insolvent debtor
cooptation	Ergänzungswahl (D: Zuwahl)	coopting a member to a board
copermutant	Tauschender	party to a barter agreement
copie certifiée conforme	beglaubigte Abschrift	certified copy
copossession	Mitbesitz	joint ownership
copropriétaire	Miteigentümer	co-owner
copropriété (art. 646 CC)	Miteigentum	co-ownership
corporation	Körperschaft	corporate body
corps certain	Speziessache	unique item, specific item (such as a work of art, as opposed to a fungible item)
corps de chauffe (F : radiateur)	Heizkörper	radiator
corps électoral	Stimmvolk	registered voters
Corps suisse d'aide humanitaire (CSA)	Schweizerisches Korps für Humanitäre Hilfe (SKH)	Swiss Humanitarian Aid Unit
correspondance commerciale	Geschäftskorrespondenz	business correspondence
corruption (art. CP 322ter CP)	Bestechung	bribery
corruption active (art. 322ter CP)	Bestechen	bribery (as opposed to taking bribes)

corruption active d'agents publics étrangers (art. 322septies CP)	Bestechung fremder Amtsträger	bribery of foreign public officials
corruption active d'agents publics suisses (art. 322ter CP)	Bestechung schweizerischer Amtsträger	bribery of Swiss public officials
corruption électorale (art. 281 CP)	Wahlbestechung	corrupt electoral practices
corruption passive (art. 322quater CP)	sich bestechen lassen	acceptance of bribes
cotation en bourse	Kotierung (D: Notierung)	listing on the stock exchange
cotation par catégorie	gattungsmässige Kotierung	listing by class
coté en bourse	börsenkotiert (D: börsennotiert)	listed on the stock exchange
coter	kotieren (D: notieren)	to list on the stock exchange
cotisation	Beitrag	contribution
cotisation à la caisse de pensions	Pensionskassenbeitrag	pension fund contribution
cotisation AVS/AI/APG	AHV/IV/EO-Beitrag	contribution to old age and survivors insurance
cotisation de l'employeur	Arbeitgeberbeitrag	employer's contribution (to social security)
cotisation de risque	Risikobeitrag	risk contribution
cotisation du travailleur	Arbeitnehmerbeitrag	employee contribution (to social security)
cotisation paritaire	paritätischer Beitrag	contribution paid in equal shares by employer and employee
coup de force	Zwängerei	blackmail
Cour AELE	EFTA-Gerichtshof	EFTA Court (in Luxembourg)
cour d'appel	Appellationsgericht	court of appeals, appellate court
Cour de cassation pénale	Kassationshof	Court of Criminal Cassation
Cour des affaires pénales	Strafkammer	Criminal Chamber of the Federal Criminal Court
Cour des plaintes du Tribunal pénal fédéral	Beschwerdekammer des Bundesstrafgerichts	Appeals Chamber of the Federal Criminal Court
cour plénière	Gesamtgericht	court sitting en banc

cour suprême	oberstes Gericht	supreme court
cour suprême du canton	Obergericht	cantonal supreme court
courant	kurant	liquid, easily marketable
courrier A	A-Post	mail delivered on the following day
courrier B	B-Post	mail delivered within three business days
cours boursier	Börsenkurs	stock market price
cours de conversion	Umrechnungskurs	translation rate
cours de formation professionnelle	Berufsausbildungskurs	vocational training course
cours de référence	Referenzkurs	reference price (price of the underlying assets on the valuation date in a derivatives transaction)
cours des intérêts (art. 209 LP)	Zinsenlauf	accrual of interest
cours en bourse	Börsenkurs	stock market price
cours fait	Abschlusskurs	trading price
courtage (art. 412-418 CO)	Mäklervertrag (D: Maklervertrag)	brokerage contract
courtier	Courtier, Mäkler (D: Makler)	broker
courtier en crédit (art. 4 LCC)	Kreditvermittler	credit broker
coût de la vie	Lebenskosten	cost of living
coût de portage	Haltekosten	cost of carry
coût de prestations de tiers	Aufwand für Drittleistungen	cost of purchased services
couverture	Deckung	coverage
couverture d'assurance	Versicherungsschutz	insurance coverage
couverture delta	dynamische Absicherung	delta hedging, dynamic hedging
couverture des coûts	Kostenübernahme	coverage of costs
couverture fixe	fixe Absicherung	fixed hedge
couvrir	absichern	to hedge
crainte fondée (F : violence) (art. 29-31 CO)	Furchterregung	duress
créance	Forderung	claim
créance accessoire	Nebenanspruch	accessory claim
créance contestée (art. 305 al. 3, al. 2 et 325 LP)	bestrittene Forderung	contested claim
créance dans la faillite	Konkursforderung	bankruptcy claim, insolvency claim

créance de valeur équivalente (art. 211 al. 1 LP)	Forderung von entsprechendem Wert	claim of equivalent value
créance écartée (art. 248 LP)	abgewiesene Forderung	dismissed claim, rejected claim
créance en poursuite	in Betreibung gesetzte Forderung	claim being enforced
créance future	künftige Forderung	future claim
créance garantie par gage (art. 151 al. 1 LP)	pfandversicherte Forderung, durch Pfand gesicherte Forderung	secured claim
créance garantie par gage mobilier (art. 140 CO)	Fahrnispfandrecht	lien on chattels
créance incontestée	unbestrittene Forderung	uncontested claim
créance inscrite au livre de la dette publique	Schuldbuchforderung	debt register claim (a claim on the state arising from a loan or credit entered in an official register of debt – no securities are issued for such claims; they are recorded solely in the register)
créance inscrite d'office (art. 246 LP)	von Amtes wegen aufgenommene Forderung	automatically registered claim
créance ne portant pas intérêt (art. 208 al. 2 LP)	unverzinsliche Forderung	non-interest-bearing claim
créance non échue (art. 208 al. 2 LP)	nicht verfallene Forderung	unmatured claim, claim not yet due
créance non produite (art. 267 LP)	nicht eingegebene Forderung	unproduced claim
créance privilégiée	privilegierte Forderung	secured claim
créance recouvrable	eintreibbare Forderung	recoverable claim
créance subordonnée à une condition suspensive (art. 131 al. 1 LP)	Forderung unter aufschiebender Bedingung	claim subject to a condition precedent
créancier	Gläubiger	creditor; obligee
créancier d'entretien viager (art. 521 CO)	Pfründer (D: Pfründner), Pfrundnehmer	beneficiary of lifelong support
créancier du failli	Konkursgläubiger	creditor of the bankrupt debtor
créancier d'une rente viagère (art. 516 CO)	Rentengläubiger	annuitant
créancier gagiste	Pfandgläubiger	pledgee
créancier participant	Anschlussgläubiger	participating creditor
créancier personnel	Privatgläubiger	personal creditor
créancier séquestrant	Arrestgläubiger	attaching creditor

crédit	Kredit	credit
crédit contre cession	Zessionskredit	assignment credit (book credit secured by the assignment of existing receivables)
crédit de construction	Baukredit	construction loan
crédit d'engagement	Verpflichtungskredit	guarantee credit (the maximum financial commitment that the Federal Council can make for a specific project)
crédit documentaire	Dokumentenakkreditiv	documentary credit
crédit hypothécaire	Hypothekarkredit (D: Hypothekenkredit)	mortgage loan
crédit saisonnier	Saisonkredit	seasonal loan
crédit supplémentaire et crédit additionnel urgent (art. 28 et 24 LFC)	dringlicher Nachtrags- und Zusatzkredit	emergency amendment and additional credit
créditeurs	Kreditoren	accounts payable
crime	Verbrechen	felony (Swiss law divides offenses into three groups: felonies [*crimes*], misdemeanors [*délits*] and infractions [*contraventions*]. The punishment for a felony is a *peine privative de liberté de plus de 3 ans.*
crime contre l'humanité (art. 264a CP)	Verbrechen gegen die Menschlichkeit	crime against humanity
crime de guerre	Kriegsverbrechen	war crime
crime organisé	organisiertes Verbrechen	organized crime
crimes dans la faillite et la poursuite pour dettes (art. 163 CP)	Betreibungsverbrechen	debt collection felonies
crimes ou délits contre la paix publique (art. 260ter ss. CP)	Verbrechen und Vergehen gegen den öffentlichen Frieden	felonies and crimes against public order
criminalistique	Kriminalistik	forensic science, criminalistics
criminalité économique	Wirtschaftskriminalität	white collar crime
criminalité enregistrée	registrierte Kriminalität	recorded crime
croissance économique	Wirtschaftswachstum	economic growth
cruauté	Grausamkeit	cruelty
cruauté envers les animaux	Tierquälerei	cruelty to animals

culpabilité (art. 14-21 CP)	Schuld	guilt
culture cinématographique (art. 5 LCin)	Filmkultur	film culture
cumul (suffrages)	Kumulieren	accumulating of votes
cumul d'actions (art. 90 CPC)	Klagenhäufung	joinder of actions
cumul officiel	Vorkumulieren	pre-cumulation (entry in duplicate of a candidate's name on a pre-printed ballot paper on the instructions of the candidate's own party)
cura in custodiendo	cura in custodiendo	supervising employees properly
cura in eligendo	cura in eligendo	selecting employees with due care
cura in instruendo	cura in instruendo	training employees properly
curatelle (art. 308 ss, 325 et 390 ss CC)	Beistandschaft (D: Pflegschaft)	curatorship
curatelle d'accompagnement (art. 393 CC)	Begleitbeistandschaft	assistance curatorship
curatelle de coopération (art. 396 CC)	Mitwirkungsbeistandschaft	advisory curatorship
curatelle de gestion (art. 394 CC)	Verwaltungsbeistandschaft	representative curatorship
curatelle de portée générale (art. 398 CC)	umfassende Beistandschaft	general curatorship
curatelle de représentation (art. 394 CC)	Vertretungsbeistandschaft	representative curatorship
curatelle volontaire	Beistandschaft auf eigenes Begehren	voluntary curatorship
curateur (art. 392-393 CC)	Beistand (D: Pfleger)	curator (unlike a guardian, a curator is appointed to deal with a specific matter or to take care of property)
cure de désintoxication	Entziehungskur	withdrawal treatment, detoxification program
curriculum vitae	Lebenslauf	résumé, CV
damnum emergens	damnum emergens	actual loss (as opposed to lost profits)
danger	Gefahr	danger
danger de mort	Lebensgefahr	mortal danger

dans les 30 jours	innert 30 Tagen (D: innerhalb von 30 Tagen)	within 30 days
dans les délais	zeitgerecht	timely
date de détachement	Ex-Dividende-Tag	ex-dividend date
dation en paiement	Hingabe an Erfüllungs Statt, Leistung an Erfüllungs Statt, Leistung an Zahlungs Statt, Leistung erfüllungshalber, Leistung zahlungshalber, Anweisung an Zahlungs Statt	accord and satisfaction
de bonne foi	gutgläubig	in good faith
de cujus	Erblasser	decedent
de réversion	anwartschaftlich	reversionary
de transmissibilité restreinte	vinkuliert	with restricted transferability
débat de groupe réduit	verkürzte Fraktionsdebatte	time-limited group debate
débat d'entrée en matière	Eintretensdebatte	preliminary discussion (to decide whether to pursue a matter further)
débat du tribunal	Gerichtsverhandlung	court hearing
débats d'instruction (art. 226 CPC)	Instruktionsverhandlung	preliminary hearing, pretrial conference
débats principaux (art. 228 ss CPC)	Hauptverhandlung	trial, main hearing
débauchage de travailleurs	Abwerbung von Arbeitnehmern	solicitation of employees
débit de dotation (art. 4 LEaux)	Dotierwassermenge	required water endowment
débit permanent (art. 4 LEaux)	ständige Wasserführung	permanent flow
débit résiduel (art. 4 LEaux)	Restwassermenge	residual flow
débiteur	Schuldner	debtor; obligor
débiteur cédé	Zessus	assigned debtor
débiteur de passage (art. 271 LP)	Schuldner auf der Durchreise	passing debtor
débiteur d'entretien viager (art. 521 CO)	Pfrundgeber	grantor of lifelong support
débiteur d'une rente viagère (art. 516 CO)	Rentenschuldner	grantor of a life annuity
débiteur non soumis à la faillite	Schuldner, der nicht der Konkursbetreibung unterliegt	debtor not subject to bankruptcy proceedings
débiteur poursuivi	Betriebene	debtor (whose debt is being collected)

débiteur saisi	Pfändungsschuldner	debtor whose assets have been seized
débiteur séquestré	Arrestschuldner	attached debtor
débiteurs solidaires	Solidarschuldner (D: Gesamtschuldner)	joint and several debtors, joint and several obligors
débours	Auslagen	expenses
débours de chancellerie	Kanzleiauslagen	expenses incurred by the court (expert fees, travel expenses, witnesses, etc.)
débours nécessaires	notwendige Auslagen	necessary outlays
début de l'activité lucrative	Aufnahme der Erwerbstätigkeit	start date of gainful employment
décharge (F : quitus)	Decharge (D: Entlastung)	"discharge" of the board of directors
décharge pour déchets urbains	Siedlungsabfalldeponie	landfill for domestic waste
déchéance	Verwirkung	forfeiture
déchets	Abfälle	waste
déchets urbains	Siedlungsabfälle	domestic waste
décision	Entscheid (D: Entscheidung), Verfügung	decision
décision au fond	Entscheid zur Hauptsache, Sachentscheid	decision on the merits
décision définitive	rechtskräftiger Entscheid	final non-appealable decision (compare *décision finale*, one which is final in the sense that it puts an end to the proceedings—as opposed to an interlocutory decision—but can then be appealed)
décision d'entrée en matière	Eintretensverfügung	order to hear the case
décision d'extension	Allgemeinverbindlicherklärung	declaration of general application
décision d'homologation du concordat (art. 306 LP)	Bestätigungsentscheid	decision ratifying the debt restructuring agreement
décision d'irrecevabilité	Nichteintretensentscheid	decision of dismissal
décision d'un tribunal international	Entscheidung eines internationalen Gerichts	decision of an international court
décision en constatation	Feststellungsverfügung	declaratory order

décision en constatation de droit	Feststellungsentscheid	declaratory judgment
décision exécutoire	vollstreckbarer Entscheid	enforceable decision
décision finale	Endentscheid	final judgment (one which is final in the sense that it puts an end to the proceedings—as opposed to an interlocutory decision—but can then be appealed; compare *décision définitive*, a final judgment that cannot be appealed)
décision incidente	Zwischenentscheid	interlocutory decision on a procedural issue (as opposed to a *décision préjudicielle*, an interlocutory decision on a substantive issue)
décision incitative	Appellentscheid	court decision asking the legislature to change the law in question
décision judiciaire	Gerichtsentscheid	court decision, judgment
décision partielle	Teilentscheid	partial decision
décision pendente lite	Verfügung pendente lite	interlocutory decision
décision préjudicielle	Vorentscheid	interlocutory decision on a substantive matter
décision présidentielle	Präsidialverfügung	order by the presiding judge
décision prise en matière de révision (art. 68 PA)	Entscheid im Rahmen einer Revision	decision in a review
décision proposée par circulaire (art. 255a al. 1 LP)	Zirkularbeschluss	decision by circular letter
décision qui met fin à la procédure	verfahrensabschliessender Entscheid	final judgment
décision sur les frais (art. 104 CPC)	Kostenentscheid	decision on costs
décision sur opposition (art. 30 al. 2 et 74 PA)	Einspracheentscheid	decision on objections

décision sur recours (art. 61 PA)	Beschwerdeentscheid	appeal decision, decision on appeal
décisions d'instruction (art. 246 CPC)	prozessleitende Verfügungen	procedural rulings
déclaration	Angabe, Erklärung	declaration, statement
déclaration d'absence (art. 21 CPC)	Verschollenerklärung	declaration of presumed death
déclaration de décès (art. 21 CPC)	Todeserklärung	declaration of death
déclaration de faillite	Konkurserkenntnis	declaration of bankruptcy
déclaration de patronage	Patronatserklärung	comfort letter
déclaration de première heure	Aussage der ersten Stunde	statement made immediately after an event
déclaration de reconnaissance	Anerkennungserklärung	acknowledgment of paternity
déclaration de volonté	Willenserklärung	declaration of intent
déclaration d'échéance	Kaduzierung	forfeiture of shares (when shareholder has not paid for new shares or is late in paying for the outstanding portion of existing shares)
déclaration d'exécution	Vollstreckbarerklärung	declaration of enforceability
déclaration d'impôt	Steuererklärung	tax return
déclaration d'insolvabilité (art. 191 LP)	Insolvenzerklärung	declaration of insolvency
déclaration du failli sur l'inventaire (art. 228 LP)	Erklärung des Schuldners zum Inventar	insolvent's statement on the inventory
déclarer	aussagen	to testify
déclassement	Auszonung	dezoning
décompte de bourse	Börsenabrechnung	securities trading statement (statement sent by a bank to its customers when securities are traded)
décompte de primes	Prämienabrechnung	premium statement
découvert en cas de créance garantie gage	Pfandausfallforderung	overdraft in the event of a secured claim
décriminalisation	Entkriminalisierung	decriminalization
décriminaliser	entkriminalisieren	to decriminalize
décryptage	Entschlüsselung	deciphering, decoding
dédit (art. 158 CO)	Reugeld	forfeit money
dédouanement	Zollabfertigung	customs clearance

déduction	Abzug	subtraction, deduction
déduction des frais d'acquisition	Abzug für Gewinnungskosten	deduction of costs of generating income
déduction des frais généraux	Unkostenabzug	deduction of overhead costs
déduction des intérêts passifs	Abzug für Schuldzinsen	deduction of interest on debt
déduction du loyer	Mietzinsabzug	deduction of rent
déduction du revenu	Abzug vom Einkommen	deduction of income
déduction du revenu déterminant	Abzug vom anrechenbaren Einkommen	deduction of creditable income
déduction pour enfant	Kinderabzug	child deduction
déduction pour frais d'entretien d'immeuble	Abzug für Liegenschaftsaufwand	deduction of costs of maintaining the building
défaillant	säumig	in default
défaut (1) (art. 147 CPC, art. 93 CPP)	Säumnis	default, failure to appear
défaut (2)	Mangel	defect
défaut à l'audience des débats principaux	Säumnis an der Hauptverhandlung	failure to attend the main hearing
défaut apparent	offener Mangel	patent defect
défaut caché	geheimer Mangel	latent defect
défaut d'avis en cas de trouvaille (art. 332 CP)	Nichtanzeigen eines Fundes	failure to report a find
défaut de construction	Baumangel	construction defect
défaut de la chose	Sachmangel	quality defect
défaut de paiement	Nichtbezahlung	default
défaut de réponse (art. 223 CPC)	versäumte Klageantwort	failure to file an answer (to the complaint)
défaut d'entretien	mangelhafter Unterhalt	defective maintenance
défaut esthétique	kosmetische Beeinträchtigung	cosmetic defect
défaut manifeste	offensichtlicher Mangel	patent defect
défendeur	Beklagter	defendant
défendeur reconventionnel	Widerbeklagte	counterclaim defendant
défense (art. 128 ss CPP)	Verteidigung	defense, defense lawyer
défense de choix (art. 129 CPP)	Wahlverteidigung	right to choose a defense lawyer
défense d'office (art. 132 CPP)	amtliche Verteidigung	duty defense lawyer
défense excusable (art. 16 CP)	entschuldbare Notwehr	mitigatory self defense

défense nécessaire (art. 130 CPP)	notwendige Verteidigung	mandatory appointment of a defense lawyer
déficit	Rückschlag	deficit
déflation	Deflation	deflation
degré de la preuve	Beweismass	degree of proof
degré de l'incapacité de travail	Arbeitsunfähigkeitsgrad	degree of disability
degré de l'invalidité	Invaliditätsgrad	degree of disability
délai	Frist	deadline, time limit
délai absolu	absolute Frist	absolute deadline
délai de carence d'une année	Karenzjahr	one-year grace period
délai de congé	Kündigungsfrist	notice period, period for giving notice
délai de garde	Aufbewahrungsfrist	minimum period for retaining records
délai de paiement (art. 137 LP)	Zahlungsfrist	payment deadline
délai de production (art. 244 LP)	Eingabefrist	filing deadline
délai de réalisation (art. 154 LP)	Verwertungsfrist	deadline for a sale
délai de recours	Beschwerdefrist, Rechtsmittelfrist	deadline for an appeal
délai d'interdiction	Sperrfrist	proscribed period
délai d'opposition au commandement de payer (art. 74 LP)	Rechtsvorschlagsfrist	deadline for objecting to the order to pay
délai fixé par le juge	richterliche Frist	deadline set by the judge
délai pour intenter action	Klagefrist	time limit for bringing a claim
délai pour la liquidation de la faillite	Frist für die Durchführung des Konkurses	deadline for liquidating the assets in a bankruptcy or insolvency
délai raisonnable	angemessene Frist	reasonable deadline
délais péremptoires (art. 129 CO)	Unabänderlichkeit der Fristen	mandatory limitation periods
délégation	Delegation	delegation
délégation administrative	Verwaltungsdelegation	administrative delegation
délégation de compétence	Zuständigkeitsübertragung	delegation of jurisdiction
délégation de possession (art. 924 al. 1 CC)	Besitzanweisung	transfer of possession with physical delivery

délégué	Delegierter	delegate
Déléguée à l'égalité	Beauftragte für Gleichstellung	Office for Gender Equality
Delémont	Delsberg	Delémont (capital of the canton of Jura)
délibération du tribunal	Gerichtsberatung	court's deliberations
délibérations	Urteilsberatung	court deliberations
délibéré	Beratung zur Urteilsfindung	deliberation
délimitation de compétence	Abgrenzung der Zuständigkeit	delimitation of jurisdiction
délimitation du terrain	Grundstücksabgrenzung	demarcation, delimitation(of land)
délinquance apparente	registrierte Kriminalität	recorded crime
délinquance juvénile	Jugendkriminalität, Jugenddelinquenz	juvenile delinquency
délinquant	Straffälliger	offender, perpetrator
délinquant anormal	geistig Abnormer	mentally ill person
délinquant d'habitude	Gewohnheitsverbrecher	habitual offender
délinquant primaire	Erstverurteilter, erstmaliger Verurteilter	first offender
délit (art. 10 al. 3 CP)	Vergehen	misdemeanor (The punishment for a misdemeanor is a *peine pécuniaire* ou a *peine de liberté n'excédant pas 3 ans*).
délit continu	Dauerdelikt	continuing crime (one whose effects last over a period of time, such as kidnapping)
délit de commission	Begehungsdelikt	crime of commission
délit de fuite (art. 92 al. 2 LCR)	Fahrerflucht	hit and run
délit d'initié	Insiderdelikt	insider trading
délit d'omission (art. 11 CP)	Unterlassungsdelikt	crime of omission
délit économique	Wirtschaftsdelikt	economic offense, white-collar crime
délit formel	Tätigkeitsdelikt	offense that is a crime even without actual harm (such as perjury, or driving without a driver's license, or illegal possession of weapons, all of which are crimes whether they cause harm or not)

délit impossible (art. 23 CP)	untauglicher Versuch	impossible attempt
délit intentionnel	Vorsatzdelikt	intentional offense, offense committed with intent
délit manqué (art. 23 CP)	vollendeter Versuch	completed attempt
délit par négligence	fahrlässiges Vergehen	misdemeanor committed through negligence
délit putatif	Wahndelikt	act wrongly assumed by perpetrator to be criminal
délit successif	fortgesetztes Delikt	continuous offense
délivrance (art. 188 CO)	Übergabe	delivery of possession
délivrance des biens (art. 559 CC)	Auslieferung der Erbschaft	release of the estate
demande (1) (art. 221 CPC)	Klage	complaint
demande (2)	Begehren	petition, motion, application
demande d'asile (art. 18 LAsi)	Asylgesuch	application for asylum
demande de concordat	Nachlassbegehren	application for debt restructuring
demande de divorce	Scheidungsbegehren	divorce petition
demande de mesures provisionnelles	Massnahmebegehren, Massnahmegesuch	petition for a preliminary injunction
demande de permis de construire	Baubewilligungsgesuch	application for a building permit
demande de protection juridique	Rechtsschutzbegehren	relief sought, legal remedy sought
demande de reconsidération	Wiedererwägungsgesuch	motion for reconsideration
demande de rectification	Berichtigungsgesuch	motion to correct the court's decision
demande de récusation (art. 49 CPC, art. 58 CPP)	Ausstandsgesuch	motion to recuse
demande de réparation morale	Gesuch um Genugtuung	application for compensation for pain and suffering
demande de séquestre	Arrestforderung	claim for attachment of assets
demande d'entraide	Rechtshilfegesuch	request for mutual assistance
demande d'indemnisation	Entschädigungsgesuch	application for compensation for financial loss

demande d'indemnisation	Gesuch um Entschädigung	application for compensation for financial loss
demande d'interprétation	Erläuterungsgesuch	motion for an explanation (of the court's decision)
demande en divorce	Klage auf Scheidung	petition for divorce
demande en révision (art. 329 CPC)	Revisionsgesuch	application for a review
demande reconventionnelle (art. 224 CPC)	Widerklage	counterclaim
demandeur	Kläger	plaintiff
demandeur reconventionnel	Widerkläger	counterclaim plaintiff
démarchage à domicile (art. 40a CO)	Haustürgeschäft	door-to-door transaction
déménager	zügeln (D: umziehen)	to move (house)
demeure (art. 102-106 CO, art. 143 LP)	Verzug, Zahlungsverzug	default
demeure du créancier (art. 91 CO)	Gläubigerverzug, Verzug des Gläubigers	default by the obligee
demeure du débiteur (art. 102 CO)	Schuldnerverzug, Verzug des Schuldners	default by the obligor
demi-rente	halbe Rente	half pension
démocratie de concordance	Konkordanzdemokratie	consotiational democracy
déni de justice (art. 17 al. 3 LP)	Rechtsverweigerung	denial of justice
deniers	Gelder	moneys
dénigrement	Anschwärzung	denigration
dénonçant (art. 78 CPC)	Streitverkünder, Litidenunziant	third-party plaintiff (in an impleader)
dénonciation	Strafanzeige	crime report, report to the authorities
dénonciation à l'autorité (art. 301 al. 1 CPP)	Strafanzeige	crime report, report to the authorities
dénonciation à l'autorité de surveillance (art. 71 PA)	Aufsichtsbeschwerde (Art. 71 VwVG)	complaint to the supervisory authority
dénonciation calomnieuse (art. 303 CP)	falsche Anschuldigung	false accusation
dénonciation d'instance (art. 193 CO, art. 78 CPC)	Streitverkündung	impleader (notice of pending litigation and request for litigation support sent by defendant to a third party)

dénonciation spontanée	Selbstanzeige	voluntary disclosure (of tax fraud)
denrée alimentaire	Lebensmittel	food
dénuement	Bedürftigkeit	neediness, poverty, indigence
déontologie	Standesrecht	code of ethics, professional ethics
département	Departement	department
Département fédéral de justice et police (DFJP)	Eidgenössisches Justiz- und Polizeidepartement (EJPD)	Federal Department of Justice and Police
Département fédéral de la défense, de la protection de la population et des sports (DDPS)	Eidgenössisches Departement für Verteidigung, Bevölkerungsschutz und Sport (VBS)	Federal Department of Defense, Civil Protection and Sport
Département fédéral de l'économie, de la formation et de la recherche (DEFR)	Eidgenössisches Departement für Wirtschaft, Bildung und Forschung (WBF)	Federal Department of Economic Affairs, Education and Research
Département fédéral de l'environnement, des transports, de l'énergie et de la communication (DETEC)	Eidgenössisches Departement für Umwelt, Verkehr, Energie und Kommunikation (UVEK)	Federal Department of the Environment, Transport, Energy and Communication
Département fédéral de l'intérieur (DFI)	Eidgenössisches Departement des Innern (EDI)	Federal Department of Home Affairs
Département fédéral des affaires étrangères (DFAE)	Eidgenössisches Departement für auswärtige Angelegenheiten (EDA)	Federal Department of Foreign Affairs
Département fédéral des finances (DFF)	Eidgenössisches Finanzdepartement (EFD)	Federal Department of Finance
dépénalisation	Entkriminalisierung	decriminalization
dépénaliser	entkriminalisieren	to decriminalize
dépendance	Sucht	addiction
dépens (art. 95 CPC)	Parteientschädigung	attorney's fees and expenses
dépense	Ausgabe	expense
dépense nécessaire	notwendige Verwendung	necessary expense
dépense somptuaire	luxuriöse Verwendung	spending on luxury items
dépense unique	einmalige Ausgabe	one-time expense
dépense utile	nützliche Verwendung	useful expense
déplacement de bornes (art. 258 CP)	Grenzverrückung	moving of boundary markers
déposant	Hinterleger	depositor
déposer	hinterlegen	to deposit, to pay into court

dépositaire (1) (art. 474 CO)	Aufbewahrer	bailee
dépositaire (2)	Verwahrer	custodian
dépositaire (3)	Verwahrstelle	securities depository
dépositaire central (art. 61 LIMF)	Zentralverwahrer	central securities depository
déposition des parties (art. 192 CPC)	Beweisaussage	giving evidence, testifying
déposition du témoin	Zeugenaussage	witness testimony
dépôt (1)	Hinterlegung	deposit
dépôt (2)	Depot	custody account
dépôt (3)	Hinterlegung	filing (of a trademark or patent registration)
dépôt (4) (art. 472 ss CO)	Hinterlegung	bailment
dépôt collectif (art. 973a CC)	Sammelverwahrung	collective custody (of securities at a central depository, as opposed to individual custody)
dépôt de la demande (art. 220 CPC)	Einreichung der Klage	filing of the complaint
dépôt de l'état de collocation (art. 147 LP)	Auflegung der Kollokationsplans	filing of the schedule of claims
dépôt de titres	Wertschriftendepot	securities account
dépôt d'épargne	Spareinlage	savings deposit
dépôt d'espèces et d'objets de prix (art. 9 LP)	Aufbewahrung von Geld oder Wertsachen	deposit of money and valuables
dépôt du public (art. 1 LB)	Publikumseinlage	deposit (from the public)
dépôt du tableau de distribution et du compte final (art. 263 LP)	Auflage von Verteilungsliste und Schlussrechnung	filing of the distribution plan and the final accounting
dépôt irrégulier (art. 481 CO)	Hinterlegung vertretbarer Sachen	bailment of fungible goods
dépôts de banques	Bankengelder	interbank funds (funds deposited by one bank in another bank)
dépourvu d'effets juridiques	rechtsunwirksam	null and void, legally ineffective, unenforceable
déréglementation	Deregulierung	deregulation
déréliction	Dereliktion	dereliction
dérivés	Derivate	derivatives
dernière instance	letzte Instanz	last resort
déroulement de la procédure	Verfahrensablauf	course of the proceedings
désarmement	Abrüstung	disarmament

désavouer	aberkennen	to disallow (a claim)
descendant	Nachkomme	descendant
descente sur les lieux	Augenscheinnahme	visual inspection of evidence by the court
description de l'ouvrage	Baubeschrieb (D: Baubeschreibung)	building description
désertion	Fahnenflucht	desertion
déshérence (art. 45 OB)	Nachrichtenlosigkeit	dormancy
désignation de fantaisie	Phantasiebezeichnung	invented name, made-up name
désignation du créancier (art. 1105 CO)	Bezeichnung des Remittenten	designation of payee (of a check)
désignation du tiré (art. 1102 CO)	passive Checkfähigkeit	capacity to act as drawee
désignation générique	Sachbezeichnung	generic designation
désintéresser	abfinden	to settle a claim, to pay off a creditor
désintéresser un créancier	befriedigen – einen Gläubiger befriedigen	to pay a creditor, to satisfy a creditor's claims
désistement (art. 23 CP)	Rücktritt	withdrawal (from completing the criminal act)
désistement d'action (art. 241 CPC)	Klagerückzug	withdrawal, dismissal of the action (by the plaintiff)
dessaisissement de fortune	Vermögensverzicht	renunciation of assets
dessein d'appropriation	Aneignungswille	intention to appropriate
dessein d'enrichissement	Bereicherungsabsicht	acting for financial gain
dessous-de-table	Schmiergeld	bribe
destinataire	Adressat	addressee
destinataire de l'acte	Zustellungsempfänger	agent for receipt of process
destinataire de l'offre	Oblat	offeree
destitution (art. 14 al. 2 LP)	Amtsentsetzung (D: Amtsenthebung)	dismissal from office
destruction	Vernichtung	destruction
désunion	Zerrüttung	irretrievable breakdown (of a marriage)
détaillant	Detaillist (D: Einzelhändler)	retailer
détaillé	einlässlich (D: ausführlich)	in detail, thorough
détenir	in Gewahrsam haben	to possess, to hold
détenteur d'animal	Tierhalter	keeper of an animal
détenteur de gage	Pfandhalter	holder of a pledge

détenteur de véhicule	Fahrzeughalter	vehicle owner
détenteur du domicile	Domizilhalter	registered agent
détention (1)	Gewahrsam	possession
détention (2)	Haft	detention
détention administrative	Administrativhaft	administrative detention
détention aux fins d'expulsion	Ausschaffungshaft	arrest for purposes of deportation
détention avant jugement (art. 110 CP)	Untersuchungshaft	pretrial detention
détention cellulaire (art. 78 CP)	Einzelhaft	solitary confinement
détention d'armes	Waffenbesitz	possession of weapons
détention de stupéfiants	Betäubungsmittelbesitz	possession of narcotics
détention extraditionnelle	Auslieferungshaft	detention pending extradition
détention préparatoire (art. 75 LEtr)	Vorbereitungshaft	preparatory custody (prior to repatriation)
détention pour des motifs de sûreté (art. 229 CPP)	Sicherheitshaft	preventive detention
détenu	Gefangener	prisoner
détérioration de données (art. 144bis CP)	Datenbeschädigung	damage to data
déterminabilité	Bestimmbarkeit	determinability
détermination	Ermittlung	investigation
déterminer – se déterminer sur (= se prononcer sur)	Stellung nehmen	to state one's opinion on
détournement de choses frappées d'un droit de gage ou de rétention (art. 145 CP)	Veruntreuung und Entzug von Pfandsachen und Retentionsgegenständen	misappropriation and removal of property subject to a pledge or lien
détournement de retenues sur les salaires (art. 159 CP)	Missbrauch von Lohnabzügen	misuse of salary deductions
détournement de valeurs patrimoniales mises sous main de justice (art. 169 CP)	Verfügung über mit Beschlag belegte Vermögenswerte	disposal of seized assets
détresse profonde	schwere Bedrängnis	dire straits
détriment des créanciers	Gläubigerbenachteiligung	fraudulent conveyance
dette	Schuld	debt
dette constatée par acte authentique	Schuld durch öffentliche Urkunde festgestellt	debt established by an authenticated deed
dette d'argent	Geldschuld	monetary debt

dette de corps certain	Stückschuld	obligation to deliver a specific thing (as opposed to a type of thing)
dette de genre	Gattungsschuld	generic item, fungible item (as opposed to a unique item such as a work of art)
dette de somme	Summenschuld	monetary obligation
dette d'impôt	Abgabeschuld	tax debt
dette d'une sorte d'argent	Geldsortenschuld	debt payable with a specific type of coin
dette durable	Dauerschuld	long-term debt
dette portable	Bringschuld	obligation to be performed at creditor's (obligee's) residence or place of business
dette quérable	Holschuld	debt collectible by the creditor, obligation to be performed at the debtor's location
dette reconnue par acte sous seing privé	Schuld durch Privaturkunde bekräftigt	debt established by private deed
dette solidaire (art. 143 CO)	Solidarschuld (D: Gesamtschuld)	joint and several obligation
développement durable	nachhaltige Entwicklung	sustainable development
devenir caduc	dahinfallen	to lapse
devis	Kostenvoranschlag	quote
devise	Devisen	foreign exchange, forex
devoir de collaboration	Mitwirkungspflicht	duty to cooperate
devoir de collaborer	Mitwirkungspflicht	duty to cooperate
devoir de diligence (art. 717 CO)	Sorgfaltspflicht	duty of care
devoir de fidélité (art. 717 CO)	Treuepflicht	duty of loyalty
devoir de récusation	Ausstandspflicht	recusal obligation, duty to recuse oneself
devoir d'information	Informationspflicht	duty of disclosure
devoir fondamental	Grundpflicht	fundamental duty
devoir moral	sittliche Pflicht	moral duty
dévolution de la succession	Erbgang	devolution of the estate, succession upon death

dévolution des sûretés (art. 240 CPP)	Verfall der Sicherheitsleistung	forfeiture of the bail payment
dévolution successorale	Erbgang	devolution of the estate, succession upon death
diffamation (art. 173 CP)	üble Nachrede	defamation
différend commercial	Handelsstreitigkeit	commercial dispute
différend relevant du droit des sociétés	gesellschaftsrechtliche Streitigkeit	dispute concerning company law, company law dispute
diffusion (1)	Verbreitung	distribution, circulation
diffusion (2)	Streuung	free float
diligence	Sorgfalt	care
dimensions de la construction	Ausmass der Baute	dimensions of the construction
diminution effective de l'actif (art. 164 CP)	Gläubigerschädigung durch Vermögensminderung	reduction of assets to the prejudice of creditors
d'intérêt général	gemeinnützig	in the public interest
direction	Geschäftsleitung	management
Direction de la politique économique (DP)	Direktion für Wirtschaftspolitik (DP)	Economic Policy Directorate
Direction de la promotion économique (DS)	Direktion für Standortförderung (DS)	Promotion Activities Directorate
Direction de l'éducation	Bildungsdirektion (D: Kultusministerium)	Department of Education
direction de l'entreprise	Betriebsleitung	company management
Direction des affaires économiques extérieures (DW)	Direktion für Aussenwirtschaft (DW)	Federal Economic Affairs Directorate
Direction des ressources (DR)	Direktion für Ressourcen (DR)	Directorate for Resources
direction des travaux	Bauleitung	site management, site supervision
Direction du développement et de la coopération (DDC)	Direktion für Entwicklung und Zusammenarbeit (DEZA)	Swiss Agency for Development and Cooperation
Direction du droit international public (DV)	Direktion für Völkerrecht (DV)	Directorate of Public International Law
direction du fonds de placement	Fondsleitung	fund management
Direction du travail (DA)	Direktion für Arbeit (DA)	Labor Directorate
directive (1)	Richtlinie	guideline
directive (2) (droit communautaire)	Richtlinie (Gemeinschaftsrecht)	directive

disagio	Abschlag, Disagio	discount (the difference between the nominal value of a security and its issue or market price)
discrimination raciale (art. 261bis CP)	Rassendiskriminierung	racial discrimination
discussion par article	Detailberatung	detailed consideration (of a bill)
disjonction de causes	Trennung von Verfahren	severance of proceedings
dispense	Dispens	exemption
dispense des frais	Kostenerlass (D: Kostenaufhebung)	waiver of costs
disponibilité au placement	Vermittlungsbereitschaft	availability for hiring
disponibilités	Disponibilitäten	cash, liquid resources
dispositif	Dispositiv (D: Tenor)	operative part of a judgment, operative provisions, holding
dispositif de la décision	Entscheiddispositiv (D: Tenor)	operative part of a judgment, operative provisions, holding
disposition (1)	Bedingung	provision
disposition (2)	Verfügung	disposition
disposition finale (disp. fin.)	Schlussbestimmung (SchlB; SchlBest.)	final provision
disposition irrévocable	nicht wieder rückgängig zu machende Disposition	irrevocable provision
disposition pour cause de mort	Verfügung von Todes wegen	testamentary disposition
disposition statutaire	Statutenbestimmung (D: Satzungsbestimmung)	provision of the bylaws, bylaw provision
disposition transitoire (disp. trans.)	Übergangsbestimmung (UeB; ÜbBest.)	transitional provision
dispositions fédérales en matière de preuve	bundesrechtliche Beweisvorschriften	federal rules of evidence
dissociation	Ausscheidung	separation of property
dissolution de la société	Auflösung der Gesellschaft	dissolution of a company or partnership
dissolution du régime matrimonial	Auflösung des Güterstandes	dissolution of the marital property regime
dissoudre : dissoudre le mariage	scheiden: die Ehe scheiden	to dissolve the marriage

distorsions de la concurrence	Wettbewerbsverzerrungen	distortion of competition
distributeur automatique	Verkaufsautomat	vending machine
distribution	Ausschüttung	distribution
distribution dissimulée de bénéfices	verdeckte Gewinnausschüttung	hidden profit distribution
distribution du courrier	Postzustellung	mail delivery
district	Bezirk	district
diversification	Risikostreuung	risk spreading, diversification
dividende	Dividende	dividend
dividende intérimaire	Abschlagsdividende	interim dividend
dividendes non perçus (art. 329 LP)	nicht erhobene Beträge	uncollected dividends
divorce (art. 111 CC)	Ehescheidung	divorce
divorce pour rupture du lien conjugal (art. 115 CC)	Scheidung wegen Unzumutbarkeit der Ehe	divorce due to irretrievable breakdown of the marriage
divorce sur demande unilatérale (art. 114 CC, art. 290 CPC)	Scheidung auf Klage eines Ehegatten	divorce at the petition of one spouse
divorce sur requête commune (art. 111 CC)	Scheidung auf gemeinsames Begehren	divorce by joint request
divulgations non opposables (art. 7b LBI)	unschädliche Offenbarungen	non-prejudicial disclosures
doctrine	Doktrin, Lehre	legal scholarship, the legal literature
doctrine dominante (1)	herrschende Lehre	prevailing opinion (in the literature)
doctrine dominante (2)	herrschende Meinung (h.M.)	prevailing opinion (in the literature and the case law)
document écrit	Schriftstück	written document
documentation	Dokumentation	documentation
d'office	von Amtes wegen	sua sponte, at the court's initiative ("ex officio" is a mistranslation)
dol (art. 28 CO)	absichtliche Täuschung	fraud
dol éventuel	Eventualvorsatz	recklessness
domaine public	Gemeingut	public domain
domicile (art. 23 CC)	Wohnsitz	domicile (place where a person resides with the intention of settling)

domicile à l'étranger	Auslandswohnsitz, Wohnsitz im Ausland	domicile abroad
domicile antérieur	bisheriger Wohnsitz	former address
domicile connu	bekannter Wohnsitz	known address
domicile du fonds	Fondsdomizil	fund domicile
domicile élu	Zustellungsdomizil	address for service
domicile fiscal	steuerrechtlicher Wohnsitz	tax domicile
domicile fixe	fester Wohnsitz	fixed domicile
domicile séparé	getrennter Wohnsitz	separate residence
dommage	Schaden	damage
dommage abstrait (art. 42 CO)	abstrakter Schaden	abstract damage
dommage actuel	aktueller Schaden	current damage
dommage causé à un tiers	Drittschaden	third party damage
dommage consécutif au défaut	Mangelfolgeschaden	consequential harm caused by a defect
dommage corporel	Personenschaden	bodily injury
dommage de guerre	Kriegsschaden	war damage
dommage direct	direkter Schaden	direct damage
dommage dû au retard	Verspätungsschaden	damage due to delay
dommage irréparable	nichtwiedergutzumachender Nachteil	irreparable harm, irreparable damage
dommage matériel	Sachschaden	property damage
dommage né de la confiance déçue	Vertrauensschaden	negative interest, damage caused by breach of contract
dommage patrimonial	Vermögensschaden	pecuniary damage, economic loss
dommage purement économique	reiner Vermögensschaden	purely economic damage
dommage supplémentaire	weiterer Schaden	additional damage
dommage total	Totalschaden	total loss, total write-off
dommages à la propriété (art. 144 CP)	Sachbeschädigung	criminal damage to property, vandalism
dommages-intérêts	Schadenersatz	damages
dommages-intérêts punitifs	Strafschadenersatz	punitive damages
don	Spende	donation
donataire (art. 241 CO)	Beschenkter	donee
donateur (art. 240 CO)	Schenker	donor
donation (art. 286 al. 1 LP; art. 239-252 CO)	Schenkung	gift
donation manuelle (art. 242 CO)	Schenkung von Hand zu Hand	gift from hand to hand
donation pour cause de mort	Schenkung von Todes wegen	testamentary gift

donnant donnant (art. 75 CO)	Zug-um-Zug-Geschäft	reciprocal and simultaneous transaction
donnant lieu à enregistrement	eintragungspflichtig	subject to registration
données personnelles	Personendaten	personal data
données sensibles	besonders schützenswerte Personendaten	sensitive data
donner suite à	Folge geben an	to take action on, to follow up on
donneur	Spender	donor
donneur d'aval	Wechselbürge	guarantor (on a bill)
donneur de leasing	Leasinggeber	lessor
donneur de licence	Lizenzgeber	licensor
donneur d'ordre	Auftraggeber	client
dossier	Akte, Aktenstelle (act.)	file, record
dossier médical	Krankengeschichte	medical history
dotation en capital	Kapitalausstattung	capital resources
douane	Zoll	customs
double imposition	Doppelbesteuerung	double taxation
double imposition intercantonale	interkantonale Doppelbesteuerung	intercantonal double taxation
double mise à prix	Doppelaufruf	double auction
double national	Doppelbürger	dual national
double oui	doppeltes Ja	double yes vote
doute sur la responsabilité de l'auteur (art. 20 CP)	zweifelhafte Schuldfähigkeit	doubt as to legal responsibility
doyen de fonction	Alterspräsident	oldest member (of the National Council)
droit (1)	Recht, Rechtsanspruch	right
droit (2)	Recht	law (the word droit is usually capitalized in French when it means law rather than right)
droit (3)	Gebühr	fee
droit à des conditions minimales d'existence	Recht auf Existenzsicherung	right to secure one's livelihood
droit à la formation	Recht auf Bildung	right to education
droit à la liberté	Schutz vor Freiheitsentzug	right to freedom
droit à la naturalisation	Anspruch auf Einbürgerung	right to naturalization
droit à la prestation d'assurance	Leistungsanspruch (Versicherung)	right to insurance benefits
droit à la réduction du prix	Minderungsrecht	right to a reduction in the purchase price
droit à la réfection de l'ouvrage	Nachbesserungsrecht	contractor's right to be given an opportunity to cure the breach

droit à la résolution du contrat	Wandelungsrecht	right to rescind the contract
droit à la santé	Recht auf Gesundheit	right to health
droit à la vie (art. 10 CF)	Recht auf Leben	right to life
droit à l'affiliation	Recht auf Mitgliedschaft	right to membership
droit à l'instruction primaire	Anspruch auf Primarschulunterricht	right to elementary education
droit à se défendre soi-même	Recht auf Selbstverteidigung	right to self defense
droit à un défenseur	Recht auf einen Verteidiger	right to a defender
droit à un enseignement de base (art. 19 CF)	Anspruch auf Grundschuldunterricht	right to basic education
droit à un enterrement décent	Anspruch auf ein schickliches Begräbnis	right to a decent burial
droit à une couverture d'assurance plus étendue	Recht auf Höherversicherung	right to supplemental insurance
droit à une expression non falsifiée de la volonté (art. 34 CF)	Anspruch auf unverfälschte Willenskundgabe	right to give genuine expression to one's intent
droit absolu	absolutes Recht	absolute right (effective erga omnes)
droit accessoire	Nebenrecht	accessory right
droit acquis	wohlerworbenes Recht	vested right
droit administratif	Verwaltungsrecht	administrative law
droit applicable	anwendbares Recht	governing law
droit au gain	Gewinnanspruch	entitlement to profits
droit au mariage (art. 14 CF)	Ehefreiheit	right to marry
droit au respect de la correspondance	Recht auf freien Briefverkehr	right to privacy of correspondence
droit au travail	Recht auf Arbeit	right to work
droit aux fruits	Anries (D: Überhangsrecht)	right to the fruits
droit bancaire	Bankenrecht	banking law
droit cantonal	kantonales Recht	cantonal law
droit civil	Zivilrecht	civil law
droit commercial	Handelsrecht	commercial law
droit communal	Gemeinderecht	municipal law
droit communautaire	Europarecht, Gemeinschaftsrecht	EU law
droit comparé	Rechtsvergleichung	comparative law
droit constitutionnel	Verfassungsrecht	constitutional law
droit constitutionnel à la protection de la bonne foi	verfassungsmässiges Recht auf Treu-und -Glaubensschutz	constitutional right to the protection of good faith
droit coutumier	Gewohnheitsrecht	customary law, custom

droit coutumier international	Völkergewohnheitsrecht	customary international law
droit d'accès	Zutrittsrecht	right of access
droit d'asile	Asylrecht	right to asylum
droit d'auteur et droits voisins	Urheberrecht und verwandte Schutzrechte	copyright and related rights
droit d'avancement à un rang antérieur	Nachrückungsrecht	right to move mortgage to higher order of priority
droit de caractère civil	zivilrechtlicher Anspruch	civil claim
droit de cité (art. 37 CF)	Bürgerrecht	citizenship
droit de cité cantonal	Kantonsbürgerrecht	cantonal citizenship
droit de cité communal	Bürgerrecht einer Gemeinde	municipal citizenship
droit de cité d'honneur	Ehrenbürgerrecht	honorary citizenship
droit de commission	Kommissionsgebühr	commission, fee
droit de compensation	Verrechnungsrecht	right of offset
droit de connaître son ascendance	Anspruch auf Kenntnis der Abstammung	right to know one's origins
droit de consignation (art. 92 CO)	Recht zur Hinterlegung	right to deposit the object (at the obligee's expense)
droit de construire en limite	Grenzbaurecht (Dienstbarkeit)	right to build on the boundary
droit de conversion	Wandelrecht	conversion right (right to convert bonds into shares or participation certificates)
droit de correction	Züchtigungsrecht	right to use corporal punishment
droit de disjonction	Aussonderungsrecht	right to withdraw one's property from the operation of bankruptcy
droit de disposer de son domicile	Hausrecht	authority over one's home
droit de fonder une famille	Recht der Familiengründung	right to start a family
droit de gage (art. 151 LP)	Pfandrecht	charge
droit de gage collectif	Gesamtpfandrecht	multiple lien (real estate lien constituted by pledging several pieces of property to secure the same debt, with each property being encumbered with the amount of the entire debt)

droit de gage enregistré	Registerpfandrecht	registered lien (no physical delivery of the pledged asset)
droit de gage subséquent (art. 886 CC)	Nachverpfändung	subordinate pledge
droit de garde	Obhut	custody
droit de garde de titres	Depotgebühren	custody charges
droit de garder le silence	Aussageverweigerungsrecht	right to remain silent
droit de la concurrence déloyale	Lauterkeitsrecht	law of fair trade, law of unfair competition
droit de la faillite	Konkursrecht	bankruptcy law, insolvency law
droit de la famille	Familienrecht	family law
droit de la guerre	Kriegsrecht	martial law
droit de la mère non mariée	Anspruch der unverheirateten Mutter	right of unmarried mothers
droit de la profession d'avocat	Anwaltsrecht	attorney liability law
droit de la propriété intellectuelle	Immaterialgüterrecht	intellectual property right
droit de l'État	Staatsrecht	constitutional and administrative law
droit de mise en circulation	Verbreitungsrecht	right of distribution
droit de passage	Wegrecht	right of way
droit de passage nécessaire	Notwegrecht	right to a necessary easement
droit de pétition (art. 33 CF)	Petitionsrecht	right to petition
droit de poser des questions	Fragerecht	right to ask questions
droit de préaffermage	Vorpachtrecht	leaseholder's right to extend the lease
droit de préemption	Vorkaufsrecht	right of first refusal
droit de préemption limité	limitiertes Vorkaufsrecht	limited right of first refusal
droit de préférence (art. 198 LP)	Vorzugsrecht des Pfandgläubigers	paramount right (of the pledgee)
droit de prélocation	Vormietrecht	lease option
droit de procédure	Prozessrecht, Verfahrensrecht	procedural law
droit de procédure pénale	Strafverfahrensrecht	criminal procedure
droit de reconstruire	Hofstattrecht	right to rebuild a destroyed building
droit de recours de l'autorité (art. 56 LPE)	Behördenbeschwerde	public authority appeal
droit de refus de collaborer	Verweigerungsrecht	right to refuse to cooperate

droit de refuser le témoignage (art. 169 CPP)	Zeugnisverweigerungsrecht	right to refuse to testify
droit de regard	Recht auf Einsichtnahme	right to inspect documents, right to examine all relevant documents
droit de réméré (art. 216 CO)	Rückkaufsrecht	right of repurchase
droit de réponse (art. 28g CC)	Gegendarstellung	reply, right of reply
droit de représentation	Aufführungsrecht	performing rights, rights to perform a play or a musical composition
droit de résolution du vendeur	Rücktrittsrechts des Verkäufers	seller's right to terminate
droit de rétention (art. 895 CC, art. 491 CO)	Retentionsrecht	possessory lien
droit de signature	Unterschriftsberechtigung	authority to sign
droit de suite (art. 216 CPP)	Recht der Nacheile	right to pursue
droit de superficie (art. 779 CC)	Baurechtsdienstbarkeit	right to construct a building on another person's land
droit de timbre de négociation	Umsatzabgabe	transfer stamp tax
droit de timbre d'émission	Emissionsabgabe	stamp tax on the issuance of securities
droit de vaine pâture	Gemeinatzung	communal grazing
droit de vendre	Selbsthilfeverkauf	self-help sale
droit de veto	Vetorecht	veto right
droit de visite	Besuchsrecht	visitation rights
droit de voisinage	Nachbarrecht	law governing neighbors
droit de vote	Stimmrecht (D: Wahlrecht)	voting right, right to vote
droit de vote des actions déposées	Depotstimmrecht	proxy voting rights
droit de vote des étrangers	Ausländerstimmrecht (D: Ausländerwahlrecht)	foreign nationals' right to vote
droit d'ébrancher (art. 687 CC)	Kapprecht	right to cut overhanging branches
droit d'emption (art. 216 CO)	Kaufsrecht	option right (to buy a piece of property at a later date on the terms set forth in the contract)

droit des assurances	Versicherungsrecht	insurance law
droit des cartels	Kartellrecht	antitrust law
droit des constructions	Baurecht	construction law
droit des contrats	Vertragsrecht	law of contracts
droit des étrangers	Ausländerrecht	immigration law
droit des obligations	Obligationenrecht (D: Schuldrecht)	law of obligations
droit des papiers-valeurs	Wertpapierrecht	securities law
droit des personnes	Personenrecht	law of persons
droit des poursuites	Betreibungsrecht	debt collection law
droit des poursuites et faillites	Schuldbetreibungs- und Konkursrecht	debt collection and bankruptcy law
droit des sociétés	Gesellschaftsrecht	company law
droit des successions	Erbrecht	law of succession
droit d'être entendu (art. 29 CF)	Anspruch auf rechtliches Gehör	right to be heard
droit d'être occupé	Beschäftigungspflicht	right to be employed (until the end of the employment agreement)
droit d'être présent à l'audience	Anspruch auf persönliche Teilnahme an der Verhandlung	right to be present at the hearing
droit d'exposition (art. 14 LDA)	Ausstellungsrecht	author's right of exhibition
droit d'habitation	Wohnrecht	right of residence
droit disciplinaire	Disziplinarrecht	disciplinary law
droit dispositif (F : droit supplétif)	dispositives Recht, ergänzendes Recht	non-mandatory legal rule (one that can be contracted out of)
droit d'obtenir une décision	Anspruch auf einen Entscheid	right to a decision
droit d'option	Optionsrecht	option right
droit douteux (art. 269 al. 3 LP)	zweifelhafter Rechtsanspruch	questionable right
droit du créancier aux versements partiels en cas de résiliation (art. 162 CO)	Verfall von Teilzahlungen	forfeiture of partial payments
droit du domicile	Wohnsitzprinzip	right of domicile
droit du public et de la presse d'assister aux débats	Publikumsöffentlichkeit	open court
droit du travail	Arbeitsrecht	labor law
droit d'usufruit	Nutzniessungsrecht	right of usufruct
droit édicté	erlassenes Recht	enacted law
droit exclusif	Ausschliesslichkeitsrecht, Sonderrecht	exclusive right
droit expectatif	Anwartschaftsrecht	reversionary interest

droit fédéral	Bundesrecht	federal law
droit fiscal	Steuerrecht, Abgaberecht	tax law
droit foncier rural	bäuerliches Bodenrecht	rural land rights
droit fondamental	Grundrecht	fundamental right
droit formel	formelles Recht	procedural law
droit héréditaire	Erbteil	share of an estate
droit impératif	zwingendes Recht	mandatory legal rule (one that can be contracted out of)
droit international privé	internationales Privatrecht	private international law (also called "conflict of laws")
droit international public	Völkerrecht	public international law, the law of nations
droit interne	Landesrecht	internal law
droit jurisprudentiel	Richterrecht	judge-made law, case law
droit maritime	Seerecht	maritime law
droit matériel	materielles Recht	substantive law (as opposed to procedural law)
droit moral	Urheberpersönlichkeitsrecht	moral right
droit national	Heimatrecht	national law
droit naturel	Naturrecht	natural right
droit objectif	objektives Recht	law (as opposed to subjektives Recht, which means 'right')
droit pénal	Strafrecht	criminal law
droit pénal administratif	Verwaltungsstrafrecht	administrative criminal law
droit pénal des mineurs	Jugendstrafrecht	juvenile criminal law
droit pénal fiscal	Steuerstrafrecht	criminal tax law
droit pénal formel	formelles Strafrecht	criminal procedure
droit pénal militaire	Militärstrafrecht	military criminal law
droit personnel	persönliches Recht	personal right
droit positif	positives Recht	positive law
droit préférentiel de souscription	Bezugsrecht	preemptive right (right granted in the context of a capital increase to subscribe for new shares so as to avoid dilution of percentage ownership)
droit prétorien	Richterrecht	judge-made law, case law
droit privé	Privatrecht	private law
droit public	öffentliches Recht	public law

droit réel limité (art. 261a CO)	beschränktes dingliches Recht	limited right in rem
droit relatif	relatives Recht	relative right (Obligations are an example of relative rights, which apply only inter partes, as opposed to absolute rights, which apply erga omnes.)
droit résultant des impenses (art. 65 CO)	Anspruch aus Verwendungen	right in respect of expenditures
droit social	soziales Grundrecht	welfare right (fundamental right that guarantees that an individual is entitled to certain social benefits from the State – note that "droit social" usually refers to "labor law" in France)
droit subjectif	subjektives Recht	right (as opposed to law, which is objektives Recht or droit objectif)
droit suisse	schweizerisches Recht	Swiss law
droit transitoire	Übergangsrecht	interim law
droits de diffusion	Senderechte	broadcasting rights
droits de douane	Zollabgabe	customs duties
droits de l'homme	Menschenrechte	human rights
droits de mutation	Handänderungssteuer (D: Grunderwerbssteuer)	real estate transfer tax
droits de timbre	Stempelabgaben	stamp duties
droits patrimoniaux	Vermögensrechte	economic rights (embodied in a share, i.e., the right to receive dividends, the right to a portion of any liquidation proceeds, and subscription rights)
droits politiques (art. 34 CF)	politische Rechte	political rights
droits réels	Sachenrecht	law of real and personal property
droits réels immobiliers	Immobiliarsachenrecht	law of real property
droits sociaux	Rechte des Gesellschafters	shareholder rights

droits strictement personnels	höchstpersönliche Rechte	strictly personal rights
droits-valeurs (art. 973c CO)	Wertrechte	uncertificated securities
ducroire (art. 430 CO)	Delkredere	del credere (special remuneration of agent who has assumed liability for performance by the debtor)
duplicata (art. 1063 ss CO)	Duplikate	duplicate of a bill of exchange
duplique	Duplik	rejoinder
durée d'activité probable	Aktivitätserwartung	expectation of activity
durée de la fonction	Amtsdauer	term of office
durée de la responsabilité	Haftungsdauer	duration of liability
durée du droit à la prestation d'assurance	Anspruchsdauer	duration of the right to insurance benefits
durée du repos	Ruhezeit	rest period
durée et horaire de travail	Arbeitszeit	working hours
durée indéterminée	unbestimmte Dauer	unlimited duration
durée réglementaire du travail	Soll-Arbeitszeit	regular working hours
durée résiduelle	Restlaufzeit	residual term
d'utilité publique	gemeinnützig	in the public interest
eau de percolation	Sickerwasser	seepage water
eau usée	Abwasser	sewage, waste water
eaux polluées (art. 4 LEaux)	verschmutztes Abwasser	polluted waste water
eaux souterraines (art. 4 LEaux)	unterirdisches Gewässer	underground water
eaux superficielles (art. 4 LEaux)	oberirdisches Gewässer	surface water
échange (art. 184-238 CO)	Tausch	barter
échange de vues (art. 8 PA)	Meinungsaustausch	exchange of views
échange d'écritures	Schriftenwechsel	exchange of written submissions
échantillon de voix (art. 262 CPP)	Sprachprobe	voice sample
échéance	Laufzeit	term
échéance principale	Hauptfälligkeit	anniversary date (of an insurance policy)
échec de la mise à l'épreuve (art. 46 CP)	Nichtbewährung	breach of probation
écolage (F : frais de scolarité)	Schulgeld	tuition fees
école de recrues	Rekrutenschule (D: militärische Grundausbildung)	recruit school

école enfantine (F : école maternelle)	Kindergarten	kindergarten
école hôtelière	Hotelfachschule	hotel management school
école juridique	Rechtsschule	law school
école primaire (F : école élémentaire)	Primarschule (D: Grundschule)	elementary school
école privée	Privatschule	private school
école secondaire	Sekundärschule	secondary school
école spéciale	Sonderschule	special school
économie	Wirtschaft	economy
économie de procédure	Prozessökonomie	procedural economy
économie privée	Privatwirtschaft	private economy
édit	Edikt	edict
éducation au travail	Arbeitserziehung	vocational training
effet	Wirkung	effect
effet à l'égard des tiers	Drittwirkung	third party effect
effet anticipé	Vorwirkung	advance effect
effet cassatoire	kassatorische Wirkung	quashing the lower court's decision without substituting the appellate court's judgment for the lower court's decision
effet de change (art. 177-189 LP)	Wechsel	bill of exchange
effet de levier	Hebelwirkung	leverage
effet déclaratif	deklaratorische Wirkung	declaratory effect
effet dévolutif	Devolutiveffekt	devolutive effect (appeal to a higher court rather than to the very judge who issued the ruling being appealed)
effet horizontal des droits constitutionnels	Drittwirkung der Grundrechte	third party effect of fundamental rights
effet juridique	Rechtswirkung	legal effect
effet suspensif du recours	aufschiebende Wirkung des Rechtsmittels	suspensive effect of an appeal (an appeal stays execution of the lower court's judgment)
effets comptables	Bucheffekte	book-entry securities
effets du divorce (art. 119-134 CC)	Scheidungsfolgen	consequences of divorce
efficacité	Wirksamkeit	effectiveness
efficience économique	Wirtschaftlichkeit	economic efficiency

effraction de véhicule	Aufbrechen eines Fahrzeugs	breaking into a vehicle
effraction de véhicule	Fahrzeugaufbruch	breaking into a vehicle
égalité dans l'illégalité	Gleichheit im Unrecht	equal treatment in illegality
égalité de rémunération	Lohngleichheit	equal pay
égalité des armes	Waffengleichheit	equal fighting power, equal fighting chance
égalité des voix	Stimmengleichheit	tied vote, tie
égalité devant la loi	Rechtsgleichheit in der Rechtsanwendung	equal protection of the law
élaboration de textes de loi	Legiferierung	lawmaking, drafting legislation
élaboration des produits	Produktegestaltung	product design
électeur	Stimmberechtigter, Stimmbürger	eligible voter
élection	Wahl	election
élection de droit	Rechtswahl	choice of law
élection de for (art. 17 CPC)	Gerichtsstandsvereinbarung	agreement on jurisdiction
élection de remplacement	Ersatzwahl	special election
élection du Conseil des Etats	Ständeratswahl	election of the Council of States
élection du Conseil fédéral	Bundesratswahlen	Federal Council election
élection pour le renouvellement général	Gesamterneuerungswahl	general election
élection tacite	stille Wahl	silent election
éléments objectifs (de la typicité)	objektiver Tatbestand	actus reus (in the definition of a crime)
éléments subjectifs (de la typicité)	subjektiver Tatbestand	mens rea (in the definition of a crime)
éligibilité	Wählbarkeit, passive Wahlfähigkeit	eligibility for election
élimination des doubles impositions	Vermeidung der Doppelbesteuerung	relief from double taxation
élimination des eaux usées	Abwasserbeseitigung	elimination of sewage
embargo	Embargo	embargo
emblème national	Hoheitszeichen	national emblem
émetteur	Emittent	issuer
émeute (art. 260 CP)	Landfriedensbruch	rioting
émission	Emission, Ausgabe	issue, issuance (sale of securities to the public and their introduction to trading)
émolument	Gebühr	fee
émolument administratif	Verwaltungsgebühr	administrative fee
émolument de justice	Gerichtsgebühr	court fee

émolument forfaitaire de conciliation (art. 95 CPC)	Pauschalen für das Schlichtungsverfahren	fee for the conciliation proceedings
émolument forfaitaire de décision (art. 95 CPC)	Entscheidgebühr, Pauschalen für den Entscheid	judgment fee, fee for the decision (this is an item of court costs)
émolument judiciaire	Gerichtsgebühr	court fee
empêchement au mariage (art. 95 CC)	Ehehindernis	impediment to marriage
empiètement	Überbau	encroachment
emplacement	Standort	location
emploi, avec dessein délictueux, d'explosifs ou de gaz toxiques (art. 224 CP)	Gefährdung durch Sprengstoffe und giftige Gase in verbrecherischer Absicht	misuse of explosives and toxic gases with criminal intent
employeur	Arbeitgeber	employer
empreinte digitale	Fingerabdruck	fingerprint
emprunt	Anleihe	bond
emprunt convertible	Wandelanleihe	convertible bond
emprunt d'État	Staatsanleihe	government bond
emprunt étranger	Auslandsanleihen	foreign bond
emprunt national	Inlandanleihen	domestic bond
emprunt par obligations	Anleihensobligation	debenture bond
emprunteur (1) (prêt à usage) (art. 305-311 CO)	Entlehner	borrower (in a loan for use)
emprunteur (2) (prêt de consommation) (art. 312-318 CO)	Borger	borrower (in a loan for consumption)
en affiliation à une bande	bandenmässig	as a member of a gang
en audience publique	an Schranken	in open court
en état d'être jugé (art. 236 CPC)	spruchreif	ripe for judgment
encaissement des créances (art. 100 et 243 LP)	Forderungseinzug	receipt of credit payments
enchérisseur	Bieter	bidder
encouragement	Förderung	promotion
encouragement à la propriété du logement (EPL)	Wohneigentumsförderung	promotion of home ownership
encouragement à la prostitution (art. 195 CP)	Förderung der Prostitution	encouraging prostitution
encouragement à l'accession à la propriété	Eigentumsförderung	promotion of home ownership
encouragement du cinéma (art. 2 LCin)	Filmförderung	film promotion

encourager : Je voudrais vous encourager à ne pas appuyer cette proposition.	beliebt machen: Ich möchte Ihnen beliebt machen, diesen Vorschlag nicht zu unterstützen.	to encourage, to urge: I would urge you not to support this proposal.
endossataire	Indossatar	indorsee
endossement (art. 1001 CO)	Indossament	indorsement
endossement en blanc	Blankoindossament	blank indorsement
endossement partiel	Teilindossament	partial indorsement
endosseur	Indossant	indorser
énergie non renouvelable	unerneuerbare Energie	nonrenewable energy
énergie renouvelable	erneuerbare Energie	renewable energy
énergie solaire	Sonnenenergie	solar energy
enfant adoptif	Adoptivkind	adopted child
enfant apatride (art. 38 CF)	staatenloses Kind	stateless child
enfant du conjoint	Stiefkind	stepchild
enfant né hors mariage	aussereheliches Kind (D: außereheliches Kind)	illegitimate child
enfant trouvé	Findelkind	foundling
engagement	Anstellung	hiring
engagement à terme strict (art. 211 al. 2bis LP)	Fixgeschäft (D: Fixhandelskauf)	commitment for a strict period
engagement de bétail (art. 885 CC)	Viehverpfändung	pledge of livestock
engagement excessif (art. 27 CC)	übermässige Bindung	excessive restriction
engin de pêche	Fischereigerät	fishing tackle
engrais de ferme (art. 4 LEaux)	Hofdünger	farm manure
enlèvement (art. 184 CP)	Entführung	abduction
enlèvement de mineur (art. 220 CP)	Entziehen von Minderjährigen	abduction of minors
enquête	Abklärung (D: Untersuchung)	investigation
enquête administrative	Administrativuntersuchung	administrative investigation
enquête parlementaire	parlamentarische Untersuchung	parliamentary investigation
enquête pénale	Strafuntersuchung	criminal investigation
enquête préalable	Vorabklärung (D: erstes informelles Sammeln von Information)	preliminary investigation
enregistrement non autorisé de conversations (art. 179ter CP)	unbefugtes Aufnehmen von Gesprächen	unauthorized recording of conversations
enregistrements non punissables (art. 179quinquies CP)	nicht strafbares Aufnehmen	legal recordings

enrichissement	Bereicherung	enrichment
enrichissement illégitime (art. 62 CO)	ungerechtfertigte Bereicherung	unjust enrichment
entente sur les prix	Preisabsprache	price fixing
entraide	Rechtshilfe	mutual assistance
entraide administrative	administrative Rechtshilfe	administrative mutual assistance
entraide en matière de police (art. 350-362 CP)	Amtshilfe im Bereich der Polizei	administrative assistance with police matters
entraide et extradition	Rechtshilfe und Auslieferung	mutual assistance and extradition
entraide judiciaire civile	Rechtshilfe in Zivilsachen	mutual assistance in civil matters
entraide judiciaire nationale (art. 43 ss CPP)	nationale Rechtshilfe	domestic mutual assistance
entraide judiciaire pénale	Rechtshilfe in Strafsachen	mutual assistance in criminal matters
entrave à la circulation publique (art. 237 CP)	Störung des öffentlichen Verkehrs	disruption of public traffic
entrave à l'action pénale	Begünstigung	aiding and abetting (an offender)
entrave au service des chemins de fer (art. 238 CP)	Störung des Eisenbahnverkehrs	disruption of rail traffic
entrave aux services d'intérêt général (art. 239 CP)	Störung von Betrieben, die der Allgemeinheit dienen	disruption of public services
entraver le service militaire (art. 278 CP)	Störung des Militärdienstes	disruption of military service
entré en force	rechtskräftig	legally effective
entrée dans un pays	Einreise	entry into a country, entering a country
entrée en vigueur	Inkrafttreten	entry into force
entrée illégale	illegale Einreise	illegal entry
entreposant	Einlagerer	depositor (of goods in a warehouse)
entrepositaire (art. 483 CO)	Lagerhalter	warehouse keeper
entrepôt	Lagergebäude	warehouse
entrepôt douanier	Zollager	inbond warehouse
entrepreneur	Unternehmer	business owner
entrepreneur en raison individuelle	Einzelkaufmann	sole proprietor
entrepreneur général	Generalunternehmer	general contractor
entrepreneur total	Totalunternehmer	turnkey contractor
entreprise agricole de plaine	Talbetrieb	low land farm

entreprise associée	verbundenes Unternehmen	associated enterprise
entreprise de construction	Bauunternehmen	construction company
entreprise de démolition de voitures	Autoabbruchbetrieb	car demolition company
entreprise dominant le marché (art. 4 LCart)	marktbeherrschendes Unternehmen	market dominant enterprise
entreprise familiale	Familienbetrieb	family-owned business
entreprise individuelle	Einzelunternehmen	sole proprietorship
entreprise téméraire	Wagnis	hazardous business, hazardous enterprise
entreprises associées	verbundene Unternehmen	associated enterprises
entreprises et menées de l'étranger contre la sécurité de la Suisse (art. 266bis CP)	Gegen die Sicherheit der Schweiz gerichtete ausländische Unternehmungen und Bestrebungen	foreign operations and activities directed against the security of Switzerland
entrer en force	in Rechtskraft erwachsen	to enter into force
entrer en matière	eintreten: auf etwas eintreten (D: auf etwas eingehen)	to address, deal with, hear, examine
entretien viager	Pfrund	support for life
environnement	Umwelt	environment
envoi d'une chose non commandée (art. 6a CO)	Zusendung einer unbestellten Sache	delivery of an unsolicited object
épargne	Ersparnis	savings
épargne de prévoyance	Vorsorgesparen	saving up for pension provision
épaves (art. 725 CC)	Zuführung	driftage
épicerie fine	Comestibles	delicatessen
époux (art. 105 CC)	Ehegatte	spouse
épuisement des instances	Erschöpfung des Instanzenzuges	exhaustion of remedies
épuration de l'état des charges	Lastenbereinigung	determination of charges
épuration des eaux usées	Abwasserreinigung	waste water treatment
équilibre écologique	ökologisches Gleichgewicht	ecological balance
équilibre financier	finanzielles Gleichgewicht	financial equilibrium
équipage du navire	Schiffsbesatzung	ship's crew
équipement de détail	Feinerschliessung	development of side roads
équipement de terrains	Erschliessung von Land	development of land
équipement général	Groberschliessung	development of main roads
équité	Billigkeit	equity, fairness
équivalence	Gleichwertigkeit	equivalence
erreur (art. 23 CO)	Irrtum	mistake
erreur de base	Grundlagenirrtum	mistake as to the basis of the contract
erreur de droit	Rechtsirrtum	error of law

erreur sur les faits	Sachverhaltsirrtum	error of fact
erreur sur l'illicéité (art. 21 CP)	Irrtum über die Rechtswidrigkeit	error as to unlawfulness
escompte	Diskont, Skonto	discount
escroquer	betrügen	to defraud
escroquerie (art. 146 CP)	Betrug	fraud
escroquerie fiscale	Steuerbetrug	tax fraud
espérance de vie	Lebenserwartung	life expectancy
espérances successorales	Erbanwartschaft	estate in expectancy
espionnage (art. 272 CP)	verbotener Nachrichtendienst	espionage
espionnage militaire au préjudice d'un Etat étranger (art. 301 CP)	Nachrichtendienst gegen fremde Staaten	military espionage against a foreign state
estimation (art. 97 al. 1 et 227 LP)	Schätzung	valuation
estimation de la mise en danger	Gefährdungsabschätzung	risk assessment
estimation des gages (art. 299 LP)	Pfandschätzung	valuation of pledges
estimer	veranschlagen	to estimate
établir la carte grise de	immatrikulieren	to register a vehicle
établissement (1)	Anstalt	establishment
établissement (2)	Niederlassung	place of business
établissement commercial (art. 50 al. 1 LP)	Geschäftsniederlassung	branch
établissement d'arrêts	Haftanstalt	detention center
établissement de semi-liberté	Halbfreiheitsheim	semi-liberty institution
établissement de soins	Pflegeheim	nursing home
établissement financier	Geldinstitut	financial institution
établissement pénitentiaire	Strafanstalt	penal institution
établissement semi-ouvert	halboffene Anstalt	semi-open institution
établissement stable	Betriebsstätte	permanent establishment
étage	Geschoss	floor, story
état	Stand	last updated on
état antérieur	Vorzustand	previous condition
état civil	Zivilstand (D: Personenstand)	marital status, civil status
état de collocation (art. 146 et 247 LP)	Kollokationsplan (D: Konkurstabelle)	schedule of accepted claims
état de droit	Rechtsstaat	(state under) the rule of law
état de fait	Sachverhalt (D: Tatbestand)	facts of the case
état de la fortune	Vermögenslage	financial position, financial condition

état de la fortune sociale	Vermögensstand	statement of assets
état de la technique	Stand der Technik	state of the art
état de nécessité	Notstand	state of emergency
état de nécessité excusable (art. 18 CP)	entschuldbarer Notstand	mitigatory act in a state of emergency
état de nécessité extérieure	äusserer Notstand	threat of invasion, threat of attack
état de nécessité intérieure	innerer Notstand	internal state of emergency
état de nécessité licite (art. 17 CP)	rechtfertigender Notstand	legitimate act in a state of emergency
état des charges (art. 140 LP et art. 125 ORFI)	Lastenverzeichnis	schedule of charges
état descriptif	Liegenschaftenbeschreibung	property description
État émetteur	ausstellender Staat	country of issue
état fédéral	Bundesstaat	federal state
état membre	Mitgliedstaat	member state
état-major général	Generalstab	general staff
étendue de la saisie (art. 97 LP)	Umfang der Pfändung	extent of the seizure
être accidenté	verunfallen, verunglücken	to have an accident
être humain	Mensch	human being
étude d'avocat	Anwaltsbüro	law firm
étude de notaire	Notariatsbüro	notary's office
études offertes	Festschrift	Festschrift
évacuation	Räumung	evacuation
évacuation des déchets	Abfallentsorgung	waste disposal
évaluation de l'invalidité	Invaliditätsbemessung	disability evaluation
évaluation préliminaire	Erstbewertung	preliminary evaluation
évasion	Entweichung	escape
évasion fiscale	Steuerumgehung	tax evasion
éventuel	allfällig (D: etwaig)	any; possible, potential
éviction (art. 195 CO)	Entwehrung	deprivation from the use of property for lack of good title
évier	Schüttstein (D: Spüle, Ausguss)	sink
évolution des prix	Preisentwicklung	price trend
examen de conduite	Führerprüfung	driver's examination
examen de l'intérieur du corps (art. 85 CP)	Untersuchung im Körperinnern	search of body cavities
examen de maturité (F : baccalauréat)	Maturitätsprüfung	high school graduation exam
examen des productions (art. 244 LP)	Prüfung der eingegebenen Forderungen	examination of productions
examen du cadavre (art. 253 ss CPP)	Untersuchungen an Leichen	examination of dead bodies

examen du risque	Risikoprüfung	risk check
excavatrice	Trax (D: Bagger, Schaufellader)	bulldozer, excavator
excédent	Überschuss	surplus
exception	Ausnahme	exception
exception opposer une exception	Einrede eine Einrede entgegensetzen	defense to assert a defense
exception appartenant aux codébiteurs (art. 145 CO)	Einrede der Schuldner	objection by the debtors
exception de litispendance	Einrede der Rechtshängigkeit	defense that the same case is pending elsewhere (sometimes called "defense of lis alibi pendens")
exception de position mal acquise	Berufung auf eigenes Unrecht	defense that the plaintiff is pleading his own immoral or illegal conduct
exception d'inexécution	Einrede des nichterfüllten Vertrages	defense that the other party has failed to perform the contract
exception du non-retour a la meilleure fortune	Einrede des mangelnden neuen Vermögens	plea of lack of improvement in the debtor's fortune
excès de vitesse	Geschwindigkeits-überschreitung	speeding
excitation	Aufregung	incitement
excitation au duel (art. 132 CP)	Aufreizung zum Zweikampf	incitement to fight a duel
exclure	wegbedingen	to exclude
exclure des preuves	Recht: aus dem Recht weisen	to exclude from evidence
exclusion (art. 199 CO)	Ausschluss, Wegbedingung	exclusion
exécutabilité	Erfüllbarkeit	enforceability
exécuteur testamentaire (art. 517 CC)	Testamentsvollstrecker, Willensvollstrecker	executor (of the will)
exécution (1)	Ausführung, Erfüllung	implementation, performance, execution
exécution (2) (procédure)	Vollstreckung	enforcement, execution
exécution de la saisie (art. 156 LP)	Pfändungsvollzug	seizure of the assets
exécution de l'obligation	Erfüllung der Obligation	performance of the obligation
exécution du séquestre (art. 275 LP)	Arrestvollzug	attachment of the assets
exécution en nature	Realerfüllung	performance in kind

exécution forcée	Zwangsvollstreckung	judicial execution, enforcement of a judgment
exécution générale (art. 159 ss LP)	Generalexekution	general enforcement (sale of the debtor's assets)
exécution par le débiteur lui-même (art. 68 CO)	persönliche Leistung	performance by the obligor in person
exécution par substitution usuelle	gewöhnliche Ersatzvornahme	substitutive measure
exécution par un tiers (art. 98 CO)	Ersatzvornahme	performance by a third party
exécution simultanée	Erfüllung Zug um Zug	simultaneous performance
exécution sous surveillance électronique	elektronisch überwachter Strafvollzug	electronic monitoring
exécution spéciale	Spezialexekution	seizure of specific assets of the debtor
exécutoire	vollstreckbar	enforceable
exemption de peine (art. 52 CP)	Strafbefreiung	exemption from punishment
exequatur	Exequatur, Vollstreckbarkeitserklärung	exequatur (declaration that a judgment is enforceable)
exercice annuel	Geschäftsjahr	fiscal year
exercice de la fonction	amtliche Tätigkeit	acting in an official capacity
exercice des droits civils (art. 54 CC)	Handlungsfähigkeit (D: Geschäftsfähigkeit)	capacity to contract
exercice du droit de vote	Stimmabgabe	voting, casting of votes
exercice illicite de la prostitution (art. 199 CP)	unzulässige Ausübung der Prostitution	unauthorized practice of prostitution
exhérédation	Enterbung	disinheritance
exhérédation punitive (art. 477 CC)	Strafenterbung	punitive disinheritance
exhéréder	enterben	to disinherit
exhibitionnisme (art. 194 CP)	Exhibitionismus	indecent conduct
exhumation (art. 254 CPP)	Exhumierung	exhumation
exigibilité	Fälligkeit	maturity
exonération de primes	Prämienbefreiung	waiver of premium
exonération d'impôt	Steuerbefreiung	tax exemption
exonération fiscale	Abgabefreiheit	tax exemption
expectative	Anwartschaft	expectancy, right of future enjoyment

expectative d'une pension	Anwartschaft auf eine Rente	expectancy of a pension
expéditeur	Absender	sender
expédition exécutoire de jugement	vollstreckbare Urteilsausfertigung	enforceable copy of a judgment
expert	Sachverständiger	expert
expert-arbitre	Schiedsgutachter	expert arbitrator
expert-comptable	Bücherexperte	certified public accountant
expert-fiduciaire	Treuhandexperte	certified fiduciary
expert-fiscal	Steuerexperte	tax expert
expertise	Begutachtung, Gutachten	expert opinion
expertise-arbitrage	Schiedsgutachtervertrag	expert arbitrator agreement
expertise ordonnée par l'administration	Administrativgutachten	government-ordered expert opinion
expertise sur pièces	Aktengutachten	expert opinion based solely on the record
expertiser	begutachten	to assess, to evaluate
explications de vote	Wahlanleitung	voting guide
exploitant à titre personnel	Selbstbewirtschafter	"self-manager" (farmer who personally works the soil and manages the farm)
exploitation de l'invention	Ausführung der Erfindung	reduction to practice of the invention
exploitation des moyens de preuves obtenus illégalement (art. 141 CPP)	Verwertbarkeit rechtswidrig erlangter Beweise	admissibility of unlawfully obtained evidence
exploitation en fermage	Pachtbetrieb	tenant farm, leased farm
exploitation viticole	Rebbaubetrieb (D: Weinbaubetrieb)	winery
explosion (art. 223 CP)	Verursachung einer Explosion	causing an explosion
exportation	Ausfuhr	export
exposé juridique	Rechtsausführungen	legal discussion
exposition	Ausstellung	exhibition
exposition à un danger (art. 127 CP)	Aussetzung	abandonment
exposition des biens à protéger	Exposition der Schutzgüter	exposure of the natural resources
expressément	ausdrücklich	expressly
expropriant	Enteigner	expropriater
expropriation	Enteignung	expropriation
expropriation partielle	Teilenteignung	partial expropriation
exproprié	Enteigneter	expropriatee

expulser	wegweisen	to expel, kick out
expulsion (1)	Räumung	eviction
expulsion (2)	Ausweisung	deportation
expulsion de locataire	Ausweisung des Mieters	eviction of a tenant
extension de la saisie	Ergänzungspfändung	seizure of additional assets
externalisation	Auslagerungen	outsourcing
extinction de la poursuite (art. 121 LP)	Erlöschen der Betreibung	lapse of insolvency proceedings
extinction d'une créance	Erlöschen einer Forderung	extinction of a claim
extourne	Umbuchung	reversal (of an entry)
extradition (art. 32 ss EIMP)	Auslieferung	extradition
extrait du casier judiciaire (art. 365 ss CP)	Strafregisterauszug	criminal record extract
extrait du compte individuel	Kontenauszug	account statement
extrait du registre	Registerauszug	register extract
extrait du registre foncier	Grundbuchauszug	land register extract
extrajudiciaire	ausserrechtlich	out-of-court
fabricant	Hersteller	manufacturer
facteur (1)	Pöstler (D: Postangestellter, Postbote)	postal employee, postman
facteur (2)	Faktor	factor
facteur étranger à l'accident	unfallfremder Faktor	factor unrelated to the accident
failli	Gemeinschuldner, Konkursit, Kridar	debtor in bankruptcy, bankrupt debtor
faillite (art. 159 ss LP)	Konkurs	insolvency, bankruptcy
faillite bancaire	Bankenkonkurs	insolvency of a bank
fainéantise	Arbeitsscheu	work shyness
faire appel	rekurrieren	to appeal
faire appel à	beiziehen (D: hinzuziehen, heranziehen)	to consult
faire évader des détenus (art. 310 CP)	Befreiung von Gefangenen	helping prisoners escape
faire valoir	geltend machen	to assert
fait d'exposer des marchandises (art. 7 CO)	Auslage von Waren	display of merchandise
faits	Tatsachen	facts
faits nouveaux	Veränderung der Verhältnisse	change of circumstances
falsification	Fälschung	forgery
falsification de la monnaie	Geldverfälschung	counterfeiting
falsification de marchandises (art. 155 CP)	Warenfälschung	counterfeiting of goods

falsification des marques officielles (art. 246 CP)	Fälschung amtlicher Zeichen	forgery of official marks
falsification des poids et mesures (art. 248 CP)	Fälschung von Mass und Gewicht	falsification of weights and measurements
falsification des timbres officiels de valeur (art. 245 CP)	Fälschung amtlicher Wertzeichen	forgery of official stamps
falsification d'ordre de mise sur pied ou d'instructions (art. 277 CP)	Fälschung von Aufgeboten oder Weisungen	forgery of military orders or instructions
famille monoparentale	Einelternfamilie	single-parent family
fardeau de la preuve	Beweislast	burden of proof, onus probandi
fausse alerte (art. 128bis CP)	falscher Alarm	false alarm
fausse déclaration d'une partie en justice	falsche Beweisaussage der Partei	giving of false evidence by a party
fausse monnaie (art. 241 CP)	Geldfälschung	counterfeiting money
fausses communications aux autorités chargées du registre du commerce (art. 153 CP)	unwahre Angaben gegenüber Handelsregisterbehörden	false statements to the commercial register authorities
faute	Verschulden	fault (either negligence or intentional misconduct)
faute de frappe	Verschrieb (D: Schreibfehler)	typo
faute d'orthographe	Verschrieb (D: Schreibfehler)	spelling mistake
faute du tiers	Drittverschulden	third party fault
faute grave	schweres Verschulden	gross negligence
faute professionnelle	Kunstfehler	malpractice
faute propre	Selbstverschulden	one's own fault
faux certificat médical (art. 318 CP)	falsches ärztliches Zeugnis	issuing a false medical certificate
faux dans les certificats (art. 252 CP)	Fälschung von Ausweisen	forgery of certificates
faux dans les titres commis dans l'exercice de fonctions publiques (art. 317 CP)	Urkundenfälschung im Amt	forgery of documents by a public official
faux intellectuel	intellektuelle Fälschung	false certification
faux intellectuel dans les titres	Falschbeurkundung	false certification
faux matériel dans les titres (art. 251 CP)	Urkundenfälschung	forgery of documents

faux rapport (art. 307 CP)	falsches Gutachten	perjury by an expert witness
faux renseignements sur des entreprises commerciales (art. 152 CP)	unwahre Angaben über kaufmännische Gewerbe	false statements about commercial business
faux témoignage (art. 307 CP)	falsches Zeugnis	perjury
favoriser	begünstigen	to favor
favoriser la débauche	Begünstigung der Unzucht	permitting the use of rented premises for professional procuring
fédéralisme	Föderalismus	federalism
fédération	Genossenschaftsverband	federation
Fédération des entreprises suisses	Verband der Schweizer Unternehmen	Swiss Business Federation
Fédération Suisse des Avocats (FSA)	Schweizerischer Anwaltsverband (SAV)	Swiss Bar Association
féries de poursuite (art. 56 ss LP)	Betreibungsferien	days exempt from debt collection proceedings
féries judiciaires (art. 89 al. 2 CPP)	Gerichtsferien	court holidays
fermage	Pachtzins	rent
fermier	Pächter	usufructuary lessee
Fête nationale	Bundesfeier	Swiss National Day (August 1)
feu rouge	Rotlicht (D: Verkehrsampel)	traffic light
feuille de maladie	Krankenschein	health insurance certificate
feuille de signatures	Unterschriftenbogen	petition form
Feuille fédérale de la Confédération suisse (FF)	Bundesblatt der Schweizerischen Eidgenossenschaft (BBl)	Federal Gazette of the Swiss Confederation
Feuille officielle	Amtsblatt	official gazette
Feuille officielle suisse du commerce (FOSC)	Schweizerisches Handelsamtsblatt (SHAB)	Swiss Trade Bulletin
feux de signalisation	Signallicht (D: Verkehrsampel)	traffic light
fiançailles (art. 90-95 CC)	Verlöbnis	engagement to marry
fidéicommettant	Begründer eines Fideikommisses	settlor (of a trust)
fidéicommis	Fideikommiss	trust
fidélité	Treue	loyalty
fidélité contractuelle	Vertragstreue	loyalty to the terms of the contract
fiduciaire	Treuhänder, Fiduziar	trustee, fiduciary, escrow agent

fiduciant (F : constituant)	Treugeber, Fiduziant	trustor, settlor (of a trust)
figurer au dossier	Recht: im Recht liegen	to be on file with
filiale mère	Zwischengesellschaft	intermediate company
filiation	Kindesverhältnis	filiation
filouterie d'auberge (art. 149 CP)	Zechprellerei	leaving a hotel, restaurant or bar without paying
fin de non-recevoir	Nichteintreten	dismissal
financement	Finanzierung	financing, funding
financement du terrorisme (art. 260quinquies CP)	Finanzierung des Terrorismus	financing terrorism
financement paritaire	paritätische Finanzierung	equal-share financing
fixation de la peine (art. 47 CP)	Strafzumessung	sentencing
fixation de l'amende	Festsetzung der Busse (D: Buße)	determination of the fine
fixation des prix	Preisansatz	pricing
fixation d'un délai (art. 107-108 CO)	Fristansetzung	setting a time limit for subsequent performance
flagrant délit	in flagranti	caught in the act
folle enchère	Reukauf	unreasonable bid
fonctionnaire	Beamter	public official
fondateur (1) (art. 635 CO) (société)	Gründer	founder
fondateur (2) (fondation)	Stifter	founder
fondation (art. 80-89 CC)	Stiftung	foundation
fondation collective	Sammelstiftung	collective foundation
fondation de libre passage	Freizügigkeitsstiftung	vested benefit policy
fondation de placement	Anlagestiftung	investment foundation
fondation de prévoyance en faveur du personnel	Personalfürsorgestiftung	company pension fund
fondation par apport en espèces	Bargründung	formation by cash subscription
fondation par apport en nature	Sachgründung	formation by in-kind contribution
Fondation patronale de prévoyance retraite	Patronale Finanzierungsstiftung (PAFI)	Pension Fund Foundation (funded by employers)
fondé de procuration (art. 721 CO)	Prokurist	authorized signatory
fonds d'allocation d'actifs	Anlagestrategiefonds	asset allocation fund
fonds de bienfaisance	Wohlfahrtsfonds	welfare fund
fonds de branche	Branchenfonds	sector fund
fonds de capitalisation	Anreicherungsfonds	growth fund
fonds de compensation	Ausgleichsfonds	compensation fund

fonds de placement	Anlagefonds (D: Investmentfonds)	investment fund
fonds de thésaurisation	Thesaurierungsfonds	capitalization fund, growth fund
fonds dominant	berechtigtes Grundstück	dominant tenement
fonds en actions	Aktienfonds	equity fund
fonds en obligations	Obligationenfonds (D: Rentenfonds)	bond fund
fonds en valeurs mobilières	Effektenfonds	securities fund
fonds faîtier	Dachfonds	umbrella fund, fund of funds
fonds immobiliers	Immobilienfonds	real estate fond
Fonds National Suisse de Garantie (FNG)	Nationaler Garantiefonds Schweiz (NGF)	Swiss National Guarantee Fund
fonds propres	Eigenkapital	equity
fonds servant	belastetes Grundstück	servient tenement
for	Gerichtsstand	jurisdiction
for de la faillite du débiteur en fuite (art. 54 LP)	Konkursort bei flüchtigem Schuldner	insolvency jurisdiction for the absconding debtor
for de la poursuite (art. 46 ss LP)	Betreibungsort	place of debt collection, competent debt collection office
for de nécessité	Notzuständigkeit	emergency jurisdiction
for impératif (art. 9 CPC)	zwingender Gerichtsstand	mandatory place of jurisdiction
force de loi	Rechtskraft	force of law
force exécutoire	Vollstreckbarkeit	enforceability
force majeure	höhere Gewalt	force majeure
force obligatoire	Verbindlichkeit	binding force, binding nature
force probante	Beweiskraft	probative force
forces aériennes	Luftwaffe	airforce
forces terrestres	Heer	army, land forces
formateur	Ausbildner (D: Ausbilder)	trainer
formation continue	Weiterbildung	continuing education
formation de séries	Gruppenbildung	constitution of series
forme écrite (art. 12 CO)	Schriftlichkeit	written form
forme écrite: exige la forme écrite	Schriftform: bedarf der Schriftform	must be in writing
forme requise par la loi (art. 14 CO)	gesetzlich vorgeschriebene Form	form required by law
forme réservée dans le contrat (art. 16 CO)	vertraglich vorbehaltene Form	form stipulated by contract
forme volontaire (art. 16 CO)	gewillkürte Form	form stipulated by contract
formule officielle	amtliches Formular	official form

formuler des objections	beanstanden	to object to, to reject
fortune	Vermögen	assets, wealth
fortune du fonds	Fondsvermögen	fund assets
fortune immobilière	unbewegliches Vermögen	real estate assets
fortune nette	Reinvermögen	net assets
fouille de personnes (art. 249-250 CPP)	Durchsuchung von Personen	search of persons
fouille d'objets (art. 249-250 CPP)	Durchsuchung von Gegenständen	search of property
fournisseur de services de télécommunication	Anbieter von Fernmeldediensten	telecommunications service provider
fourniture de sûretés (art. 238 CPP)	Sicherheitsleistung	payment of bail money
foyer pour femmes battues	Frauenhaus	battered women's shelter
frais (art. 95 CPC)	Kosten, Prozesskosten Die Kosten fallen ausser Ansatz.	costs, court costs No order is made as to costs.
frais accessoires (art. 257a CO)	Nebenkosten	ancillary costs
frais administratifs	Verwaltungskosten	administrative costs
frais d'achat de titres	Titelankaufsspesen	securities purchase fees
frais d'acquisition	Anschaffungskosten	cost of acquisition
frais d'acquisition du revenu	Gewinnungskosten (D: Betriebsausgaben und Werbungskosten)	business and other income-related expenses
frais de bureau	Bürounkosten	office expenses
frais de chancellerie	Kanzleigebühren	clerk's fee for copies, excerpts, transmittals, etc.
frais de construction	Baukosten	construction costs
frais de couverture	Absicherungskosten	hedging costs
frais de démolition	Abbruchkosten	demolition costs
frais de détention	Haftkosten	detention costs
frais de formation	Ausbildungskosten	training costs
frais de la procédure (art. 262 LP)	Verfahrenskosten	cost of the proceedings
frais de poursuite (art. 68 LP)	Betreibungskosten	costs of debt collection proceedings
frais de présidence	Präsidialgebühr	fee for case being heard by a single judge
frais de production	Herstellungskosten	manufacturing costs
frais de sommation	Mahngebühr	reminder fee
frais d'écriture	Schreibgebühren	document preparation fees
frais d'entretien	Unterhaltskosten	maintenance costs

frais d'établissement	Ausstattung	endowment
frais d'expertise	Sachverständigenkosten	expert witness fees
frais d'exploitation	Betriebskosten	operating expenses, business expenses
frais du séquestre (art. 281 al. 2 LP)	Arrestkosten	costs of attaching the assets
frais et les dépens	Kosten- und Entschädigungsfolge	court costs and attorney's fees
frais généraux	Unkosten	overhead costs
frais judiciaires (art. 95 CPC)	Gerichtskosten	court costs
frais médicaux	Heilungskosten	medical expenses
franchise	Franchise, Selbstbehalt	deductible (in an insurance policy)
franchisé	Franchisenehmer	franchisee
franchise de port	Portofreiheit	exemption from postage
franchise douanière	Zollbefreiung	customs exemption
franchiseur	Franchisegeber	franchisor
franc-tireur	Franktireur	sniper
fraude à la loi	Rechtsumgehung, Gesetzesumgehung	evasion of the law
fraude dans la saisie (art. 163 CP)	Pfändungsbetrug	fraud against seizure
fraude électorale (art. 282 CP)	Wahlfälschung	electoral fraud
fraude fiscale	Abgabebetrug	tax fraud
frein à l'endettement	Schuldenbremse	debt brake
frein aux dépenses	Ausgabenbremse	spending brake
fréteur	Vercharterer	charterer
Fribourg	Freiburg	Fribourg (city and canton)
friche	Brachfläche	derelict land
frontière	Grenze	border
fruit civil	zivile Frucht	civil fruit
fruits naturels (art. 643 CC)	natürliche Früchte	natural fruits, natural proceeds
fuite	Flucht	escape
funérailles	Abdankung (D: Trauerfeier)	funeral service
fusion	Fusion	merger
gage (art. 37 al. 3 LP)	Pfand	pledge, mortgage
gage collectif	Gesamtpfand	multiple lien
gage immobilier (art. 793-823 CC)	Grundpfand	real estate security interest
gage mobilier (art. 884-894 CC)	Fahrnispfand	chattel pledge
gain en capital	Kapitalgewinn	investment income

gain immobilier	Grundstückgewinn	real estate gains
gain intermédiaire	Zwischenverdienst	work while registered as unemployed
garantie bancaire	Bankgarantie	bank guaranty
garantie complémentaire	Aufstockungssicherheit	top-up collateral
garantie de la propriété (art. 26 CF)	Eigentumsgarantie	protection of the private ownership of property
garantie de l'accès au juge (art. 29a CF)	Rechtsweggarantie	guarantee of access to the courts
garantie de l'institution	Institutsgarantie	institutional guarantee
garantie d'exécution	Erfüllungsgarantie	warranty of performance
garantie en cas d'éviction (art. 192 ss CO)	Rechtsgewährleistung, Gewährleistung des veräusserten Rechtes	warranty of good title
garantie en raison des défauts de la chose (art. 197 ss CO)	Sachgewährleistung	warranty against defects in the item purchased
garantie indépendante	selbstständige Garantie	independent guarantee, stand-alone guarantee
garantie pour les défauts	Mängelhaftung	warranty against defects
garanties	Sicherheiten	collateral
garde	Obhut	custody
garde alternée	alternative Obhut	shared custody (of children after divorce)
garde du courrier	Postrückbehaltung	hold mail
garde-chasse	Jagdaufseher	game warden
garde-frontière	Grenzwächter	border guard
garderie	Kinderkrippe	day care center
gardien	Abwart (D: Hausmeister)	janitor, caretaker
gardien de prison	Strafanstaltspersonal	prison guard
génération d'entrée	Eintrittsgeneration	initial generation
Genève	Genf	Geneva (canton and city)
génocide (art. 264 CP)	Völkermord	genocide
genre de délit	Deliktsart	type of offense
gérance d'immeubles	Liegenschaftsverwaltung	property management
gérant (1)	Geschäftsführer	manager, managing director
gérant (2) (fonds de placement)	Sachwalter (Anlagefonds)	manager
gérant de fortune	Vermögensverwalter	asset manager
gestion d'affaires	Geschäftsführung ohne Auftrag (GoA)	agency without authority

gestion de fortune	Vermögensverwaltung	asset management
gestion déloyale (art. 158 CP)	ungetreue Geschäftsbesorgung	criminal mismanagement
gestion déloyale des intérêts publics (art. 314 CP)	ungetreue Amtsführung	misconduct in public office
gestion des déchets	Abfallbewirtschaftung	waste management
gestion des finances (art. 126 CF)	Haushaltsführung	financial management
gestion des risques	Risikomanagement	risk management
gestion des sites contaminés	Altlastenbearbeitung	contaminated site management
gestion fautive (art. 165 CP)	Misswirtschaft	mismanagement
Glaris	Glarus	Glarus (canton and city)
glissement de terrain (art. 660 CC)	Bodenverschiebung	landslide
gouvernement	Regierung	government
grâce	Begnadigung	pardon, clemency
grâce conditionnelle	bedingte Begnadigung	conditional pardon
gracier	begnadigen	to pardon
grand conseil	Kantonsrat	cantonal parliament
grand livre	Hauptbuch	general ledger
gratuité	Unentgeltlichkeit	non-commercialism
gratuité de la procédure	kostenloses Verfahren	proceedings are free of charge
gravité de la faute	Grad des Verschuldens	degree of fault
gravité d'un délit	Deliktsschwere	gravity, seriousness of an offense
greffe du tribunal de district	Bezirksgerichtskanzlei	registry of the district court
greffe du Tribunal des mineurs	Jugendgerichtskanzlei	Registry of the Juvenile Court
greffier	Gerichtsaktuar, Gerichtsschreiber	court clerk
greffier du tribunal de district	Bezirksgerichtsschreiber	clerk of the district court
grenier	Estrich (D: Dachboden)	attic
grève	Streik	strike
grève de la faim	Hungerstreik	hunger strike
grèvement	Belastung	encumbrance
grief constitutionnel	Verfassungsrüge	constitutional claim
Grisons	Graubünden	Graubünden (canton)
gros œuvre	Rohbau	shell, external structure of an unfinished building

grossiste	Grossist	wholesaler
groupe d'actionnaires	Aktionärsgruppe	group of shareholders
groupe de sociétés	Konzern	group of companies
groupe parlementaire	Fraktion	parliamentary group
groupements illicites (art. 275ter CP)	rechtswidrige Vereinigung	unlawful association
gymnase (F : lycée)	Gymnasium	academic high school
habitations (CO 253a)	Wohnräume	residential premises
harcèlement psychologique	Mobbing	bullying
harmonisation fiscale	Steuerharmonisierung	tax harmonization
Haute école de gestion de Zurich	Hochschule für Wirtschaft Zürich (HWZ)	Zurich University of Applied Sciences in Business Administration
haute surveillance	Oberaufsicht	overall supervision
haute trahison (art. 265 CP)	Hochverrat	high treason
héritier (art. 457 ss CC)	Erbe	heir
héritier appelé (art. 488 CC)	Nacherbe	remainderman
héritier grevé	Vorerbe	encumbered heir
héritier institué	eingesetzter Erbe	named heir
héritier légal	gesetzlicher Erbe	intestate heir
héritier réservataire	Pflichtteilserbe	forced heir
héritier substitué	Ersatzerbe	contingent beneficiary
heures d'appoint	Mehrarbeit	overtime
heures de travail supplémentaires	Überstundenarbeit	overtime work
hoirie	Erbe	heir
homicide	Tötung	homicide
homicide par négligence (art. 117 CP)	fahrlässige Tötung	negligent homicide
homologation du concordat (art. 306 LP)	Bestätigung des Nachlassvertrages	ratification of the debt restructuring agreement
honoraires	Honorar	fees
honoraires calculés en fonction du résultat positif	Erfolgshonorar	contingency fee
hôpital	Spital (D: Krankenhaus)	hospital
hôpital cantonal	Kantonsspital	cantonal hospital
horaire de travail mobile (art. 64 OPers)	gleitende Arbeitszeit	flexible working hours
horaire de travail modulable	flexible Arbeitszeit	flexible work schedule

horizon de placement	Anlagehorizont	investment horizon (the period of time for which investors want to commit part of their assets)
horloger	Uhrmacher	watchmaker
huis clos prononcer le huis clos	Ausschluss der Öffentlichkeit die Öffentlichkeit ausschliessen	holding a hearing in camera to hold a hearing in camera
huissier	Weibel (D: Gerichtsvollzieher)	bailiff, process server
huissier aux poursuites	Betreibungsweibel	process server in debt collection proceedings
huissier exploitant	Gerichtsvollzieher	process server
hypothèque (art. 824 ss CC)	Grundpfandverschreibung (D: Hypothek)	mortgage
hypothèque légale	gesetzliches Grundpfandrecht	statutory lien on real property
hypothèque légale des artisans et entrepreneurs (art. 837 al. 1 lit. 3 et al. 2, art. 839 ss CC)	Bauhandwerkerpfandrecht	building contractor's lien
hypothèque maximale	Maximalhypothek	maximum amount mortgage
hypothèque mobilière enregistrée	Fahrnisverschreibung	nonpossessory security interest (the debtor remains in possession of the chattel, e.g., ships and aircraft)
hypothèque sur aéronef	Luftfahrzeugverschreibung	mortgage on an aircraft
identificateur personnel	Personenidentifikator	personal identifier
identité	Identität	identity
identité des créances (art. 120 al. 1 CO)	Gleichartigkeit der Forderungen	identical nature of the claims (for claims to be offset, they must be identical)
identité des demandes	Identität der Klagen	identical nature of the claims
ignorance de la loi (art. 3 al. 2 CC)	Rechtsunkenntnis	ignorance of the law
illégal	rechtswidrig, widerrechtlich	unlawful, illegal
illégalité	Rechtswidrigkeit, Widerrechtlichkeit	unlawfulness, illegality
illicéité	Rechtswidrigkeit, Widerrechtlichkeit	unlawfulness

illicite	rechtswidrig, widerrechtlich	unlawful
imitation (propriété intellectuelle)	Nachahmung (geistiges Eigentum)	imitation
imitation de billets de banque, de pièces de monnaies ou de timbres officiels de valeur sans dessein de faux (art. 243 CP)	Nachmachen von Banknoten, Münzen oder amtlichen Wertzeichen ohne Fälschungsabsicht	imitation of bank notes, coins or official stamps without intent to commit forgery
immeuble (art. 655 CC)	Grundstück	property, real property, real estate
immeuble de base	Stammgrundstück	original parcel
immeuble de rapport	Renditeliegenschaft	commercial property (built or bought as a capital investment rather than for use by the owner)
immeuble dépendant (art. 655a CC)	Anmerkungsgrundstück	dependent property
immeuble d'habitation	Wohnhaus	residential building
immigration	Zuwanderung	immigration
immission	Immission	exposure
immunité	Immunität	immunity
immunité de l'Etat	Immunität des Staates	sovereign immunity
immunité diplomatique	diplomatische Immunität	diplomatic immunity
impact sur l'environnement	Umweltverträglichkeit	impact on the environment
implication	Einbezug (D: Einbeziehung)	inclusion, involvement
importance minime	Geringfügigkeit	immateriality
importation	Einfuhr	import
importation, acquisition et prise en dépôt de fausse monnaie (art. 244 CP)	Einführen, Erwerben, Lagern falschen Geldes	import, acquisition and storage of counterfeit money
imposition selon la capacité économique	Besteuerung nach wirtschaftlicher Leistungsfähigkeit	taxation in accordance with ability to pay
impossibilité	Unmöglichkeit	impossibility
impossibilité initiale	ursprüngliche Unmöglichkeit	initial impossibility
impossibilité objective	objektive Unmöglichkeit	objective impossibility
impossibilité subséquente (art. 119 CO)	nachträgliche Unmöglichkeit	subsequent impossibility (e.g. an animal sold before birth is stillborn)
impôt	Steuer	tax
impôt à la source	Quellensteuer (QS)	withholding tax
impôt annuel	Jahressteuer	annual tax

impôt anticipé (IA) (F : retenue à la source)	Verrechnungssteuer (VSt) (D: Quellensteuer)	withholding tax
impôt cantonal	Staatssteuer	cantonal tax
impôt cantonal et communal (ICC)	Kantons- und Gemeindesteuer	cantonal and municipal tax
impôt communal	Gemeindesteuer	municipal tax
impôt de consommation	Verbrauchssteuer	consumption tax
impôt d'orientation	Lenkungssteuer	steering tax (a tax imposed on the consumption of certain resources to reduce such consumption)
impôt écologique	Umweltsteuer	environmental tax
impôt fédéral direct	direkte Bundessteuer	direct federal tax (levied on individual income and profits and net assets of corporations and other legal entities)
impôt foncier	Liegenschaftssteuer	property tax
impôt sur la fortune	Vermögenssteuer, Steuer vom Vermögen, Reichensteuer	wealth tax
impôt sur le revenu	Einkommensteuer, Steuer vom Einkommen	income tax
impôt sur l'énergie	Energiesteuer	energy tax
impôt sur les bateaux	Schiffsteuer	ship tax
impôt sur les bénéfices en capital	Kapitalgewinnsteuer (D: Kapitalertragsteuer)	investment income tax
impôt sur les biens	Objektsteuer	tax levied on specific property
impôt sur les billets d'entrée	Billettsteuern	ticket tax, tax on admission tickets
impôt sur les boissons	Getränkesteuer	beverage tax
impôt sur les gains immobiliers	Grundstückgewinnsteuer	real estate gains tax, tax on the profit from the sale of real estate
impôt sur les gains sur participation	Beteiligungsgewinnsteuer	capital gains tax on corporate equity
impôt sur les huiles minérales	Mineralölsteuer	gas tax (tax on oil, gasoline and kerosene)
impôt sur les successions et les donations	Erbschafts- und Schenkungssteuer	inheritance and gift tax
impotence	Hilflosigkeit	incapacitation
impotence grave	schwere Hilflosigkeit	severe disability
imprescriptibilité de l'action pénale	Unverjährbarkeit der Strafverfolgung	no time limit for criminal prosecution

imputabilité	Zurechenbarkeit	imputability
imputable	zurechenbar	imputable
imputation	Anrechnung	charge
imputation de la détention avant jugement (art. 51 CP)	Anrechnung der Untersuchungshaft	credit for time served
imputation des pertes	Verlustverrechnung	offsetting of losses
imputer	zurechnen	to impute
incapacité de gain	Erwerbsunfähigkeit	inability to work
incapacité de procéder (art. 69 CPC)	Unvermögen der Partei	inability to appear
incapacité de travail	Arbeitsunfähigkeit	disability
incapacité du failli de disposer (art. 204 LP)	Verfügungsunfähigkeit des Schuldners	insolvent's lack of capacity to dispose of his assets
incarcérer	einweisen	to incarcerate, to imprison
incendie intentionnel (art. 221 CP)	Brandstiftung	arson
incendie par négligence (art. 222 CP)	fahrlässige Verursachung einer Feuersbrunst	negligent arson
inceste (art. 213 CP)	Inzest	incest
incinération des déchets	Abfallverbrennung	incineration of waste
incitation au suicide (art. 115 CP)	Verleitung zum Selbstmord	inciting suicide
incomber : La preuve incombe au demandeur.	obliegen: Der Beweis obliegt dem Kläger.	The burden of proof is on the plaintiff.
incompatibilité	Unvereinbarkeit	incompatibility
incontesté	unbestritten	undisputed, uncontested
inconvénients	Umtriebe	trouble, time and expense (associated with something difficult)
indemnisation en nature	Realersatz	compensation in kind
indemniser	abfinden	to settle a claim, to pay off a creditor
indemnité (1)	Abfindung	settlement
indemnité (2)	Entschädigung	compensation
indemnité au témoin	Zeugenentschädigung	witness fee
indemnité de chômage	Arbeitslosenentschädigung (D: Arbeitslosengeld)	unemployment benefit
indemnité de départ (art. 339b CO)	Abgangsentschädigung	severance pay
indemnité de résidence	Ortszuschlag	cost-of-living allowance
indemnité d'usure	Entschädigung für Abnützung	compensation for wear and tear

indemnité en cas d'intempéries	Schlechtwetterentschädigung	bad weather compensation
indemnité équitable pour les démarches effectuées (art. 95 CPC)	angemessene Umtriebsentschädigung	reasonable compensation for personal efforts when a party is not represented by a lawyer
indemnité journalière	Taggeld (D: Tagegeld)	daily sick pay
indemnité pour atteinte à l'intégrité (art. 24-25 LAA)	Integritätsentschädigung	impairment compensation
indemnité pour changement d'occupation	Übergangsentschädigung	severance benefit
indemnité pour travail consacré à la famille (art. 334 CC)	Lidlohn	compensation to which adult children and grandchildren are entitled if they live with their parents and contribute their labor or income
indemnités (1)	Entschädigungsfolgen	damages
indemnités (2)	Vergütungen	compensation, remuneration
indemnités journalières de maladie	Krankentaggeld (KTG)	daily health insurance benefits
indexation	Indexierung	indexing
indication de la source	Quellenangabe	indication of the source
indication des voies de droit	Rechtsmittelbelehrung	instructions regarding appeal, instructions regarding legal remedies
indications de provenance (art. 47 LPM)	Herkunftsangaben	indications of source
indice	Indiz	circumstantial evidence
indice boursier	Börsenindex	stock exchange index
indice d'actions	Aktienindex	equity index
indice des prix à la consommation (IPC)	Index der Konsumentenpreise	Consumer Price Index (CPI)
indignité successorale (art. 540 CC)	Erbunwürdigkeit	unworthiness to inherit
indivision (art. 46 al. 3 LP)	Gemeinderschaft	undivided shares
indivision de famille (art. 132 al. 1 LP)	Gemeinderschaft	undivided family shares
indu	Nichtschuld	nonexistent debt, amount not owed

induction de la justice en erreur (art. 304 CP)	Irreführung der Rechtspflege	misleading the judicial authorities
industrie de la construction	Baugewerbe	construction industry
industrie de l'isolation	Isoliergewerbe	insulation industry
industrie horlogère	Uhrenindustrie	watch- and clockmaking industry
inexécution	Ausbleiben der Erfüllung	failure to perform
infanticide (art. 116 CP)	Kindestötung	infanticide
information d'initié	Insiderinformation	insider information
infraction	strafbare Handlung	offense
infraction à l'interdiction d'exercer une activité, à l'interdiction de contact ou à l'interdiction géographique (art. 294 CP)	Missachtung eines Tätigkeitsverbots oder eines Kontakt- und Rayonverbots	breach of an activity prohibition order or a contact prohibition and exclusion order
infraction commise à distance	Distanzdelikt	offense committed under a different jurisdiction
infraction commise contre le droit des gens	Verletzung des Völkerrechts	violation of international law
infraction commise par négligence (art. 12 al. 3 CP)	Fahrlässigkeitsdelikt	offense committed through negligence
infraction dans la poursuite pour dettes	Betreibungsdelikt	debt collection offense
infraction de commission	Handlungsdelikt	offense committed by an act (rather than an omission)
infraction de mise en danger	Gefährdungsdelikt	endangerment offense
infraction de résultat	Erfolgsdelikt	offense that must cause harm to be a crime
infraction d'importance mineure (art. 172ter CP)	geringfügiges Vermögensdelikt	minor offense against property
infraction donnant lieu à extradition (art. 35 EIMP)	Auslieferungsdelikt	extraditable offense
infraction douanière	Zollwiderhandlung	customs violation
infraction extraditionnelle (art. 35 EIMP)	Auslieferungsdelikt	extraditable offense
infraction initiale (art. 160 CP)	Vortat	original offense
infraction intentionnelle	Vorsatzdelikt	intentional offense, offense committed with intent
infraction liée à l'acquisition de stupéfiants	Beschaffungsdelikt	drug-related offense
infraction mineure	Bagatelldelikt	petty offense

infraction poursuivie d'office	Offizialdelikt	criminal offense prosecuted regardless of whether the victim brings charges (such as murder)
infraction poursuivie sur autorisation	Ermächtigungsdelikt	offense prosecuted on official authorization
infraction poursuivie sur plainte	Antragsdelikt	offense prosecuted only at the victim's request (such as negligent assault)
infraction spéciale (art. 26 CP)	Sonderdelikt	special offense
infractions au devoir de servir (art. 84 CPM)	Verletzung der Pflicht zur Dienstleistung	violation of the duty to serve
infractions contre la défense nationale	Straftaten gegen die Landesverteidigung	violations against the national defense
infractions contre la famille	Straftaten gegen die Familie	violations against the family
infractions contre la liberté	Straftaten gegen die Freiheit	violations against liberty
infractions contre la santé publique	Straftaten gegen die öffentliche Gesundheit	violations against public health
infractions contre la sécurité des rapports juridiques	Straftaten gegen die Sicherheit des Rechtsverkehrs	violations against the security of legal relationships
infractions contre la vie et l'intégrité corporelle (art. 111-136 CP)	Straftaten gegen Leib und Leben	violations against life and limb
infractions contre la volonté populaire	Straftaten gegen den Volkswillen	violations against the will of the people
infractions contre l'administration de la justice	Straftaten gegen die Rechtspflege	violations against the administration of justice
infractions contre l'autorité publique	Straftaten gegen die öffentliche Gewalt	violations against public authority
infractions contre le patrimoine (art. 137-172ter CP)	strafbare Handlungen gegen das Vermögen	offenses against property
infractions contre les communications publiques	Straftaten gegen den öffentlichen Verkehr	violations against public traffic
infractions contre les devoirs de fonction	Straftaten gegen die Amts- und Berufspflicht	violations against official or professional duty
infractions contre l'honneur	Straftaten gegen die Ehre	violations against honor

infractions contre l'intégrité sexuelle (art. 187-212 CP)	Straftaten gegen die sexuelle Integrität	violations against sexual integrity
infractions créant un danger collectif	gemeingefährliche Straftaten	offenses creating a public danger
infractions en matière informatique	Computerstraftaten	computer-related offenses
infrastructure des marchés financiers	Finanzmarktinfrastruktur	financial market infrastructure
initiation à la profession	Anlehre (D: berufliche Kurzausbildung)	vocational training for young people who have not done an apprenticeship
initiative constitutionnelle	Verfassungsinitiative	constitutional initiative
initiative déposée par un canton	Ständeinitiative	cantonal initiative
initiative des cantons	Standesinitiative	cantonal initiative
initiative législative	Gesetzesinitiative	legislative initiative (whereby voters begin the legislative procedure by submitting a draft bill to the parliament of the canton)
initiative parlementaire	parlamentarische Initiative	parliamentary initiative
initiative populaire	Volksinitiative	popular initiative
initié	Insider	insider
injure (art. 177 CP)	Beschimpfung	insult
injure grave	Ehrenkränkung	libel (written), slander (oral), defamation (superordinate term covering both libel and slander)
inobservation des prescriptions légales sur la comptabilité (art. 325 CP)	ordnungswidrige Führung der Geschäftsbücher	failure to comply with accounting regulations
inobservation du contrat	Vertragsverletzung	breach of contract
insaisissabilité	Unpfändbarkeit	unseizability
insaisissable	unpfändbar	unseizable
inscription	Eintragung	registration
inscription à l'ordre du jour (art. 699-701 CO)	Traktandierung	inclusion on the agenda
inscription au registre du commerce (art. 640 CO)	Eintragung ins Handelsregister	entry in the Commercial Register
insécurité juridique	Rechtsunsicherheit	legal uncertainty
insolvabilité	Zahlungsunfähigkeit	insolvency

insoumission (militaire)	Dienstversäumnis	absence without leave (AWOL)
insoumission à une décision de l'autorité (art. 292 CP)	Ungehorsam gegen amtliche Verfügungen	contempt of official orders
inspection locale (art. 181-182 CPC)	Augenschein	on-site inspection by the court
inspections (art. 14 LP)	Geschäftsprüfung	inspections
installation d'épuration	Kläranlage	sewage treatment plant, waste water treatment plant
installation pour services accessoires du chemin de fer	Anlage für Bahnnebenbetrieb	facilities for railroad station kiosks
instance de recours	Rechtsmittelinstanz	appellate court
instance unique	einzige Instanz	single instance
instigation (art. 24 CP)	Anstiftung	incitement, instigation
instigation à un faux témoignage	Zeugenbestechung	bribing a witness
Institut du Fédéralisme	Institut für Föderalismus	Institute of Federalism
Institut fédéral de la propriété intellectuelle (IPI)	Eidgenössisches Institut für Geistiges Eigentum (IGE)	Swiss Federal Institute of Intellectual Property
Institut suisse de droit comparé (ISDC)	Schweizerisches Institut für Rechtsvergleichung (SIRG)	Swiss Institute of Comparative Law
institution de libre passage	Freizügigkeitseinrichtung	vested benefits institution
institution de prévoyance	Vorsorgeeinrichtung	pension institution, pension fund
institution de prévoyance de droit public	öffentlich-rechtliche Vorsorgeeinrichtung	public law pension institution
institution de prévoyance enregistrée	registrierte Vorsorgeeinrichtung	registered pension institution
institution de prévoyance enveloppante	umhüllende Vorsorgeeinrichtung	comprehensive pension institution
institution de prévoyance non enregistrée	nichtregistrierte Vorsorgeeinrichtung	unregistered pension institution
institution de privation de liberté	Institution des Freiheitsentzugs	penal institution
institution d'héritier (art. 483 ss CC)	Erbeinsetzung	appointment of an heir
institution supplétive	Auffangeinrichtung	substitute occupational benefit institution
instruments financiers dérivés	derivative Finanzinstrumente	derivative financial instruments, derivatives

insubordination (art. 63-64 CPM)	Verletzung der Pflicht der militärischen Unterordnung	insubordination
insuffisance du gage	Pfandausfall	insufficient pledge
insulte	Beleidigung	insult
intégrité corporelle	körperliche Integrität	bodily integrity
intégrité sexuelle	sexuelle Integrität	sexual integrity
intention (1)	Vorsatz	intent
intention (2)	Absicht	intention
intention de faire une libéralité	Schenkungsabsicht	intention to make a gift
intention de se marier	Heiratsabsicht	intention to marry
intention de s'établir	Absicht dauernden Verbleibens	intention to settle
intercantonal	interkantonal	intercantonal
interdiction (1)	Verbot	prohibition
interdiction (2)	Entmündigung	making someone a ward of the court
interdiction d'accepter des dons	Verbot der Annahme von Geschenken	prohibition on accepting gifts
interdiction de bâtir	Bauverbot	ban on construction
interdiction de circuler (art. 67e CP)	Fahrverbot	disqualification from driving
interdiction de contact (art. 67 CC)	Kontaktverbot	contact prohibition
interdiction de cumuler la protection (art. 140 LBI)	Verbot des Doppelschutzes	prohibition of double patenting
interdiction de démolir	Abbruchverbot	prohibition on demolition
interdiction de la cession	Zessionsverbot	prohibition of assignment
interdiction de la contrainte par corps	Verbot des Schuldverhafts	prohibition of debtor's prison
interdiction de la double poursuite (art. 11 CPP)	Verbot der doppelten Strafverfolgerung	prohibition of double jeopardy
interdiction de la torture	Folterverbot	prohibition on torture
interdiction de parquer	Parkverbot	parking ban, no parking
interdiction de payer	Zahlungsverbot	injunction against payment
interdiction de pénétrer dans une zone	Ausgrenzung	prohibition on entering an area
interdiction de quitter une région	Eingrenzung	restriction order, order not leave a specific area
interdiction des traitements inhumains (art. 10 al. 3 CF)	Verbot unmenschlicher Behandlung	prohibition of inhuman treatment

interdiction d'exercer une activité (art. 67 CP)	Tätigkeitsverbot	prohibition on engaging in an activity
interdiction d'exercer une profession	Berufsverbot	prohibition on practicing a profession
interdiction du commerce	Verbot des Handels	prohibition of trade
interdiction du travail forcé	Verbot der Zwangsarbeit	prohibition of forced labor
interdiction géographique	Rayonverbot	exclusion order
intérêt	Zins	interest
intérêt actuel	aktuelles Interesse	current interest
intérêt couru mais non échu	Marchzins	accrued interest
intérêt de l'enfant	Kindeswohl	best interests of the child
intérêt débiteur	Schuldzins	interest on debt
intérêt digne de protection (art. 156 CPC)	schutzwürdiges Interesse	legitimate interest
intérêt économique	wirtschaftliches Interesse	economic interest
intérêt fiscal	fiskalisches Interesse	fiscal interest
intérêt hypothécaire	Hypothekarzins (D: Hypothekenzins)	mortgage interest
intérêt important du pays	Landesinteressen	national interests
intérêt juridique (procédure civile)	Rechtsschutzinteresse (Zivilprozess)	legitimate interest
intérêt juridiquement protégé	rechtlich geschütztes Interesse	legally protected interest
intérêt moratoire	Verzugszins	default interest
intérêt rémunératoire (art. 61 LTVA)	Vergütungszins	refund interest
intérêts composés	Zinseszins	compound interest
intérêts créditeurs	Habenzins	creditor interest (rate); deposit rate
intérêts débiteurs	Sollzins	debtor interest (rate); lending rate
intérêts intercalaires (art. 627 CO)	Bauzinsen	interest paid to shareholder until commencement of company's operations
intérêts public prépondérants	überwiegende öffentliche Interessen	compelling public interests
intergroupe parlementaire	parlamentarische Gruppen	cross-party groups
intermédiaire	Vermittler	justice of the peace
intermédiaire financier	Finanzintermediär	financial intermediary
intermédiaire financier sans statut bancaire	nichtbankmässige Finanzintermediär	nonbank financial intermediary
internement (art. 56 ss CP)	Verwahrung	incarceration, imprisonment

internement à vie (art. 64 CP)	lebenslängliche Verwahrung	lifelong imprisonment
internement des délinquants d'habitude (art. 42 CP)	Verwahrung von Gewohnheitsverbrechern	incarceration of habitual offenders
interpellateur	Interpellant	interpellator
interpellation (art. 102 al. 1 CO)	Mahnung	formal reminder to pay
interpellation par le tribunal (art. 56 CPC)	gerichtliche Fragepflicht	court's duty to question insufficient or unclear allegations made by the parties
interpellation parlementaire	Interpellation	interpellation
interprétation (1)	Auslegung	interpretation, construction (of a law or contract)
interprétation (2) (art. 69 PA)	Erläuterung	explanatory statement
interprétation conforme à la constitution	verfassungskonforme Auslegung	constitutional interpretation
interprétation de la loi	Gesetzesauslegung	statutory construction
interprétation littérale	grammatikalische Auslegung	literal interpretation
interprétation systématique	systematische Auslegung	systematic interpretation
interprétation téléologique	teleologische Auslegung	teleological interpretation
interprétation uniforme	einheitliche Auslegung	uniform interpretation
interrogation d'une partie (art. 191 CPC)	Parteibefragung (D: Parteivernehmung)	examination of a party
interrogatoire	Verhör	examination, questioning
interrogatoire par le président du tribunal	Präsidialverhör	examination by the presiding judge (as opposed to cross examination)
interroger	einvernehmen (D: vernehmen)	to examine, interrogate
interruption	Unterbruch (D: Unterbrechung)	interruption
interruption de grossesse non punissable (art. 119 CP)	strafloser Schwangerschaftsabbruch	legal abortion
interruption de grossesse punissable (art. 118 CP)	strafbarer Schwangerschaftsabbruch	illegal abortion
interruption de la grossesse (art. 118 CP)	Schwangerschaftsabbruch	abortion

interruption de la prescription (art. 135-138 CO)	Unterbrechung der Verjährung	interruption of the limitation period
interruption de l'exploitation	Betriebsunterbruch (D: Betriebsunterbrechung)	business interruption
interruption du délai	Fristunterbrechung	interruption of a period of time
intervenant (1) (art. 76 CPC)	intervenierende Person	intervenor
intervenant (2)	Votant (D: Diskussionsredner im Parlament)	speaker
intervenir (1)	intervenieren	to intervene
intervenir (2)	votieren (D:Stellung nehmen)	to speak
intervention (1) (art. 73 CPC)	Intervention	third-party intervention
intervention (2)	Votum(D: Diskussionsbeitrag)	speech
intervention (3) (papier-valeur)	Ehreneintritt	intervention
intervention accessoire (art. 74 CPC)	Nebenintervention	accessory intervention (a third party supports either the plaintiff's claim or the defendant's claim)
intervention fédérale	Bundesintervention	federal intervention
intervention parlementaire	Vorstoss, parlamentarischer Vorstoss	parliamentary procedural request
intervention principale (art. 73 CPC)	Hauptintervention	principal intervention (a third party asserts his own claim in the lawsuit)
interventions ultérieures	Nachsorge	continuous monitoring
intimé	Beschwerdegegner, Rekursgegner	appellee
intoxication	Vergiftung	poisoning
intracantonal	innerkantonal	intracantonal
invalidité	Invalidität	disability
invalidité partielle	Teilinvalidität	partial disability
invalidité permanente	Dauerinvalidität	permanent disability
inventaire	Inventar	inventory
inventaire communal	kommunales Inventar	inventory of cultural assets in a municipality
inventaire des biens	Güterverzeichnis	inventory
Inventaire fédéral des paysages, sites et monuments naturels	Bundesinventar der Landschaften und Naturdenkmäler	Federal Inventory of Landscapes and Natural Monuments
inventaire fiscal	Steuerinventar	tax inventory

inventeur	Erfinder	inventor
invention	Erfindung	invention
invention brevetable	patentierbare Erfindung	patentable invention
invention dépendante (art. 36 LBI)	abhängige Erfindung	dependant invention
investigation de détail	Detailuntersuchung	detailed investigation
investigation secrète (art. 285a CPP)	verdeckte Ermittlung	undercover investigation
investissement	Anlage, Investition	investment
investisseur	Anleger	investor
inviolabilité du domicile	Unverletzlichkeit der Wohnung	inviolability of the home
irrecevabilité	Unzulässigkeit	inadmissibility
irresponsabilité (art. 19 CP)	Schuldunfähigkeit	absence of legal responsibility due to a mental disorder
irresponsabilité fautive (art. 263 CPP)	selbstverschuldete Unzurechnungsfähigkeit	voluntarily induced mental incapacity
isolation	Isolation	insulation
jeton de présence	Sitzungsgeld	directors' fee, attendance fee
Jeûne fédéral	Eidgenössischer Dank, Buss- und Bettag	Federal Day of Thanksgiving, Repentance and Prayer
jeux d'argent (art. 106 CF)	Geldspiele	gambling
jonction de causes	Vereinigung von Verfahren	joinder of cases
jouissance des droits civils (art. 53 CC)	Rechtsfähigkeit	legal capacity
jour-amende	Tagessatz	daily penalty unit
jour férié	Feiertag	public holiday
jour ouvrable	Werktag	working day
jour ouvrable bancaire	Bankarbeitstag	banking day
journal	Tagebuch	journal (accounting)
judiciaire	richterlich	judicial
juge	Richter	judge
juge arbitre	Schiedsrichter	arbitrator
juge assesseur	Beisitzer (BS)	advisor
juge de la détention	Haftrichter	committing magistrate
juge de la faillite	Konkursrichter	bankruptcy judge
juge de l'arrestation	Haftgericht	committal court
juge de paix	Friedensrichter, Sühnbeamter, Vermittleramt	justice of the peace
juge de renvoi	Überweisungsrichter	remand judge

juge d'instruction pénale	Verhörrichter, Untersuchungsrichter	investigating magistrate (no longer exists in Swiss law – criminal investigations are now conducted by the prosecutor)
juge du concordat (art. 293a LP)	Nachlassgericht	debt restructuring court
juge du fond	Sachrichter	trial judge, judge who decided the merits of the case
juge laïc	Laienrichter	lay judge
juge suppléant	Ersatzrichter	substitute judge
juge unique	Einzelrichter	single judge (as opposed to a panel of judges)
jugement	Urteil	judgment
jugement au fond	Sachentscheid	judgment on the merits
jugement contradictoire	streitiges Urteil	judgment in a defended action
jugement de débouté	Abweisung	judgment for the defendant
jugement de divorce	Scheidungsurteil, Ehescheidungsurteil	divorce decree
jugement par défaut	Abwesenheitsurteil	default judgment
Jura	Jura	Jura (canton)
juré	Geschworener	juror
juridiction arbitrale	Schiedsgerichtsbarkeit	arbitral jurisdiction
juridiction cantonale	kantonale Gerichtsbarkeit	cantonal jurisdiction
juridiction constitutionnelle	Verfassungsgerichtsbarkeit	constitutional jurisdiction
juridiction fédérale	Bundesgerichtsbarkeit	federal jurisdiction
juridiction gracieuse (art. 19 CPC)	freiwillige Gerichtsbarkeit	noncontentious matters
jurisprudence	Judikatur, Rechtsprechung, Richterrecht	case law, judge-made law
Jurisprudence des autorités administratives de la Confédération (JAAC)	Verwaltungsentscheide der Bundesbehörden (VEB)	Decisions of the Administrative Authorities of the Confederation
jurisprudence fédérale	Bundesrechtsprechung	federal case law
juriste	Jurist	law graduate, person with a law degree
jury civil	Ziviljury	civil jury
jusqu'à nouvel ordre	auf Zusehen hin	until further notice
jusqu'à présent	bis anhin (D: bis jetzt)	until now

juste motif	wichtiger Grund	good cause
justice	Gerechtigkeit	justice
justice propre	Selbsthilfe	self-help (taking the law into one's own hands)
justice vehmique	Femegericht	kangaroo court
label de qualité	Gütezeichen	certification mark
lacune (législation)	Lücke (Rechtssetzung)	gap
lacune du contrat	Vertragslücke	matter as to which a contract is silent
landamman	Landammann (D: Regierungschef eines Kantons)	head of cantonal government
langage juridique	Rechtssprache	legal language
langue nationale	Landessprache	national language
langue officielle (art. 70 CP)	Amtssprache	official language
latoisage	Streichung (Wahlliste)	voter's deletion of candidates from a list
légalisation	Beglaubigung	certification
légalité	Gesetzmässigkeit, Rechtsmässigkeit	legality
légataire	Legatar, Vermächtnisnehmer	legatee
légèreté	Leichtsinn	carelessness
légiférer	legiferieren (D: Gesetze erlassen)	to legislate, to make legislation
législateur	Gesetzgeber	legislator
législation	Gesetzgebung, Rechtssetzung	legislation
législation cadre	Rahmengesetzgebung	framework legislation
législation fédérale	Bundesgesetzgebung	federal legislation
législature	Legislatur, Legislaturperiode	legislative period
légitimation active	Aktivlegitimation	plaintiff's standing
légitimation passive	Passivlegitimation	defendant's standing, standing to be sued
légitime défense (art. 15-16 CP)	Notwehr (Art. 15-16 StGB)	self-defense
legs (art. 484 CC)	Legat, Vermächtnis	legacy
legs d'une chose déterminée (art. 526 CC)	Vermächtnis einer einzelnen Sache	specific legacy
legs préciputaire	Vorausvermächtnis, Prälegat	advance legacy
lésé (art. 115 CPP)	geschädigte Person	aggrieved person (person whose rights have been directly violated by the criminal offense)
lésion (1)	Läsion	injury
lésion (2) (art. 21 CO)	Übervorteilung (Art. 21 OR)	unconscionable bargain

lésion corporelle (art. 122 CP)	Körperverletzung	assault
lésion corporelle assimilée à un accident	unfallähnliche Körperschädigung	accident-like bodily harm
lésion corporelle grave (art. 122 CP)	schwere Körperverletzung	aggravated assault
lésion corporelle par négligence (art. 125 CP)	fahrlässige Körperverletzung	negligent assault
lésion corporelle simple (art. 123 CP)	einfache Körperverletzung	common assault
lettre de change (art. 991-1085 CO)	gezogener Wechsel	bill of exchange
lettre de change à un certain délai de vue (art. 1013 CO)	Nachsichtwechsel	bill payable at a fixed period after sight
lettre de change à vue (art. 1024 CO)	Sichtwechsel	bill payable on demand
lettre de change domiciliée (art. 994 CO)	Domizilwechsel	domiciled bill of exchange
lettre de chargement	Ladeschein	bill of lading
lettre de confirmation	Bestätigungsschreiben	letter of confirmation
lettre de crédit (art. 407 CO)	Kreditbrief	letter of credit
lettre de gage	Pfandbrief	mortgage bond
lettre de voiture	Frachtbrief	waybill
lettre signature	Einschreiben	registered letter
levée du corps	Wegnahme der Leiche	removal of the body
liaisons interopérables	interoperable Verbindungen	interoperability agreements
libéralités (art. 286 LP)	Zuwendungen	gifts
libéralités entre vifs (art. 475 CC)	Zuwendungen unter Lebenden	inter vivos gifts
libéralités entre vifs faites à titre d'avancement d'hoirie	Zuwendungen auf Anrechnung an den Erbteil	advances against a person's share of an inheritance
libération (1)	Entlassung	release
libération (2)	Liberierung (D: Einzahlung)	payment in full (for shares)
libération conditionnelle (art. 62 CP)	bedingte Entlassung (Art. 62 StGB)	parole
libération de dette	Aberkennung der Forderung	lifting of a debt
libération des apports (art. 633, 652a CO)	Leistung der Einlagen	making capital contributions
libération des sûretés (art. 239 CPP)	Freigabe der Sicherheitsleistung	return of the bail payment
libération du paiement des primes	Prämienbefreiung	waiver of premium

libération en espèces	Barliberierung	payment in cash
libération judiciaire d'une servitude (art. 736 CC)	Ablösung einer Dienstbarkeit durch den Richter	termination of an easement by the court
libération ultérieure (art. 634 CO)	nachträgliche Leistung	subsequent payment in full (when share capital has only been partially paid in)
libéré	liberiert (D: eingezahlt)	fully paid-in
libérer (1)	liberieren (D: einzahlen)	to pay for shares
libérer (2)	entlassen	to release
libérer conditionnellement	bedingt entlassen	to release on parole
liberté	Freiheit	freedom, liberty
liberté contractuelle (art. 19 al. 1 CO)	Vertragsfreiheit	freedom of contract
liberté d'association (art. 23 CF)	Vereinigungsfreiheit	freedom of association
liberté de conscience et de croyance (art. 15 CF)	Glaubens- und Gewissensfreiheit	freedom of religion and conscience
liberté de consommation	Konsumfreiheit	freedom of consumption
liberté de contracter	Abschlussfreiheit	freedom of contract
liberté de culte	Kultusfreiheit	freedom of religion
liberté de disposer	Verfügungsfreiheit	freedom to dispose of assets
liberté de la concurrence	Wettbewerbsfreiheit	freedom of competition
liberté de la langue (art. 18 CF)	Sprachenfreiheit	freedom to use any language
liberté de la presse	Pressefreiheit	freedom of the press
liberté de la recherche	Forschungsfreiheit	freedom to conduct research
liberté de la science (art. 20 CF)	Wissenschaftsfreiheit	academic freedom
liberté de l'art (art. 21 CF)	Kunstfreiheit	freedom of artistic expression
liberté de manifestation	Demonstrationsfreiheit	freedom to demonstrate, freedom of demonstration
liberté de parole	Redefreiheit	freedom of speech
liberté de réunion (art. 22 CF)	Versammlungsfreiheit	freedom of assembly
liberté des médias (art. 17 CF)	Medienfreiheit	freedom of the media
liberté d'établissement (art. 24 CF)	Niederlassungsfreiheit	freedom of domicile
liberté d'étude et d'enseignement	Lehr- und Lernfreiheit	academic freedom

liberté d'expression	Meinungsäusserungsfreiheit	freedom of expression
liberté d'expression et d'information (art. 16 CV)	Meinungs- und Informationsfreiheit	freedom of expression and of information
liberté d'information	Informationsfreiheit	freedom of information
liberté économique (art. 27 CF)	Wirtschaftsfreiheit	economic freedom
liberté syndicale (art. 28 CF)	Koalitionsfreiheit	right to form professional associations
libre appréciation des preuves	freie Beweiswürdigung	principle of free interpretation of evidence
libre circulation des capitaux	Kapitalverkehrsfreiheit	free circulation of capital
libre circulation des marchandises	freier Warenverkehr	free movement of goods
libre passage (art. 70 al. 4 LFMal)	Zügerrecht	right to transfer from a group health insurance policy to an individual policy upon termination of employment
libre passage (assurances)	Freizügigkeit (Versicherung)	vested benefits
licence	Lizenz	license
licence temporaire	befristete Lizenz	temporary license
licenciement collectif	Massenentlassung	mass layoff
licenciement économique	wirtschaftlich bedingte Entlassung	layoff for economic reasons
lieu d'accident	Unfallstandort	accident site
lieu de commission (art. 8 CP)	Begehungsort	place of commission (of a crime)
lieu de destination	Bestimmungsort	place of destination
lieu de l'exécution (art. 74 CO)	Erfüllungsort	place of performance
lieu de provenance	Herkunftsort	place of origin
lieu de résultat	Erfolgsort	place of performance
lieu de séjour	Aufenthaltsort	place of residence
lieu de travail	Arbeitsort	place of work
lieu d'origine	Bürgerort, Heimatort	place of origin
limitation	Beschränkung	limitation
limitation de la transmissibilité	Vinkulierung	restricted transferability
limitation du nombre des étrangers	Begrenzung der Zahl der Ausländer	limitation on the number of foreigners
limite d'âge	Altersgrenze	age limit

limites : dans les limites de la loi et des règles de la profession	Schranken: in den Schranken von Gesetz und Standesregeln	subject to the restrictions laid down by law and in the code of professional practice
liquidateur (art. 317 ss LP)	Liquidator	liquidator
liquidation	Liquidation	liquidation
liquidation de la succession	Abwicklung eines Nachlasses	settlement of an estate
liquidation du régime matrimonial	güterrechtliche Auseinandersetzung	marital property settlement
liquidation en espèces	Barabgeltung, Barabrechnung	cash settlement
liquidités	flüssige Mittel	cash and cash equivalents
liste des annexes	Beilagenverzeichnis	list of exhibits (to a document)
liste des hôpitaux	Spitalliste (D: Krankenhausliste)	list of hospitals
litige	Rechtsstreit	legal dispute, litigation
litige en matière de contribution publique	Abgabestreitigkeit	tax dispute
litige en matière de frontière	Grenzstreitigkeit zwischen Staaten	border dispute
litige en matière de tarif	Tarifstreit	wage dispute
litige patrimonial	vermögensrechtliche Streitigkeit	financial dispute
litispendance (art. 62 ss CPC)	Rechtshängigkeit	pendency (of a lawsuit)
litispendant	rechtshängig	pending
livraison	Lieferung	delivery
livre de caisse	Kassabuch	cash book
livres comptables	Geschäftsbücher	accounting books and records
livret de cours	Testatbuch	course attendance booklet
livret de famille	Familienbüchlein	family record book
livret de service (F : livret militaire)	Dienstbüchlein (D: Wehrpass)	military record
livret d'épargne	Sparheft	savings passbook
livret d'étudiant	Testat	course attendance record
livret pour étrangers	Ausländerausweis	foreign national identity card
local de vote	Stimmlokal (D: Wahllokal)	voting location
local des sapeurs-pompiers	Feuerwehrlokal	fire station
localité	Ort	place, city (in an address)
locataire	Mieter	tenant, renter, lessee

locataire de remplacement	Ersatzmieter	substitute tenant
location-vente	Miet-Kauf-Vertrag	installment plan
locaux commerciaux (art. 253a CO)	Geschäftsräume	business premises
lock-out	Aussperrung	lock-out
logement	Wohnraum	residence
logement de la famille (art. 151 al. 1 lit. b et 153 al. 2 lit. b LP)	Familienwohnung, Wohnung der Familie	family residence, family home
Loi cantonale sur l'aménagement du territoire	Kantonales Raumplanungsgesetz	Cantonal Act on Spatial Planning
loi d'application	Einführungsgesetz	introductory act
loi fédérale	Bundesgesetz	federal act
Loi fédérale concernant la constitution de gages sur les chemins de fer et de navigation et la liquidation forcée de ces entreprises (LGEL)	Bundesgesetz über die Verpfändung und Zwangsliquidation von Eisenbahn- und Schifffahrtsunternehmungen (VZEG)	Federal Act on the Attachment and Administrative Receivership of Railroad and Shipping Companies
Loi fédérale concernant la surveillance des prix (LSPr)	Preisüberwachungsgesetz (PüG)	Price Supervision Act
Loi fédérale contre la concurrence déloyale (LCD)	Bundesgesetz gegen den unlauteren Wettbewerb (UWG)	Federal Act on Unfair Competition
Loi fédérale de procédure civile fédérale (PCF)	Bundesgesetz über den Bundeszivilprozess (BZP)	Federal Act on Federal Civil Procedure
Loi fédérale instituant des mesures visant au maintien de la sûreté intérieure (LMSI)	Bundesgesetz über Massnahmen zur Wahrung der inneren Sicherheit (BWIS)	Internal Security Act
Loi fédérale permettant d'étendre le champ d'application de la convention collective de travail (LECCT)	Bundesgesetz über die Allgemeinverbindlicherklärung von Gesamtarbeitsverträgen (AVEG)	Federal Act on the Declaration of the General Application of Collective Employment Agreements
Loi fédérale régissant la condition pénale des mineurs (DPMin)	Bundesgesetz über das Jugendstrafrecht (JStG)	Federal Act on the Criminal Law applicable to Juveniles; Juvenile Criminal Law Act
Loi fédérale régissant la taxe sur la valeur ajoutée (LTVA)	Bundesgesetz über die Mehrwertsteuer (MWSTG)	Federal Value Added Tax Act

Loi fédérale relative au traité conclu avec les États-Unis d'Amérique sur l'entraide judiciaire en matière pénale (LTEJUS)	Bundesgesetz zum Staatsvertrag mit den Vereinigten Staaten von Amerika über gegenseitige Rechtshilfe in Strafsachen (BG-RVUS)	Federal Act on the Treaty concluded with the United States of America on Mutual Assistance in Criminal Matters
Loi fédérale sur la circulation des véhicules automobiles et des cycles	Bundesgesetz über den Motorfahrzeug- und Fahrradverkehr (MFG)	Federal Act on Motor Vehicle and Cycle Traffic
Loi fédérale sur la circulation routière (LCR)	Strassenverkehrsgesetz (SVG)	Road Traffic Act
Loi fédérale sur la constitution de réserves de crise bénéficiant d'allégements fiscaux (LCRC)	Bundesgesetz über die Bildung steuerbegünstigter Arbeitsbeschaffungsreserven (ABRG)	Federal Act on the Establishment of Tax Privileged Job Creation Reserves
Loi fédérale sur la formation professionnelle (LFPr)	Bundesgesetz über die Berufsbildung (BBG)	Federal Act on Vocational and Professional Education and Training
Loi fédérale sur la libre circulation des avocats (LLCA)	Bundesgesetz über die Freizügigkeit der Anwältinnen und Anwälte (BGFA)	Federal Act on the Free Movement of Lawyers
Loi fédérale sur la partie générale du droit des assurances sociales (LPGA)	Bundesgesetz über den allgemeinen Teil des Sozialversicherungsrechts (ATSG)	Federal Act on General Aspects of Social Security Law
Loi fédérale sur la pêche (LFSP)	Bundesgesetz über die Fischerei (BGF)	Federal Act on Fish and Fisheries
Loi fédérale sur la péréquation financière et la compensation des charges (PFCC)	Bundesgesetz über den Finanz- und Lastenausgleich (FiLaG)	Federal Act on Fiscal Equalization and Cost Compensation
Loi fédérale sur la poste (LPO)	Postgesetz (PG)	Postal Services Act
Loi fédérale sur la poursuite pour dettes et la faillite (LP)	Bundesgesetz über Schuldbetreibung und Konkurs (SchKG)	Debt Collection and Bankruptcy Act
Loi fédérale sur la prévoyance professionnelle vieillesse, survivants et invalidité (LPP)	Bundesgesetz über die berufliche Alters-, Hinterlassenen- und Invalidenvorsorge (BVG)	Swiss Federal Occupational Retirement, Survivors and Disability Pension Plan Act
Loi fédérale sur la procédure administrative (PA)	Bundesgesetz über das Verwaltungsverfahren (VwVG)	Federal Act on Administrative Procedure; Administrative Procedure Act

Loi fédérale sur la procédure de consultation (LCo)	Vernehmlassungsgesetz (VlG)	Federal Act on the Consultation Procedure
Loi fédérale sur la procréation médicalement assistée (LPMA)	Bundesgesetz über die medizinisch unterstützte Fortpflanzung (FMedG)	Reproductive Medicine Act
Loi fédérale sur la protection de la nature et du paysage (LPN)	Bundesgesetz über den Natur- und Heimatschutz (NHG)	Nature and Cultural Heritage Act
Loi fédérale sur la protection des designs (LDes)	Bundesgesetz über den Schutz von Design (DesG)	Federal Act on the Protection of Designs; Designs Act
Loi fédérale sur la protection des données (LPD)	Bundesgesetz über den Datenschutz (DSG)	Federal Act on Data Protection; Data Protection Act
Loi fédérale sur la protection des marques et des indications de provenance (LPM)	Bundesgesetz über den Schutz von Marken und Herkunftsangaben (MSchG)	Federal Act on the Protection of Trademarks and Indications of Source
Loi fédérale sur la radio et la télévision (LRTV)	Bundesgesetz über Radio und Fernsehen (RTVG)	Radio and Television Act
Loi fédérale sur la responsabilité du fait des produits (LRFP)	Bundesgesetz über die Produktehaftpflicht (PrHG)	Product Liability Act
Loi fédérale sur la signature électronique (SCSE)	Bundesgesetz über die elektronische Signatur (ZertES)	Federal Act on Electronic Signatures
Loi fédérale sur la statistique fédérale (LSF)	Bundesstatistikgesetz (BStatG)	Federal Statistics Act
Loi fédérale sur la surveillance de la correspondance par poste et télécommunication (LSCPT)	Bundesgesetz betreffend die Überwachung des Post- und Fernmeldeverkehrs (BÜPF)	Federal Act on the Surveillance of Post and Telecommunications
Loi fédérale sur la surveillance des assurances (LSA)	Versicherungsaufsichtsgesetz (VAG)	Insurance Supervision Act
Loi fédérale sur la taxe d'exemption de l'obligation de servir (LTEO)	Bundesgesetz über die Wehrpflichtersatzabgabe (WPEG)	Federal Act on the Military Service Exemption Tax
Loi fédérale sur la transparence de l'administration (LTrans)	Bundesgesetz über die Öffentlichkeit der Verwaltung (BGÖ)	Freedom of Information Act
Loi fédérale sur la transplantation	Transplantationsgesetz	Transplantation Act

Loi fédérale sur l'acquisition d'immeubles par des personnes à l'étranger (LFAIE)	Bundesgesetz über den Erwerb von Grundstücken durch Personen im Ausland (BewG)	Federal Act on the Acquisition of Real Estate in Switzerland by Non-Residents
Loi fédérale sur l'aide aux victimes d'infractions (LAVI)	Opferhilfegesetz (OHG)	Victim Support Act
Loi fédérale sur l'alcool (Lalc)	Bundesgesetz über die gebrannten Wasser (AlKG)	Alcohol Act
Loi fédérale sur l'aménagement du territoire (LAT)	Bundesgesetz über die Raumplanung (RPG)	Federal Spatial Planning Act
Loi fédérale sur l'assurance militaire (LAM)	Militärversicherungsgesetz (MVG)	Military Insurance Act
Loi fédérale sur l'assurance-accidents (LAA)	Bundesgesetz über die Unfallversicherung (UVG)	Accident Insurance Act
Loi fédérale sur l'assurance-invalidité (LAI)	Bundesgesetz über die Invalidenversicherung (IVG)	Disability Insurance Act
Loi fédérale sur l'assurance-maladie	Krankenversicherungsgesetz (KVG)	Swiss Federal Health Insurance Act
Loi fédérale sur l'assurance-maladie (LFMal)	Bundesgesetz über die Krankenversicherung (KVG)	Federal Health Insurance Act
Loi fédérale sur l'aviation (LA)	Bundesgesetz über die Luftfahrt (LFG)	Federal Aviation Act
Loi fédérale sur l'entraide pénale internationale (EIMP)	Bundesgesetz über internationale Rechtshilfe in Strafsachen (IRSG)	Federal Act on Mutual Assistance in Criminal Matters
Loi fédérale sur le blocage et la restitution des valeurs patrimoniales d'origine illicite de personnes politiquement exposées à l'étranger (LVP)	Bundesgesetz über die Sperrung und die Rückerstattung unrechtmässig erworbener Vermögenswerte ausländischer politisch exponierter Personen (SRVG)	Federal Act on the Freezing and Restitution of Illicit Assets held by Foreign Politically Exposed Persons
Loi fédérale sur le crédit à la consommation (LCC)	Bundesgesetz über den Konsumkredit (KKG)	Federal Act on Consumer Credit; Consumer Credit Act
Loi fédérale sur le droit d'auteur (LDA)	Urheberrechtsgesetz (URG)	Copyright Act
Loi fédérale sur le droit foncier rural (LDFR)	Bundesgesetz über das bäuerliche Bodenrecht (BGBB)	Federal Act on Rural Land Rights
Loi fédérale sur le droit international privé (LDIP)	Bundesgesetz über das internationale Privatrecht (IPRG)	Federal Act on International Private Law
Loi fédérale sur le droit pénal administratif (DPA)	Bundesgesetz über das Verwaltungsstrafrecht (VStrR)	Federal Act on Administrative Criminal Law

Loi fédérale sur le marché intérieur (LMI)	Bundesgesetz über den Binnenmarkt (BGBM)	Federal Act on the Internal Market; Internal Market Act
Loi fédérale sur le matériel de guerre (LFMG)	Kriegsmaterialgesetz (KMG)	War Material Act
Loi fédérale sur le régime des allocations pour perte de gain (LAPG)	Bundesgesetz über die Erwerbsersatzordnung (EOG)	Loss of Earnings Compensation Act
Loi fédérale sur le service civil (LSC)	Zivildienstgesetz (ZDG)	Federal Civil Service Act
Loi fédérale sur le service de l'emploi et la location de services (LSE)	Bundesgesetz über die Arbeitsvermittlung und den Personalverleih (AVG)	Federal Act on Recruitment and the Hiring of Services; Recruitment Act
Loi fédérale sur le transfert de biens culturels (LTBC)	Kulturgütertransfergesetz (KGTG)	Cultural Property Transfer Act
Loi fédérale sur le travail dans les fabriques	Bundesgesetz betreffend die Arbeit in den Fabriken	Federal Act on Work in Factories
Loi fédérale sur le tribunal fédéral (LTF)	Bundesgerichtgesetz (BGG)	Federal Supreme Court Act
Loi fédérale sur les aides financières et les indemnités (LSu)	Bundesgesetz über Finanzhilfen und Abgeltungen (SuG)	Federal Act on Financial Aids and Grants
Loi fédérale sur les allocations familiales (LAFam)	Bundesgesetz über die Familienzulagen (FamZG)	Family Allowances Act
Loi fédérale sur les amendes d'ordre (LAO)	Ordnungsbussengesetz (OBG)	Fixed Penalties Act
Loi fédérale sur les banques et les caisses d'épargne (LB)	Bundesgesetz über die Banken und Sparkassen (BankG)	Federal Act on Banks and Savings Banks
Loi fédérale sur les bourses et les valeurs mobilières (LBVM)	Bundesgesetz über die Börsen und den Effektenhandel (BEHG)	Federal Act on Stock Exchanges and Securities Trading
Loi fédérale sur les cartels et autres restrictions à la concurrence (LCart)	Bundesgesetz über Kartelle und andere Wettbewerbs-beschränkungen (KG)	Federal Act on Cartels and Other Restraints of Competition
Loi fédérale sur les chemins de fer (LCdF)	Eisenbahngesetz (EBG)	Railroads Act
Loi fédérale sur les chemins pour piétons et les chemins de randonnée pédestre (LCPR)	Bundesgesetz über Fuss- und Wanderwege (FWG)	Federal Act on Footpaths and Hiking Trails
Loi fédérale sur les droits de timbre (LT)	Bundesgesetz über die Stempelabgaben (StG)	Stamp Duties Act
Loi fédérale sur les entraves techniques au commerce (LETC)	Bundesgesetz über die technischen Handelshemmnisse (THG)	Federal Act on Technical Barriers to Trade

Loi fédérale sur les étrangers (LEtr)	Bundesgesetz über die Ausländerinnen und Ausländer (AuG)	Federal Act on Foreign Nationals
Loi fédérale sur les loteries et les paris professionnels	Bundesgesetz betreffend die Lotterien und die gewerbsmässigen Wetten	Federal Act on Lotteries and Commercial Gambling
Loi fédérale sur les marchés publics (LMP)	Bundesgesetz über das öffentliche Beschaffungswesen (BöB)	Government Procurement Act
Loi fédérale sur les placements collectifs de capitaux (LPCC)	Bundesgesetz über die kollektiven Kapitalanlagen (KAG)	Federal Act on Collective Investment Schemes
Loi fédérale sur les prestations complémentaires (LPC)	Bundesgesetz über die Ergänzungsleistungen (ELG)	Supplementary Benefits Act
Loi fédérale sur les services de certification dans le domaine de la signature électronique (SCSE)	Bundesgesetz über Zertifizierungsdienste im Bereich der elektronischen Signatur (ZertES)	Federal Act on Electronic Signatures
Loi fédérale sur les stupéfiants (LStup)	Betäubungsmittelgesetz (BetmG)	Narcotics Act
Loi fédérale sur les voyages à forfait	Bundesgesetz über Pauschalreisen	Federal Act on Package Travel
Loi fédérale sur l'harmonisation des impôts directs des cantons et des communes (LHID)	Bundesgesetz über die Harmonisierung der direkten Steuern der Kantone und Gemeinden (StHG)	Direct Taxation Harmonization Act
Loi fédérale sur l'impôt fédéral direct (LIFD)	Bundesgesetz über die direkte Bundessteuer (DGB)	Federal Act on Direct Federal Taxation
Loi fédérale sur l'unité monétaire et les moyens de paiement	Bundesgesetz über die Währung und die Zahlungsmittel (WZG)	Federal Act on Currency and Payment Instruments
Loi fédérale sur l'utilisation des forces hydrauliques (LFH)	Bundesgesetz über die Nutzbarmachung der Wasserkräfte (WRG)	Federal Act on the Use of Hydraulic Power (Water Rights Act)
loi formelle	Gesetz	statute
Loi sur la banque nationale (LBN)	Nationalbankgesetz (NBG)	National Bank Act
Loi sur la fusion (LFus)	Fusionsgesetz (FusG)	Merger Act
Loi sur la géoinformation (LGéo)	Geoinformationsgesetz (GeoIG)	Geoinformation Act
Loi sur la nationalité (LN)	Bürgerrechtsgesetz (BüG)	Swiss Citizenship Act
Loi sur la participation	Mitwirkungsgesetz	Codetermination Act
Loi sur la police	Polizeigesetz	Police Act
Loi sur la protection de la nature et du paysage (LPN)	Natur- und Heimatschutzgesetz (NHG)	Nature and Cultural Heritage Act
Loi sur la protection de l'environnement (LPE)	Umweltschutzgesetz (USG)	Environmental Protection Act

Loi sur la protection des eaux (LEaux)	Gewässerschutzgesetz (GSchG)	Waters Protection Act
Loi sur la protection des marques (LPM)	Markenschutzgesetz (MSchG)	Trademark Protection Actd
Loi sur la radioprotection (LRaP)	Strahlenschutzgesetz (StSG)	Radiological Protection Act
Loi sur la responsabilité (LRCF)	Verantwortlichkeitsgesetz (VG)	Government Liability Act
Loi sur l'aménagement du territoire (LAT)	Raumplanungsgesetz (RPG)	Spatial Planning Act
Loi sur l'approvisionnement du pays (LAP)	Landesversorgungsgesetz	National Economic Supply Act
Loi sur l'asile (LAsi)	Asylgesetz	Asylum Act
Loi sur l'assurance-accidents (LAA)	Unfallversicherungsgesetz (UVG)	Swiss Federal Accident Insurance Act (similar to workers' compensation)
Loi sur l'assurance-chômage (LACI)	Arbeitslosenversicherungsgesetz (AVIG)	Unemployment Insurance Act
Loi sur le blanchiment d'argent (LBA)	Geldwäschereigesetz (GwG)	Money Laundering Act
Loi sur le cinéma (LCin)	Filmgesetz (FiG)	Film Act
Loi sur le contrat d'assurance (LCA)	Versicherungsvertragsgesetz (VVG)	Insurance Policies Act
Loi sur le contrôle des biens (LCB)	Güterkontrollgesetz (GKG)	Goods Control Act
Loi sur le libre passage (LFLP) / Loi fédérale sur le libre passage dans la prévoyance professionnelle vieillesse, survivants et invalidité	Freizügigkeitsgesetz (FZG) / Bundesgesetz über die Freizügigkeit in der beruflichen Alters-, Hinterlassenen- und Invalidenvorsorge	Swiss Federal Law on Vested Benefits in Occupational Old Age, Survivors and Disability Benefit Plans
Loi sur le notariat (LNot)	Notariatsgesetz (NG)	Notary Act
Loi sur le Parlement (LParl)	Parlamentsgesetz (ParlG)	Parliament Act
Loi sur le partenariat (LPart)	Partnerschaftsgesetz (PartG)	Same-Sex Partnership Act
Loi sur le personnel de la Confédération (LPers)	Bundespersonalgesetz (BPG)	Federal Personnel Act
Loi sur le service de l'emploi et la location de services (LSE)	Arbeitsvermittlungsgesetz (AVG)	Recruitment Act
Loi sur le travail	Arbeitsgesetz	Labor Act
Loi sur le Tribunal fédéral des brevets (LTFB)	Patentgerichtsgesetz (PatGG)	Patent Court Act
Loi sur l'égalité (LEg)	Gleichstellungsgesetz (GIG)	Gender Equality Act

Loi sur l'entraide pénale internationale (EIMP)	Rechtshilfegesetz (IRSG)	Mutual Assistance Act
Loi sur les armes (LArm)	Waffengesetz (WG)	Weapons Act
Loi sur les bourses (LBVM)	Börsengesetz (BEHG)	Stock Exchange Act
Loi sur les brevets (LBI)	Patentgesetz (PatG)	Patents Act
Loi sur les cartels (LCart)	Kartellgesetz (KG)	Cartel Act
Loi sur les denrées alimentaires (LDAl)	Lebensmittelgesetz (LMG)	Foodstuffs Act
Loi sur les droits de timbre	Stempelabgabengesetz	Stamp Duties Act
Loi sur les embargos (LEmb)	Embargogesetz (EmbG)	Embargo Act
Loi sur les épizooties	Tierseuchengesetz	Animal Diseases Act
Loi sur les explosifs (LExpl)	Sprengstoffgesetz (SprstG)	Explosives Act
Loi sur les installations électriques (LIE)	Elektrizitätsgesetz (EleG)	Electricity Act
Loi sur les placements collectifs (LPCC)	Kollektivanlagengesetz (KAG)	Collective Investment Schemes Act
Loi sur les produits chimiques (LChim)	Chemikaliengesetz (ChemG)	Chemicals Act
Loi sur les produits thérapeutiques	Heilmittelgesetz	Therapeutic Products Act
Loi sur les professions médicales (LPMéd)	Medizinalberufegesetz (MedBG)	Medical Professions Act
Loi sur les subventions (LSu)	Subventionsgesetz (SuG)	Subsidies Act
Loi sur les titres intermédiés	Bucheffektengesetz	Federal Act on the Custody and Transfer of Securities Held with an Intermediary
Loi sur les topographies (LTo)	Topographiengesetz (ToG)	Topographies Act
Loi sur l'impôt anticipé (LIA)	Verrechnungssteuergesetz (VStG)	Withholding Tax Act
Loi sur l'infrastructure des marchés financiers (LIMF)	Finanzmarktinfrastrukturgesetz (FinfraG)	Financial Market Infrastructure Act
Loi sur l'organisation des autorités pénales (LOAP)	Strafbehördenorganisationsgesetz (StBOG)	Criminal Justice Authorities Act
Loi sur l'organisation du gouvernement et de l'administration (LOGA)	Regierungs- und Verwaltungsorganisations-gesetz (RVOG)	Government and Administration Organization Act
loyale échute (art. 496 CC)	lediger Anfall	ineffective renunciation (of an inheritance)
loyer (art. 253 CO)	Miete, Mietzins	rent
loyer abusif (art. 253b CO)	missbräuchlicher Mietzins	abusive rent
loyer contrôlé	Mietzinsüberwachung	rent control
loyer échelonné	gestaffelter Mietzins	graduated rent

loyer fondé sur les coûts	Kostenmiete	rent that covers costs
loyer fondé sur les prix du marché	Marktmiete	market rent
loyer indexé	indexierter Mietzins	indexed rent
loyer initial	Anfangsmietzins	initial rent
Lucerne	Luzern	Lucerne (canton and city)
lucrum cessans	lucrum cessans	lost profits
lutte contre le blanchiment d'argent	Geldwäschereibekämpfung	anti-money laundering
magasin	Verkaufsgeschäft (D: Verkaufsstelle)	store
magasin de détail	Detailgeschäft (D: Einzelhandelsgeschäft)	retail store
magistrat	Richter	judge
mainlevée définitive (art. 82 LP)	definitive Rechtsöffnung	final dismissal of debtor's objection
mainlevée d'opposition (art. 80 ss LP)	Rechtsöffnung	court order dismissing debtor's objection
mainlevée provisoire (art. 82 LP)	provisorische Rechtsöffnung	preliminary dismissal of debtor's objection
maire	Gemeindepräsident, Stadtammann, Gemeindeammann	mayor
maison à colombages	Riegelhaus (D: Fachwerkhaus)	half-timbered house
maison d'arrêts	Haftanstalt	detention center
maison d'éducation au travail	Arbeitserziehungsanstalt	vocational training institution
maison de jeu	Spielbank	casino
maître d'apprentissage	Lehrmeister	master
maître d'ouvrage	Bauherr	project owner (if a private company); contracting authority (if a government agency)
majorité (1)	Mehr (D: Mehrheit)	majority
majorité (2) (art. 14 CC)	Mündigkeit	age of majority
majorité absolue	absolutes Mehr (D: absolute Mehrheit)	absolute majority
majorité des cantons	Ständemehr	majority of the cantons
majorité des voix	Stimmenmehr (D: Stimmenmehrheit)	majority of votes
majorité du peuple	Volksmehr	popular majority, majority of those voting

majorité pénale	Strafmündigkeit	age of criminal responsibility
majorité pénale limitée	bedingte Strafmündigkeit	limited criminal responsibility
majorité qualifiée	qualifiziertes Mehr (D: qualifizierte Mehrheit)	qualified majority
majorité relative	relatives Mehr (D: relative Mehrheit)	relative majority
majorité simple	einfaches Mehr (D: einfache Mehrheit)	simple majority
malade mental	Geisteskranker	mentally ill person
maladie mentale	Geisteskrankheit	mental illness
mandant	Auftraggeber	principal
mandat (art. 394-406 CO)	Auftrag	agency contract
mandat commercial (art. 458-465 CO)	Handlungsvollmacht	commercial power of attorney
mandat d'amener (art. 208 CPP)	Vorführungsbefehl	warrant for an enforced appearance
mandat d'arrêt	Haftbefehl	arrest warrant
mandat d'arrêt aux fins d'extradition (art. 48 al. 2 EIMP)	Auslieferungshaftbefehl	arrest warrant with a view to extradition
mandat de comparution (art. 201 CPP)	Vorladung	summons
mandat de gestion de fortune	Vermögensverwaltungsauftrag	asset management mandate
mandat de légiférer	Gesetzgebungsauftrag	mandate to legislate
mandat de perquisition	Durchsuchungsbefehl	search warrant
mandat de poste (MP)	Postanweisung (PA)	postal money order
mandat de prestations	Leistungsauftrag	public service agreement
mandat de puissance protectrice	Schutzmachtmandat	protecting power mandate
mandat de recherches (art. 201 CPP)	Fahndung	search for a fugitive, APB (all persons bulletin)
mandat de répression (art. 64 DPA)	Strafbescheid	sentence order
mandat pour cause d'inaptitude (art. 360 CC)	Vorsorgeauftrag	advance care directive
mandat proprement dit (art. 394 CO)	einfacher Auftrag	simple agency
mandataire	Beauftragter	agent, representative
mandataire commercial	Handlungsbevollmächtigter	commercial agent
manifestation de volonté	Willensäusserung	statement of intent
manipulation de cours	Kursmanipulation	price manipulation
marché à terme	Terminbörse	futures market

marché au comptant	Kassamarkt	spot market, cash market
marché commun	gemeinsamer Markt	common market
marché des capitaux	Kapitalmarkt	capital market
marché du travail	Arbeitsmarkt	labor market
marché hypothécaire	Hypothekarmarkt (D: Hypothekenmarkt)	mortgage market
marché intérieur	Binnenmarkt	internal market
marché locatif	Wohnungsmarkt	housing market
mariage (art. 94 ss CC)	Ehe	marriage
mariage coutumier	gewohnheitsrechtliche Ehe	customary marriage
mariage de nationalité	Ausländerrechtsehe	marriage entered into to obtain a residence permit
mariage forcé (art. 181a CP)	Zwangsheirat	forced marriage
mariage inexistant	Nichtehe	void marriage
mariage religieux	religiöse Eheschliessung	church wedding
marque (art. 1 LPM)	Marke	trademark
marque antérieure (art. 3 LPM)	ältere Marke	earlier trademark
marque associée	begleitende Marke	associated trademark
marque collective (art. 22 LPM)	Kollektivmarke	collective mark
marque de garantie (art. 21 LPM)	Garantiemarke	guarantee mark
marque de haute renommée (art. 15 LPM)	berühmte Marke	famous trademark
marque de réserve	Vorratsmarke	reserve mark, reserve trademark
marque de service	Dienstleistungsmarke	service mark
marque défensive	Defensivmarke	defensive trademark (can be applied for by a trademark owner of a well-known trademark for goods or services that are not intended to be used by that owner)
marque figurative	Bildmarke	figurative mark (the part of a brand that appears in the form of a symbol, picture, design, or distinctive color)
marque géographique (art. 27a LPM)	geographische Marke	geographical mark

marque notoirement connue (art. 3 LPM)	notorisch bekannte Marke	well-known trademark (Well-known trademarks are protected whether they are registered or not.)
marque qui s'est imposée au public	durchgesetzte Marke	mark that has acquired distinctiveness
marque verbale	Wortmarke	word mark
masse en faillite (art. 197 LP)	Konkursmasse	bankrupt estate
masse sous gestion	verwaltete Vermögen	assets under management (AuM)
masse successorale	Erbmasse	estate
matérialisé	verbrieft	certificated
matériaux d'excavation	Aushubmaterial	excavated material
matériaux terreux	Bodenaushub	excavated soil
matière commerciale	Handelssache	commercial case, commercial matter
maturité (F : baccalauréat)	Matura (D: Abitur)	high school graduation exam
maturité professionnelle	Berufsmaturität	diploma of vocational training
mauvais traitement	Misshandlung	mistreatment
mauvais traitements envers les enfants	Kindesmisshandlung	child abuse
mauvaise exécution	Schlechterfüllung	defective performance
mauvaises odeurs (art. 684 CC)	übler Geruch	noxious vapors
maxime des débats	Verhandlungsmaxime	rule that the parties control the subject matter of the proceedings and may present the case as they see fit
maxime d'office (art. 58 CPC)	Offizialgrundsatz	principle that no statement of any kind is binding on the judge unless he himself is convinced that the fact occurred as asserted
maxime éventuelle	Eventualmaxime	principle that the parties have a certain time in which to file briefs, and may not file them after that time
méchanceté	Bosheit	cruelty

médecin conseil	Vertrauensarzt	independent medical examiner
médecine de pointe	Spitzenmedizin	advanced medical science
média	Medien	media
médiation	Mediation	mediation
mélanges	Festschrift	Festschrift
membre	Mitglied	member
membre de la famille	Familienangehöriger	family member
mémoire	Rechtsschrift (D: Schriftsatz)	brief
mémoire d'appel	Berufungsschrift	appellate brief
mémoire de recours	Beschwerdeschrift	appellate brief
mémoire préventif (art. 270 CPC)	Schutzschrift	protective letter (in an ex parte situation)
menace	Drohung	threat
menace alarmant la population (art. 258 CP)	Schreckung der Bevölkerung	causing fear and alarm among the general public
menaces (art. 180 CP)	Drohung	threatening behavior
ménage	Haushalt	household
ménagement dans l'exercice du droit	schonende Rechtsausübung	moderation in the exercise of legal rights
mendicité	Bettel (D: Betteln)	begging
mention	Anmerkung	indication
mention de l'acceptation (art. 1065 CO)	Annahmevermerk	mention of acceptance
mention de l'impôt (art. 27 LTVA)	Steuerausweis	VAT details
mercenaire	Söldner	mercenary
message du Conseil Fédéral	Botschaft des Bundesrates	Federal Council Dispatch (report and opinion on a bill)
mesure anticipée d'exécution par substitution	antizipierte Ersatzvornahme	anticipated substitutive measure
mesure architectonique	bauliche Änderung	structural alteration
mesure de contrainte (1) (art. 343 CPC)	Zwangsmassnahme	compulsory measure (such as taking away the chattel or vacating real property) in civil procedure
mesure de contrainte (2) (art. 50 CPP)	Zwangsmassnahme	coercive measure (such as arrest or detention) in criminal procedure

mesure de réadaptation	Eingliederungsmassnahme	rehabilitation measure (to promote reintegration of the disabled)
mesure de sûreté (art. 98 ss et 223 LP)	Sicherungsmassnahme	safety measure
mesure d'instruction	Abklärungsmassnahme	investigation, investigatory measure
mesure disciplinaire (art. 14 LP)	Disziplinarmassnahme	disciplinary measure
mesure en matière d'exécution (art. 41 al. 1 PA)	Vollstreckungsverfügung	enforcement measure
mesure provisionnelle (art. 261 ss CPC)	vorsorgliche Massnahme (D: einstweilige Verfügung)	preliminary injunctive relief
mesure superprovisionnelle (art. 265 CPC)	superprovisorische Massnahme	ex parte preliminary injunctive relief
mesures de sécurité	Sicherheitsvorkehrungen	security precautions
mesures de substitution (art. 237 CPP)	Ersatzmassnahmen	alternative measures
mesures de surveillance secrètes (art. 269 ss CPP)	geheime Überwachungsmassnahmen	covert surveillance measures
mesures protectrices de l'union conjugale (art. 172-179 CC)	Eheschutzmassnahmen	measures to protect the marital union
mesures superprovisionnelles (art. 265 CPC)	superprovisorische Massnahmen	ex parte preliminary injunctive relief
mesures urgentes	Sofortmassnahmen	immediate measures
métaux précieux (art. 128 LP)	Edelmetall	precious metal
méthode de capitalisation	Anwartschaftsdeckungsverfahren	capitalization method
méthodes d'administration des preuves interdites (art. 140 CPP)	verbotene Beweiserhebungsmethoden	prohibited methods of taking evidence
méthodologie du droit	Rechtsmethodik	legal methodology
metteur en gage	Verpfänder	pledgor
meurtre (art. 111 CP)	vorsätzliche Tötung	intentional homicide
meurtre passionnel (art. 113 CP)	Totschlag	manslaughter
meurtre sur la demande de la victime (art. 114 CP)	Tötung auf Verlangen	homicide at the request of the victim
minimum vital	Existenzminimum, Notbedarf	vital minimum
ministère public	Staatsanwaltschaft	public prosecutor

Ministère public de la Confédération (MPC)	Bundesanwaltschaft (BA)	Office of the Attorney General of Switzerland
Ministère public des mineurs	Jugendanwaltschaft	Office of the Juvenile Prosecutor
minoration de capital	Kapitalherabsetzung	capital reduction
minorité (1)	Minderheit	minority
minorité (2)	Minderjährigkeit	minority, being underage, being a minor
minorité de blocage	Sperrminorität	blocking minority
mise à la retraite	Pensionierung	retirement
mise au secret	Isolationshaft	solitary confinement
mise en accusation	Anklageerhebung	bringing of charges
mise en circulation	Inverkehrbringen	marketing
mise en circulation de fausse monnaie (art. 242 CP)	in Umlaufsetzen falschen Geldes	tendering counterfeit money
mise en circulation de fourrages altérés (art. 236 CP)	Inverkehrbringen von gesundheitsschädlichem Futter	marketing of harmful animal feed
mise en circulation et réclame en faveur d'appareils d'écoute, de prise de son et de prise de vues (art. 179sexies CP)	Inverkehrbringen und Anpreisen von Abhör-, Ton- und Bildaufnahmegeräten	marketing and promotion of devices for unlawful listening or sound or image recording
mise en danger de la sécurité publique au moyen d'armes (art. 260quater CP)	Gefährdung der öffentlichen Sicherheit mit Waffen	endangering public safety with weapons
mise en danger de la vie d'autrui (art. 129 CP)	Gefährdung des Lebens	endangering life
mise en danger de l'ordre constitutionnel (art. 275 CP)	Gefährdung der verfassungsmässigen Ordnung	endangering the constitutional order
mise en liberté définitive	definitive Freilassung	permanent release
mise en liberté provisoire	vorläufige Freilassung	temporary release
mise en œuvre du droit communautaire	Umsetzung des Gemeinschaftsrechts	transposition of EU law
mise sous régie	Zwangsverwaltung	receivership
mise sous scellés (art. 248 CPP)	Siegelung	sealing of evidence
mitoyenneté	Grenzgemeinschaft	co-ownership of a party wall
mobile	Beweggrund	motive
mobilier	Hausrat	furnishings, household effects

mode de réalisation (art. 256 LP)	Verwertungsmodus	means of selling the assets
mode de signature	Zeichnungsart	type of signature required (individual or joint)
modification	Änderung, Abänderung	amendment
modification de charges foncières	Änderung von Grundlasten	modification of real estate charges
modification de la demande (art. 227 CPC)	Klageänderung	amendment of the complaint
modification de droits personnels annotés	Änderung von vorgemerkten persönlichen Rechten	modification of registered personal rights
modification de gages immobiliers	Änderung von Grundpfandrechten	modification of mortgages
modification de servitudes	Änderung von Dienstbarkeiten	modification of easements
modification des statuts (art. 647 CO)	Statutenänderung (D: Satzungsänderung)	amendment of the bylaws, bylaw amendment
modifier	ändern, abändern	to amend
mœurs	Sitte	customs, mores
moins-value (art. 205 CO)	Minderwert	decrease in the object's value
moins-value sur le prix des premières enchères (art. 129 al. 4 et 143 al. 2 LP)	Ausfall	depreciation of the price reached at a first auction
monnaie (1)	Retourgeld (D: Wechselgeld)	change
monnaie (2)	Währung	currency
monnaie comptable	Rechnungswährung	account currency
monnaie de placement	Anlagewährung	investment currency
monnaie de référence	Referenzwährung	reference currency
monnaie du pays	Landesmünze	national currency
monnaie électronique	elektronisches Geld	electronic money
monnaie étrangère	fremde Währung	foreign currency
monopole de droit	rechtliches Monopol	legal monopoly
monopole de fait	faktisches Monopol	de facto monopoly
montant nominal	Nennbetrag	nominal amount
montant exempté	Freibetrag	exempt amount
moquette	Spannteppich (D: Teppichboden)	wall-to-wall carpet
moralité	Sittlichkeit	morality
Morat	Murten	Murten (municipality)
moratoire	Moratorium	moratorium
morcellement (art. 833 CC)	Zerstückelung	parceling, division
mort	Tod	death

mort suspecte (art. 253 CPP)	aussergewöhnliche Todesfälle	unnatural death
motif	Grund	ground, reason
motif d'asile	Asylgrund	ground for asylum
motif de détention	Haftgrund	ground for detention
motif de réclamation	Klagegrund	grounds for a claim
motif de récusation (art. 47 CPC)	Ausstandsgrund	ground for recusal
motif de révision (art. 328 CPC)	Revisionsgrund	ground for review
motif d'expulsion	Ausweisungsgrund	grounds for deportation (of a foreign national), grounds for eviction (of a tenant)
motif du recours	Beschwerdegrund	ground for the appeal
motion	Motion	parliamentary motion asking the government to legislate (as opposed to a motion requiring the government to legislate, cf. *postulat*)
motivation de la décision	Begründung des Entscheids	grounds for the decision
motivation de la demande	Begründung der Eingabe	grounds for the request
motiver	motivieren (D: begründen)	to state the reasons (for something)
moyen de contrainte	Zwangsmittel	enforcement measure
moyen de droit (1)	rechtliches Vorbringen	point of law, legal argument
moyen de droit (2)	Rechtsmittel	legal remedy
moyen de fait	tatsächliches Vorbringen	factual argument, argument based on the facts
moyen de paiement	Zahlungsmittel	means of payment
moyen de preuve	Beweismittel	evidence
moyen de transport	Transportmittel	means of transportation
moyens d'appel	Appellationsbegründung	grounds for appeal
mutation	Handänderung	transfer of property
mutilation d'organes génitaux féminins (art. 124 CP)	Verstümmelung weiblicher Genitalien	female genital mutilation
mutinerie (art. 63 CPM)	Meuterei	mutiny

mutinerie de détenus (art. 311 CP)	Meuterei von Gefangenen	prison mutiny
mutualité	Gegenseitigkeit	mutuality
mutuum	Mutuum	loan (for consumption, such as a loan of money, as opposed to loan for use, such as a loan of a painting)
nantissement (art. 884-894 CC)	Faustpfand	pledge of chattels, possessory security interest in chattels (such as securities or insurance policies)
nasciturus (art. 544 al. 1 CC)	Nasciturus	unborn child
natel (F : téléphone portable)	Handy	cell phone, mobile phone
nationalisation	Verstaatlichung	nationalization
nationalité	Staatsangehörigkeit	nationality
nationalité suisse	Schweizer Bürgerrecht	Swiss nationality
naturalisation	Einbürgerung	naturalization
naturalisation facilitée	erleichterte Einbürgerung	simplified naturalization
nature juridique	Rechtsnatur	legal status
navigation	Schifffahrt	navigation
ne bis in idem	ne bis in idem	rule against double jeopardy
nécessité	Erforderlichkeit	necessity
négligence	Fahrlässigkeit	negligence
négligence consciente	bewusste Fahrlässigkeit	recklessness, willful negligence
négligence grave	grobe Fahrlässigkeit	gross negligence
négligence inconsciente	unbewusste Fahrlässigkeit	unconscious negligence
négligence légère	leichte Fahrlässigkeit	slight negligence
négoce de valeurs mobilières	Effektenhandel	securities trading
négoce pour compte propre	Eigenhandel	proprietary trading
négociant en valeurs mobilières	Effektenhändler	securities dealer
négociation à la criée	Parketthandel, Zuruf-System	open outcry trading
Neuchâtel	Neuenburg	Neuchatel (canton and city)
neutralité	Neutralität	neutrality
Nidwald	Nidwalden	Nidwalden (canton)
niveau de vie	Lebensstandard	standard of living

nom commercial	Handelsname	trade name
nom d'alliance	Allianzname	hyphenated last name
nom de famille	Familienname	family name
nommer	brevetieren	to appoint
non-activité	Nichterwerbstätigkeit	economic inactivity
non-courant	unkurant	not easily marketable, illiquid (e.g., the shares of a family-owned business)
non-entrée en matière	Nichtanhandnahme	abandonment, discontinuation of criminal proceedings (by the prosecutor)
non-respect de l'assistance de probation ou des règles de conduite (art. 295 CP)	Missachtung von Bewährungshilfe oder Weisungen	failure to comply with probation assistance or instructions
non-usage de la marque	Nichtgebrauch der Marke	failure to use the mark
norme	Norm	standard
norme potestative	Kann-Vorschrift	discretionary rule
norme SIA (Société suisse des Ingénieurs et des Architectes)	SIA-Norm (Schweizerischer Ingenieur- und Architektenverein)	Swiss Society of Engineers and Architects
notaire	Notar	notary
notation	Rating	rating
note marginale	Randbemerkung	marginal note, note in the margin
notification (1)	Eröffnung	notice, notification
notification (2)	Zustellung	service (of process)
notification de la décision	Eröffnung des Entscheids	notice of a decision
notification de l'ordonnance pénale (art. 353 CPP)	Eröffnung des Strafbefehls	notice of the summary penalty order
notification écrite	schriftliche Eröffnung	written notice
notification irrégulière (art. 38 PA)	mangelhafte Eröffnung	defective notification
notification judiciaire (art. 136 CPC)	gerichtliche Zustellung	service of process
notification orale	mündliche Eröffnung	oral notice
notification par huissier	Zustellung durch den Weibel	service by a process server
notification par voie diplomatique	Eröffnung auf diplomatischem Weg	notification through diplomatic channels
notification par voie électronique (art. 86 CPP)	elektronische Zustellung	electronic service
notifier (1)	eröffnen	to notify

notifier (2)	zustellen	to serve something on someone, to serve someone with something
notion de double imposition	Begriff der Doppelbesteuerung	concept of double taxation
notion juridique	Rechtsbegriff	legal concept
nouveauté de l'invention (art. 7 LBI)	Neuheit der Erfindung	novelty of the invention
nouveaux arrivants	Zuzüger (D: Zugezogene)	newcomer
nouvelle construction	Neubau	new construction
nouvelle demande	Neuanmeldung	new application
nouvelle fondation	Neugründung	business start-up
novas improprement dits (art. 229 CPC)	unechte Noven	improper new facts and evidence (facts or evidence that existed before the close of the exchange of written submissions or before the last hearing but could have not been submitted despite reasonable diligence)
novas proprement dits (art. 229 CPC)	echte Noven	proper new facts and evidence (facts and evidence that occurred or were discovered after the exchange of written submissions or after the last hearing)
novation (art. 116-117 CO)	Novation, Neuerung	novation
novelle (loi spéciale modifiant le contenu d'anciennes lois)	Novelle	amendment (to prior laws)
novum (faits nouveaux ou preuves nouvelles) (art. 99 LTF)	Novum, Noven (neue Tatsachen oder Beweismittel)	new facts or evidence
nul	nichtig, rechtsunwirksam	null and void, legally ineffective, unenforceable
nullité (art. 20 CO)	Nichtigkeit	nullity
nullité des promesses faites en sus des stipulations du concordat (art. 312 LP)	Nichtigkeit von Nebenversprechen	nullity of the promises made in addition to the debt restructuring agreement
nullité partielle	Teilnichtigkeit	severability
numéro de valeur	Valorennummer (D: Wertpapierkennnummer)	security number

numéro postal d'acheminement (NPA) (F : code postal)	Postleitzahl (PLZ)	postal code
objecteur de conscience	Dienstverweigerer	conscientious objector
objection	Einwendung	objection
objet (1)	Gegenstand	subject, subject matter
objet (2)	Gegenstand	object, item
objet de la poursuite (art. 38 LP)	Gegenstand der Schuldbetreibung	subject of debt collection proceedings
objet de l'expropriation	Gegenstand der Enteignung	subject of the expropriation
objet de prix	Wertsache	object of value
objet du litige	Prozesssache, Streitgegenstand	matter in dispute, subject matter of the dispute
objet en vente	Steigerungsgegenstand	item for sale (at auction)
objet insaisissable (art. 224 LP)	Kompetenzstück	bare necessity good
objet séquestré	Arrestgegenstand	attached asset
objets ayant une valeur scientifique (art. 724 CC)	wissenschaftliche Gegenstände	objects of scientific value
objets de remplacement qui ont la même valeur d'usage (art. 92 al. 3 LP)	Ersatzgegenstände von gleichem Gebrauchswert	substitution of goods of equal value
obligation (1)	Obligation	obligation
obligation (2)	Obligation	bond
obligation à terme	befristete Verbindlichkeit	obligation subject to a time limit
obligation alternative (art. 72 CO)	Wahlobligation	obligation involving choice of performance
obligation avec faculté alternative	Alternativermächtigung	obligation that can be performed in a different manner than originally agreed (such as paying in local currency even though the obligation was in foreign currency)
obligation avec options	Optionsanleihe	option bond, bond with options
obligation d'accepter une fonction	Amtszwang	obligation to accept an office
obligation d'annoncer	Meldepflicht	obligation to report
obligation d'assurance	Versicherungspflicht	insurance obligation

obligation de borner (art. 669 CC)	Abgrenzungspflicht	duty to establish boundaries, duty to demarcate
obligation de caisse	Kassenobligation	medium-term notes issued by banks
obligation de compenser	Abrechnungspflicht	clearing duty
obligation de construire	Baupflicht	duty to build
obligation de cotiser	Beitragspflicht	duty to contribute
obligation de faire ou de ne pas faire (art. 98 CO)	Verbindlichkeit zu einem Tun oder Nichttun	obligation to act or refrain from action
obligation de fournir des prestations accessoires	Nebenleistungspflicht	obligation to make additional material contributions
obligation de motiver	Begründungspflicht	obligation to state the grounds (for a decision)
obligation de poser des questions	Fragepflicht	duty to question
obligation de produire des pièces	Editionspflicht	duty to produce documents
obligation de reconstruire	Wiederaufbaupflicht	obligation to rebuild
obligation de réduire le dommage	Schadenminderungspflicht	duty to mitigate damage
obligation de rendre comptes	Rechenschaftspflicht	accountability
obligation de renseigner	Auskunftspflicht	duty to inform
obligation de renseigner et de remettre (art. 222 LP)	Auskunfts- und Herausgabepflicht	duty to provide information and deliver assets
obligation de supporter les frais	Kostentragungspflicht	obligation to bear costs
obligation de témoigner (art. 163 CPP)	Zeugnispflicht	duty to testify
obligation de tolérer les réparations et inspections de la chose	Duldungspflicht	duty to tolerate
obligation de verser le revenu	Abgabepflicht	tax obligation
obligation d'entretien (art. 276-294 CC)	Unterhaltspflicht	maintenance obligation, duty of maintenance
obligation divisible	teilbare Leistung	divisible obligation
obligation indivisible (art. 70 CO)	unteilbare Leistung	indivisible obligation
obligation juridique	Rechtspflicht	legal obligation
obligation militaire	Wehrpflicht	compulsory military service

obligation naturelle	Naturalobligation	natural obligation, obligation not enforceable at law
obligation sans terme (art. 75 CO)	unbefristete Verbindlichkeit	open-ended obligation
obligations communes du failli (art. 215 LP)	Mitverpflichtungen des Schuldners	common obligations of the insolvent debtor
obtenir gain de cause	obsiegen	to prevail, to win, to be successful
obtenir par fraude	ertrügen (D: betrügerisch erlangen)	to obtain fraudulently
obtention frauduleuse d'un concordat judiciaire (art. 170 CP)	Erschleichung eines gerichtlichen Nachlassvertrages	obtaining a judicial debt restructuring agreement by fraud
obtention frauduleuse d'une constatation fausse (art. 253 CP)	Erschleichung einer falschen Beurkundung	obtaining a false certificate by fraud
obtention frauduleuse d'une prestation (art. 150 CP)	Erschleichen einer Leistung	obtaining a service without payment
Obwald	Obwalden	Obwalden (canton)
occupation (art. 658 CC)	Aneignung	appropriation
octroi des pouvoirs	Bevollmächtigung	grant of a power of attorney
octroi du sursis (art. 295 LP)	Bewilligung der Nachlassstundung	granting of the stay
octroi d'un avantage (art. 322quinquies CP)	Vorteilsgewährung	granting an advantage
œuvre (droit d'auteur)	Werk (Urheberrecht)	work
œuvre de prévoyance	Vorsorgewerk	pension organization
œuvre dérivée	Werk zweiter Hand	derivative work
offense	Verfehlung	offense
Office AI	IV-Stelle	Disability Insurance Office
Office AI pour les assurés résidant à l'étranger (OAIE)	IV-Stelle für Versicherte im Ausland	Disability Insurance Office for People Living Abroad
Office cantonal de conciliation	Kantonales Einigungsamt	Cantonal Office for Conciliation in Labor Disputes
office de consultation conjugale (art. 171 CC)	Eheberatungsstelle	marital counseling agency
office des faillites (art. 2 LP)	Konkursamt	bankruptcy office
office des poursuites (art. 2 LP)	Betreibungsamt	debt collection authority

office d'état civil	Zivilstandsamt (D: Standesamt)	civil registry, office of vital records
office du travail	Arbeitsamt	employment office
Office fédéral	Bundesamt	Federal Office
Office fédéral de la communication (OfCom)	Bundesamt für Kommunikation (BAKOM)	Federal Office of Communications
Office fédéral de la culture (OFC)	Bundesamt für Kultur (BAK)	Federal Office for Culture
Office fédéral de la formation professionnelle et de la technologie (OFFT)	Bundesamt für Berufsbildung und Technologie (BBT)	Federal Office for Professional Education and Technology
Office fédéral de la justice (OFJ)	Bundesamt für Justiz (BJ)	Federal Office of Justice
Office fédéral de la protection de la protection (OFPP)	Bundesamt für Bevölkerungsschutz (BABS)	Federal Office for Civil Protection
Office fédéral de la santé publique (OFSP)	Bundesamt für Gesundheit (BAG)	Federal Office of Public Health
Office fédéral de la statistique (OFS)	Bundesamt für Statistik (BFS)	Federal Statistical Office
Office fédéral de l'agriculture (OFAG)	Bundesamt für Landwirtschaft (BLW)	Federal Office for Agriculture
Office fédéral de l'aviation civile (OFAC)	Bundesamt für Zivilluftfahrt (BAZL)	Federal Office for Civil Aviation
Office fédéral de l'éducation et de la science	Bundesamt für Bildung und Wissenschaft (BBW)	Federal Office for Education and Science
Office fédéral de l'énergie (OFE)	Bundesamt für Energie (BFE)	Swiss Federal Office of Energy
Office fédéral de l'environnement (OFEV)	Bundesamt für Umwelt (BAFU)	Federal Office for the Environment
Office fédéral de l'état civil (OFEC)	Eidgenössisches Amt für das Zivilstandswesen (EAZW)	Federal Civil Status Office
Office fédéral de l'informatique et de la télécommunication (OFIT)	Bundesamt für Informatik und Telekommunikation (BIT)	Federal Office of Information Tech-nology, Systems and Telecommunication
Office fédéral de météorologie et de climatologie (MétéoSuisse)	Bundesamt für Meteorologie und Klimatologie (MeteoSchweiz)	Federal Office of Meteorology and Climatology
Office fédéral de métrologie (METAS)	Bundesamt für Metrologie (METAS)	Federal Office of Metrology
Office fédéral de topographie (swisstopo)	Bundesamt für Landestopographie (swisstopo)	Federal Office of Topography
Office fédéral des assurances privées (OFAP)	Bundesamt für Privatversicherungen (BPV)	Federal Office of Private Insurance
Office fédéral des assurances sociales (OFAS)	Bundesamt für Sozialversicherung (BSV)	Federal Social Insurance Office

Office fédéral des constructions et de la logistique (OFCL)	Bundesamt für Bauten und Logistik (BBL)	Federal Office for Buildings and Logistics
Office fédéral des migrations (OFM)	Bundesamt für Migration (BFM)	Federal Office for Migration
Office fédéral des routes (OFROU)	Bundesamt für Strassen (ASTRA)	Federal Roads Office
Office fédéral des transports (OFT)	Bundesamt für Verkehr (BAV)	Federal Office of Transport
Office fédéral du développement territorial (ARE)	Bundesamt für Raumentwicklung (ARE)	Federal Office for Spatial Development
Office fédéral du logement (OFL)	Bundesamt für Wohnungswesen (BWO)	Federal Office for Housing
Office fédéral du personnel (OFPER)	Eidgenössisches Personalamt (EPA)	Federal Personnel Office
Office fédéral du sport	Bundesamt für Sport (BASPO)	Federal Office of Sport
Office fédéral pour l'approvisionnement économique du pays (OFAE)	Bundesamt für wirtschaftliche Landesversorgung (BWL)	Federal Office for National Economic Supply
Office Régional de l'AI	IV-Regionalstelle	Regional Disability Insurance Office
office régional de placement	regionales Arbeitsvermittlungszentrum	regional employment center
Office vétérinaire fédéral (OVF)	Bundesamt für Veterinärwesen (BVET)	Federal Veterinary Office
officier de l'état civil	Zivilstandsbeamte (D: Standesbeamte)	civil registrar, vital records official
offre	Offerte, Kostenvoranschlag (D: Angebot)	quote (estimated price of goods or services)
offre avec délai pour accepter (art. 3 CO)	Antrag mit Annahmefrist	offer with time limit for acceptance
offre de contracter	Antrag zu Vertragsabschluss	offer to contract
offre de preuve	Beweiseofferte (BO)	offer of evidence
offre de travailler	Angebot der Arbeitsleistung	offer to work
offre et acceptation	Antrag und Annahme	offer and acceptance (to form a contract)
offre publique (art. 7 CO)	Auskündung	announcement of prices
offre publique d'acquisition	öffentliche Kaufangebote	tender offer, takeover bid
offre réelle	Realoblation	actual offer, effective offer
offre sans engagement (art. 7 CO)	Antrag ohne Verbindlichkeit	nonbinding offer

offre sous réserve de retrait	Antrag mit Vorbehalt des Widerrufs	offer subject to withdrawal
offre verbale	Verbaloblation	oral offer
Ombudsman des banques suisses	Schweizerische Bankenombudsman	Swiss Banking Ombudsman
omettre d'installer des appareils protecteurs (art. 230 CP)	Nichtanbringung von Sicherheitsvorrichtungen	non-installation of safety devices
omission	Unterlassung	omission, failure
omission de prêter secours (art. 128 CP)	Unterlassung der Nothilfe	failure to offer aid in an emergency
omission illicite de rejoindre	unerlaubtes Wegbleiben	absence without leave (AWOL)
opérateur	Marktteilnehmer	market participant
opération à terme	Termingeschäft	futures trading
opération à terme sur devises	Devisentermingeschäft	forward foreign exchange transaction
opération à terme sur métaux précieux	Edelmetalltermingeschäft	forward precious metal transaction
opération boursière	Börsengeschäft	stock market transaction
opération de couverture	Absicherungsgeschäft	hedge, hedging
opération de liquidation	Glattstellungsgeschäft, Glattstellungstransaktion	closing trade
opération d'initié	Insidergeschäft	insider transaction
opération sur devises	Devisengeschäft	foreign exchange transaction, forex transaction
opération sur devises au comptant	Devisenkassengeschäft	foreign exchange spot transaction
opération sur métaux précieux	Edelmetallsgeschäft	precious metal transaction
opération sur métaux précieux au comptant	Edelmetallkassageschäft	precious metal spot transaction
opération swap sur devises	Devisenswapgeschäft	currency swap transaction
opérations sur dérivés	Derivatgeschäfte	derivatives transactions
opérations transfrontalières	grenzüberschreitende Geschäfte	cross-border transactions
opinion	Meinung	opinion
opinion dissidente	abweichende Meinung	dissenting opinion
opinion juridique	Rechtsauffassung	legal opinion
opinion minoritaire	Minderheitsmeinung	minority opinion
opportunité (1)	Angemessenheit	appropriateness
opportunité (2)	Zweckmässigkeit	expediency

opposable aux tiers	wirksam gegenüber Dritten	enforceable against third parties
opposition (1)	Einsprache	objection
opposition (2) (art. 31 LPM)	Widerspruch	opposition (to registration of a trademark)
opposition à l'ordonnance de séquestre (art. 278 CP)	Einsprache gegen den Arrestbefehl	objection to the attachment order
opposition à un acte de l'autorité (art. 286 CP)	Hinderung einer Amtshandlung	prevention of an official act
opposition au commandement de payer (art. 74 LP)	Rechtsvorschlag (D:~Widerspruch)	debtor's objection to the order to pay
opposition au séquestre	Arresteinsprache	objection to the attachment of assets
opposition tardive	nachträglicher Rechtsvorschlag	belated objection (when there is a change of creditors)
option cotée en bourse	börsengehandelte Option	exchange-traded option, listed option
option couverte	Stillhalteroption	covered option
option de change, option sur devises	Devisenoption	currency option, forex option, FX option
option de collaborateur	Mitarbeiteroption	employee option
option inscrite à la cote	börsengehandelte Option	exchange-traded option, listed option
option sur actions	Aktienoption	stock option
ordonnance (1)	Verordnung	ordinance
ordonnance (2)	Anordnung	order
ordonnance administrative	Verwaltungsverordnung	administrative ordinance
Ordonnance de l'Assemblée fédérale sur l'organisation de l'armée (OOrgA)	Verordnung der Bundesversammlung über die Organisation der Armee (AO)	Ordinance of the Federal Assembly on the Organization of the Armed Forces
ordonnance de non-entrée en matière (art. 310 CPP)	Nichtanhandnahmeverfügung	order to abandon the criminal proceedings
ordonnance de séquestre (art. 274 LP)	Arrestbefehl	attachment order
ordonnance dépendante	unselbständige Verordnung	dependent ordinance
Ordonnance du Tribunal fédéral sur la faillite de la société coopérative (OFCoop)	Verordnung des Bundesgerichts über den Genossenschaftskonkurs (VGeK)	Ordinance of the Federal Supreme Court on the Bankruptcy of a Cooperative

Ordonnance du Tribunal fédéral sur la réalisation forcée des immeubles (ORFI)	Verordnung des Bundesgerichts über die Zwangsverwertung von Grundstücken (VZG)	Ordinance of the Federal Supreme Court on the Forced Sale of Real Estate
ordonnance fédérale	Bundesverordnung	federal ordinance
ordonnance indépendante	selbständige Verordnung	independent ordinance
ordonnance pénale (art. 352 CPP)	Strafbefehl	summary penalty order
Ordonnance relative à la haute surveillance en matière de poursuite et de faillite (OHS-LP)	Verordnung betreffend die Oberaufsicht über Schuldbetreibung und Konkurs (OAV-SchKG)	Ordinance on the Oversight of Debt Collection and Bankruptcy Matters
Ordonnance relative à l'état-major Centrale nationale d'alarme du Conseil fédéral (O EM CF CENAL)	Verordnung über den Stab Bundesrat Nationale Alarmzentrale (V Stab BR NAZ)	Ordinance on the Federal Council National Emergency Operations Centre Staff
Ordonnance relative à l'étude de l'impact sur l'environnement (OEIE)	Verordnung über die Umweltverträglichkeitsprüfung (UVPV)	Environmental Impact Assessment Ordinance
Ordonnance relative aux émoluments liés au trafic des animaux (OEmol-TA)	Verordnung über die Gebühren für den Tierverkehr (GebV-TVD)	Ordinance on Animal Movement Fees
Ordonnance son et laser (OSLa)	Schall- und Laserverordnung (SLV)	Noise and Laser Ordinance
Ordonnance sur contrôle des stupéfiants (OCStup)	Betäubungsmittelkontroll-verordnung (BetmKV)	Narcotics Control Ordinance
Ordonnance sur la conservation des espèces (OCE)	Artenschutzverordnung (ASchV)	Species Protection Ordinance
Ordonnance sur la pharmacopée (OPha)	Pharmakopöeverordnung (PhaV)	Pharmacopoeia Ordinance
Ordonnance sur la progression à froid (OPFr)	Verordnung über die kalte Progression (VKP)	Bracket Creep Ordinance
Ordonnance sur la protection contre le bruit (OPB)	Lärmschutz-Verordnung (LSV)	Noise Abatement Ordinance
Ordonnance sur la protection de l'air (OPair)	Luftreinhalte-Verordnung (LRV)	Ordinance on Air Pollution Control
Ordonnance sur la protection des eaux (OEaux)	Gewässerschutzverordnung (GSchV)	Waters Protection Ordinance
Ordonnance sur la protection des travailleurs contre les risques liés aux microorganismes (OPTM)	Verordnung über den Schutz der Arbeitnehmerinnen und Arbeitnehmer vor Gefährdung durch Mikroorganismen (SAMV)	Ordinance on Protection of Employees from Dangerous Microorganisms

Ordonnance sur la radioprotection (ORaP)	Strahlenschutzverordnung (StSV)	Radiological Protection Ordinance
Ordonnance sur la signalisation routière (OSR)	Signalisationsverordnung (SSV)	Road Signs Ordinance
Ordonnance sur l'administration des offices de faillite (OAOF)	Verordnung über die Geschäftsführung der Konkursämter (KOV)	Ordinance on Procedures for Bankruptcy Offices
Ordonnance sur l'aide aux victimes d'infractions (OAVI)	Opferhilfeverordnung (OHV)	Victim Support Ordinance
Ordonnance sur l'assurance des véhicules (OAV)	Verkehrsversicherungsverordnung (VVV)	Vehicles Insurance Ordinance
Ordonnance sur l'assurance-accidents (OLAA)	Verordnung über die Unfallversicherung (UVV)	Accident Insurance Ordinance
Ordonnance sur l'assurance-chômage (OACI)	Arbeitslosenversicherungsverordnung (AVIV)	Unemployment Insurance Ordinance
Ordonnance sur le contrôle des biens (OCB)	Güterkontrollverordnung (GKV)	Goods Control Ordinance
Ordonnance sur le droit d'auteur (ODAu)	Urheberrechtsverordnung (URV)	Copyright Ordinance
Ordonnance sur le matériel de guerre (OMG)	Kriegsmaterialverordnung (KMV)	War Material Ordinance
Ordonnance sur le personnel de la Confédération (OPers)	Bundespersonalverordnung (BPV)	Federal Personnel Ordinance
Ordonnance sur le registre du commerce (ORC)	Handelsregisterverordnung (HRegV)	Commercial Register Ordinance
Ordonnance sur le service civil	Zivildienstverordnung	Civil Service Ordinance
Ordonnance sur le service de l'emploi (OSE)	Arbeitsvermittlungsverordnung (AVV)	Recruitment Ordinance
Ordonnance sur le traitement des déchets (OTD)	Technische Verordnung über Abfälle (TVA)	Technical Ordinance on Waste
Ordonnance sur le transfert des biens culturels (OTBC)	Kulturgütertransferverordnung (KGTV)	Cultural Property Transfer Ordinance
Ordonnance sur les accidents majeurs (OPAM)	Störfallverordnung (StFV)	Major Accidents Ordinance
Ordonnance sur les amendes d'ordre (OAO)	Ordnungsbussenverordnung (OBV)	Fixed Penalties Ordinance
Ordonnance sur les atteintes portées aux sols (OSol)	Verordnung über Belastungen des Bodens (VBBo)	Soil Pollution Ordinance

Ordonnance sur les banques (OB)	Bankenverordnung (BankV)	Banking Ordinance
Ordonnance sur les bourses (OBVM)	Börsenverordnung (BEHV)	Stock Exchange Ordinance
Ordonnance sur les brevets (OBI)	Patentverordnung (PatV)	Patents Ordinance
Ordonnance sur les chemins de fer (OCF)	Eisenbahnverordnung (EBV)	Railroads Ordinance
Ordonnance sur les contrôles de sécurité relatifs aux personnes (OCSP)	Verordnung über die Personensicherheitsprüfungen (PSPV)	Ordinance on Personnel Security Screening
Ordonnance sur les contrôles de sécurité relatifs aux personnes (OCSP)	Verordnung über die Personensicherheitsprüfungen (PSPV)	Ordinance on Personnel Security Screening
Ordonnance sur les denrées alimentaires et les objets usuels (ODAIOUs)	Lebensmittel- und Gebrauchsgegenständeverordnung (LGV)	Ordinance on Foodstuffs and Utility Articles
Ordonnance sur les droits de timbre (OT)	Stempelabgabenverordnung (StV)	Stamp Duties Ordinance
Ordonnance sur les importations agricoles (OIAgr)	Agrareinfuhrverordnung (AEV)	Agricultural Imports Ordinance
Ordonnance sur les installations de transport à câbles (OICa)	Seilbahnverordnung (SebV)	Cableways Ordinance
Ordonnance sur les maisons de jeu (OLMJ)	Spielbankenverordnung (VSBG)	Gambling Ordinance
Ordonnance sur les mouvements de déchets (OMD)	Verordnung über den Verkehr mit Abfällen (VeVA)	Waste Movements Ordinance
Ordonnance sur les règles de la circulation routière (OCR)	Verkehrsregelnverordnung (VRV)	Traffic Regulations Ordinance
Ordonnance sur les sites contaminés (OSites)	Altlastenverordnung (AltlV)	Contaminated Sites Ordinance
Ordonnance sur les topographies (OTo)	Topographienverordnung (ToV)	Topographies Ordinance
Ordonnance sur les travailleurs détachés en Suisse (Odét)	Verordnung über die in die Schweiz entsandten Arbeitnehmerinnen und Arbeitnehmer (EntsV)	Ordinance on Workers posted to Switzerland
Ordonnance sur l'état civil (OEC)	Zivilstandsverordnung (ZStV)	Civil Status Ordinance
Ordonnance sur l'impôt anticipé (OIA)	Verrechnungssteuerverordnung (VStV)	Withholding Tax Ordinance

ordre de crédit (art. 408 CO)	Kreditauftrag	credit order
ordre de démolition	Abbruchbefehl	demolition order
ordre de paiement	Zahlungsauftrag	payment order (by check, wire transfer, etc.)
ordre de saisie (art. 95 LP)	Reihenfolge der Pfändung	order of the seizure
ordre des créanciers (art. 219 LP)	Rangordnung der Gläubiger	order of creditors
ordre d'évacuation	Räumungsbefehl	evacuation order
ordre du jour	Traktandenliste (D: Tagesordnung)	agenda
ordre limité	limitierter Auftrag	limit order
ordure ménagère	Hauskehricht (D: Hausmüll)	domestic waste
organe de publication	Publikationsorgan	publication medium
organe de révision (art. 727 ss CO)	Revisionsstelle	auditor
organisation	Organisation	organization
organisation criminelle	kriminelle Organisation	criminal organization
organisation d'utilité publique	gemeinnützige Organisation	charitable organization, charity
organisation non gouvernementale	nichtstaatliche Organisation	non-governmental organization (NGO)
organisme d'autorégulation (OAR)	Selbstregulierungsorganisation (SRO)	self-regulatory organization (SRO)
orientation professionnelle	Berufsberatung	career counseling
otage	Geisel	hostage
outrages à des institutions interétatiques (art. 297 CP)	Beleidigung zwischenstaatlicher Organisationen	insulting an international organization
outrages aux États étrangers (art. 296 CP)	Beleidigung eines fremden Staates	insulting a foreign state
ouverture	Eröffnung	opening
ouverture de la faillite (art. 171 LP)	Konkurseröffnung	declaration of insolvency
ouverture de la procédure	Eröffnung des Verfahrens	opening of a proceeding
ouverture du testament (art. 559 CC)	Testamentseröffnung, Eröffnung der letztwilligen Verfügung	probate of a will, probate proceedings
ouvrage public	öffentliches Werk	public work
ouvrier du bâtiment	Bauarbeiter	construction worker
ouvrir	eröffnen	to open
pacte d'actionnaires	Aktionärbindungsvertrag (ABV)	shareholders' agreement
pacte de préemption (art. 216 CO)	Vorkaufsvertrag	contract conferring a right of first refusal

pacte de renonciation à succession à titre onéreux (art. 495 CC)	Erbauskauf	compensation in lieu of future inheritance
pacte successoral (art. 512 CC)	Erbvertrag	contract of inheritance (a bilateral contract between the testator and another person, which cannot be revoked unilaterally)
pacte successoral de renonciation	Erbverzichtsvertrag	agreement renouncing one's claim to an estate
paiement	Ausrichtung, Zahlung, Auszahlung	payment
paiement comptant	Barzahlung	cash payment
paiement de l'arriéré	Nachzahlung	payment of arrears
paiement de l'indu (art. 63 CO)	Zahlung einer Nichtschuld	payment of a non-existent debt
paiement direct	Direktzahlung	direct payment
paiement par intervention	Ehrenzahlung	payment by intervention
paiement partiel	Teilzahlung	partial payment
paix des morts (art. 262 CP)	Totenfrieden	the peace of the dead
Palais du Parlement	Parlamentsgebäude	Parliament Building (in Bern)
panachage	panaschieren	splitting the vote
panache de pollution	Verschmutzungsfahne	pollution plume
papier de légitimation	Ausweispapier	identification paper
papier-valeur (art. 965 CO) (F : valeur mobilière)	Wertpapier	security
par ouï-dire	Hörensagen	hearsay
paraphe	Visum (D: Namenszeichnen)	initials
pardon	Verzeihung	pardon
parenté	Verwandtschaft	relationship, kinship
parentèle (art. 457 CC)	Parentel (D: Stammgruppe)	statutory heir (The relatives of the deceased person are divided into groups of statutory heirs. These are based on the natural order in which the generations succeed each other. A group includes all persons who descend from a common ancestor.)

parentèle des grands-parents	grosselterlicher Stamm	grandparental line
parentèle des père et mère	elterlicher Stamm	parental line
parents adoptifs	Adoptiveltern	adoptive parents
parents nourriciers (art. 294 CC)	Pflegeeltern	foster parents
parité	Parität	equal representative of management and labor
parlement	Parlament	parliament
parlement cantonal	Kantonales Parlament	cantonal parliament
parlement communal	Gemeindeparlament	municipal parliament
parlementaire	Parlamentarier	member of parliament
paroi antibruit	Lärmschutzwand	noise barrier
parquer (F : stationner)	parkieren (D: parken)	to park
parrain	Götti (D: Taufpate)	godfather
parraine	Gotte (D: Taufpatin)	godmother
part	Betreffnis (D: Quote, Betrag)	portion, share, amount
part de bénéfice	Gewinnanteil	share of the profit
part sociale (1) (société coopérative)	Genossenschaftsanteil	share of a cooperative
part sociale (2) (société à responsabilité limitée)	Stammeinlage	share in a limited liability company
partage de la prévoyance professionnelle	Vorsorgeausgleich	pension splitting
partage matériel	Realteilung	physical division of property
partage successoral (art. 602 CC)	Erbschaftsteilung	distribution of the estate (among coheirs)
partenaire enregistré	eingetragener Partner	registered partner, domestic partner
partenariat enregistré	eingetragene Partnerschaft	registered partnership, domestic partnership
parti politique	politische Partei	political party
participant	Partizipant (D: Teilnehmer)	participant
participation (1)	Beteiligung, Teilnahme	participation
participation (2)	Mitwirkung (D: Mitbestimmung)	codetermination
participation à des troubles	Teilnahme an Unruhen	participation in civil unrest
participation à la saisie (art. 110 LP)	Pfändungsanschluss	participation in the seizure
participation à l'infraction	Teilnahme an der Straftat	participation in an offense (e.g. instigation and complicity)

participation au capital	Kapitalbeteiligung	equity interest
participation aux acquêts (art. 196 ss CC)	Errungenschaftsbeteiligung, Errungenschaftsgemeinschaft (D: Zugewinngemeinschaft)	participation in accrued gains
participation aux élections	Stimmbeteiligung (D: Wahlbeteiligung)	voter turnout
participation aux frais	Kostenbeteiligung	contribution to costs
participation aux pertes	Verlustanteil	participation in losses, share of the losses
participation obligatoire	Zwangsmitgliedschaft	mandatory participation
participations aux excédents	Überschussbeteiligung	surplus sharing
partie adverse	Gesuchsgegner (D: Antragsgegner)	respondent (in an administrative law case)
partie au contrat	Vertragspartei	party to the contract
partie intégrante	Bestandteil	integral part
partie plaignante (art. 118 CPP)	Privatklägerschaft	private claimant
partie qui obtient gain de cause	obsiegende Partei	successful party, prevailing party
partie qui succombe	unterliegende Partei	losing party
passage nécessaire (art. 694 CC)	Notweg	necessary easement
passage sous voie	Unterführung	underpass
passer en force de chose jugée	in Rechtskraft erwachsen (D: rechtskräftig werden)	to be res judicata
passible de droits de douane	zollpflichtig	dutiable
passifs transitoires	transitorische Passiven	accrued liabilities
paternité	Vaterschaft	paternity
patrimoine administratif	Verwaltungsvermögen	administrative assets
patrimoine génétique	Erbgut	genetic make-up
patrimoine naturel	Naturgut	natural heritage site
patrimoine organisé	organisierte Vermögenseinheiten	organized units of assets
patronage (art. 47 CP)	Schutzaufsicht	surveillance
payable	zahlbar	payable
payer	ausrichten (D: zahlen, auszahlen)	to pay
pays d'origine	Heimatstaat	country of origin
pays en voie de développement	Entwicklungsland	developing country
pêche	Fischerei	fishing
peine	Strafe	penalty, punishment
peine accessoire	Nebenstrafe	additional penalty

peine de mort (art. 10 CF)	Todesstrafe	death penalty, capital punishment
peine d'ensemble (art. 34 al. 3 CPP)	Gesamtstrafe	cumulative sentence
peine maximale	Höchststrafe	maximum sentence
peine pécuniaire (art. 34 CP)	Geldstrafe	monetary penalty
peine privative de liberté (art. 40 CP)	Freiheitsstrafe	custodial sentence
peine privative de liberté de substitution (art. 36 CP)	Ersatzfreiheitsstrafe	alternative custodial sentence
peine privative de liberté suspendue	aufgeschobene Freiheitstrafe	suspended custodial sentence
peine résolutoire	Wandelpön	penalty for termination
peine suspendue	aufgeschobene Strafe, Strafaufschub	suspended sentence
peines et mesures	Strafen und Massnahmen	penalties and measures
pelle mécanique	Trax (D: Bagger, Schaufellader)	bulldozer, excavator
pendant : affaires pendantes au 1er janvier	hängig (D: anhängig): am 1. Januar hängige Angelegenheiten	pending: cases pending on January 1
pendant la journée	untertags (D: tagsüber)	during the day
pendulaire (F : personne qui fait la navette)	Pendler	commuter
pénitencier	Zuchthaus	penitentiary
pensionnaire d'un établissement	Anstaltsinsasse	prison inmate
pensions (art. 93 al. 1 LP)	Pensionen	pensions
pénurie de logements	Wohnungsnot	housing shortage
pénurie de main d'œuvre	Arbeitskräftemangel	labor shortage, tight labor market
perception	Erhebung	levy (of taxes)
perception de l'impôt	Steuerbezug	tax collection
perception des droits douaniers	Zollerhebung	collection of customs duties
perception d'une contribution	Abgabeerhebung	levying of taxes
percevoir	erheben	to levy
péremption	Verwirkung	forfeiture
péréquation financière	Finanzausgleich	fiscal equalization
péril en la demeure	Gefahr im Verzug	danger in delay
périmer	erlöschen	to expire
période d'attente	Wartezeit	waiting period
période de calcul	Berechnungsperiode	calculation period
période de cotisation (AC)	Beitragszeit, Beitragsperiode	contribution period

période de présence obligatoire	Blockzeit	period of mandatory presence
période d'essai	Probezeit	trial period
période législative	Legislatur, Legislaturperiode	legislative period
période mobile	Gleitzeit	flextime
période suspecte	Verdachtsperiode, Verdachtsfrist	reach-back period (in bankruptcy)
période transitoire	Übergangszeit	transitional period
permis de chasse	Jagdpatent	hunting permit
permis de circulation	Fahrzeugausweis (D: Fahrzeugbrief)	vehicle title
permis de conduire	Führerausweis (D: Führerschein)	driver's license
permis de construire	Baubewilligung (D: Baugenehmigung)	building permit
permis de démolir	Abbruchbewilligung	demolition permit
permis de pêche	Fischereipatent	fishing license
permis de port d'armes	Waffentragschein	weapons permit
permis d'élève conducteur	Lernfahrausweis	learner's permit
permis d'habiter	Wohnbewilligung	housing permit
permis d'importation	Einfuhrbewilligung	import permit
perquisition de documents et enregistrements (art. 246-247 CPP)	Durchsuchung von Aufzeichnungen	search of records and recordings
perquisition de papiers	Durchsuchung von Papieren	search of papers
perquisition domiciliaire (art. 244 CPP)	Hausdurchsuchung	search of premises
persécution	Verfolgung	persecution
personnalité	Persönlichkeit	personality
personnalité juridique	Rechtspersönlichkeit	legal personality
personne	Person	person
personne à l'assistance	Armengenössiger (D: Sozialhilfeempfänger)	welfare recipient
personne âgée	Betagter	elderly person
personne assistée	betreute Person, Bretreuter	probationer
personne autorisée à signer	Unterschriftsberechtigter	person authorized to sign, authorized signatory
personne ayant qualité pour signer	Zeichnungsberechtigter (ZB)	authorized signatory, person with power to sign
personne concernée	betroffene Person	person in question
personne de confiance (art. 432 CC)	Vertrauensperson	authorized representative
personne détenue	Eingewiesene, inhaftierte Person	inmate, prisoner
personne morale	juristische Person	legal entity

personne physique	natürliche Person	natural person, individual
personne privée	Privatperson	private person
personne proche	nahestehende Person	related party
personne remariée	wiederverheiratete Person	remarried person
personne retraitée	Pensionierter	pensioner, retiree
personne sans activité lucrative	Nichterwerbstätiger	person without gainful employment
personne servant dans la protection civile	Zivilschutzangehöriger	person serving in the civil defense
personne seule	alleinstehende Person	single person
personne soumise au secret professionnel	Berufsgeheimnisträger	person subject to a professional duty of confidentiality
personne sous surveillance électronique	elektronisch überwachte Person	electronically monitored person, tagged person
personne tenue de fournir une prestation	Realleistungspflichtiger	person obligated to take measures
personne tenue de supporter les frais	Kostentragungspflichtiger	person liable to bear costs
perte	Verlust	loss
perte comptable	Buchverlust	book loss
perte de gain	Erwerbsausfall, Verdienstausfall	loss of earnings
perte de soutien	Versorgerschaden	loss of upkeep
perte de travail	Arbeitsausfall	loss of working hours
perte de travail due aux intempéries	wetterbedingter Arbeitsausfall	loss of working hours due to bad weather
perte d'une chance	verlorene Chance	loss of a chance
pertinent, important pour la procédure	rechtserheblich	relevant from a legal standpoint
perturbateur	Störer	polluter
perturbateur par comportement	Verhaltensstörer	polluter by virtue of misconduct
perturbateur par situation	Zustandsstörer	polluter by virtue of situation
petite délinquance	Bagatelldelinquenz	petty crime
petit-enfant	Grosskind (D: Enkelkind)	grandchild
petites et moyennes entreprises (PME)	kleine und mittlere Unternehmen (KMU)	small and medium-sized enterprises (SME)
pétition	Bittschrift	petition
philosophie du droit	Rechtsphilosophie	jurisprudence, legal philosophy
pièce comptable	Buchungsbeleg	accounting record
pierre précieuse	Edelstein	precious stone, jewel, gem

pillage	Plünderung	plundering
piraterie aérienne	Flugzeugentführung	hijacking
place de dépôt	Deponie	disposal site, dump
place de parc (F : place de stationnement)	Parkierplatz (D: Parkplatz)	parking place, parking space
place de travail (F : emploi)	Arbeitsplatz	job
placement chez des parents nourriciers	Familienpflege	placement with foster parents
placement dans une maison d'éducation	Heimeinweisung, Heimversorgung	placement in a children's home
placement de personnel	Arbeitsvermittlung	recruitment
placement d'enfants	Aufnahme von Pflegekindern	placement of children in foster homes
placement d'enfants en vue d'adoption	Adoptionsvermittlung	adoption placement
placements sur le marché monétaire	Geldmarktanlage	money market funds
plagiat	Plagiat	plagiarism
plaidoiries finales (art. 232 CPC)	Schlussvortrage	closing arguments
plaignant	Strafantragsteller	criminal complainant
plainte (1) (LP)	Beschwerde (SchKG)	complaint
plainte (2) (art. 304 CPP)	Strafantrag	criminal complaint
plainte à l'autorité de surveillance (art. 71 PA)	Aufsichtsbeschwerde (Art. 71 VwVG)	complaint to the supervisory authority
plainte à l'autorité supérieure de surveillance (art. 18 LP)	Beschwerde an die obere Aufsichtsbehörde	complaint to the higher supervisory authority
plainte pénale (art. 30-33 CP, art. 304 CPP)	Strafantrag	criminal complaint
plan de mensuration	Vermessungsplan	survey plan
plan de quote-part de logements	Wohnanteilplan	plan reserving a certain percentage for residences
plan de zones	Zonenplan (D: Flächennutzungsplan)	zoning plan
plan d'épargne	Sparplan	savings plan
plan d'épargne en fonds de placement	Fondssparplan	fund savings plan
plan social (art. 335h CO)	Sozialplan	social plan (an agreement in which an employer and employees indicate measures to avoid layoffs or to reduce their numbers and mitigate their effects)

planification de la gestion des déchets	Abfallplanung	waste management planning
planification fiscale	Steuerplanung	tax planning
planification hospitalière	Spitalplanung (D: Krankenhausplanung)	hospital planning
plante protégée	geschützte Pflanze	protected plant
plate-forme de négociation	Handelsplatz	trading venue
pluralité de mariages (art. 215 CP)	mehrfache Ehe	bigamy
plus ou moins value	Mehr- oder Minderwert	increase or decrease in value
plus subsidiairement encore	subeventualiter (D: weiter hilfsweise)	in the further alternative
plus-value	Mehrwert	value added
pneu	Pneu (D: Autoreifen, Fahrradreifen)	tire
point central de contact	zentrale Anlaufstelle	single point of contact
point de base	Basispunkt	basis point (100 basis points are equal to 1%, so 1 basis point = 0.01%)
points de l'ordre du jour	Traktanden, Regularien (D: Tagesordnungspunkte)	agenda items
police	Polizei	police
police cantonale	Kantonspolizei (Kapo)	cantonal police
police d'assurance	Versicherungspolice	insurance policy
police des denrées alimentaires	Lebensmittelpolizei	food police
police du commerce, police économique	Gewerbepolizei (D: Gewerbeaufsichtsamt)	trade inspection agency
police du feu	Feuerpolizei	fire marshal
police judiciaire	Gerichtspolizei	judicial police
Police judiciaire fédérale (PJF)	Bundeskriminalpolizei (BKP)	Federal Criminal Police
politique	Politik	policy
politique agricole	Agrarpolitik	agricultural policy
politique conjoncturelle (art. 100 CF)	Konjunkturpolitik	economic policy
politique culturelle	Kulturpolitik	cultural policy
politique d'asile	Asylpolitik	asylum policy
politique de placement	Anlagepolitik	investment policy
politique des étrangers	Ausländerpolitik	immigration policy
politique douanière	Zollpolitik	customs policy
politique du personnel	Personalpolitik	personnel policy
politique économique extérieure (art. 101 CF)	Aussenwirtschaftspolitik (D: Außenwirtschaftspolitik)	foreign economic policy

politique en matière de chômage	Arbeitslosenpolitik	unemployment policy
politique en matière de formation	Bildungspolitik	educational policy
politique en matière de prix	Preispolitik	pricing policy
politique en matière de stupéfiants	Drogenpolitik	drug policy
politique environnementale	Umweltpolitik	environmental policy
politique extérieure	Aussenpolitik (D: Außenpolitik)	foreign policy
politique familiale	Familienpolitik	family policy
politique fiscale	Steuerpolitik	tax policy
politique foncière	Bodenpolitik	land policy
politique monétaire	Geldpolitik	monetary policy
politique pénitentiaire	Strafvollzugspolitik	prison policy
politique régionale	Regionalpolitik	regional policy
politique structurelle (art. 103 CF)	Strukturpolitik	structural policy
pollueur	Verursacher	polluter
pollution (art. 4 LEaux)	Verunreinigung	pollution
pollution de l'air	Luftverunreinigung	air pollution
pool d'assurances	Versicherungspool	insurance pool
population	Bevölkerung	population
pornographie (art. 197 CP)	Pornografie	pornography
pornographie qualifiée (art. 197 CP)	qualifizierte Pornografie	aggravated pornography
port obligatoire de la ceinture de sécurité	Gurtentrageobligatorium (D: Anschnallpflicht)	mandatory wearing of seatbelts
portefeuille collectif interne de la banque	bankinternes Sondervermögen	separate assets within a bank
porte-fort (art. 111 CO)	Vertrag zu Lasten eines Dritten	guarantee of performance by third party
porter une affaire devant le tribunal	eine Sache beim Gericht anhängig machen	to file a case with a court
porteur d'une procuration non-commerciale	Trager nichtkaufmännischer Prokura (TnkProk)	holder of a noncommercial power of attorney
position dominante	beherrschende Stellung	dominant position
positivisme juridique	Rechtspositivismus	legal positivism
possesseur	Besitzer	possessor
possesseur pour autrui	Besitzdiener	possessor's agent
possession (art. 919-941 CC)	Besitz	possession
possession commune	Gesamtbesitz	common ownership
possession médiate	mittelbarer Besitz	indirect ownership

poste restante	postlagernde Sendung	poste restante
postposition	Rangrücktritt	subordination
postulat	Postulat	parliamentary motion asking the government to legislate (as opposed to a motion requiring the government to legislate, cf. *motion*)
potentiel de pollution	Schadstoffpotenzial	pollution potential
pour le surplus	im Übrigen	in other respects
pourparlers	Vertragsverhandlung	contract negotiations
poursuite	Betreibung (D: Beitreibung)	debt collection (legal action to enforce payment in cash or the provision of cash coverage by a debtor who fails to meet his payment obligations)
poursuite en réalisation de gage (art. 151 ss LP)	Betreibung auf Pfandverwertung	debt collection via sale of pledged assets (legal action to enforce debt recovery under claims secured by pledged collateral, requiring the sale of the property in question)
poursuite par voie de faillite (art. 159 LP)	Konkursbetreibung, Betreibung auf Konkurs	debt collection via bankruptcy proceedings (legal action to enforce the sale of all assets of a debtor who fails to meet his payment obligations)
poursuite par voie de saisie (art. 89 LP)	Betreibung auf Pfändung	debt collection via seizure of assets
poursuite pénale (art. 302 CP)	Strafverfolgung	prosecution
poursuite pour dettes	Schuldbetreibung	debt collection, debt collection
poursuite pour effets de change (art. 177 ss LP)	Wechselbetreibung	enforcement of bills of exchange
poursuivre	betreiben (D: beitreiben)	to collect, to sue to recover

pourvoi en nullité (art. 228 CPC)	Nichtigkeitsbeschwerde (D: Revision)	appeal to the Supreme Court on a point of law, similar to *cassation* in France and *Revision* in Germany
pousser	stossen (D: drücken)	to push
pouvoir d'achat	Kaufkraft	purchasing power
pouvoir d'appréciation du juge (art. 4 CC)	richterliches Ermessen, gerichtliches Ermessen	judicial discretion
pouvoir de disposer	Verfügungsmacht	power to dispose of assets
pouvoir de représentation	Vertretungsmacht	power of representation
pouvoir judiciaire	Judikative	judicial power
pouvoirs discrétionnaires	Ermessensspielraum	discretion
préambule (préamb.)	Präambel, Ingress (Ingr.)	preamble
précédent	Präzedenzfall	precedent
préemption	Vorkauf	right of first refusal
préfecture	Statthalteramt, Regierungsstatthalteramt	Chancellery of State
préfet	Statthalter, Regierungsstatthalter	Chancellor of State (representative of the Cantonal Government responsible for the administration of the district)
préjudice financier	Steuerausfall	loss of tax
prélèvements sur les biens de l'enfant (art. 320 CC)	Anzehrung des Kindesvermögens	drawing on the child's assets
premier ministre	Ministerpräsident	prime minister
première instance	erste Instanz	first instance
preneur d'assurance	Versicherungsnehmer	the insured
preneur de leasing	Leasingnehmer	lessee
preneur de licence	Lizenznehmer	licensee
prénom	Vorname	first name, given name
préposé à la protection des données	Datenschutzbeauftragter	data protection commissioner
préposé au registre du commerce	Handelsregisterführer	Commercial Registrar
préposé aux faillites (art. 2 LP)	Konkursbeamter	bankruptcy official
préposé aux poursuites (art. 2 LP)	Betreibungsbeamter	debt collection official

Préposé fédéral à la protection des données et à la transparence (PFPDT)	Eidgenössischer Datenschutz- und Öffentlichkeitsbeauftragte (EDÖB)	Federal Data Protection and Information Commissioner
prescription (art. 127-138 CO)	Verjährung	statute of limitations, limitation period (the basic one is 10 years)
prescription acquisitive (art. 661 ss CC)	Ersitzung	adverse possession
prescription acquisitive ordinaire (art. 661 CC)	ordentliche Ersitzung	ordinary adverse possession
prescription extraordinaire (art. 662 CC)	ausserordentliche Ersitzung	extraordinary adverse possession
présence	Anwesenheit	presence
présentation à vue (art. 1099 CO)	Vorlegung zur Sichtnahme	presentment at sight
présentation de faits	Tatsachendarstellung	presentation of the facts
présentation des moyens de preuve (art. 73 LP)	Vorlage der Beweismittel	presentation of evidence
présentation d'un produit	Ausstattung (gewerblicher Rechtsschutz)	trade dress
présentation d'une lettre de change (art. 1011 CO)	Vorlegung eines Wechsels	presentment of a draft/bill of exchange
président	Präsident	president, chairman
Président de la Confédération	Bundespräsident	President of the Swiss Confederation
président de la direction	Vorsitzender der Geschäftsleitung (D: ~Vorstandsvorsitzender)	chairman of the board of managers (CEO)
président du conseil d'administration	Präsident des Verwaltungsrates (D: ~Aufsichtsratsvorsitzender)	chairman of the board of directors
président du Conseil d'Etat	Regierungspräsident	president of the Council of State
président du tribunal	Gerichtspräsident, vorsitzender Richter	presiding judge
président du tribunal de district	Bezirksgerichtspräsident	president of the district court
président d'un groupe parlementaire	Fraktionspräsident	president of a parliamentary group, chairman of a parliamentary group
présomption	Vermutung	presumption
présomption de la paternité du mari (art. 255-258 CC)	Vermutung der Vaterschaft des Ehemannes	presumption of the paternity of the husband

présomption de paternité	Vaterschaftsvermutung	presumption of paternity
présomption d'innocence (art. 10 CPP)	Unschuldsvermutung, Vermutung der Schuldlosigkeit	presumption of innocence
prestation (1)	Leistung	performance
prestation (2)	Leistung	supply (in the VAT context)
prestation (3)	Leistung	benefit (in the insurance context)
prestation appréciable en argent	geldwerte Leistung	payment in kind
prestation complémentaire (PC)	Ergänzungsleistung (EL)	supplementary benefit
prestation d'assistance	Sozialhilfeleistung	welfare benefit
prestation d'assurance	Versicherungsleistung	insurance benefit
prestation de libre passage	Freizügigkeitsleistung	vested benefit
prestation de prévoyance	Vorsorgeleistung	pension benefit
prestation de services	Dienstleistung	provision of services
prestation de sortie	Austrittsleistung	termination benefits
prestation de vieillesse	Altersleistung	pension benefits
prestation d'invalidité	Invalidenleistung	disability benefits
prestation en argent	Geldleistung	payment in money
prestation en capital	Kapitalabfindung	cash settlement
prestation en cas de maternité	Mutterschaftsleistung	maternity benefit
prestation en nature	Sachleistung	payment in kind, benefit in kind
prestation pour survivants	Hinterlassenenleistung	surviving dependents' benefit
prestation propre	Eigenleistung	"sweat equity," work by the owner
prestations de risque	Risikoleistungen	risk benefits
prestations écologiques requises (PER)	Ökologischer Leistungsnachweis (ÖLN)	proof of ecological performance
prestations sociales	Sozialleistungen	social insurance benefits
prêt (art. 305 ss CO)	Leihe	loan
prêt à usage (art. 305-311 ss CO)	Gebrauchsleihe	loan for use (as opposed to a loan for consumption)
prêt de consommation (art. 312-318 ss CO)	Darlehen	loan (for consumption, as opposed to a loan for use)
prêt sur gage (art. 907 ss CC)	Versatzpfand	pawn, pawning
prétendre	behaupten	to claim, to allege

prétention de droit public	öffentlich-rechtliche Forderung	public law claim
prétention de tiers	Drittansprache	third-party claim
prétention fondée sur l'enrichissement illégitime	Bereicherungsanspruch	claim based on unjust enrichment
prêteur (1) (prêt à usage) (art. 305-311 ss CO)	Verleiher	lender (loan for use)
prêteur (2) (prêt de consommation) (art. 312-318 ss CO)	Darleiher	lender
prétraitement des eaux usées	Abwasservorbehandlung	pretreatment of sewage
prêts consentis	Aktivdarlehen	loans granted
prêts sur gage	Forderungen der Pfandleihanstalten	pawning
preuve	Beweis	proof, evidence
preuve à futur (art. 158 CPC)	vorsorgliche Beweisführung	precautionary taking of evidence, preservation of evidence
preuve de la qualité de réfugié (art. 7 LAsi)	Nachweis der Flüchtlingseigenschaft	proof of refugee status
preuve de la vérité	Wahrheitsbeweis	proof of the truth
preuve illicite	Beweisverwertungsverbot	unlawful evidence
preuve libératoire	Entlastungsbeweis	exonerating evidence
preuve par indices	Indizienbeweis	circumstantial evidence
prévention des accidents	Unfallverhütung	accident prevention
prévenu (art. 111 CPP)	Beschuldigter	person charged, the accused, defendant
prévisibilité	Voraussehbarkeit, Vorhersehbarkeit	foreseeability
prévisions concernant un préjudice	Nachteilsprognose	likelihood of irreparable harm if preliminary injunctive relief is not granted
prévoyance individuelle	individuelle Vorsorge	individual pension plan
prévoyance professionnelle (art. 113 CF)	berufliche Vorsorge	pension plan (A company pension plan is mandatory for all employees and is the second pillar of the Swiss social security system. The fund may be operated by the company, a professional association or an insurance company.)

prévoyance vieillesse	Altersvorsorge	provision for old age
primauté des cotisations	Beitragsprimat	defined contribution plan (financing system in which the pension plan's benefits are based on contributions equaling a certain percentage of the pensionable salary)
primauté des prestations	Leistungsprimat	defined benefit plan
primauté du droit fédéral (art. 49 CF)	Vorrang des Bundesrechts	supremacy of federal law
primauté du droit international	derogatorische Kraft internationalen Rechts	primacy of international law
prime (1)	Agio, Aufgeld	premium (difference between the nominal value of a security and its issue or market price)
prime (2)	Prämie	premium
prime d'assurance	Versicherungsprämie	insurance premium
prime d'assurance-accidents	Unfallversicherungsprämie	accident insurance premium (similar to workers' compensation premium)
prime d'assurance-maladie	Krankenversicherungsprämie	health insurance premium
prime de risque	Risikoprämie	risk premium
prime irrécouvrable	uneinbringliche Prämie	irrecoverable premium
prime unique	Einmalprämie	single premium
principe constitutionnel	verfassungsmässiger Grundsatz	constitutional principle
principe d'allégation (art. 106 al. 2 LTF)	Rügeprinzip	principle that a constitutional claim must be raised in the trial court and cannot be raised for the first time on appeal
principe de causalité (art. 3a LEaux)	Verursacherprinzip	"polluter pays" principle
principe de désunion	Zerrütungsprinzip	principle of irretrievable breakdown

principe de disposition (art. 58 CPC)	Dispositionsgrundsatz	principle of non ultra petita (principle that a judge may not award more than a party claims or less than the other party recognizes, nor may the judge's judgment be different in kind from that sought)
principe de l'accession	Akzessionsprinzip	principle of accession
principe de l'accusation (art. 9 CPP)	Anklagegrundsatz	principle of no judgment without a charge
principe de la bonne foi	Grundsatz von Treu und Glauben	good faith principle
principe de la célérité	Beschleunigungsgebot	right to a speedy trial
principe de la confiance	Vertrauensprinzip	principle of good faith
principe de la convention unique	Tarifeinheit	principle of one collective bargaining agreement per business
principe de la double incrimination	Grundsatz der beidseitigen Strafbarkeit	principle of double criminality (a requirement in the extradition law of many countries whereby a suspect can be extradited from one country to stand trial for breaking a second country's laws only when a similar law exists in the extraditing country)
principe de la liberté de la preuve	Freibeweis	principle that all types of evidence are admissible (as opposed to the system in the US, where evidence is evaluated by a lay jury, and therefore there are strict rules governing admissibility of evidence)

principe de la territorialité	Territorialitätsprinzip	principle of territoriality (a person who commits a crime in Switzerland is subject to the jurisdiction of the Swiss courts)
principe de la transparence	Öffentlichkeitsprinzip	principle of transparency
principe de légalité (art. 1 CP)	Legalitätsprinzip	principle of legality, principle of previously defined conduct
principe de l'épuisement	Erschöpfungsgrundsatz	principle of exhaustion
principe de l'équivalence	Äquivalenzprinzip	benefit principle
principe de l'estoppel	Estoppel-Prinzip	principle of estoppel
principe de l'immédiat	Unmittelbarkeitsprinzip	principle of immediacy
principe de l'offre suffisante (art. 126 LP)	Deckungsprinzip	sufficient bid principle (bid for the item being auctioned is sufficient to cover the claims of secured creditors)
principe de l'opportunité des poursuites	Opportunitätsprinzip	principle of prosecutorial discretion
principe du pays de destination	Bestimmungslandprinzip	taxation in the destination country
principe d'universalité	Universalitätsprinzip	principle of universality (bankrupt estate includes all of debtor's assets, including those located abroad)
principe juridique	Rechtsgrundsatz	legal principle
principes d'investissement	Anlagegrundsätze	investment principles
priorité	Vortritt (D: Vorfahrt)	right of way (in traffic)
priorité découlant du dépôt (art. 6 LPM)	Hinterlegungspriorität	right of priority
prise de sang	Blutprobe	blood sample
prise d'inventaire	Inventaraufnahme	taking of inventory
prise d'otages (art. 185 CP)	Geiselnahme	hostage taking, taking of hostages
prise d'une activité lucrative	Aufnahme einer Erwerbstätigkeit	taking up gainful employment
prise en charge préalable	Vorleistungspflicht	advance performance obligation
privation de liberté (art. 31 CF)	Freiheitsentzug	deprivation of liberty

privation de lumière	Entzug von Tageslicht	deprivation of daylight
privation d'ensoleillement (art. 684 CC)	Entzug von Besonnung	deprivation of sunlight
privatisation	Privatisierung	privatization
privilège	Vorrecht	preferential right
privilège dans la faillite	Konkursprivileg	preferential right in bankruptcy proceedings
prix	Preis	price
prix coûtant	Einstandspreis	cost price
prix d'achat	Kaufpreis	purchase price
prix d'appel	Lockvogel	loss leader
prix de base	Ausgangspreis	base price
prix de détail	Detailpreis (D: Einzelhandelspreis)	retail price
prix de gros	Grosshandelspreis	wholesale price
prix de transfert	Transferpreis (D: Verrechnungspreis)	transfer pricing
prix d'émission	Ausgabepreis, Emissionspreis	issue price
prix d'exercice	Ausübungspreis	exercise price, strike price
prix du marché	Marktpreis	market price
prix ferme	fester Preis	firm price
prix imposés	Preisbindung	retail price maintenance
procédé de fabrication	Herstellungsverfahren	manufacturing process
procédé téméraire (art. 128 CPC)	mutwillige Prozessführung	frivolous litigation, vexatious litigation
procédure	Verfahren	procedure, proceedings
procédure accélérée	beschleunigtes Verfahren	accelerated procedure
procédure administrative	Verwaltungs- und Verwaltungsgerichtsverfahren	administrative procedure
procédure administrative de recours	Verwaltungsbeschwerde-verfahren	administrative appeal procedure
procédure amiable	Verständigungsverfahren	mutual agreement procedure
procédure arbitrale	schiedsrichterliches Verfahren	arbitration proceeding
procédure cantonale	kantonales Verfahren	cantonal procedure
procédure civile	Zivilprozess	civil procedure
procédure concordataire (art. 293 ss LP)	Nachlassverfahren	debt restructuring proceedings
procédure contentieuse	streitige Gerichtsbarkeit	adversary proceedings
procédure contradictoire	kontradiktorisches Verfahren	adversary proceedings
procédure d'adoption	Adoptionsverfahren	adoption procedure
procédure d'appel	Berufungsverfahren	appellate procedure
procédure d'asile	Asylverfahren	asylum procedure

procédure d'assainissement	Sanierungsverfahren	reorganization procedure
procédure d'autorisation	Bewilligungsverfahren	authorization procedure
procédure de conciliation (art. 202 ss CPC)	Einigungsverfahren, Schlichtungsverfahren, Sühnverfahren	conciliation proceedings
procédure de consultation	Vernehmlassungsverfahren	consultation procedure (the phase in the preparation of legislation in which bills (draft laws) are verified by the cantons, parties, associations and sometimes other stakeholders throughout Switzerland, in order to determine the likelihood of their adoption)
procédure de faillite (art. 221 ss LP)	Konkursverfahren	bankruptcy proceedings
procédure de la justice militaire	Militärstrafrechtspflege	administration of military justice
procédure de mainlevée (art. 84 LP)	Rechtsöffnungsverfahren	procedure for dismissal of debtor's objection
procédure de réalisation (art. 155 ss LP)	Verwertungsverfahren	sale procedure
procédure de recours	Beschwerdeverfahren	appellate proceedings
procédure de revendication (art. 106-109 LP)	Widerspruchsverfahren	third party objection procedure
procédure d'épuration de l'état des charges (art. 140 al. 2 LP)	Lastenbereinigungsverfahren	proceedings to determine charges
procédure d'estimation	Schätzungsverfahren	valuation procedure
procédure d'exécution	Vollstreckungsverfahren	enforcement
procédure d'inscription	Anmeldeverfahren	registration procedure
procédure d'instruction de la demande	Abklärungsverfahren	investigation proceedings
procédure diplomatique	diplomatisches Verfahren	diplomatic procedure
procédure disciplinaire	Disziplinarverfahren	disciplinary procedure
procédure disciplinaire militaire	Militärdisziplinarrechtspflege	administration of military discipline
procédure d'opposition (1)	Einspracheverfahren	objections procedure

procédure d'opposition (2) (art. 31 LPM)	Widerspruchsverfahren	opposition proceedings (to registration of a trademark)
procédure écrite	schriftliches Verfahren	written procedure
procédure en rappel d'impôt	Nachsteuerverfahren	additional tax assessment
procédure législative	Rechtssetzungsverfahren	legislative procedure
procédure orale	mündliches Verfahren	oral procedure
procédure ordinaire (art. 219 ss CPC)	ordentliches Verfahren	ordinary procedure
procédure par défaut	Kontumatialverfahren	proceedings for a default judgment
procédure par voie de circulation	Zirkulationsverfahren	circulation procedure
procédure pénale	Strafprozess	criminal procedure
procédure pénale administrative	Verwaltungsstrafverfahren	administrative criminal proceedings
Procédure pénale applicable aux mineurs (PPMin)	Jugendstrafprozessordnung (JStPO)	Juvenile Criminal Procedure Code
procédure pénale des mineurs	Jugendstrafverfahren	juvenile criminal procedure
procédure pénale fiscale	Steuerstrafverfahren	criminal tax procedure
procédure pénale militaire	Militärstrafprozess	military criminal procedure
procédure préliminaire (art. 299 ss CPP)	Vorverfahren	preliminary proceedings
procédure principale	Hauptsacheverfahren	trial on the merits, proceedings on the merits
procédure probatoire	Beweisverfahren	evidentiary proceedings
procédure simplifiée (1) (art. 243 ss CPC)	vereinfachtes Verfahren	simplified procedure (applies in financial disputes where the amount in controversy does not exceed CHF 30,000)
procédure simplifiée (2) (art. 358-362 CPP)	abgekürztes Verfahren	accelerated proceedings (in plea bargaining cases)
procédure sommaire (art. 248 ss CPC, art. 231 LP)	summarisches Verfahren	summary proceedings
procédures judiciaires (art. 30 CF)	gerichtliche Verfahren	judicial proceedings

procès devenu sans objet (art. 242 CPC)	Gegenstandslosigkeit	proceedings made groundless
processus d'élimination des divergences	Differenzbereinigungsverfahren	procedure for the resolution of differences (when the National Council and Council of States have differing opinions of a bill)
procès-verbal (1)	Protokoll	minutes
procès-verbal (2)	Protokoll	record
procès-verbal de procédure (art. 77 CPP)	Verfahrensprotokoll	record of proceedings
procès-verbal de saisie (art. 112 LP)	Pfändungsurkunde	seizure report
procès-verbal de séquestre (art. 276 LP)	Arresturkunde	attachment certificate (listing the frozen assets and their estimated value)
procès-verbal des auditions (art. 78 CPP)	Einvernahmeprotokoll	record of examination hearings
procès-verbal des enchères	Steigerungsprotokoll	auction record
procuration	Vollmacht	power of attorney
procuration apparente	Rechtsscheinvollmacht	apparent authority
procuration individuelle (art. 459 II CO)	Einzelvollmacht, Einzelprokura	individual power of attorney
procureur des mineurs	Jugendanwalt	juvenile prosecutor
prodigalité	Verschwendung	profligacy
production de créance	Forderungseingabe	production of the claim
production de documents	Edition	production of documents
productions	Konkurseingaben	creditors' claims in bankruptcy
produire	anmelden	to produce
produire en justice	edieren	to produce documents
produit de l'infraction	Deliktsgut	proceeds of a crime
produit de réalisation	Erlös	proceeds of sale
produit fini	Endprodukt	end product, final product
produit importé	Importpräparat	imported product
produit intermédiaire	Zwischenprodukt	intermediate product
produit mi-fini	Halbfabrikat	half-finished product
produit net des livraisons et de prestations	Nettoerlös aus Lieferungen und Leistungen	net sales
produits d'exploitation	Betriebsertrag	operating income
produits financiers	Finanzertrag	finance income

produits hors exploitation	betriebsfremder Ertrag	nonoperating income
profession	Beruf	profession
profil d'ADN	DNA-Profil	DNA profile
profil de la personnalité	Persönlichkeitsprofil	personality profile
programme d'enseignement	Lehrplan	curriculum
prohibition de concurrence (art. 340 CO)	Konkurrenzverbot	covenant not to compete
prohibition des loteries	Lotterieverbot	prohibition of lotteries
projet d'assainissement	Sanierungsprojekt	remediation project
projet de constitution	Verfassungsentwurf	draft constitution
projet de convention	Konventionsvorschlag	proposed divorce agreement
projet de décision	Entscheidentwurf	draft decision, draft judgment
projet de loi	Gesetzesentwurf	bill
projet rédigé de toutes pièces	ausgearbeiteter Entwurf	specific draft provision (as opposed to a general one)
prolongation	Erstreckung	extension
prolongation du délai	Fristerstreckung (D: Fristverlängerung)	extension of the deadline, extension of the time limit
prolonger – Les délais légaux ne peuvent pas être prolongés.	erstreckbar – Gesetzliche Fristen sind nicht erstreckbar.	Statutory deadlines cannot be extended.
promesse de contracter, précontrat (art. 22 CO)	Vorvertrag	contract creating an obligation for one or both parties to enter into a contract in the future
promesse de donner (art. 243 CO)	Schenkungsversprechen	promise to make a gift
promesse de payer	Zahlungsversprechen	promise to pay
promesse de porte-fort (art. 111 CO)	Vertrag zu Lasten eines Dritten	guarantee of performance by third party
promesse publique (art. 8 CO)	Auslobung	publicly promised remuneration
promettant	Promittent	promisor
promotion	Aktion (D: Sonderangebot)	promotion, special sale
promotion de la presse	Presseförderung	promotion of the press
pronostic favorable sur le fond	Hauptsachenprognose	likelihood of success on the merits
propagande subversive (art. 275bis CP)	staatsgefährliche Propaganda	subversive propaganda

propagation d'une épizootie (art. 232 CP)	Verbreiten von Tierseuchen	transmission of epizootic diseases
propagation d'une maladie de l'homme (art. 231 CP)	Verbreiten menschlicher Krankheiten	transmission of human diseases
propension au risque	Risikoneigung	risk appetite
proportionnalité	Verhältnismässigkeit	proportionality
proposition	Vorschlag	proposal
proposition conçue en termes généraux	allgemeine Anregung	general proposal
proposition d'arrangement	Vergleichsvorschlag	proposed settlement
proposition de candidat	Wahlvorschlag	candidate list
proposition de conciliation	Schlichtungsvorschlag	conciliation proposal
proposition de jugement (art. 210 CPC)	Urteilsvorschlag	proposed judgment
proposition de réexamen	Rückkommensantrag	proposal for reconsideration
proposition subsidiaire	Eventualbegehren (D: Hilfsantrag)	alternative petition, petition in the alternative
propres actions	eigene Aktien	own shares
propriétaire	Eigentümer	owner
propriétaire d'entreprise	Betriebsinhaber	business owner
propriétaire d'immeuble	Grundeigentümer	landowner
propriétaire d'ouvrage	Werkeigentümer	property owner
propriété	Eigentum	ownership
propriété collective (art. 646 CC)	gemeinschaftliches Eigentum	collective ownership
propriété commune (art. 652 ss CC)	Gesamteigentum	collective ownership
propriété exclusive	Alleineigentum	sole ownership
propriété foncière (art. 655 ss CC)	Grundeigentum	land ownership
propriété mobilière	Fahrniseigentum	ownership of chattels
propriété par étages (PPE) (art. 712a CC)	Stockwerkeigentum (StWE)	condominium
propriété quiritaire	dominium ex iure quiritium	full ownership
prospectus d'émission (art. 652a CO)	Emissionsprospekt	issue prospectus
protection civile (art. 61 CF)	Zivilschutz	civil defense
protection de l'union conjugale	Eheschutz, Schutz der ehelichen Gemeinschaft	protection of the marital union
protection des consommateurs	Verbraucherschutz	consumer protection
protection des données	Datenschutz	data protection
protection juridique	Rechtsschutz	legal protection
protêt	Protest	protest

protêt faute d'acceptation	Protest mangels Annahme	protest on nonacceptance
protêt faute de paiement	Protest mangels Zahlung	protest on nonpayment
protocole d'élection	Wahlprotokoll	election record
provision	Rückstellung	provision
provisions pour impôts	Steuerrückstellungen	tax provisions
provocation publique au crime ou à la violence (art. 259 CP)	öffentliche Aufforderung zu Verbrechen oder zur Gewalttätigkeit	public incitement to commit a felony or act of violence
prud'homme	Arbeitsrichter	labor court judge
publication	Bekanntgabe, Bekanntmachung	publication, public notice
publication de débats officiels secrets (art. 293 CP)	Veröffentlichung amtlicher geheimer Verhandlungen	publication of secret official proceedings
publication de l'ouverture de la faillite (art. 232 LP)	Bekanntmachung der Konkurseröffnung	public notice of the opening of bankruptcy proceedings
publication électronique	elektronische Veröffentlichung	electronic publication
publicité	Werbung	advertising
punir	bestrafen	to punish
punissabilité	Strafbarkeit	criminal liability
punition	Bestrafung	punishment
punition corporelle	Körperstrafe	corporal punishment
pupille	Mündel	ward
purge hypothécaire	einseitige Ablösung eines Grundpfandrechts	unilateral redemption of a mortgage
quai	Perron (D: Bahnsteig)	platform
qualification juridique	rechtliche Qualifikation	applying the law to the facts
qualification professionnelle	berufliche Fähigkeit	professional qualification
qualité de salarié	Arbeitnehmereigenschaft	capacity as employee
qualité pour agir	Klageberechtigung	right to bring action
qualité pour agir et recourir	Legitimation	standing to sue
qualité pour poursuivre (LP)	Betreibungsfähigkeit (SchKG)	standing to sue
qualité pour recourir	Beschwerdebefugnis, Beschwerdelegitimation	standing to appeal, right to appeal
quartier	Quartier (D: Stadtviertel)	neighborhood

question	Anfrage	question (a request by a member of Parliament to the Federal Council for information about important domestic or foreign affairs)
question de droit	Rechtsfrage	legal issue (as opposed to an issue of fact)
question de fait	Tatfrage	issue of fact
question juridique de principe	Rechtsfrage von grundsätzlicher Bedeutung	legal question of fundamental importance
question préjudicielle	Vorfrage	incidental question
quittance	Quittung	receipt
quorum	Quorum	quorum
quote-part	Bruchteil	fraction (of a fund unit)
quote-part fiscale	Fiskalquote	tax ratio (ratio of taxes to GNP)
quotité disponible (art. 470 CC)	verfügbarer Teil	disposable portion (of an estate, i.e., the part that the testator may freely dispose of; it is subordinate to the amount of each heir's compulsory portion)
rabais	Rabatt	discount
rabais de réinvestissement	Wiederanlagerabatt	reinvestment discount
rachat (1)	Einkauf	purchase
rachat (2)	Rückkauf	redemption
radiation au registre du commerce	Löschung im Handelsregister	deletion from the Commercial Register
radiation de l'enregistrement (art. 35 LPM)	Löschung der Eintragung	cancellation of trademark registration
radiation du rôle	Streichung	striking from the docket
rafraîchissement (F : refroidissement)	Kühlung	cooling
raison de commerce	Firma, Geschäftsfirma	company name
raison individuelle	Einzelfirma	sole proprietorship
rançon	Lösegeld	ransom
rang des créanciers (art. 146 LP)	Rangfolge der Gläubiger	ranking of creditors
rapatriement	Heimschaffung	repatriation

rapide	beförderlich (D: beschleunigt, rasch)	quick, fast
rapport (1)	Bericht	report
rapport (2)	Verhältnis	relationship, ratio
rapport annuel	Jahresbericht (D: Geschäftsbericht)	annual report
rapport d'activité (art. 330 LP)	Rechenschaftsbericht	report of activities
rapport d'assurance	Versicherungsverhältnis	insurance relationship
rapport d'augmentation (art. 652e CO)	Kapitalerhöhungsbericht	capital increase report
rapport de couverture	Deckungsverhältnis	contractual relationship between the promisor and the promisee (in a third-party beneficiary contract)
rapport de droit	Rechtsverhältnis	legal relationship
rapport de fondation (art. 631 CO)	Gründungsbericht	organizational report
rapport de prestation	Leistungsverhältnis	relationship between the promisor and the third party beneficiary
rapport de représentation (art. 29 CP)	Vertretungsverhältnisse	agency relationships
rapport de révision	Revisionsbericht	audit report
rapport de valeur	Valutaverhältnis	underlying debt relationship (relationship between the promise and the beneficiary)
rapport d'impact sur l'environnement	Umweltverträglichkeitsbericht	environmental impact report
rapport du commissaire (art. 304 LP)	Sachwertbericht	administrator's report
rapport explicatif (traité international)	erläuternder Bericht (Staatsvertrag)	explanatory report (international treaty)
rapport final	Schlussbericht	final report
rapport successoral (art. 626 ss CC)	Ausgleichung	bringing into hotchpot (statutory heirs are required to bring into hotchpot anything that the decedent gave them during his lifetime by way of an advance on their inheritance)
rapporteur	Berichterstatter	reporter

rapports externes	Aussenverhältnis (D: Außenverhältnis)	relationships with third parties
ratification (1)	Ratifikation	ratification (of a treaty)
ratification (2) (art. 38 CO)	Genehmigung	ratification (by the principal of the agent's acts)
ratification du contrat (art. 31 CO)	Genehmigung des Vertrags	ratification of the contract
rattachement spécial	Sonderanknüpfung	special rule
rayonnements (art. 684 CC)	Strahlung	radiation
réalisation	Verwertung	sale
réalisation de gage (art. 156 LP)	Pfandverwertung	proceeds of the pledge, proceeds of the collateral
réalisation des droits fondamentaux (art. 35 CF)	Verwirklichung der Grundrechte	upholding of fundamental rights
réalisation d'une infraction	Erfüllung des Tatbestands	meeting the definition of a crime
réalisation d'urgence (art. 243 LP)	Notverkauf	emergency sale
réalisation forcée	Zwangsverwertung	forced sale
réaliser	verwerten	to sell
réassurance	Rückversicherung, Rückdeckung	reinsurance
reboisement	Aufforstung	reforestation
recel (art. 160 CP)	Hehlerei	receiving stolen goods, "fencing"
recel par métier (art. 160 CP)	gewerbsmässige Hehlerei	receiving stolen goods for commercial gain
récemment	letzthin (D: kürzlich)	recently
recensement	Volkszählung	census
récépissé	Empfangsschein	deposit slip
réception de l'ouvrage	Abnahme des Werkes	acceptance of the work
recevabilité du recours	Zulässigkeit der Berufung	admissibility of the appeal
recherche sur l'être humain (art. 118b CF)	Forschung an Menschen	research on human beings
récidive (art. 93 CP)	Rückfall, Rückfälligkeit	recidivism
réciprocité	Gegenrecht, Gegenseitigkeit	reciprocity
reclassement	Umzonung	rezoning
récolte de signatures	Unterschriftensammlung	petition
récolte des fruits (art. 103 LP)	Einheimsen der Früchte	fruit harvest, harvesting of fruit
recommandation de vote	Abstimmungsempfehlung	voting recommendation

recommandation de vote de l'autorité	Abstimmungsbotschaft	authority's recommendation on how to vote
Recommandations pour la présentation des comptes (RPC)	Fachempfehlungen zur Rechnungslegung (FER)	Swiss Accounting and Reporting Recommendations
récompense	Belohnung	reward
reconnaissance de dette (art. 17 CO)	Schuldbekenntnis, Schuldanerkennung	acknowledgment of debt
reconnaissance de dette abstraite (art. 17 CO)	abstraktes Schuldbekenntnis	acknowledgment of debt that does not state the cause of the obligation
reconnaissance de paternité (art. 260-260c CC)	Anerkennung der Vaterschaft, Vaterschaftsanerkennung	acknowledgment of paternity
reconnaissance d'états	Anerkennung von Staaten	recognition of states
reconnaissance d'un enfant	Anerkennung eines Kindes	acknowledgment of an illegitimate child
reconversion professionnelle	Umschulung	retraining
recourable	rekurabel	appealable, subject to appeal
recourant	Beschwerdeführer	appellant
recourir	weiterziehen	to appeal
recours (1)	Regress	recourse
recours (2)	Rechtsbehelf	remedy
recours (3) (art. 319-327a CPC) interjeter recours	Beschwerde eine Beschwerde einlegen	appeal (to the Federal Supreme Court) to file an appeal
recours à l'autorité tutélaire	Beschwerde an die Vormundschaftsbehörde	appeal to the guardianship authority
recours administratif	Verwaltungsbeschwerde	administrative appeal
recours cantonal en matière de droit de vote	kantonale Stimmrechtsbeschwerde	cantonal appeal on a matter related to voting rights
recours constitutionnel	Verfassungsbeschwerde	constitutional appeal
recours contre la décision du conservateur du registre foncier	Grundbuchbeschwerde	appeal from the decision of the land registrar
recours de change	Wechselregress	recourse against guarantors of a bill of exchange
recours de droit administratif	Verwaltungsgerichtsbeschwerd e	administrative court appeal

recours de droit public	staatsrechtliche Beschwerde (D: Verfassungsbeschwerde)	public law appeal, constitutional complaint (a general remedy against constitutional rights, including those set forth in the ECHR)
recours direct	Sprungrekurs	leapfrog appeal
recours disciplinaire	Disziplinarbeschwerde	disciplinary appeal
recours en carence	Untätigkeitsklage	action on grounds of administrative inaction
recours en grâce	Begnadigungsgesuch	petition for clemency
recours en manquement	Vertragsverletzungsklage	action for breach of contract
recours en matière civile	Beschwerde in Zivilsachen	appeal in civil cases
recours en matière de droit public	Beschwerde in öffentlich-rechtlichen Angelegenheiten	public law appeal
recours en matière pénale	Beschwerde in Strafsachen	appeal in criminal cases
recours joint	Anschlussbeschwerde	cross appeal (to the Federal Supreme Court)
recours procédurier (art. 42 al. 7 LTF)	querulatorische Beschwerde	querulous appeal, frivolous appeal
recouvrement	Inkasso	collection
recouvrement des créances (art. 100 et 243 LP)	Forderungseinzug	receipt of credit payments
recrutement	Aushebung (D: Einberufung)	conscription
rectification	Berichtigung	correction
rectification de frontière	Grenzbereinigung	rectification of boundaries
recueil d'arrêts	Entscheidsammlung	court reports
recueil des lois	Gesetzessammlung	compendium of laws
Recueil officiel du droit fédéral (RO)	Amtliche Sammlung des Bundesrechts (AS)	Official Compilation of Swiss Federal Legislation
récusation (art. 10 LP) Le juge se récuse.	Ausstand Der Richter tritt in Ausstand.	recusal The judge recuses himself.
récusation des arbitres (art. 180 LDIP)	Ablehnung eines Schiedsrichters	recusal of arbitrators
récusation d'un juge	Richterablehnung	recusal of a judge
recyclage de déchets	Recycling	recycling
recyclage de terrains en friche	Brachflächenrecycling	recycling of derelict land

rédacteur du procès-verbal	Protokollführer	person taking the minutes
reddition de comptes	Rechenschaftsablegung	rendering of accounts
redevance	Lizenzgebühr	royalty, license fee
réduction	Ermässigung	reduction
réduction de capital	Kapitalherabsetzung	capital reduction
réduction de la peine	Herabsetzung der Strafe	reduction of the penalty
réduction de la prestation d'assurance	Versicherungsleistungskürzung	reduction of the insurance benefit
réduction du traitement	Herabsetzung des Gehalts	salary reduction, pay cut
réduire	herabsetzen	to reduce, to abate
rééchelonnement de dettes	Umschuldung	debt rescheduling
réélection	Wiederwahl	reelection
réexpédition	Rücksendung	return
références à l'existence d'une protection (art. 11 LBI)	Hinweise auf Patentschutz	marking of patented products
referendum	Referendum	referendum
référendum demandé par l'autorité	Behördenreferendum	referendum requested by the authorities
référendum facultatif	fakultatives Referendum	optional referendum
référendum législatif	Gesetzesreferendum	legislative referendum
référendum obligatoire	obligatorisches Referendum	mandatory referendum
référentiel central (art. 74 LIMF)	Transaktionsregister	trade repository
refoulement	Ausschaffung	deportation
réfugié (art. 3 LAsi)	Flüchtling	refugee
refus d'acheter des marchandises	Bezugssperre	refusal to purchase goods
refus de l'entraide	Ablehnung der Rechtshilfe	refusal of mutual assistance
refus de livrer des marchandises	Liefersperre	refusal to supply goods
refus de payer	Zahlungsverweigerung	refusal to pay
refus de statuer	Rechtsverweigerung im engeren Sinne	refusal to rule
refus d'entretenir des relations commerciales (art. 7 LCart)	Verweigerung von Geschäftsbeziehungen	refusal to do business
refus d'homologation du concordat (art. 309 LP)	Ablehnung des Nachlassvertrags	refusal to ratify the debt restructuring agreement

refus d'un travail convenable	Ablehnung zumutbarer Arbeit	refusal of a reasonable job
régale des mines	Bergregal	right of ownership of untapped mineral resources
régale des postes	Postregal	postal regale
régale du sel	Salzregal	salt monopoly, salt tax
Régie fédérale des alcools (RFA)	Eidgenössische Alkoholverwaltung (EAV)	Swiss Alcohol Board
régime matrimonial	Güterrecht, Ehegüterrecht	marital property system
région à forte concentration urbaine	Agglomeration (D: Ballungsgebiet)	urban center
région périphérique	Randgebiet	border region
registre de la prévoyance professionnelle	Register für berufliche Vorsorge	Register for Occupational Pension Provision
registre de l'état civil	Zivilstandsregister (D: Personenstandsregister)	civil register, vital records register
registre de l'impôt	Steuerregister	tax register
registre des actions (art. 686 CO)	Aktienbuch	stock ledger
registre des bateaux	Schiffsregister	ship register
registre des brevets	Patentregister	patent register
registre des décès	Todesregister	register of deaths
registre des électeurs	Stimmregister	list of registered voters
registre des familles	Familienregister	family register
registre des mariages	Eheregister	marriage register
registre des marques	Markenregister	trademark register
registre des pactes de réserve de propriété	Eigentumsvorbehaltsregister	register of retention of title
registre des poursuites (LP)	Betreibungsregister (SchKG)	debt collection register
registre des reconnaissances	Anerkennungsregister	register of acknowledgments of paternity
registre du commerce	Handelsregister	Commercial Register
registre foncier	Grundbuch	land register
règle de conflit	Kollisionsregel	conflicts of law rule
règle de consolidation	Konsolidierungsregel	rule of consolidation
règle de droit	Rechtsnorm, Rechtssatz	legal rule
règle de la circulation	Verkehrsregel	traffic rule

règle de l'insolite	Ungewöhnlichkeitsregel	rule regarding unusual clauses (A party cannot be expected to have agreed to a clause contained in a text to which the main contract or another document refers if the content of such clause is unusual, i.e., if it departs from a reasonable person would expect in the same circumstances.)
règle de saisie	Erfassungsregel	recording rule
règlement	Abwicklung	settlement
règlement (droit communautaire)	Verordnung (Gemeinschaftsrecht)	regulation
règlement amiable des dettes	einvernehmliche Private Schuldenbereinigung	amicable settlement of debts
règlement d'arbitrage	Schiedsreglement	arbitration rules, rules of arbitration
règlement d'assurance	Versicherungsreglement	insurance regulations
règlement de fonds de placement	Fondsreglement	fund regulations
règlement d'entreprise	Betriebsordnung	internal company regulations
règlement des dettes	Schuldenbereinigung	debt settlement
règlement d'exécution	Vollziehungsverordnung (VV)	implementing order
règlement d'organisation (art. 716b CO)	Organisationsreglement (Art. 716b OR)	organizational regulations
Règlement du Tribunal Fédéral (RTF)	Reglement für das Bundesgericht (BGerR)	Federal Supreme Court Regulations
Règlement du Tribunal pénal fédéral sur les activités accessoires (RAATPF)	Nebenbeschäftigungsreglement Bundesstrafgericht (BStGerNR)	Federal Criminal Court Secondary Employment Regulations
règlement en espèces	Barabgeltung, Barabrechnung	cash settlement
réglementation fiscale	Steuerordnung	tax regulation
règles de comportement	Verhaltensregeln	rules of conduct
règles de conduite	Weisungen	specific orders as to conduct
règles de conduite sur le marché	Marktverhaltensregeln (FINMA)	market conduct rules
regroupement familial	Familiennachzug	family reunion
régularité	Ordnungsmässigkeit	regularity
régulation	Korrektion (D: Regulierung)	regulation

réhabilitation	Rehabilitation	rehabilitation
réinscription	Wiedereintragung	re-entry
réintégrande (art. 927 CC)	Besitzesentziehungsklage, Klage aus Besitzesentziehung	action to recover possession (by someone who has been unlawfully dispossessed)
réintégration des biens (art. 284 LP)	Rückschaffung von Gegenstände	forced deliverance of assets
réintégration professionnelle	beruflicher Wiedereinstieg	rejoining the workforce
réinvestissement	Wiederanlage	reinvestment
rejet de la demande	Abweisung der Klage	dismissal of the claim, dismissal of the action
rejet de la réquisition de faillite (art. 172 LP)	Abweisung des Konkursbegehrens	rejection of the insolvency petition
rejeter : rejeter un recours rejeter une demande	abweisen: eine Beschwerde abweisen ein Gesuch abweisen	to dismiss: to dismiss an appeal to dismiss a claim
relation d'affaires	Geschäftsbeziehung	business relationship
relation de clientèle	Kundenbeziehung	customer relationship
relation de dépendance	Abhängigkeitsverhältnis	relationship of dependency
relation interne	Binnenbeziehung	internal relationship
relations personnelles (art. 273 CC)	persönlicher Verkehr	personal access to, contact with (children)
reliquat	Restanz (D: Restbetrag)	outstanding balance
remaniement parcellaire	Landumlegung	reorganization of land
rembours	Rembours	drawback
remboursement	Abgaberückerstattung	tax refund
remboursement anticipé	vorzeitige Rückzahlung	early repayment
remboursement de frais	Auslagenersatz, Kostenvergütung	cost reimbursement, reimbursement of costs/expenses
remboursement des droits de douane	Zollrückerstattung	refund of customs duties
remise	Aushändigung	delivery
remise à des enfants de substances pouvant mettre en danger leur santé (CP 136)	Verabreichen gesundheitsgefährdender Stoffe an Kinder	administering substances capable of causing injury to children
remise à l'encaissement	Anweisung zur Eintreibung	handover of a security (for debt collection)
remise conventionnelle (art. 115 CO)	Aufhebung durch Übereinkunft (Art. 115 OR)	extinction by agreement
remise conventionnelle de dette	Schulderlass	debt remission

remise de loyer	Mietzinserlass	rent abatement
remise de peine	Straferlass	remission of penalty (or sentence)
remise de sûretés	Bestellung von Sicherheit	provision of collateral, furnishing of collateral
remise des clés	Schlüsselübergabe	handover of the keys
remise des droits de douane	Zollnachlass	abatement of customs duty
remise d'impôt	Steuererlass	tax abatement, tax remission
remise d'objets ou de valeurs (art. 59 EIMP)	Sachauslieferung	handing over of objects and assets
remise en main propre	eigenhändige Abgabe	personal delivery
remise partielle	Teilerlass	forgiveness of part of the debt
remise temporaire (art. 58 EIMP)	vorübergehende Zuführung	provisional surrender
remplacement de la chose vendue (art. 206 CO)	Ersatzleistung	substitute performance
rémunération (art. 83 CP)	Arbeitsentgelt	wages
rémunérer	salarieren	to remunerate, to pay a salary to
renchérissement	Teuerung	inflation
rendement à l'échéance	Verfallrendite	yield to maturity
rendement brut	Bruttoertrag	gross yield
rendement de distribution	Ausschüttungsrendite	distribution yield (ratio of distributed income to the current market price)
rendement des participations	Beteiligungsertrag	income from investments
rendement du placement	Anlagerendite	investment yield
rendement net	Nettoertrag	net yield
rendre vraisemblable	glaubhaft machen	to present prima facie evidence (in order to obtain preliminary injunctive relief)
renoncement à des créances	Forderungsverzicht	waiver of claims
renonciation	Verzicht	waiver
renonciation à la réalisation (art. 127 et 142a LP)	Verzicht auf die Verwertung	waiver of realization
renonciation à succession	Erbverzicht	renunciation of one's claim to an estate
renonciation aux fors légaux (art. 35 CPC)	Verzicht auf die gesetzlichen Gerichtsstände	waiver of statutory jurisdiction

renouvellement de l'autorisation	Erneuerung der Bewilligung	renewal of the permit
rénovation d'immeuble	Erneuerung der Baute	renovation of a building
renseignement erroné	unrichtige Auskunft	erroneous information
rentabilité	Wirtschaftlichkeit	profitability
rente de survivant	Hinterlassenenrente	survivor's pension
rente de veuf	Witwerrente	widower's pension
rente de veuve	Witwenrente	widow's pension
rente de vieillesse	Altersrente	old-age pension, retirement pension
rente de vieillesse pour couple	Ehepaar-Altersrente	old age pension for couples
rente dégressive	abgestufte Rente	graduated pension
rente d'enfant d'invalide	Invaliden-Kinderrente	disable persons' children's pension
rente d'invalidité	Invalidenrente	disability pension
rente d'invalidité pour couple	Ehepaar-Invalidenrente	disability pension for couples
rente d'orphelin	Waisenrente	orphan's benefit, orphan's allowance
rente d'orphelin de mère	Mutterwaisenrente	pension for a child whose mother has died
rente d'orphelin double	Vollwaisenrente	orphan's pension
rente du droit de superficie (art. 779i CC)	Baurechtszins	remuneration for the building right
rente pour atteinte à l'intégrité	Integritätsrente	impairment pension
rente pour cas pénible	Härtefallrente	hardship pension
rente pour perte de gain	Erwerbsunfähigkeitsrente	disability benefits
rente temporaire	befristete Rente	temporary annuity
rente viagère (art. 516-520 CO)	Leibrente	life annuity
rente viagère à paiement différé	Anwartschaftsrente	reversionary annuity
rente-pont	Überbrückungsrente	interim pension
renversement du fardeau de la preuve	Beweislastumkehr, Umkehr der Beweislast	reversal of the burden of proof
renvoi (1)	Verweisung (1)	reference
renvoi (2) (art. 14 LDIP)	Rückverweisung	renvoi (conflict of laws rule)
renvoi (3) (droit des étrangers)	Wegweisung (Ausländerrecht)	expulsion
renvoi dans un hôpital ou un hospice	Einweisung in eine Heil- oder Pflegeanstalt	admission to a hospital or hospice
renvoi d'un projet	Rückweisung	referral for review

renvoi préjudiciel	Vorlagen zur Vorabentscheidung	reference for a preliminary ruling
réparation (art. 53 CP)	Wiedergutmachung	reparation
répartition des sièges	Sitzverteilung	allotment of seats (in the National Council)
répartition des tâches	Aufgabenteilung	distribution of tasks
répartition du bénéfice	Gewinnverwendung	appropriation of profit
répartition intercantonale	Steuerausscheidung	tax apportionment
répartition provisoire (art. 144 al. 2 et 266 LP)	Abschlagsverteilung	interim distribution, provisional distribution
répartitions (art. 123 al. 3, 326 et 348 al. 1 lit. 1 LP)	Abschlagszahlungen	down payments, installment payments
repentir actif (art. 23 CP)	tätige Reue	active repentance
repentir sincère (art. 48 CP)	aufrichtige Reue	genuine remorse
répétition	Rückforderung	claim for return of an amount paid in error
réplique	Replik	reply
réponse (1) (art. 222 CPC)	Klageantwort	answer (to the complaint)
réponse (2) (art. 312 CPC)	Berufungsantwort (BA)	respondent's answer on appeal
réponse au recours	Beschwerdeantwort	answer to the appeal
report (1)	Agio, Aufgeld	premium (difference between the nominal value of a security and its issue or market price)
report (2)	Verschiebung	postponement, deferral
report de l'imposition	Steueraufschub	tax deferral
report de solde	Saldovortrag	balance carried forward
reportage	Berichterstattung	reporting
reprenant (art. 175-183 CO)	Schuldübernehmer	debt acquirer
représailles	Repressalien	retaliation
représentant	Vertreter	representative
représentant commun (art. 72 CPC)	gemeinsame Vertretung	joint representation
représentant de la communauté héréditaire	Erbenvertreter	representative of the community of heirs
représentant de la succession	Erbschaftsvertreter	representative of the estate
représentant légal	Rechtsvertreter	legal representative

représentation (art. 32-40 CO)	Stellvertretung	agency
représentation de la violence (art. 135 CP)	Gewaltdarstellung	representation of acts of violence
représentation des parties (art. 68 CPC)	Parteivertretung	representation of the parties
représentation diplomatique	diplomatische Vertretung	diplomatic representation
représentation en procédure	Prozessvertretung	procedural representation
représentation par un avocat	anwaltliche Vertretung	representation by a lawyer, representation by counsel
représentation par un dépositaire	Depotvertreter	representation by a custodian
représentation par un membre d'un organe	Organvertreter	governing officer as representative
représentation sans pouvoirs	Vertretung ohne Vollmacht	unauthorized agency
représenté (art. 38 CO)	Vertretener	the principal
représenter	vertreten	to represent
réprimande (art. 14 al. 2 lit. 1 LP)	Rüge, Verweis	reprimand
repris à la page 10	Übertrag auf Seite 10	continued on page 10
repris de la page 10	Übertrag von Seite 10	continued from page 10
reprise cumulative de dette	kumulative Schuldübernahme	cumulative assumption of indebtedness
reprise de biens (art. 628 CO)	Sachübernahme	acquisition of assets
reprise de dette (art. 175-183 CO)	Schuldübernahme	assumption of indebtedness
reprise de saisie (art. 145 LP)	Nachpfändung von Amtes wegen	resumption of seizure
répudiation d'une personne	Verstossung	repudiation of a person
répudiation d'une succession (art. 566 CC)	Erbschaftsausschlagung, Ausschlagung einer Erbschaft	disclaimer of an inheritance
réputation	Leumund	reputation
requérant (1)	Rekurrent	appellant
requérant (2)	Gesuchsteller (D: Antragsteller)	applicant (in an administrative law case)
requérant du brevet	Patentbewerber	patent applicant
requérants	Asylsuchende	asylum seekers

requête	Begehren, Gesuch	petition, motion, application
requête additionnelle	Ergänzungsklage	supplementary petition
requête de mainlevée	Rechtsöffnungsbegehren	motion for court order dismissing debtor's objection
requête en intervention (art. 75 CPC)	Interventionsgesuch	application for intervention
requête exploratoire	Beweisausforschung	fishing expedition
requête fondée sur le droit du mariage (art. 23 CPC)	eherechtliches Gesuch	application based on marital law
requête populaire	Volksbegehren	popular request
réquisition	Begehren	petition, motion, application
réquisition de continuer la poursuite	Fortsetzungsbegehren	motion to continue with the debt collection proceedings (in one of three ways: saisie, faillite or réalisation de gage)
réquisition de faillite (art. 166 LP)	Konkursbegehren	insolvency petition, bankruptcy petition
réquisition de participation	Teilnahmebegehren	request to participate
réquisition de poursuite (art. 67 et 151 LP)	Betreibungsbegehren	debt collection petition, petition to open debt collection proceedings
réquisition de procéder à la saisie	Pfändungsbegehren	application for seizure of assets
réquisition de réaliser	Verwertungsbegehren	request for a sale
réquisition de séquestre	Arrestbegehren, Arrestgesuch	application for attachment of assets
réquisitoire	Antrag des Staatsanwaltes	oral arguments by the prosecutor
réseau de télécommunication	Fernmeldenetz	telecommunications network
réservataire	Pflichtteilsberechtigter	forced heir
réservé – Les traités internationaux sont réservés.	vorbehalten – Völkerrechtliche Verträge sind vorbehalten.	take precedence – International treaties take precedence.
réserve d'assurance	Versicherungsvorbehalt	insurance reserve
réserve de fluctuation	Schwankungsreserve	fluctuation reserve
réserve de la législation cantonale	Vorbehalt der kantonalen Gesetzgebung	reservation of cantonal law

réserve de propriété (CO 217)	Eigentumsvorbehalt	retention of title (despite physical transfer, until purchase price is paid in full)
réserve de réévaluation (art. 671b CO)	Aufwertungsreserve	revaluation reserve
réserve latente	stille Reserve	hidden reserve
réserve légale	gesetzliche Reserve	statutory reserve
réserve mathématique	Deckungskapital	actuarial reserve
réserve naturelle	Schongebiet	nature reserve
réserve successorale (art. 470 CC)	Pflichtteil	forced heir's share
résidence habituelle	gewöhnlicher Aufenthalt	usual place of residence
résidence ininterrompue	ununterbrochener Aufenthalt	uninterrupted residence
résidence secondaire	Zweitwohnung	secondary residence
résiliation	Kündigung	termination
résiliation abusive	missbräuchliche Kündigung	wrongful termination
résiliation anticipée	vorzeitige Kündigung	early termination
résiliation en cas de perte de la chose (art. 207 CO)	Wandelung bei Untergang der Sache	rescission when the object is destroyed
résiliation en temps inopportun (art. 336c CO)	Kündigung zur Unzeit	termination at an inopportune juncture (such as during pregnancy or military service)
résiliation immédiate	fristlose Kündigung	termination without notice, immediate termination
résolution du contrat (art. 190 CO)	Rücktritt vom Vertrag	termination of the contract
résolutions d'urgence	Beschlüsse über dringliche Frage	decisions on urgent matters
respect de la vie familiale	Achtung des Familienlebens	respect for family life
respect de la vie privée	Achtung des Privatlebens	respect for privacy
respect des règles de la bonne foi (art. 2 al. 1 CC, art. 52 CPC)	Handeln nach Treu und Glauben	acting in good faith
respectivement (resp.) (F : ou)	beziehungsweise (bzw.)	or

responsabilité (pénale)	Zurechnungsfähigkeit	soundness of mind (consists of the ability to understand one's acts and to govern one's conduct accordingly)
responsabilité aquilienne	deliktische Haftung	tort liability, liability in tort (liability based on fault – either negligence or intentional misconduct)
responsabilité causale	Kausalhaftung	vicarious liability and strict liability
responsabilité civile	Haftpflicht, zivilrechtliche Haftung	civil liability
responsabilité contractuelle	Vertragshaftung	contractual liability
responsabilité de dommages-intérêts	Schadenersatzpflicht	liability for damages
responsabilité de la Confédération	Bundeshaftung	federal liability under the Military Insurance Act
responsabilité de la personne incapable de discernement (art. 54 CO)	Haftung des Urteilsunfähigen	liability of persons lacking capacity to consent
responsabilité de l'employeur (art. 55 CO)	Geschäftsherrenhaftung, Haftung des Geschäftsherrn	vicarious liability of employers
responsabilité de l'État	Staatshaftung	liability of the State (The State is only liable for damage caused by government officials if liability is provided for by a special law. If there is no law, or liability is excluded, the State does not have to compensate for damages caused by government officials.)
responsabilité de l'institution d'assurance	Haftung des Versicherungsträgers	liability of the insurer
responsabilité découlant du principe de la transparence	Durchgriff	piercing the corporate veil
responsabilité délictuelle	Haftung aus unerlaubter Handlung, Deliktshaftung	tort liability

responsabilité du chef de famille (art. 333 CC)	Haftung des Familienhauptes	liability of the head of the family
responsabilité du détenteur d'animal (art. 56-57 CO)	Tierhalterhaftung	liability of the keeper of an animal
responsabilité du détenteur d'animaux (art. 56-57 CO)	Haftung des Tierhalters	liability of the keeper of an animal
responsabilité du fait des produits	Produktehaftpflicht	products liability
responsabilité du propriétaire d'immeuble (art. 678 et 684 CC)	Grundeigentümerpflicht	landowner liability
responsabilité du propriétaire d'ouvrage	Werkeigentümerhaftung	liability of the property owner
responsabilité du propriétaire d'un bâtiment (art. 58-59 CO)	Haftung des Werkeigentümers	liability of property owners
responsabilité en matière de clé de signature (art. 59a CO)	Haftung für Signaturschlüssel	liability in respect of electronic signatures
responsabilité fondée sur la confiance	Vertrauenshaftung	liability based on creating trust
responsabilité fondée sur le droit public	Haftung aus öffentlichem Recht	public law liability
responsabilité illimitée	unbeschränkte Haftung	unlimited liability
responsabilité limitée	beschränkte Haftung	limited liability
responsabilité objective	verschuldensunabhängige Haftung	strict liability, liability without fault, no-fault liability
responsabilité objective	Gefährdungshaftung	strict liability, no-fault liability (as opposed to liability based on fault)
responsabilité objective simple	einfache Kausalhaftung	simple causal third party liability
responsabilité partagée de la victime	Opfermitverantwortung	joint liability of the victim
responsabilité partielle	Teilhaftung	partial liability
responsabilité pour faute	Verschuldenshaftung	liability based on fault, fault-based liability (as opposed to no-fault liability, known as "strict liability")
responsabilité pour le prospectus d'émission (art. 752 CO)	Prospekthaftung	prospectus liability
responsabilité pour les auxiliaires	Haftung für Hilfspersonen	vicarious liability

responsabilité pour les organes (art. 722 CO)	Haftung der Organe	directors' and officers' liability, D&O liability
responsabilité restreinte	verminderte Schuldfähigkeit	diminished responsibility
responsabilité solidaire	Solidarhaftung (D: solidarische Haftung)	joint and several liability
ressortissant étranger	Ausländer	foreign national
ressource d'adressage	Adressierungselement	addressing resource
ressources humaines	menschliche Ressourcen	human resources (HR)
restitution	Rückerstattung	restitution, refund
restitution anticipée de la chose (art. 264 CO)	vorzeitige Rückgabe der Sache	early return of the premises
restitution de l'impôt	Steuerrückerstattung	tax refund
restitution des apports	Einlagerückgewähr	refund of contributions
restitution des biens donnés (art. 249 CO)	Rückforderung der Schenkung	claim for return of a gift
restitution des délais (art. 148 CPC)	Wiederherstellung	restitution of deadlines
restitution du prix (art. 202 LP)	Herausgabe des Kaufpreises	restitution of the price
restitution du titre de la créance (art. 150 LP)	Herausgabe der Forderungsurkunde	return of the deed of claim
restriction à la concurrence	Wettbewerbsbeschränkung, Wettbewerbsbehinderung	restraint of competition
restriction à la propriété	Eigentumsbeschränkung	restriction on ownership
restriction des droits des créanciers	Eingriffe in die Gläubigerrechte	encroachment on creditors' rights
restriction d'utilisation du sol	Nutzungseinschränkung beim Boden	restrictions on soil use
restrictions illicites à la concurrence (art. 5 LCart)	unzulässige Wettbewerbsbeschränkungen	unlawful restraints of competition
restructuration	Umstrukturierung	restructuring
résultat du vote	Abstimmungsresultat	result of the vote
résumé	Regeste (D: Zusammenfassung)	summary (of important points in a decision—this part is always in three languages)
rétablissement de la situation conforme au droit	Wiederherstellung des rechtmässigen Zustandes	remedy of any violations
retard	Verspätung	delay
retard injustifié (art. 17 al. 3 LP)	Rechtsverzögerung	delay of justice

retardement du rapatriement de prisonniers de guerre (art. 264i CP)	verzögerte Heimschaffung von Kriegsgefangenen	delayed repatriation of prisoners of war
retenue sur le salaire	Lohnrückbehalt	withholding from salary
retour	Rückkehr	return
retour des objets donnés (art. 247 CO)	Rückfall der geschenkten Sache	reversion of the gift
retrait d'admonestation	Warnungsentzug	temporary suspension of a driver's license
retrait de l'autorisation	Bewilligungsentzug	withdrawal of the authorization, withdrawal of the permit
retrait de permis	Ausweisentzug	revocation of a driver's license
retrait des objets soumis à délibération (art. 73 LParl)	Rückzug eines Beratungsgegenstandes	withdrawal of an item of business from the agenda
retrait du droit de déterminer le lieu de résidence (art. 310 CC)	Aufhebung des Aufenthaltsbestimmungsrechts	revocation of the right to decide on place of residence
retrait du permis de conduire	Führerausweisentzug	suspension of driver's license
retrait du recours	Beschwerderückzug	withdrawal of the appeal
retrait d'une initiative populaire	Rückzug einer Volksinitiative	withdrawal of a popular initiative
retraite (art. 1049 CO)	Rückwechsel	redraft, re-exchange bill
retraite anticipée	vorzeitige Pensionierung	early retirement
rétribuer	salarieren	to remunerate, to pay a salary to
rétroactivité	Rückwirkung	retroactivity
rétrocession	Rückübertragung	retransfer, back transfer, reassignment
réunion aux acquêts (art. 208 CC)	Hinzurechnung	addition
réussir	reüssieren (D: gelingen)	to succeed
revendication (1)	Ansprache	recovery, replevin
revendication (2) (brevet)	Patentanspruch	patent claim
revendication de la masse en faillite	Admassierung	recovery, replevin
revendication de propriété	Eigentumsansprache	recovery of property, replevin
revendiquer	ansprechen	to reclaim, to recover

revente	Wiederverkauf	resale
revenu	Einkommen	income
revenu accessoire	Nebeneinkommen	additional income
revenu annuel moyen	durchschnittliches Jahreseinkommen	average annual income
revenu de la fortune	Vermögensertrag	investment income
revenu déterminant	anrechenbares Einkommen	creditable income
revenu d'invalide	Invalideneinkommen	disability income
revenu d'une activité lucrative	Erwerbseinkommen	income from gainful employment, earned income
revenu en nature	Naturaleinkommen	income in kind
revenu exonéré d'impôt	steuerfreie Einkünfte	tax-exempt income
revenu immobilier	Liegenschaftsertrag	property income
revenu net	Reineinkommen	net income
revenus immobiliers	Einkünfte aus unbeweglichem Vermögen	income from real property
réviseur	Revisor	auditor
révision (1) (art. 397 CP)	Wiederaufnahme	motion for a retrial
révision (2)	Wirtschaftsprüfung	audit
révision (3) (art. 328-333 CPC)	Revision	review
révision bancaire	Bankenrevision	bank audit
révocation (1)	Abberufung	removal, dismissal (of a person from office)
révocation (2)	Widerruf	revocation
révocation d'actes juridiques (art. 331 LP)	Anfechtung von Rechtshandlungen	revocation of legal transactions
révocation de la faillite (art. 195 ss LP)	Widerruf des Konkurses	revocation of the insolvency proceedings
révocation de l'adjudication (art. 143 al. 1 LP)	Widerruf des Zuschlags	revocation of the auction sale
révocation du concordat (art. 305 LP)	Widerruf des Nachlassvertrags	revocation of the debt restructuring agreement
révocation d'une libéralité (art. 286 et 291 LP)	Schenkungsanfechtung, Schenkungspauliana	challenge of gifts (made by the debtor)
révocation d'une personne	Amtsentlassung	removal of a person from office
révocation pour cause de surendettement (art. 287 LP)	Überschuldungsanfechtung, Überschuldungspauliana	challenge of overindebtedness
révoquer	abberufen	to remove, to dismiss (a person from office)
risque assuré	versichertes Risiko	insured risk

risque de change	Wechselkursrisiko	exchange rate risk
risque de collusion	Kollusionsgefahr	risk of collusion
risque de confusion (art. 3 LPM)	Verwechslungsgefahr	likelihood of confusion
risque de contrepartie	Gegenparteirisiko	counterparty risk
risque de crédit	Kreditrisiko	credit risk
risque de fuite	Fluchtgefahr	risk of escape
risque de récidive	Wiederholungsgefahr	danger of recidivism
risque de solvabilité	Bonitätsrisiko	credit rating risk
risque d'exploitation	Betriebsrisiko	operational risk
risque du marché	Marktrisiko	market risk
risque écologique	Umweltrisiko	environmental risk
risque inhérent à l'emploi	Betriebsgefahr	inherent risk, inherent danger
risques cumulés	Klumpenrisiko	cluster risk
riverain	Anstösser (D: Anlieger)	resident
rixe (art. 133 CP)	Raufhandel	brawling
rôle des biens-fonds	Liegenschaftenverzeichnis	property list
route	Strasse (D: Straße)	road, street
route cantonale	Kantonsstrasse	cantonal road
route nationale	Nationalstrasse (D: Bundesstraße)	federal highway
rupture de ban (art. 291 CP)	Verweisungsbruch	breach of an expulsion order
rupture irrémédiable	unheilbare Zerrüttung	irretrievable breakdown
saillie	Anbaute (D: Anbau)	extension
Saint-Gall	St. Gallen	St. Gallen (canton and city)
saisie (art. 89 ss LP)	Pfändung	seizure
saisie complémentaire (art. 145 LP)	Nachpfändung	seizure of additional assets
saisie de permis	Abnahme des Ausweises	taking away someone's driver's license
saisie de salaire (art. 93 LP)	Lohnpfändung	garnishment
saisie des données signalétiques (art. 260 CPP)	erkennungsdienstliche Erfassung	recording identification data
saisie par voie rogatoire	Requisitorialpfändung	seizure by way of judicial cooperation
saisine du tribunal	Anrufung des Gerichts	bringing case before a court, filing a case with a court
saisir	pfänden	to seize
saisir le juge	Richter: den Richter anrufen	to bring a matter before the court, to file suit

saisir un tribunal	eine Sache beim Gericht abhängig machen	to file a case with a court
saisissabilité	Pfändbarkeit	seizability
saisissable	pfändbar	subject to seizure
saisonnier	Saisonnier (D: Saisonarbeiter)	seasonal worker
salaire	Lohn	salary
salaire à la tâche (art. 319 CO)	Akkordlohn	piecework wage
salaire annuel	Jahreslohn	annual salary
salaire brut	Bruttolohn	gross salary
salaire coordonné	koordinierter Lohn	coordinated wage
salaire déterminant	massgebender Lohn	relevant wage (all elements of annual compensation that must be taken into account for the occupational pension plan)
salaire en nature	Naturallohn	wages in kind
salaire fixé d'après le temps (art. 319 CO)	Zeitlohn	wage paid on the basis of time worked
salaire horaire	Stundenlohn	hourly wage
salaire journalier	Tageslohn	daily wage
salaire mensuel	Monatslohn	monthly wage, monthly salary
salaire minimum	Minimallohn	minimum wage
salaire moyen	Durchschnittslohn	average wage
salaire net	Nettolohn	net wage
salaire nominal	Nominallohn	nominal wages
sauf-conduit	freies Geleit	safe-conduct
sauf riverains	Zubringerdienst gestattet	access for residents only
sauvegarde du secret	Geheimhaltung	confidentiality
sceau	Siegel	seal
Schaffhouse	Schaffhausen	Schaffhausen (canton and city)
Schwyz	Schwyz	Schwyz (canton)
scission	Spaltung, Aufspaltung	demerger
scrutateur	Stimmenzähler	teller (of elections)
séance du tribunal	Gerichtssitzung	court hearing
séance extraordinaire	Extrasitzung	special session
séance plénière	Plenarsitzung	plenary session
sécession	Sezession	secession
second échange d'écritures	zweiter Schriftenwechsel	second round of written submissions
secret bancaire	Bankgeheimnis	bank secrecy

secret d'affaires	Geschäftsgeheimnis	business secret, trade secret
secret de fonction	Amtsgeheimnis	official secrecy
secret de vote	Stimmgeheimnis	secrecy of voting
secret des télécommunications	Fernmeldegeheimnis	secrecy of telecommunications
secret postal	Postgeheimnis	secrecy of the mail
secret professionnel	Berufsgeheimnis	professional privilege
secret professionnel du banquier	Bankkundengeheimnis	bank-client confidentiality
secrétaire	Sekretär, Aktuar (D: Schriftführer)	secretary
secrétaire communal	Gemeindeschreiber	municipal secretary
secrétaire d'état	Staatssekretär	state secretary
Secrétariat d'État à la formation, à la recherche et à l'innovation (SEFRI)	Staatssekretariat für Bildung, Forschung und Innovation (SBFI)	State Secretariat for Education, Research and Innovation
Secrétariat d'État à l'économie (SECO)	Staatssekretariat für Wirtschaft (SECO)	State Secretariat for Economic Affairs
Secrétariat d'État aux migrations (SEM)	Staatssekretariat für Migration (SEM)	State Secretariat for Migration
Secrétariat d'État aux questions financières internationales (SFI)	Staatssekretariat für internationale Finanzfragen (SIF)	State Secretariat for International Financial Matters
Secrétariat général	Generalsekretariat	General Secretariat (of the Swiss Federal Supreme Court)
secteur	Rayon (D: Dienstbezirk)	district
sécurité de la circulation	Verkehrssicherheit	traffic safety
sécurité des données	Datensicherheit	data security
sécurité du droit	Rechtssicherheit	legal certainty
sécurité du travail	Arbeitssicherheit	safety at work
sécurité sociale	soziale Sicherheit	social security
séjour	Aufenthalt	stay
séjour à l'hôpital	Spitalaufenthalt (D: Krankenhausaufenthalt)	hospital stay
séjour dans un établissement	Anstaltsaufenthalt	stay in an establishment
séjour hebdomadaire	Wochenaufenthalt	weekly residence
séjour illégal	illegaler Aufenthalt	illegal stay
selon la jurisprudence du Tribunal fédéral	bundesgerichtlich	pursuant to the case law of the Federal Supreme Court
selon l'usage de la place	ortsüblich	as provided for by local custom
semainier	Wochenaufenthalter	weekly resident

semi-détention (art. 77b CP)	Halbgefangenschaft	semi-detention
semi-liberté	Halbfreiheit	semi-liberty
sentence	Urteilsspruch	judgment, verdict
sentence arbitrale (art. 381-388 CPC)	Schiedsspruch, Schiedsentscheid	arbitral award
séparation	Abspaltung	spin-off
séparation de biens (art. 247-251 CC)	Gütertrennung	separate property regime
séparation de corps (art. 116 CC)	Ehetrennung, Trennung statt Scheidung	legal separation
séparation de l'état et de l'église	Trennung von Staat und Kirche	separation of church and state
séparation des pouvoirs	Gewaltentrennung	separation of powers
séquestrabilité	Arrestierbarkeit	attachability
séquestration (art. 184 CP)	Freiheitsberaubung	false imprisonment
séquestre (1) (art. 271 LP)	Arrest	attachment of assets
séquestre (2) (mesure provisionnelle)	Beschlagnahme	seizure, confiscation
séquestre (3) (art. 480 CO)	Sequester	escrow agent
séquestre investigatoire	Sucharrest	fishing expedition, attachment to determine what assets the debtor has (this is not allowed in Swiss law)
séquestrer	verarrestieren	to attach (assets)
série de créanciers saisissants	Pfändungsgruppe	group of seizing creditors
serment	Eid	oath
serment du témoin	Zeugeneid	witness oath
serveuse	Serviertochter (D: Kellnerin)	waitress
service civil	Zivildienst	civil service
service dans la protection civile	Zivilschutzdienst	civil defense service
service d'appui (art. 67 LAAM)	Assistenzdienst	assistance of civil authorities by the army
service d'avancement	Beförderungsdienst	promotion service
Service de la protection de l'environnement	Umweltschutzfachstelle	environmental protection agency
service de permanence	Bereitschaftsdienst	after-hours service
service de probation	Bewährungshilfestelle	probation service
service de protection des témoins	Zeugenschutzstelle	witness protection agency
service de renseignements économiques (art. 273 CP)	wirtschaftlicher Nachrichtendienst	industrial espionage

service de renseignements militaires (art. 274 CP)	militärischer Nachrichtendienst	military espionage
Service des naturalisations	Bürgerrechtsdienst	Naturalization Service
Service fédéral de sécurité (SFS)	Bundessicherheitsdienst (BSD)	Federal Security Service
service juridique	Rechtsdienst	legal department
service militaire	Militärdienst	military service
Services du Parlement	Parlamentsdienste	Parliamentary Services
services intercantonaux	interkantonale Stellen	intercantonal offices
servitude (art. 730 ss CC)	Servitut, Dienstbarkeit	easement
servitude de conduite	Durchleitungsrecht	right for pipe, cables and conduits to traverse an adjoining parcel of land
servitude de fontaine nécessaire (art. 710 CC)	Notbrunnenrecht	right to use an essential water source
servitude de non-bâtir	Bauverbotsdienstbarkeit	easement not to build
servitude de source (art. 780 CC)	Quellenrecht	spring rights
servitude d'empiétement	Überbaurecht	encroachment easement
servitude d'État	Staatsdienstbarkeit	state easement
servitude foncière (art. 730-744 CC) (F : servitude prédiale)	Grunddienstbarkeit	easement that runs with the land
servitude légale	Legalservitut	statutory easement
servitude négative	negative Dienstbarkeit	negative easement
servitude personnelle	Personaldienstbarkeit	personal easement
seuil de détection	Nachweisgrenze	limit of detection (LOD)
siège	Sitz	headquarters, registered office
signature	Unterschrift	signature
signature collective	Kollektivunterschrift	requirement of more than one signature
signature collective à deux	Kollektivunterschrift zu zweien	two signatures required
signature électronique qualifiée (art. 14 CO)	qualifizierte elektronische Unterschrift	authenticated electronic signature
signature individuelle	Einzelunterschrift	authority to represent the company signing alone
signature manuscrite (art. 14 CO)	eigenhändige Unterschrift	handwritten signature
signature numérique	digitale Unterschrift	digital signature
signe appartenant au domaine public	gemeinfreies Zeichen	sign in the public domain

signe d'identification du producteur (art. 51 LPM)	Produzentenkennzeichen	producer identification mark
signe distinctif	Kennzeichen	distinctive sign
signe propre à induire en erreur (art. 2 LPM)	irreführendes Zeichen	misleading sign
silence qualifié	qualifiziertes Schweigen	qualified silence
simulation (art. 18 CO)	Simulation	failure to express one's real intent, false representation
Sion	Sitten	Sion/Sitten
site contaminé	Altlast	contaminated site
site de stockage définitif	Ablagerungsstandort	waste disposal site
site pollué	belasteter Standort	polluted site
site pollué avec projet de construction	Bauherrenaltlast	polluted excavated material within construction projects
situation juridique	Rechtsstellung	legal status, legal position
société	Gesellschaft	company or partnership
société à responsabilité limitée (Sàrl) (art. 772 ss CO)	Gesellschaft mit beschränkter Haftung (GmbH)	limited liability company
société anonyme (SA) (art. 620 CO)	Aktiengesellschaft (AG)	corporation
société commerciale	Handelsgesellschaft	commercial company
société coopérative (art. 828 ss CO)	Genossenschaft	cooperative
société coopérative d'habitation	Wohnbaugenossenschaft	residential building cooperative
société d'allmend	Allmendgenossenschaft	commons
société de capitaux	Kapitalgesellschaft	capital company
société de domicile	Domizilgesellschaft	mailbox company
société de fait	faktische Gesellschaft	de facto company
société de famille	Familiengesellschaft	family-owned company
société de gestion des droits d'auteur	Verwertungsgesellschaft	copyright collecting agency, copyright collective
société de personnes	Personengesellschaft	partnership
société de renflouement	Auffanggesellchaft	rescue company
société de tir	Schützenverein	shooting club, shooting range
société en commandite (art. 594 ss CO)	Kommanditgesellschaft (KmG)	limited partnership

société en commandite par actions (SCmA) (art. 764 ss CO)	Kommanditaktiengesellschaft (KmAG) (D: Kommandit-gesellschaft auf Aktien)	partnership limited by shares
société en nom collectif (SNC) (art. 552 ss CO)	Kollektivgesellschaft (KG)	general partnership
société exerçant une activité commerciale (art. 552 CO)	kaufmännische Gesellschaft	commercial partnership
société fictive	Scheingesellschaft	sham company
société fiduciaire	Treuhandgesellschaft	accounting firm
société fille	Tochtergesellschaft	subsidiary
société holding	Holdinggesellschaft	holding company
société mère	Muttergesellschaft	parent company
société n'exerçant pas une activité commerciale (art. 553 CO)	nichtkaufmännische Gesellschaft	noncommercial partnership
société publique	Publikumsgesellschaft	publicly-held company
société simple (art. 530-551 CO)	einfache Gesellschaft (eG)	simple partnership
société sœur	Schwestergesellschaft	sister company
Société suisse de radiodiffusion et télévision (SSR)	Schweizerische Radio- und Fernsehgesellschaft (SRG)	Swiss Broadcasting Corporation
Société suisse des ingénieurs et des architectes (SIA)	Schweizerischer Ingenieurs- und Architektenverein (SIA)	Swiss Society of Engineers and Architects
société tacite	stille Gesellschaft	silent partnership
société unipersonnelle	Einmanngesellschaft	single-member company
soins à domicile	Hauspflege	home care
soins médicaux	Krankenpflege	nursing
soins médicaux de base (art. 117a CF)	medizinische Grundversorgung	primary medical care
sol	Boden	soil
sol dégradé (art. 7 al. 4bis LPE)	belasteter Boden	polluted soil
solde de la dette	Restschuld	residual debt, balance due
solde de la peine	Reststrafe	remaining sentence
solde militaire	Sold	soldier's pay
solder	saldieren	to balance (an account)
Soleure	Solothurn	Solothurn (canton and city)
solidarité	Solidarität	joint and several liability

solidarité active (art. 150 CO)	Solidargläubigerschaft	joint and several creditors
solidarité fiscale	Steuersolidarität	tax solidarity
solidarité imparfaite	unechte Solidarität	"imperfect" joint and several liability(the tortfeasors do not act jointly but their negligence results in the same harm)
solidarité parfaite	echte Solidarität	"perfect" joint and several liability (the tortfeasors act jointly and directly)
solidarité passive (art. 143-149 CO)	Solidarschuldnerschaft (D: Gesamtschuldnerschaft)	joint and several liability
solutions consacrées par la doctrine	bewährte Lehre	settled legal scholarship
solvabilité (1)	Bonität	credit rating (of a fund)
solvabilité (2)	Zahlungsfähigkeit	solvency
solvable	zahlungsfähig	solvent
sommation de payer	Zahlungsaufforderung	request for payment
sommation publique (art. 582 CC)	Rechnungsruf	formal call to account (to register all debts and claims)
somme assurée	Versicherungssumme	sum insured, amount insured
sortie	Austritt	departure, resignation
sortie illégale	illegale Ausreise	illegal departure
soumission à la législation du lieu de travail	Erwerbsortsprinzip	application of the law of the place where the person works
soumissionnaire	Submittent	bidder, tenderer
soupçon	Verdacht	suspicion
source	Quelle	source
source accessible à tous	allgemein zugängliche Quelle	generally accessible source
source du droit	Rechtsquelle	source of law
sous-assurance	Unterversicherung	underinsurance
sous-contrat	Untervertrag	subcontract
souscription	Zeichnung	signature
souscription d'actions (art. 630 CO)	Aktienzeichnung	share subscription
sous-jacent	Basiswert	underlying instrument
sous-licence	Unterlizenz	sublicense
sous-locataire	Untermieter	subtenant
sous-location (art. 262 CO)	Untermiete	sublease

sous-sol (1)	Untergeschoss	basement
sous-sol (2)	Untergrund	substratum, subsoil
soustraction de données	unbefugte Datenbeschaffung	obtaining data without authorization
soustraction de données personnelles (art. 179novies CP)	unbefugtes Beschaffen von Personendaten	obtaining personal data without authorization
soustraction d'énergie (art. 142 CP)	unrechtmässige Entziehung von Energie	unlawful abstraction of energy
soustraction d'impôts (F : évasion fiscale)	Steuerhinterziehung, Abgabenhinterziehung	tax evasion
soustraction d'objets mis sous main de l'autorité (art. 289 CP)	Bruch amtlicher Beschlagnahme	removal of seized property
soustraction d'une chose mobilière (art. 141 CP)	Sachentziehung	removal of property
soustraction d'une contribution	Hinterziehung	evasion
sous-traitant	Subakkordant, Subunternehmer	subcontractor
souveraineté	Souveränität	sovereignty
souveraineté fiscale	Steuerhoheit	tax sovereignty
spéculation	Spekulation	speculation
spéculation foncière	Bodenspekulation	land speculation
sphère privée	Privatbereich	private sphere
sphère publique	Gemeinbereich	public sphere
stage	Praktikum	internship
stage d'information professionnelle	Schnupperlehre	internship
stand de foire	Messestand	tradeshow booth
stand de marché	Marktstand	market stall
station d'épuration (STEP) (art. 10 LEaux)	Abwasserreinigungsanlage (ARA)	sewage treatment plant
statuer	entscheiden	to decide, to rule
statutaire	statutarisch (D: satzungsgemäß)	pursuant to the bylaws
statuts	Statuten (D: Satzung)	bylaws
stipulant	Promissar	promisee (in a third-party beneficiary contract)
stipulation pour autrui (art. 112 CO)	Vertrag zugunsten Dritter	third-party beneficiary contract (contract conferring rights on third parties)
stipulation pour autrui imparfaite	unechter Vertrag zugunsten Dritter	contract in favor of an incidental beneficiary

stipulation pour autrui parfaite (art. 112 al. 2 CO)	echter Vertrag zugunsten Dritter	contract in favor of an intended beneficiary
stock	Vorrat	inventory
strangulation	Strangulation	strangulation
stupéfiant	Betäubungsmittel	narcotic
subdélégation	Subdelegation	subdelegation
subjectif	subjektiv	subjective
subornation dans l'exécution forcée (art. 168 CP)	Bestechung bei Zwangsvollstreckung	subornation in enforcement proceedings
subrogation	Subrogation	subrogation
subsidiairement	eventualiter (D: hilfsweise)	alternatively, in the alternative
substances dangereuses pour l'environnement	umweltgefährdende Stoffe	substances hazardous to the environment
substitution de partie (art. 83 CPC)	Parteiwechsel	substitution of a party
substitution fidéicommissaire (CC 488)	Nacherbeneinsetzung	appointment of a remainderman
substitution fiscale (art. 17 LTVA)	Steuersubstitution	tax substitution
substitution vulgaire (art. 487 CC)	Ersatzverfügung	substitution (A testator can appoint one or more persons to take the inheritance or legacy if one or more heirs or legatees predecease him or disclaim their inheritance or legacy.)
subvention	Beitrag, Subvention, Zuschuss	subsidy
subvention pour la construction	Baubeitrag	construction subsidy
subvention pour l'emploi temporaire	Beschäftigungsbeitrag	subsidy for temporary employment
succès de la mise à l'épreuve (art. 45 CP)	Bewährung	successful completion of probation
succès de la réadaptation	Eingliederungserfolg	success of the rehabilitation
succession (art. 457 ss CC)	Erbschaft	inheritance
succession fiscale (art. 16 LTVA)	Steuernachfolge	succession to tax liability
succession juridique	Rechtsnachfolge	legal succession
succession légale (art. 457-466 CC)	gesetzliche Erbfolge	intestate succession

succession universelle	Universalsukzession	universal succession (all of the decedent's assets go to the heirs)
succomber	unterliegen	to lose
succursale (art. 641 CO)	Zweigniederlassung	branch
suffrage de parti	Parteistimme	party vote
suffrage nominatif	Kandidatenstimme	candidate vote
suicide	Suizid	suicide
suite d'un accident	Unfallfolge	result of an accident
suivi	Nachkontrolle	aftercare
sujet de droit	Rechtssubjekt	person recognized by law as having rights and obligations
sujet de l'impôt	Steuersubjekt	taxable person
superficiaire	Bauberechtigter	building right holder
suppléant	Ersatzmann, Suppleant	deputy, substitute
supplément	Zuschlag	surcharge, additional fee
supplément de droits de douane	Zollnachforderung	additional customs duty
supplément de prime	Prämienzuschlag	premium supplement
supplément de salaire	Lohnzuschlag	wage supplement, extra pay
suppression de la prestation d'assurance	Versicherungsleistungsentzug	elimination of the insurance benefit
suppression de titres (art. 254 CP)	Unterdrückung von Urkunden	suppression of documents
supprimer des appareils protecteurs (art. 230 CP)	Beseitigung von Sicherheitsvorrichtungen	removal of safety devices
supputation	Berechnung	calculation
suprématie de la loi	Gesetzesvorrang	the rule of law
sur le plan fédéral	auf Bundesebene	at the federal level
surcharge de travail	Arbeitsüberlastung	overwork
surenchérir	überbieten	to outbid
surendettement (art. 725 al. 2 CO)	Überschuldung	overindebtedness
sûreté en garantie des dépens (art. 99 CPC)	Sicherheit für die Parteientschädigung	security for attorney's fees and expenses
sûretés fournies par le locataire (art. 257e CO)	Sicherheiten durch den Mieter	collateral furnished by the tenant
surface	Fläche	surface
sursis (art. 1166 CO)	Aufschub, Stundung	stay, moratorium
sursis à la réalisation (art. 123 LP)	Aufschub der Verwertung	deferred sale
sursis à l'exécution de la peine (art. 42 CP)	bedingte Strafe, bedingter Strafvollzug	suspended sentence

sursis au paiement	Zahlungsaufschub	extension of the time in which to pay a debt
sursis aux enchères (art. 14 LP)	Aussetzen der Versteigerung	postponement of the auction
sursis concordataire (art. 293 ss LP)	Nachlassstundung	debt restructuring moratorium
sursis extraordinaire (art. 337 ss LP)	Notstundung	extraordinary moratorium
sursis partiel à l'exécution de la peine (art. 43 CP)	teilbedingte Strafe	partially suspended sentence
surveillance	Überwachung	monitoring
surveillance administrative	administrative Aufsicht	administrative supervision
surveillance des banques	Bankenaufsicht	bank supervision
surveillance des bourses	Börsenaufsicht	stock market supervision
surveillance étatique	behördliche Aufsicht	regulatory supervision
surveillance téléphonique	Telefonabhörung	phone tapping
surveillant des prix	Preisüberwacher	price watchdog
survenance du cas d'assurance	Eintritt des Versicherungsfalls	occurrence of the insured event
survenance du dommage	Eintritt des Schadens	occurrence of the damage, occurrence of the harm
survivant	Hinterlassener	survivor, surviving dependent
suspect	verdächtig	suspicious
suspendre suspendre quelqu'un de ses fonctions	einstellen jemanden in etwas einstellen	to stay, to suspend to suspend someone's duties
suspendre la procédure	sistieren: das Verfahren sistieren	to stay, suspend the proceedings
suspension	Sistierung	suspension, stay
suspension dans la profession	Einstellung im Beruf	suspension from the profession
suspension de la faillite faute d'actifs	Einstellung des Konkursverfahrens mangels Aktiven	suspension of insolvency proceedings for lack of assets
suspension de la poursuite (art. 85 LP)	Einstellung der Betreibung	suspension of the debt collection proceedings
suspension de la prestation d'assurance	Sistierung der Versicherungsleistung	suspension of insurance benefits
suspension de la procédure	Sistierung des Verfahrens	stay, suspension of the proceedings

suspension de la réalisation des gages immobiliers (art. 306a LP)	Einstellung der Verwertung von Grundpfändern	suspension of the sale of mortgaged property
suspension de la vie commune (art. 175 CC)	Aufhebung des gemeinsamen Haushaltes	suspension of cohabitation
suspension des poursuites (art. 57-62 LP)	Rechtsstillstand	suspension, stay of debt collection (e.g. during military service, a death in the debtor's family, severe illness of the debtor)
suspension des procès civils et des procédures administratives (art. 207 LP)	Einstellung von Zivilprozessen und Verwaltungsverfahren	suspension of civil court actions and administrative proceedings
suspension des travaux	Baustop	suspension of construction work
suspension du délai	Frist每stillstand	suspension of the deadline
swap de taux d'intérêt	Zinsswap	interest rate swap
syndic (Vaud et Fribourg)	Stadtpräsident	mayor
syndicat de révision	Revisionsverband	audit committee
système de distribution	Vertriebssystem	distribution system
système de la capitalisation	Kapitaldeckungsverfahren	funding system
système de la répartition	Umlageverfahren	pay-as-you-go system (payment of benefits from the contributions collected in the same period)
système de négociation électronique	elektronisches Handelssystem	electronic trading system
système de paiement (art. 81 LIMF)	Zahlungssystem	payment system
système des trois piliers	Drei-Säulen-Konzept	three-pillar system
système majoritaire	Majorzwahl (D: Mehrheitswahl)	election by a simple majority
système multilatéral de négociation	multilaterales Handelssystem	multilateral trading system
système parlementaire	parlamentarisches System	parliamentary system
système proportionnel	Proporzwahl (D: Verhältniswahl)	election based on proportional representation
tableau d'affichage	Anschlagsbrett (D: Anschlagbrett)	bulletin board
tables de capitalisation	Barwerttafeln	capitalization tables
talus	Bord (D: Böschung)	embankment
tampon	Stempel	stamp

tantième (art. 627 CO)	Tantieme	director profit-sharing
tarif	Tarif	rate
tarif échelonné	abgestufter Tarif	graduated rate
taux de conversion	Umwandlungssatz	conversion rate
taux de couverture	Deckungsgrad	cover ratio
taux de participation électorale	Wahlbeteiligung	voter turnout
taux d'élucidation	Aufklärungsrate	detection rate (percentage of offenses with respect to which one or more suspects have been identified)
taux d'intérêt	Zinssatz, Zinsfuss	interest rate
taux d'occupation (travail)	Beschäftigungsgrad	level of employment
taux technique	technischer Zins	actuarial interest
taux usurier	Wucherzins	usurious interest
taxation (1)	Bonitierung	land appraisal
taxation (2)	Veranlagung	assessment
taxation d'office	Ermessensveranlagung	administrative assessment (of taxes)
taxation intermédiaire	Zwischenveranlagung	interim assessment
taxe	Abgabe	tax
taxe compensatoire	Ersatzabgabe	exemption tax (e.g. tax payable by people who are exempted from military or fire brigade service)
taxe d'abattage	Schlachtgebühr	slaughtering fee
taxe de raccordement	Anschlussgebühr, Anschlussbeitrag	hook-up fee, connection fee
taxe de ramassage des ordures	Kehrichtgebühr	garbage collection fee
taxe d'exemption au service de feu	Feuerwehrsteuer	fire service tax (paid by all community members who are not yet active members of the local fire service—may be a percentage of basic tax or a lump sum, depending on the canton)

taxe d'incitation	Lenkungsabgabe	steering tax (a tax imposed on the consumption of certain resources to reduce such consumption)
taxe d'inscription	Einschreibgebühr	registration fee
taxe d'inscription au registre	Registereintragungsgebühr	registration fee
taxe d'orientation	Lenkungsabgabe	steering tax (a tax imposed on the consumption of certain resources to reduce such consumption)
taxe d'utilisation de place de parc	Parkplatzbenutzungsgebühr	parking place fee
taxe hospitalière	Spitaltaxe	hospital tax
taxe incitative	Lenkungsabgabe	steering tax (a tax imposed on the consumption of certain resources to reduce such consumption)
taxe militaire	Militärpflichtersatz	exemption tax
taxe poids lourd (art. 85 CF)	Schwerverkehrsabgabe	heavy vehicle charge
taxe sacs de poubelle	Abfallsackgebühr	trash bag fee
taxe sur la valeur ajoutée (TVA)	Mehrwertsteuer (MWST)	value-added tax
technicien géomètre	Vermessungstechniker	surveying technician, topographer
technique de télécommunication	Fernmeldetechnik	telecommunications
technique législative	Gesetzestechnik	legislative technique
technologie de pointe	Spitzentechnologie	state-of-the-art technology
technologie génétique	Gentechnologie	genetic engineering
télécommunication	Fernmeldeverkehr	telecommunication
témoignage (art. 169 ff CPC)	Zeugnis	witness testimony
témoin	Zeuge	witness
témoin à charge	Belastungszeuge	witness for the prosecution
témoin à décharge	Entlastungszeuge	defense witness, witness for the defense

témoin oculaire	Augenzeuge	eyewitness
temps inopportun	zur Unzeit	at an inopportune juncture
tentative (art. 22 CP)	Versuch	attempt
tentative de suicide	Suizidversuch	suicide attempt, attempted suicide
tentative simple (art. 21 CP)	unvollendeter Versuch	uncompleted attempt
tenue des dossiers	Aktenführung	file management
terme comminatoire (art. 102 al. 2 CO)	Verfalltag	deadline for performance
terrain à bâtir	Bauland	building site
Tessin	Tessin	Ticino (canton)
test d'aptitude	Eignungsabklärung (D: Eignungsprüfung)	aptitude test
testament (art. 498-511 CC)	letztwillige Verfügung, Testament	last will and testament
testament olographe (art. 505 CC)	eigenhändiges Testament	holographic will
testament oral (art. 505-511 CC)	mündliches Testament	nuncupative will, oral will
testament public (art. 498-504 CC)	öffentliches Testament	will in the form of a notarial instrument
tester	testieren	to make a will
texte soumis à la votation	Abstimmungsvorlage	proposal submitted to the people
théorie générale du droit	allgemeine Rechtslehre	general theory of law
thésaurisation	Thesaurierung	capitalization
Thurgovie	Thurgau	Thurgau (canton)
tierce partie	Nebenpartei	third-party intervenor
tiers	Dritter	third party
tiers appelé à fournir des renseignements	Auskunftsperson	person providing information
tiers appelé en cause (art. 81 CPC)	Streitberufener, Litisdenunziat	third-party defendant (the impleaded party)
tiers débiteur	Drittschuldner	third-party debtor
tiers dénoncé (art. 81 CPC)	Streitberufener, Litisdenunziat	third-party defendant (the impleaded party)
tiré	Bezogener	drawee (of a check or draft)
tireur	Aussteller	drawer (of a check or draft)
titre	Titel	title
titre à ordre (art. 1145 ss CO)	Ordrepapier	order paper
titre au porteur (art. 978 ss CO)	Inhaberpapier	bearer paper

titre au porteur boiteux	hinkendes Inhaberpapier	restricted bearer instrument
titre de gage	Pfandtitel	mortgage certificate
titre de mainlevée (art. 80 LP)	Rechtsöffnungstitel	automatically enforceable document
titre de part social	Anteilschein	unit certificate
titre de preuve (art. 784 CO)	Beweisurkunde	evidentiary document
titre de transport	Fahrkarte	ticket
titre final (tit. fin.)	Schlusstitel	final title
titre global	Sammeltitel	collective security
titre juridique	Rechtsgrund	legal basis
titre marginal (tit. marg.)	Randtitel (RandT)	margin title
titre nominatif (art. 974 CO)	Namenpapier	registered paper
titre préliminaire	Einleitungstitel	introductory title
titre représentatif de marchandises	Warenpapier	title document (document of title to goods)
titre universitaire	Universitätstitel	university degree
titres à rémunération fixe	festverzinsliche Wertpapiere	fixed interest-bearing securities
titres analogues aux effets de change (art. 1147 CO)	wechselähnliche Papiere	bill-like securities
titulaire du brevet	Patentinhaber	patent holder
titulaire du droit de préemption	Vorkaufsberechtigter	holder of a right of first refusal
toile à sac	Emballage (D: Sackleinen)	burlap
toile d'emballage	Emballage (D: Sackleinen)	burlap
tort moral	Genugtuung (D: Schmerzensgeld)	pain and suffering
total du bilan	Bilanzsumme	total assets
tournus	Turnus	rotation
traduire en justice	Recht: ins Recht fassen	to sue
trafic de matériel séquestré ou réquisitionné par l'armée (art. 330 CP)	Handel mit militärisch beschlagnahmtem Material	trading in material requisitioned by the armed forces
trafic des paiements	Zahlungsverkehr	payment transactions
trahison diplomatique (art. 267 CP)	diplomatischer Landesverrat	diplomatic treason
trahison du pays	Landesverrat	treason
train de vie	Lebensaufwand	lifestyle
traité	Abkommen	treaty, convention
traite d'êtres humains (art. 182 CP)	Menschenhandel	trafficking in human beings
traité international	Staatsvertrag, völkerrechtlicher Vertrag	international treaty

traitement ambulatoire (art. 63 CP)	ambulante Behandlung	outpatient treatment
traitement des addictions (art. 60 CP)	Suchtbehandlung	treatment of addiction
traitement des troubles mentaux (art. 59 CP)	Behandlung von psychischen Störungen	treatment of mental disorders
traitement hospitalier	Spitalbehandlung (D: Krankenhausbehandlung)	hospital treatment
traitement préférentiel des créanciers	Gläubigerbegünstigung, Gläubigerbevorzugung	preferential treatment of creditors
trajet pour se rendre au travail	Arbeitsweg	commute, way to work
transaction à risques accrus	Transaktion mit erhöhten Risiken	high-risk transaction
transaction couplée (art. 254 CO)	Koppelungsgeschäft	linked transaction, tie-in transaction
transaction de clôture	Glattstellungsgeschäft, Glattstellungstransaktion	closing trade
transaction d'ouverture	Eröffnungsgeschäft	opening trade
transaction financière	Transaktion	transaction
transaction judiciaire	gerichtlicher Vergleich	in-court settlement
transaction: transiger	Vergleich: einen Vergleich schliessen	settlement to settle
transactions en bourse	börsliche Abschlüsse	on-order-book trades
transactions hors bourse	ausserbörsliche Abschlüsse	off-order-book trades
transférabilité	Überwälzbarkeit	transferability
transfert	Übertragung	transfer
transfert de la propriété	Eigentumsübergang	passing of title
transfert de la provision (art. 1053 CO)	Übergang der Deckung	transfer of cover
transfert de l'impôt (art. 6 LTVA)	Steuerüberwälzung	passing on of the tax
transfert de patrimoine	Vermögensübertragung	asset transfer, transfer of assets
transfert de technologie	Technologietransfer	technology transfer
transfert d'une créance	Übergang einer Forderung	transfer of a claim
transformation de la société	Umwandlung der Gesellschaft	transformation of the company (change of corporate form)
transformation de l'entreprise	Umwandlung der Unternehmung	transformation of the company (change of corporate form)
transit	Durchlieferung	transit
transmissibilité	Übertragbarkeit	transferability
transmissibilité par succession	Vererblichkeit	transferability by succession

transport des marchandises	Transport der Güter	forwarding of the goods
transports en agglomération	Agglomerationsverkehr	urban transport
travail	Arbeit	work, labor
travail à la tâche	Akkordarbeit	piecework
travail à plein temps	Vollzeitbeschäftigung	full-time work
travail à temps partiel	Teilzeitarbeit	part-time work, part-time employment
travail au noir	Schwarzarbeit	illegal employment
travail auxiliaire	Aushilfsarbeit	temporary work
travail de remplacement	Ersatzarbeit	replacement work
travail des enfants	Kinderarbeit	child labor
travail d'intérêt général (art. 37 CP)	gemeinnützige Arbeit	community service
travail du dimanche	Sonntagsarbeit	work on Sunday
travail intellectuel	geistige Arbeit	brain work, intellectual work
travail par équipes	Schichtarbeit	shift work
travail pénible	Schwerarbeit	heavy labor
travail supplémentaire	Überzeit	overtime
travail sur appel	Arbeit auf Abruf	shift-based work
travail temporaire	Temporärarbeit	temporary work, temporary employment
travailleur	Arbeitnehmer	employee
travailleur à domicile	Heimarbeitnehmer	homeworker
travaux de construction (art. 647c CC)	Bauarbeit, bauliche Massnahmen	construction work
travaux de réfection (art. 647d CC)	Erneuerungsarbeiten	renovation work
travaux de réparation (art. 259 CO)	Ausbesserungen	repairs
travaux préparatoires	Materialien (Gesetzesmaterialien)	legislative history, drafting history
travaux soumis à autorisation	bewilligungspflichtige Arbeit	work subject to authorization
treizième salaire	dreizehnter Monatslohn	13th month salary
très subsidiairement	supereventualiter (D: hoechstvorsorglich)	in the further alternative
tribunal	Gericht	court
tribunal administratif	Verwaltungsgericht	administrative court
Tribunal administratif fédéral (TAF)	Bundesverwaltungsgericht (BVGer)	Federal Administrative Court (in St. Gallen)
tribunal arbitral (art. 179 LDIP)	Schiedsgericht	arbitral tribunal

tribunal cantonal	Kantonsgericht	cantonal court (court of first instance in AR, AI, OW, SH and ZG; court of appeals in FR, GR, NW, SZ and VS)
tribunal civil	Zivilgericht	civil court
tribunal constitutionnel	Verfassungsgericht	constitutional court
Tribunal criminel	Blutgericht	criminal court
tribunal de commerce (art. 6 CPC)	Handelsgericht	commercial court (exists in four cantons)
tribunal de district	Bezirksgericht	district court (civil court of first instance in AR, AI, BI, FR, GR SG, SZ, TG, ZH)
tribunal de police	Polizeigericht	police court
tribunal de première instance (art. 13 CPP)	erstinstanzliches Gericht	court of first instance
tribunal des baux	Mietgericht	landlord-tenant court
tribunal des mesures de contrainte (art. 13 CPP)	Zwangsmassnahmengericht	coercive measures court
tribunal des mineurs	Jugendgericht	juvenile court
tribunal des prud'hommes	Arbeitsgericht	Labor Court
tribunal d'exception	Ausnahmegericht	special tribunal
tribunal disciplinaire	Disziplinargericht	disciplinary tribunal
Tribunal fédéral (TF)	Bundesgericht (BGer), Lausanner Richter	Swiss Federal Supreme Court
Tribunal fédéral des brevets (TFB)	Bundespatentgericht (BPatGer)	Federal Patent Court
tribunal militaire	Militärgericht	court martial
Tribunal militaire d'appel (TMA)	Militärappellationsgericht (MAG)	Military Court of Appeals
Tribunal militaire de cassation (TMC)	Militärkassationsgericht (MKG)	Military Supreme Court
tribunal pénal	Strafgericht	criminal court
Tribunal pénal fédéral (TPF)	Bundesstrafgericht (BStGer)	Federal Criminal Court (based in Bellinzona)
troc	Umtausch	barter, exchange
tromperie	Täuschung	fraud
trouble de la possession	Besitzesstörung (D: Besitzstörung)	trespass, disturbance of possession
tutelle (art. 360-456 CC)	Vormundschaft	guardianship
tuteur (art. 358 CC)	Vormund	guardian
typicité	Tatbestandsmässigkeit (D: Tatbestandsmäßigkeit)	fulfillment of the elements of the offense, meeting the statutory definition of a crime

unanimité	Einstimmigkeit	unanimity
unification du droit	Rechtsvereinheitlichung	unification of law
union conjugale (art. 159 CC)	eheliche Gemeinschaft	marital union
union des biens	Güterverbindung	union of property system
union douanière	Zollunion	customs union
Union intercantonale de réassurance (UIR)	Interkantonaler Rückversicherungsverband (IRV)	Intercantonal Union of Reinsurance
union personnelle	Personalunion	one person doing two things
Unité de pilotage informatique de la Confédération (UPIC)	Informatiksteuerungsorgan des Bundes (ISB)	Federal IT Steering Unit
unité d'une propriété par étages	Stockwerkeinheit	condominium unit
Unité fédérale pour la filière alimentaire (UFAL)	Bundeseinheit für die Lebensmittelkette (BLK)	Federal Food Chain Unit
urbanisme	Städtebau	urban development
Uri	Uri	Uri (canton)
urne électorale	Abstimmungsurne	ballot box
usage abusif de permis et de plaques	Missbrauch von Ausweisen und Schildern	misuse of driver's licenses and license plates
usage antérieur	Vorbenutzung	prior use
usage commercial	Handelsgebrauch	business practice, trade practice
usage frauduleux d'une marque (art. 62 LPM)	betrügerischer Markengebrauch	fraudulent use of a trademark
usage local	Ortsgebrauch	local usage
usage personnel	Eigengebrauch	personal use
usance du marché	Usanz (D: Usance)	market practice
usufruit (art. 745-755 CC)	Nutzniessung (D: Nießbrauch)	usufruct, life estate
usufruitier	Nutzniesser, Nutzniessungsberechtigter	usufructuary, life tenant
usure (1) (art. 157 CP)	Wucher	profiteering
usure (2) (détérioration)	Abnützung (D: Abnutzung)	wear and tear
usurier	Wucherer	profiteer, usurer
usurpation de fonction (art. 287 CP)	Amtsanmassung	usurpation of office
usurpation de titre	Titelanmassung	abuse of title
usurpation d'un nom (art. 29 al. 2 CC)	Namensanmassung	wrongful use of another person's name
utilisateur autorisé	Nutzungsberechtigter	authorized user
utilisation	Benützung (D: Benutzung)	use

utilisation abusive d'une installation de télécommunication (art. 179septies CP)	Missbrauch einer Fernmeldeanlage	misuse of a telecommunications installation
utilisation frauduleuse d'un ordinateur (art. 147 CP)	betrügerischer Missbrauch einer Datenverarbeitungsanlage	computer fraud
utilisation sans droit de valeurs patrimoniales (CP 141bis)	unrechtmässige Verwendung von Vermögenswerten	unlawful use of financial assets
utilité publique	Gemeinnutzen	public interest
vacances non payées	unbezahlter Urlaub	unpaid vacation
Valais	Wallis	Valais (canton)
valeur	Wert	value
valeur à neuf	Neuwert	value when new
valeur affective de l'animal (art. 43 al. 1bis CO)	Affektionswert (eines Haustiers)	sentimental value of a pet
valeur capitalisée	Kapitalwert	capitalized value
valeur comptable	Buchwert	book value
valeur d'affection	Erinnerungswert	sentimental value
valeur d'assurance	Versicherungswert	insurance value
valeur de liquidation	Liquidationswert	liquidation value
valeur de rachat	Rückkaufswert	redemption value
valeur de remplacement	Ersatzwert	replacement value
valeur d'imputation	Anrechnungswert	imputed value
valeur du cours	Kurswert	market price
valeur intrinsèque	innerer Wert	intrinsic value (of an option)
valeur limite	Grenzwert	limit, limiting value
valeur litigieuse (art. 91-94 CPC)	Streitwert	amount in controversy
valeur locative	Mietwert, Eigenmietwert	rental value
valeur monétaire	Geldwert	monetary value
valeur nette d'inventaire	Nettoinventarwert	net asset value (NAV)
valeur nominale	Nennwert	par value
valeur officielle	amtlicher Wert	official value
valeur réelle	Realwert	real value
valeur résiduelle	Zeitwert	current value
valeur vénale	Verkehrswert	market value
valeur vénale du droit exproprié	Verkehrswert des enteigneten Rechts	market value of the expropriated right
valeurs mobilières	Effekten	securities
validation de séquestre (art. 279 LP)	Arrestprosequierung, Prosequierung des Arrests	ratification of the attachment of assets
valider	prosequieren	to validate
validité	Geltung	validity

validité juridique	Rechtswirksamkeit	legal validity, enforceability
valorisation des déchets	Abfallverwertung	waste recycling
Vaud	Waadt	Vaud (canton)
vélo	Velo (D: Fahrrad)	bicycle, bike
vendeur	Verkäufer	seller
vendeur de call couvert	gedeckter Stillhalter	covered writer
vendre aux enchères	versteigern	to auction off
vente (art. 184-238 CO)	Kauf	sale
vente à découvert	Leerverkauf	short sale
vente à distance	Distanzkauf	distance selling
vente à l'essai ou à l'examen (art. 223 CO)	Kauf auf Probe oder auf Besicht	sale on trial or approval
vente à tempérament	Teilzahlungsgeschäft	installment sale, sale on the installment plan
vente au comptant	Barkauf	cash sale
vente aux enchères	Versteigerung	auction
vente aux enchères forcées (art. 234 CO)	Zwangsversteigerung	mandatory auction sale
vente avec paiements préalables (CO 227a)	Vorauszahlungsvertrag	contract with payment in advance
vente commerciale	Kauf im kaufmännischen Verkehr	commercial sale
vente de gré à gré	Freihandverkauf, Verkauf aus freier Hand	private sale (as opposed to a public auction)
vente d'un corps certain	Stückkauf	sale of a specific thing (as opposed to sale of a type of thing)
vente d'une chose de genre	Gattungskauf	sale of a type of thing (as opposed to a sale of a specific thing)
vente fictive	Scheinkauf	sham purchase, fictitious purchase
vente immobilière (art. 655 CC)	Grundstückkauf	land purchase
vente mobilière (art. 187 CO)	Fahrniskauf	sale of chattels
vente par acomptes	Abzahlungsgeschäft	installment sale
vente simulée	Scheinkauf	sham purchase, fictitious purchase
vente sur échantillon	Kauf nach Muster	purchase based on a sample
ventes commerciales	kaufmännischer Verkehr	commercial transactions

vérification de la chose et avis au vendeur (art. 201 CO)	Mängelrüge	notice of defects
vérification d'écriture	Schriftprobe	handwriting sample
vérification des créances (art. 244 ss LP)	Erwahrung der Konkursforderungen	claim examination
versement en mains d'un tiers	Drittauszahlung	payment to a third party
versement supplémentaire	Nachschusspflicht	obligation to make additional contribution
verser comme preuve au dossier	Recht: ins Recht legen	to file with the court, to submit as evidence
vibrations (art. 684 CC)	Erschütterung	vibrations
vice	Mangel	defect
vice de construction	Baumangel, fehlerhafte Anlage	construction defect
vice de forme	Formmangel	procedural defect
vice du consentement	Willensmangel, Mangel des Vertragsabschlusses	defect in consent (defense to contract formation)
vices de forme (art. 132 CPC)	mangelhafte Eingaben	defective pleadings, defective submissions
victime (art. 116 CPP)	Opfer	victim (person who suffered physical, sexual or mental harm from a criminal offense)
victime d'un accident	Verunfallte (D: Unfallopfer)	accident victim
vie séparée	Getrenntleben	living separately
vignette autoroutière	Autobahnvignette	highway sticker
viol (art. 190 CP)	Vergewaltigung	rape
violation de domicile (art. 186 CP)	Hausfriedensbruch	unlawful entry
violation de la souveraineté territoriale de la Suisse (art. 269 CP)	Verletzung schweizerischer Gebietshoheit	violation of Swiss territorial sovereignty
violation de la souveraineté territoriale étrangère (art. 299 CP)	Verletzung fremder Gebietshoheit	violation of foreign territorial sovereignty
violation de l'obligation d'annoncer	Meldepflichtverletzung	breach of the obligation to report
violation de l'obligation de tenir une comptabilité (art. 166 CP)	Unterlassung der Buchführung	failure to keep proper accounts
violation de secrets militaires	Verletzung militärischer Geheimnisse	violation of military secrets
violation de secrets privés (art. 179 CP)	Verletzung des Schriftgeheimnisses	breach of the privacy of a sealed document

violation des devoirs en cas d'accident (art. 92 LCR)	pflichtwidriges Verhalten bei Unfall	violation of duties in the event of an accident
violation des lois de la guerre	Verletzung kriegsrechtlicher Bestimmungen	violations of the law of war
violation des règles de la circulation	Verletzung der Verkehrsregeln	traffic violation
violation des règles de l'art de construire (art. 229 CP)	Gefährdung durch Verletzung der Regeln der Baukunde	violation of construction regulations
violation du brevet	Patentverletzung	patent infringement
violation du devoir d'assistance ou d'éducation (art. 219 CP)	Verletzung der Fürsorge- oder Erziehungspflicht	neglect of duties of care, supervision or education
violation du domaine secret ou du domaine privé au moyen d'un appareil de prise de vues (art. 179quater CP)	Verletzung des Geheim- oder Privatbereichs durch Aufnahmegeräte	breach of secrecy or privacy through the use of an image-carrying device
violation du droit	Rechtsverletzung	legal violation
violation du droit à la marque (art. 61 LPM)	Markenrechtsverletzung	infringement of a trademark
violation du droit cantonal	Verletzung kantonalen Rechts	violation of cantonal law
violation du droit d'auteur	Urheberrechtsverletzung	copyright infringement
violation du droit fédéral	Bundesrechtsverletzung	violation of federal law
violation du secret de fabrication ou commercial (art. 162 CP)	Verletzung des Fabrikations- oder Geschäftsgeheimnisses	breach of manufacturing or trade secrecy
violation du secret de fonction (art. 320 CP)	Verletzung des Amtsgeheimnisses	breach of official secrecy
violation du secret du vote (art. 283 CP)	Verletzung des Abstimmungs- und Wahlgeheimnisses	breach of voting secrecy
violation du secret professionnel (art. 321 CP)	Verletzung des Berufsgeheimnisses	breach of professional confidentiality
violation d'une obligation d'entretien (CP 217)	Vernachlässigung von Unterhaltspflichten	neglect of duty to support the family
violation positive du contrat	positive Vertragsverletzung	positive breach of contract
violence	Gewalt	violence
violence domestique	häusliche Gewalt	domestic violence
violence ou menace contre les autorités et les fonctionnaires (art. 285 CP)	Gewalt und Drohung gegen Behörden und Beamte	violence and threats against public authorities and public officials

violences (art. 279 CP)	Störung und Hinderung von Wahlen und Abstimmungen	disruption and obstruction of elections and votes
virement	Überweisung	wire transfer
visite corporelle	körperliche Durchsuchung	body search
visite de travail	Arbeitsbesuch	working visit
visite d'État	Staatsbesuch	state visit
viticulteur	Rebbauer (D: Weinbauer)	winegrower
viticulture	Rebbau (D: Weinbau)	wine growing
vocation successorale	Erbberechtigung	succession rights
voie de contamination	Wirkungspfad	pollution path
voie de droit	Rechtsvorkehr	legal channel
voies de fait (art. 126 CP)	Tätlichkeiten	acts of aggression
voiture d'occasion	Occasion (D: Gebrauchtwagen)	used car
voiturier	Frachtführer	carrier
voix consultative	beratende Stimme	advisory capacity
voix prépondérante	Stichentscheid	deciding vote, tie-breaking vote
vol (art. 139 CP)	Diebstahl	theft
vol à l'arraché	Entreissdiebstahl	theft by snatching, mugging
vol au préjudice d'un colocataire	Familiengenossendiebstahl	theft from a cotenant
vol par introduction clandestine	Einschleichdiebstahl	theft by secretly entering an unsecured place
vol par métier (art. 139 CP)	gewerbsmässiger Diebstahl	theft for commercial gain
vol qualifié (art. 172ter CP)	qualifizierter Diebstahl	aggravated theft
volonté	Wille	will
volonté de recourir	Anfechtungswille	intent to challenge
votation (1)	Urnengang	going to the polls, voter turnout
votation (2)	Abstimmung	voting
votation consultative	Konsultativabstimmung	nonbinding vote
votation éventuelle (art. 79 LParl)	Eventualabstimmung	elimination vote, elimination procedure
votation populaire	Volksabstimmung	popular vote, popular ballot
vote	Abstimmung	vote
vote à bulletins secrets	geheime Abstimmung	voting by secret ballot
vote à l'appel nominal	Abstimmung unter Namensaufruf	vote by roll call
vote à main levée	Abstimmung durch Handaufheben	vote by show of hands
vote à main levée acquis à la majorité simple	Handmehr	majority vote by a show of hands

vote électronique	elektronische Abstimmung	electronic voting
vote final	Schlussabstimmung	final vote
vote obligatoire	Stimmzwang	mandatory voting
vote par correspondance	briefliche Stimmabgabe	postal voting
vote par procuration	Vertretung bei der Stimmabgabe	proxy voting
voter	stimmen gehen (D: wählen gehen)	to vote
voter à main levée	abmehren (D: durch Handerheben abstimmen)	to vote by show of hands
voter la décharge (F : donner quitus)	Decharge erteilen (D: entlasten)	to grant "discharge" to the members of the board of directors
voué à l'échec	aussichtslos	hopeless, pointless, having no prospect of success
voyageur de commerce	Handelsreisender	traveling salesman
vraisemblance de l'usage (art. 32 LPM)	Glaubhaftmachung des Gebrauchs	providing prima facie evidence of use (of the trademark)
zone	Zone	area, zone
zone à bâtir	Bauzone	building zone
zone agricole	Landwirtschaftszone	agricultural area
zone alluviale	Auengebiet	wetland, flood plain
zone de bruit	Lärmzone	noise zone
zone de gisement	Abbauzone	mining district, mining region
zone d'habitation	Wohnzone	residential area
zone en amont	Oberstrombereich	upstream groundwater
zone en aval	Abstrombereich	downstream groundwater
zone franche	Freizone	free trade zone
zone non saturée	ungesättigte Zone	unsaturated zone
zone tampon	Pufferzone	buffer zone
zone viticole	Rebbauzone (D: Weinbauzone)	wine-growing area
Zoug	Zug	Zug (canton and city)
Zurich	Zürich	Zurich (canton and city)

Abréviations françaises

A.	arrêté
AC	assurance-chômage
ACF	arrêté du Conseil fédéral
Adm. féd.	Administration fédérale
AF	arrêté fédéral
AFC	Administration fédérale des contributions
AFD	Administration fédérale des douanes
AFF	Administration fédérale des finances
AFS	Archives fédérales suisses
AI	assurance-invalidité
al.	alinéa
art.	article
Ass. féd.	Assemblée fédérale
ATF	Arrêts du Tribunal fédéral
AVS	assurance-vieillesse et survivants
BNS	Banque Nationale Suisse
c.	contre
cant.	canton
CC	Code civil
CCT	convention collective de travail
CF	Conseil fédéral ; Constitution fédérale
CG	conditions générales
ch.	chiffre
chap.	chapitre
CN	Conseil national
CNA	Caisse nationale suisse d'assurance en cas d'accidents
CO	Code des obligations
conc.	concordat
CP	Code pénal
CPC	Code de procédure civile
CPM	Code pénal militaire
CPP	Code de procédure pénale
cpr.	comparer
ct.	canton
CTT	contrat-type de travail
D	décision
dép.	département
DG	direction générale
DIP	droit international privé
dir.	directives
disp. fin.	disposition(s) finale(s)
disp. trans.	disposition(s) transitoire(s)
édit.	éditeur
EIMP	Loi fédérale sur l'entraide pénale internationale
env.	environ
EPF	École polytechnique fédérale

F	feuille
FF	Feuille fédérale
i.f.	in fine
i.i.	in initio
ISDC	Institut suisse de droit comparé
L	loi
LAA	Loi sur l'assurance-accidents
LBA	Loi sur le blanchiment d'argent
LCR	Loi fédérale sur la circulation routière
LDIP	Loi fédérale sur le droit international privé
LF	loi fédéral
LP	Loi fédérale sur la poursuite pour dettes et la faillite
LPM	Loi fédérale sur la protection des marques et des indications de provenance
LPP	Loi fédérale sur la prévoyance professionnelle vieillesse, survivants et invalidité
mél.	mélanges
Mess.	Message du Conseil fédéral à l'Assemblée fédérale
n.	note
n.p.	non publié
NS	Nouvelle série
O	ordonnance
OCF	ordonnance du Conseil fédéral
OCFIM	Office central fédéral des imprimes et du matériel
O d'ex.	ordonnance d'exécution
P	projet
par.	paragraphe
PC	procédure civile
PG	partie générale
phr.	phrase
PP	procédure pénale
pres.	prescription
prot.	protocole
PS	partie spéciale
R	règlement
R d'ex.	règlement d'exécution
rem.	remarque
resp.	respectivement
Rev.	Revue
RgC	registre du commerce
RgF	registre foncier
RO	Recueil officiel des lois fédérales
RS	Recueil systématique des lois fédérales
s.	et suivant(s)
s.a.	sine anno
sc.	scilicet
s.d.	sine dato
s.ed.	sine editore
SIA	Société suisse des ingénieurs et des architectes

s.l.	sine loco
ss	suivant(e)
SSJ	Société suisse des juristes
TA	Tribunal administratif
TAF	Tribunal administratif fédéral
TC	tribunal cantonal
TF	Tribunal fédéral
th.	thèse
tit.	titre
tit.fin.	titre final
tit.marg.	titre marginal
tr.	traité
UIR	Union intercantonale de réassurance
UPIC	Unité de pilotage informatique de la Confédération
UFAL	Unité fédérale pour la filière alimentaire

Aargau (AG)	Argovie (AG)	Aargau (canton)
abändern	modifier	to amend
Abänderung	modification	amendment
Abbauzone	zone de gisement	mining district, mining region
abberufen	révoquer	to remove, to dismiss (a person from office)
Abberufung	révocation	removal, dismissal (of a person from office)
Abbruchbefehl	ordre de démolition	demolition order
Abbruchbewilligung	permis de démolir	demolition permit
Abbruchkosten	frais de démolition	demolition costs
abbruchreife Baute	construction en ruines	condemned building
Abbruchverbot	interdiction de démolir	prohibition on demolition
Abdankung (D: Trauerfeier)	funérailles	funeral service
aberkennen	désavouer	to disallow (a claim)
Aberkennung der Forderung	libération de dette	lifting of a debt
Aberkennungsklage (Art. 83 SchKG)	action en libération de dette	action for a declaratory judgment that a debt does not exist
Abfallbewirtschaftung	gestion des déchets	waste management
Abfälle	déchets	waste
Abfallentsorgung	évacuation des déchets	waste disposal
Abfallplanung	planification de la gestion des déchets	waste management planning
Abfallsackgebühr	taxe sacs de poubelle	trash bag fee
Abfallverbrennung	incinération des déchets	incineration of waste
Abfallverwertung	valorisation des déchets	waste recycling
abfinden	désintéresser, indemniser	to settle a claim, to pay off a creditor
Abfindung	indemnité	settlement
Abgabe	taxe	tax
Abgabebetrug	fraude fiscale	tax fraud

Abgabeerhebung	perception d'une contribution	levying of taxes
Abgabefreiheit	exonération fiscale	tax exemption
Abgabenhinterziehung	soustraction d'impôts (F : évasion fiscale)	tax evasion
Abgabepflicht	obligation de verser le revenu	tax obligation
Abgabepflichtiger	contribuable	taxpayer
Abgaberecht	droit fiscal	tax law
Abgaberückerstattung	remboursement	tax refund
Abgabeschuld	dette d'impôt	tax debt
Abgabestreitigkeit	litige en matière de contribution publique	tax dispute
Abgangsentschädigung (Art. 339b OR)	indemnité de départ	severance pay
abgekürztes Verfahren (Art. 358-362 StPO)	procédure simplifiée	accelerated proceedings (in plea bargaining cases)
abgestufte Rente	rente dégressive	graduated pension
abgestufter Tarif	tarif échelonné	graduated rate
abgewiesene Forderung (Art. 248 SchKG)	créance écartée	dismissed claim, rejected claim
Abgrenzung der Zuständigkeit	délimitation de compétence	delimitation of jurisdiction
Abgrenzungspflicht (Art. 669 ZGB)	obligation de borner	duty to establish boundaries, duty to demarcate
abhanden gekommene Sache	chose perdue ou volée	lost or stolen item
abhängige Erfindung (Art. 36 PatG)	invention dépendante	dependent invention
Abhängigkeitsverhältnis	relation de dépendance	relationship of dependency
Abklärung (D: Untersuchung)	enquête	investigation
Abklärungsmassnahme	mesure d'instruction	investigation, investigatory measure
Abklärungsverfahren	procédure d'instruction de la demande	investigation proceedings
Abkommen	traité, convention	treaty, convention
Ablagerungsstandort	site de stockage définitif	waste disposal site
Ablehnung der Rechtshilfe	refus de l'entraide	refusal of mutual assistance

Ablehnung des Nachlassvertrags (Art. 309 SchKG)	refus d'homologation du concordat	refusal to ratify the debt restructuring agreement
Ablehnung eines Schiedsrichters (Art. 180 IPRG)	récusation des arbitres	recusal of arbitrators
Ablehnung zumutbarer Arbeit	refus d'un travail convenable	refusal of a reasonable job
Ablösung einer Dienstbarkeit durch den Richter (Art. 736 ZGB)	libération judiciaire d'une servitude	termination of an easement by the court
Abmahnung	avis formel	formal notice
abmehren (D: durch Handerheben abstimmen)	voter à main levée	to vote by show of hands
Abnahme der Jahresrechnung (D: Billigung des Jahresabschlusses)	approbation des comptes annuels	approval of the annual financial statements
Abnahme des Ausweises	saisie de permis	taking away someone's driver's license
Abnahme des Werkes	réception de l'ouvrage	acceptance of the work
Abnützung (D: Abnutzung)	usure (détérioration)	wear and tear
Abrechnung	compensation	clearing
Abrechnungspflicht	obligation de compenser	clearing duty
Abrechnungsstelle	chambre de compensation	clearing house
Abredeversicherung	assurance par convention	interim accident insurance
Abrüstung	désarmement	disarmament
Abschlag	disagio, déport	discount (the difference between the nominal value of a security and its issue or market price)
Abschlagsdividende	dividende intérimaire	interim dividend
Abschlagsverteilung (Art. 144 Abs. 2 und 266 SchKG)	répartition provisoire	interim distribution, provisional distribution
Abschlagszahlungen (Art. 123 Abs. 3, 326 und 348 Abs. 1 Ziff. 1 SchKG)	acomptes, répartitions	down payments, installment payments
abschliessen	conclure	to enter into (a contract)
Abschluss des Rechtshilfeverfahrens	clôture de la procédure d'entraide	completion of the mutual assistance procedure
Abschluss des Vertrages	conclusion du contrat	entry into the contract
Abschlussbilanz	bilan de clôture	closing balance sheet

Abschlussfreiheit	liberté de contracter	freedom of contract
Abschlusskurs	cours fait	trading price
Abschreibung	amortissement	depreciation (of tangible assets); amortization (of intangible assets)
Abschreibung eines Entlassentwurfes	classement d'un projet d'acte	abandoning a bill
Abschreibung eines Vorstosses	classement d'une intervention	abandoning a procedural request
Absender	expéditeur	sender
Absenz (D: Nichterscheinen, Abwesenheit)	absence	absence
absichern	couvrir	to hedge
Absicherungsgeschäft	opération de couverture	hedge, hedging
Absicherungskosten	frais de couverture	hedging costs
Absicht dauernden Verbleibens	intention de s'établir	intention to settle
absichtliche Täuschung (Art. 28 OR)	dol	fraud
Absichtsanfechtung (Art. 288 SchKG)	action en révocation d'actes dolosifs	challenge of a debtor's fraudulent conveyance of assets
absolute Frist	délai absolu	absolute deadline
absolutes Mehr (D: absolute Mehrheit)	majorité absolue	absolute majority
absolutes Recht	droit absolu	absolute right (effective erga omnes)
Abspaltung	séparation	spin-off
Abstimmung (1) (politische Rechte)	votation (droits politiques)	voting
Abstimmung (2) (Versammlung)	vote (assemblée)	vote
Abstimmung der Zahlungen	appariement des paiements	reconciliation of payments
Abstimmung durch Handaufheben	vote à main levée	vote by show of hands
Abstimmung unter Namensaufruf	vote à l'appel nominal	vote by roll call
Abstimmungsbotschaft	recommandation de vote de l'autorité	authority's recommendation on how to vote
Abstimmungsempfehlung	recommandation de vote	voting recommendation
Abstimmungskampf	campagne	campaign
Abstimmungsparole	consigne de vote	voting recommendation

Abstimmungsresultat	résultat du vote	result of the vote
Abstimmungsurne	urne électorale	ballot box
Abstimmungsvorlage	texte soumis à la votation	proposal submitted to the people
abstrakter Schaden (Art. 42 OR)	dommage abstrait	abstract damage
abstraktes Schuldbekenntnis (Art. 17 OR)	reconnaissance de dette abstraite	acknowledgment of debt that does not state the cause of the obligation
Abstrombereich	zone en aval	downstream groundwater
Abtretbarkeit	cessibilité (créance)	assignability
Abtretung durch Vertrag	cession contractuelle	assignment by contract
Abtretung einer Forderung (Art. 164 OR)	cession de créance	assignment of a claim
Abtretung von Rechtsansprüchen der Masse	cession des droits de la masse	assignment of the rights of creditors
Abverdienen einer Busse (D: Buße)	compensation d'une amende	working off of a fine
Abwart (D: Hausmeister)	concierge, gardien	janitor, caretaker
Abwasser	eau usée	sewage, waste water
Abwasserbeseitigung	évacuation des eaux usées	disposal of sewage, disposal of waste water
Abwasserreinigung	épuration des eaux usées	sewage treatment, waste water treatment
Abwasserreinigungsanlage (ARA) (Art. 10 GschG)	station d'épuration (STEP)	sewage treatment plant, waste water treatment plant
Abwasservorbehandlung	prétraitement des eaux usées	pretreatment of sewage, pretreatment of waste water
Abwehrhandlung	acte de légitime défense	self-defense
Abwehrklage	action défensive	action to quiet title
abweichende Meinung	opinion dissidente	dissenting opinion
abweisen: eine Beschwerde abweisen ein Gesuch abweisen	rejeter rejeter un recours rejeter une demande	to dismiss: to dismiss an appeal to dismiss a claim
Abweisung	jugement de débouté	judgment for the defendant
Abweisung der Klage	rejet de la demande	dismissal of the claim, dismissal of the action

Abweisung des Konkursbegehrens (Art. 172 SchKG)	rejet de la réquisition de faillite	rejection of the insolvency petition
Abwerbung von Arbeitnehmern	débauchage de travailleurs	solicitation of employees
Abwesenheit	absence	absence
Abwesenheitsurteil	jugement par défaut	default judgment
Abwicklung	règlement	settlement
Abwicklung eines Nachlasses	liquidation de la succession	settlement of an estate
Abzahlungsgeschäft	vente par acomptes	installment sale
Abzahlungsvertrag	contrat de vente par acomptes	installment sales agreement
Abzug	déduction	subtraction, deduction
Abzug für Gewinnungskosten	déduction des frais d'acquisition	deduction of costs of generating income
Abzug für Liegenschaftsaufwand	déduction pour frais d'entretien d'immeuble	deduction of costs of maintaining the building
Abzug für Schuldzinsen	déduction des intérêts passifs	deduction of interest on debt
Abzug vom anrechenbaren Einkommen	déduction du revenu déterminant	deduction of creditable income
Abzug vom Einkommen (Steuerrecht)	déduction du revenu (droit fiscal)	deduction of income
Achtung des Familienlebens	respect de la vie familiale	respect for family life
Achtung des Privatlebens	respect de la vie privée	respect for privacy
adäquate Kausalität	causalité adéquate	proximate cause
Adhäsionsklage	constitution de partie civile	filing a civil action for damages as part of a criminal action
Adhäsionspartei	partie civile	party claiming damages in a criminal action
Admassierung	revendication de la masse en faillite	recovery, replevin
administrative Aufsicht	surveillance administrative	administrative supervision

administrative Rechtshilfe	entraide administrative	administrative mutual assistance
Administrativgutachten	expertise ordonnée par l'administration	government-ordered expert opinion
Administrativhaft	détention administrative	administrative detention
Administrativuntersuchung	enquête administrative	administrative investigation
Adoption	adoption	adoption
Adoption Entmündigter	adoption d'interdits	adoption of incapacitated persons
Adoption Unmündiger	adoption de mineurs	adoption of minors
Adoptionsverfahren	procédure d'adoption	adoption procedure
Adoptionsvermittlung	placement d'enfants en vue d'adoption	adoption placement
Adoptiveltern	parents adoptifs	adoptive parents
Adoptivkind	enfant adoptif	adopted child
Adressat	destinataire	addressee
Adressierungselement	ressource d'adressage	addressing resource
Advokat (D: Rechtsanwalt)	avocat	lawyer
Advokatenprüfungsbehörde	Commission d'examen des avocats	Lawyers Examination Board
Advokaturbüro (D: Anwaltskanzlei)	cabinet d'avocats	law firm
Affektionswert eines Haustiers (Art. 43 Abs. 1bis OR)	valeur affective de l'animal	sentimental value of the pet
Agent	agent	agent
Agenturvertrag (Art. 418a ff. OR)	contrat d'agence	agency agreement
Agglomeration (D: Ballungsgebiet)	région à forte concentration urbaine, conurbation	urban center
Agglomerationsverkehr	transports en agglomération	urban transport
Agio	agio, prime, report	premium (difference between the nominal value of a security and its issue or market price)
Agrareinfuhrverordnung (AEV)	Ordonnance sur les importations agricoles (OIAgr)	Agricultural Imports Ordinance
Agrarpolitik	politique agricole	agricultural policy

Agrément eines Botschafters	agrément d'un ambassadeur	agrément of an ambassador (Diplomatic courtesy requires that before a state appoints a new chief of diplomatic mission to represent it in another state, it must be first ascertained whether the proposed appointee is acceptable to the receiving state. The acquiescence of the receiving state is signified by its granting its agrément to the appointment.)
AHV (Alters- und Hinterlassenenversicherung)	AVS (assurance vieillesse et survivants)	old age and survivors insurance
AHV/IV/EO-Beitrag	cotisation AVS/AI/APG	contribution to old age and survivors insurance
AHV/IV-Kommission	commission de l'AVS/AI	old age and survivors insurance commission
AHV-Ausgleichskasse	caisse de compensation AVS	old age and survivors insurance compensation fund
Akkordarbeit	travail à la tâche	piecework
Akkordlohn (Art. 319 OR)	salaire à la tâche	piecework wage
Akkreditierung	accréditation	accreditation
Akkreditierung von Medienschaffenden	accréditation des médias	journalist accreditation
Akkreditiv	accréditif	letter of credit (L/C)
Akte	dossier	file
Aktenaufbewahrung	conservation des documents	archiving
Akteneinsicht	consultation du dossier	inspection of the record
Aktenführung	tenue des dossiers	file management
Aktengutachten	expertise sur pièces	expert opinion based solely on the record
Aktenstelle (act.)	dossier	record
aktenwidrig	contraire aux pièces	contrary to the record, error apparent on the face of the record
Aktie	action	share, share of stock
Aktienbuch (Art. 686 OR)	registre des actions	stock ledger
Aktienfonds	fonds en actions	equity fund
Aktiengesellschaft (AG) (Art. 620 ff. OR)	société anonyme (SA)	corporation

Aktienindex	indice d'actions	equity index
Aktienkapital (D: Grundkapital)	capital-actions (F : capital social)	share capital, capital stock
Aktienoption	option sur actions	stock option
Aktienzeichnung (Art. 630 OR)	souscription d'actions	share subscription
Aktienzertifikat (D: Aktienurkunde)	certificat d'actions	share certificate, stock certificate
Aktion (D: Sonderangebot)	promotion	promotion, special sale
Aktionär	actionnaire	shareholder
Aktionärbindungsvertrag (ABV)	convention d'actionnaires, pacte d'actionnaires	shareholders' agreement
Aktionariat	actionnariat	shareholders
Aktionärsgruppe	groupe d'actionnaires	group of shareholders
Aktivbürger	citoyen actif	citizen who is eligible to vote
Aktivdarlehen	prêts consentis	loans granted
aktives Wahlrecht	capacité civique active, droit de vote	right to vote
Aktivierung	activation	capitalization
Aktivitätserwartung	durée d'activité probable	expectation of activity
Aktivlegitimation	légitimation active	plaintiff's standing
Aktuar (D: Schriftführer)	secrétaire	secretary
aktueller Schaden	dommage actuel	current damage
aktuelles Interesse	intérêt actuel	current interest
Akzessionsprinzip	principe de l'accession	principle of accession
Akzessorietät	accessoriété	accessoriness
Alibi	alibi	alibi
Alleinaktionär	actionnaire unique	sole shareholder, single shareholder
Alleineigentum	propriété exclusive	sole ownership
alleinstehende Person	personne seule	single person
Alleintäter	agent solitaire	lone offender
Alleinvertreter	concessionnaire exclusif	sole agent, sole representative
Alleinvertriebsvertrag	contrat de représentation exclusive	exclusive distribution agreement
allfällig (D: etwaig)	éventuel	any; possible, potential

Allfinanz	bancassurance	one-stop financial service center
allgemein gekreuzter Check (Art. 1124 OR)	chèque à barrement général	generally crossed check
allgemein zugängliche Quelle	source accessible à tous	generally accessible source
allgemeine Anregung	proposition conçue en termes généraux	general proposal
allgemeine Gütergemeinschaft	communauté universelle	general community of property
allgemeine Rechtslehre	théorie générale du droit	general theory of law
allgemeine Vertragsbedingungen	conditions générales du contrat	general terms and conditions
Allgemeinverbindlicherklärung	décision d'extension	declaration of general application
Allgemeinverfügung	acte de portée générale	general ruling
Allianzname	nom d'alliance	hyphenated last name
Allmendgenossenschaft	société d'allmend	commons
alltägliche Lebensverrichtung	acte ordinaire de la vie	daily chores
Alpenkonvention	Convention alpine	Alpine Convention (an international treaty between the Alpine countries (Austria, France, Germany, Italy, Liechtenstein, Monaco, Slovenia and Switzerland) and the EU, aimed at promoting sustainable development in the Alpine area and at protecting the interests of its inhabitants)
ältere Marke (Art. 3 MSchG)	marque antérieure	earlier trademark
alternative Obhut	garde alternée	shared custody (of children after divorce)
Alternativermächtigung	obligation avec faculté alternative	obligation that can be performed in a different manner than originally agreed (such as paying in local currency even though the obligation was in foreign currency)

Alters- und Hinterlassenenversicherung (AHV)	Assurance-vieillesse et survivants (AVS)	Old Age and Survivors Insurance
Altersgrenze	limite d'âge	age limit
Altersguthaben	avoir de vieillesse	retirement savings
Altersgutschrift	bonification de vieillesse	retirement pension credit
Alterskapital	capital-vieillesse	endowment sum for old age
Altersleistung	prestation de vieillesse	pension benefits
Alterspräsident	doyen de fonction	oldest member (of the National Council)
Altersrente	rente de vieillesse	old-age pension, retirement pension
Altersvorsorge	prévoyance vieillesse	provision for old age
Alterszulage	allocation d'ancienneté	superannuation allowance
Altlast	site contaminé	contaminated site
Altlastenbearbeitung	gestion des sites contaminés	contaminated site management
Altlastenverordnung (AltlV)	Ordonnance sur les sites contaminés (OSites)	Contaminated Sites Ordinance
ambulante Behandlung (Art. 63 StGB)	traitement ambulatoire	outpatient treatment
Amnestie	amnistie	amnesty
Amtliche Sammlung des Bundesrechts (AS)	Recueil officiel du droit fédéral (RO)	Official Compilation of Swiss Federal Legislation
amtliche Tätigkeit	exercice de la fonction	acting in an official capacity
amtliche Verteidigung (Art. 132 StPO)	défense d'office	duty defense lawyer
amtlicher Wert	valeur officielle	official value
Amtliches Bulletin der Bundesversammlung (Amtl. Bull.; AB)	Bulletin officiel de l'Assemblée fédérale (BO)	Official Bulletin of the Federal Assembly
amtliches Formular	formule officielle	official form
Amtsanmassung (Art. 287 StGB)	usurpation de fonction	usurpation of office
Amtsblatt	Feuille officielle	official gazette
Amtsdauer	durée de la fonction	term of office

Amtsentlassung	révocation d'une personne	removal of a person from office
Amtsentsetzung (Art. 14 Abs. 2 Ziff. 4 SchKG) (D: Amtsenthebung)	destitution	dismissal from office
Amtsgeheimnis	secret de fonction	official secrecy
Amtshilfe im Bereich der Polizei (Art. 350-362 StGB)	entraide en matière de police	administrative assistance with police matters
Amtsmissbrauch (Art. 312 StGB)	abus d'autorité	abuse of public office
Amtssprache (Art. 70 BV)	langue officielle	official language (the three official languages of Switzerland are French, German and Italian; compare national language)
Amtszwang	obligation d'accepter une fonction	obligation to accept an office
an Schranken: Die Parteien geben an Schranken die Prozesserklärung ab, dass sie auf eine Appellation verzichten.	en audience publique	in open court
Anbaute (D: Anbau)	saillie	extension
Anbieter von Fernmeldediensten	fournisseur de services de télécommunication	telecommunications service provider
Änderung	modification	amendment
Änderung von Dienstbarkeiten	modifications de servitudes	modification of easements
Änderung von Grundlasten	modifications de charges foncières	modification of real estate charges
Änderung von Grundpfandrechten	modifications de gages immobiliers	modification of mortgages
Änderung von vorgemerkten persönlichen Rechten	modifications de droits personnels annotés	modification of registered personal rights
Änderungskündigung	congé-pression	notice of termination pending a change of contract
Aneignung (Art. 658 ZGB)	occupation	appropriation
Aneignungswille	dessein d'appropriation	intention to appropriate
Anerkennung der Vaterschaft (Art. 260-260c ZGB)	reconnaissance de paternité	acknowledgment of paternity
Anerkennung eines Kindes	reconnaissance d'un enfant	acknowledgment of an illegitimate child

Anerkennung von Staaten	reconnaissance d'états	recognition of states
Anerkennungserklärung	déclaration de reconnaissance	acknowledgment of paternity
Anerkennungsklage (Art. 79 SchKG)	action en reconnaissance de dette	action for the recognition of a claim
Anerkennungsregister	registre des reconnaissances	register of acknowledgments of paternity
Anfangsmietzins	loyer initial	initial rent
anfechtbare Rechtshandlungen	actes révocables	revocable transactions
Anfechtbarkeit	annulabilité	voidability
anfechten	attaquer, contester, s'en prendre à	to challenge, to contest, to object to
Anfechtung der Anerkennung des Kindes	contestation de la reconnaissance de l'enfant	contesting the acknowledgment of the child (born out of wedlock)
Anfechtung der Ehelicherklärung	contestation de la légitimation	contesting a declaration of legitimacy
Anfechtung der Vermutung der Vaterschaft	action en désaveu	contesting the presumption of paternity
Anfechtung eines Testaments	contestation d'un testament	challenge of a will, contest of a will
Anfechtung von Rechtshandlungen (Art. 331 SchKG)	révocation d'actes juridiques	revocation of legal transactions
Anfechtungsklage (SchKG)	action en contestation, action révocatoire (LP)	avoidance action (action by creditors to void a fraudulent conveyance)
Anfechtungswille	volonté de recourir	intent to challenge
Anfrage	question	question (a request by a member of Parliament to the Federal Council for information about important domestic or foreign affairs)
Angabe	déclaration	statement
Angebot der Arbeitsleistung	offre de travailler	offer to work
angemessene Entschädigung	indemnité équitable	appropriate compensation
angemessene Frist	délai raisonnable	reasonable deadline
Angemessenheit	opportunité	appropriateness
Angriff (Art. 134 StGB)	agression	attack

Angriffe auf die sexuelle Freiheit und Ehre (Art. 129 StGB)	atteinte à la liberté et l'honneur sexuels	offenses against sexual liberty and honor
Angriffe auf die Unabhängigkeit der Eidgenossenschaft (Art. 266 StGB)	atteinte à l'indépendance de la Confédération	attacks on the independence of the Confederation
Angriffe auf die verfassungsmässige Ordnung (Art. 275 StGB)	atteintes à l'ordre constitutionnel	attacks on the constitutional order
Anhaltung	appréhension	power to stop
Anhang (zur Jahresrechnung)	annexe (aux comptes annuels)	notes (to the financial statements)
anhängig machen	porter une affaire devant le tribunal	to bring to court, to file with a court
Anhörung des Kindes	audition de l'enfant	hearing of the child
Anhörung eines Elternteils	audition d'un parent	hearing of a parent
Anklage	accusation	indictment
Anklageerhebung	mise en accusation	bringing of charges
Anklagegrundsatz (Art. 9 StPO)	principe de l'accusation	principle of no judgment without a charge
anklagen	accuser	to indict
Anklageschrift (Art. 360 StPO)	acte d'accusation	indictment
Anlage (1)	investissement, placement	investment
Anlage (2)	installation	facilities
Anlage für Bahnnebenbetrieb	installation pour services accessoires du chemin de fer	facilities for railroad station kiosks
Anlageberatung	conseil en placement	portfolio management
Anlagefonds (D: Investmentfonds)	fonds de placement	investment fund
Anlagegrundsätze	principes d'investissement	investment principles
Anlagehorizont	horizon de placement	investment horizon (the period of time for which investors want to commit part of their assets)
Anlagepolitik	politique de placement	investment policy

Anlagerendite	rendement du placement	investment yield
Anlagestiftung	fondation de placement	investment foundation
Anlagestrategiefonds	fonds d'allocation d'actifs	asset allocation fund
Anlagevermögen	actif immobilisé	fixed assets
Anlagewährung	monnaie de placement	investment currency
Anleger	investisseur	investor
Anlehre	initiation à la profession	vocational training for young people who have not done an apprenticeship
Anleihe	emprunt	bond
Anleihensobligation	emprunt par obligations	debenture bond
anmelden	produire	to produce
Anmeldeverfahren	procédure d'inscription	registration procedure
Anmerkung	mention	indication
Anmerkungsgrundstück (Art. 655a ZGB)	immeuble dépendant	dependent property
Annahme des Antrags	acceptation de l'offre	acceptance of the offer
Annahmevermerk (Art. 1065 OR)	mention de l'acceptation	mention of acceptance
Annuität	annuité	annuity
anrechenbares Einkommen	revenu déterminant	creditable income
Anrechnung	imputation	charge
Anrechnung der Untersuchungshaft (Art. 51 StGB)	imputation de la détention avant jugement	credit for time served
Anrechnungswert	valeur d'imputation	imputed value
Anreicherungsfonds	fonds de capitalisation	growth fund
Anries (D: Überhangsrecht)	droit aux fruits	right to the fruits
Anrufung des Gerichts	saisine du tribunal	bringing case before a court, filing a case with a court
Anschaffungskosten	frais d'acquisition	cost of acquisition
Anschlagsbrett (D: Anschlagbrett)	tableau d'affichage	bulletin board
Anschluss	participation	participation

Anschlussbeitrag	taxe de raccordement	hook-up fee, connection fee
Anschlussberufung (Art. 313 ZPO)	appel joint	cross appeal
Anschlussbeschwerde	recours joint	cross appeal (to the Federal Supreme Court)
Anschlussgebühr	taxe de raccordement	connection fee
Anschlussgläubiger	créancier participant	participating creditor
Anschlussklage (Art. 111 SchKG)	action en participation	action for participation
Anschlusspfändung	participation à la saisie	subordinate seizure
Anschwärzung	dénigrement	denigration
Ansprache	revendication	recovery, replevin
ansprechen	revendiquer	to reclaim, to recover
Anspruch auf Einbürgerung	droit à la naturalisation	right to naturalization
Anspruch auf ein schickliches Begräbnis	droit à un enterrement décent	right to a decent burial
Anspruch auf einen Entscheid	droit d'obtenir une décision	right to a decision
Anspruch auf Grundschuldunterricht (Art. 19 BV)	droit à un enseignement de base	right to basic education
Anspruch auf Kenntnis der Abstammung	droit de connaître son ascendance	right to know one's origins
Anspruch auf persönliche Teilnahme an der Verhandlung	droit d'être présent à l'audience	right to be present at the hearing
Anspruch auf Primarschulunterricht	droit à l'instruction primaire	right to elementary education
Anspruch auf rechtliches Gehör (Art. 29 BV)	droit d'être entendu	right to be heard
Anspruch auf unverfälschte Willenskundgabe (Art. 34 BV)	droit à une expression non falsifiée de la volonté	right to give genuine expression to one's intent
Anspruch aus Verwendungen (Art. 65 OR)	droit résultant des impenses	right in respect of expenditures
Anspruch der unverheirateten Mutter	droit de la mère non mariée	right of unmarried mothers

Anspruchsdauer	durée du droit à la prestation d'assurance	duration of the right to insurance benefits
Anspruchsvoraussetzung	condition du droit à la prestation d'assurance	prerequisite to the right to insurance benefits
Anstalt	établissement	establishment
Anstaltsaufenthalt	séjour dans un établissement	stay in an establishment
Anstaltsinsasse	pensionnaire d'un établissement	prison inmate
Anstellung	engagement	hiring
Anstiftung (Art. 24 StGB)	instigation	incitement, instigation
Anstösser (D: Anlieger)	riverain	resident
Anteilschein	titre de part social	unit certificate
antizipierte Beweiswürdigung	appréciation anticipée des preuves	anticipated assessment of the evidence (the court can refuse evidence when it feels that it is sufficiently informed and anticipates that the evidence offered would not change its opinion)
antizipierte Ersatzvornahme	mesure anticipée d'exécution par substitution	anticipated substitutive measure
Antrag des Staatsanwaltes	réquisitoire	oral arguments by the prosecutor
Antrag mit Annahmefrist (Art. 3 OR)	offre avec délai pour accepter	offer with time limit for acceptance
Antrag mit Vorbehalt des Widerrufs	offre sous réserve de retrait	offer subject to withdrawal
Antrag ohne Verbindlichkeit (Art. 7 OR)	offre sans engagement	nonbinding offer
Antrag und Annahme	offre et acceptation	offer and acceptance (to form a contract)
Antrag zu Vertragsabschluss	offre de contracter	offer to contract
Antragsdelikt	infraction poursuivie sur plainte	offense prosecuted only at the victim's request (such as negligent assault)
Antragsteller (Offerent) (Art. 7 OR)	auteur de l'offre	offeror
anvertraute Sache	chose confiée	entrusted item of property
anwaltliche Vertretung	représentation par un avocat	representation by a lawyer, representation by counsel

Anwaltsbüro	étude d'avocat	law firm
Anwaltskammer	chambre des avocats	bar association
Anwaltspatent (D: Anwaltszulassung)	brevet d'avocat	admission to the bar, license to practice law
Anwaltsrecht	droit de la profession d'avocat	attorney liability law
Anwartschaft	expectative	expectancy, right of future enjoyment
Anwartschaft auf eine Rente	expectative d'une pension	expectancy of a pension
anwartschaftlich	de réversion	reversionary
Anwartschaftsdeckungsverfahren	méthode de capitalisation	capitalization method
Anwartschaftsrecht	droit expectatif	reversionary interest
Anwartschaftsrente	rente viagère à paiement différé	reversionary annuity
Anweisender (Art. 467 OR)	assignant	principal
Anweisung (Art. 466-471 OR)	assignation	payment instruction, authorization to pay a third party
Anweisung an Zahlungsstatt (Art. 131 Abs. 1 SchKG)	dation en paiement	donation in lieu of payment, accord and satisfaction
Anweisung zur Eintreibung	remise à l'encaissement	handover of a security (for debt collection)
Anweisungsempfänger (Art. 467 OR)	assignataire	payee
anwendbares Recht	droit applicable	governing law
Anwendbarkeit	applicabilité	applicability
Anwesenheit	présence	presence
Anzahlung	acompte	payment on account, down payment
Anzehrung des Kindesvermögens (Art. 320 ZGB)	prélèvements sur les biens de l'enfant	drawing on the child's assets
Anzeige	avis	notice, notification
Anzeige an den Schuldner (Art. 120 SchKG)	avis au débiteur	notice to the debtor
Anzeige an die Beteiligten (Art. 139 SchKG)	avis aux intéressés	notice to the interested parties
Anzeige an die Gläubiger (Art. 233 SchKG)	avis aux créanciers	notice to creditors
Anzeige an Mieter und Pächter (Art. 152 SchKG)	avis aux locataires et aux fermiers	notice to lessees

Anzeigepflicht	avis obligatoire	duty of disclosure, duty to give notice, duty to notify
A-Post	courrier A	mail delivered on the following day
Apostille	apostille	apostille
Appellation	appel	appeal
Appellationsbegründung	moyens d'appel	grounds for appeal
Appellationsgericht	cour d'appel	court of appeals, appellate court
appellatorisch	appellatoire	unsubstantiated
Appellentscheid	décision incitative	court decision asking the legislature to change the law in question
Appenzell Ausserrhoden (AR)	Appenzell Rhodes-Extérieures (AR)	Appenzell Outer Rhodes (canton)
Appenzell Innerrhoden (AI)	Appenzell Rhodes-Intérieures (AI)	Appenzell Inner Rhodes (canton)
Äquivalenzprinzip	principe de l'équivalence	benefit principle
Arbeit	travail	work, labor
Arbeit auf Abruf	travail sur appel	shift-based work
Arbeitgeber	employeur	employer
Arbeitgeberbeitrag	cotisation de l'employeur	employer's contribution (to social security)
Arbeitgeberbescheinigung	attestation de l'employeur	employer's certificate
Arbeitgeberhaftung	responsabilité de l'employeur (AVS)	employer liability
Arbeitgeberverband	association d'employeurs	employers association
Arbeitnehmer	travailleur	employee
Arbeitnehmeraktie	action remise au salarié	employee share, employee stock
Arbeitnehmerbeitrag	cotisation du travailleur	employee contribution (to social security)
Arbeitnehmereigenschaft	qualité de salarié	capacity as employee
Arbeitsamt	office du travail	employment office
Arbeitsausfall	perte de travail	loss of working hours
Arbeitsbedingungen	conditions de travail	working conditions
Arbeitsbesuch	visite de travail	working visit
Arbeitsbewilligung	autorisation de travail	work permit
Arbeitsentgelt (Art. 83 StGB)	rémunération	wages

Arbeitserziehung	éducation au travail	vocational training
Arbeitserziehungsanstalt	maison d'éducation au travail	vocational training institution
Arbeitsgericht	tribunal des prud'hommes	Labor Court
Arbeitsgesetz	Loi sur le travail	Labor Act
Arbeitskräftemangel	pénurie de main d'œuvre	labor shortage, tight labor market
Arbeitslosenentschädigung (D: Arbeitslosengeld)	indemnité de chômage	unemployment benefit
Arbeitslosenkasse	caisse de chômage	unemployment office
Arbeitslosenpolitik	politique en matière de chômage	unemployment policy
Arbeitslosenversicherung (ALV)	assurance-chômage (AC)	unemployment insurance (mandatory for all employees and withheld from monthly paycheck)
Arbeitslosenversicherungsgesetz (AVIG)	Loi sur l'assurance-chômage (LACI)	Unemployment Insurance Act
Arbeitslosenversicherungsverordnung (AVIV)	Ordonnance sur l'assurance-chômage (OACI)	Unemployment Insurance Ordinance
Arbeitslosigkeit	chômage	unemployment
Arbeitsmarkt	marché du travail	labor market
Arbeitsort	lieu de travail	place of work
Arbeitsplatz	place de travail (F : emploi)	job
Arbeitsrecht	droit du travail	labor law
Arbeitsrichter	prud'homme	labor court judge
Arbeitsscheu	fainéantise	work shyness
Arbeitssicherheit	sécurité du travail	safety at work
Arbeitsüberlastung	surcharge de travail	overwork
Arbeitsunfähigkeit	incapacité de travail	disability
Arbeitsunfähigkeitsgrad	degré de l'incapacité de travail	degree of disability
Arbeitsvermittlung	placement de personnel	recruitment

Arbeitsvermittlungsgesetz (AVG)	Loi sur le service de l'emploi et la location de services (LSE)	Recruitment Act
Arbeitsvermittlungsverordnung (AVV)	Ordonnance sur le service de l'emploi (OSE)	Recruitment Ordinance
Arbeitsvertrag (Art. 319-362 OR)	contrat de travail	employment agreement
Arbeitsweg	trajet pour se rendre au travail	commute, way to work
Arbeitszeit	durée et horaire de travail	working hours
Arbeitszeugnis	certificat de travail	certificate of employment
Arbitrage (Börse)	arbitrage	arbitrage
Arglist	astuce	malice, fraud
arglistige Vermögensschädigung (Art. 151 StGB)	atteinte astucieuse aux intérêts pécuniaires	maliciously causing financial loss to another
Armee (Art. 58 BV)	armée	armed forces
Armengenössiger (D: Sozialhilfeempfänger)	personne à l'assistance	welfare recipient
Arrest (Art. 271 ff. SchKG)	séquestre	attachment (of money in a bank account)
Arrestaufhebungsklage (Art. 279 SchKG)	action en contestation du cas de séquestre	action challenging the attachment
Arrestbefehl (Art. 274 SchKG)	ordonnance de séquestre	attachment order
Arrestbegehren	réquisition de séquestre	application for attachment
Arrestbehörde	autorité de séquestre	attachment authority
Arrestbewilligung (Art. 272 SchKG)	autorisation de séquestre	authorization to attach
Arresteinsprache	opposition au séquestre	objection to an attachment
Arrestforderung	demande de séquestre	claim for attachment of assets
Arrestgegenstand	objet séquestré	attached asset
Arrestgesuch	réquisition de séquestre	application for attachment of assets
Arrestgläubiger	créancier séquestrant	attaching creditor
Arrestgrund (Art. 271 SchKG)	cas de séquestre	ground for attachment
Arrestierbarkeit	séquestrabilité	attachability

Arrestkosten (Art. 281 Abs. 2 SchKG)	frais du séquestre	costs of attachment
Arrestprosequierung (Art. 279 SchKG)	validation de séquestre	ratification of the attachment
Arrestprosequierungsklage	action en validation de séquestre	action for ratification of the attachment
Arrestschuldner	débiteur séquestré	attached debtor
Arresturkunde (Art. 276 SchKG)	procès-verbal de séquestre	attachment certificate (listing the attached assets and their estimated value)
Arrestvollzug (Art. 275 SchKG)	exécution du séquestre	attachment of the assets
Artenschutzverordnung (ASchV)	Ordonnance sur la conservation des espèces (OCE)	Species Protection Ordinance
Artikel	article	section
Assistenzdienst (Art. 67 MG)	service d'appui	assistance of civil authorities by the army
Assistenzentschädigung	allocation d'assistance	personal assistance benefits for disabled persons
Asylgesetz (AsylG)	Loi sur l'asile (LAsi)	Asylum Act
Asylgesuch (Art. 18 AsylG)	demande d'asile	application for asylum
Asylgrund	motif d'asile	ground for asylum
Asylpolitik	politique d'asile	asylum policy
Asylrecht	droit d'asile	right to asylum
Asylsuchende	requérants	asylum seekers
Asylverfahren	procédure d'asile	asylum procedure
Attentat	attentat	attack
Auditor (Militärgericht)	accusation (tribunal militaire)	prosecutor
Auengebiet	zone alluviale	wetland, flood plain
auf Bundesebene	sur le plan fédéral	at the federal level
auf eigene Gefahr	à ses risques et périls	at one's own risk
auf Gesuch hin	à demande	upon request
auf Lebenszeit	à vie	for life
auf Widerruf	à bien plaire (F : à titre précaire)	revocable
auf Zusehen hin	jusqu'à nouvel ordre	until further notice
Aufbewahrer (Art. 474 OR)	dépositaire	bailee

Aufbewahrung	conservation	safekeeping
Aufbewahrung von Geld oder Wertsachen (Art. 9 SchKG)	dépôt d'espèces et d'objets de prix	deposit of money and valuables
Aufbewahrungsfrist	délai de garde	minimum period for retaining records
Aufbrechen eines Fahrzeugs	effraction de véhicule	breaking into a vehicle
Aufenthalt	séjour	stay
Aufenthaltsbewilligung (D: Aufenthaltserlaubnis)	autorisation de séjour (F : carte de séjour)	residence permit
Aufenthaltsort	lieu de séjour	place of residence
Auffangeinrichtung	institution supplétive	substitute occupational benefit institution
Auffanggesellchaft	société de renflouement	rescue company
Aufforstung	reboisement	reforestation
Aufführungsrecht	droit de représentation	performing rights, rights to perform a play or a musical composition
Aufgabe der Erwerbstätigkeit	cessation de l'activité lucrative	stopping work
Aufgabenteilung	répartition des tâches	distribution of tasks
Aufgeld	agio, prime, report	premium (difference between the nominal value of a security and its issue or market price)
aufgeschobene Freiheitstrafe	peine privative de liberté suspendue	suspended custodial sentence
aufgeschobene Strafe	peine suspendue	suspended sentence
Aufhebung der Betreibung (Art. 85 SchKG)	annulation de la poursuite	annulment of the insolvency proceeding
Aufhebung des Aufenthaltsbestimmungsrechts (Art. 310 ZGB)	retrait du droit de déterminer le lieu de résidence	revocation of the right to decide on place of residence
Aufhebung des gemeinsamen Haushaltes (Art. 175 ZGB)	suspension de la vie commune	suspension of cohabitation
Aufhebung durch Übereinkunft (Art. 115 OR)	remise conventionnelle	extinction by agreement
Aufklärungsrate	taux d'élucidation	detection rate (percentage of offenses with respect to which one or more suspects have been identified)

Auflage (Verpflichtung)	charge (obligation)	condition
Auflage von Verteilungsliste und Schlussrechnung (Art. 263 SchKG)	dépôt du tableau de distribution et du compte final	filing of the distribution plan and the final accounting
Auflegung der Kollokationsplans (Art. 147 SchKG)	dépôt de l'état de collocation	filing of the schedule of claims
Auflösung der Gesellschaft	dissolution de la société	dissolution of a company or partnership
Auflösung des Güterstandes	dissolution du régime matrimonial	dissolution of the marital property regime
Aufnahme der Erwerbstätigkeit	début de l'activité lucrative	start date of gainful employment
Aufnahme einer Erwerbstätigkeit	prise d'une activité lucrative	taking up gainful employment
Aufnahme von Pflegekindern	placement d'enfants	placement of children in foster homes
äufnen (D: ansammeln, aufstocken, vermehren)	accumuler	to accumulate
Aufregung	excitation	incitement
Aufreizung zum Zweikampf (Art. 132 StGB)	excitation au duel	incitement to fight a duel
aufrichtige Reue (Art. 48 StGB)	repentir sincère	genuine remorse
aufschiebende Wirkung des Rechtsmittels	effet suspensif du recours	suspensive effect of an appeal (an appeal stays execution of the lower court's judgment)
Aufschub	sursis	stay, moratorium
Aufschub der Verwertung (Art. 123 SchKG)	sursis à la réalisation	deferred sale
Aufschub des Entscheides	ajournement de la décision	postponement of the decision
Aufsichtsbehörde	autorité de surveillance	supervisory authority
Aufsichtsbeschwerde (Art. 71 VwVG)	dénonciation, plainte à l'autorité de surveillance	complaint to the supervisory authority
Aufspaltung	scission	demerger
Aufstockungssicherheit	garantie complémentaire	top-up collateral
Auftrag (Art. 394-406 OR)	mandat	agency contract
Auftraggeber (1)	donneur d'ordre	client
Auftraggeber (2)	mandant	principal
Auftraggeber (3)	adjudicateur	contracting authority

Aufwand für Drittleistungen	coût de prestations de tiers	cost of purchased services
Aufwertungsgewinn	bénéfice de réévaluation	revaluation gain
Aufwertungsreserve (Art. 671b OR)	réserve de réévaluation	revaluation reserve
Aufzonung	augmentation des possibilités d'utilisation du sol	increasing the permissible uses of land
Augenschein (Art. 181-182 ZPO)	inspection locale	on-site inspection by the court
Augenscheinnahme	descente sur les lieux	visual inspection of evidence by the court
Augenzeuge	témoin oculaire	eyewitness
Ausbesserungen (Art. 259 OR)	travaux de réparation	repairs
Ausbildner (D: Ausbilder)	formateur	trainer
Ausbildungsbeitrag (Art. 66 BV)	aide à la formation	educational grant
Ausbildungskosten	frais de formation	training costs
Ausbildungszuschuss	allocation de formation	training allowance
Ausbleiben	défaut	default, failure to appear
Ausbleiben der Erfüllung	inexécution	failure to perform
ausdrücklich	expressément	expressly
Ausfall (Art. 129 Abs. 4 und 143 Abs. 2 SchKG)	moins-value sur le prix des premières enchères	depreciation of the price reached at a first auction
Ausfuhr	exportation	export
Ausführung	exécution	implementation, execution
Ausführung der Erfindung	exploitation de l'invention	reduction to practice of the invention
Ausgabe (Geld)	dépense	expense
Ausgabe (Wertpapier)	émission (papier-valeur)	issuance (of securities)
Ausgabenbewilligungskompetenz	compétence d'autoriser les dépenses	authority to authorize expenses
Ausgabenbremse	frein aux dépenses	spending brake
Ausgabepreis	prix d'émission	issue price
Ausgangspreis	prix de base	base price

ausgearbeiteter Entwurf	projet rédigé de toutes pièces	specific draft provision (as opposed to a general one)
Ausgleichsfonds	fonds de compensation	compensation fund
Ausgleichskasse	caisse de compensation	pension fund
Ausgleichung (Erbrecht) (Art. 626 ff ZGB)	rapport successoral	bringing into hotchpot (statutory heirs are required to bring into hotchpot anything that the decedent gave them during his lifetime by way of an advance on their inheritance)
Ausgrenzung	interdiction de pénétrer dans une zone	prohibition on entering an area
Aushändigung	remise	delivery
Aushebung (D: Einberufung)	recrutement	conscription
Aushilfsarbeit	travail auxiliaire	temporary work
Aushubmaterial	matériaux d'excavation	excavated material
Auskündung (Art. 7 OR)	offre publique	announcement of prices
Auskunfts- und Herausgabepflicht (Art. 222 SchKG)	obligation de renseigner et de remettre	duty to provide information and deliver assets
Auskunftsperson	tiers appelé à fournir des renseignements	person providing information
Auskunftspflicht	obligation de renseigner	duty to inform
Auslage von Waren (Art. 7 OR)	fait d'exposer des marchandises	display of merchandise
Auslagen	débours	expenses
Auslagenersatz	remboursement de frais	reimbursement of expenses
Auslagerungen	externalisation	outsourcing
Ausländer	ressortissant étranger	foreign national
Ausländerausweis	livret pour étrangers	foreign national identity card
Ausländerpolitik	politique des étrangers	immigration policy
Ausländerrecht	droit des étrangers	immigration law
Ausländerrechtsehe	mariage de nationalité	marriage entered into to obtain a residence permit

Ausländerstimmrecht (D: Ausländerwahlrecht)	droit de vote des étrangers	foreign nationals' right to vote
Auslandgeschäft	activités à l'étranger	international business
Auslandsanleihen	emprunt étranger	foreign bond
Auslandstaten (Art. 264m StGB)	actes commis à l'étranger	acts carried out abroad
Auslandswohnsitz	domicile à l'étranger	residence abroad
Auslandszulage	allocation de séjour à l'étranger	foreign assignment allowance
Auslegung	interprétation	interpretation, construction (of a law or contract)
Auslieferung (Art. 32 ff IRSG)	extradition	extradition
Auslieferung der Erbschaft (Art. 559 ZGB)	délivrance des biens	release of the estate
Auslieferungsdelikt (Art. 35 IRSG)	infraction donnant lieu à extradition, infraction extraditionnelle	extraditable offense
Auslieferungshaft	détention extraditionnelle	detention pending extradition
Auslieferungshaftbefehl (Art. 48 Abs. 2 IRSG)	mandat d'arrêt aux fins d'extradition	arrest warrant with a view to extradition
Auslobung (Art. 8 OR)	promesse publique	publicly promised remuneration
Ausmass der Baute	dimensions de la construction	dimensions of the construction
Ausnahme	exception	exception
Ausnahmegericht	tribunal d'exception	special tribunal
Ausnützung der Notlage (Art. 193 StGB)	abus de la détresse	exploitation of a person in a position of need or dependency
ausrichten (D: zahlen, auszahlen)	payer	to pay
Ausrichtung (D: Zahlung, Auszahlung)	paiement	payment
Aussage der ersten Stunde	déclaration de première heure	statement made immediately after an event
aussagen	déclarer	to testify
Aussageverweigerungsrecht	droit de garder le silence	right to remain silent
Ausschaffung	refoulement	deportation

Ausschaffungshaft	détention aux fins d'expulsion	arrest for purposes of deportation
Ausscheidung	dissociation	separation of property
Ausschlagung einer Erbschaft (Art. 566 ZGB)	répudiation d'une succession	disclaimer of an inheritance
ausschliessliche Zuständigkeit	compétence exclusive	exclusive jurisdiction
Ausschliesslichkeitsrecht	droit exclusif	exclusive right
Ausschluss	exclusion	exclusion
Ausschluss der Öffentlichkeit die Öffentlichkeit ausschliessen	huis clos prononcer le huis clos	holding a hearing in camera to hold a hearing in camera
Ausschreibung	appel d'offres (marchés publics)	request for proposals (RFP)
Ausschuss	comité	committee
Ausschüttung	distribution	distribution
Ausschüttungsrendite	rendement de distribution	distribution yield (ratio of distributed income to the current market price)
Aussenhandel (D: Außenhandel)	commerce extérieur	foreign trade
Aussenpolitik (D: Außenpolitik)	politique extérieure	foreign policy
Aussenverhältnis (D: Außenverhältnis)	rapports externes	relationships with third parties
Aussenwirtschaftspolitik (D: Außenwirtschaftspolitik) (Art. 101 BV)	politique économique extérieure	foreign economic policy
Ausserbetriebnahme	cessation de l'exploitation	decommissioning
ausserbörsliche Abschlüsse	transactions hors bourse	off-order-book trades
aussereheliches Kind (D: außereheliches Kind)	enfant né hors mariage	illegitimate child
äusserer Notstand	état de nécessité extérieure	threat of invasion, threat of attack
aussergewöhnliche Todesfälle (Art. 253 StPO)	mort suspecte	unnatural death
ausserordentliche Ersitzung (Art. 662 ZGB)	prescription extraordinaire	extraordinary adverse possession
ausserordentliche Generalversammlung (D: außerordentliche Hauptversammlung)	assemblée générale extraordinaire	special meeting of shareholders
Ausserordentlichkeit	caractère extraordinaire	exceptionality

ausserorts	à l'extérieur des localités	out of town
ausserparlamentarische Kommission	commission extra-parlementaire	extraparliamentary committee
ausserrechtlich	extrajudiciaire	out-of-court
ausserschulische Jugendarbeit	activités de jeunesse extra-scolaires	extracurricular youth activities
Aussetzen der Versteigerung (Art. 14 SchKG)	sursis aux enchères	postponement of the auction
Aussetzung (Art. 127 StGB)	exposition à un danger	abandonment
aussichtslos	voué à l'échec	hopeless, pointless, having no prospect of success
Aussonderungsklage (Art. 242 SchKG)	action en revendication de tiers	third party action
Aussonderungsrecht	droit de disjonction	right to withdraw one's property from the operation of bankruptcy
Aussperrung	lock-out	lock-out
Ausstand (Art. 47-51 ZPO, Art. 10 SchKG) Der Richter tritt in Ausstand.	récusation Le juge se récuse.	recusal The judge recuses himself.
Ausstandsgesuch (Art. 492 ZPO, Art. 58 StPO)	demande de récusation	motion to recuse
Ausstandsgrund (Art. 47 ZPO)	motif de récusation	ground for recusal
Ausstandspflicht	devoir de récusation	recusal obligation, duty to recuse oneself
Ausstattung (1)	frais d'établissement	endowment
Ausstattung (2)	présentation d'un produit	trade dress
ausstellender Staat	État émetteur	country of issue
Aussteller	tireur	drawer (of a check or draft)
Ausstellung	exposition	exhibition
Ausstellungsrecht (Art. 14 URG)	droit d'exposition	author's right of exhibition
Austritt	sortie	departure, resignation
Austrittsleistung	prestation de sortie	termination benefits
Ausübungspreis	prix d'exercice	exercise price, strike price
auswärtige Angelegenheiten (Art. 54 BV)	affaires étrangères	foreign affairs
Ausweis (D: Führerschein)	permis	driver's license

Ausweisentzug (D: Entziehung der Fahrerlaubnis)	retrait de permis	revocation of a driver's license
Ausweispapier	papier de légitimation	identification paper
Ausweisung	expulsion	deportation
Ausweisung des Mieters	expulsion de locataire	eviction of a tenant
Ausweisungsgrund	motif d'expulsion	grounds for deportation (of a foreign national), grounds for eviction (of a tenant)
Auszonung	déclassement	dezoning
Autoabbruchbetrieb	entreprise de démolition de voitures	car demolition company
Autobahnvignette	vignette autoroutière	highway sticker
Avis-Bank	banque notificatrice	advising bank (in documentary credit business, the bank that informs the beneficiary of the credit that the credit has been opened)
avisieren (D: benachrichtigen)	notifier	to notify, to advise
avisierende Bank	banque notificatrice	advising bank (in documentary credit business, the bank that informs the beneficiary of the credit that the credit has been opened)
Bagatelldelikt	infraction mineure	petty offense
Bagatelldelinquenz	petite délinquance	petty crime
Bagatellunfall	accident anodin	minor accident
Bande	bande	gang
bandenmässig	en affiliation à une bande	as a member of a gang
Bandenmässigkeit	affiliation à une bande	membership in a gang
Bankarbeitstag	jour ouvrable bancaire	banking day
Bankbürgschaft	cautionnement bancaire	bank guaranty
Bankcheck	chèque bancaire	bank check
Bankenaufsicht	surveillance des banques	bank supervision
Bankendebitoren auf Sicht	avoirs en banque à vue	sight deposits with banks

Bankendebitoren auf Zeit	avoirs en banque à terme	term deposits with banks
Bankengelder	dépôts de banques	interbank funds (funds deposited by one bank in another bank)
Bankenkonkurs	faillite bancaire	insolvency of a bank
Bankenrecht	droit bancaire	banking law
Bankenrevision	révision bancaire	bank audit
Bankenverordnung (BankV)	Ordonnance sur les banques (OB)	Banking Ordinance
Bankgarantie	garantie bancaire	bank guaranty
Bankgeheimnis	secret bancaire	bank secrecy
Bankguthaben	avoirs bancaires	bank balance
Bankier	banquier	banker
bankinternes Sondervermögen	portefeuille collectif interne de la banque	separate assets within a bank
Bankkonto	compte bancaire	bank account
Bankkundengeheimnis	secret professionnel du banquier	bank-client confidentiality
banklagernd	banque restante	held-mail service at banks
Banknote	billet de banque	banknote
Bankomat (D: Geldautomat)	bancomat (F : distributeur automatique de billets)	ATM
Barabgeltung	règlement en espèces, liquidation en espèces	cash settlement
Barabrechnung	règlement en espèces, liquidation en espèces	cash settlement
Bargründung	fondation par apport en espèces	formation by cash subscription
Barkauf	vente au comptant	cash sale
Barliberierung	libération en espèces	payment in cash
Barwerttafeln	tables de capitalisation	capitalization tables
Barzahlung	paiement comptant	cash payment

Basel-Landschaft (BL)	Bâle-Campagne (BL)	Basel-Landschaft (canton)
Basel-Stadt (BS)	Bâle-Ville (BS)	Basel-Stadt (canton)
Basispunkt	point de base	basis point (100 basis points are equal to 1%, so 1 basis point = 0.01%)
Basiswert	sous-jacent	underlying instrument
Bauarbeit	travaux de construction	construction work
Bauarbeiter	ouvrier du bâtiment	construction worker
Baubeitrag	subvention pour la construction	construction subsidy
Bauberechtigter	superficiaire	building right holder
Baubeschrieb (D: Baubeschreibung)	description de l'ouvrage	building description
Baubewilligung (D: Baugenehmigung)	permis de construire	building permit
Baubewilligungsgesuch	demande de permis de construire	application for a building permit
bäuerliches Bodenrecht	droit foncier rural	rural land rights
Baufreigabe	autorisation de commencer les travaux	authorization to commence construction work
Bauführer	chef de chantier	construction site manager
Baugewerbe	industrie de la construction	construction industry
Bauhandwerkerpfandrecht (Art. 837 Abs. 1 Ziff. 3 und Abs. 2, Art. 839 ff ZGB)	hypothèque légale des artisans et entrepreneurs	building contractor's lien
Bauherr	maître d'ouvrage	project owner (if a private company); contracting authority (if a government agency)
Bauherrenaltlast	site pollué avec projet de construction	polluted excavated material within construction projects
Baujahr	année de construction	year built
Baukosten	frais de construction	construction costs
Baukostenplan (BKP)	Code des frais de construction (CFC)	construction cost budget

Baukredit	crédit de construction	construction loan
Bauland	terrain à bâtir	building site
Bauleitung	direction des travaux	site management, site supervision
bauliche Änderung	mesure architectonique	structural alteration
bauliche Massnahmen (Art. 647c ZGB)	travaux de construction	construction work
Baulinie	alignement	building line
Baumangel	défaut de construction, vice de construction	construction defect
Baupflicht	obligation de construire	duty to build
Baurecht (1)	droit des constructions	construction law
Baurecht (2)	droit de superficie	building right
Baurechtsdienstbarkeit (Art. 779 ZGB)	droit de superficie	right to construct a building on another person's land
Baurechtszins (Art. 779i ZGB)	rente du droit de superficie	remuneration for the building right
Bausparvertrag	contrat d'épargne-logement	building loan agreement
Baustop	suspension des travaux	suspension of construction work
Baute (D: Bauwerk)	construction	building
Bauunternehmen	entreprise de construction	construction company
Bauverbot	interdiction de bâtir	ban on construction
Bauverbotsdienstbarkeit	servitude de non-bâtir	easement not to build
Bauwerkvertrag	contrat de construction	construction agreement
Bauwesenversicherung	assurance des risques de la construction	builders' risk insurance
Bauzinsen (Art. 627 OR)	intérêts intercalaires	interest paid to shareholder until commencement of company's operations
Bauzone	zone à bâtir	building zone
Beamter	fonctionnaire	public official

beanstanden	s'opposer, formuler des objections	to object to, to reject
Beauftragte für Gleichstellung	Déléguée à l'égalité	Office for Gender Equality
Beauftragter	mandataire	agent, representative
bedingt entlassen	libérer conditionnellem ent	to release on parole
bedingte Begnadigung	grâce conditionnelle	conditional pardon
bedingte Busse (D: Buße)	amende avec sursis	suspended fine
bedingte Entlassung (Art. 62 StGB)	libération conditionnelle	parole
bedingte Kapitalerhöhung (Art. 653 OR)	augmentation conditionnelle	contingent capital increase
bedingte Strafe (Art. 42 StGB)	sursis à l'exécution de la peine	suspended sentence
bedingte Strafmündigkeit	majorité pénale limitée	limited criminal responsibility
bedingte Verurteilung	condamnation avec sursis	conviction with suspended sentence
bedingter Strafvollzug	sursis à l'exécution de la peine	suspended sentence
Bedingung	condition	condition
Bedürfnis	besoin	need
Bedürftigkeit	dénuement	neediness, poverty, indigence
befinden – über etwas befinden	se prononcer sur quelque chose	to decide, to rule on something
beförderlich (D: beschleunigt, rasch)	rapide	quick, fast
Beförderungsdienst	service d'avancement	promotion service
Befreiung von Gefangenen (Art. 310 StGB)	faire évader des détenus	helping prisoners escape
befriedigen – einen Gläubiger befriedigen	désintéresser un créancier	to pay a creditor, to satisfy a creditor's claims
befristete Lizenz	licence temporaire	temporary license
befristete Rente	rente temporaire	temporary annuity
befristete Verbindlichkeit	obligation à terme	obligation subject to a time limit

befristeter Vertrag	contrat de durée déterminée (F : contrat à durée déterminée	fixed-term employment agreement
Begehren	requête, demande, réquisition	petition, motion, application
Begehungsdelikt	délit de commission	crime of commission
Begehungsort (Art. 8 StGB)	lieu de commission	place of commission (of a crime)
beglaubigte Abschrift	copie certifiée conforme	certified copy
Beglaubigung	légalisation, attestation authentique	certification
Begleitbeistandschaft (Art. 393 ZGB)	curatelle d'accompagnem ent	assistance curatorship
begleitende Marke	marque associée	associated trademark
begnadigen	gracier	to pardon
Begnadigung	grâce	pardon, clemency
Begnadigungsgesuch	recours en grâce	petition for clemency
Begrenzung der Zahl der Ausländer	limitation du nombre des étrangers	limitation on the number of foreigners
Begriff	notion	concept
Begriff der Doppelbesteuerung	notion de double imposition	concept of double taxation
Begründer eines Fideikommisses	fidéicommettant	settlor (of a trust)
begründeter Verdacht	bonnes raisons de soupçonner	justified suspicion
Begründung der Eingabe	motivation de la demande	grounds for the request
Begründung des Entscheids	motivation de la décision	grounds for the decision
Begründungspflicht	obligation de motiver	obligation to state the grounds (for a decision)
begünstigen	favoriser	to favor
Begünstigter	bénéficiaire	beneficiary
Begünstigung (1) (Gabe)	libéralité	gift
Begünstigung (2) (Strafrecht)	entrave à l'action pénale	aiding and abetting (an offender)
Begünstigung der Unzucht	favoriser la débauche	permitting the use of rented premises for professional procuring
begutachten	expertiser	to assess, to evaluate

Begutachtung	expertise	expert opinion
Behandlung von psychischen Störungen (Art. 59 StGB)	traitement des troubles mentaux	treatment of mental disorders
Behandlungsvertrag	contrat de soins	treatment contract
behaupten	affirmer, alléguer, prétendre	to claim, to allege
Behelf (D: Anleitung)	aide-mémoire	instructions, guide
beherrschende Stellung	position dominante	dominant position
Behörde	autorité	authority
Behördenbeschwerde (Art. 56 USG)	droit de recours de l'autorité	public authority appeal
Behördenreferendum	référendum demandé par l'autorité	referendum requested by the authorities
behördliche Aufsicht	surveillance étatique	regulatory supervision
Beihilfe zum Selbstmord (Art. 115 StGB)	assistance au suicide	assisted suicide
Beilage (D: Anlage)	annexe	exhibit (to a document)
Beilagenverzeichnis	liste des annexes	list of exhibits (to a document)
Beirat	conseil consultatif	board of advisors
Beisitzer (BS)	juge assesseur	advisor
Beisitzer des Friedengerichts	assesseur de la justice de paix	assessor to the justice of the peace
Beistand (D: Pfleger) (Art. 392-393 ZGB)	curateur	curator (unlike a guardian, a curator is appointed to deal with a specific matter or to take care of property)
Beistandschaft (D: Pflegschaft) (Art. 308 f., 325 und 390 ff. ZGB)	curatelle	curatorship
Beistandschaft auf eigenes Begehren	curatelle volontaire	voluntary curatorship
Beitrag (1)	cotisation	contribution
Beitrag (2) (D: Zuschuss)	subvention	subsidy
Beitragsperiode	période de cotisations	contribution period
Beitragspflicht	obligation de cotiser	duty to contribute

Beitragsprimat	primauté des cotisations	defined contribution plan (financing system in which the pension plan's benefits are based on contributions equaling a certain percentage of the pensionable salary)
Beitragszeit (ALV)	période de cotisation (AC)	contribution period
beiziehen (D: hinzuziehen, heranziehen)	faire appel à	to consult
Beizug (D: Hinzuziehung)	appel à, recours à	consultation of
bekannter Wohnsitz	domicile connu	known address
Bekanntgabe	publication	publication, public notice
Bekanntmachung	publication	publication, public notice
Bekanntmachung der Konkurseröffnung (Art. 232 SchKG)	publication de l'ouverture de la faillite	public notice of the opening of bankruptcy proceedings
Beklagter	défendeur	defendant
beklagtische Beilage (BB)	annexe du défendeur	defendant's exhibit
belasteter Boden (Art. 7 Abs. 4bis USG)	sol dégradé	polluted soil
belasteter Standort	site pollué	polluted site
belastetes Grundstück	fonds servant	servient tenement
Belastung	grèvement	encumbrance
Belastungszeuge	témoin à charge	witness for the prosecution
Beleidigung	insulte	insult
Beleidigung eines fremden Staates (Art. 296 StGB)	outrages aux États étrangers	insulting a foreign state
Beleidigung zwischenstaatlicher Organisationen (Art. 297 StGB)	outrages à des institutions interétatiques	insulting an international organization
beliebt machen: ich möchte Ihnen beliebt machen, diesen Vorschlag nicht zu unterstützen.	encourager : je voudrais vous encourager à ne pas appuyer cette proposition.	to encourage, to urge: I would encourage (urge) you not to support this proposal.
Belohnung	récompense	reward
Bemessung der Kausalabgabe	calcul de la contribution causale	calculation of tax for services rendered
Benützung (D: Benutzung)	utilisation	use
beratende Stimme	voix consultative	advisory capacity
Beratung zur Urteilsfindung	délibéré	deliberation

Beratungsvertrag	contrat de consultant	consultant agreement
berechnen	calculer	to calculate
Berechnung	calcul, supputation	calculation
Berechnungsgrundlage	base de calcul	basis for calculation
Berechnungsperiode	période de calcul	calculation period
berechtigtes Grundstück	fonds dominant	dominant tenement
Bereicherung	enrichissement	enrichment
Bereicherungsabsicht	dessein d'enrichissement	acting for financial gain
Bereicherungsanspruch	prétention fondée sur l'enrichissement illégitime	claim based on unjust enrichment
Bereicherungsklage	action en enrichissement illégitime	action based on unjust enrichment
Bereitschaftsdienst	service de permanence	after-hours service
Bergregal	régale des mines	right of ownership of untapped mineral resources
Bergwerk	mine	mine
Bericht	rapport	report
Berichterstatter	rapporteur	reporter
Berichterstattung	reportage	reporting
Berichtigung	rectification	correction
Berichtigungsgesuch	demande de rectification	motion to correct the court's decision
Berichtigungsklage	action en rectification	action to have an employment record corrected
Bern (BE)	Berne (BE)	Bern (canton and city)
Beruf	profession	profession
berufliche Fähigkeit	qualification professionnelle	professional qualification
berufliche Vorsorge (Art. 113 BV)	prévoyance professionnelle	pension plan (A company pension plan is mandatory for all employees and is the second pillar of the Swiss social security system. The fund may be operated by the company, a professional association or an insurance company.)
beruflicher Wiedereinstieg	réintégration professionnelle	rejoining the workforce

Berufsausbildungskurs	cours de formation professionnelle	vocational training course
Berufsausübungsbewilligung	autorisation d'exercer	license to practice a profession
Berufsberatung	orientation professionnelle	career counseling
Berufsgeheimnis	secret professionnel	professional privilege
Berufsgeheimnisträger	personne soumise au secret professionnel	person subject to a professional duty of confidentiality
Berufs-Haftpflichtversicherung	assurance de responsabilité civile professionnelle	professional liability insurance
Berufslehre	apprentissage (formation professionnelle)	apprenticeship
Berufsmaturität	maturité professionnelle	diploma of vocational training
Berufsunfall	accident professionnel	occupational accident
Berufsverband	association professionnelle	trade association
Berufsverbot	interdiction d'exercer une profession	prohibition on practicing a profession
Berufswechsel	changement de profession	change of profession
Berufung (Art. 308-318 ZPO) Die Berufung steht offen	appel L'appel est ouvert	appeal The appeal lies
Berufung auf eigenes Unrecht	exception de position mal acquise	defense that the plaintiff is pleading his own immoral or illegal conduct
Berufungsantwort (BA) (Art. 312 ZPO)	réponse	respondent's answer on appeal
berufungsfähig	appelable	appealable
Berufungskläger	appelant	appellant
Berufungsschrift	mémoire d'appel	appellate brief
Berufungsverfahren	procédure d'appel	appellate procedure
berühmte Marke (Art. 15 MSchG)	marque de haute renommée	famous trademark

Beschaffungsdelikt	infraction liée à l'acquisition de stupéfiants	drug-related offense
Beschäftigungsbeitrag	subvention pour l'emploi temporaire	subsidy for temporary employment
Beschäftigungsgrad	taux d'occupation	level of employment
Beschäftigungspflicht	droit d'être occupé	right to be employed (until the end of the employment agreement)
Bescheinigung	attestation	certificate
Beschenkter (Art. 241 OR)	donataire	donee
Beschimpfung (Art. 177 StGB)	injure	insult
Beschlagnahme	séquestre (mesure provisionnelle)	seizure, confiscation
beschleunigtes Verfahren	procédure accélérée	accelerated procedure
Beschleunigungsgebot	principe de la célérité	right to a speedy trial
Beschlüsse über dringliche Frage (Art. 238 SchKG)	résolutions d'urgence	decisions on urgent matters
beschränkte Haftung	responsabilité limitée	limited liability
beschränktes dingliches Recht (Art. 261a OR)	droit réel limité	limited right in rem
Beschränkung	limitation	limitation
Beschuldigter (Art. 111 StPO)	prévenu	person charged, defendant, the accused
Beschwerde (1) (D: Revision) (Art. 319-327a ZPO) eine Beschwerde einlegen	recours interjeter recours	appeal (to the Federal Supreme Court) to file an appeal
Beschwerde (2) (SchKG)	plainte (LP)	complaint
Beschwerde an die Aufsichtsbehörde (Art. 17 SchKG)	plainte à l'autorité de surveillance	complaint to the supervisory authority
Beschwerde an die obere Aufsichtsbehörde (Art. 18 SchKG)	plainte à l'autorité supérieure de surveillance	complaint to the higher supervisory authority
Beschwerde an die Vormundschaftsbehörde	recours à l'autorité tutélaire	appeal to the guardianship authority
Beschwerde in öffentlich-rechtlichen Angelegenheiten	recours en matière de droit public	public law appeal

Beschwerde in Strafsachen	recours en matière pénale	appeal in criminal cases
Beschwerde in Zivilsachen	recours en matière civile	appeal in civil cases
Beschwerdeantwort	réponse au recours	answer to the appeal
Beschwerdebefugnis	qualité pour recourir	standing to appeal, right to appeal
Beschwerdeentscheid (Art. 61 VwVG)	décision sur recours	appeal decision, decision on appeal
Beschwerdefrist	délai de recours	deadline for an appeal
Beschwerdeführer	recourant	appellant
Beschwerdegegner	intimé	appellee
Beschwerdegrund	motif du recours	ground for the appeal
Beschwerdeinstanz	autorité de recours	appellate authorities
Beschwerdekammer des Bundesstrafgerichts	Cour des plaintes du Tribunal pénal fédéral	Appeals Chamber of the Federal Criminal Court
Beschwerdelegitimation	qualité pour recourir	standing to appeal
Beschwerderückzug	retrait du recours	withdrawal of the appeal
Beschwerdeschrift	mémoire de recours	appellate brief
Beschwerdeverfahren	procédure de recours	appellate proceedings
Beseitigung von Sicherheitsvorrichtungen (Art. 230 StGB)	supprimer des appareils protecteurs	removal of safety devices
Beseitigungsklage (Art. 28a Abs. 1 ZGB)	action en cessation de trouble	action to have violence, threats or harassment cease
Besitz (Art. 919-941 ZGB)	possession	possession
Besitzanweisung (Art. 924 Abs. 1 ZGB)	délégation de possession	transfer of possession with physical delivery
Besitzdiener	possesseur pour autrui	possessor's agent
Besitzer	possesseur	possessor
Besitzerwerb	acquisition de la possession	acquisition of possession
Besitzesentziehungsklage (Art. 927 ZGB)	réintégrande	action to recover possession (by someone who has been unlawfully dispossessed)
Besitzesstörung (D: Besitzstörung)	trouble de la possession	trespass, disturbance of possession

Besitzvertrag	contrat possessoire	possessory contract
besondere Zuständigkeit	compétence spéciale	special jurisdiction
besonders gekreuzter Check (Art. 1124 OR)	chèque à barrement spécial	specially crossed check
besonders schützenswerte Personendaten	données sensibles	sensitive data
besorgt: für etwas besorgt sein (D: für etwas sorgen)	s'occuper de quelque chose	to take care of something
Besserungsschein	bon de récupération	debtor warrant (written promise from a debtor to make periodic payments to a creditor, with the payments being contingent on the profits generated by the debtor's company, thus compensating the creditor for not enforcing his right to have a restructuring program imposed on the debtor)
Bestandteil	partie intégrante	integral part
bestätigende Bank	banque confirmatrice	confirming bank
Bestätigung des Nachlassvertrages (Art. 306 SchKG)	homologation du concordat	ratification of the debt restructuring agreement
Bestätigung, dass keine Beschwerde eingegangen ist	attestation de non-recours	certificate that no appeal has been filed
Bestätigungsentscheid (Art. 306 ff. SchKG)	décision d'homologation du concordat	decision ratifying the debt restructuring agreement
Bestätigungsschreiben	lettre de confirmation	letter of confirmation
bestechen – sich bestechen lassen (Art. 322quater StGB)	corruption passive	acceptance of bribes
Bestechen (Art. 322ter StGB)	corruption active	bribery
Bestechung (Art. 322ter StGB)	corruption	bribery
Bestechung bei Zwangsvollstreckung (Art. 168 StGB)	subornation dans l'exécution forcée	subornation in enforcement proceedings
Bestechung fremder Amtsträger (Art. 322septies StGB)	corruption active d'agents publics étrangers	bribery of foreign public officials
Bestechung schweizerischer Amtsträger (Art. 322ter StGB)	corruption active d'agents publics suisses	bribery of Swiss public officials

bestehende Baute	construction existante	existing construction
Bestelltalon	bulletin de commande	order form
Bestellung	commande	order
Bestellung von Sicherheit	remise de sûretés	provision of collateral, furnishing of collateral
Besteuerung nach wirtschaftlicher Leistungsfähigkeit	imposition selon la capacité économique	taxation in accordance with ability to pay
Bestimmbarkeit	déterminabilité	determinability
Bestimmungslandprinzip	principe du pays de destination	taxation in the destination country
Bestimmungsort	lieu de destination	place of destination
bestrafen	punir	to punish
Bestrafung	punition	punishment
bestreiten	contester	to challenge
Bestreitung	contestation	challenge
Bestreitung der Verrechnung (Art. 214 SchKG)	contestation de la compensation	challenge to the setoff
Bestreitung der Verwertung (Art. 132a SchKG)	contestation de la réalisation	challenge to the realization
Bestreitung des Kollokationsplans (Art. 148 und 250 SchKG)	contestation de l'état de collocation	challenge to the schedule of claims
Bestreitung des Lastenverzeichnisses	contestation de l'état des charges	challenge to the schedule of charges
bestrittene Forderung (Art. 305 Abs. 3, Abs. 2 und 325 SchKG)	créance contestée	contested claim
Besuchsrecht	droit de visite	visitation rights
Betagter	personne âgée	elderly person
Betäubungsmittel	stupéfiant	narcotic
Betäubungsmittelbesitz	détention de stupéfiants	possession of narcotics
Betäubungsmittelgesetz (BetmG)	Loi fédérale sur les stupéfiants (LStup)	Narcotics Act
Betäubungsmittelkonsum	consommation de stupéfiants	consumption of narcotics
Betäubungsmittelkontroll-verordnung (BetmKV)	Ordonnance sur contrôle des stupéfiants (OCStup)	Narcotics Control Ordinance
Betäubungsmittelmissbrauch	abus de stupéfiants	abuse of narcotics

Beteiligung	participation	participation
Beteiligungsertrag	rendement des participations	income from investments
Beteiligungsgewinnsteuer	impôt sur les gains sur participation	capital gains tax on corporate equity
Betrag	montant	amount
Betreffnis (D: Quote, Betrag)	part, montant	portion, share, amount
betreiben (D: beitreiben)	poursuivre	to collect, to sue to recover
Betreibung (D: Beitreibung)	poursuite	debt collection (legal action to enforce payment in cash or the provision of cash coverage by a debtor who fails to meet his payment obligations)
Betreibung auf Konkurs (Art. 159 ff. SchKG)	poursuite par voie de faillite	debt collection via bankruptcy proceedings (legal action to enforce the sale of all assets of a debtor who fails to meet his payment obligations)
Betreibung auf Pfändung (Art. 89 ff. SchKG)	poursuite par voie de saisie	debt collection via seizure of assets
Betreibung auf Pfandverwertung (Art. 151 ff. SchKG)	poursuite en réalisation de gage	debt collection via sale of pledged assets (legal action to enforce debt recovery under claims secured by pledged collateral, requiring the sale of the property in question)
Betreibungsamt (Art. 2 SchKG)	office des poursuites	debt collection authority
Betreibungsbeamter (Art. 2 SchKG)	préposé aux poursuites	debt collection official
Betreibungsbegehren (Art. 67 und 151 SchKG)	réquisition de poursuite	debt collection petition, petition to open debt collection proceedings
Betreibungsdelikt	infraction dans la poursuite pour dettes	debt collection offense
Betreibungsfähigkeit (SchKG)	qualité pour poursuivre	standing to sue
Betreibungsferien (Art. 56 ff. SchKG)	féries de poursuite	days exempt from debt collection proceedings
Betreibungshandlung (Art. 56 SchKG)	acte de poursuite	debt collection proceeding
Betreibungskosten (Art. 68 SchKG)	frais de poursuite	costs of debt collection proceedings

Betreibungskreis (Art. 1 ff. SchKG)	arrondissement de poursuite	district
Betreibungsort (Art. 46 ff. SchKG)	for de la poursuite	place of debt collection, competent debt collection office
Betreibungsrecht	droit des poursuites	debt collection law
Betreibungsregister (SchKG)	registre des poursuites	debt collection register
Betreibungsverbrechen (Art. 163 StGB)	crimes dans la faillite et la poursuite pour dettes	debt collection felonies
Betreibungsweibel	huissier aux poursuites	process server in debt collection proceedings
Betreuer	agent de probation	probation officer
betreute Person	personne assistée	probationer
Betreuung	assistance, encadrement social	social assistance
Betriebene	débiteur poursuivi	debtor (whose debt is being collected)
betrieblicher Nebenerfolg	autres produits d'exploitation	other operating income
Betriebsaufwand	charges d'exploitation	operating expenses
Betriebsertrag	produits d'exploitation	operating income
betriebsfremder Aufwand	charges hors exploitation	nonoperating expenses
betriebsfremder Ertrag	produits hors exploitation	nonoperating income
Betriebsgefahr	risque inhérent à l'emploi	inherent risk, inherent danger
Betriebs-Haftpflichtversicherung	assurance de responsabilité civile d'entreprise	business third-party insurance
Betriebsinhaber	propriétaire d'entreprise	business owner
Betriebskosten	frais d'exploitation	operating expenses, business expenses
Betriebsleitung	direction de l'entreprise	company management
Betriebsordnung	règlement d'entreprise	internal company regulations

Betriebsrisiko	risque d'exploitation	operational risk
Betriebsstandort	aire d'exploitation	company site
Betriebsstätte	établissement stable	permanent establishment
Betriebsunterbrechungs-Versicherung	assurance d'interruption d'exploitation	business interruption insurance
Betriebsunterbruch (D: Betriebsunterbrechung)	interruption de l'exploitation	business interruption
betroffene Person	personne concernée	person in question
Betrug (Art. 146 StGB)	escroquerie	fraud
betrügen	escroquer	to defraud
betrügerischer Konkurs (Art. 163 StGB)	banqueroute frauduleuse	fraudulent bankruptcy
betrügerischer Markengebrauch (Art. 62 MSchG)	usage frauduleux d'une marque	fraudulent use of a trademark
betrügerischer Missbrauch einer Datenverarbeitungsanlage (Art. 147 StGB)	utilisation frauduleuse d'un ordinateur	computer fraud
Bettag	Jeûne fédéral	Federal Day of Thanksgiving, Repentance and Prayer
Bettel (D: Betteln)	mendicité	begging
Bevölkerung	population	population
Bevollmächtigung	octroi des pouvoirs	grant of a power of attorney
Bevorzugung eines Gläubigers (Art. 167 StGB)	avantage accordé à un créancier	undue preference of a creditor
bewaffneter Konflikt	conflit armé	armed conflict
bewährte Lehre	solutions consacrées par la doctrine	settled legal scholarship
Bewährung (Art. 45 StGB)	succès de la mise à l'épreuve	successful completion of probation
Bewährungshelfer	agent de probation	probation officer
Bewährungshilfestelle	service de probation	probation service
Beweggrund	mobile	motive
bewegliche Sache	chose mobilière	chattel, movable property
Beweis	preuve	proof, evidence
Beweisabnahme (Art. 231 ZPO)	administration des preuves	taking evidence, taking of evidence
Beweisantrag	offre de preuve	offer of evidence

Beweisausforschung	requête exploratoire	fishing expedition
Beweisaussage (Art. 192 ZPO)	déposition des parties	giving evidence, testifying
Beweiseofferte (BO)	offre de preuve	offer of evidence
Beweiskraft	force probante	probative force
Beweislast	fardeau de la preuve, charge de la preuve	burden of proof, onus probandi
Beweislasterleichterung	allègement du fardeau de la preuve	reduced burden of proof
Beweislastumkehr	renversement du fardeau de la preuve	reversal of the burden of proof
Beweismass	degré de la preuve	degree of proof
Beweismittel	moyen de preuve	evidence
Beweissicherung	conservation de la preuve	preservation of evidence
Beweisurkunde (Art. 784 OR)	titre de preuve	evidentiary document
Beweisverfahren	procédure probatoire	evidentiary proceedings
Beweisverwertungsverbot	preuve illicite	unlawful evidence
Beweiswürdigung	appréciation des preuves	evaluation of the evidence
Bewilligung	autorisation, octroi	authorization, grant
Bewilligung der Nachlassstundung (Art. 295 SchKG)	octroi du sursis	granting of the stay
Bewilligungsentzug	retrait de l'autorisation	withdrawal of the authorization, withdrawal of the permit
bewilligungspflichtige Arbeit	travaux soumis à autorisation	work subject to authorization
Bewilligungsverfahren	procédure d'autorisation	authorization procedure
bewusste Fahrlässigkeit	négligence consciente	recklessness, willful negligence
Bezeichnung des Remittenten (Art. 1105 OR)	désignation du créancier	designation of payee (of a check)
beziehungsweise (bzw.)	respectivement (resp.) (F : ou)	or
Bezirk	district	district

Bezirksgericht	tribunal de district	district court (civil court of first instance in AR, AI, BI, FR, GR, SG, SZ, TG, ZH)
Bezirksgerichtskanzlei	greffe du tribunal de district	registry of the district court
Bezirksgerichtskasse	caisse du tribunal de district	office of the district court cashier
Bezirksgerichtspräsident	président du tribunal de district	president of the district court
Bezirksgerichtsschreiber	greffier du tribunal de district	clerk of the district court
Bezogener	tiré	drawee (of a check or draft)
Bezugsrecht	droit préférentiel de souscription	preemptive right (right granted in the context of a capital increase to subscribe for new shares so as to avoid dilution of percentage ownership)
Bezugssperre	refus d'acheter des marchandises	refusal to purchase goods
Biel	Bienne	Biel/Bienne
Bieter (Versteigerung)	enchérisseur	bidder
Bijou (D: Juwel, Kleinod)	bijou	jewel
Bijoutier (D: Juwelier)	bijoutier	jeweler
Bilanz	bilan	balance sheet
Bilanzsumme	total du bilan	total assets
Bildmarke	marque figurative	figurative mark (the part of a brand that appears in the form of a symbol, picture, design, or distinctive color)
Bildungsdirektion (D: Kultusministerium)	Direction de l'éducation	Department of Education
Bildungspolitik	politique en matière de formation	educational policy
Billettsteuern	impôts sur les billets d'entrée	ticket taxes, taxes on admission tickets
Billigkeit	équité	equity, fairness
Binnenbeziehung	relation interne	internal relationship
Binnenmarkt	marché intérieur	internal market
bis anhin (D: bis jetzt)	jusqu'à présent	until now

bisheriger Wohnsitz	domicile antérieur	former address
Bittschrift	pétition	petition
Blankett	blanc-seing	blank form, blank document
Blankettnorm	blankettnorm	blanket provision of the law
Blankoindossament	endossement en blanc	blank indorsement
Blockade	blocus	blockade
Blockzeit	période de présence obligatoire	period of mandatory presence
Blutgericht	Tribunal criminel	criminal court
Blutprobe	prise de sang	blood sample
Boden	sol	soil
Bodenaushub	matériaux terreux	excavated soil
Bodenbelastung	charge du sol en polluants	soil pollution
Bodenpolitik	politique foncière	land policy
Bodenspekulation	spéculation foncière	land speculation
Bodenverschiebung (Art. 660 ZGB)	glissement de terrain	landslide
Bonität	solvabilité	credit rating (of a fund)
Bonitätsrisiko	risque de solvabilité	credit rating risk
Bonitierung	taxation	land appraisal
Bord (D: Böschung)	talus	embankment
Borger (Art. 312-318 OR)	emprunteur	borrower
Börse	bourse	stock market, stock exchange
Börsenabrechnung	décompte de bourse	securities trading statement (statement sent by a bank to its customers when securities are traded)
Börsenaufsicht	surveillance des bourses	stock market supervision
börsengehandelte Option	option cotée en bourse, option inscrite à la cote	exchange-traded option, listed option
Börsengeschäft	opération boursière	stock market transaction
Börsengesetz (BEHG)	Loi sur les bourses (LBVM)	Stock Exchange Act
Börsenindex	indice boursier	stock exchange index
börsenkotiert (D: börsennotiert)	coté en bourse	listed on the stock exchange

Börsenkurs	cours boursier, cours en bourse	stock market price
Börsenverordnung (BEHV)	Ordonnance sur les bourses (OBVM)	Stock Exchange Ordinance
börsliche Abschlüsse	transactions en bourse	on-order-book trades
Bosheit	méchanceté	cruelty
Botschaft des Bundesrates	message du Conseil Fédéral	Federal Council Dispatch (report and opinion on a bill)
Boykott	boycott	boycott
B-Post	courrier B	mail delivered within three business days
Brachfläche	friche	derelict land
Brachflächenrecycling	recyclage de terrains en friche	recycling of derelict land
Branchenfonds	fonds de branche	sector fund
Brandstiftung (Art. 221 StGB)	incendie intentionnel	arson
Bretreuter	personne assistée	probationer
Brevet	acte de nomination	appointment
brevetieren	nommer	to appoint
briefliche Stimmabgabe	vote par correspondance	postal voting
Bringschuld	dette portable	obligation to be performed at creditor's (obligee's) residence or place of business
Bruch amtlicher Beschlagnahme (Art. 289 StGB)	soustraction d'objets mis sous main de l'autorité	removal of seized property
Bruchteil	quote-part	fraction (of a fund unit)
Bruttoertrag	rendement brut	gross yield
Bruttolohn	salaire brut	gross salary
Bucheffekte	effets comptables	book-entry securities
Bucheffektengesetz	Loi sur les titres intermédiés	Federal Act on the Custody and Transfer of Securities Held with an Intermediary
Bücherexperte	expert-comptable	certified public accountant
Buchgewinn	bénéfice comptable	book profit
Buchhalter	comptable	accountant, bookkeeper

Buchhaltung	comptabilité	accounting, bookkeeping
Buchungsbeleg	pièce comptable	accounting record
Buchungsfehler	comptabilisation erronée	accounting error
Buchverlust	perte comptable	book loss
Buchwert	valeur comptable	book value
Budget	budget	budget
Bund	Confédération	Confederation
Bundesamt	Office fédéral	Federal Office
Bundesamt für Bauten und Logistik (BBL)	Office fédéral des constructions et de la logistique (OFCL)	Federal Office for Buildings and Logistics
Bundesamt für Berufsbildung und Technologie (BBT)	Office fédéral de la formation professionnelle et de la technologie (OFFT)	Federal Office for Professional Education and Technology
Bundesamt für Bevölkerungsschutz (BABS)	Office fédéral de la protection de la protection (OFPP)	Federal Office for Civil Protection
Bundesamt für Bildung und Wissenschaft (BBW)	Office fédéral de l'éducation et de la science	Federal Office for Education and Science
Bundesamt für Energie (BFE)	Office fédéral de l'énergie (OFE)	Swiss Federal Office of Energy
Bundesamt für Gesundheit (BAG)	Office fédéral de la santé publique (OFSP)	Federal Office of Public Health
Bundesamt für Informatik und Telekommunikation (BIT)	Office fédéral de l'informatique et de la télécommunicati on (OFIT)	Federal Office of Information Technology, Systems and Telecommunication
Bundesamt für Justiz (BJ)	Office fédéral de la justice (OFJ)	Federal Office of Justice
Bundesamt für Kommunikation (BAKOM)	Office fédéral de la communi- cation (OfCom)	Federal Office of Communications
Bundesamt für Kultur (BAK)	Office fédéral de la culture (OFC)	Federal Office for Culture
Bundesamt für Landestopographie (swisstopo)	Office fédéral de topographie (swisstopo)	Federal Office of Topography

Bundesamt für Landwirtschaft (BLW)	Office fédéral de l'agriculture (OFAG)	Federal Office for Agriculture
Bundesamt für Meteorologie und Klimatologie (MeteoSchweiz)	Office fédéral de météorologie et de climatologie (MétéoSuisse)	Federal Office of Meteorology and Climatology
Bundesamt für Metrologie (METAS)	Office fédéral de métrologie (METAS)	Federal Office of Metrology
Bundesamt für Migration (BFM)	Office fédéral des migrations (OFM)	Federal Office for Migration
Bundesamt für Privatversicherungen (BPV)	Office fédéral des assurances privées (OFAP)	Federal Office of Private Insurance
Bundesamt für Raumentwicklung (ARE)	Office fédéral du développement territorial (ARE)	Federal Office for Spatial Development
Bundesamt für Sozialversicherung (BSV)	Office fédéral des assurances sociales (OFAS)	Federal Social Insurance Office
Bundesamt für Sport (BASPO)	Office fédéral du sport	Federal Office of Sport
Bundesamt für Statistik (BFS)	Office fédéral de la statistique (OFS)	Federal Statistical Office
Bundesamt für Strassen (ASTRA)	Office fédéral des routes (OFROU)	Federal Roads Office
Bundesamt für Umwelt (BAFU)	Office fédéral de l'environnement (OFEV)	Federal Office for the Environment
Bundesamt für Verkehr (BAV)	Office fédéral des transports (OFT)	Federal Office of Transport
Bundesamt für Veterinärwesen (BVET)	Office vétérinaire fédéral (OVF)	Federal Veterinary Office
Bundesamt für wirtschaftliche Landesversorgung (BWL)	Office fédéral pour l'approvisionnement économique du pays (OFAE)	Federal Office for National Economic Supply
Bundesamt für Wohnungswesen (BWO)	Office fédéral du logement (OFL)	Federal Office for Housing

Bundesamt für Zivilluftfahrt (BAZL)	Office fédéral de l'aviation civile (OFAC)	Federal Office for Civil Aviation
Bundesanwaltschaft (BA)	Ministère public de la Confédération (MPC)	Office of the Attorney General of Switzerland
Bundesarchiv (BAR)	Archives fédérales (AFS)	Swiss Federal Archives
Bundesbehörde	autorité fédérale	federal authority
Bundesbeschluss (BB)	arrêté fédéral (AF)	federal decree
Bundesblatt der Schweizerischen Eidgenossenschaft (BBl)	Feuille fédérale de la Confédération suisse (FF)	Federal Gazette of the Swiss Confederation
Bundeseinheit für die Lebensmittelkette (BLK)	Unité fédérale pour la filière alimentaire (UFAL)	Federal Food Chain Unit
Bundesfeier	Fête nationale	Swiss National Day (August 1)
Bundesgericht (BGer)	Tribunal fédéral (TF)	Swiss Federal Supreme Court
Bundesgerichtgesetz (BGG)	Loi fédérale sur le tribunal fédéral (LTF)	Federal Supreme Court Act
bundesgerichtlich	selon la jurisprudence du Tribunal fédéral	pursuant to the case law of the Federal Supreme Court
Bundesgerichtsbarkeit	juridiction fédérale	federal jurisdiction
Bundesgerichtsentscheide (BGE)	Arrêts du Tribunal fédéral (ATF)	Supreme Court Reports
Bundesgerichtskanzlei	chancellerie du Tribunal fédéral	Chancellery of the Federal Supreme Court
Bundesgesetz	loi fédérale	federal act
Bundesgesetz betreffend die Arbeit in den Fabriken	Loi fédérale sur le travail dans les fabriques	Federal Act on Work in Factories
Bundesgesetz betreffend die Lotterien und die gewerbsmässigen Wetten	Loi fédérale sur les loteries et les paris professionnels	Federal Act on Lotteries and Commercial Gambling

Bundesgesetz betreffend die Überwachung des Post- und Fernmeldeverkehrs (BÜPF)	Loi fédérale sur la surveillance de la correspondance par poste et télécommunication (LSCPT)	Federal Act on the Surveillance of Post and Telecommunications
Bundesgesetz gegen den unlauteren Wettbewerb (UWG)	Loi fédérale contre la concurrence déloyale (LCD)	Federal Act on Unfair Competition
Bundesgesetz über das bäuerliche Bodenrecht (BGBB)	Loi fédérale sur le droit foncier rural (LDFR)	Federal Act on Rural Land Rights
Bundesgesetz über das internationale Privatrecht (IPRG)	Loi fédérale sur le droit international privé (LDIP)	Federal Act on International Private Law
Bundesgesetz über das Jugendstrafrecht (JStG)	Loi fédérale régissant la condition pénale des mineurs (DPMin)	Federal Act on the Criminal Law applicable to Juveniles; Juvenile Criminal Law Act
Bundesgesetz über das öffentliche Beschaffungswesen (BöB)	Loi fédérale sur les marchés publics (LMP)	Government Procurement Act
Bundesgesetz über das Verwaltungsstrafrecht (VStrR)	Loi fédérale sur le droit pénal administratif (DPA)	Federal Act on Administrative Criminal Law
Bundesgesetz über das Verwaltungsverfahren (VwVG)	Loi fédérale sur la procédure administrative (PA)	Federal Act on Administrative Procedure; Administrative Procedure Act
Bundesgesetz über den allgemeinen Teil des Sozialversicherungsrechts (ATSG)	Loi fédérale sur la partie générale du droit des assurances sociales (LPGA)	Federal Act on General Aspects of Social Security Law
Bundesgesetz über den Binnenmarkt (BGBM)	Loi fédérale sur le marché intérieur (LMI)	Federal Act on the Internal Market; Internal Market Act
Bundesgesetz über den Bundeszivilprozess (BZP)	Loi fédérale de procédure civile fédérale (PCF)	Federal Act on Federal Civil Procedure
Bundesgesetz über den Datenschutz (DSG)	Loi fédérale sur la protection des données (LPD)	Federal Act on Data Protection; Data Protection Act

Bundesgesetz über den Erwerb von Grundstücken durch Personen im Ausland (BewG)	Loi fédérale sur l'acquisition d'immeubles par des personnes à l'étranger (LFAIE)	Federal Act on the Acquisition of Real Estate in Switzerland by Non-Residents
Bundesgesetz über den Finanz- und Lastenausgleich (FiLaG)	Loi fédérale sur la péréquation financière et la compensation des charges (PFCC)	Federal Act on Fiscal Equalization and Cost Compensation
Bundesgesetz über den Konsumkredit (KKG)	Loi fédérale sur le crédit à la consommation (LCC)	Federal Act on Consumer Credit; Consumer Credit Act
Bundesgesetz über den Motorfahrzeug- und Fahrradverkehr (MFG)	Loi fédérale sur la circulation des véhicules automobiles et des cycles	Federal Act on Motor Vehicle and Cycle Traffic
Bundesgesetz über den Natur- und Heimatschutz (NHG)	Loi fédérale sur la protection de la nature et du paysage (LPN)	Nature and Cultural Heritage Act
Bundesgesetz über den Schutz von Design (DesG)	Loi fédérale sur la protection des designs (LDes)	Federal Act on the Protection of Designs; Designs Act
Bundesgesetz über den Schutz von Marken und Herkunftsangaben (MSchG)	Loi fédérale sur la protection des marques et des indications de provenance (LPM)	Federal Act on the Protection of Trademarks and Indications of Source
Bundesgesetz über die Allgemeinverbindlicherklärung von Gesamtarbeitsverträgen (AVEG)	Loi fédérale permettant d'étendre le champ d'application de la convention collective de travail (LECCT)	Federal Act on the Declaration of the General Application of Collective Employment Agreements
Bundesgesetz über die Arbeitsvermittlung und den Personalverleih (AVG)	Loi fédérale sur le service de l'emploi et la location de services (LSE)	Federal Act on Recruitment and the Hiring of Services; Recruitment Act

Bundesgesetz über die Ausländerinnen und Ausländer (AuG)	Loi fédérale sur les étrangers (LEtr)	Federal Act on Foreign Nationals
Bundesgesetz über die Banken und Sparkassen (BankG)	Loi fédérale sur les banques et les caisses d'épargne (LB)	Federal Act on Banks and Savings Banks
Bundesgesetz über die berufliche Alters-, Hinterlassenen- und Invalidenvorsorge (BVG)	Loi fédérale sur la prévoyance professionnelle vieillesse, survivants et invalidité (LPP)	Swiss Federal Occupational Retirement, Survivors and Disability Pension Plan Act
Bundesgesetz über die Berufsbildung (BBG)	Loi fédérale sur la formation professionnelle (LFPr)	Federal Act on Vocational and Professional Education and Training
Bundesgesetz über die Bildung steuerbegünstigter Arbeitsbeschaffungsreserven (ABRG)	Loi fédérale sur la constitution de réserves de crise bénéficiant d'allégements fiscaux (LCRC)	Federal Act on the Establishment of Tax Privileged Job Creation Reserves
Bundesgesetz über die Börsen und den Effektenhandel (BEHG)	Loi fédérale sur les bourses et les valeurs mobilières (LBVM)	Federal Act on Stock Exchanges and Securities Trading
Bundesgesetz über die direkte Bundessteuer (DGB)	Loi fédérale sur l'impôt fédéral direct (LIFD)	Federal Act on Direct Federal Taxation
Bundesgesetz über die elektronische Signatur (ZertES)	Loi fédérale sur la signature électronique (SCSE)	Federal Act on Electronic Signatures
Bundesgesetz über die Ergänzungsleistungen (ELG)	Loi fédérale sur les prestations complémentaire s (LPC)	Supplementary Benefits Act
Bundesgesetz über die Erwerbsersatzordnung (EOG)	Loi fédérale sur le régime des allocations pour perte de gain (LAPG)	Loss of Earnings Compensation Act
Bundesgesetz über die Familienzulagen (FamZG)	Loi fédérale sur les allocations familiales (LAFam)	Family Allowances Act

Bundesgesetz über die Fischerei (BGF)	Loi fédérale sur la pêche (LFSP)	Federal Act on Fish and Fisheries
Bundesgesetz über die Freizügigkeit der Anwältinnen und Anwälte (BGFA)	Loi fédérale sur la libre circulation des avocats (LLCA)	Federal Act on the Free Movement of Lawyers
Bundesgesetz über die gebrannten Wasser (AlkG)	Loi fédérale sur l'alcool (Lalc)	Alcohol Act
Bundesgesetz über die Harmonisierung der direkten Steuern der Kantone und Gemeinden (StHG)	Loi fédérale sur l'harmonisation des impôts directs des cantons et des communes (LHID)	Direct Taxation Harmonization Act
Bundesgesetz über die Invalidenversicherung (IVG)	Loi fédérale sur l'assurance-invalidité (LAI)	Disability Insurance Act
Bundesgesetz über die kollektiven Kapitalanlagen (KAG)	Loi fédérale sur les placements collectifs de capitaux (LPCC)	Federal Act on Collective Investment Schemes
Bundesgesetz über die Krankenversicherung (KVG)	Loi fédérale sur l'assurance-maladie (LFMal)	Federal Health Insurance Act
Bundesgesetz über die Luftfahrt (LFG)	Loi fédérale sur l'aviation (LA)	Federal Aviation Act
Bundesgesetz über die medizinisch unterstützte Fortpflanzung (FMedG)	Loi fédérale sur la procréation médicalement assistée (LPMA)	Reproductive Medicine Act
Bundesgesetz über die Mehrwertsteuer (MWSTG)	Loi fédérale régissant la taxe sur la valeur ajoutée (LTVA)	Federal Value Added Tax Act
Bundesgesetz über die Nutzbarmachung der Wasserkräfte (WRG)	Loi fédérale sur l'utilisation des forces hydrauliques (LFH)	Federal Act on the Use of Hydraulic Power (Water Rights Act)
Bundesgesetz über die Öffentlichkeit der Verwaltung (BGÖ)	Loi fédérale sur la transparence de l'administration (LTrans)	Freedom of Information Act

Bundesgesetz über die Produktehaftpflicht (PrHG)	Loi fédérale sur la responsabilité du fait des produits (LRFP)	Product Liability Act
Bundesgesetz über die Raumplanung (RPG)	Loi fédérale sur l'aménagement du territoire (LAT)	Federal Spatial Planning Act
Bundesgesetz über die Sperrung und die Rückerstattung unrechtmässig erworbener Vermögenswerte ausländischer politisch exponierter Personen (SRVG)	Loi fédérale sur le blocage et la restitution des valeurs patrimoniales d'origine illicite de personnes politiquement exposées à l'étranger (LVP)	Federal Act on the Freezing and Restitution of Illicit Assets held by Foreign Politically Exposed Persons
Bundesgesetz über die Stempelabgaben (StG)	Loi fédérale sur les droits de timbre (LT)	Stamp Duties Act
Bundesgesetz über die technischen Handelshemmnisse (THG)	Loi fédérale sur les entraves techniques au commerce (LETC)	Federal Act on Technical Barriers to Trade
Bundesgesetz über die Unfallversicherung (UVG)	Loi fédérale sur l'assurance-accidents (LAA)	Accident Insurance Act
Bundesgesetz über die Verpfändung und Zwangsliquidation von Eisenbahn- und Schifffahrtsunternehmungen (VZEG)	Loi fédérale concernant la constitution de gages sur les chemins de fer et de navigation et la liquidation forcée de ces entreprises (LGEL)	Federal Act on the Attachment and Administrative Receivership of Railroad and Shipping Companies
Bundesgesetz über die Währung und die Zahlungsmittel (WZG)	Loi fédérale sur l'unité monétaire et les moyens de paiement	Federal Act on Currency and Payment Instruments
Bundesgesetz über die Wehrpflichtersatzabgabe (WPEG)	Loi fédérale sur la taxe d'exemption de l'obligation de servir (LTEO)	Federal Act on the Military Service Exemption Tax

Bundesgesetz über Finanzhilfen und Abgeltungen (SuG)	Loi fédérale sur les aides financières et les indemnités (LSu)	Federal Act on Financial Aids and Grants
Bundesgesetz über Fuss- und Wanderwege (FWG)	Loi fédérale sur les chemins pour piétons et les chemins de randonnée pédestre (LCPR)	Federal Act on Footpaths and Hiking Trails
Bundesgesetz über internationale Rechtshilfe in Strafsachen (IRSG)	Loi fédérale sur l'entreaide internationale en matière pénale (EIMP)	Federal Act on International Mutual Assistance in Criminal Matters
Bundesgesetz über Kartelle und andere Wettbewerbs-beschränkungen (KG)	Loi fédérale sur les cartels et autres restrictions à la concurrence (LCart)	Federal Act on Cartels and Other Restraints of Competition
Bundesgesetz über Massnahmen zur Wahrung der inneren Sicherheit (BWIS)	Loi fédérale instituant des mesures visant au maintien de la sûreté intérieure (LMSI)	Internal Security Act
Bundesgesetz über Pauschalreisen	Loi fédérale sur les voyages à forfait	Federal Act on Package Travel
Bundesgesetz über Radio und Fernsehen (RTVG)	Loi fédérale sur la radio et la télévision (LRTV)	Radio and Television Act
Bundesgesetz über Schuldbetreibung und Konkurs (SchKG)	Loi fédérale sur la poursuite pour dettes et la faillite (LP)	Debt Collection and Bankruptcy Act
Bundesgesetz über Zertifizierungsdienste im Bereich der elektronischen Signatur (ZertES)	Loi fédérale sur les services de certification dans le domaine de la signature électronique (SCSE)	Federal Act on Electronic Signatures

Bundesgesetz zum Staatsvertrag mit den Vereinigten Staaten von Amerika über gegenseitige Rechtshilfe in Strafsachen (BG-RVUS)	Loi fédérale relative au traité conclu avec les États-Unis d'Amérique sur l'entraide judiciaire en matière pénale (LTEJUS)	Federal Act on the Treaty concluded with the United States of America on Mutual Assistance in Criminal Matters
Bundesgesetzgebung	législation fédérale	federal legislation
Bundeshaftung	responsabilité de la Confédération	federal liability under the Military Insurance Act
Bundesintervention	intervention fédérale	federal intervention
Bundesinventar der Landschaften und Naturdenkmäler	Inventaire fédéral des paysages, sites et monuments naturels	Federal Inventory of Landscapes and Natural Monuments
Bundeskanzlei (BK)	Chancellerie fédérale (ChF)	Federal Chancellery
Bundeskanzler	Chancelier fédéral	Federal Chancellor
Bundeskriminalpolizei (BKP)	Police judiciaire fédérale (PJF)	Federal Criminal Police
Bundeslagezentrum (BLZ)	Centre fédéral de situation (CFS)	National Intelligence Centre
Bundesordner (D: Leitz-Ordner)	classeur à levier	ring binder
Bundespatentgericht (BPatGer)	Tribunal fédéral des brevets (TFB)	Federal Patent Court
Bundespersonalgesetz (BPG)	Loi sur le personnel de la Confédération (LPers)	Federal Personnel Act
Bundespersonalverordnung (BPV)	Ordonnance sur le personnel de la Confédération (OPers)	Federal Personnel Ordinance
Bundespräsident	Président de la Confédération	President of the Swiss Confederation
Bundesrat (BR) (D: Bundesregierung)	Conseil fédéral (CF)	Federal Council
Bundesratswahlen	élection du Conseil fédéral	Federal Council election
Bundesrecht	droit fédéral	federal law

bundesrechtliche Beweisvorschriften	dispositions fédérales en matière de preuve	federal rules of evidence
Bundesrechtsprechung	jurisprudence fédérale	federal case law
Bundesrechtsverletzung	violation du droit fédéral	violation of federal law
Bundesreisezentrale (BRZ)	Centrale des voyages de la Confédération (CVC)	Swiss Government Travel Centre
Bundessicherheitsdienst (BSD)	Service fédéral de sécurité (SFS)	Federal Security Service
Bundesstaat	état fédéral	federal state
Bundesstadt (D: Bundeshauptstadt)	capitale fédérale	federal capital
Bundesstatistikgesetz (BStatG)	Loi fédérale sur la statistique fédérale (LSF)	Federal Statistics Act
Bundesstrafgericht (BStGer)	Tribunal pénal fédéral (TPF)	Federal Criminal Court (based in Bellinzona)
Bundesverfassung (BV) (D: Grundgesetz)	Constitution fédérale (CF)	Swiss Federal Constitution
Bundesverordnung	ordonnance fédérale	federal ordinance
Bundesversammlung (BVers)	Assemblée fédérale (Ass. féd.)	Federal Assembly (the Swiss legislature, made up of two houses: the National Council and the Council of States)
Bundesverwaltung (BVerw)	Administration fédérale (Adm. féd.)	Federal Administration
Bundesverwaltungsgericht (BVGer)	Tribunal administratif fédéral (TAF)	Federal Administrative Court (in St. Gallen)
Bürge	caution (partie au cautionnement)	guarantor
Bürgergemeinde	commune bourgeoise, bourgeosie	citizens' community
Bürgergemeinderat	conseil bourgeoisial	citizens' council
Bürgergemeindeversammlung	assemblée bourgeoisiale	citizens' assembly
Bürgerort	lieu d'origine	place of origin
Bürgerrecht (Art. 37 BV)	droit de cité	citizenship

Bürgerrechtsdienst	Service des naturalisations	Naturalization Service
Bürgerrechtsgesetz (BüG)	Loi sur la nationalité (LN)	Swiss Citizenship Act
Bürgschaft (Art. 492-512 OR)	cautionnement	surety
Bürgschaftserklärung	acte de cautionnement	guarantee commitment
Bürgschaftsvertrag (Art. 492 ff. OR)	contrat de cautionnement	contract of surety
Büro der Vereinigten Bundesversammlung	Bureau de l'Assemblée fédérale	Office of the United Federal Assembly
Büro des Nationalrates	Bureau du Conseil national	Office of the National Council
Büro des Ständerates	Bureau du Conseil des États	Office of the Council of States
Bürounkosten	frais de bureau	office expenses
Busse (D: Buße)	amende	fine
Bussenumwandlung (D: Bußenumwandlung)	conversion de l'amende	conversion of the fine
Charterer	affréteur	charterer
Chartervertrag	contrat d'affrètement	charter agreement
Check (D: Scheck) (Art. 1100 ff OR)	chèque	check
Checkkartenmissbrauch (Art. 148 StGB)	abus de cartes-chèques	misuse of a check card
Chemikaliengesetz (ChemG)	Loi sur les produits chimiques (LChim)	Chemicals Act
Coiffeurlehre (D: Friseurlehre)	apprentissage de coiffeur	hairdresser apprenticeship
Comestibles	épicerie fine	delicatessen
Computerstraftaten	infractions en matière informatique	computer-related offenses
Congé-Vente-Kündigung	congé-vente	termination of a lease to force the tenant to purchase the premises
Courtier (D: Makler)	courtier	broker
cura in custodiendo	cura in custodiendo	supervising employees properly
cura in eligendo	cura in eligendo	selecting employees with due care
cura in instruendo	cura in instruendo	training employees properly
Dachfonds	fonds faîtier	umbrella fund, fund of funds

Dachgeschoss	comble	top floor, attic floor
Dachverband	association faîtère	umbrella association
dahinfallen	devenir caduc	to lapse
Dahinfallen des Arrests (Art. 280 SchKG)	caducité du séquestre	lapsing of the attachment
Dahinfallen des Schuldübernahmevertrages (Art. 180 OR)	annulation du contrat de reprise de dette	failure of debt assumption contract
damnum emergens	damnum emergens	actual loss (as opposed to lost profits)
Darlehen (Art. 312-318 OR)	prêt de consommation	loan (for consumption, as opposed to a loan for use)
Darleiher (D: Darlehensgeber) (Art. 312-218 OR)	prêteur	lender
Datenaufbewahrung	conservation des données	data retention
Datenbeschädigung (Art. 144bis StGB)	détérioration de données	damage to data
Datenschutz	protection des données	data protection
Datenschutzbeauftragter	préposé à la protection des données	data protection commissioner
Datensicherheit	sécurité des données	data security
Dauer	durée	duration
Dauerdelikt	délit continu	continuing crime (one whose effects last over a period of time, such as kidnapping)
Dauerinvalidität	invalidité permanente	permanent disability
Dauerschuld	dette durable	long-term debt
Decharge (D: Entlastung)	décharge (F : quitus)	"discharge" of the board of directors
Decharge erteilen (D: entlasten)	voter la décharge (F : donner quitus)	to grant "discharge" to the members of the board of directors
Deckung	couverture	coverage
Deckungsgrad	taux de couverture	cover ratio
Deckungskapital	réserve mathématique	actuarial reserve
Deckungskauf	achat de couverture	hedge buying

Deckungsprinzip (Art. 126 SchKG)	principe de l'offre suffisante	sufficient bid principle (bid for the item being auctioned is sufficient to cover the claims of secured creditors)
Deckungsverhältnis	rapport de couverture	contractual relationship between the promisor and promisee (in a third-party beneficiary contract)
Defensivmarke	marque défensive	defensive trademark (can be applied for by a trademark owner of a well known trademark for goods or services that are not intended to be used by that owner)
definitive Freilassung	mise en liberté définitive	permanent release
definitive Rechtsöffnung (Art. 82 SchKG)	mainlevée définitive	final dismissal of debtor's objection
Deflation	déflation	deflation
deklaratorische Wirkung	effet déclaratif	declaratory effect
Delegation	délégation	delegation
Delegiertenversammlung	assemblée des délégués	meeting of delegates
Delegierter	délégué	delegate
deliktische Haftung	responsabilité aquilienne	tort liability, liability in tort (liability based on fault – either negligence or intentional misconduct)
Deliktsart	genre de délit	type of offense
Deliktsfähigkeit	capacité délictuelle	capacity to commit a tort
Deliktsgut	produit de l'infraction	proceeds of a crime
Deliktshaftung	responsabilité délictuelle	tort liability
Deliktspauliana (Anfechtungsklage)	action en contestation, action révocatoire	avoidance action (action by creditors to void a fraudulent conveyance)
Deliktsschwere	gravité d'un délit	gravity, seriousness of an offense
Delkredere (Art. 430 OR)	ducroire	del credere (special remuneration of agent who has assumed liability for performance by the debtor)
Delsberg	Delémont	Delémont (capital of the canton of Jura)

Demonstrationsfreiheit	liberté de manifestation	freedom to demonstrate, freedom of demonstration
Departement	département	department
Deponie	place de dépôt	disposal site, dump
Deponiebewilligung	autorisation de déposer	authorization to dump
Depositenanstalt (Art. 9, 24, 264 Abs. 3 und 329 Abs. 1 SchKG)	caisse des dépôts et consignations	deposit and consignment office
Depot (1)	dépôt	custody account
Depot (2) (D: Flaschenpfand)	consigne	deposit
Depotbank	banque dépositaire	custodian bank
Depotgebühren	droit de garde de titres	custody charges
Depotstimmrecht	droit de vote des actions déposées	proxy voting rights
Depotvertrag	contrat de dépôt bancaire	deposit agreement
Depotvertreter (Art. 689d OR)	représentation par un dépositaire	representation by a custodian
der Öffentlichkeit zugängliche Baute	bâtiment ouvert au public	building open to the public
Deregulierung	déréglementa-tion	deregulation
Dereliktion	déréliction	dereliction
Derivate	dérivés	derivatives
Derivatgeschäfte	opérations sur dérivés	derivatives transactions
derivative Finanzinstrumente	instruments financiers dérivés	derivative financial instruments, derivatives
derivativer Erwerb	acquisition dérivée	derivative acquisition
derogatorische Kraft internationalen Rechts	primauté du droit international	primacy of international law
Detailberatung	discussion par article	detailed consideration (of a bill)
Detailgeschäft (D: Einzelhandelsgeschäft)	magasin de détail	retail store
Detailhandel (D: Einzelhandel)	commerce de détail	retail trade
Detaillist (D: Einzelhändler)	détaillant	retailer
Detailpreis (D: Einzelhandelspreis)	prix de détail	retail price
Detailuntersuchung	investigation de détail	detailed investigation

Devisen	devise	foreign exchange, forex
Devisengeschäft	opération sur devises	foreign exchange transaction, forex transaction
Devisenkassengeschäft	opération sur devises au comptant	foreign exchange spot transaction
Devisenoption	option de change, option sur devises	currency option, forex option, FX option
Devisenswapgeschäft	opération swap sur devises	currency swap transaction
Devisentermingeschäft	opération à terme sur devises	forward foreign exchange transaction
Devolutiveffekt	effet dévolutif	devolutive effect (appeal to a higher court rather than to the very judge who issued the ruling being appealed)
devolutives Rechtsmittel	appel dévolutif	appeal to a higher court (rather than to the court that handed down the ruling)
Diebstahl (Art. 139 StGB)	vol	theft
Diebstahlversicherung	assurance-vol	theft insurance
Dienstalter	ancienneté de service	seniority
Dienstbarkeit (Art. 730 ff. ZGB)	servitude	easement
Dienstbarkeitsvertrag	contrat de servitude	easement agreement
Dienstbüchlein (D: Wehrpass)	livret de service (F : livret militaire)	military record
Dienstleistung	prestation de services	provision of services
Dienstleistungsmarke	marque de service	service mark
Dienstleistungsvertrag	contrat de prestation de services	contract to provide services
Diensttauglichkeit	aptitude au service	fitness for duty
Dienstversäumnis	insoumission (militaire)	absence without leave (AWOL)
Dienstverweigerer	objecteur de conscience	conscientious objector
Differenzausgleich	compensation de la différence	offset of the difference

Differenzbereinigungsverfahren	processus d'élimination des divergences	procedure for the resolution of differences (when the National Council and Council of States have differing opinions of a bill)
digitale Unterschrift	signature numérique	digital signature
dingliche Klage (Art. 29 ZPO)	action réelle	action in rem
dinglicher Vertrag	contrat réel	contract related to real property rights
diplomatische Immunität	immunité diplomatique	diplomatic immunity
diplomatische Vertretung	représentation diplomatique	diplomatic representation
diplomatischer Landesverrat (Art. 267 StGB)	trahison diplomatique	diplomatic treason
diplomatisches Verfahren	procédure diplomatique	diplomatic procedure
direkte Bundessteuer	impôt fédéral direct	direct federal tax (levied on individual income and profits and net assets of corporations and other legal entities)
direkte Zuständigkeit	compétence directe	direct jurisdiction
direkter Gegenentwurf	contre-projet direct	direct counterproposal
direkter Schaden	dommage direct	direct damage
Direktion für Arbeit (DA)	Direction du travail (DA)	Labor Directorate
Direktion für Aussenwirtschaft (DW)	Direction des affaires économiques extérieures (DW)	Federal Economic Affairs Directorate
Direktion für Entwicklung und Zusammenarbeit (DEZA)	Direction du développement et de la coopération (DDC)	Swiss Agency for Development and Cooperation
Direktion für Ressourcen (DR)	Direction des ressources (DR)	Directorate for Resources
Direktion für Standortförderung (DS)	Direction de la promotion économique (DS)	Promotion Activities Directorate
Direktion für Völkerrecht (DV)	Direction du droit international public (DV)	Directorate of Public International Law

Direktion für Wirtschaftspolitik (DP)	Direction de la politique économique (DP)	Economic Policy Directorate
Direktversicherung	assurance directe	direct insurance
Direktzahlung	paiement direct	direct payment
Diskont	escompte (opération bancaire)	discount
Dispens	dispense	exemption
Disponibilitäten	disponibilités	cash, liquid resources
Dispositionsgrundsatz (Art. 58 ZPO)	principe de disposition	principle of non ultra petita (principle that a judge may not award more than a party claims or less than the other party recognizes, nor may the judge's judgment be different in kind from that sought)
Dispositiv (D: Tenor)	dispositif	operative part of a judgment, operative provisions, holding
dispositives Recht	droit dispositif (F : droit supplétif)	non-mandatory legal rule (one that can be contracted out of)
Distanzdelikt	infraction commise à distance	offense committed under a different jurisdiction
Distanzkauf	vente à distance	distance selling
Disziplinarbehörde	autorité disciplinaire	disciplinary authority
Disziplinarbeschwerde	recours disciplinaire	disciplinary appeal
Disziplinargericht	tribunal disciplinaire	disciplinary tribunal
Disziplinarkommission	commission disciplinaire	disciplinary commission
Disziplinarmassnahme (Art. 14 SchKG)	mesure disciplinaire	disciplinary measure
Disziplinarrecht	droit disciplinaire	disciplinary law
Disziplinarverfahren	procédure disciplinaire	disciplinary procedure
Dividende	dividende	dividend
Dividendenvergleich	concordat-dividendes	debt restructuring agreement on dividends
DNA-Profil	profil d'ADN	DNA profile
Doktrin	doctrine	legal scholarship, the legal literature
Dokumentation	documentation	documentation

Dokumentenakkreditiv	crédit documentaire	documentary credit
dominium ex iure quiritium	propriété quiritaire	full ownership
Domizilcheck (Art. 1107 OR)	chèque domicilié	domiciled check
Domizilgesellschaft	société de domicile	mailbox company
Domizilhalter	détenteur du domicile	registered agent
Domizilwechsel (Art. 994 OR)	lettre de change domiciliée	domiciled bill of exchange
Dopingkontrolle	contrôle antidopage	anti-doping control
Doppelaufruf (Art. 142 SchKG)	double mise à prix	double auction
Doppelbesteuerung	double imposition	double taxation
Doppelbesteuerungsabkommen (DBA)	accord de double imposition (ADI)	double taxation treaty
Doppelbürger	double national	dual national
doppeltes Ja	double oui	double yes vote
Dotierwassermenge (Art. 4 GSchG)	débit de dotation	required water endowment
Drei-Säulen-Konzept	système des trois piliers	three-pillar system
dreizehnter Monatslohn	treizième salaire	13th month salary
dringlicher Bundesbeschluss	arrêté fédéral urgent	urgent federal decree
dringlicher Nachtrags- und Zusatzkredit (Art. 28 und 24 FHG)	crédit supplémentaire et crédit additionnel urgent	emergency amendment and additional credit
Drittansprache	prétention de tiers	third-party claim
Drittauszahlung	versement en mains d'un tiers	payment to a third party
Dritter	tiers	third party
Dritthilfe	aide d'autrui	assistance by a third party
Drittschaden	dommage causé à un tiers	third party damage
Drittschuldner	tiers débiteur	third party debtor
Drittverschulden	faute du tiers	third party fault
Drittwirkung	effet à l'égard des tiers	third party effect
Drittwirkung der Grundrechte	effet horizontal des droits constitutionnels	third party effect of fundamental rights

Drogenpolitik	politique en matière de stupéfiants	drug policy
Drohung (Art. 180 StGB)	menaces	threatening behavior
Duldungspflicht	obligation de tolérer les réparations et inspections de la chose	duty to tolerate
Duplik	duplique	rejoinder
Duplikate (Art. 1063 ff OR)	duplicata	duplicate of a bill of exchange
durch Pfand gesicherte Forderung (Art. 151 Abs. 1 SchKG)	créance garantie par gage	secured claim
durchgesetzte Marke	marque qui s'est imposée au public	mark that has acquired distinctiveness
Durchgriff	responsabilité découlant du principe de la transparence	piercing the corporate veil
Durchleitungsrecht	servitude de conduite	right for pipe, cables and conduits to traverse an adjoining parcel of land
Durchlieferung	transit	transit
durchschnittliches Jahreseinkommen	revenu annuel moyen	average annual income
Durchschnittslohn	salaire moyen	average wage
Durchsuchung von Aufzeichnungen (Art. 246-247 StPO)	perquisition de documents et enregistrements	search of records and recordings
Durchsuchung von Gegenständen (Art. 249-250 StPO)	fouille d'objets	search of property
Durchsuchung von Papieren	perquisition de papiers	search of papers
Durchsuchung von Personen (Art. 249-250 StPO)	fouille de personnes	search of persons
Durchsuchungsbefehl	mandat de perquisition	search warrant
dynamische Absicherung	couverture delta	delta hedging, dynamic hedging
echte Noven (Art. 229 ZPO)	novas proprement dits	proper new facts and evidence (facts and evidence that occurred or were discovered after the exchange of written submissions or after the last hearing)

echte Solidarität	solidarité parfaite	"perfect" joint and several liability (the tortfeasors act jointly and directly)
echter Vertrag zugunsten Dritter (Art. 112 Abs. 2 OR)	stipulation pour autrui parfaite	contract in favor of an intended beneficiary
Echtheit	authenticité	authenticity
Edelmetall (Art. 128 SchKG)	métaux précieux	precious metal
Edelmetallkassageschäft	opération sur métaux précieux au comptant	precious metal spot transaction
Edelmetallsgeschäft	opération sur métaux précieux	precious metal transaction
Edelmetalltermingeschäft	opération à terme sur métaux précieux	forward precious metal transaction
Edelstein	pierre précieuse	precious stone, jewel, gem
edieren (D: vorlegen)	produire en justice	to produce documents
Edikt	édit	edict
Edition	production de documents	production of documents
Editionspflicht	obligation de produire des pièces	duty to produce documents
Effekten	valeurs mobilières	securities
Effektenfonds	fonds en valeurs mobilières	securities fund
Effektenhandel	négoce de valeurs mobilières	securities trading
Effektenhändler	négociant en valeurs mobilières	securities dealer
EFTA-Gerichtshof	Cour AELE	EFTA Court (in Luxembourg)
Ehe (Art. 94 ff. ZGB)	mariage	marriage
Eheberatungsstelle (Art. 171 ZGB)	office de consultation conjugale	marital counseling agency
Ehefähigkeit (Art. 94 ZGB)	capacité matrimoniale	capacity to marry
Ehefreiheit	droit au mariage	right to marry
Ehegatte (Art. 105 ff. ZGB)	conjoint, époux	spouse
Ehegüterrecht	régime matrimonial	marital property system
Ehehindernis (Art. 95 ZGB)	empêchement au mariage	impediment to marriage

eheliche Gemeinschaft (Art. 159 ZGB)	union conjugale	marital union
Ehepaar-Altersrente	rente de vieillesse pour couple	old age pension for couples
Ehepaar-Invalidenrente	rente d'invalidité pour couple	disability pension for couples
eherechtliche Klage (Art. 23 ZPO)	action fondée sur le droit du mariage	action based on marital law
eherechtliches Gesuch (Art. 23 ZPO)	requête fondée sur le droit du mariage	application based on marital law
Eheregister	registre des mariages	marriage register
Ehescheidung (Art. 111 ff. ZGB)	divorce	divorce
Ehescheidungsurteil	jugement de divorce	divorce decree
Eheschein (D: Heiratsurkunde)	certificat de mariage	marriage certificate
Eheschliessung	conclusion du mariage	marriage
Eheschutz	protection de l'union conjugale	protection of the marital union
Eheschutzmassnahmen (Art. 172-179 ZGB)	mesures protectrices de l'union conjugale	measures to protect the marital union
Ehetrennung (Art. 116 ZGB)	séparation de corps	legal separation
Eheungültigkeit (Art. 104-110 ZGB)	annulation du mariage	annulment of marriage
Ehevertrag	contrat de mariage	prenuptial agreement
Ehrenbürgerrecht	droit de cité d'honneur	honorary citizenship
Ehreneintritt	intervention (papier-valeur)	intervention
Ehrenkränkung	injure grave	libel (written), slander (oral), defamation (superordinate term covering both libel and slander)
Ehrenzahlung	paiement par intervention	payment by intervention
Ehrverletzung (Art. 173-178 StGB)	atteinte à l'honneur	crime against personal honor
Eid	serment	oath
Eidgenossenschaft	confédération	confederation

Eidgenössische Alkoholverwaltung (EAV)	Régie fédérale des alcools (RFA)	Swiss Alcohol Board
Eidgenössische Arzneimittelkommission (EAK)	Commission fédérale des médicaments (CFM)	Federal Medicines Commission
Eidgenössische Ausgleichskasse (EAK)	Caisse de compensation fédérale (CFC)	Federal Compensation Office
Eidgenössische Berufsbildungskommission (EBBK)	Commission fédérale de la formation professionnelle (CFFP)	Federal Commission for Vocational and Professional Education and Training
Eidgenössische Berufsmaturitätskommission (EBMK)	Commission fédérale de la maturité professionnelle (CFMP)	Federal Vocational Baccalaureate Commission
Eidgenössische Designkommission (EDnK)	Commission fédérale du design (CFD)	Federal Design Commission
Eidgenössische Finanzkontrolle (EFK)	Contrôle fédéral des finances (CDF)	Swiss Federal Audit Office
Eidgenössische Finanzmarktaufsicht (FINMA)	Autorité fédérale de surveillance des marchés financiers (FINMA)	Swiss Financial Market Supervisory Authority (FINMA)
Eidgenössische Finanzverwaltung (EFV)	Administration fédérale des finances (AFF)	Federal Finance Administration
Eidgenössische Kommission für Alkoholfragen (EKAL)	Commission fédérale pour les problèmes liés à l'alcool (CFAL)	Federal Commission for Alcohol-Related Issues
Eidgenössiche Kommission für Drogenfragen (EKDF)	Commission fédérale pour les problèmes liés aux drogues (CFPD)	Federal Commission for Drug-Related Issues
Eidgenössische Räte	Conseils fédéraux	Federal Councils (the two houses of Parliament, i.e., the National Council and the Council of States)

Eidgenössische Steuerverwaltung (ESTV)	Administration fédérale des contributions (AFC)	Swiss Federal Tax Administration
Eidgenössische Zollverwaltung (EZV)	Administration fédérale des douanes (AFD)	Federal Customs Administration
Eidgenössischer Dank, Buss- und Bettag	Jeûne fédéral	Federal Day of Thanksgiving, Repentance and Prayer
Eidgenössischer Datenschutz- und Öffentlichkeitsbeauftragte (EDÖB)	Préposé fédéral à la protection des données et à la transparence (PFPDT)	Federal Data Protection and Information Commissioner
Eidgenössisches Amt für das Zivilstandswesen (EAZW)	Office fédéral de l'état civil (OFEC)	Federal Civil Status Office
Eidgenössisches Büro für die Gleichstellung von Frau und Mann (EBG)	Bureau fédéral de l'égalité entre femmes et hommes (BFEG)	Federal Office for Gender Equality
Eidgenössisches Büro für die Gleichstellung von Menschen mit Behinderungen (EBGB)	Bureau fédéral de l'égalité pour les personnes handicapées (BFEG)	Federal Office for the Equality of People with Disabilities
Eidgenössisches Departement des Innern (EDI)	Département fédéral de l'intérieur (DFI)	Federal Department of Home Affairs
Eidgenössisches Departement für auswärtige Angelegenheiten (EDA)	Département fédéral des affaires étrangères (DFAE)	Federal Department of Foreign Affairs
Eidgenössisches Departement für Umwelt, Verkehr, Energie und Kommunikation (UVEK)	Département fédéral de l'environnement, des transports, de l'énergie et de la communi-cation (DETEC)	Federal Department of the Environment, Transport, Energy and Communication
Eidgenössisches Departement für Verteidigung, Bevölkerungsschutz und Sport (VBS)	Département fédéral de la défense, de la protection de la population et des sports (DDPS)	Federal Department of Defense, Civil Protection and Sport

Eidgenössisches Departement für Wirtschaft, Bildung und Forschung (WBF)	Département fédéral de l'économie, de la formation et de la recherche (DEFR)	Federal Department of Economic Affairs, Education and Research
Eidgenössisches Finanzdepartement (EFD)	Département fédéral des finances (DFF)	Federal Department of Finance
Eidgenössisches Institut für Geistiges Eigentum (IGE)	Institut fédéral de la propriété intellectuelle (IPI)	Swiss Federal Institute of Intellectual Property
Eidgenössisches Justiz- und Polizeidepartement (EJPD)	Département fédéral de justice et police (DFJP)	Federal Department of Justice and Police
Eidgenössisches Personalamt (EPA)	Office fédéral du personnel (OFPER)	Federal Personnel Office
eigene Aktien	propres actions	own shares
Eigengebrauch	usage personnel	personal use
Eigengut (Art. 198 ZGB)	biens propres	personal property
Eigenhandel	négoce pour compte propre	proprietary trading
eigenhändige Abgabe	remise en main propre	personal delivery
eigenhändige Unterschrift (Art. 14 OR)	signature manuscrite	handwritten signature
eigenhändiges Testament (Art. 505 ZGB)	testament olographe	holographic will
Eigenkapital	fonds propres	equity
Eigenleistung	prestation propre	"sweat equity," work by the owner
Eigenmietwert	valeur locative	rental value
Eigenständigkeit der Kantone (Art. 47 BV)	autonomie des cantons	autonomy of the cantons
Eigentum (Art. 641 ff. ZGB)	propriété	ownership
Eigentümer	propriétaire	owner
Eigentumsansprache	revendication de propriété	recovery of property, replevin
Eigentumsbeschränkung	restriction à la propriété	restriction on ownership
Eigentumserwerb	acquisition de la propriété	acquisition of ownership
Eigentumsförderung	encouragement à l'accession à la propriété	promotion of home ownership

Eigentumsfreiheitsklage	action négatoire	action to establish the nonexistence of an easement
Eigentumsgarantie (Art. 26 BV)	garantie de la propriété	protection of the private ownership of property
Eigentumsklage	action en revendication	action to establish ownership
Eigentumsübergang	transfert de la propriété	passing of title
Eigentumsvorbehalt (Art. 217 OR)	réserve de propriété	retention of title (despite physical transfer, until purchase price is paid in full)
Eigentumsvorbehaltsregister	registre des pactes de réserve de propriété	register of retention of title
Eigenwechsel (Art. 1096-1099 OR)	billet à ordre	promissory note
Eignungsabklärung (D: Eignungsprüfung)	test d'aptitude	aptitude test
einberufen	convoquer	to convene
Einberufung	convocation	convening meeting
Einberufung der Gläubigerversammlung (Art. 301 SchKG)	convocation de l'assemblée des créanciers	notice of the creditor's meeting
Einbezug (D: Einbeziehung)	implication	inclusion, involvement
Einbürgerung	naturalisation	naturalization
Einelternfamilie	famille monoparentale	single-parent family
einfache Bürgschaft (Art. 495 OR)	cautionnement simple	simple surety
einfache Gesellschaft (eG) (Art. 530-551 OR)	société simple	simple partnership
einfache Kausalhaftung	responsabilité objective simple	simple causal third party liability
einfache Körperverletzung (Art. 123 StGB)	lésion corporelle simple	common assault
einfache Streitgenossenschaft (Art. 71 ZPO)	consorité simple	voluntary joinder
einfacher Auftrag (Art. 394 OR)	mandat proprement dit	simple agency
einfacher Raub	brigandage simple	common robbery
einfaches Mehr (D: einfache Mehrheit)	majorité simple	simple majority
Einfriedung	clôture	fence, enclosure
Einfuhr	importation	import
Einfuhrbewilligung	permis d'importation	import permit

Einführen, Erwerben, Lagern falschen Geldes (Art. 244 StGB)	importation, acquisition et prise en dépôt de fausse monnaie	import, acquisition and storage of counterfeit money
Einführungsgesetz	loi d'application	introductory act
Einfuhrzertifikat	certificat d'importation	import certificate
Eingabe	demande	petition
Eingabefrist (Art. 244 SchKG)	délai de production	filing deadline
Eingaben der Parteien (Art. 130 ZPO)	actes de parties	pleadings, submissions of the parties
eingeschränkte Revision (Art. 727a OR)	contrôle restreint	limited audit
eingesetzter Erbe	héritier institué	named heir
eingetragene Partnerschaft	partenariat enregistré	registered partnership, domestic partnership
eingetragener Partner	partenaire enregistré	registered partner, domestic partner
Eingewiesene	personne détenue	inmate
Eingliederungserfolg	succès de la réadaptation	success of the rehabilitation
Eingliederungsmassnahme	mesure de réadaptation	rehabilitation measure (to promote reintegration of the disabled)
Eingliederungsstätte	centre de réadaptation	rehabilitation center
Eingrenzung	interdiction de quitter une région	restriction order, order not leave a specific area
Eingriffe in das Stimm- und Wahlrecht (Art. 280 StGB)	atteinte au droit de vote	attacks on the right to vote
Eingriffe in die Gläubigerrechte	restriction des droits des créanciers	encroachment on creditors' rights
Einheimsen der Früchte (Art. 103 SchKG)	récolte des fruits	fruit harvest, harvesting of fruit
einheitliche Auslegung	interprétation uniforme	uniform interpretation
Einigungsverfahren	procédure de conciliation	conciliation proceedings
Einkauf	rachat	purchase
Einkommen	revenu	income
Einkünfte aus unbeweglichem Vermögen	revenus immobiliers	income from real property

Einlage	apport	contribution
Einlagerer	entreposant	depositor (of goods in a warehouse)
Einlagerückgewähr	restitution des apports	refund of contributions
einlässlich (D: ausführlich)	détaillé, en détail	in detail, thorough
Einlassung (Art. 18 ZPO)	acceptation tacite de compétence	acceptance by appearance
Einleitungstitel	titre préliminaire	introductory title
einmalige Ausgabe	dépense unique	one-time expense
Einmalprämie	prime unique	single premium
Einmanngesellschaft	société unipersonnelle	single-member company
Einrede eine Einrede entgegensetzen	exception opposer une exception	defense to assert a defense
Einrede der Rechtshängigkeit	exception de litispendance	defense that the same case is pending elsewhere (sometimes called "defense of lis alibi pendens")
Einrede der Schuldner (Art. 145 OR)	exception appartenant aux codébiteurs	objection by the debtors
Einrede des mangelnden neuen Vermögens	exception du non-retour a la meilleure fortune	plea of lack of improvement in the debtor's fortune
Einrede des nichterfüllten Vertrages	exception d'inexécution	defense that the other party has failed to perform the contract
Einreichung der Klage (Art. 220 ZPO)	dépôt de la demande	filing of the complaint
Einreise	entrée dans un pays	entry into a country, entering a country
Einschleichdiebstahl	vol par introduction clandestine	theft by secretly entering an unsecured place
Einschreiben	lettre signature	registered letter
Einschreibgebühr	taxe d'inscription	registration fee
einseitige Ablösung eines Grundpfandrechts	purge hypothécaire	unilateral redemption of a mortgage
einseitiger Vertrag	contrat unilatéral	unilateral contract
einseitiges Rechtsgeschäft	acte unilatéral	unilateral transaction (such as making a last will and testament)
Einsprache	opposition	objection

Einsprache gegen den Arrestbefehl (Art. 278 SchKG)	opposition à l'ordonnance de séquestre	objection to the attachment order
Einspracheentscheid (Art. 30 Abs. 2 und 74 VwVG)	décision sur opposition	decision on objections
Einspracheverfahren	procédure d'opposition	objections procedure
Einstandspreis	prix coûtant	cost price
einstellen jemanden in etwas einstellen	suspendre suspendre quelqu'un de ses fonctions	to stay, to suspend to suspend someone's duties
Einstellung der Betreibung (Art. 85 SchKG)	suspension de la poursuite	suspension of the debt collection proceedings
Einstellung der Verwertung von Grundpfändern (Art. 306a SchKG)	suspension de la réalisation des gages immobiliers	suspension of the sale of mortgaged property
Einstellung des Konkursverfahrens mangels Aktiven	suspension de la faillite faute d'actifs	suspension of insolvency proceedings for lack of assets
Einstellung des Verfahrens (Art. 319 StPO)	classement de la procédure	abandonment of the proceedings
Einstellung im Beruf	suspension dans la profession	suspension from the profession
Einstellung von Zivilprozessen und Verwaltungsverfahren (Art. 207 SchKG)	suspension des procès civils et des procédures administratives	suspension of civil court actions and administrative proceedings
Einstimmigkeit	unanimité	unanimity
Eintragung	inscription	registration
Eintragung ins Handelsregister (Art. 640-642 OR)	inscription au registre du commerce	entry in the commercial register
eintragungspflichtig	donnant lieu à enregistrement	subject to registration
eintreibbare Forderung	créance recouvrable	recoverable claim
eintreten: auf etwas eintreten (D: auf etwas eingehen)	entrer en matière	to address, deal with, hear, examine
Eintretensdebatte	débat d'entrée en matière	preliminary discussion (to decide whether to pursue a matter further)
Eintretensverfügung	décision d'entrée en matière	order to hear the case
Eintritt des Schadens	survenance du dommage	occurrence of the damage, occurrence of the harm

Eintritt des Versicherungsfalls	survenance du cas d'assurance	occurrence of the insured event
Eintrittsalter	âge d'entrée	age at entry
Eintrittsgeneration	génération d'entrée	initial generation
Einvernahme (D: Vernehmung)	audition	examination, interrogation
Einvernahmeprotokoll (Art. 78 StPO)	procès-verbal des auditions	record of examination hearings
einvernehmen (D: vernehmen)	interroger	to examine, interrogate
einvernehmliche Private Schuldenbereinigung	règlement amiable des dettes	amicable settlement of debts
einweisen	incarcérer	to incarcerate, to imprison
einweisende Behörde	autorité d'incarcération	authority responsible for incarceration
Einweisung in eine Heil- oder Pflegeanstalt	renvoi dans un hôpital ou un hospice	admission to a hospital or hospice
Einwendung	objection	objection
Einwilligung	assentiment, consentement	consent
Einwilligung des Verletzten	consentement du lésé	consent of the injured party
Einzahlungsschein (D: Zahlkarte)	bulletin de versement (F : mandat-poste)	giro transfer form
Einzeladoption	adoption par une personne seule	adoption by a single person
Einzelarbeitsvertrag	contrat individuel de travail	(individual) employment agreement (as opposed to a collective bargaining agreement)
Einzelfallweise	cas par cas	on a case-by-case basis
Einzelfirma	raison individuelle	sole proprietorship
Einzelhaft (Art. 78 StGB)	détention cellulaire	solitary confinement
Einzelkaufmann	entrepreneur en raison individuelle	sole proprietor
Einzelprokura (Art. 459 II OR)	procuration individuelle	single power of attorney
Einzelrichter	juge unique	single judge (as opposed to a panel of judges)
Einzelunternehmen	entreprise individuelle	sole proprietorship

Einzelunterschrift	signature individuelle	authority to represent the company signing alone
Einzelvollmacht	procuration individuelle	individual power of attorney
einziehen	confisquer	to confiscate
Einziehung (Art. 69, 249 StGB)	confiscation	forfeiture
einzige Instanz	instance unique	single instance
Einzonung	classement (zone)	zoning
Eisenbahngesetz (EBG)	Loi fédérale sur les chemins de fer (LCdF)	Railroads Act
Eisenbahnverordnung (EBV)	Ordonnance sur les chemins de fer (OCF)	Railroads Ordinance
Elektrizitätsgesetz (EleG)	Loi sur les installations électriques (LIE)	Electricity Act
elektronisch überwachte Person	personne sous surveillance électronique	electronically monitored person, tagged person
elektronisch überwachter Strafvollzug	exécution sous surveillance électronique	electronic monitoring
elektronische Abstimmung	vote électronique	electronic voting
elektronische Börse	bourse électronique	automated exchange
elektronische Veröffentlichung	publication électronique	electronic publication
elektronische Zustellung (Art. 86 StPO)	notification par voie électronique	electronic service
elektronisches Geld	monnaie électronique	electronic money
elektronisches Handelssystem	système de négociation électronique	electronic trading system
elterliche Sorge (früher "elterliche Gewalt" genannt) (Art. 296-297 ZGB)	autorité parentale	parental authority (the authority of the father and mother over their children)
elterlicher Stamm	parentèle des père et mère	parental line
Emballage (D: Sackleinen)	toile d'emballage, toile à sac	burlap
Embargo	embargo	embargo

Embargogesetz (EmbG)	Loi sur les embargos (LEmb)	Embargo Act
Emission	émission	issue (sale of securities to the public and their introduction to trading)
Emissionsabgabe	droit de timbre d'émission	stamp tax on the issuance of securities
Emissionsbank	banque émettrice	issuing bank
Emissionspreis	prix d'émission	issue price
Emissionsprospekt (Art. 652a OR)	prospectus d'émission	issue prospectus
Emittent	émetteur	issuer
Empfangs- und Verfahrenszentrum (Art. 26 AsylG)	centre d'enregistrement et de procédure	reception and processing center
Empfangsschein	récépissé	deposit slip
Endentscheid (Art. 90 BGG)	décision finale	final judgment (one which is final in the sense that it puts an end to the proceedings—as opposed to an interlocutory decision—but can then be appealed; compare rechtskräftiger Entscheid, a final judgment that cannot be appealed)
Endprodukt	produit fini	end product, final product
Energiesteuer	impôt sur l'énergie	energy tax
Enteigner	expropriant	expropriater
Enteigneter	exproprié	expropriatee
Enteignung	expropriation	expropriation
enterben	exhéréder	to disinherit
Enterbung	exhérédation	disinheritance
Entführung (Art. 184 StGB)	enlèvement	abduction
Entgelt	contre-prestation	consideration, good and valuable consideration
Entgeltlichkeit	caractère onéreux	compensation, monetary consideration, remunerative nature
entkriminalisieren	décriminaliser, dépénaliser	to decriminalize
Entkriminalisierung	décriminalisation, dépénalisation	decriminalization
entlassen	libérer	to release

Entlassenenhilfe	assistance aux personnes libérées	aftercare
Entlassung	libération	release
Entlassung auf Bewährung	libération conditionnelle	parole, release on parole
Entlastungsbeweis	preuve libératoire	exonerating evidence
Entlastungszeuge	témoin à décharge	defense witness, witness for the defense
Entlehner (Art. 305-211 OR)	emprunteur	borrower
Entmündigung	interdiction	making someone a ward of the court
Entreicherung	appauvrissement	impoverishment
Entreissdiebstahl	vol à l'arraché	theft by snatching, mugging
Entschädigung	indemnité	compensation
Entschädigung für Abnützung	indemnité d'usure	compensation for wear and tear
Entschädigungsfolgen	indemnités	compensation, damages
Entschädigungsgesuch	demande d'indemnisation	application for compensation for financial loss
Entscheid (D: Entscheidung)	décision, arrêt	decision
Entscheid im Rahmen einer Revision (Art. 68 VwVG)	décision prise en matière de révision	decision in a review
Entscheid zur Hauptsache	décision au fond	decision on the merits
Entscheiddispositiv (D: Tenor)	dispositif de la décision	operative part of a judgment, operative provisions, holding
entscheiden	statuer	to decide, to rule
Entscheidentwurf	projet de décision	draft decision, draft judgment
Entscheidgebühr (Art. 95 ZPO)	émolument forfaitaire de décision	judgment fee, fee for the decision (this is an item of court costs)
Entscheidgründe	considérants	grounds for the decision
Entscheidsammlung	recueil d'arrêts	court reports
Entscheidung eines internationalen Gerichts	décision d'un tribunal international	decision of an international court
Entschlüsselung	décryptage	deciphering, decoding
entschuldbare Notwehr (Art. 16 StGB)	défense excusable	mitigatory self defense
entschuldbarer Notstand (Art. 18 StGB)	état de nécessité excusable	mitigatory act in a state of emergency
entsprechende Anwendung finden	s'appliquer par analogie	to apply by analogy

Entwehrung (Art. 195 OR)	éviction	deprivation from the use of property for lack of good title
entweichen	s'évader	to escape
Entweichenlassen von Gefangenen (Art. 319 StGB)	assistance à l'évasion	assistance by a public official in the escape of prisoners
Entweichung	évasion	escape
Entwicklungshilfe	aide au développement	foreign aid
Entwicklungsland	pays en voie de développement	developing country
Entziehen von Minderjährigen (Art. 220 StGB)	enlèvement de mineur	abduction of minors
Entziehungskur	cure de désintoxication	withdrawal treatment, detoxification program
Entzug von Besonnung (Art. 684 ZGB)	privation d'ensoleillement	deprivation of sunlight
Entzug von Tageslicht	privation de lumière	deprivation of daylight
Erbanwartschaft	espérances successorales	estate in expectancy
Erbauskauf (Art. 495 ZGB)	pacte de renonciation à succession à titre onéreux	compensation in lieu of future inheritance
Erbberechtigung	vocation successorale	succession rights
Erbbescheinigung	certificat d'héritier	certificate of inheritance
Erbe (Art. 457 ff. ZGB)	héritier	heir
Erbeinsetzung (Art. 483 ff. ZGB)	institution d'héritier	appointment of an heir
Erbeinsetzungsvertrag (Art. 494 ZGB)	contrat d'institution d'héritier	contract appointing heirs
Erbenausschlussklause	clause d'exclusion des héritiers	heir exclusion clause
Erbengemeinschaft	hoirie, communauté héréditaire	community of heirs
Erbenvertreter	représentant de la communauté héréditaire	representative of the community of heirs
Erbgang	dévolution de la succession, dévolution successorale	devolution of the estate, succession upon death

Erbgut	patrimoine génétique	genetic make-up
Erblasser	de cujus	decedent
Erbmasse	masse successorale	estate
Erbrecht	droit des successions	law of succession
Erbschaft (Art. 457 ff. ZGB)	succession	inheritance
Erbschafts- und Schenkungssteuer	impôt sur les successions et les donations	inheritance and gift tax
Erbschaftsannahme	acceptation d'héritage	acceptance of an inheritance
Erbschaftsausschlagung	répudiation d'une succession	disclaimer of an inheritance
Erbschaftsklage	action en pétition d'hérédité	action for recovery of an inheritance
Erbschaftsteilung (Art. 602 ff ZGB)	partage successoral	division of the estate
Erbschaftsvertreter	représentant de la succession	representative of the estate
Erbschaftsverwalter	administrateur officiel de la succession	administrator of the estate
Erbschaftsverwaltung	administration d'office de la succession	administration of an estate
Erbteil	droit héréditaire	share of an estate
Erbteilung	partage successoral	distribution of the estate (among coheirs)
Erbteilungsklage	action en partage successoral	action for distribution of an estate
Erbteilungsvertrag	acte de partage successoral	contract between heirs regarding the distribution of the estate
Erbunwürdigkeit (Art. 540 ZGB)	indignité successorale	unworthiness to inherit
Erbvertrag (Art. 494 ff. und 512 ff. ZGB)	pacte successoral	contract of inheritance (a bilateral contract between the testator and another person, which cannot be revoked unilaterally)
Erbverzicht	renonciation à succession	renunciation of one's claim to an estate

Erbverzichtsvertrag	pacte successoral de renonciation	agreement renouncing one's claim to an estate
Erbvorbezug	avancement d'hoirie	advance on an inheritance
Erfassungsregel	règle de saisie	recording rule
Erfinder	inventeur	inventor
Erfindung	invention	invention
Erfindungspatent	brevet d'invention	patent
Erfolgsdelikt	infraction de résultat	offense that must cause harm to be a crime
Erfolgshonorar	honoraires calculés en fonction du résultat positif	contingency fee
Erfolgsort	lieu de résultat	place of performance
Erfolgsrechnung (D: G.u.V.-Rechnung)	compte de profits et pertes	income statement
Erforderlichkeit	nécessité	necessity
Erfüllbarkeit	exécutabilité	enforceability
Erfüllung der Obligation	exécution de l'obligation	performance of the obligation
Erfüllung des Tatbestands	réalisation d'une infraction	meeting the definition of a crime
Erfüllung Zug um Zug	exécution simultanée	simultaneous performance
Erfüllungsgarantie	garantie d'exécution	warranty of performance
Erfüllungsort (Art. 74 OR)	lieu de l'exécution	place of performance
ergänzendes Recht	droit dispositif	non-mandatory legal rule (one that can be contracted out of)
Ergänzungsklage	requête additionnelle	supplementary petition
Ergänzungsleistung (EL)	prestation complémentaire (PC)	supplementary benefit
Ergänzungspfändung	extension de la saisie	seizure of additional assets
Ergänzungswahl (D: Zuwahl)	cooptation	coopting a member to a board
erheben	percevoir	to levy
Erhebung	perception	levy (of taxes)
Erhöhung	augmentation	increase

Erhöhung des Aktienkapitals (Art. 650-656 OR)	augmentation du capital-actions	capital increase
Erinnerungswert	valeur d'affection	sentimental value
erkennungsdienstliche Erfassung (Art. 260 StPO)	saisie des données signalétiques	recording identification data
Erklärung	déclaration	declaration, statement
Erklärung des Schuldners zum Inventar (Art. 228 SchKG)	déclaration du failli sur l'inventaire	insolvent's statement on the inventory
Erlass	acte législatif	legislation, enactment (in the sense of "something that has been enacted")
Erlasse der Bundesversammlung	actes édictés par l'Assemblée fédérale	enactments of the Federal Assembly
erlassenes Recht	droit édicté	enacted law
erläuternder Bericht (Staatsvertrag)	rapport explicatif (traité international)	explanatory report (international treaty)
Erläuterung (Art. 69 VwVG)	interprétation	explanatory statement
Erläuterungsgesuch	demande d'interprétation	motion for an explanation (of the court's decision)
erleichterte Einbürgerung	naturalisation facilitée	simplified naturalization
Erlös	produit de réalisation	proceeds of sale
erlöschen	périmer	to expire
Erlöschen der Betreibung (Art. 121 SchKG)	extinction de la poursuite	lapse of insolvency proceedings
Erlöschen einer Forderung	extinction d'une créance	extinction of a claim
Ermächtigung zur Strafverfolgung	autorisation de la poursuite pénale	authorization to prosecute
Ermächtigungsdelikt	infraction poursuivie sur autorisation	offense prosecuted on official authorization
Ermässigung	réduction	reduction
Ermessensspielraum	pouvoirs discrétionnaires	discretion
Ermessensveranlagung	taxation d'office	administrative assessment (of taxes)
Ermittlung	détermination	investigation
Ernährung	alimentation	food, nutrition

erneuerbare Energie	énergie renouvelable	renewable energy
Erneuerung der Baute	rénovation d'immeuble	renovation of a building
Erneuerung der Bewilligung	renouvellement de l'autorisation	renewal of the permit
Erneuerungsarbeiten (Art. 647d ZGB)	travaux de réfection	renovation work
eröffnen (1)	ouvrir	to open
eröffnen (2)	notifier	to notify, to serve notice
Eröffnung (1)	ouverture	opening
Eröffnung (2)	notification	notice, notification
Eröffnung auf diplomatischem Weg	notification par voie diplomatique	notification through diplomatic channels
Eröffnung der letztwilligen Verfügung (Art. 559 ZGB)	ouverture du testament	probate of a will, probate proceedings
Eröffnung des Entscheids	notification de la décision	notice of a decision
Eröffnung des Strafbefehls (Art. 353 StPO)	notification de l'ordonnance pénale	notice of the summary penalty order
Eröffnung des Verfahrens	ouverture de la procédure	opening of a proceeding
Eröffnungsgeschäft	transaction d'ouverture	opening trade
Erpressung (Art. 156 StGB)	chantage	extortion, blackmail
Errichtung eines dinglichen Rechts	constitution d'un droit réel	creation of a right in rem
Errichtungsakt (Art. 629 OR)	acte constitutif	charter
Errungenschaft (Art. 197 ZGB)	acquêt	property acquired during marriage
Errungenschaftsbeteiligung (D: Zugewinngemeinschaft) (Art. 196 ff. ZGB)	participation aux acquêts	participation in accrued gains
Errungenschaftsgemeinschaft (D: Zugewinngemeinschaft)	participation aux acquêts	participation in accrued gains
Ersatzabgabe	contribution de remplacement, taxe compensatoire	exemption tax (e.g. tax payable by people who are exempted from military or fire brigade service)
Ersatzanschaffung	bien acquis en remploi	replacement acquisition
Ersatzarbeit	travail de remplacement	replacement work

Ersatzbeisitzer des Friedensgerichts	assesseur suppléant de la justice de paix	Deputy Assessor to the Justice of the Peace
Ersatzerbe	héritier substitué	contingent beneficiary
Ersatzfreiheitsstrafe (Art. 36 StGB)	peine privative de liberté de substitution	alternative custodial sentence
Ersatzgegenstände von gleichem Gebrauchswert (Art. 92 Abs. 3 SchKG)	objets de remplacement qui ont la même valeur d'usage	substitution of goods of equal value
Ersatzleistung (Art. 206 OR)	remplacement de la chose vendue	substitute performance
Ersatzmann	suppléant	substitute
Ersatzmassnahmen (Art. 237 StPO)	mesures de substitution	alternative measures
Ersatzmieter	locataire de remplacement	substitute tenant
Ersatzrichter	juge suppléant	substitute judge
Ersatzverfügung (Art. 487 ZGB)	substitution vulgaire	substitution (A testator can appoint one or more persons to take the inheritance or legacy if one or more heirs or legatees predecease him or disclaim their inheritance or legacy.)
Ersatzvornahme (Art. 98 OR)	exécution par un tiers	performance by a third party
Ersatzwahl	élection de remplacement	special election
Ersatzwert	valeur de remplacement	replacement value
Erschleichen einer Leistung (Art. 150 StGB)	obtention frauduleuse d'une prestation	obtaining a service without payment
Erschleichung einer falschen Beurkundung (Art. 253 StGB)	obtention frauduleuse d'une constatation fausse	obtaining a false certificate by fraud
Erschleichung eines gerichtlichen Nachlassvertrages (Art. 170 StGB)	obtention frauduleuse d'un concordat judiciaire	obtaining a judicial debt restructuring agreement by fraud
Erschliessung von Land	équipement de terrains	development of land

Erschöpfung des Instanzenzuges	épuisement des instances	exhaustion of remedies
Erschöpfungsgrundsatz	principe de l'épuisement	principle of exhaustion
Erschütterung (Art. 684 ZGB)	vibrations	vibrations
erschwerende Umstände (Art. 184 StGB)	circonstances aggravantes	aggravating circumstances
Ersitzung (Art. 661 ff ZGB)	prescription acquisitive	adverse possession
Ersparnis	épargne	savings
Erstbewertung	évaluation préliminaire	preliminary evaluation
erste Instanz	première instance	first instance
Ersteigerer	adjudicataire	successful bidder
erstmaliger Verurteilter	délinquant primaire	first offender
erstreckbar – Gesetzliche Fristen sind nicht erstreckbar (D: können nicht verlängert werden).	prolongeable - Les délais légaux ne peuvent pas être prolongés.	Statutory deadlines cannot be extended.
Erstreckung	prolongation	extension
Erstverurteilter	délinquant primaire	first offender
ertrügen (D: betrügerisch erlangen)	obtenir par fraude	to obtain fraudulently
Erwägungen	considérations	court's findings (set forth in the decision)
Erwahrung der Konkursforderungen (Art. 244 ff. SchKG)	vérification des créances	claim examination
Erwerb ohne Besitz (Art. 717 ZGB)	constitut possessoire	acquisition without possession
Erwerbsausfall	perte de gain	loss of earnings
Erwerbseinkommen	revenu d'une activité lucrative	income from gainful employment, earned income
Erwerbsersatz	allocation pour perte de gain	unemployment benefits
Erwerbsortsprinzip	soumission à la législation du lieu de travail	application of the law of the place where the person works
Erwerbstätigkeit	activité lucrative	gainful employment
Erwerbsunfähigkeit	incapacité de gain	inability to work
Erwerbsunfähigkeitsrente	rente pour perte de gain	disability benefits

Erziehungsgutschrift	bonification pour tâches éducatives	parenting credit
Estoppel-Prinzip	principe de l'estoppel	principle of estoppel
Estrich (D: Dachboden)	grenier	attic
Ethikkommission	commission d'éthique	ethics commission
Europarecht	droit communautaire	EU law
Eventualabstimmung (Art. 79 ParlG)	votation éventuelle	elimination vote, elimination procedure
Eventualbegehren (D: Hilfsantrag)	proposition subsidiaire	alternative petition, petition in the alternative
eventualiter (D: hilfsweise)	subsidiairement	alternatively, in the alternative
Eventualmaxime	maxime éventuelle	principle that the parties have a certain time in which to file briefs, and may not file them after that time
Eventualvorsatz	dol éventuel	recklessness
eventualvorsätzlich	commis avec dol éventuel	recklessly
Ex-Dividende-Tag	date de détachement	ex-dividend date
Exekutive	autorité exécutive	executive authority
Exequatur	exequatur	exequatur
Exhibitionismus (Art. 194 StGB)	exhibitionnisme	indecent conduct
Exhumierung (Art. 254 StPO)	exhumation	exhumation
Existenzminimum	minimum vital	vital minimum
Exposition der Schutzgüter	exposition des biens à protéger	exposure of the natural resources
Extrasitzung	séance extraordinaire	special session
Fachempfehlungen zur Rechnungslegung (FER)	Recommandations pour la présentation des comptes (RPC)	Swiss Accounting and Reporting Recommendations
Fachstelle für die Gleichstellung von Frauen und Männern	Bureau de l'égalité entre femmes et hommes	Office for Gender Equality
Factoringvertrag	contrat d'affacturage	factoring agreement

Fähigkeitsausweis (D: Gesellenbrief)	certificat de capacité	certificate of qualification (for passing final examination in apprenticeship)
Fahndung (Art. 201 StPO)	mandat de recherches	search for a fugitive, APB (all persons bulletin)
Fahnenflucht	désertion	desertion
Fahren in angetrunkenem Zustand (FiaZ)	conduite en état d'ivresse	drunk driving
Fahren ohne Fahrzeugausweis	circulation sans permis de circulation	driving without a vehicle title
Fahren ohne Führerausweis	circulation sans permis de conduire	driving without a license
Fahrerflucht (Art. 92 Abs. 2 SVG)	délit de fuite	hit and run
Fahrfähigkeit	capacité de conduire	driving ability, ability to drive
Fahrhabe (D: Fahrnis)	bien meuble	chattel
Fahrkarte	titre de transport	ticket
fahrlässige Körperverletzung (Art. 125 StGB)	lésion corporelle par négligence	negligent assault
fahrlässige Tötung (Art. 117 StGB)	homicide par négligence	negligent homicide
fahrlässige Verursachung einer Feuersbrunst (Art. 222 StGB)	incendie par négligence	negligent arson
fahrlässiges Vergehen	délit par négligence	misdemeanor committed through negligence
Fahrlässigkeit	négligence	negligence
Fahrlässigkeitsdelikt (Art. 12 Abs. 3 StGB)	infraction commise par négligence	offense committed through negligence
Fahrnisbaute (Art. 266b OR)	construction mobilière	movable construction
Fahrniseigentum	propriété mobilière	ownership of chattels
Fahrniskauf (Art. 187 OR)	vente mobilière	sale of chattels
Fahrnispfand (Art. 884-894 ZGB)	gage mobilier	pledge of chattels, possessory security interest in chattels (such as securities or insurance policies)
Fahrnispfandrecht (Art. 140 OR)	créance garantie par gage mobilier	lien on chattels
Fahrnisverschreibung	hypothèque mobilière enregistrée	nonpossessory security interest (the debtor remains in possession of the chattel, e.g., ships and aircraft)

Fahrverbot (Art. 67e StGB)	interdiction de circuler	disqualification from driving
Fahrzeugaufbruch	effraction de véhicule	breaking into a vehicle
Fahrzeugausweis (D: Fahrzeugbrief)	permis de circulation	vehicle title
Fahrzeugführer	conducteur	driver
Fahrzeughalter	détenteur de véhicule	vehicle owner
faktische Gesellschaft	société de fait	de facto company
faktisches Monopol	monopole de fait	de facto monopoly
fakultatives Referendum	référendum facultatif	optional referendum
Fälligkeit	exigibilité	maturity
Falschbeurkundung	faux intellectuel dans les titres	false certification
falsche Anschuldigung (Art. 303 StGB)	dénonciation calomnieuse	false accusation
falsche Beweisaussage der Partei	fausse déclaration d'une partie en justice	giving of false evidence by a party
falscher Alarm (Art. 128bis StGB)	fausse alerte	false alarm
falsches ärztliches Zeugnis (Art. 318 StGB)	faux certificat médical	issuing a false medical certificate
falsches Gutachten (Art. 307 StGB)	faux rapport	perjury by an expert witness
falsches Zeugnis (Art. 307 StGB)	faux témoignage	perjury
Fälschung	falsification	forgery
Fälschung amtlicher Wertzeichen (Art. 245 StGB)	falsification des timbres officiels de valeur	forgery of official stamps
Fälschung amtlicher Zeichen (Art. 246 StGB)	falsification des marques officielles	forgery of official marks
Fälschung von Aufgeboten oder Weisungen (Art. 277 StGB)	falsification d'ordre de mise sur pied ou d'instructions	forgery of military orders or instructions
Fälschung von Ausweisen (Art. 252 StGB)	faux dans les certificats	forgery of certificates
Fälschung von Mass und Gewicht (Art. 248 StGB)	falsification des poids et mesures	falsification of weights and measurements
Fälschungsgeräte; unrechtmässiger Gebrauch von Geräten (Art. 247 StGB)	appareils de falsification et emploi illicite d'appareils	counterfeiting equipment and unlawful use of equipment

Familienangehöriger	membre de la famille	family member
Familienausweis (D: Familienstammbuch)	certificat de famille	family certificate
Familienbetrieb	entreprise familiale	family-owned business
Familienbüchlein	livret de famille	family record book
Familiengenossendiebstahl	vol au préjudice d'un colocataire	theft from a cotenant
Familiengesellschaft	société de famille	family-owned company
Familienhaupt	chef de famille	head of the family
Familiennachzug	regroupement familial	family reunion
Familienname	nom de famille	family name
Familienpflege	placement chez des parents nourriciers	placement with foster parents
Familienpolitik	politique familiale	family policy
Familienrecht	droit de la famille	family law
Familienregister	registre des familles	family register
Familienvermögen	biens de famille	family assets
Familienwohnung (Art. 151 Abs. 1 lit. b und 153 Abs. 2 lit. b SchKG)	logement de la famille	family residence
Familienzulage	allocation familiale	family allowance
Faustpfand (Art. 884-894 ZGB, Art. 37 Abs. 2 SchKG)	nantissement	pledge of chattels, possessory security interest in chattels (such as securities or insurance policies)
fehlerhafte Anlage	vice de construction	construction defect
Feiertag	jour férié	public holiday
Feindseligkeiten gegen einen Kriegführenden oder fremde Truppen (StGB 300)	actes d'hostilité contre un belligérant ou des troupes étrangères	hostility towards a country at war or foreign troops
Feinerschliessung	équipement de détail	development of side roads
Femegericht	justice vehmique	kangaroo court
Ferienwohnung	appartement de vacances	vacation apartment

Fernheizung	chauffage à distance	district heating
Fernmeldegeheimnis	secret des télécommunications	secrecy of telecommunications
Fernmeldenetz	réseau de télécommunication	telecommunications network
Fernmeldetechnik	technique de télécommunication	telecommunications
Fernmeldeverkehr	télécommunication	telecommunication
Fernunterrichtsvertrag	contrat d'enseignement à distance	distance learning agreement
fester Preis	prix ferme	firm price
fester Wohnsitz	domicile fixe	fixed domicile
Festnahme (Art. 217 StPO)	arrestation	arrest
Festschrift	mélanges, études offertes	Festschrift
Festsetzung der Busse (D: Buße)	fixation de l'amende	determination of the fine
Feststellung des neuen Vermögens (Art. 265a SchKG)	constatation du retour à meilleure fortune	recognition of an improvement in the debtor's fortune
Feststellung des Sachverhaltes	constatation des faits	establishing the facts of the case
Feststellungsentscheid	décision en constatation de droit	declaratory judgment
Feststellungsklage (Art. 84 ZPO)	action en constatation de droit	action for a declaratory judgment
Feststellungsverfügung	décision en constatation	declaratory order
festverzinsliche Wertpapiere	titres à rémunération fixe	fixed interest-bearing securities
Festvorschuss	avance ferme	fixed advance (a short-term loan)
Feuerpolizei	police du feu	fire marshal
Feuerwehrlokal	local des sapeurs-pompiers	fire station

Feuerwehrsteuer	taxe d'exemption au service de feu	fire service tax (paid by all community members who are not yet active members of the local fire service—may be a percentage of basic tax or a lump sum, depending on the canton)
Fideikommiss	fidéicommis	trust
Fiduziant	fiduciant (F : constituant)	trustor, settlor (of a trust)
Fiduziar	fiduciaire	trustee, fiduciary, escrow agent
Filmförderung (Art. 2 FiG)	encouragement du cinéma	film promotion
Filmgesetz (FiG)	Loi sur le cinéma (LCin)	Film Act
Filmkultur (Art. 5 FiG)	culture cinématographiq ue	film culture
Finanzanalytiker	analyste financier	financial analyst
Finanzaufwand	charges financières	finance expenses
Finanzausgleich	péréquation financière	fiscal equalization
Finanzbuchhaltung (FIBU)	comptabilité financière (COFI)	financial accounting
Finanzchef	chef des finances	chief financial officer (CFO)
Finanzertrag	produits financiers	finance income
Finanzhilfe	aide financière	financial aid
finanzielles Gleichgewicht	équilibre financier	financial equilibrium
Finanzierung	financement	financing, funding
Finanzierung des Terrorismus (Art. 260quinquies StGB)	financement du terrorisme	financing terrorism
Finanzintermediär	intermédiaire financier	financial intermediary
Finanzmarktinfrastruktur	infrastructure des marchés financiers	financial market infrastructure
Finanzmarktinfrastrukturgesetz (FinfraG)	Loi sur l'infrastructure des marchés financiers (LIMF)	Financial Market Infrastructure Act
Finanz-Termingeschäft	contrat à terme d'instruments financiers	financial future

Findelkind	enfant trouvé	foundling
Fingerabdruck	empreinte digitale	fingerprint
Firma	raison de commerce	company name
Fischerei	pêche	fishing
Fischereigerät	engin de pêche	fishing tackle
Fischereipatent	permis de pêche	fishing license
Fiskalabgabe	charge fiscale	fiscal duty, tax
fiskalisches Interesse	intérêt fiscal	fiscal interest
Fiskalquote	quote-part fiscale	tax ratio (ratio of taxes to GNP)
fixe Absicherung	couverture fixe	fixed hedge
Fixgeschäft (D: Fixhandelskauf) (Art. 211 Abs. 2bis SchKG)	engagement à terme strict	commitment for a strict period
Fläche	surface	surface
flexible Arbeitszeit	horaire de travail modulable	flexible work schedule
Flucht	fuite	escape
Fluchtgefahr	risque de fuite	risk of escape
Flüchtling (Art. 3 AsylG)	réfugié	refugee
Flüchtlingshilfe	aide aux réfugiés	aid to refugees
Flugzeugentführung	piraterie aérienne	hijacking
flüssige Mittel	liquidités	cash and cash equivalents
Föderalismus	fédéralisme	federalism
Folge geben an	donner suite à	to take action on, to follow up on
Folterverbot	interdiction de la torture	prohibition on torture
Fondsdomizil	domicile du fonds	fund domicile
Fondsleitung	direction du fonds de placement	fund management
Fondsreglement	règlement de fonds de placement	fund regulations
Fondssparplan	plan d'épargne en fonds de placement	fund savings plan
Fondsvermögen	fortune du fonds	fund assets
Forderung	créance	claim
Förderung	encouragement	promotion
Förderung der Prostitution (Art. 195 StGB)	encouragement à la prostitution	encouraging prostitution

Forderung unter aufschiebender Bedingung (Art. 131 Abs. 1 SchKG)	créance subordonnée à une condition suspensive	claim subject to a condition precedent
Forderung von entsprechendem Wert (Art. 211 Abs. 1 SchKG)	créance de valeur équivalente	claim of equivalent value
Forderungen der Pfandleihanstalten	prêts sur gage	pawning
Forderungseingabe	production de créance	production of the claim
Forderungseinzug (Art. 100 und 243 SchKG)	encaissement des créances, recouvrement des créances	receipt of credit payments
Forderungsverzicht	renoncement à des créances	waiver of claims
formelles Recht	droit formel	procedural law
formelles Strafrecht	droit pénal formel	criminal procedure
Formmangel	vice de forme	procedural defect
Forschung an Menschen (Art. 118b BV)	recherche sur l'être humain	research on human beings
Forschungsfreiheit	liberté de la recherche	freedom to conduct research
fortgesetztes Delikt	délit successif	continuous offense
Fortsetzung der Betreibung (Art. 88 SchKG)	continuation de la poursuite	continuation of debt collection proceedings
Fortsetzung des Handels oder Gewerbes (Art. 237 Abs. 3 Ziff. 3 SchKG)	continuation du commerce ou de l'industrie	continuation of business
Fortsetzungsbegehren	réquisition de continuer la poursuite	motion to continue with the debt collection proceedings (in one of three ways: Pfändung, Konkurs or Pfandverwertung)
Frachtbrief	lettre de voiture	waybill
Frachtführer	voiturier	carrier
Frachtvertrag (Art. 440-457 OR)	contrat de transport de marchandises	contract of carriage
Fragepflicht	obligation de poser des questions	duty to question
Fragerecht	droit de poser des questions	right to ask questions
Fraktion	groupe parlementaire	parliamentary group

Fraktionspräsident	président d'un groupe parlementaire	president of a parliamentary group, chairman of a parliamentary group
Franchise (D: Selbstbehalt)	franchise	deductible
Franchisegeber	franchiseur	franchisor
Franchisenehmer	franchisé	franchisee
Franchisevertrag	contrat de franchisage	franchise agreement
Frankatur	affranchissement postal	postage
Franktireur	franc-tireur	sniper
Frauenhaus	foyer pour femmes battues	battered women's shelter
Freibetrag	montant exempté	exempt amount
Freibeweis	principe de la liberté de la preuve	principle that all types of evidence are admissible (as opposed to the system in the US, where evidence is evaluated by a lay jury, and therefore there are strict rules governing admissibility of evidence)
Freiburg (FR)	Fribourg (FR)	Fribourg (canton)
freie Beweiswürdigung	libre appréciation des preuves	principle of free interpretation of evidence
freier Mitarbeiter	collaborateur libre	independent contractor
freier Warenverkehr	libre circulation des marchandises	free movement of goods
freies Geleit	sauf-conduit	safe-conduct
Freigabe der Sicherheitsleistung (Art. 239 StPO)	libération des sûretés	return of the bail payment
Freihaltebedürfnis	besoin de rester à libre disposition	public interest (against exclusive use)
Freihandverkauf	vente de gré à gré	private sale (as opposed to a public auction)
Freiheit	liberté	freedom, liberty
Freiheitsberaubung (Art. 184 StGB)	séquestration	false imprisonment
Freiheitsentzug (Art. 31 BV)	privation de liberté	deprivation of liberty
Freiheitsstrafe (Art. 40 StGB)	peine privative de liberté	custodial sentence
Freispruch	acquittement	acquittal

freiwillig	à titre volontaire	voluntarily
freiwillige Gerichtsbarkeit (Art. 19 ZPO)	juridiction gracieuse	noncontentious matters
Freizone	zone franche	free trade zone
Freizügigkeit (Versicherung)	libre passage (assurances)	vested benefits
Freizügigkeitsabkommen (FZA)	Accord sur la libre circulation des personnes (ALCP)	Agreement on the Free Movement of Persons
Freizügigkeitseinrichtung	institution de libre passage	vested benefits institution
Freizügigkeitsgesetz (FZG) / Bundesgesetz über die Freizügigkeit in der beruflichen Alters-, Hinterlassenen- und Invalidenvorsorge	Loi sur le libre passage (LFLP) / Loi fédérale sur le libre passage dans la prévoyance professionnelle vieillesse, survivants et invalidité	Swiss Federal Law on Vested Benefits in Occupational Old Age, Survivors and Disability Benefit Plans
Freizügigkeitskonto	compte de libre passage	vested benefits account
Freizügigkeitsleistung	prestation de libre passage	vested benefit
Freizügigkeitsstiftung	fondation de libre passage	vested benefit policy
fremde Sache	bien appartenant à autrui	object belonging to someone else
fremde Währung	monnaie étrangère	foreign currency
Friedensbürgschaft (Art. 66 StGB)	cautionnement préventif	good behavior bond
Friedensrichter	juge de paix	justice of the peace
friedliche Koexistenz	coexistence pacifique	peaceful coexistence
Frist	délai	deadline, time limit
Frist für die Durchführung des Konkurses	délai pour la liquidation de la faillite	deadline for liquidating the assets in a bankruptcy or insolvency
Fristansetzung (Art. 107-108 OR)	fixation d'un délai	setting a time limit for subsequent performance
Fristberechnung	calcul du délai	calculation of the deadline, calculation of the time limit
Fristerstreckung (D: Fristverlängerung)	prolongation du délai	extension of the deadline, extension of the time limit

fristlose Kündigung	résiliation immédiate	termination without notice, immediate termination
Friststillstand	suspension du délai	suspension of the deadline
Fristunterbrechung	interruption du délai	interruption of a period of time
Führerausweis (D: Führerschein)	permis de conduire	driver's license
Führerausweisentzug	retrait du permis de conduire	suspension of driver's license
Führerprüfung	examen de conduite	driver's examination
Fund	chose trouvée	find
Fünferbesetzung der Kammer	collège de cinq juges	presence of five judges on the bench
funktionelle Zuständigkeit (Art. 4 ZPO)	compétence à raison de la fonction	functional jurisdiction
Furchterregung (Art. 29-31 OR)	crainte fondée (F : violence)	duress
Fürsorger	agent de probation	probation officer
Fürsprecher	avocat et notaire	lawyer and notary
Fusion	fusion	merger
Fusionsgesetz (FusG)	Loi sur la fusion (LFus)	Merger Act
Gabelung des Rechtsweges	bifurcation de la voie de droit	bifurcation of appeals
Ganzarbeitslosigkeit	chômage complet	full unemployment
Garantiemarke (Art. 21 MSchG)	marque de garantie	guarantee mark
Garantievertrag	porte-fort	guarantee agreement
Gattungskauf	vente d'une chose de genre	sale of a type of thing (as opposed to a sale of a specific thing)
gattungsmässige Kotierung	cotation par catégorie	listing by class
Gattungssache	chose de genre	type of thing
Gattungsschuld	dette de genre	generic item, fungible item (as opposed to a unique item such as a work of art)
Gebrauchsleihe (Art. 305 ff. OR)	prêt à usage	loan for use (as opposed to a loan for consumption)
Gebühr	émolument, droit	fee

Gebührenüberforderung (Art. 313 StGB)	concussion	overcharging of taxes
Geburtsschein (D: Geburtsurkunde)	acte de naissance	birth certificate
gedeckter Stillhalter	vendeur de call couvert	covered writer
Gefahr	danger	danger
Gefahr im Verzug	péril en la demeure	danger in delay
Gefährdung der öffentlichen Sicherheit mit Waffen (Art. 260quater StGB)	mise en danger de la sécurité publique au moyen d'armes	endangering public safety with weapons
Gefährdung der verfassungsmässigen Ordnung (Art. 275 StGB)	mise en danger de l'ordre constitutionnel	endangering the constitutional order
Gefährdung des Lebens (Art. 129 StGB)	mise en danger de la vie d'autrui	endangering life
Gefährdung durch Sprengstoffe und giftige Gase in verbrecherischer Absicht (Art. 224 StGB)	emploi, avec dessein délictueux, d'explosifs ou de gaz toxiques	misuse of explosives and toxic gases with criminal intent
Gefährdung durch Verletzung der Regeln der Baukunde (Art. 229 StGB)	violation des règles de l'art de construire	violation of construction regulations
Gefährdungsabschätzung	estimation de la mise en danger	risk assessment
Gefährdungsdelikt	infraction de mise en danger	endangerment offense
Gefährdungshaftung	responsabilité objective	strict liability, no-fault liability (as opposed to liability based on fault)
gefälschter Check (Art. 1132 OR)	chèque falsifié	forged check
Gefangener	détenu	prisoner
Gegen die Sicherheit der Schweiz gerichtete ausländische Unternehmungen und Bestrebungen (Art. 266bis StGB)	entreprises et menées de l'étranger contre la sécurité de la Suisse	foreign operations and activities directed against the security of Switzerland
Gegenangebot	contre-offre	counteroffer
Gegenanwalt	avocat de la partie adverse	opposing counsel
Gegendarstellung (Art. 28g ZGB)	droit de réponse	reply, right of reply
Gegenleistung	contre-prestation	consideration
Gegenmehr	contre-épreuve	votes against something

Gegenofferte	contre-offre	counteroffer
Gegenparteirisiko	risque de contrepartie	counterparty risk
Gegenrecht	réciprocité	reciprocity
Gegenseitigkeit (1)	mutualité	mutuality
Gegenseitigkeit (2)	réciprocité	reciprocity
Gegenstand (1)	objet	subject, subject matter
Gegenstand (2)	objet	object, item
Gegenstand der Enteignung	objet de l'expropriation	subject of the expropriation
Gegenstand der Schuldbetreibung (Art. 38 SchKG)	objet de la poursuite	subject of debt collection proceedings
Gegenstandslosigkeit (Art. 242 ZPO)	procès devenu sans objet	proceedings made groundless
gegenüberstellen	confronter	to compare
Konfrontation (Art. 174 ZPO)	confrontation	confrontation (of witnesses)
geheime Abstimmung	vote à bulletins secrets	voting by secret ballot
geheime Überwachungsmassnahmen (Art. 269 ff StPO)	mesures de surveillance secrètes	covert surveillance measures
geheimer Mangel	défaut caché	latent defect
Geheimhaltung	sauvegarde du secret	confidentiality
Gehilfenschaft (Art. 25 StGB)	complicité	complicity
Geisel	otage	hostage
Geiselnahme (Art. 185 StGB)	prise d'otages	hostage taking, taking of hostages
Geisteskranker	malade mental	mentally ill person
Geisteskrankheit	maladie mentale	mental illness
geistig Abnormer	délinquant anormal	mentally ill person
geistige Arbeit	travail intellectuel	brain work, intellectual work
gekreuzter Check (Art. 1123 OR)	chèque barré	crossed check
Geldbusse (D: Geldbuße)	peine pécuniaire	monetary penalty
Geldeinlage (Art. 631 OR)	apport en espèces	cash contribution
Gelder	deniers	moneys
Geldfälschung (Art. 241 StGB)	fausse monnaie	counterfeiting money
Geldinstitut	établissement financier	financial institution
Geldleistung	prestation en argent	payment in money
Geldmarktanlage	placements sur le marché monétaire	money market funds

Geldpolitik	politique monétaire	monetary policy
Geldschuld	dette d'argent	monetary debt
Geldsortenschuld	dette d'une sorte d'argent	debt payable with a specific type of coin
Geldspiele (Art. 106 BV)	jeux d'argent	gambling
Geldstrafe (Art. 34 StGB)	peine pécuniaire	monetary penalty
Geldverfälschung	falsification de la monnaie	counterfeiting
Geldwäscherei (D: Geldwäsche)	blanchiment d'argent	money laundering
Geldwäschereibekämpfung (D: Geldwäschebekämpfung)	lutte contre le blanchiment d'argent	anti-money laundering
Geldwäschereigesetz (GwG)	Loi sur le blanchiment d'argent (LBA)	Money Laundering Act
Geldwert	valeur monétaire	monetary value
geldwerte Leistung	prestation appréciable en argent	payment in kind
geltend machen	faire valoir	to assert
Geltung	validité	validity
Geltungsbereich	champ d'application	scope
Gemässigkeit	conformité	compliance, conformity
Gemeinatzung	droit de vaine pâture	communal grazing
Gemeinbereich	sphère publique	public sphere
Gemeinde (Art. 50 BV)	commune	municipality
Gemeindeammann	maire, président du conseil communal	mayor
Gemeindekanzlei	chancellerie municipale	municipal chancellery
Gemeindeparlament	parlement communal	city parliament
Gemeindepräsident	maire	mayor
Gemeinderat	conseil exécutif	municipal council
Gemeinderecht	droit communal	municipal law
Gemeinderschaft (Art. 132 Abs. 1 SchKG)	indivision de famille	undivided family shares
Gemeindeschreiber	secrétaire communal	municipal secretary
Gemeindesteuer	impôt communal	municipal tax
Gemeindeversammlung	assemblée communale	municipal assembly

gemeinfreies Zeichen	signe appartenant au domaine public	sign in the public domain
gemeingefährliche Straftaten	infractions créant un danger collectif	offenses creating a public danger
Gemeingut	domaine public	public domain
Gemeinnutzen	utilité publique	public interest
gemeinnützig	d'intérêt général, d'utilité publique	in the public interest
gemeinnützige Arbeit (Art. 37 StGB)	travail d'intérêt général	community service
gemeinnützige Organisation	organisation d'utilité publique	charitable organization, charity
gemeinsame Vertretung (Art. 72 ZPO)	représentant commun	joint representation
gemeinsamer Markt	marché commun	common market
Gemeinschaft der Stockwerkeigentümer (Art. 46 Abs. 4 SchKG)	communauté des propriétaires par étages	community of condominium owners
gemeinschaftliches Eigentum (Art. 646 ZGB)	propriété collective	collective ownership
Gemeinschaftsrecht	droit communautaire	EU law
Gemeinschuldner	failli	debtor in bankruptcy, bankrupt debtor
Gemeinwesen (Art. 12 MWSTG)	collectivité publique	public authority
Genehmigung (Art. 38 OR)	ratification	ratification (by the principal of the agent's acts)
Genehmigung des Vertrags (Art. 31 OR)	ratification du contrat	ratification of the contract
Generalexekution (Art. 159 ff SchKG)	exécution générale	general enforcement (sale of the debtor's assets)
Generalsekretariat	Secrétariat général	General Secretariat (of the Swiss Federal Supreme Court)
Generalstab	état-major général	general staff
Generalunternehmer	entrepreneur général	general contractor
Generalunternehmervertrag	contrat d'entreprise générale	general contractor agreement
Generalversammlung (D: Hauptversammlung)	assemblée générale	shareholders' meeting
Genf (GE)	Genève (GE)	Geneva (canton and city)

Genossenschaft (Art. 828 ff OR)	société coopérative	cooperative
Genossenschaftsanteil	part sociale	share of a cooperative
Genossenschaftsverband	fédération	federation
Gentechnologie	technologie génétique	genetic engineering
Genugtuung (D: Schmerzensgeld)	tort moral	pain and suffering
Genugtuungsklage	action en réparation du tort moral	action for pain and suffering
Genussschein (Art. 657 OR)	bon de jouissance	dividend rights certificate
Geoinformationsgesetz (GeoIG)	Loi sur la géoinformation (LGéo)	Geoinformation Act
Gerechtigkeit	justice	justice
Gericht	tribunal	court
gerichtliche Fragepflicht (Art. 56 ZPO)	interpellation par le tribunal	court's duty to question insufficient or unclear allegations made by the parties
gerichtliche Hinterlegung	consignation en justice	deposit into court
gerichtliche Verfahren (Art. 30 BV)	procédures judiciaires	judicial proceedings
gerichtliche Zustellung (Art. 136 ZPO)	notification judiciaire	service of process
gerichtlicher Nachlassvertrag (Art. 171 StGB)	concordat judiciaire	judicial debt restructuring agreement
gerichtlicher Vergleich	transaction judiciaire	in-court settlement
gerichtliches Ermessen (Art. 4 ZGB)	pouvoir d'appréciation du juge	judicial discretion
Gerichtsaktuar	greffier	court clerk
Gerichtsberatung	délibération du tribunal	court's deliberations
Gerichtsentscheid (D: Gerichtsurteil)	décision judiciaire	court decision, judgment
Gerichtsferien (Art. 89 Abs. 2 StPO)	féries judiciaires	court holidays
Gerichtsgebühr	émolument de justice, émolument judiciaire	court fee
Gerichtskasse	caisse du tribunal	court cashier's office
Gerichtskosten (Art. 95 ZPO)	frais judiciaires	court costs

Gerichtspolizei	police judiciaire	judicial police
Gerichtspräsident	président du tribunal	presiding judge
Gerichtsschreiber	greffier	court clerk
Gerichtssitzung	séance du tribunal	court hearing
Gerichtsstand	for	jurisdiction
Gerichtsstandsklausel	clause d'élection de for (F : clause attributive de compétence)	forum selection clause
Gerichtsstandsvereinbarung (Art. 17 ZPO)	élection de for	agreement on jurisdiction
Gerichtsverhandlung	débat du tribunal	court hearing
Gerichtsverwaltung	administration du tribunal	court administration
Gerichtsvollzieher	huissier exploitant	process server
geringfügiges Vermögensdelikt (Art. 172ter StGB)	infraction d'importance mineure	minor offense against property
Geringfügigkeit	importance minime	immateriality
Gesamtarbeitsvertrag (GAV) (D: Tarifvertrag)	convention collective de travail (CCT)	collective bargaining agreement
Gesamtbesitz	possession commune	common ownership
Gesamteigentum (Art. 652 ff ZGB)	propriété commune	collective ownership
Gesamteigentümer (Art. 653 ZGB)	communiste	collective owner
Gesamterneuerungswahl	élection pour le renouvellement général	general election
Gesamtgericht	cour plénière	court sitting en banc
Gesamtpfand	gage collectif	multiple lien
Gesamtpfandrecht	droit de gage collectif	multiple lien (real estate lien constituted by pledging several pieces of property to secure the same debt, with each property being encumbered with the amount of the entire debt)
Gesamtstrafe (Art. 34 Abs. 3 StPO)	peine d'ensemble	cumulative sentence

geschädigte Person (Art. 115 StPO)	lésé	aggrieved person (person whose rights have been directly violated by the criminal offense)
geschäftlich	commercial	commercial, business-related
geschäftlicher Aufwand	charges commerciales	business expenses
Geschäftsbeziehung	relation d'affaires	business relationship
Geschäftsbücher	livres comptables	accounting books and records
Geschäftsfirma	raison de commerce	company name
geschäftsführender Gesellschafter	associé gérant	managing partner, managing shareholder
Geschäftsführer	gérant	manager, managing director
Geschäftsführung ohne Auftrag (GoA)	gestion d'affaires	agency without authority
Geschäftsgeheimnis	secret d'affaires	business secret, trade secret
Geschäftsherrenhaftung (Art. 55 OR)	responsabilité de l'employeur	vicarious liability of employers
Geschäftsjahr	exercice annuel	fiscal year
Geschäftskorrespondenz	correspondance commerciale	business correspondence
Geschäftsleitung	direction	management
Geschäftsniederlassung (Art. 50 Abs. 1 SchKG)	établissement commercial	branch
Geschäftsprüfung (Art. 14 SchKG)	inspections	inspections
Geschäftsräume (Art. 253a OR)	locaux commerciaux	business premises
Geschoss	étage	floor, story
geschützte Pflanze	plante protégée	protected plant
geschütztes Rechtsgut	bien juridique protégé	object of legal protection
Geschwindigkeitsüberschreitung	excès de vitesse	speeding
Geschworener	juré	juror
Gesellschaft	société	company or partnership
Gesellschaft mit beschränkter Haftung (GmbH) (Art. 772 ff OR)	société à responsabilité limitée (Sàrl)	limited liability company
Gesellschafter	associé	partner, shareholder
Gesellschaftskapital	capital social	share capital
Gesellschaftsrecht	droit des sociétés	company law
gesellschaftsrechtliche Streitigkeit	différend relevant du droit des sociétés	dispute concerning company law, company law dispute

Gesetz	loi formelle	statute
Gesetzesauslegung	interprétation de la loi	statutory construction
Gesetzesentwurf	projet de loi	bill
Gesetzesinitiative	initiative législative	legislative initiative (whereby voters begin the legislative procedure by submitting a draft bill to the parliament of the canton)
Gesetzesreferendum	référendum législatif	legislative referendum
Gesetzessammlung	recueil des lois	compendium of laws
Gesetzestechnik	technique législative	legislative technique
Gesetzesumgehung	fraude à la loi	evasion of the law
Gesetzesvorrang	suprématie de la loi	the rule of law
Gesetzgeber	législateur	legislator
Gesetzgebung	législation	legislation
Gesetzgebungsauftrag	mandat de légiférer	mandate to legislate
gesetzlich vorgeschriebene Form (Art. 14 OR)	forme requise par la loi	form required by law
gesetzliche Erbfolge (Art. 457-466 ZGB)	succession légale	intestate succession
gesetzliche Reserve	réserve légale	statutory reserve
gesetzlicher Erbe	héritier légal	intestate heir
gesetzliches Grundpfandrecht (Art. 836 ff ZGB)	hypothèque légale	statutory lien on real property
Gesetzmässigkeit	légalité	legality
gestaffelter Mietzins	loyer échelonné	graduated rent
Gestaltungsklage (Art. 87 ZPO)	action formatrice	action to modify a legal relationship
Geständnis	aveu	confession
Gesuch	requête	application
Gesuch um Entschädigung	demande d'indemnisation	application for compensation for financial loss
Gesuch um Genugtuung	demande de réparation morale	application for compensation for pain and suffering
Gesuchsgegner (D: Antragsgegner)	partie adverse	respondent (in an administrative law case)
Gesuchsteller (D: Antragsteller)	requérant	applicant (in an administrative law case)
Getränkesteuer	impôt sur les boissons	beverage tax
getrennter Wohnsitz	domicile séparé	separate residence

Getrenntleben	vie séparée	living separately
Gewährleistung des veräusserten Rechtes (Art. 192 OR)	garantie en cas d'éviction	warranty of good title
Gewahrsam	détention	possession
Gewalt	violence	violence
Gewalt und Drohung gegen Behörden und Beamte (Art. 285 StGB)	violence ou menace contre les autorités et les fonctionnaires	violence and threats against public authorities and public officials
Gewaltdarstellung (Art. 135 StGB)	représentation de la violence	representation of acts of violence
Gewaltentrennung	séparation des pouvoirs	separation of powers
Gewaltmissbrauch	abus de pouvoir	abuse of power
Gewässerschutzgesetz (GSchG)	Loi sur la protection des eaux (LEaux)	Waters Protection Act
Gewässerschutzverordnung (GSchV)	Ordonnance sur la protection des eaux (OEaux)	Waters Protection Ordinance
Gewerbepolizei (D: Gewerbeaufsichtsamt)	police du commerce, police économique	trade inspection agency
gewerbliche Verrichtungen	actes se rattachant à l'exercice d'une industrie	commercial duties
gewerbsmässige Hehlerei	recel par métier	receiving stolen goods for commercial gain
gewerbsmässiger Diebstahl	vol par métier	theft for commercial gain
gewillkürte Form (Art. 16 OR)	forme volontaire	form stipulated by contract
Gewinnanspruch	droit au gain	entitlement to profits
Gewinnanteil	part de bénéfice	share of the profit
Gewinnherausgabe (Art. 423 OR)	action en remise de gain	restitution
Gewinnsucht: aus Gewinnsucht handeln	agir dans un dessein de lucre	to act with motives of financial gain
Gewinnungskosten (D: Betriebsausgaben und Werbungskosten)	frais d'acquisition du revenu	business and other income-related expenses
Gewinnverwendung	répartition du bénéfice	appropriation of profit
Gewohnheitsrecht	droit coutumier	customary law, custom
gewohnheitsrechtliche Ehe	mariage coutumier	customary marriage

Gewohnheitsverbrecher	délinquant d'habitude	habitual offender
gewöhnliche Ersatzvornahme	exécution par substitution usuelle	substitutive measure
gewöhnlicher Aufenthalt	résidence habituelle	usual place of residence
gezogener Wechsel (Art. 991-1085 OR)	lettre de change	bill of exchange
Glarus	Glaris	Glarus (canton)
Glasversicherung	assurance contre le bris de glaces	glass insurance, plate glass insurance
Glattstellungsgeschäft	transaction de clôture, opération de liquidation	closing trade
Glattstellungstransaktion	transaction de clôture, opération de liquidation	closing trade
Glaubens- und Gewissensfreiheit (Art. 15 BV)	liberté de conscience et de croyance	freedom of religion and conscience
glaubhaft machen	rendre vraisemblable, commencer à faire la preuve	to present prima facie evidence (in order to obtain preliminary injunctive relief)
Glaubhaftmachung	commencement de preuve	presentation of prima facie evidence
Glaubhaftmachung des Gebrauchs (Art. 32 MSchG)	vraisemblance de l'usage	providing prima facie evidence of use (of the trademark)
Gläubiger	créancier	creditor; obligee
Gläubigerausschuss (Art. 237 Abs. 3 SchKG)	commission de surveillance	supervisory commission
Gläubigerbegünstigung	traitement préférentiel des créanciers	preferential treatment of creditors
Gläubigerbenachteiligung	détriment des créanciers	fraudulent conveyance
Gläubigerbevorzugung	traitement préférentiel des créanciers	preferential treatment of creditors
Gläubigergemeinschaft	communauté des créanciers	community of creditors
Gläubigerschädigung durch Vermögensminderung (Art. 164 StGB)	diminution effective de l'actif	reduction of assets to the prejudice of creditors

Gläubigerversammlung (Art. 232 Abs. 2 Ziff. 5, 252 ff SchKG)	assemblée des créanciers	creditors meeting
Gläubigerwechsel (Art. 77 SchKG)	changement de créancier	change of creditor
Gleichartigkeit der Forderungen (Art. 120 Abs. 1 OR)	identité des créances	identical nature of the claims (for claims to be offset, they must be identical)
Gleichheit im Unrecht	égalité dans l'illégalité	equal treatment in illegality
Gleichstellungsgesetz (GIG)	Loi sur l'égalité (LEg)	Gender Equality Act
Gleichwertigkeit	équivalence	equivalence
gleichzeitige Auslieferungsgesuche	concours de requêtes d'extradition	concurrent extradition requests
gleitende Arbeitszeit (Art. 64 BPV)	horaire de travail mobile	flexible working hours
Gleitzeit	période mobile	flextime
Globalurkunde (Art. 973b ZGB)	certificat global	global certificate
Globalzession	cession globale	assignment of all outstanding receivables as security for a loan
Gotte (D: Taufpatin)	parraine	godmother
Götti (D: Taufpate)	parrain	godfather
Grad des Verschuldens	gravité de la faute	degree of fault
grammatikalische Auslegung	interprétation littérale	literal interpretation
Gratisaktie	action gratuite	bonus share
Graubünden (GR)	Grisons (GR)	Graubünden (canton)
Grausamkeit	cruauté	cruelty
Grenzanbau	construction à la limite	zero lot line building (construction of a building directly on a property line)
Grenzbaurecht (Dienstbarkeit)	droit de construire en limite	right to build on the boundary
Grenzbereinigung	rectification de frontière	rectification of boundaries
Grenze	frontière	border
Grenzgängerbewilligung	autorisation de frontalier	cross-border commuter permit
Grenzgemeinschaft	mitoyenneté	co-ownership of a party wall
Grenzscheidungsklage	action en bornage	action for demarcation
Grenzstreitigkeit zwischen Staaten	litige en matière de frontière	border dispute

grenzüberschreitende Geschäfte	opérations transfrontalières	cross-border transactions
Grenzverrückung (Art. 258 StGB)	déplacement de bornes	moving of boundary markers
Grenzwächter	garde-frontière	border guard
Grenzwert	valeur limite	limit, limiting value
grobe Fahrlässigkeit	négligence grave	gross negligence
Groberschliessung	équipement général	development of main roads
grosselterlicher Stamm	parentèle des grands-parents	grandparental line
Grosshandelspreis	prix de gros	wholesale price
Grossist	grossiste	wholesaler
Grosskind (D: Enkelkind)	petit-enfant	grandchild
Grund	motif	ground, reason
Grundbuch	registre foncier	land register
Grundbuchauszug	extrait du registre foncier	land register extract
Grundbuchberichtigungsklage	action en rectification du registre foncier	action to correct the land register
Grundbuchbeschwerde	recours contre la décision du conservateur du registre foncier	appeal from the decision of the land registrar
Grundbuchführer	conservateur du registre foncier	land registrar
Grundbuchkreis	arrondissement du registre foncier	land register district
Grundbuchsperre	blocage du registre foncier	prohibition on recording in the land register
Grundbuchverwalter	conservateur du registre foncier	land registrar
Grunddienstbarkeit (Art. 730-744 ZGB)	servitude foncière	easement that runs with the land
Grundeigentum (Art. 655 ff ZGB)	propriété foncière	land ownership
Grundeigentümer	propriétaire d'un immeuble	landowner
Grundeigentümerpflicht (Art. 678 und 684 ZGB)	responsabilité du propriétaire d'immeuble	landowner liability
Gründer (Art. 635 OR)	fondateur	founder
Grundlagenirrtum	erreur de base	mistake as to the basis of the contract
Grundlast (Art. 782-792 ZGB)	charge foncière	real estate charge

Grundpfand (Art. 793-823 ZGB)	gage immobilier	real estate security interest
Grundpfandverschreibung (D: Hypothek) (Art. 824 ff ZGB)	hypothèque	mortgage (The difference between a *Grundpfandverschreibung* and a *Schuldbrief* is that mortgage notes can be transferred by delivering them, whereas mortgages can only be transferred by written assignment.)
Grundpflicht	devoir fondamental	fundamental duty
Grundrecht	droit fondamental	fundamental right
Grundrechtseingriff	atteinte à un droit constitutionnel	constitutional right violation
Grundsatz der beidseitigen Strafbarkeit	principe de la double incrimination	principle of double criminality (a requirement in the extradition law of many countries whereby a suspect can be extradited from one country to stand trial for breaking a second country's laws only when a similar law exists in the extraditing country)
Grundsatz von Treu und Glauben	principe de la bonne foi	good faith principle
Grundstück (Art. 655 ZGB)	immeuble	property, real property, real estate
Grundstückgewinn	gain immobilier	real estate gains
Grundstückgewinnsteuer	impôt sur les gains immobiliers	real estate gains tax, tax on the profit from the sale of real estate
Grundstückkauf (Art. 655 ZGB)	vente immobilière	land purchase
Grundstücksabgrenzung	délimitation du terrain	demarcation, delimitation(of land)
Gründung der Gesellschaft	constitution de la société	organization of a company
Gründungsbericht (Art. 631 OR)	rapport de fondation	organizational report
Gruppenbildung	formation de séries	constitution of series
Gurtentrageobligatorium (D: Anschnallpflicht)	port obligatoire de la ceinture de sécurité	mandatory wearing of seatbelts

Gutachten	expertise	expert opinion
gute Dienste	bons offices	good offices (a dispute settlement procedure in which a respected third party or a neutral State acting on request or at its own discretion seeks through diplomatic means to persuade the disputing parties to meet and resume direct negotiation)
guter Glaube (Art. 3 ZGB)	bonne foi	good faith
Gütergemeinschaft (Art. 221-246 ZGB)	communauté de biens	community property
Güterkontrollgesetz (GKG)	Loi sur le contrôle des biens (LCB)	Goods Control Act
Güterkontrollverordnung (GKV)	Ordonnance sur le contrôle des biens (OCB)	Goods Control Ordinance
Güterrecht	régime matrimonial	marital property system
güterrechtliche Auseinandersetzung	liquidation du régime matrimonial	marital property settlement
Gütertrennung (Art. 247-251 ZGB)	séparation de biens	separate property regime
Güterumschlag	chargement de marchandises	handling of goods, cargo handling
Güterverbindung	union des biens	union of property system
Güterverzeichnis	inventaire des biens	inventory
Gütezeichen	label de qualité	certification mark
gutgläubig	de bonne foi	in good faith
gutheissen	admettre	to admit
Gutheissung	admission de la demande	admission of the complaint
Gutheissung der Beschwerde	admission du recours	granting the appeal
Gymnasium	gymnase (F : lycée)	academic high school
Habenzins	intérêts créditeurs	creditor interest (rate); deposit rate
Haft	détention	detention
Haft- und Reugeld (Art. 158 OR)	arrhes et dédit	earnest money and forfeit money

Haftanstalt	maison d'arrêts, établissement d'arrêts	detention center
Haftbefehl	mandat d'arrêt	arrest warrant
Haftgeld (Art. 158 OR)	arrhes	earnest money
Haftgericht	juge de l'arrestation	committal court
Haftgrund	motif de détention	ground for detention
Haftkosten	frais de détention	detention costs
Haftpflicht	responsabilité civile	legal liability
Haftpflichtversicherer	assureur responsabilité civile	liability insurer
Haftpflichtversicherung	assurance de responsabilité civile	liability insurance
Haftrichter	juge de la détention	committing magistrate
Haftung aus öffentlichem Recht	responsabilité fondée sur le droit public	public law liability
Haftung aus unerlaubter Handlung	responsabilité délictuelle	tort liability
Haftung der Organe (Art. 722 OR)	responsabilité pour les organes	directors' and officers' liability, D&O liability
Haftung des Familienhauptes (Art. 333 ZGB)	responsabilité du chef de famille	liability of the head of the family
Haftung des Geschäftsherrn (Art. 55 OR)	responsabilité de l'employeur	vicarious liability of employers
Haftung des Tierhalters (Art. 56-57 OR)	responsabilité du détenteur d'animaux	liability of the keeper of an animal
Haftung des Urteilsunfähigen (Art. 54 OR)	responsabilité de la personne incapable de discernement	liability of persons lacking capacity to consent
Haftung des Versicherungsträgers	responsabilité de l'institution d'assurance	liability of the insurer
Haftung des Werkeigentümers (Art. 58-59 OR)	responsabilité du propriétaire d'un bâtiment	liability of property owners
Haftung für Hilfspersonen	responsabilité pour les auxiliaires	vicarious liability

Haftung für Signaturschlüssel (Art. 59a OR)	responsabilité en matière de clé de signature	liability in respect of electronic signatures
Haftungsdauer	durée de la responsabilité	duration of liability
Haftungskonkurrenz	concours de responsabilités	joint liability
Hagelversicherung	assurance contre la grêle	hail insurance
halbe Rente	demi-rente	half pension
Halbfabrikat	produit mi-fini	half-finished product
Halbfreiheit	semi-liberté	semi-liberty
Halbfreiheitsheim	établissement de semi-liberté	semi-liberty institution
Halbgefangenschaft (Art. 77b StGB)	semi-détention	semi-detention
halboffene Anstalt	établissement semi-ouvert	semi-open institution
Haltekosten	coût de portage	cost of carry
Handänderung	mutation	transfer of property
Handänderungssteuer (D: Grunderwerbssteuer)	droits de mutation	real estate transfer tax
Handel mit Betäubungsmitteln	commerce de stupéfiants	narcotics trade
Handel mit militärisch beschlagnahmtem Material (Art. 330 StGB)	trafic de matériel séquestré ou réquisitionné par l'armée	trading in material requisitioned by the armed forces
Handeln nach Treu und Glauben (Art. 2 Abs. 1 ZGB, Art. 52 ZPO)	respect des règles de la bonne foi	acting in good faith
Handelsgebrauch	usage commercial	business practice, trade practice
Handelsgericht (Art. 6 ZPO)	tribunal de commerce	commercial court (exists in four cantons)
Handelsgesellschaft	société commerciale	commercial company
Handelskammer	chambre de commerce	chamber of commerce
Handelsname	nom commercial	trade name
Handelsplatz	plate-forme de négociation	trading venue
Handelsrecht	droit commercial	commercial law
Handelsregister	registre du commerce	Commercial Register
Handelsregisterführer	préposé au registre du commerce	Commercial Registrar

Handelsregisterverordnung (HRegV)	Ordonnance sur le registre du commerce (ORC)	Commercial Register Ordinance
Handelsreisender	voyageur de commerce	traveling salesman
Handelsreisendervertrag	contrat d'engagement des voyageurs de commerce	traveling salesman agreement
Handelssache	matière commerciale	commercial case, commercial matter
Handelsstreitigkeit	différend commercial	commercial dispute
Handgelübde	attestation solennelle	affirmation (taken without swearing an oath)
Handlungsbevollmächtigter	mandataire commercial	commercial agent
Handlungsdelikt	infraction de commission	offense committed by an act (rather than an omission)
Handlungsfähigkeit (Art. 54 ZGB) (D: Geschäftsfähigkeit)	exercice des droits civils	capacity to contract
Handlungsvollmacht (Art. 458-465 OR)	mandat commercial	commercial power of attorney
Handmehr	vote à main levée acquis à la majorité simple	majority vote by a show of hands
Handy	natel (F : téléphone portable)	cell phone, mobile phone
hängig (D: anhängig) am 1. Januar hängige Angelegenheiten	pendant affaires pendantes au 1er janvier	pending cases pending on January 1
Härtefall	cas de rigueur	hardship case
Härtefallrente	rente pour cas pénible	hardship pension
Hauptbuch	grand livre	general ledger
Hauptfälligkeit	échéance principale	anniversary date (of an insurance policy)
Hauptintervention (Art. 73 ZPO)	intervention principale	principal intervention (a third party asserts his own claim)
Hauptsachenprognose	pronostic favorable sur le fond	likelihood of success on the merits
Hauptsacheverfahren	procédure principale	trial on the merits, proceedings on the merits
Hauptverhandlung (Art. 228 ff ZPO)	débats principaux	trial, main hearing

Hausdurchsuchung (Art. 244 StPO)	perquisition domiciliaire	search of premises
Hausfriedensbruch (Art. 186 StGB)	violation de domicile	unlawful entry
Haushalt	ménage	household
Haushaltsführung (Art. 126 BV)	gestion des finances	financial management
Haushaltungszulage	allocation de ménage	household allowance
Hausieren	colportage	peddling, door-to-door selling
Hauskehricht (D: Hausmüll)	ordure ménagère	domestic waste
häusliche Gewalt	violence domestique	domestic violence
Hauspflege	soins à domicile	home care
Hausrat	mobilier	furnishings, household effects
Hausrecht	droit de disposer de son domicile	authority over one's home
Haustürgeschäft (Art. 40a OR)	démarchage à domicile	door-to-door transaction
Hebelwirkung	effet de levier	leverage
Heer	forces terrestres	army, land forces
Hehlerei (Art. 160 StGB)	recel	receiving stolen goods, "fencing"
Heilmittelgesetz	Loi sur les produits thérapeutiques	Therapeutic Products Act
Heilungskosten	frais médicaux	medical expenses
Heimarbeitnehmer	travailleur à domicile	homeworker
Heimarbeitsvertrag (Art. 351 OR)	contrat de travail à domicile	work-at-home agreement
Heimatgemeinde	commune d'origine	municipality of origin
Heimatort	lieu d'origine	place of origin
Heimatrecht	droit national	national law
Heimatschein	acte d'origine	certificate of family origin
Heimatstaat	pays d'origine	country of origin
Heimeinweisung	placement dans une maison d'éducation	placement in a children's home
Heimschaffung	rapatriement	repatriation
Heimversorgung	placement dans une maison d'éducation	placement in a children's home

Heiratsabsicht	intention de se marier	intention to marry
Heiratsgut	dot	wedding gift
Heizkörper	corps de chauffe (F : radiateur)	radiator
herabsetzen	réduire	to reduce, to abate
Herabsetzung der Strafe	réduction de la peine	reduction of the penalty
Herabsetzung des Gehalts	réduction du traitement	salary reduction, pay cut
Herabsetzungsklage (Art. 522 ZGB)	action en réduction	action in abatement
Herausgabe (Art. 194 OR)	abandon de la chose	relinquishment
Herausgabe der Forderungsurkunde (Arg. 150 SchKG)	restitution du titre de la créance	return of the deed of claim
Herausgabe des Kaufpreises (Art. 202 SchKG)	restitution du prix	restitution of the price
Herkunftsangaben (Art. 47 MSchG)	indications de provenance	indications of source
Herkunftsort	lieu de provenance	place of origin
herrenlos werdende Tiere (Art. 719 ZGB)	animaux échappés	escaped animals
herrenlose Sache (Art. 664 ZGB)	chose sans maître	res nullius
herrschende Lehre	doctrine dominante	prevailing opinion (in the literature)
herrschende Meinung (h.M.)	doctrine dominante	prevailing opinion (in the literature and the case law)
Herstellen von gesundheitsschädlichem Futter (Art. 235 StGB)	altération de fourrages	production of harmful animal feed
Hersteller	fabricant	manufacturer
Herstellungskosten	frais de production	manufacturing costs
Herstellungsverfahren	procédé de fabrication	manufacturing process
Hilfeleistung	assistance	assistance
Hilflosenentschädigung (HE) (Art. 26-27 UVG)	allocation pour impotent	incapacitation compensation
Hilflosigkeit	impotence	incapacitation
Hinderung einer Amtshandlung (Art. 286 StGB)	opposition à un acte de l'autorité	prevention of an official act
Hinfälligkeit	caducité du séquestre	lapsing of the attachment

Hingabe an Erfüllungs statt	dation en paiement	accord and satisfaction
hinkendes Inhaberpapier	titre au porteur boiteux	restricted bearer instrument
Hinterlassenenleistung	prestation pour survivants	surviving dependents' benefit
Hinterlassenenrente	rente de survivant	survivor's pension
Hinterlassener	survivant	survivor, surviving dependent
hinterlegen	déposer	to pay into court
Hinterleger (1)	déposant	depositor
Hinterleger (2) (Art. 473 OR)	déposant	bailor
Hinterlegung (1)	dépôt	deposit
Hinterlegung (2)	dépôt	filing (of a trademark or patent registration)
Hinterlegung (3) (Art. 473 OR)	dépôt	bailment
Hinterlegung der Miete	consignation de loyer	deposit of rent (by tenant when landlord fails to repair defects in the lease premises)
Hinterlegung sicherheitshalber	consignation à titre de sûreté	escrow, placing in escrow
Hinterlegung vertretbarer Sachen (Art. 481 OR)	dépôt irrégulier	bailment of fungible goods
Hinterlegungspriorität (Art. 6 MSchG)	priorité découlant du dépôt	right of priority
Hinterlegungsvertrag (Art. 472-491 OR)	contrat de dépôt	contract of bailment; deposit agreement
Hinterziehung	soustraction d'une contribution	evasion
Hinweise auf Patentschutz (Art. 11 PatG)	références à l'existence d'une protection	marking of patented products
Hinzurechnung (Art. 208 ZGB)	réunion aux acquêts	addition
Hochschule für Wirtschaft Zürich (HWZ)	Haute école de gestion de Zurich	Zurich University of Applied Sciences in Business Administration
höchstpersönliche Rechte	droits strictement personnels	strictly personal rights
Höchststrafe	peine maximale	maximum sentence
Hochverrat (Art. 265 StGB)	haute trahison	high treason
Hofdünger (Art. 4 GSchG)	engrais de ferme	farm manure
Hofstattrecht	droit de reconstruire	right to rebuild a destroyed building

hoheitliche Tätigkeit	activité relevant de la puissance publique	sovereign activity
Hoheitszeichen	emblème national	national emblem
höhere Gewalt	force majeure	force majeure
Holdinggesellschaft	société holding	holding company
Holschuld	dette quérable	debt collectible by the creditor, obligation to be performed at the debtor's location
Honorar	honoraires	fees
Hörensagen	par ouï-dire	hearsay
Hotelfachschule	école hôtelière	hotel management school
Hungerstreik	grève de la faim	hunger strike
Hypothekarkredit (D: Hypothekenkredit)	crédit hypothécaire	mortgage loan
Hypothekarmarkt (D: Hypothekenmarkt)	marché hypothécaire	mortgage market
Hypothekarzins (D: Hypothekenzins)	intérêt hypothécaire	mortgage interest
Hypothekenbank	banque hypothécaire	mortgage bank
Hypothekenversicherung	assurance des hypothèques	mortgage insurance
Idealkonkurrenz	concours idéal	commission of a single act that results in several criminal offenses (multiple offenses committed by one act)
Identität	identité	identity
Identität der Klagen	identité des demandes	identical nature of the claims
Identitätskarte (D: Personalausweis)	carte d'identité	identity card
illegale Ausreise	sortie illégale	illegal departure
illegale Einreise	entrée illégale	illegal entry
illegaler Aufenthalt	séjour illégal	illegal stay
im Übrigen	pour le surplus	in other respects
Immaterialgut	bien immatériel	intangible asset
Immaterialgüterrecht	droit de la propriété intellectuelle	intellectual property right
Immatrikulation	carte grise	vehicle registration
immatrikulieren	établir la carte grise de	to register a vehicle
Immission	immission	exposure

Immobiliarsachenrecht	droits réels immobiliers	law of real property
Immobilienfonds	fonds immobiliers	real estate fond
Immobilienhändler	agent immobilier	real estate agent, realtor
Immunität	immunité	immunity
Immunität des Staates	immunité de l'Etat	sovereign immunity
Importpräparat	produit importé	imported product
in Betreibung gesetzte Forderung	créance en poursuite	claim being enforced
in flagranti	flagrant délit	caught in the act
in Gewahrsam haben	détenir	to possess, to hold
in Rechtskraft erwachsen	entrer en force	to enter into force
in Umlaufsetzen falschen Geldes (Art. 242 StGB)	mise en circulation de fausse monnaie	tendering counterfeit money
Index der Konsumentenpreise	indice des prix à la consommation (IPC)	Consumer Price Index (CPI)
indexierter Mietzins	loyer indexé	indexed rent
Indexierung	indexation	indexing
individuelle Vorsorge	prévoyance individuelle	individual pension plan
individuelles Konto	compte individuel	individual account
Indiz	indice	circumstantial evidence
Indizienbeweis	preuve par indices	circumstantial evidence
Indossament (Art. 1001 OR)	endossement	indorsement
Indossant	endosseur	indorser
Indossatar	endossataire	indorsee
Informatiksteuerungsorgan des Bundes (ISB)	Unité de pilotage informatique de la Confédération (UPIC)	Federal IT Steering Unit
Informationsfreiheit	liberté d'information	freedom of information
Informationspflicht	devoir d'information	duty of disclosure
Ingress (Ingr.)	préambule (préamb.)	preamble
Inhaberaktie (Art. 683 OR)	action au porteur	bearer share
Inhaberpapier (Art. 978 ff OR)	titre au porteur	bearer paper
Inhaberpartizipationsschein	bon de participation au porteur	bearer participation certificate

inhaftierte Person	personne détenue	prisoner
Initiant	auteur/promoteur d'une initiative	initiator
Inkasso	recouvrement	collection
Inkrafttreten	entrée en vigueur	entry into force
Inlandanleihen	emprunt national	domestic bond
innerer Notstand	état de nécessité intérieure	internal state of emergency
innerer Wert	valeur intrinsèque	intrinsic value (of an option)
innerkantonal	intracantonal	intracantonal
innerorts	à l'intérieur des localités	in an urban area
innert 30 Tagen (D: innerhalb von 30 Tagen)	dans les 30 jours	within 30 days
Innominatvertrag (D: atypischer Vertrag)	contrat innommé	innominate contract (one not provided for by the code)
Insider	initié	insider
Insiderdelikt	délit d'initié	insider trading
Insidergeschäft	opération d'initié	insider transaction
Insiderinformation	information d'initié	insider information
Insolvenzerklärung (Art. 191 SchKG)	déclaration d'insolvabilité	declaration of insolvency
Inspektorat der Bezirksschreibereien	Autorité de surveillance du registre foncier	Land Register Inspectorate
Inspektorat für die Notariate, Grundbuch- und Konkursämter	Autorité de surveillance du registre foncier	Land Register Inspectorate
Institut für Föderalismus	Institut du Fédéralisme	Institute of Federalism
Institution des Freiheitsentzugs	institution de privation de liberté	penal institution
Institutsgarantie	garantie de l'institution	institutional guarantee
Instruktionsrichter	juge délégué à l'instruction	investigating judge
Instruktionsverhandlung (Art. 226 ZPO)	débats d'instruction	preliminary hearing, pretrial conference

Integritätsentschädigung (Art. 24-25 UVG)	indemnité pour atteinte à l'intégrité	impairment compensation
Integritätsrente	rente pour atteinte à l'intégrité	impairment pension
Integritätsschaden	atteinte à l'intégrité	impairment
intellektuelle Fälschung	faux intellectuel	false certification
Interessenkonflikt	conflit d'intérêts	conflict of interest
Interimsschein	certificat intérimaire	interim certificate
interkantonal	intercantonal	intercantonal
interkantonale Behörde	autorité intercantonale	intercantonal authority
interkantonale Doppelbesteuerung	double imposition intercantonale	intercantonal double taxation
interkantonale Stellen	services intercantonaux	intercantonal offices
Interkantonaler Rückversicherungsverband (IRV)	Union intercantonale de réassurance (UIR)	Intercantonal Union of Reinsurance
Internationale Energieagentur	Agence internationale de l'énergie	International Energy Agency
Internationale Handelskammer (IHK)	Chambre de commerce internationale (CCI)	International Chamber of Commerce (ICC)
internationales Privatrecht	droit international privé	private international law (also called "conflict of laws")
interoperable Verbindungen	liaisons interopérables	interoperability agreements
Interpellant	interpellateur	interpellator
Interpellation	interpellation parlementaire	interpellation
intervenierende Person (Art. 76 ZPO)	intervenant	intervenor
Intervention (Art. 73 ZPO)	intervention	third-party intervention
Interventionsgesuch (Art. 75 ZPO)	requête en intervention	application for intervention
Invalideneinkommen	revenu d'invalide	disability income
Invaliden-Kinderrente	rente d'enfant d'invalide	disable persons' children's pension

Invalidenleistung	prestation d'invalidité	disability benefits
Invalidenrente	rente d'invalidité	disability pension
Invalidenversicherung (IV)	assurance-invalidité (AI)	disability insurance
Invalidität	invalidité	disability
Invaliditätsbemessung	évaluation de l'invalidité	disability evaluation
Invaliditätsgrad	degré de l'invalidité	degree of disability
Inventar	inventaire	inventory
Inventaraufnahme	prise d'inventaire	taking of inventory
Inverkehrbringen	mise en circulation	marketing
Inverkehrbringen und Anpreisen von Abhör-, Ton- und Bildaufnahmegeräten (Art. 179sexies StGB)	mise en circulation et réclame en faveur d'appareils d'écoute, de prise de son et de prise de vues	marketing and promotion of devices for unlawful listening or sound or image recording
Inverkehrbringen von gesundheitsschädlichem Futter (Art. 236 StGB)	mise en circulation de fourrages altérés	marketing of harmful animal feed
Inzest (Art. 213 StGB)	inceste	incest
irreführendes Zeichen (Art. 2 MSchG)	signe propre à induire en erreur	misleading sign
Irreführung der Rechtspflege (Art. 304 StGB)	induction de la justice en erreur	misleading the judicial authorities
Irrtum (Art. 23 OR)	erreur	mistake
Irrtum über die Rechtswidrigkeit (Art. 21 StGB)	erreur sur l'illicéité	error as to unlawfulness
Isolation (Baute)	isolation	insulation
Isolation (Krankheit)	isolement (maladie)	isolation
Isolationshaft	mise au secret	solitary confinement
Isoliergewerbe	industrie de l'isolation	insulation industry
IV-Regionalstelle	Office Régional de l'AI	Regional Disability Insurance Office
IV-Stelle	Office AI	Disability Insurance Office
IV-Stelle für Versicherte im Ausland	Office AI pour les assurés résidant à l'étranger (OAIE)	Disability Insurance Office for People Living Abroad
Jagdaufseher	garde-chasse	game warden

Jagdpatent	permis de chasse	hunting permit
Jahresbericht (D: Geschäftsbericht)	rapport annuel	annual report
Jahresgewinn	bénéfice de l'exercice	profit for the year
Jahreslohn	salaire annuel	annual salary
Jahresrechnung (D: Jahresabschluss)	comptes annuels	annual financial statements
Jahressteuer	impôt annuel	annual tax
Judikative	pouvoir judiciaire	judicial power
Judikatur (D: Rechtsprechung)	jurisprudence	case law
Jugendanwalt	procureur des mineurs	juvenile prosecutor
Jugendanwaltschaft	Ministère public des mineurs	Office of the Juvenile Prosecutor
Jugenddelinquenz	délinquance juvénile	juvenile delinquency
Jugendgericht	tribunal des mineurs	juvenile court
Jugendgerichtskammer	Chambre des mineurs	Juvenile Court of Appeals
Jugendgerichtskanzlei	greffe du Tribunal des mineurs	Registry of the Juvenile Court
Jugendgerichtskommission	Commission du Tribunal des mineurs	Juvenile Court Commission
Jugendkriminalität	délinquance juvénile	juvenile delinquency
Jugendstrafprozessordnung (JStPO)	Procédure pénale applicable aux mineurs (PPMin)	Juvenile Criminal Procedure Code
Jugendstrafrecht	droit pénal des mineurs	juvenile criminal law
Jugendstrafverfahren	procédure pénale des mineurs	juvenile criminal procedure
Jura (JU)	Jura (JU)	Jura (canton)
Jurist	juriste	law graduate, person with a law degree
juristische Person	personne morale	legal entity
Kadermitarbeiter	cadre	management employee
Kaderversicherung	assurance pour cadres	executive management insurance

Kaduzierung	déclaration d'échéance	forfeiture of shares (when shareholder has not paid for new shares or is late in paying for the outstanding portion of existing shares)
Kammer	chambre	chamber (of a court)
Kandidatenstimme	suffrage nominatif	candidate vote
Kann-Vorschrift	norme potestative	discretionary rule
Kanton	canton	canton
Kantonalbank	banque cantonale	cantonal bank
Kantonale Amtsstelle	autorité cantonale	cantonal authority
kantonale Behörde	autorité cantonale	cantonal authority
kantonale Gerichtsbarkeit	juridiction cantonale	cantonal jurisdiction
kantonale Stimmrechtsbeschwerde	recours cantonal en matière de droit de vote	cantonal appeal on a matter related to voting rights
Kantonales Einigungsamt	Office cantonal de conciliation	Cantonal Office for Conciliation in Labor Disputes
Kantonales Parlament	parlement cantonal	cantonal parliament
Kantonales Raumplanungsgesetz	Loi cantonale sur l'aménagement du territoire	Cantonal Act on Spatial Planning
kantonales Recht	droit cantonal	cantonal law
kantonales Verfahren	procédure cantonale	cantonal procedure
Kantonales Verwaltungsrechtspflegegesetz	code de procédure administrative cantonal	Cantonal Code of Administrative Procedure
Kantons- und Gemeindesteuer	impôt cantonal et communal (ICC)	cantonal and municipal tax
Kantonsbürgerrecht	droit de cité cantonal	cantonal citizenship
Kantonsgericht	tribunal cantonal	cantonal court (court of first instance in AR, AI, OW, SH and ZG; court of appeals in FR, GR, NW, SZ and VS)
Kantonspolizei (Kapo)	police cantonale	cantonal police
Kantonsrat	grand conseil	cantonal parliament

Kantonsspital	hôpital cantonal	cantonal hospital
Kantonsstrasse	route cantonale	cantonal road
Kantonsverfassung (KV) (Art. 51 BV)	constitution cantonale	cantonal constitution
Kanzlei	chancellerie	office of the court clerk
Kanzleiauslagen	débours de chancellerie	expenses incurred by the court (expert fees, travel expenses, witnesses, etc.)
Kanzleigebühren	frais de chancellerie	clerk's fee for copies, excerpts, transmittals, etc.
Kapitalabfindung	prestation en capital	cash settlement
Kapitalausstattung	dotation en capital	capital resources
Kapitalbeteiligung	participation au capital	equity interest
Kapitaldeckungsverfahren	système de la capitalisation	funding method, funding system
Kapitalerhöhungsbericht (Art. 652e OR)	rapport d' augmentation	capital increase report
Kapitalgesellschaft	société de capitaux	capital company
Kapitalgewinn	gain en capital	investment income
Kapitalgewinnsteuer (D: Kapitalertragsteuer)	impôt sur les bénéfices en capital	investment income tax
Kapitalherabsetzung	réduction de capital, minoration de capital	capital reduction
Kapitalhilfe	aide en capital	capital injection
Kapitalmarkt	marché des capitaux	capital market
Kapitalverkehrsfreiheit	libre circulation des capitaux	free circulation of capital
Kapitalwert	valeur capitalisée	capitalized value
Kapprecht (Art. 687 ZGB)	droit d'ébrancher	right to cut overhanging branches
Karenzjahr	délai de carence d'une année	one-year grace period
Kartell	cartel	cartel
Kartellgesetz (KG)	Loi sur les cartels (LCart)	Cartel Act
Kartellrecht	droit des cartels	antitrust law
Kassabuch	livre de caisse	cash book
Kassamarkt	marché au comptant	spot market, cash market

Kassationshof	Cour de cassation pénale	Court of Criminal Cassation
kassatorische Wirkung	effet cassatoire	quashing the lower court's decision without substituting the appellate court's judgment for the lower court's decision
Kassenobligation	obligation de caisse	medium-term notes issued by banks
Kassier (D: Kassierer)	caissier	treasurer; cashier
Kataster	cadastre	cadaster
Kataster der belasteten Standorte	cadastre des sites pollués	register of polluted sites
Kauf (Art. 184-238 OR)	vente	sale
Kauf auf Probe oder auf Besicht (Art. 223 OR)	vente à l'essai ou à l'examen	sale on trial or approval
Kauf im kaufmännischen Verkehr	vente commerciale	commercial sale
Kauf nach Muster	vente sur échantillon	purchase based on a sample
Käufer	acheteur	buyer, purchaser
Kaufkraft	pouvoir d'achat	purchasing power
Kaufmann	commerçant	merchant
kaufmännische Buchführung (Art. 957 OR)	comptabilité commerciale	commercial accounting
kaufmännische Gesellschaft (Art. 552 CO)	société exerçant une activité commerciale	commercial partnership
kaufmännischer Verkehr	ventes commerciales	commercial transactions
Kaufpreis	prix d'achat	purchase price
Kaufsache (D: Kaufgegenstand)	chose vendue	item sold
Kaufsrecht (Art. 216 OR)	droit d'emption	option right (to buy a piece of property at a later date on the terms set forth in the contract)
Kaufvertrag (Art. 184-221 OR)	contrat de vente	sales agreement
Kausalabgabe	contribution causale	tax for services rendered
Kausalhaftung	responsabilité causale	vicarious liability and strict liability
Kausalität	causalité	causation
Kehrichtgebühr	taxe de ramassage des ordures	garbage collection fee
Kennzeichen	signe distinctif	distinctive sign

Kinder- und Erwachsenenschutzbehörde (KESB)	Autorité` de protection de l'enfant et de l'adulte (APEA)	Child and Adult Protection Authority
Kinderabzug	déduction pour enfant	child deduction
Kinderarbeit	travail des enfants	child labor
Kindergarten	école enfantine (F : école maternelle)	kindergarten
Kinderkrippe	garderie	day care center
Kinderzulage	allocation pour enfant	child allowance
Kindesannahme	adoption	adoption
Kindesmisshandlung	mauvais traitements envers les enfants	child abuse
Kindestötung (Art. 116 StGB)	infanticide	infanticide
Kindesverhältnis	filiation	filiation
Kindeswohl	intérêt de l'enfant	best interests of the child
Kirchenpflege	conseil de paroisse	parish council
Kirchensteuer	contribution ecclésiastique	church tax
Klage (1)	action en justice	lawsuit, court action
Klage (2) (Art. 221 ZPO)	demande	complaint (the document filed by the plaintiff to commence the lawsuit)
Klage auf Abtretung des Patentgesuchs	action en cession de la demande de brevet	action for assignment of a patent
Klage auf Anerkennung der Forderung (Art. 153a Abs. 1 SchKG)	action en constatation de la créance	action for recognition of the claim
Klage auf Bestreitung des neuen Vermögens (Art. 265a Abs. 4 SchKG)	action en constatation du non-retour à la meilleure fortune	action for recognition of a lack of improvement in the debtor's fortune
Klage auf Feststellung des neuen Vermögens (Art. 265a Abs. 4 SchKG)	action en constatation du retour à la meilleure fortune	action for recognition of an improvement in the debtor's fortune

Klage auf Feststellung des Pfandrechts (Art. 153a Abs. 1 SchKG)	action en constatation du droit de gage	action for recognition of a pledge
Klage auf Rückschaffung von Retentionsgegenständen (Art. 284 SchKG)	action en réintégration des biens soumis au droit de rétention	action to recover items subject to a right of retention
Klage auf Scheidung	demande en divorce	petition for divorce
Klage auf Übertragung der Marke (Art. 53 MSchG)	action en cession du droit à la marque	action for assignment of the trademark
Klage auf Zahlung (Art. 184 Abs. 2 SchKG)	action en paiement	action for payment
Klage aus Besitzesentziehung (Art. 927 ZGB)	réintégrande	action to recover possession (by someone who has been unlawfully dispossessed)
Klage aus Besitzesstörung (Art. 928 ZGB)	action en raison du trouble de la possession	action for trespass
Klage aus unerlaubter Handlung (Art. 36 ZPO)	action fondée sur un acte illicite	action in tort, action sounding in tort
Klage aus Vertrag (Art. 31 ZPO)	action découlant d'un contrat	action in contract, action sounding in contract
Klageänderung (Art. 227 ZPO)	modification de la demande	amendment of the complaint
Klageanerkennung (Art. 241 ZPO)	acquiescement	acceptance of the plaintiff's claim (by the defendant)
Klageantwort (Art. 222 ZPO)	réponse	answer (to the complaint)
Klageberechtigung	qualité pour agir	right to bring action
Klagebewilligung (Art. 209 ZPO)	autorisation de procéder	conciliation authority's authorization to proceed
Klagefrist	délai pour intenter action	time limit for bringing a claim
Klagegrund	motif de réclamation	grounds for a claim
Klagenhäufung (Art. 90 ZPO)	cumul d'actions	joinder of actions
Kläger	demandeur	plaintiff
Klagerückzug (Art. 241 ZPO)	désistement d'action	withdrawal, dismissal of the action (by the plaintiff)
Klageschrift	demande	complaint
Kläranlage	installation d'épuration	sewage treatment plant, waste water treatment plant

Kleinanwalt	agent d'affaires	professional who represents parties in cases such as bankruptcy, employment disputes and landlord-tenant disputes
kleine und mittlere Unternehmen (KMU)	petites et moyennes entreprises (PME)	small and medium-sized enterprises (SME)
Kleinhandel	commerce de détail	retail trade
Klumpenrisiko	risques cumulés	cluster risk
Koalitionsfreiheit (BV 28)	liberté syndicale	right to form professional associations
Kollektivanlagengesetz (KAG)	Loi sur les placements collectifs (LPCC)	Collective Investment Schemes Act
Kollektivanlagevertrag	contrat de placement collectif	collective investment agreement
Kollektivarbeitsstreitigkeit	conflit collectif du travail	collective bargaining dispute
Kollektivgesellschaft (KG) (Art. 552 ff OR)	société en nom collectif (SNC)	general partnership
Kollektivmarke (Art. 22 MSchG)	marque collective	collective mark
Kollektivunterschrift	signature collective	requirement of more than one signature
Kollektivunterschrift zu zweien	signature collective à deux	two signatures required
Kollektivversicherung	assurance collective	group insurance
Kollisionsregel	règle de conflit	conflicts of law rule
Kollokation (Art. 247 ff SchKG)	collocation	schedule of admission of the accepted claims
Kollokationsklage (Art. 148 und 250 SchKG)	action en contestation de l'état de collocation	action to challenge the schedule of claims
Kollokationsplan (D: Konkurstabelle) (Art. 146 und 247 SchKG)	état de collocation	schedule of accepted claims
Kollozierung (Art. 247 ff SchKG)	collocation	schedule of admission of the accepted claims
Kollusionsgefahr	risque de collusion	risk of collusion
Kolonnenverkehr	circulation en file	line of traffic
Komitee	comité	committee

Kommanditaktiengesellschaft (KmAG) (D: Kommanditgesellschaft auf Aktien) (Art. 764 ff OR)	société en commandite par actions (SCmA)	partnership limited by shares
Kommanditär (D: Kommanditist) (Art. 600 OR)	commanditaire	limited partner
Kommanditgesellschaft (KmG) (Art. 594 ff OR)	société en commandite	limited partnership
Kommanditsumme (Art. 609 OR)	commandite	limited partner's contribution
Kommentar (1) (Bemerkung)	commentaire (remarque)	comment
Kommentar (2) (Werk)	commentaire (ouvrage)	commentary
Kommission (Art. 425-439 OR)	commission	commission contract
Kommissionär	commissionnaire	commission agent
Kommissionsgebühr	droit de commission	commission, fee
Kommissionsgut (Art. 426 OR)	choses formant l'objet du contrat de commission	goods for sale on commission
Kommissionsverhältnis	contrat de commission	commission agency relationship
Kommittent (Art. 425 OR)	commettant	principal
kommunales Inventar	inventaire communal	inventory of cultural assets in a municipality
Kompetenzattraktion	attraction de compétence	ancillary jurisdiction (power of a court to take jurisdiction over matters that are normally outside its jurisdiction, in order to settle all claims in one court)
Kompetenz-Kompetenz	compétence de la compétence	power of a court or tribunal to decide questions concerning its own jurisdiction
Kompetenzkonflikt	conflit de compétences	jurisdictional conflict
Kompetenzstück (Art. 224 SchKG)	bien de stricte nécessité, objet insaisissable	bare necessity good
Komplementär	associé indéfiniment responsable	general partner
Kondukteur (D: Schaffner)	contrôleur	ticket collector
Konfrontation (Art. 174 ZPO)	confrontation	confrontation (of witnesses)
Konjunktur	conjoncture	the economy, economic climate, economic conditions, the overall economic picture

Konjunkturpolitik (Art. 100 BV)	politique conjoncturelle	economic policy
konkludentes Verhalten	acte concluant	implicit, implicitly, implied contract
Konkordanzdemokratie	démocratie de concordance	consotiational democracy
Konkordat (1) (Vertrag mit dem Apostolischen Stuhl)	concordat (traité avec le siège apostolique)	concordat (convention with the Holy See)
Konkordat (2) (Vertrag zwischen Kantonen)	concordat (traité entre cantons)	treaty between cantons
Konkubinat	concubinage, union libre	cohabitation
Konkurrent	concurrent	competitor
konkurrenzieren (D: mit jemandem oder etwas konkurrieren)	concourir avec	to compete with
Konkurrenzverbot (Art. 340 OR)	prohibition de concurrence	covenant not to compete
Konkurs (Art. 159 ff SchKG)	faillite	insolvency, bankruptcy
Konkursamt (Art. 2 SchKG)	office des faillites	bankruptcy office
Konkursandrohung (Art. 159 SchG)	commination de faillite	threat of bankruptcy, threat of insolvency, bankruptcy warning, insolvency warning
Konkursaufschub (Art. 173 Abs. 1, 173a und 331 Abs. 2 SchKG)	ajournement de la faillite	stay of insolvency proceedings, stay of bankruptcy proceedings
Konkursbeamter (Art. 2 SchKG)	préposé aux faillites	bankruptcy official
Konkursbegehren (Art. 166 SchKG)	réquisition de faillite	insolvency petition, bankruptcy petition
Konkursbetreibung (Art. 159 ff SchKG)	poursuite par voie de faillite	debt collection via bankruptcy proceedings (legal action to enforce the sale of all assets of a debtor who fails to meet his payment obligations)
Konkurseingaben	productions	creditors' claims in bankruptcy
Konkurserkenntnis	déclaration de faillite	declaration of bankruptcy
Konkurseröffnung (Art. 171 SchKG)	ouverture de la faillite	declaration of insolvency
Konkursforderung	créance dans la faillite	bankruptcy claim, insolvency claim
Konkursgläubiger	créancier du failli	creditor of the bankrupt debtor
Konkursit	failli	bankrupt debtor

Konkursmasse (Art. 197 SchKG)	masse en faillite	bankrupt estate
Konkursort bei flüchtigem Schuldner (Art. 54 SchKG)	for de la faillite du débiteur en fuite	insolvency jurisdiction for the absconding debtor
Konkursprivileg	privilège dans la faillite	preferential right in bankruptcy proceedings
Konkursrecht	droit de la faillite	bankruptcy law, insolvency law
Konkursrichter	juge de la faillite	bankruptcy judge
Konkursverfahren (Art. 221 ff SchKG)	procédure de faillite	bankruptcy proceedings
Konkursverhandlung (Art. 168 SchKG)	audience de faillite	bankruptcy hearing
Konkursverlustschein	acte de défaut de biens après faillite	certificate of unpaid debt established after bankruptcy
Konkursverwalter	administrateur de la faillite	administrator in bankruptcy or liquidation
Konkursverwaltung (Art. 240 SchKG)	administration de la faillite	bankruptcy administration
Konnossement	connaissement	bill of lading
Konsens (Art. 1 Abs. 1 OR)	accord de volontés	meeting of the minds
Konsolidierungsregel	règle de consolidation	rule of consolidation
Konsortium	consortium	consortium
konstituieren: Der Verwaltungsrat konstituiert sich selbst.	constituer : Le conseil se constitue lui-même.	The board shall organize itself internally [i.e., the directors decide who does what].
konstitutive Generalversammlung	assemblée générale constitutive	organizational meeting
Konsultativabstimmung	votation consultative	nonbinding vote
Konsultativversammlung	assemblée consultative	organizational meeting
Konsum	consommation	consumption
Konsument	consommateur	consumer
Konsumfreiheit	liberté de consommation	freedom of consumption
Konsumkreditvertrag	contrat de crédit à la consommation	consumer credit agreement
Konsumkreditvertrag (Art. 1 KKG)	contrat de crédit à la consommation	consumer credit contract

Kontaktverbot (Art. 67 StGB)	interdiction de contact	contact prohibition
Kontenauszug	extrait du compte individuel	account statement
Kontokorrent	compte courant	checking account
Kontokorrentguthaben bei der Bank	avoirs en comptes courants auprès de banques	cash in bank, checking account balance
kontradiktorisches Verfahren	procédure contradictoire	adversary proceedings
Kontumatialverfahren	procédure par défaut	proceedings for a default judgment
Konventionalstrafe (D: Vertragsstrafe) (Art. 160 OR)	clause pénale	liquidated damages
Konventionsvorschlag	projet de convention	proposed divorce agreement
Konzern	groupe de sociétés	group of companies
Konzernrechnung (D: Konzernabschluss)	comptes de groupe	consolidated financial statements
Konzession	concession	concession
Konzessionär	concessionnaire	concessionaire
koordinierter Lohn	salaire coordonné	coordinated wage
Koppelungsgeschäft (Art. 254 OR)	transaction couplée	linked transaction, tie-in transaction
körperliche Durchsuchung	visite corporelle	body search
körperliche Integrität	intégrité corporelle	bodily integrity
Körperschaft	corporation	corporate body
Körperstrafe	punition corporelle	corporal punishment
Körperverletzung (Art. 122 StGB)	lésion corporelle	assault
Korrektion (D: Regulierung)	régulation	regulation
Korrespondenzbank	banque correspondante	correspondent bank
kosmetische Beeinträchtigung	défaut esthétique	cosmetic defect
Kosten Die Kosten fallen ausser Ansatz.	frais	costs No order is made as to costs.
Kosten- und Entschädigungsfolge	frais et les dépens	court costs and attorney's fees
Kostenbeteiligung	participation aux frais	contribution to costs

Kostenentscheid (Art. 104 ZPO)	décision sur les frais	decision on costs
Kostenerlass (D: Kostenaufhebung)	dispense des frais	waiver of costs
kostenloses Verfahren	gratuité de la procédure	proceedings are free of charge
Kostenmiete	loyer fondé sur les coûts	rent that covers costs
Kostentragungspflicht	obligation de supporter les frais	obligation to bear costs
Kostentragungspflichtiger	personne tenue de supporter les frais	person liable to bear costs
Kostenübernahme	couverture des coûts	coverage of costs
Kostenvergleich	comparaison des coûts	cost comparison
Kostenvergütung	remboursement de frais	cost reimbursement
Kostenvoranschlag	devis	quote
Kostenvorschuss (Art. 98 ZPO)	avance de frais	advance payment of court costs
kotieren (D: notieren)	coter	to list on the stock exchange
Kotierung (D: Notierung)	cotation en bourse	listing on the stock exchange
Kotierungsreglement (KR)	règlement de cotation	listing rules
Kraftloserklärung	annulation (papier-valeur)	cancellation
Kranken- und Unfallversicherung (KUV) (Art. 117 BV)	assurance-maladie et accidents	health and accident insurance
Krankengeschichte	dossier médical	medical history
Krankenkasse	caisse maladie	health insurance
Krankenpflege	soins médicaux	nursing
Krankenschein	feuille de maladie	health insurance certificate
Krankentaggeld (KTG)	indemnités journalières de maladie	daily health insurance benefits
Krankentaggeldversicherung	assurance d'indemnités journalières en cas de maladie	daily benefit health insurance
Krankenversicherer	assureur-maladie	health insurer

Krankenversicherung	assurance-maladie	health insurance
Krankenversicherungsgesetz (KVG)	Loi fédérale sur l'assurance-maladie	Swiss Federal Health Insurance Act
Krankenversicherungsprämie	prime d'assurance-maladie	health insurance premium
Krankheitsfall	cas de maladie	case of illness
Kredit	crédit	credit
Kreditauftrag (Art. 408 OR)	ordre de crédit	credit order
Kreditbrief (Art. 407 OR)	lettre de crédit	letter of credit
Kreditfähigkeit	capacité de crédit	creditworthiness
Kreditkarte	carte de crédit	credit card
Kreditoren	créditeurs	accounts payable
Kreditrisiko	risque de crédit	credit risk
Kreditvermittler (Art. 4 KKG)	courtier en crédit	credit broker
Kreditversicherung	assurance-crédit	credit insurance
Kreisschreiben	circulaire	circular
Kridar	failli	bankrupt debtor
Kriegsmaterialgesetz (KMG)	Loi fédérale sur le matériel de guerre (LFMG)	War Material Act
Kriegsmaterialverordnung (KMV)	Ordonnance sur le matériel de guerre (OMG)	War Material Ordinance
Kriegsrecht	droit de la guerre	martial law
Kriegsschaden	dommage de guerre	war damage
Kriegsverbrechen	crime de guerre	war crime
Kriminalistik	criminalistique	forensic science, criminalistics
kriminelle Organisation	organisation criminelle	criminal organization
Kühlung	rafraîchissement (F : refroidisse-ment)	cooling
Kulturgut (Art. 196a OR)	bien culturel	cultural property, cultural heritage site
Kulturgütertransfergesetz (KGTG)	Loi fédérale sur le transfert de biens culturels (LTBC)	Cultural Property Transfer Act

Kulturgütertransferverordnung (KGTV)	Ordonnance sur le transfert des biens culturels (OTBC)	Cultural Property Transfer Ordinance
Kulturpolitik	politique culturelle	cultural policy
Kultusfreiheit	liberté de culte	freedom of religion
kumulative Schuldübernahme	reprise cumulative de dette	cumulative assumption of indebtedness
Kumulieren	cumul (suffrages)	accumulating of votes
Kundenbeziehung	relation de clientèle	customer relationship
Kündigung	résiliation	termination
Kündigung zur Unzeit (Art. 336c OR)	résiliation en temps inopportun	termination at an inopportune juncture (such as during pregnancy or military service)
Kündigungsfrist	délai de congé	notice period, period for giving notice
Kundschaft	clientèle	clientele
künftige Forderung	créance future	future claim
Kunstfehler	faute professionnelle	malpractice
Kunstfreiheit (Art. 21 BV)	liberté de l'art	freedom of artistic expression
kurant	courant	liquid, easily marketable
Kursmanipulation	manipulation de cours	price manipulation
Kurswert	valeur du cours	market price
kurzfristiges Fremdkapital	capitaux étrangers à court terme	short-term liabilities
Ladeschein	lettre de chargement	bill of lading
lädieren (D: beschädigen, verletzen)	blesser	to damage, to injure
Lagergebäude	entrepôt	warehouse
Lagerhalter (Art. 483 OR)	entrepositaire	warehouse keeper
Lagerschein	certificat de dépôt	warehouse receipt
Laienrichter	juge laïc	lay judge
Landammann (D: Regierungschef eines Kantons)	landamman	head of cantonal government
Landesinteressen	intérêt important du pays	national interests

Landesmünze	monnaie du pays	national currency
Landesrecht	droit interne	internal law
Landessprache	langue nationale	national language
Landesunglück (Art. 62 SchKG)	calamité publique	public calamity
Landesverrat	trahison du pays	treason
Landesversorgung (Art. 102 BV)	approvisionnement du pays	national economic supply
Landesversorgungsgesetz (LVG)	Loi sur l'approvisionnement du pays (LAP)	National Economic Supply Act
Landfriedensbruch (Art. 260 StGB)	émeute	rioting
Landumlegung	remaniement parcellaire	reorganization of land
landwirtschaftliche Pacht (Art. 276a OR)	bail agricole	agricultural lease
Landwirtschaftszone	zone agricole	agricultural area
Lärm (Art. 684 ZGB)	bruit	noise
Lärmbelastungskataster	cadastre de bruit	register of noise pollution
Lärmschutz-Verordnung (LSV)	Ordonnance sur la protection contre le bruit (OPB)	Noise Abatement Ordinance
Lärmschutzwand	paroi antibruit	noise barrier
Lärmzone	zone de bruit	noise zone
Läsion	lésion	injury
Lastenbereinigung	épuration de l'état des charges	determination of charges
Lastenbereinigungsverfahren (Art. 140 Abs. 2 SchKG)	procédure d'épuration de l'état des charges	proceedings to determine charges
Lastenverzeichnis (Art. 140 SchKG und Art. 125 VZG)	état des charges	schedule of charges
Laufzeit	échéance	term
Lausanner Richter	Tribunal fédéral (TF)	Swiss Federal Supreme Court
Lauterkeitsrecht	droit de la concurrence déloyale	law of fair trade, law of unfair competition
Leasinggeber	donneur de leasing	lessor
Leasingnehmer	preneur de leasing	lessee

Leasingvertrag	contrat de leasing	leasing agreement
Lebensaufwand	train de vie	lifestyle
Lebenserwartung	espérance de vie	life expectancy
Lebensgefahr	danger de mort	mortal danger
Lebenskosten	coût de la vie	cost of living
lebenslängliche Verwahrung (Art. 64 StGB)	internement à vie	lifelong imprisonment
Lebenslauf	curriculum vitae	résumé, CV
Lebensmittel	denrée alimentaire	food
Lebensmittel- und Gebrauchsgegenständeverordnung (LGV)	Ordonnance sur les denrées alimentaires et les objets usuels (ODAlOUs)	Ordinance on Foodstuffs and Utility Articles
Lebensmittelgesetz (LMG)	Loi sur les denrées alimentaires (LDAl)	Foodstuffs Act
Lebensmittelpolizei	police des denrées alimentaires	food police
Lebensstandard	niveau de vie	standard of living
Lebensversicherung	assurance-vie	life insurance
lediger Anfall (Art. 496 ZGB)	loyale échute	ineffective renunciation (of an inheritance)
leerer Stimmzettel	bulletin blanc	blank ballot
leerer Wahlzettel	bulletin blanc	blank ballot
Leerverkauf	vente à découvert	short sale
Legalitätsprinzip (Art. 1 StGB)	principe de légalité	principle of legality, principle of previously defined conduct
Legalservitut	servitude légale	statutory easement
Legalzession	cession légale	transfer by operation of law
Legat (D: Vermächtnis)	legs	legacy
Legatar (D: Vermächtnisnehmer)	légataire	legatee
legiferieren (D: Gesetze erlassen)	légiférer	to legislate, to make legislation
Legiferierung	élaboration de textes de loi	lawmaking, drafting legislation
Legislatur	législature, période législative	legislative period
Legislaturperiode	législature, période législative	legislative period

Legitimation	qualité pour agir et recourir	standing to sue
Legitimationskarte (D: Studentenausweis)	carte d'étudiant	student ID
Lehr- und Lernfreiheit	liberté d'étude et d'enseignement	academic freedom
Lehre	doctrine	legal scholarship
Lehrling	apprenti	apprentice
Lehrmeister	maître d'apprentissage	master
Lehrplan	programme d'enseignement	curriculum
Lehrvertrag (D: Berufsausbildungsvertrag) (Art. 344a OR)	contrat d'apprentissage	apprenticeship contract
Leibrente (Art. 516-520 OR)	rente viagère	life annuity
Leibrentenvertrag (Art. 516-520 OR)	contrat de rente viagère	life annuity agreement
leichte Fahrlässigkeit	négligence légère	slight negligence
Leichtsinn	légèreté	carelessness
Leihe (Art. 305 ff OR)	prêt	loan
Leistung (1)	prestation	performance
Leistung (2) (Art. 18 ff MWSTG)	prestation	supply (in the VAT context)
Leistung (3)	prestation	benefit (in the insurance context)
Leistung an Erfüllungs Statt	dation en paiement	accord and satisfaction
Leistung an Zahlungs Statt	dation en paiement	accord and satisfaction
Leistung der Eingaben (Art. 633, 652c OR)	libération des apports	making capital contributions
Leistung erfüllungshalber	dation en paiement	accord and satisfaction
Leistung zahlungshalber	dation en paiement	accord and satisfaction
Leistungsanspruch (Versicherung)	droit à la prestation d'assurance	right to insurance benefits
Leistungsauftrag	mandat de prestations	public service agreement
Leistungskatalog	catalogue de prestations	list of insurance benefits

Leistungsklage (Art. 84 ZPO)	action condamnatoire, action en exécution d'une prestation	action for performance
Leistungsprimat	primauté des prestations	defined benefit plan
Leistungsverhältnis	rapport de prestation	relationship between the promisor and the third party beneficiary
Leitschein	acte de non-conciliation	certificate from justice of the peace that the case was not able to be settled
Lenkungsabgabe	taxe d'orientation, taxe incitative, taxe d'incitation	steering tax (a tax imposed on the consumption of certain resources to reduce such consumption)
Lenkungssteuer	impôt d'orientation	steering tax (a tax imposed on the consumption of certain resources to reduce such consumption)
Lernfahrausweis	permis d'élève conducteur	learner's permit
letzte Instanz	dernière instance	last resort
letzthin (D: kürzlich)	récemment	recently
letztwillige Verfügung (Art. 498 ff. ZGB)	testament	last will and testament
Leumund	réputation	reputation
Leumundszeugnis	certificat de bonne vie et mœurs	character reference
liberiert (D: eingezahlt)	libéré	fully paid-in
Liberierung (D: Einzahlung)	libération	payment in full (for shares)
Lidlohn (Art. 334 ZGB)	indemnité pour travail consacré à la famille	compensation to which adult children and grandchildren are entitled if they live with their parents and contribute their labor or income
Liefersperre	refus de livrer des marchandises	refusal to supply goods
Lieferung	livraison	delivery
Liegenschaft	bien-fonds	property
Liegenschaftenbeschreibung	état descriptif	property description
Liegenschaftenverzeichnis	rôle des biens-fonds	property list

Liegenschaftsertrag	revenu immobilier	property income
Liegenschaftssteuer	impôt foncier	property tax
Liegenschaftsverwaltung	gérance d'immeubles	property management
Liegenschaftverwaltungsvertrag	contrat de gérance d'immeubles	property management agreement
limitierter Auftrag	ordre limité	limit order
limitiertes Vorkaufsrecht	droit de préemption limité	limited right of first refusal
Liquidation	liquidation	liquidation
Liquidationswert	valeur de liquidation	liquidation value
Liquidator (Art. 317 ff SchKG)	liquidateur	liquidator
Listenverbindung	apparentement de listes	list combination
Litisdenunziant (Art. 78 ZPO)	dénonçant	third-party plaintiff (in an impleader)
Litisdenunziat (Art. 78 ZPO)	appelé en cause	third-party defendant (in an impleader)
Lizenz	licence	license
Lizenzgeber	donneur de licence	licensor
Lizenzgebühr	redevance	royalty, license fee
Lizenznehmer	preneur de licence	licensee
Lizenzvertrag	contrat de licence	license agreement
Lockvogel	prix d'appel	loss leader
Lohn	salaire	salary
Lohnausweis	attestation de salaire	annual salary statement
Lohngleichheit	égalité de rémunération	equal pay
Lohngutschrift	bonification du salaire	wife's compensation (for working in her husband's business)
Lohnpfändung (Art. 93 SchKG)	saisie de salaire	garnishment
Lohnrückbehalt	retenue sur le salaire	withholding from salary
Lohnzuschlag	supplément de salaire	wage supplement, extra pay
Lokalbank	banque locale	local bank
Löschung der Eintragung (Art. 35 MSchG)	radiation de l'enregistrement	cancellation of trademark registration

Löschung im Handelsregister	radiation au registre du commerce	deletion from the Commercial Register
Lösegeld	rançon	ransom
Lotterieverbot	prohibition des loteries	prohibition of lotteries
Lücke (Rechtssetzung)	lacune	gap
lucrum cessans	lucrum cessans	lost profits
Luftfahrtversicherung	assurance aérienne	aviation insurance
Luftfahrzeugverschreibung	hypothèque sur aéronef	mortgage on an aircraft
Luftreinhalte-Verordnung (LRV)	Ordonnance sur la protection de l'air (OPair)	Ordinance on Air Pollution Control
Luftverunreinigung	pollution de l'air	air pollution
Luftwaffe	forces aériennes	airforce
luxuriöse Verwendung	dépense somptuaire	spending on luxury items
Luzern (LU)	Lucerne (LU)	Lucerne (canton and city)
Mahngebühr	frais de sommation	reminder fee
Mahnung (Art. 102 Abs. 1 OR)	interpellation	formal reminder to pay
Majorzwahl (D: Mehrheitswahl)	système majoritaire	election by a simple majority
Mäkler (D: Makler)	courtier	broker
Mäklervertrag (Art. 412-418 OR) (D: Maklervertrag)	courtage	brokerage contract
Mangel	défaut, vice	defect
Mangel des Vertragsabschlusses	vice du consentement	defect in consent (defense to contract formation)
Mangelfolgeschaden	dommage consécutif au défaut	consequential harm caused by a defect
mangelhafte Eingaben (Art. 132 ZPO)	vices de forme	defective pleadings, defective submissions
mangelhafte Eröffnung (Art. 38 VwVG)	notification irrégulière	defective notification
mangelhafter Unterhalt	défaut d'entretien	defective maintenance
Mängelhaftung	garantie pour les défauts	warranty against defects
Mängelrüge (Art. 201 OR)	vérification de la chose et avis au vendeur	notice of defects
Marchzins	intérêt couru mais non échu	accrued interest

Marke (Art. 1 MSchG)	marque	trademark
Markenartikel	article de marque	brand item
Markenrechtsverletzung (Art. 61 MSchG)	violation du droit à la marque	infringement of a trademark
Markenregister	registre des marques	trademark register
Markenschutzgesetz (MSchG)	Loi sur la protection des marques (LPM)	Trademark Protection Actd
marktbeherrschendes Unternehmen (Art. 4 KG)	entreprise dominant le marché	market dominant enterprise
Marktkapitalisierung	capitalisation de marché	market capitalization
Marktmiete	loyer fondé sur les prix du marché	market rent
Marktpreis	prix du marché	market price
Marktrisiko	risque du marché	market risk
Marktstand	stand de marché	market stall
Marktverhalten	comportement sur le marché	market conduct
Marktverhaltensregeln (FINMA)	règles de conduite sur le marché	market conduct rules
Masse	masse	bankrupt estate
Massenentlassung	licenciement collectif	mass layoff
massgebender Lohn	salaire déterminant	relevant wage (all elements of annual compensation that must be taken into account for the occupational pension plan)
Massivbaute (D: Massivbau)	construction massive	massive construction
Massnahmebegehren	demande de mesures provisionnelles	petition for a preliminary injunction
Massnahmegesuch	demande de mesures provisionnelles	petition for a preliminary injunction
Materialien (Gesetzesmaterialien)	travaux préparatoires	legislative history, drafting history
materielles Recht	droit matériel	substantive law (as opposed to procedural law)

Matura (D: Abitur)	maturité (F : baccalauréat)	high school graduation exam
Maturitätsausweis	certificat de maturité	certificate of passing the high school graduation exam
Maturitätsprüfung (D: Abitur)	examen de maturité (F : baccalauréat)	high school graduation exam
Maturitätszeugnis (D: Zeugnis der allgemeinen Hochschulreife)	certificat de maturité	certificate of high school graduation
Maximalhypothek	hypothèque maximale	maximum amount mortgage
Mediation	médiation	mediation
Medien	média	media
Medienfreiheit (Art. 17 BV)	liberté des médias	freedom of the media
Medizinalberufegesetz (MedBG)	Loi sur les professions médicales (LPMéd)	Medical Professions Act
Medizinalberufekommission (MEBEKO)	Commission des professions médicales (MEBEKO)	Commission for Medical Professions
medizinische Grundversorgung (Art. 117a BV)	soins médicaux de base	primary medical care
Mehr (D: Mehrheit)	majorité	majority
Mehr- oder Minderwert	plus ou moins value	increase or decrease in value
Mehrarbeit	heures d'appoint	overtime
Mehrfachbeschäftigung	activité au service de plusieurs employeurs	working for several employers at the same time
mehrfache Ehe (Art. 215 StGB)	pluralité de mariages	bigamy
Mehrfachkandidatur	candidature multiple	multiple candidacy
Mehrheitsaktionär	actionnaire majoritaire	majority shareholder
Mehrwert	plus-value	value added
Mehrwertsteuer (MWST)	taxe sur la valeur ajoutée (TVA)	value-added tax
Meinung	avis, opinion	opinion
Meinungs- und Informationsfreiheit (Art. 16 BV)	liberté d'expression et d'information	freedom of expression and of information

Meinungsäusserungsfreiheit	liberté d'expression	freedom of expression
Meinungsaustausch (Art. 8 VwVG)	échange de vues	exchange of views
Meistbegünstigungsklausel	clause de la nation la plus favorisée	MFN clause, most favored nation clause
Meldepflicht	obligation d'annoncer	obligation to report
Meldepflichtverletzung	violation de l'obligation d'annoncer	breach of the obligation to report
Meldestelle für Geldwäscherei (MROS)	Bureau de communication en matière de blanchiment d'argent (MROS)	Money Laundering Reporting Office Switzerland (MROS)
Mensch	être humain	human being
Menschenhandel (Art. 182 StGB)	traite d'êtres humains	trafficking in human beings
Menschenrechte	droits de l'homme	human rights
menschliche Ressourcen	ressources humaines	human resources (HR)
Messestand	stand de foire	tradeshow booth
Meuterei (Art. 63 MStG)	mutinerie	mutiny
Meuterei von Gefangenen (Art. 311 StGB)	mutinerie de détenus	prison mutiny
Miete (Art. 253-304 OR)	loyer	rent
Mieter	locataire	tenant, renter, lessee
Mieterverband	association de locataires	tenant association
Mietgericht	tribunal des baux	landlord-tenant court
Miet-Kauf-Vertrag	location-vente	installment plan
Mietsache	chose louée	rented premises, demised premises
Mietverhältnis	contrat de bail	landlord-tenant relationship, tenancy
Mietvertrag (Art. 253-304 OR)	bail à loyer	lease agreement, rental agreement
Mietwert	valeur locative	rental value
Mietzins (Art. 253-304 OR)	loyer	rent
Mietzinsabzug	déduction du loyer	deduction of rent
Mietzinserlass	remise de loyer	rent abatement
Mietzinsüberwachung	loyer contrôlé	rent control
Militärappellationsgericht (MAG)	Tribunal militaire d'appel (TMA)	Military Court of Appeals

Militärdienst	service militaire	military service
Militärdisziplinarrechtspflege	procédure disciplinaire militaire	administration of military discipline
Militärgericht	tribunal militaire	court martial
militärischer Nachrichtendienst (Art. 274 StGB)	service de renseignements militaires	military espionage
Militärkassationsgericht (MKG)	Tribunal militaire de cassation (TMC)	Military Supreme Court
Militärpflichtersatz	taxe militaire	exemption tax
Militärstrafgesetz (MStG)	Code pénal militaire (CPM)	Military Criminal Code
Militärstrafprozess	procédure pénale militaire	military criminal procedure
Militärstrafrecht	droit pénal militaire	military criminal law
Militärstrafrechtspflege	procédure de la justice militaire	administration of military justice
Militärversicherungsgesetz (MVG)	Loi fédérale sur l'assurance militaire (LAM)	Military Insurance Act
Minderheit	minorité	minority
Minderheitsaktionär	actionnaire minoritaire	minority shareholder
Minderheitsmeinung	opinion minoritaire	minority opinion
Minderjährigkeit	minorité	minority, being underage, being a minor
Minderungsklage (Art. 205 OR)	action en réduction du prix	claim to a reduction in the purchase price
Minderungsrecht	droit à la réduction du prix	right to a reduction in the purchase price
Minderwert (Art. 205 OR)	moins-value	reduction in value, decrease in value
Mindesteinlage (Art. 632 OR)	apport minimum	minimum contribution (to a company's capital)
Mineralölsteuer	impôt sur les huiles minérales	gas tax (tax on oil, gasoline and kerosene)
Minimallohn	salaire minimum	minimum wage
Ministerpräsident	premier ministre	prime minister
Ministerrat	conseil des ministres	Council of Ministers

Missachtung eines Tätigkeitsverbots oder eines Kontakt- und Rayonverbots (Art. 294 StGB)	infraction à l'interdiction d'exercer une activité, à l'interdiction de contact ou à l'interdiction géographique	breach of an activity prohibition order or a contact prohibition and exclusion order
Missachtung von Bewährungshilfe oder Weisungen (Art. 295 StGB)	non-respect de l'assistance de probation ou des règles de conduite	failure to comply with probation assistance or instructions
Missbrauch des Ermessens	abus du pouvoir d'appréciation	abuse of discretionary powers
Missbrauch einer Fernmeldeanlage (Art. 179septies StGB)	utilisation abusive d'une installation de télécommunicati on	misuse of a telecommunications installation
Missbrauch von Ausweisen und Schildern	usage abusif de permis et de plaques	misuse of driver's licenses and license plates
Missbrauch von Lohnabzügen (Art. 159 StGB)	détournement de retenues sur les salaires	misuse of salary deductions
missbräuchliche Kündigung	résiliation abusive	wrongful termination
missbräuchlicher Mietzins (Art. 253b OR)	loyer abusif	abusive rent
Misshandlung	mauvais traitement	mistreatment
Misswirtschaft (Art. 165 StGB)	gestion fautive	mismanagement
Mitarbeiter	collaborateur	employee
Mitarbeiteroption	option de collaborateur	employee option
Mitbesitz	copossession	joint ownership
Mitbürgschaft (Art. 497 OR)	cautionnement conjoint	co-surety
Miteigentum (Art. 646 ZGB)	copropriété	co-ownership
Miteigentümer	copropriétaire	co-owner
Miteigentümergemeinschaft	communauté des copropriétaires	community of co-owners
Mitglied	membre	member

Mitgliedschaftsrecht	affiliation (groupement de personnes et de capitaux)	membership right (the rights of the shareholder, as embodied in the share, to participate in shareholders' meetings and in votes and elections, and to receive information, as well as rights of inspection)
Mitgliedstaat	état membre	member state
Mitmieter	colocataire	cotenant
Mitschuldner (Art. 70 Abs. 2 SchKG)	codébiteurs	joint debtors
Mittäter	coauteur	co-offender
mittelbarer Besitz	possession médiate	indirect ownership
mittelbarer Täter	auteur médiat	indirect offender (a person who commits an offense by using another person to unwillingly perform the criminal act)
Miturheber	coauteur	coauthor
Mitvermieter	cobailleur	colandlord
Mitverpflichteter (Art. 217 Abs. 1 und 303 Abs. 1 SchKG)	coobligé	co-obligor
Mitverpflichtungen des Schuldners (Art. 215 SchKG)	obligations communes du failli	common obligations of the insolvent debtor
Mitwirkung (D: Mitbestimmung)	participation	codetermination
Mitwirkung des Schuldners (Art. 229 SchKG)	coopération du failli	cooperation by the insolvent debtor
Mitwirkungsbeistandschaft (Art. 396 ZGB)	curatelle de coopération	advisory curatorship
Mitwirkungsgesetz	Loi sur la participation	Codetermination Act
Mitwirkungspflicht	devoir de collaborer, devoir de collaboration	duty to cooperate
Mobbing	harcèlement psychologique	bullying
Monatslohn	salaire mensuel	monthly wage, monthly salary
Moratorium	moratoire	moratorium
Mord (Art. 112 StGB)	assassinat	murder

Motion	motion	parliamentary motion asking the government to legislate (as opposed to a motion requiring the government to legislate, cf. *Postulat*)
motivieren (D: begründen)	motiver	to state the reasons (for something)
multilaterales Handelssystem	système multilatéral de négociation	multilateral trading system
Mündel	pupille	ward
Mündelvermögen	bien du pupille	ward's asset
Mündigkeit (Art. 14 ZGB)	majorité	age of majority
mündliche Eröffnung	notification orale	oral notice
mündliches Testament (Art. 506-511 ZGB)	testament oral	nuncupative will, oral will
mündliches Verfahren	procédure orale	oral procedure
Murten	Morat	Murten (municipality)
Muttergesellschaft	société mère	parent company
Mutterschaftsentschädigung	allocation de maternité	maternity allowance
Mutterschaftsleistung	prestation en cas de maternité	maternity benefit
Mutterschaftsurlaub	congé de maternité	maternity leave
Mutterschaftsversicherung	assurance-maternité	maternity insurance
Mutterwaisenrente	rente d'orphelin de mère	pension for a child whose mother has died
Mutuum	mutuum	loan (for consumption, such as a loan of money, as opposed to loan for use, such as a loan of a painting)
mutwillige Prozessführung (Art. 128 ZPO)	procédé téméraire	frivolous litigation, vexatious litigation
Nachahmung (geistiges Eigentum)	imitation (propriété intellectuelle)	imitation
Nachbarrecht	droit de voisinage	law governing neighbors
Nachbesserungsrecht	droit à la réfection de l'ouvrage	contractor's right to be given an opportunity to cure the breach
Nachbürge (Art. 498 OR)	certificateur de caution	collateral surety
Nachbürgschaft (Art. 498 OR)	certificateur de caution	collateral surety

Nacheile (Art. 216 StPO)	droit de suite	pursuit, hot pursuit
Nacherbe (Art. 488 ZGB)	héritier appelé	remainderman
Nacherbeneinsetzung (Art. 488 ZGB)	substitution fidéicommissaire	appointment of a remainderman
nachhaltige Entwicklung	développement durable	sustainable development
Nachkomme	descendant	descendant
Nachkontrolle	suivi	aftercare
Nachlass	succession, héritage	estate
Nachlassbegehren	demande de concordat	application for debt restructuring
Nachlassbehörde	autorité concordataire	debt restructuring authority
Nachlassgericht (Art. 293a SchKG)	juge du concordat	debt restructuring court
Nachlassstundung (Art. 293 ff SchKG)	sursis concordataire	debt restructuring moratorium
Nachlassverfahren (Art. 293 ff SchKG)	procédure concordataire	debt restructuring proceedings
Nachlassvertrag (D: Zwangsvergleich) (Art. 293 ff SchKG)	concordat	debt restructuring agreement
Nachlassvertrag im Konkurs (Art. 332 SchKG)	concordat dans la procédure de faillite	debt restructuring agreement in bankruptcy
Nachlassvertrag mit Vermögensabtretung (Art. 317 ff. SchKG)	concordat par abandon d'actif	debt restructuring agreement with assignment of assets
nachträgliche Leistung (Art. 634a OR)	libération ultérieure	subsequent payment in full (when share capital has only been partially paid in)
Nachmachen von Banknoten, Münzen oder amtlichen Wertzeichen ohne Fälschungsabsicht (Art. 243 StGB)	imitation de billets de banque, de pièces de monnaies ou de timbres officiels de valeur sans dessein de faux	imitation of bank notes, coins or official stamps without intent to commit forgery
Nachpfändung (Art. 145 SchKG)	saisie complémentaire	seizure of additional assets
Nachpfändung von Amtes wegen (Art. 145 SchKG)	reprise de saisie	resumption of seizure
Nachrichtendienst gegen fremde Staaten (Art. 301 StGB)	espionnage militaire au préjudice d'un Etat étranger	military espionage against a foreign state

nachrichtenlose Vermögenswerte	avoirs sans nouvelles	dormant assets
nachrichtenloses Vermögen	avoir en déshérence	dormant asset
Nachrichtenlosigkeit (Art. 45 BankV)	déshérence	dormancy
Nachrückungsrecht	droit d'avancement à un rang antérieur	right to move mortgage to higher order of priority
Nachschusspflicht	versement supplémentaire	obligation to make additional contribution
Nachsichtwechsel (Art. 1013 OR)	lettre de change à un certain délai de vue	bill payable at a fixed period after sight
Nachsorge	interventions ultérieures	continuous monitoring
Nachsteuerverfahren	procédure en rappel d'impôt	additional tax assessment
nachteilige Einwirkung (Art. 4 GSchG)	atteinte nuisible	detrimental effect
Nachteilsprognose	prévisions concernant un préjudice	likelihood of irreparable harm if preliminary injunctive relief is not granted
Nachtrag	codicille	codicil (to a will)
nachträgliche Bewilligung	autorisation subséquente	subsequent authorization
nachträgliche Unmöglichkeit (Art. 119 OR)	impossibilité subséquente	subsequent impossibility (e.g. an animal sold before birth is stillborn)
nachträglicher Rechtsvorschlag	opposition tardive	belated objection (when there is a change of creditors)
Nachverpfändung (Art. 886 ZGB)	droit de gage subséquent	subordinate pledge
Nachweis der Flüchtlingseigenschaft (Art. 7 AsylG)	preuve de la qualité de réfugié	proof of refugee status
Nachweisgrenze	seuil de détection	limit of detection (LOD)
Nachzahlung	paiement de l'arriéré	payment of arrears
nahestehende Person	personne proche	related party
Namenaktie (Art. 684 OR) (D: Namensaktie)	action nominative	registered share
Namenpapier (Art. 974 OR)	titre nominatif	registered paper

Namenpartizipationsschein	bon de participation nominatif	registered participation certificate
Namensanmassung (Art. 29 Abs. 2 ZGB)	usurpation d'un nom	wrongful use of another person's name
Nasciturus (Art. 544 Abs. 1 ZGB)	nasciturus	unborn child
Nationalbank	banque nationale	national bank
Nationalbankgesetz (NBG)	Loi sur la banque nationale (LBN)	National Bank Act
Nationale Alarmzentrale (NAZ)	Centrale nationale d'alarme (CCENAL)	National Emergency Operations Center
nationale Rechtshilfe (Art. 43 ff StPO)	entraide judiciaire nationale	domestic mutual assistance
Nationaler Garantiefonds Schweiz (NGF)	Fonds National Suisse de Garantie (FNG)	Swiss National Guarantee Fund
Nationales Versicherungsbüro Schweiz (NVB)	Bureau National Suisse d'Assurance (BNA)	Swiss National Bureau of Insurance
Nationalrat	Conseil national	National Council (lower house of the Federal Assembly)
Nationalstrasse (D: Bundesstraße)	route nationale	federal highway
Natur- und Heimatschutzgesetz (NHG)	Loi sur la protection de la nature et du paysage (LPN)	Nature and Cultural Heritage Act
Naturaleinkommen	revenu en nature	income in kind
Naturallohn	salaire en nature	wages in kind
Naturalobligation	obligation naturelle	natural obligation, obligation not enforceable at law
Naturgut	patrimoine naturel	natural heritage site
natürliche Früchte (Art. 643 ZGB)	fruits naturels	natural fruits, natural proceeds
natürliche Kausalität	causalité naturelle	necessary causation
natürliche Person	personne physique	natural person, individual
Naturrecht	droit naturel	natural right
Naturschutzobjekt	objet (protection de la nature)	nature conservation asset

ne bis in idem	ne bis in idem	rule against double jeopardy
Nebenanspruch	créance accessoire	accessory claim
Nebenbaute	construction annexe	outbuilding, annex
Nebenbeschäftigung	activité accessoire	secondary employment
Nebenbeschäftigungsreglement Bundesstrafgericht (BStGerNR)	Règlement du Tribunal pénal fédéral sur les activités accessoires (RAATPF)	Federal Criminal Court Secondary Employment Regulations
Nebenbürgschaft (Art. 497 OR)	cautionnement indépendant	independent surety
Nebeneinkommen	revenu accessoire	additional income
Nebenintervention (Art. 74 ZPO)	intervention accessoire	accessory intervention (a third party supports either the plaintiff's claim or the defendant's claim)
Nebenkosten (Art. 257a OR)	frais accessoires	ancillary costs
Nebenleistungspflicht	obligation de fournir des prestations accessoires	obligation to make additional material contributions
Nebenpartei	tierce partie	third-party intervenor
Nebenrecht	droit accessoire	accessory right
Nebenstrafe	peine accessoire	additional penalty
negative Dienstbarkeit	servitude négative	negative easement
Nennbetrag	montant nominal	nominal amount
Nennwert	valeur nominale	par value
Nettoerlös aus Lieferungen und Leistungen	produit net des livraisons et de prestations	net sales
Nettoertrag	rendement net	net yield
Nettoinventarwert	valeur nette d'inventaire	net asset value (NAV)
Nettolohn	salaire net	net wage
Neuanmeldung	nouvelle demande	new application
Neubau	nouvelle construction	new construction
Neuenburg (NE)	Neuchâtel (NE)	Neuchatel (canton and city)
Neuerung (Art. 116 OR)	novation	novation

Neugründung	nouvelle fondation	business start-up
Neuheit der Erfindung (Art. 7 PatG)	nouveauté de l'invention	novelty of the invention
neutraler Aufwand	charge neutre	non-operating expense
Neutralität	neutralité	neutrality
Neuwert	valeur à neuf	value when new
Neuwertversicherung	assurance de la valeur à neuf	replacement value insurance
nicht eingegebene Forderung (Art. 267 SchKG)	créance non produite	unproduced claim
nicht erhobene Beträge (Art. 329 SchKG)	dividendes non perçus	uncollected dividends
nicht gesichert	chirographaire	unsecured
nicht strafbares Aufnehmen (Art. 179quinquies StGB)	enregistrements non punissables	legal recordings
nicht verfallene Forderung (Art. 208 Abs. 2 SchKG)	créance non échue	unmatured claim, claim not yet due
nicht wieder rückgängig zu machende Disposition	disposition irrévocable	irrevocable provision
Nichtanbringung von Sicherheitsvorrichtungen (Art. 230 StGB)	omettre d'installer des appareils protecteurs	non-installation of safety devices
Nichtanhandnahme	non-entrée en matière	abandonment, discontinuation of criminal proceedings (by the prosecutor)
Nichtanhandnahmeverfügung (Art. 310 StPO)	ordonnance de non-entrée en matière	order to abandon the criminal proceedings
Nichtanzeigen eines Fundes (Art. 332 StGB)	défaut d'avis en cas de trouvaille	failure to report a find
nichtbankmässiger Finanzintermediär	intermédiaire financier sans statut bancaire	nonbank financial intermediary
Nichtberufsunfall	accident non professionnel	accident that is not work-related
Nicht-Betriebs-Unfall-Versicherung	assurance contre les accidents non professionnels	insurance covering accidents that are not work-related
Nichtbewährung (Art. 46 StGB)	échec de la mise à l'épreuve	breach of probation
Nichtbezahlung	défaut de paiement	default
Nichtehe	mariage inexistant	void marriage

Nichteintreten	fin de non-recevoir	dismissal
Nichteintretensentscheid	décision d'irrecevabilité	decision of dismissal
Nichterwerbstätiger	personne sans activité lucrative	person without gainful employment
Nichterwerbstätigkeit	non-activité	economic inactivity
Nichtgebrauch der Marke	non-usage de la marque	failure to use the mark
nichtig	nul	null and void
Nichtigkeit (Art. 20 OR)	nullité	nullity
Nichtigkeit von Nebenversprechen (Art. 312 SchKG)	nullité des promesses faites en sus des stipulations du concordat	nullity of the promises made in addition to the debt restructuring agreement
Nichtigkeitsbeschwerde (Art. 228 ZPO) (D: Revision)	pourvoi en nullité	appeal to the Supreme Court on a point of law, similar to *cassation* in France and *Revision* in Germany
nichtkaufmännische Gesellschaft (Art. 553 OR)	société n'exerçant pas une activité commerciale	noncommercial partnership
nichtregistrierte Vorsorgeeinrichtung	institution de prévoyance non enregistrée	unregistered pension institution
Nichtschuld	indu	nonexistent debt, amount not owed
nichtstaatliche Organisation	organisation non gouverne-mentale (ONG)	non-governmental organization (NGO)
nichtverkehrsfähige Sache	chose hors commerce	thing not subject to contract or exchange (such as the human body)
nichtwiedergutzumachender Nachteil	dommage irréparable	irreparable harm, irreparable damage
Nidwalden (NW)	Nidwald (NW)	Nidwalden (canton)
Niederlassung	établissement	place of business
Niederlassungsausweis	certificat de domicile	certificate of residence
Niederlassungsbewilligung	autorisation d'établissement	residence permit (for foreign nationals to live in Switzerland)
Niederlassungsfreiheit (Art. 24 BV)	liberté d'établissement	freedom of domicile
Nominallohn	salaire nominal	nominal wages

Nominationsausschuss	comité de nomination	nominating committee
Nominatvertrag (D: typischer Vertrag)	contrat nommé	nominate contract (one provided for by the code)
Norm	norme	standard
Normalarbeitsvertrag (NAV)	contrat-type de travail (CTT)	standard form employment agreement
Normenkontrolle	contrôle des normes	judicial review
Notar	notaire	notary
Notariatsbüro	étude de notaire	notary's office
Notariatsgesetz (NG)	Loi sur le notariat (LNot)	Notary Act
Notbedarf	minimum vital	vital minimum
Notbrunnenrecht (Art. 710 ZGB)	servitude de fontaine nécessaire	right to use an essential water source
Notenbank	banque d'émission	issuing bank, bank of issue
Nötigung (Art. 181 StGB)	contrainte	coercion
notorisch bekannte Marke (Art. 3 MSchG)	marque notoirement connue	well-known trademark (Well-known trademarks are protected whether they are registered or not.)
Notstand	état de nécessité	state of emergency
Notstundung (Art. 337 ff SchKG)	sursis extraordinaire (LP)	extraordinary moratorium
Notverkauf (Art. 243 SchKG)	réalisation d'urgence	emergency sale
Notweg (Art. 694 ZGB)	passage nécessaire	necessary easement
Notwegrecht	droit de passage nécessaire	right to a necessary easement
Notwehr (Art. 15-16 StGB)	légitime défense	self-defense
notwendige Auslagen	débours nécessaires	necessary outlays
notwendige Streitgenossenschaft (Art. 70 ZPO)	consorité nécessaire	necessary joinder
notwendige Verteidigung (Art. 130 StPO)	défense nécessaire	mandatory appointment of a defense lawyer
notwendige Verwendung	dépense nécessaire	necessary expense
Notzuständigkeit	for de nécessité	emergency jurisdiction
Novation (Art. 116-117 OR)	novation	novation

Novelle	novelle (loi spéciale modifiant le contenu d'anciennes lois)	amendment (to prior laws)
Novum, Noven (neue Tatsachen oder Beweismittel) (Art. 99 BGG)	novum (faits nouveaux ou preuves nouvelles)	new facts or evidence
Nummernkonto	compte numéroté	numbered account
nützliche Verwendung	dépense utile	useful expense
Nutzniesser	usufruitier	usufructuary, life tenant
Nutzniessung (D: Nießbrauch) (Art. 745-775 ZGB)	usufruit	usufruct, life estate
Nutzniessungsberechtigter	usufruitier	usufructuary, life tenant
Nutzniessungsrecht	droit d'usufruit	right of usufruct
Nutzungsberechtigter	utilisateur autorisé	authorized user
Nutzungseinschränkung beim Boden	restriction d'utilisation du sol	restrictions on soil use
Oberaufsicht	haute surveillance	overall supervision
Obergericht	cour suprême du canton	cantonal supreme court
oberirdisches Gewässer (Art. 4 GSchG)	eaux superficielles	surface water
oberstes Gericht	cour suprême	supreme court
Oberstrombereich	zone en amont	upstream groundwater
Obhut	garde, droit de garde	custody
objektive Unmöglichkeit	impossibilité objective	objective impossibility
objektiver Tatbestand	éléments objectifs (de la typicité)	actus reus (in the definition of a crime)
objektives Recht	droit objectif	law (as opposed to subjektives Recht, which means 'right')
Objektsteuer	impôt sur les biens	tax levied on specific property
Oblat	destinataire de l'offre	offeree
obliegen: Der Beweis obliegt dem Kläger.	incomber : La preuve incombe au demandeur.	The burden of proof is on the plaintiff.

Obligation (1)	obligation	obligation
Obligation (2)	obligation	bond
Obligationenfonds (D: Rentenfonds)	fonds en obligations	bond fund
Obligationenrecht (1) (D: Schuldrecht)	droit des obligations	law of obligations
Obligationenrecht (OR) (2) AT = allgemeiner Teil BT = besonderer Teil	Code des obligations (CO) PG = partie générale PS = partie spéciale	Code of Obligations general part special part
obligatorische Versicherung	assurance obligatoire	mandatory insurance
obligatorisches Referendum	référendum obligatoire	mandatory referendum
obschon (D: obwohl)	bien que	although
obsiegen	obtenir gain de cause	to prevail, to win, to be successful
obsiegende Partei	partie qui obtient gain de cause	successful party, prevailing party
Obwalden (OW)	Obwald (OW)	Obwalden (canton)
Occasion (D: Gebrauchtwagen)	voiture d'occasion	used car
offener Mangel	défaut apparent	patent defect
offensichtlicher Mangel	défaut manifeste	patent defect
öffentliche Abgaben	contributions publiques	public levies
öffentliche Aufforderung zu Verbrechen oder zur Gewalttätigkeit (Art. 259 StGB)	provocation publique au crime ou à la violence	public incitement to commit a felony or act of violence
öffentliche Kaufangebote	offre publique d'acquisition	tender offer, takeover bid
öffentliches Amt	charge publique	public office
öffentliches Recht	droit public	public law
öffentliches Testament (Art. 498-504 ZGB)	testament public	will in the form of a notarial instrument
öffentliches Werk	ouvrage public	public work
Öffentlichkeitsprinzip	principe de la transparence	principle of transparency
öffentlich-rechtliche Forderung	prétention de droit public	public law claim
öffentlich-rechtliche Streitigkeit	contestation de droit public	public law dispute

öffentlich-rechtliche Vorsorgeeinrichtung	institution de prévoyance de droit public	public law pension institution
Offerent	auteur de l'offre	offeror
Offertanfrage	appel d'offres	request for proposals (RFP)
Offerte (D: Angebot) eine Offerte unterbreiten	offre, devis soumettre une offre	quote to give a quote
Offertgarantie (D: Bietungsgarantie)	cautionnement de soumission	bid bond
Offizialanwalt	avocat d'office	court-appointed attorney
Offizialdelikt	infraction poursuivie d'office	criminal offense prosecuted regardless of whether the victim brings charges (such as murder)
Offizialgrundsatz (Art. 58 ZPO)	maxime d'office, maxime officielle	principle that no statement of any kind is binding on the judge unless he himself is convinced that the fact occurred as asserted
öko-Beitrag	contribution écologique	ecological contribution
ökologischer Ausgleich	compensation écologique	ecological compensation
Ökologischer Leistungsnachweis (ÖLN)	prestations écologiques requises (PER)	proof of ecological performance
ökologisches Gleichgewicht	équilibre écologique	ecological balance
Opfer (Art. 116 StPO)	victime	victim (person who suffered physical, sexual or mental harm from a criminal offense)
Opferhilfe	aide aux victimes	victim support
Opferhilfegesetz (OHG)	Loi fédérale sur l'aide aux victimes d'infractions (LAVI)	Victim Support Act
Opferhilfeverordnung (OHV)	Ordonnance sur l'aide aux victimes d'infractions (OAVI)	Victim Support Ordinance
Opfermitverantwortung	responsabilité partagée de la victime	joint liability of the victim

Opportunitätsprinzip	principe de l'opportunité des poursuites	principle of prosecutorial discretion
Optionsanleihe	obligation avec options	option bond, bond with options
Optionsrecht	droit d'option	option right
ordentliche Ersitzung (Art. 661 ZGB)	prescription acquisitive ordinaire	ordinary adverse possession
ordentliche Generalversammlung (D: ordentliche Hauptversammlung)	assemblée générale ordinaire	annual shareholders' meeting
ordentliche Revision (Art. 728 OR)	contrôle ordinaire	ordinary audit
ordentlicher Nachlassvertrag (Art. 314 SchKG)	concordat ordinaire	ordinary debt restructuring agreement
ordentliches Verfahren (Art. 219 ff ZPO)	procédure ordinaire	ordinary procedure
Ordnungsbusse (1) (D: Ordnungsstrafe)	amende d'ordre	fixed penalty
Ordnungsbusse (2) (D: Ordnungsstrafe) (Art. 128 ZPO)	amende disciplinaire	disciplinary fine
Ordnungsbussengesetz (OBG)	Loi fédérale sur les amendes d'ordre (LAO)	Fixed Penalties Act
Ordnungsbussenverordnung (OBV)	Ordonnance sur les amendes d'ordre (OAO)	Fixed Penalties Ordinance
Ordnungsmässigkeit	régularité	regularity
ordnungswidrige Führung der Geschäftsbücher (Art. 325 StGB)	inobservation des prescriptions légales sur la comptabilité	failure to comply with accounting regulations
Ordreklausel	clause à ordre	order clause
Ordrepapier (Art. 1145 ff OR)	titre à ordre	order paper
Organisation	organisation	organization
Organisationsreglement (Art. 716b OR)	règlement d'organisation	organizational regulations
organisierte Vermögenseinheiten	patrimoine organisé	organized units of assets
organisiertes Verbrechen	crime organisé	organized crime
Organvertreter (Art. 689c OR)	représentation par un membre d'un organe	governing officer as representative
Ort	localité	place, city (in an address)
örtliche Verhältnisse	circonstances locales	local circumstances

örtliche Zuständigkeit (Art. 9 ff ZPO)	compétence ratione loci, compétence à raison du lieu	territorial jurisdiction
Ortsgebrauch	usage local	local usage
ortsüblich	selon l'usage de la place	as provided for by local custom
Ortszuschlag	indemnité de résidence	cost-of-living allowance
Pacht (Art. 275 ff OR)	bail à ferme	usufructuary lease
Pachtbetrieb	exploitation en fermage	tenant farm, leased farm
Pächter	fermier	usufructuary lessee
Pachtzins	fermage	rent
panaschieren	panachage	splitting the vote
Parentel (Art. 457 ff ZGB) (D: Stammgruppe)	parentèle	statutory heir (The relatives of the deceased person are divided into groups of statutory heirs. These are based on the natural order in which the generations succeed each other. A group includes all persons who descend from a common ancestor.)
Parität	parité	equal representative of management and labor
paritätische Finanzierung	financement paritaire	equal-share financing
paritätische Verwaltung (BVG)	administration paritaire (LPP)	equal representation management
paritätischer Beitrag	cotisation paritaire	contribution paid in equal shares by employer and employee
Parkbusse (D: Geldbuße für falsches Parken)	amende de stationnement	parking fine
Parketthandel	négociation à la criée	open outcry trading
parkieren (D: parken)	parquer (F : stationner)	to park
Parkierplatz (D: Parkplatz)	place de parc (F : place de stationnement)	parking place
Parkplatzbenutzungsgebühr	taxe d'utilisation de place de parc	parking place fee
Parkverbot	interdiction de parquer	parking ban, no parking
Parlament	parlement	parliament

Parlamentarier	parlementaire	member of parliament
parlamentarische Gruppen	intergroupe parlementaire	cross-party groups
parlamentarische Initiative	initiative parlementaire	parliamentary initiative
parlamentarische Untersuchung	enquête parlementaire	parliamentary investigation
parlamentarische Untersuchungskommission (PUK)	Commission d'enquête parlementaire (CEP)	parliamentary investigation committee
parlamentarische Verwaltungskontrolle (PVK)	Contrôle parlementaire de l'administration (CPA)	parliamentary control of the administration
parlamentarischer Vorstoss (PV)	intervention parlementaire	parliamentary procedural request
parlamentarisches System	système parlementaire	parliamentary system
Parlamentsdienste	Services du Parlement	Parliamentary Services
Parlamentsgebäude	Palais du Parlement	Parliament Building (in Bern)
Parlamentsgesetz (ParlG)	Loi sur le Parlement (LParl)	Parliament Act
Parteibefragung (D: Parteivernehmung) (Art. 191 ZPO)	interrogation d'une partie	examination of a party
Parteientschädigung (Art. 95 ZPO)	dépens	attorney's fees and expenses
Parteifähigkeit (Art. 66 ZPO)	capacité d'être partie	capacity to be a party
Parteistimme	suffrage de parti	party vote
Parteivertretung (Art. 68 ZPO)	représentation des parties	representation of the parties
Parteiwechsel (Art. 83 ZPO)	substitution de partie	substitution of a party
Partizipant (D: Teilnehmer)	participant	participant
Partizipationskapital (Art. 656b OR)	capital-participation	participation certificate capital
Partizipationsschein (Art. 656a-656g OR)	bon de participation	participation certificate
Partnerschaftsgesetz (PartG)	Loi sur le partenariat (LPart)	Same-Sex Partnership Act
passive Checkfähigkeit (Art. 1102 OR)	désignation du tiré	capacity to act as drawee
passive Wahlfähigkeit	éligibilité	eligibility for election

passives Wahlrecht	capacité civique passive, éligibilité	right to be elected
Passivlegitimation	légitimation passive	defendant's standing, standing to be sued
Patentanspruch	revendication (brevet)	patent claim
Patentanwalt	agent en brevets	patent agent
Patentbewerber	requérant	patent applicant
Patentfähigkeit	brevetabilité	patentability
Patentgerichtsgesetz (PatGG)	Loi sur le Tribunal fédéral des brevets (LTFB)	Patent Court Act
Patentgesetz (PatG)	Loi sur les brevets (LBI)	Patents Act
patentierbare Erfindung	invention brevetable	patentable invention
Patentinhaber	titulaire du brevet	patent holder
Patentregister	registre des brevets	patent register
Patentverletzung	violation du brevet	patent infringement
Patentverordnung (PatV)	Ordonnance sur les brevets (OBI)	Patents Ordinance
Patronale Finanzierungsstiftung (PAFI)	Fondation patronale de prévoyance retraite	Pension Fund Foundation (funded by employers)
Patronatserklärung	déclaration de patronage	comfort letter
paulianische Anfechtung	action révocatoire	avoidance action (action by creditors to void a fraudulent conveyance)
pauschale Verwaltungskommission	commission forfaitaire de gestion	all-in fee
Pauschalen für das Schlichtungsverfahren (Art. 95 ZPO)	émolument forfaitaire de conciliation	fee for the conciliation proceedings
Pauschalen für den Entscheid (Art. 95 ZPO)	émolument forfaitaire de décision	judgment fee, fee for the decision
Pendler	pendulaire (F : personne qui fait la navette)	commuter

Pendlerkostenbeitrag	contribution aux frais de déplacement	commuting costs contribution
Pensionen (Art. 93 Abs. 1 SchKG)	pensions	pensions
Pensionierter	personne retraitée	pensioner, retiree
Pensionierung	mise à la retraite	retirement
Pensionierungsalter	âge de la retraite	retirement age
Pensionskasse des Bundes (PUBLICA)	Caisse fédérale de pensions (PUBLICA)	Federal Pension Fund
Pensionskassenbeitrag	cotisation à la caisse de pensions	pension fund contribution
per Nachnahme	contre remboursement	cash on delivery (COD)
Perron (D: Bahnsteig)	quai	platform
Personaldienstbarkeit	servitude personnelle	personal easement
Personalfürsorgestiftung	fondation de prévoyance en faveur du personnel	company pension fund
Personalpolitik	politique du personnel	personnel policy
Personalunion	union personnelle	one person doing two things
Personendaten	données personnelles	personal data
Personengesellschaft	société de personnes	partnership
Personenidentifikator	identificateur personnel	personal identifier
Personenrecht	droit des personnes	law of persons
Personenschaden	dommage corporel	bodily injury
persönliche Leistung (Art. 68 OR)	exécution par le débiteur lui-même	performance by the obligor in person
persönliche Verhältnisse (Art. 27 StGB)	circonstances personnelles	personal circumstances
persönlicher Verkehr (ZGB 273)	relations personnelles	personal access to, contact with (children)
persönliches Erscheinen	comparution personnelle	personal appearance
persönliches Recht	droit personnel	personal right

Persönlichkeit	personnalité	personality
Persönlichkeitsprofil	profil de la personnalité	personality profile
Petitionsrecht (Art. 33 BV)	droit de pétition	right to petition
Pfand (Art. 37 Abs. 3 SchKG)	gage	pledge, mortgage
Pfandausfall	insuffisance du gage	insufficient pledge
Pfandausfallforderung	découvert en cas de créance garantie gage	overdraft in the event of a secured claim
Pfandausfallschein	certificat d'insuffisance de gage	insufficient pledge certificate
pfändbar	saisissable	subject to seizure
Pfändbarkeit	saisissabilité	seizability
Pfandbrief	lettre de gage	mortgage bond
Pfandbriefbank	banque d'émission de lettres de gage	mortgage bond bank
pfänden	saisir	to seize (assets)
Pfandgegenstände (Art. 262 Abs. 2 SchKG)	biens remis en gage	pledged assets
Pfandgläubiger	créancier gagiste	pledgee
Pfandhalter	détenteur de gage	holder of a pledge
Pfandrecht (Art. 151 SchKG)	droit de gage	charge
Pfandschätzung (Art. 299 SchKG)	estimation des gages	valuation of pledges
Pfandtitel	titre de gage	mortgage certificate
Pfändung (Art. 89 ff. SchKG)	saisie	seizure
Pfändungsankündigung	avis de saisie	notice of seizure
Pfändungsanschluss (Art. 110 SchKG)	participation à la saisie	participation in the seizure
Pfändungsbegehren	réquisition de procéder à la saisie	application to seize assets
Pfändungsbetrug (Art. 163 StGB)	fraude dans la saisie	fraud against seizure
Pfändungsgruppe	série de créanciers saisissants	group of seizing creditors
Pfändungsschuldner	débiteur saisi	debtor whose assets have been seized
Pfändungsurkunde (Art. 112 ff SchKG)	procès-verbal de saisie	attachment report
Pfändungsvollzug (Art. 156 SchKG)	exécution de la saisie	performance of the attachment

pfandversicherte Forderung (Art. 151 Abs. 1 SchKG)	créance garantie par gage	secured claim
Pfandvertrag	contrat de constitution de gage	pledge agreement
Pfandverwertung (Art. 156 SchKG)	réalisation de gage	proceeds of the pledge, proceeds of the collateral
Pflegebedürftigkeit	besoin de soins	need of nursing care
Pflegebeitrag	contribution aux frais de soins	contribution to the costs of care
Pflegeeltern (Art. 294 ZGB)	parents nourriciers	foster parents
Pflegeheim	établissement de soins	nursing home
Pflegepersonal	personnel infirmier	nursing staff
Pflichtenheft	cahier des charges	performance specifications
Pflichtteil (Art. 470 ZGB)	réserve successorale	forced heir's share
Pflichtteilsberechtigter	réservataire	forced heir
Pflichtteilserbe	héritier réservataire	forced heir
pflichtwidriges Verhalten bei Unfall (Art. 92 SVG)	violation des devoirs en cas d'accident	violation of duties in the event of an accident
Pfrund (Art. 521-529 OR)	entretien viager	support for life
Pfrundanstalt (D: Pfründhaus)	asile	retirement home, old-age home
Pfründer (D: Pfründner) (Art. 521 OR)	créancier d'entretien viager	beneficiary of lifelong support
Pfrundgeber (Art. 521 OR)	débiteur d'entretien viager	grantor of lifelong support
Pfrundnehmer (Art. 521 OR)	créancier d'entretien viager	beneficiary of lifelong support
Phantasiebezeichnung	désignation de fantaisie	invented name, made-up name
Pharmakopöeverordnung (PhaV)	Ordonnance sur la pharmacopée (OPha)	Pharmacopoeia Ordinance
Plagiat	plagiat	plagiarism
Plenarsitzung	séance plénière	plenary session
Plünderung	pillage	plundering

Pneu (D: Autoreifen, Fahrradreifen)	pneu	tire
Politik (1)	politique	policy
Politik (2)	politique	politics
politische Partei	parti politique	political party
politische Rechte (Art. 34 BV)	droits politiques	political rights
Polizei	police	police
Polizeigericht	tribunal de police	police court
Polizeigesetz	Loi sur la police	Police Act
polizeiliche Anhaltung (Art. 215 StPO)	appréhension	police power to stop
polizeiliche Einvernahme (Art. 159 StPO)	audition menée par la police	police examination
Popularbeschwerde	action populaire	popular complaint
Pornografie (Art. 197 StGB)	pornographie	pornography
Portofreiheit	franchise de port	exemption from postage
positive Vertragsverletzung	violation positive du contrat	positive breach of contract
positives Recht	droit positif	positive law
Postanweisung (PA)	mandat de poste (MP)	postal money order
Postcheck	chèque postal	postal check
Postfach	case postale (F : boîte postale)	post office box
Postgeheimnis	secret postal	secrecy of the mail
Postgesetz (PG)	Loi fédérale sur la poste (LPO)	Postal Services Act
postlagernde Sendung	poste restante	poste restante
Postleitzahl (PLZ)	numéro postal d'acheminement (NPA) (F : code postal)	postal code
Pöstler (D: Postangestellter, Postbote)	facteur	postal employee, postman
Postregal	régale des postes	postal regale
Postrückbehaltung	garde du courrier	hold mail
Postulat	postulat	parliamentary motion asking the government to legislate (as opposed to a motion requiring the government to legislate, cf. *Motion*)
Postzustellung	distribution du courrier	mail delivery
Potestativbedingung (D: Willensbedingung)	condition potestative	discretionary condition
Präambel	préambule	preamble

Praktikum	stage	internship
Prälegat	legs préciputaire	advance legacy
Prämie	prime	premium
Prämienabrechnung	décompte de primes	premium statement
Prämienbefreiung	libération du paiement des primes, exonération de primes	waiver of premium
Prämienzuschlag	supplément de prime	premium supplement
Präsident	président	president, chairman
Präsident des Verwaltungsrates (D: ~Aufsichtsratsvorsitzender)	président du conseil d'administration	chairman of the board of directors
Präsidentenkonferenz	Conférence des présidents	Presidents' Conference (of the Swiss Federal Supreme Court)
Präsidialgebühr	frais de présidence	fee for case being heard by a single judge
Präsidialverfügung	décision présidentielle	order by the presiding judge
Präsidialverhör	interrogatoire par le président du tribunal	examination by the presiding judge (as opposed to cross examination)
Präsidium (Art. 34 ParlG)	collège présidentiel	presiding college
Präzedenzfall	précédent	precedent
Preis	prix	price
Preisabsprache	entente sur les prix	price fixing
Preisansatz	fixation des prix	pricing
Preisbindung	prix imposés	retail price maintenance
Preisentwicklung	évolution des prix	price trend
Preiskontrolle	contrôle des prix	price control
Preismissbrauch	abus de prix	unfair pricing
Preispolitik	politique en matière de prix	price policy
Preisüberwacher	surveillant des prix	price watchdog
Preisüberwachungsgesetz (PüG)	Loi fédérale concernant la surveillance des prix (LSPr)	Price Supervision Act

Preisvergleich	comparaison de prix	price comparison
Presseagentur	agence de presse	press agency
Presseförderung	promotion de la presse	promotion of the press
Pressefreiheit	liberté de la presse	freedom of the press
Pressemitteilung	communiqué de presse	press release
Primarschule (D: Grundschule)	école primaire (F : école élémentaire)	elementary school
Privatautonomie	autonomie privée	freedom of contract
Privatbank	banque privée	private bank
Privatbereich	sphère privée	private sphere
Privatgläubiger	créancier personnel	personal creditor
Privatisierung	privatisation	privatization
Privatklägerschaft (Art. 118 StPO)	partie plaignante	private claimant
Privatpatientenversicherung	assurance pour patient privé	private patient insurance
Privatperson	personne privée	private person
Privatrecht	droit privé	private law
Privatschule	école privée	private school
Privatversicherer	assureur privé	private insurer
Privatversicherung	assurance privée	private insurance
Privatwirtschaft	économie privée	private economy
privilegierte Forderung	créance privilégiée	secured claim
Probezeit	période d'essai	trial period
Produktegestaltung	élaboration des produits	product design
Produktehaftpflicht	responsabilité du fait des produits	products liability
Produzentenkennzeichen (Art. 51 MSchG)	signe d'identification du producteur	producer identification mark
Prokurist (Art. 721 OR)	fondé de procuration	authorized signatory
Promissar	stipulant	promisee (in a third-party beneficiary contract)
Promittent	promettant	promisor
Proporzwahl (D: Verhältniswahl)	système proportionnel	election based on proportional representation
prosequieren	valider	to validate

Prosequierung des Arrests (Art. 279 SchKG)	validation du séquestre	ratification of the attachment
Prospekthaftung (Art. 752 OR)	responsabilité pour le prospectus d'émission	prospectus liability
Protest	protêt	protest
Protest mangels Annahme	protêt faute d'acceptation	protest on nonacceptance
Protest mangels Zahlung	protêt faute de paiement	protest on nonpayment
Protokoll	procès-verbal	minutes
Protokollführer	rédacteur du procès-verbal	person taking the minutes
protokollieren	consigner au procès-verbal	to record
provisorische Rechtsöffnung (Art. 82 SchKG)	mainlevée provisoire	preliminary dismissal of debtor's objection
Prozessfähigkeit (Art. 67 ZPO, Art. 106 StPO)	capacité d'ester en justice	capacity to act, capacity to take legal action
Prozesskosten (Art. 95 ZPO)	frais	procedural costs (include court costs and attorney's fees)
prozessleitende Verfügungen (Art. 246 ZPO)	décisions d'instruction	procedural rulings
Prozessleitung	conduite du procès	judicial control of the proceedings
Prozessökonomie	économie de procédure	procedural economy
Prozessrecht	droit de procédure	procedural law
Prozesssache	objet du litige	matter in dispute
Prozessvertretung	représentation en procédure	
Prozessvoraussetzungen	conditions à l'ouverture de l'action	procedural requirements
Prüfung der eingegebenen Forderungen (Art. 244 SchKG)	examen des productions	examination of productions
Prüfungsausschuss	comité de contrôle	audit committee
Prüfungsbestätigung (Art. 635a OR)	attestation de vérification	audit confirmation
PS-Kapital (Partizipationsschein-Kapital)	capital-participation	participation certificate capital
Publikationsorgan	organe de publication	publication medium

Publikumseinlage (Art. 1 BankG)	dépôt du public	deposit (from the public)
Publikumsgesellschaft	société publique	publicly-held company
Publikumsöffentlichkeit	droit du public et de la presse d'assister aux débats	open court
Pufferzone	zone tampon	buffer zone
qualifizierte elektronische Unterschrift (Art. 14 OR)	signature électronique qualifiée	authenticated electronic signature
qualifizierte Pornografie (Art. 197 Abs. 3 und 4 StGB)	pornographie qualifiée	aggravated pornography
qualifizierter Diebstahl (Art. 172ter Abs. 2 StGB)	vol qualifié	aggravated theft
qualifiziertes Mehr (D: qualifizierte Mehrheit)	majorité qualifiée	qualified majority
qualifiziertes Schweigen	silence qualifié	qualified silence
Quartier (D: Stadtviertel)	quartier	neighborhood
Quelle	source	source
Quellenangabe	indication de la source	indication of the source
Quellenrecht (Art. 780 ZGB)	servitude de source	spring rights
Quellensteuer (QS)	impôt à la source	withholding tax
querulatorische Beschwerde (Art. 42 Abs. 7 BGG)	recours procédurier	querulous appeal, frivolous appeal
querulatorische Eingaben (Art. 132 ZPO)	actes introduits de manière procédurière	querulous pleadings, querulous submissions
Quittung	quittance	receipt
Quorum	quorum	quorum
Rabatt	rabais	discount
Rahmenbewilligung	autorisation générale	general authorization
Rahmengesetzgebung	législation cadre	framework legislation
Rahmenvertrag	contrat-cadre	framework agreement
Randbemerkung	note marginale	marginal note, note in the margin
Randgebiet	région périphérique	border region
Randtitel (RandT)	titre marginal (tit. marg.)	margin title
Randziffer	chiffre marginal	margin number
Rangfolge der Gläubiger (Art. 146 SchKG)	rang des créanciers	ranking of creditors
Rangordnung der Gläubiger (Art. 219 SchKG)	ordre des créanciers	order of creditors

Rangrücktritt	postposition	subordination
Rappen	centime	cent
Rassendiskriminierung (Art. 261bis StGB)	discrimination raciale	racial discrimination
Ratifikation	ratification	ratification (of a treaty)
Rating	notation	rating
Raub (Art. 140 StGB)	brigandage	robbery
Räuber	brigand	robber
Raufhandel (Art. 133 StGB)	rixe	brawling
Raumplanung	aménagement du territoire	spatial planning
Raumplanungsgesetz (RPG)	Loi sur l'aménagement du territoire (LAT)	Spatial Planning Act
Räumung	évacuation, expulsion	evacuation, eviction
Räumungsbefehl	ordre d'évacuation	evacuation order
Räumungsklage	action en déguerpisse-ment, action en expulsion	action to evict a holdover tenant
Rauschtat (Art. 263 StGB)	acte commis en état d'irresponsabilité fautive	offense committed while intoxicated
Rayon (D: Dienstbezirk)	secteur	district
Rayonverbot	interdiction géographique	exclusion order
Realakt	acte matériel	physical act
Realerfüllung	exécution en nature	performance in kind
Realersatz	indemnisation en nature	compensation in kind
Realkonkurrenz	concours réel	series of offenses prosecuted jointly (one person commits two or more crimes)
Realleistungspflichtiger	personne tenue de fournir une prestation	person obligated to take measures
Realoblation	offre réelle	actual offer, effective offer
Realteilung	partage matériel	physical division of property
Realwert	valeur réelle	real value
Rebbau (D: Weinbau)	viticulture	wine growing
Rebbaubetrieb (D: Weinbaubetrieb)	exploitation viticole	winery

Rebbauer (D: Weinbauer)	viticulteur	winegrower
Rebbauzone (D: Weinbauzone)	zone viticole	wine-growing area
Rechenschaftsablegung	reddition de comptes	rendering of accounts
Rechenschaftsbericht (Art. 330 SchKG)	rapport d'activité	report of activities
Rechenschaftspflicht	obligation de rendre comptes	accountability
Rechnungsführer	comptable	accountant
Rechnungsruf (Art. 582 ZGB)	sommation publique	formal call to account (to register all debts and claims)
Rechnungswährung	monnaie comptable	account currency
Recht (1)	droit	right
Recht (2)	Droit	law
Recht auf Arbeit	droit au travail	right to work
Recht auf Bildung	droit à la formation	right to education
Recht auf einen Verteidiger	droit à un défenseur	right to a defender
Recht auf Einsichtnahme	droit de regard	right to inspect documents, right to examine all relevant documents
Recht auf Existenzsicherung	droit à des conditions minimales d'existence	right to secure one's livelihood
Recht auf freien Briefverkehr	droit au respect de la correspondance	right to privacy of correspondence
Recht auf Gesundheit	droit à la santé	right to health
Recht auf Höherversicherung	droit à une couverture d'assurance plus étendue	right to supplemental insurance
Recht auf Leben	droit à la vie	right to life
Recht auf Mitgliedschaft	droit à l'affiliation	right to membership
Recht auf Selbstverteidigung	droit à se défendre soi-même	right to self defense
Recht der Familiengründung	droit de fonder une famille	right to start a family
Recht zur Hinterlegung (Art. 92 OR)	droit de consignation	right to deposit the object (at the obligee's expense)
Recht: aus dem Recht weisen	exclure des preuves	to exclude from evidence

Recht: im Recht liegen	figurer au dossier	to be on file with
Recht: ins Recht fassen	traduire en justice	to sue
Recht: ins Recht legen	verser comme preuve au dossier	to file with the court, to submit as evidence
Rechte des Gesellschafters	droits sociaux	shareholder rights
rechtfertigende Notwehr (Art. 15 StGB)	légitime défense	legitimate self defense
rechtfertigender Notstand (Art. 17 StGB)	état de nécessité licite	legitimate act in a state of emergency
rechtlich geschütztes Interesse	intérêt juridiquement protégé	legally protected interest
rechtliche Qualifikation	qualification juridique	applying the law to the facts
rechtlicher Konsens	accord de droit	legal consensus
rechtliches Monopol	monopole de droit	legal monopoly
rechtliches Vorbringen	moyen de droit	point of law, legal argument
Rechtsanspruch	droit	right
Rechtsanwalt	avocat	lawyer, attorney
Rechtsanwaltschaft	barreau	bar
Rechtsanwendung	application du droit	application of the law
Rechtsanwendung von Amts wegen	application du droit d'office	sua sponte application of the law
Rechtsauffassung	conception juridique, opinion juridique	legal opinion
Rechtsausführungen	exposé juridique	legal discussion
Rechtsbegehren	conclusions	prayer for relief, demand for relief
Rechtsbegriff	notion juridique	legal concept
Rechtsbeistand (Art. 127 StPO)	conseil juridique	legal advisor (appointed by the accused or the private claimant to safeguard their interests)
Rechtsberater	conseiller juridique	legal counsel, legal adviser
Rechtsdienst	service juridique	legal department
rechtserheblich	pertinent, important pour la procédure	relevant from a legal standpoint
Rechtsfähigkeit (Art. 53 ZGB)	jouissance des droits civils	legal capacity

Rechtsfolge	conséquence juridique	legal result
Rechtsfrage	question de droit	legal issue (as opposed to an issue of fact)
Rechtsfrage von grundsätzlicher Bedeutung	question juridique de principe	legal question of fundamental importance
Rechtsgeschäft	acte juridique	legal transaction
Rechtsgeschäft unter Lebenden	acte entre vifs	inter vivos transaction
Rechtsgeschäft von Todes wegen	acte pour cause de mort	transaction causa mortis
Rechtsgewährleistung (Art. 192 ff OR)	garantie en cas d'éviction	warranty of good title
Rechtsgleichheit in der Rechtsanwendung	égalité devant la loi	equal protection of the law
Rechtsgrund	titre juridique, cause juridique	legal basis
Rechtsgrundsatz	principe juridique	legal principle
Rechtshandlungen (Art. 204 Abs. 1 SchKG)	actes de disposition	disposals
rechtshängig	litispendant, pendant, en instance	pending
Rechtshängigkeit (Art. 62 ff ZPO)	litispendance	pendency (of a lawsuit)
Rechtshilfe	entraide	mutual assistance
Rechtshilfe in Strafsachen	entraide judiciaire pénale	mutual assistance in criminal matters
Rechtshilfe in Zivilsachen	entraide judiciaire civile	mutual assistance in civil matters
Rechtshilfe und Auslieferung	entraide et extradition	mutual assistance and extradition
Rechtshilfeersuchen	commission rogatoire	letters rogatory
Rechtshilfegesetz (IRSG)	Loi sur l'entraide pénale internationale (EIMP)	Mutual Assistance Act
Rechtshilfegesuch	demande d'entraide	request for mutual assistance
Rechtsirrtum	erreur de droit	error of law
Rechtskollision	conflit de lois	conflict of laws
Rechtskraft – in Rechtskraft erwachsen (D: rechtskräftig werden)	passer en force de chose jugée	to be res judicata
Rechtskraft (1)	chose jugée	res judicata
Rechtskraft (2)	force de loi	force of law

rechtskräftig	entré en force, ayant force de chose jugée	legally effective; non-appealable, res judicata
rechtskräftiger Entscheid	décision définitive	final non-appealable decision (compare *décision finale*, one which is final in the sense that it puts an end to the proceedings—as opposed to an interlocutory decision—but can then be appealed)
Rechtskunde	connaissances juridiques	legal fundamentals (name of a course)
Rechtsmässigkeit	légalité	legality
Rechtsmethodik	méthodologie du droit	legal methodology
Rechtsmissbrauch (Art. 2 Abs. 2 ZGB)	abus de droit	abuse of a right
rechtsmissbräuchliche Eingaben (Art. 132 ZPO)	actes abusifs	abusive pleadings, abusive submissions
Rechtsmittel	moyen de droit	legal remedy
Rechtsmittelbelehrung	indication des voies de droit	instructions regarding appeal, instructions regarding legal remedies
Rechtsmittelfrist	délai de recours	deadline for appeal
Rechtsmittelinstanz	instance de recours	appellate court
Rechtsnachfolge	succession juridique	legal succession
Rechtsnachfolger	ayant-cause	legal successor
Rechtsnatur	nature juridique	legal status
Rechtsnorm	règle de droit	legal rule
Rechtsöffnung (Art. 80 ff. SchKG)	mainlevée d'opposition	court order dismissing debtor's objection
Rechtsöffnungsbegehren	requête de mainlevée	motion for court order dismissing debtor's objection
Rechtsöffnungstitel (Art. 80 SchKG)	titre de mainlevée	automatically enforceable document
Rechtsöffnungsverfahren (Art. 84 SchKG)	procédure de mainlevée	procedure for dismissal of debtor's objection
Rechtspersönlichkeit	personnalité juridique	legal personality
Rechtspflicht	obligation juridique	legal obligation
Rechtsphilosophie	philosophie du droit	jurisprudence, legal philosophy
Rechtspositivismus	positivisme juridique	legal positivism

Rechtsquelle	source du droit	source of law
Rechtssatz	règle de droit	legal rule
Rechtsschein	apparence de droit	color of law
Rechtsscheinvollmacht	procuration apparente	apparent authority
Rechtsschrift (D: Schriftsatz)	mémoire	brief
Rechtsschule	école juridique	law school
Rechtsschutz	protection juridique	legal protection
Rechtsschutzbegehren	demande de protection juridique	relief sought, legal remedy sought
Rechtsschutzfall	cas de protection juridique	insured event
Rechtsschutzinteresse (Zivilprozess)	intérêt juridique (procédure civile)	legitimate interest
Rechtsschutzversicherung	assurance de protection juridique	legal expenses insurance (LEI), legal protection insurance (LPI)
Rechtssetzung	législation	legislation
Rechtssetzungsverfahren	procédure législative	legislative procedure
Rechtssicherheit	sécurité du droit	legal certainty
Rechtssprache	langage juridique	legal language
Rechtsstaat	état de droit	(state under) the rule of law
Rechtsstellung	situation juridique	legal status, legal position
Rechtsstillstand (Art. 57-62 SchKG)	suspension des poursuites	suspension, stay of debt collection (e.g. during military service, a death in the debtor's family, severe illness of the debtor)
Rechtsstreit	litige	legal dispute, litigation
Rechtssubjekt	sujet de droit	person recognized by law as having rights and obligations
Rechtsumgehung	fraude à la loi	evasion of the law
Rechtsunkenntnis (Art. 3 Abs. 2 ZGB)	ignorance de la loi	ignorance of the law
Rechtsunsicherheit	insécurité juridique	legal uncertainty
rechtsunwirksam	dépourvu d'effets juridiques, nul	null and void, legally ineffective, unenforceable
Rechtsvereinheitlichung	unification du droit	unification of law

Rechtsvergleichung	droit comparé	comparative law
Rechtsverhältnis	rapport de droit	legal relationship
Rechtsverletzung	violation du droit	legal violation
Rechtsvertreter	représentant légal	legal representative
Rechtsverweigerung (Art. 17 Abs. 3 SchKG)	déni de justice	denial of justice
Rechtsverweigerung im engeren Sinne	refus de statuer	refusal to rule
Rechtsverzögerung (Art. 17 Abs. 3 SchKG)	retard injustifié	delay of justice
Rechtsvorkehr	voie de droit	legal channel
Rechtsvorschlag (Art. 74 SchKG) (D:~Widerspruch)	opposition au commandement de payer	debtor's objection to the order to pay
Rechtsvorschlagsfrist (Art. 74 SchKG)	délai d'opposition au commandement de payer	deadline for objecting to the order to pay
Rechtswahl	élection de droit	choice of law
Rechtsweggarantie (Art. 29a BV)	garantie de l'accès au juge	guarantee of access to the courts
Rechtswegsgabelung	bifurcation de la voie de droit	bifurcation of appeals
rechtswidrig	illicite, illégal	unlawful
rechtswidrige Vereinigung (Art. 275ter StGB)	groupements illicites	unlawful association
Rechtswidrigkeit	illicéité, illégalité	unlawfulness
Rechtswirksamkeit	validité juridique	legal validity, enforceability
Rechtswirkung	effet juridique	legal effect
Rechtswohltat des Nachlassvertrags	bénéfice du concordat	benefit of a debt restructuring agreement
Recycling	recyclage de déchets	recycling
Redefreiheit	liberté de parole	freedom of speech
Referendum	referendum	referendum
Referent (Instruktionsrichter)	juge délégué à l'instruction	investigating judge
Referenzkurs	cours de référence	reference price (price of the underlying assets on the valuation date in a derivatives transaction)
Referenzwährung	monnaie de référence	reference currency
Regeste (D: Zusammenfassung)	résumé	summary (of important points in a decision—this part is always in three languages)

Regierung	gouvernement	government
Regierungs- und Verwaltungsorganisationsgesetz (RVOG)	Loi sur l'organisation du gouvernement et de l'administration (LOGA)	Government and Administration Organization Act
Regierungspräsident	président du Conseil d'Etat	president of the Council of State
Regierungsrat	Conseil d'Etat	Council of State (government of one of the French-speaking cantons, except for the République et Canton du Jura, whose government is called le Gouvernement)
Regierungsstatthalter	préfet	Chancellor of State
Regierungsstatthalteramt	préfecture	Chancellery of State
regionales Arbeitsvermittlungszentrum	office régional de placement	regional employment center
Regionalpolitik	politique régionale	regional policy
Register für berufliche Vorsorge	registre de la prévoyance professionnelle	Register for Occupational Pension Provision
Registerauszug	extrait du registre	register extract
Registereintragungsgebühr	taxe d'inscription au registre	registration fee
Registerpfandrecht	droit de gage enregistré	registered lien (no physical delivery of the pledged asset)
registrierte Kriminalität	criminalité enregistrée, délinquance apparente	recorded crime
registrierte Vorsorgeeinrichtung	institution de prévoyance enregistrée	registered pension institution
Reglement für das Bundesgericht (BGerR)	Règlement du Tribunal Fédéral (RTF)	Federal Supreme Court Regulations
Regress	recours	recourse
Regressklage (D: Rückgriffsklage)	action récursoire	recourse against those who are secondarily liable
Regularien (D: Tagesordnungspunkte)	points de l'ordre du jour	agenda items
Reichtumssteuer	impôt sur la richesse	wealth tax

Reihenfolge der Pfändung (Art. 95 SchKG)	ordre de saisie	sequence of attachment
Reineinkommen	revenu net	net income
reiner Vermögensschaden	dommage purement économique	purely economic damage
Reingewinn	bénéfice net	net profit
Reinvermögen	fortune nette	net assets
Rekrutenschule (D: militärische Grundausbildung)	école de recrues	recruit school
Rektaklausel	clause non à ordre	not to order clause
rekurabel	recourable	appealable, subject to appeal
Rekurrent	appelant, requérant	appellant
rekurrieren	faire appel	to appeal
Rekursgegner	intimé, partie intimée	appellee
Rekurskommission	commission de recours	appeals commission
relatives Mehr (D: relative Mehrheit)	majorité relative	relative majority
relatives Recht	droit relatif	relative right (Obligations are an example of relative rights, which apply only inter partes, as opposed to absolute rights, which apply erga omnes.)
religiöse Eheschliessung	mariage religieux	church wedding
Rembours	rembours	drawback
Renditeliegenschaft	immeuble de rapport	commercial property (built or bought as a capital investment rather than for use by the owner)
Rentengläubiger (Art. 516 OR)	créancier d'une rente viagère	annuitant
Rentenschuldner (Art. 516 OR)	débiteur d'une rente viagère	grantor of a life annuity
Replik	réplique	reply
Repressalien	représailles	retaliation
Requisitorialpfändung	saisie par voie rogatoire	attachment by way of judicial cooperation
Resolutivbedingung (D: auflösende Bedingung)	condition résolutoire	condition subsequent
Restanz (D: Restbetrag)	reliquat	outstanding balance
Restlaufzeit	durée résiduelle	residual term
Restschuld	solde de la dette	residual debt, balance due

Reststrafe	solde de la peine	remaining sentence
Restwassermenge (Art. 4 GSchG)	débit résiduel	residual flow
Retentionsrecht (Art. 895 ZGB, Art. 491 OR)	droit de rétention	possessory lien
Retourgeld (D: Wechselgeld)	monnaie	change
Reugeld (Art. 158 OR)	dédit	forfeit money
Reukauf	folle enchère	unreasonable bid
reüssieren (D: gelingen)	réussir	to succeed
Revision (1)	contrôle	audit
Revision (2) (D: Wiederaufnahme des Verfahrens) (Art. 328-333 ZPO)	révision	review
Revisionsbericht	rapport de révision	audit report
Revisionsgesuch (Art. 329 ZPO)	demande en révision	application for a review
Revisionsgrund (Art. 328 ZPO)	motif de révision	ground for review
Revisionsstelle (Art. 727 ff OR)	organe de révision	auditor
Revisionsverband	syndicat de révision	audit committee
Revisor	réviseur	auditor
Richter	juge	judge
Richter: den Richter anrufen	saisir le juge	to bring a matter before the court, to file suit
Richterablehnung	récusation d'un juge	recusal of a judge
richterlich	judiciaire	judicial
richterliche Behörde	autorité judiciaire	judicial authority
richterliche Frist	délai fixé par le juge	deadline set by the judge
richterliches Ermessen	pouvoir d'appréciation du juge	judicial discretion
Richterrecht	droit jurisprudentiel, droit prétorien, jurisprudence	judge-made law, case law
Richtfest	bouquet de chantier	topping-out ceremony (in a construction project)
Richtlinie (1)	directive	guideline
Richtlinie (2) (Gemeinschaftsrecht)	directive (droit communautaire)	directive
Riegelhaus (D: Fachwerkhaus)	maison à colombages	half-timbered house
Risikoanalyse	analyse des risques	risk analysis

Risikobeitrag	cotisation de risque	risk contribution
Risikofähigkeit	capacité de risque	risk capability
Risikokapital	capital risque	venture capital
Risikoleistungen	prestations de risque	risk benefits
Risikomanagement	gestion des risques	risk management
Risikoneigung	propension au risque	risk appetite
Risikoprämie	prime de risque	risk premium
Risikoprüfung	examen du risque	risk check
Risikostreuung	diversification	risk spreading, diversification
Rohbau	gros œuvre	shell, external structure of an unfinished building
Rotlicht (D: Verkehrsampel)	feu rouge	traffic light
Rückbürgschaft (Art. 498 OR)	arrière-caution	counter-surety
Rückdeckung	réassurance	reinsurance
Rückerstattung	restitution	restitution
Rückfall (Art. 93 StGB)	récidive	recidivism
Rückfall der geschenkten Sache (Art. 247 OR)	retour des objets donnés	reversion of the gift
Rückfälligkeit (Art. 93 StGB)	récidive	recidivism
Rückforderung	répétition	claim for return of an amount paid in error
Rückforderung der Schenkung (Art. 249 OR)	restitution des biens donnés	claim for return of a gift
Rückforderungsklage	action en répétition de l'indu	action to recover an amount paid in error
Rückkauf	rachat	redemption
Rückkaufsrecht (Art. 216 OR)	droit de réméré	right of repurchase
Rückkaufswert	valeur de rachat	redemption value
Rückkehr	retour	return
Rückkehrhilfe	aide au retour	aiding immigrants to return to their home country
Rückkommensantrag	proposition de réexamen	proposal for reconsideration
Rückschaffung von Gegenstände (Art. 284 SchKG)	réintégration des biens	forced deliverance of assets
Rückschlag	déficit	deficit
Rücksendung	réexpédition	return
Rückstellung	provision	provision
Rücktritt (Art. 23 StGB)	désistement	withdrawal (from completing the criminal act)

Rücktritt vom Vertrag (Art. 190 OR)	résolution du contrat	termination of the contract
Rücktrittsrechts des Verkäufers (Art. 212 SchKG)	droit de résolution du vendeur	seller's right to terminate
Rückübertragung	rétrocession	retransfer, back transfer, reassignment
Rückversicherung	réassurance	reinsurance
Rückverweisung (Art. 14 IPRG)	renvoi	renvoi (conflict of laws rule)
Rückwechsel (Art. 1049 OR)	retraite	redraft, re-exchange bill
Rückweisung	renvoi d'un projet	referral for review
Rückwirkung	rétroactivité	retroactivity
Rückzug einer Volksinitiative	retrait d'une initiative populaire	withdrawal of a popular initiative
Rückzug eines Beratungsgegenstandes (Art. 73 ParlG)	retrait des objets soumis à délibération	withdrawal of an item of business from the agenda
Rückzugsklausel	clause de retrait	withdrawal clause
Rüge (1) (Art. 14 Abs. 2 Ziff. 1 SchKG)	réprimande	reprimand
Rüge (2)	grief	constitutional claim
Rügeprinzip (Art. 106 Abs. 2 BGG)	principe d'allégation	principle that a constitutional claim must be raised in the trial court and cannot be raised for the first time on appeal
Ruhezeit	durée du repos	rest period
Sachauslieferung (Art. 59 IRSG)	remise d'objets ou de valeurs	handing over of objects and assets
Sachbereichskommission	commission thématique	specialized committee
Sachbeschädigung (Art. 144 StGB)	dommages à la propriété	criminal damage to property, vandalism
Sachbezeichnung	désignation générique	generic designation
Sache	chose	thing, item
Sache von geringem Wert (D: geringwertige Sache) (Art. 138 und 142 StGB)	chose de peu de valeur	low-value item
Sacheinlage	apport en nature	contribution in kind
Sachenrecht	droits réels	law of real and personal property

Sachentscheid	jugement au fond, jugement sur le fond, décision au fond	judgment on the merits
Sachentziehung (Art. 141 StGB)	soustraction d'une chose mobilière	removal of property
Sachgewährleistung (Art. 197 ff OR)	garantie en raison des défauts de la chose	warranty against defects in the item purchased
Sachgründung	fondation par apport en nature	formation by in-kind contribution
Sachleistung	prestation en nature	payment in kind, benefit in kind
sachliche Zuständigkeit (Art. 4 ZPO, Art. 22 ff StPO)	compétence matérielle, compétence ratione materiae, compétence à raison de la matière	subject matter jurisdiction
Sachmangel	défaut de la chose	quality defect
Sachrichter	juge du fond	trial judge, judge who decided the merits of the case
Sachschaden	dommage matériel	property damage
Sachübernahme (Art. 628 OR)	reprise de biens	acquisition of assets
Sachverhalt (D: Tatbestand)	état de fait	facts of the case
Sachverhaltsfeststellung	constatation des faits	finding of facts
Sachverhaltsirrtum	erreur sur les faits	error of fact
Sachverständigenkosten	frais d'expertise	expert witness fees
Sachverständiger	expert	expert
Sachwalter (Anlagefonds)	gérant (fonds de placement)	manager
Sachwalter (Art. 239 ff und 334 ff SchKG)	commissaire (règlement amiable des dettes)	administrator
Sachwalter (Nachlassvertrag)	commissaire (concordat)	administrator
Sachwertbericht (Art. 304 SchKG)	rapport du commissaire	administrator's report

Sachwertklausel	clause de valeur réelle	material value clause
Saisonkredit	crédit saisonnier	seasonal loan
Saisonnier (D: Saisonarbeiter)	saisonnier	seasonal worker
Salärausfallversicherung	assurance salaire	salary continuation insurance (disability insurance)
salarieren	rémunérer, rétribuer	to remunerate, to pay a salary to
saldieren	solder	to balance (an account)
Saldovortrag	report de solde	balance carried forward
Salzregal	régale du sel	salt monopoly, salt tax
Sammelstiftung	fondation collective	collective foundation
Sammeltitel	titre global	collective security
Sammelverwahrung (Art. 973a ZGB)	dépôt collectif	collective custody (of securities at a central depository, as opposed to individual custody)
Sanierung (1)	assainissement	reorganization
Sanierung (2)	assainissement	remediation
Sanierungsprojekt	projet d'assainissement	remediation project
Sanierungsverfahren	procédure d'assainissement	reorganization procedure
säumig	défaillant	in default
Säumnis (Art. 147 ZPO, Art. 93 StPO)	défaut	default
Säumnis an der Hauptverhandlung	défaut à l'audience des débats principaux	failure to attend the main hearing
Schaden	dommage	damage
Schadenberechnung	calcul des dommages-intérêts	calculation of damages
Schadenersatz	dommages-intérêts	damages
Schadenersatzklage	action en dommages-intérêts	action for damages
Schadenersatzpflicht	responsabilité de dommages-intérêts	liability for damages
Schadenminderungspflicht	obligation de réduire le dommage	duty to mitigate damage

Schadlosbürgschaft	cautionnement pour le découvert	conditional surety
Schadstoffpotenzial	potentiel de pollution	pollution potential
Schaffhausen (SH)	Schaffhouse (SH)	Schaffhausen (canton and city)
Schall- und Laserverordnung (SLV)	Ordonnance son et laser (OSLa)	Noise and Laser Ordinance
Schändung (Art. 191 StGB)	acte d'ordre sexuel sur un incapable de discernement	sexual acts with persons incapable of judgment or resistance
Schätzung (Art. 97 Abs. 1 und 227 SchKG)	estimation	valuation
Schätzungskommission	commission d'estimation	valuation committee
Schätzungskommission für die Enteignung	Commission d'estimation en matière d'expropriation	Compulsory Purchase Tribunal
Schätzungsverfahren	procédure d'estimation	valuation procedure
scheiden: die Ehe scheiden	dissoudre : dissoudre le mariage	to dissolve the marriage
Scheidung auf gemeinsames Begehren (Art. 111 ZGB)	divorce sur requête commune	divorce by joint request
Scheidung auf Klage eines Ehegatten (Art. 114 ZGB)	divorce sur demande unilatérale	divorce at the petition of one spouse
Scheidung wegen Unzumutbarkeit der Ehe (Art. 115 ZGB)	divorce pour rupture du lien conjugal	divorce due to irretrievable breakdown of the marriage
Scheidungsbegehren	demande de divorce	divorce petition
Scheidungsfolgen (Art. 119-134 ZGB)	effets du divorce	consequences of divorce
Scheidungsgrund	cause de divorce	ground for divorce
Scheidungsklage (Art. 290 ZPO)	divorce sur demande unilatérale	petition for divorce
Scheidungsurteil	jugement de divorce	divorce decree
Scheingesellschaft	société fictive	sham company
Scheinkauf	vente simulée, vente fictive	sham purchase, fictitious purchase

Schenker (Art. 240 OR)	donateur	donor
Schenkung (Art. 286 Abs. 1 SchKG, Art. 239-252 OR)	donation	gift
Schenkung von Hand zu Hand (Art. 242 OR)	donation manuelle	gift from hand to hand
Schenkung von Todes wegen	donation pour cause de mort	testamentary gift
Schenkungsabsicht	intention de faire une libéralité	intention to make a gift
Schenkungsanfechtung (Art. 286 und 291 SchKG)	révocation d'une libéralité	challenge to a gift made by the debtor
Schenkungspauliana	révocation d'une libéralité	challenge to a gift made by the debtor
Schenkungsversprechen (Art. 243 OR)	promesse de donner	promise to make a gift
Schichtarbeit	travail par équipes	shift work
Schiedsentscheid	sentence arbitrale	arbitral award
Schiedsfähigkeit (Art. 177 IPRG)	arbitrabilité	arbitrability
Schiedsgericht (Art. 179 IPRG)	tribunal arbitral	arbitral tribunal
Schiedsgerichtsbarkeit	juridiction arbitrale	arbitral jurisdiction
Schiedsgutachter	expert-arbitre	expert arbitrator
Schiedsgutachtervertrag	expertise-arbitrage	expert arbitrator agreement
Schiedsreglement	règlement d'arbitrage	arbitration rules, rules of arbitration
Schiedsrichter	juge arbitre	arbitrator
schiedsrichterliches Verfahren	procédure arbitrale	arbitration proceeding
Schiedsspruch (Art. 381-388 ZPO)	sentence arbitrale	arbitral award
Schiedsvereinbarung (Art. 61 ZPO)	convention d'arbitrage	arbitration agreement, agreement to arbitrate
Schiedsverfahren	arbitrage	arbitration
Schifffahrt	navigation	navigation
Schiffsbesatzung	équipage du navire	ship's crew
Schiffsführer	conducteur de bateau	skipper
Schiffsregister	registre des bateaux	ship register
Schiffsteuer	impôt sur les bateaux	ship tax
Schlachtgebühr	taxe d'abattage	slaughtering fee

Schlechterfüllung	mauvaise exécution	defective performance
Schlechtwetterentschädigung	indemnité en cas d'intempéries	bad weather compensation
Schlichtungsbehörde	autorité de conciliation	conciliation authority
Schlichtungsverfahren (Art. 202 ff ZPO)	procédure de conciliation	conciliation procedure
Schlichtungsvorschlag	proposition de conciliation	conciliation proposal
Schlussabstimmung	vote final	final vote
Schlussalter	age terme	final age
Schlussbericht	rapport final	final report
Schlussbestimmung (SchlB; SchlBest.)	disposition finale (disp. fin.)	final provision
Schlüsselübergabe	remise des clés	handover of the keys
schlussfertig (D: schlüsselfertig)	clés en main	turnkey
Schlussrechnung	compte final	final account
Schlusstitel	titre final (tit. fin.)	final title
Schlussvortrage (Art. 232 ZPO)	plaidoiries finales	closing arguments
Schmiergeld	dessous-de-table	bribe
Schnupperlehre	stage d'information professionnelle	internship
schonende Rechtsausübung	ménagement dans l'exercice du droit	moderation in the exercise of legal rights
Schongebiet	réserve naturelle	nature reserve
Schranken: in den Schranken von Gesetz und Standesregeln	limites : dans les limites de la loi et des règles de la profession	subject to the restrictions laid down by law and in the code of professional practice
Schrankfach	compartiment de coffre-fort	safe deposit box
Schreckung der Bevölkerung (Art. 258 StGB)	menace alarmant la population	causing fear and alarm among the general public
Schreibgebühren	frais d'écriture	document preparation fees
Schriftenwechsel	échange d'écritures	exchange of written submissions
Schriftform: bedarf der Schriftform	forme écrite: exige la forme écrite	must be in writing
schriftliche Eröffnung	notification écrite	written notice

schriftliches Verfahren	procédure écrite	written procedure
Schriftlichkeit (Art. 12 OR)	forme écrite	written form
Schriftprobe	vérification d'écriture	handwriting sample
Schriftstück	document écrit	written document
Schuld (1)	dette	debt
Schuld (2) (Art. 14-21 StGB)	culpabilité	guilt
Schuld durch öffentliche Urkunde festgestellt	dette constatée par acte authentique	debt established by an authenticated deed
Schuld durch Privaturkunde bekräftigt	dette reconnue par acte sous seing privé	debt established by private deed
Schuldanerkennung (Art. 82 Abs. 1 SchKG)	reconnaissance de dette	acknowledgment of debt
Schuldanerkennungsklage	action en reconnaissance de dette	action for acknowledgment of debt
Schuldbekenntnis (Art. 17 OR)	reconnaissance de dette	acknowledgment of debt
Schuldbetreibung	poursuite pour dettes	debt collection, debt collection
Schuldbetreibungs- und Konkursrecht	droit des poursuites et faillites	debt collection and bankruptcy law
Schuldbrief (Art. 842 ff ZGB)	cédule hypothécaire	mortgage note (a written promise to repay a mortgage loan plus interest)
Schuldbuchforderung	créance inscrite au livre de la dette publique	debt register claim (a claim on the state arising from a loan or credit entered in an official register of debt – no securities are issued for such claims; they are recorded solely in the register)
Schuldenbereinigung	règlement des dettes	debt settlement
Schuldenbremse	frein à l'endettement	debt brake
Schuldenruf (Art. 232 Abs. 2 Ziff. 2 und 300 Art. 1 SchKG)	appel aux créanciers	call to creditors
Schulderlass	remise conventionnelle de dette	debt remission
Schuldhaft	contrainte par corps	debtor's prison (abolished by Swiss Constitution of 1874)
schuldloser Ehegatte	conjoint innocent	innocent spouse

Schuldner	débiteur	debtor; obligor
Schuldner auf der Durchreise (Art. 271 SchKG)	débiteur de passage	passing debtor
Schuldner der nicht der Konkursbetreibung unterliegt	débiteur non soumis à la faillite	debtor not subject to bankruptcy proceedings
Schuldnerverzug (Art. 102 OR)	demeure du débiteur	default by the obligor
Schuldnerwechsel	changement de débiteur	change of debtor
schuldrechtliche Bestimmung	clause obligationnelle	obligation clause
Schuldübernahme (Art. 175-183 OR)	reprise de dette	assumption of indebtedness
Schuldübernehmer (Art. 175-183 OR)	reprenant	debt acquirer
Schuldunfähigkeit (Art. 19 StGB)	irresponsabilité	absence of legal responsibility due to a mental disorder
Schuldzins	intérêt débiteur	interest on debt
Schulgeld	écolage (F : frais de scolarité)	tuition fees
Schulpflege	commission scolaire	school board
Schulsack (D: Ranzen)	cartable	school bag
Schulzeugnis	bulletin scolaire	report card
Schüttstein (D: Spüle, Ausguss)	évier	sink
Schutz der ehelichen Gemeinschaft	protection de l'union conjugale	protection of the marital union
Schutz vor Freiheitsentzug	droit à la liberté	right to freedom
Schutzaufsicht (Art. 47 StGB)	patronage	surveillance
Schützenverein	société de tir	shooting club, shooting range
Schutzgut	bien à protéger	subject of protection, protected entity
Schutzmachtmandat	mandat de puissance protectrice	protecting power mandate
Schutzschrift (Art. 270 ZPO)	mémoire préventif	protective letter (in an ex parte situation)
schutzwürdiges Interesse (Art. 156 ZPO)	intérêt digne de protection	legitimate interest
Schwägerschaft	alliance	kinship by marriage
Schwangerschaftsabbruch (Art. 118 StGB)	interruption de la grossesse	abortion
Schwankungsreserve	réserve de fluctuation	fluctuation reserve
Schwarzarbeit	travail au noir	illegal employment

schwebende Bedingung	condition en suspens	condition that has not yet occurred
Schweizer Armee	Armée suisse	Swiss Armed Forces
Schweizer Bürgerrecht	nationalité suisse	Swiss nationality
Schweizerische Ausgleichskasse	Caisse suisse de compensation	Swiss Compensation Office
Schweizerische Bankenombudsman	Ombudsman des banques suisses	Swiss Banking Ombudsman
Schweizerische Eisenbahnen (SBB)	Chemins de fer suisses (CSS)	Swiss Railroads
Schweizerische Nationalbank (SNB)	Banque nationale suisse	Swiss National Bank (Switzerland's central bank)
Schweizerische Radio- und Fernsehgesellschaft (SRG)	Société suisse de radiodiffusion et télévision (SSR)	Swiss Broadcasting Corporation
Schweizerische Strafprozessordnung (StPO)	Code de procédure pénale suisse (CPP)	Swiss Criminal Procedure Code
Schweizerischer Anwaltsverband (SAV)	Fédération Suisse des Avocats (FSA)	Swiss Bar Association
Schweizerischer Ingenieurs- und Architektenverein (SIA)	Société suisse des ingénieurs et des architectes (SIA)	Swiss Society of Engineers and Architects
Schweizerisches Bundesarchiv (BAR)	Archives fédérales suisses (AFS)	Swiss Federal Archives
Schweizerisches Handelsamtsblatt (SHAB)	Feuille officielle suisse du commerce (FOSC)	Swiss Trade Bulletin
Schweizerisches Institut für Rechtsvergleichung (SIRG)	Institut suisse de droit comparé (ISDC)	Swiss Institute of Comparative Law
Schweizerisches Korps für Humanitäre Hilfe (SKH)	Corps suisse d'aide humanitaire (CSA)	Swiss Humanitarian Aid Unit
schweizerisches Recht	droit suisse	Swiss law
Schwerarbeit	travail pénible	heavy labor
schwere Bedrängnis	détresse profonde	dire straits
schwere Hilflosigkeit	impotence grave	severe disability
schwere Körperverletzung (Art. 122 StGB)	lésion corporelle grave	aggravated assault
schweres Verschulden	faute grave	gross negligence

Schwerverkehrsabgabe (Art. 85 BV)	taxe poids lourd	heavy vehicle charge
Schwestergesellschaft	société sœur	sister company
Schwyz (SZ)	Schwyz (SZ)	Schwyz (canton)
Seekonnossement	connaissement maritime	maritime bill of lading
Seerecht	droit maritime	maritime law
Seeversicherung	assurance maritime	maritime insurance
Seilbahnverordnung (SebV)	Ordonnance sur les installations de transport à câbles (OICa)	Cableways Ordinance
Sekretär	secrétaire	secretary
Sekretariat	bureau	presiding officers (at a meeting)
Sekundärschule	école secondaire	secondary school
selbständige Erwerbstätigkeit	activité lucrative indépendante	self-employment
selbständige Verordnung	ordonnance indépendante	independent ordinance
Selbstanzeige	dénonciation spontanée	voluntary disclosure (of tax fraud)
Selbstbehalt	franchise	deductible (in an insurance policy)
Selbstbewirtschafter	exploitant à titre personnel	"self-manager" (farmer who personally works the soil and manages the farm)
Selbsteintritt (Art. 436 OR)	contrat avec soi-même	self-dealing
Selbsthilfe	justice propre	self-help (taking the law into one's own hands)
Selbsthilfeverkauf	droit de vendre	self-help sale
Selbstregulierung	autoréglementa-tion	self-regulation
Selbstregulierungsorganisation (SRO)	organisme d'autorégulation (OAR)	self-regulatory organization (SRO)
selbstständige Garantie	garantie indépendante	independent guarantee, stand-alone guarantee
Selbstverschulden	faute propre	one's own fault
selbstverschuldete Unzurechnungsfähigkeit (Art. 263 StGB)	irresponsabilité fautive	voluntarily induced mental incapacity
Senderechte	droits de diffusion	broadcasting rights
Sequester (Art. 480 OR)	séquestre	escrow agent
serbeln (D: kränkeln)	être maladif	to be sickly

Serviertochter (D: Kellnerin)	serveuse	waitress
Servitut (D: Grunddienstbarkeit)	servitude	easement
sexuelle Belästigungen (Art. 198 StGB)	confrontation à un acte d'ordre sexuel	sexual harassment
sexuelle Handlung	acte d'ordre sexuel	sexual act
sexuelle Handlung mit einem Abhängigen (Art. 188 StGB)	acte d'ordre sexuel avec une personne dépendante	sexual act with a dependent person
sexuelle Handlung mit einem Gefangenen (Art. 192 StGB)	acte d'ordre sexuel avec une personne détenue	sexual act with a prisoner
sexuelle Handlung mit einem Kind (Art. 187 StGB)	acte d'ordre sexuel avec un enfant	sexual act with a child
sexuelle Handlung mit Minderjährigen gegen Entgelt (Art. 196 StGB)	acte d'ordre sexuel avec des mineurs contre rémunération	sexual act with minors against payment
sexuelle Integrität	intégrité sexuelle	sexual integrity
sexuelle Nötigung (Art. 189 StGB)	contrainte sexuelle	indecent assault
Sezession	sécession	secession
SIA-Norm (Schweizerischer Ingenieur- und Architektenverein)	norme SIA (Société suisse des Ingénieurs et des Architectes)	Swiss Society of Engineers and Architects
Sicherheit für die Parteientschädigung (Art. 99 ZPO)	sûreté en garantie des dépens	security for attorney's fees and expenses
Sicherheiten	garanties	collateral
Sicherheiten durch den Mieter (Art. 257e OR)	sûretés fournies par le locataire	collateral furnished by the tenant
Sicherheitshaft (Art. 229 StPO)	détention pour des motifs de sûreté	preventive detention
Sicherheitshinterlegung	consignation à titre de sûreté	escrow, placing in escrow
Sicherheitsleistung (Art. 238 StPO)	fourniture de sûretés	payment of bail money
Sicherheitsvorkehrungen	mesures de sécurité	security precautions
Sicherung	confinement	containment
Sicherungsmassnahme (Art. 98 ff und 223 SchKG)	mesure de sûreté	safety measures

Sichtguthaben	avoirs à vue	demand deposit
Sichtwechsel (Art. 1024 OR)	lettre de change à vue	bill payable on demand
Sickerwasser	eau de percolation	seepage water
Siedlungsabfälle	déchets urbains	domestic waste
Siedlungsabfalldeponie	décharge pour déchets urbains	landfill for domestic waste
Siegel	sceau	seal
Siegelbruch (Art. 290 StGB)	bris de scellés	breaking seals
Siegelung (Art. 248 StPO)	mise sous scellés	sealing of evidence
Signalisationsverordnung (SSV)	Ordonnance sur la signalisation routière (OSR)	Road Signs Ordinance
Signallicht (D: Verkehrsampel)	feux de signalisation	traffic light
Signaturschlüssel (Art. 59a OR)	clé de signature	signature key
Simulation (Art. 18 OR)	simulation	failure to express one's real intent, false representation
sistieren: das Verfahren sistieren	suspendre la procédure	to stay, suspend the proceedings
Sistierung	suspension	suspension, stay
Sistierung der Versicherungsleistung	suspension de la prestation d'assurance	suspension of insurance benefits
Sistierung des Verfahrens	suspension de la procédure	stay, suspension of the proceedings
Sitte	mœurs	customs, mores
Sitten	Sion	Sion/Sitten
sittliche Pflicht	devoir moral	moral duty
Sittlichkeit	moralité	morality
Sitz	siège	headquarters, registered office
Sitzungsgeld	jeton de présence	directors' fee, attendance fee
Sitzverteilung	répartition des sièges	allotment of seats (in the National Council)
Skonto	escompte	discount
Soforthilfe	aide immédiate	immediate aid
Sofortmassnahmen	mesures urgentes	immediate measures
Sold	solde militaire	soldier's pay
Söldner	mercenaire	mercenary
Solidarbürgschaft (Art. 496 OR)	cautionnement solidaire	joint and several surety
Solidargläubigerschaft (Art. 150 OR)	solidarité active	joint and several creditors

Solidarhaftung (D: solidarische Haftung)	responsabilité solidaire	joint and several liability
Solidarität	solidarité	joint and several liability
Solidarschuld (D: Gesamtschuld) (Art. 143 OR)	dette solidaire	joint and several obligation
Solidarschuldner (D: Gesamtschuldner)	débiteurs solidaires	joint and several debtors, joint and several obligors
Solidarschuldnerschaft (D: Gesamtschuldnerschaft) (Art. 143-149 OR)	solidarité passive	joint and several liability
Soll-Arbeitszeit	durée réglementaire du travail	regular working hours
Sollzins	intérêts débiteurs	debtor interest (rate); lending rate
Solothurn (SO)	Soleure (SO)	Solothurn (canton)
Sömmerungsbeitrag	contribution d'estivage	summer grazing contribution
Sonderanknüpfung	rattachement spécial	special rule
Sonderdelikt (Art. 26 StGB)	infraction spéciale	special offense
Sonderrecht	droit exclusif (propriété par étages)	exclusive right
Sonderschulbedürftigkeit	besoin d'une formation scolaire spéciale	need for a special school
Sonderschule	école spéciale	special school
Sonnenenergie	énergie solaire	solar energy
Sonntagsarbeit	travail du dimanche	work on Sunday
Sorgfalt	diligence	care
Sorgfaltspflicht (Art. 717 OR)	devoir de diligence	duty of care
Souveränität	souveraineté	sovereignty
Sozialabgaben	charges sociales	social security contributions
Sozialarbeiter	assistant social	social worker
soziale Sicherheit	sécurité sociale	social security
soziales Grundrecht	droit social	welfare right (fundamental right that guarantees that an individual is entitled to certain social benefits from the State)
Sozialhilfe	assistance publique	welfare

Sozialhilfeleistung	prestation d'assistance	welfare benefit
Sozialleistungen	prestations sociales	social insurance benefits
Sozialplan (Art. 335h OR)	plan social	social plan (an agreement in which an employer and employees indicate measures to avoid layoffs or to reduce their numbers and mitigate their effects)
Sozialversicherung	assurance sociale	social insurance
Spaltung	scission	demerger
Spannteppich (D: Teppichboden)	moquette	wall-to-wall carpet
Spareinlage	dépôt d'épargne	savings deposit
Sparheft	livret d'épargne	savings passbook
Sparkasse	caisse d'épargne	savings bank
Sparkonto	compte d'épargne	savings account
Sparplan	plan d'épargne	savings plan
Spediteur	commissionnaire -expéditeur	forwarding agent
Speditionsvertrag (Art. 439 OR)	contrat d'expédition	forwarding contract
Spekulation	spéculation	speculation
Spende	don	donation
Spender	donneur	donor
Sperrfrist	délai d'interdiction	proscribed period
Sperrkonto	compte bloqué	blocked account
Sperrminorität	minorité de blocage	blocking minority
Spezialexekution	exécution spéciale	seizure of specific assets of the debtor
Speziessache	corps certain	unique item, specific item (such as a work of art, as opposed to a fungible item)
Spielautomat	appareil automatique servant au jeu	slot machine
Spielbank	maison de jeu	casino
Spielbankenverordnung (VSBG)	Ordonnance sur les maisons de jeu (OLMJ)	Gambling Ordinance
Spital (D: Krankenhaus)	hôpital	hospital
Spitalaufenthalt (D: Krankenhausaufenthalt)	séjour à l'hôpital	hospital stay

Spitalbehandlung (D: Krankenhausbehandlung)	traitement hospitalier	hospital treatment
Spitalliste (D: Krankenhausliste)	liste des hôpitaux	list of hospitals
Spitalplanung (D: Krankenhausplanung)	planification hospitalière	hospital planning
Spitaltaxe	taxe hospitalière	hospital tax
Spitzenmedizin	médecine de pointe	advanced medical science
Spitzentechnologie	technologie de pointe	state-of-the-art technology
Sprachenfreiheit (Art. 18 BV)	liberté de la langue	freedom to use any language
Sprachprobe (Art. 262 StPO)	échantillon de voix	voice sample
Sprengstoffgesetz (SprstG)	Loi sur les explosifs (LExpl)	Explosives Act
spruchreif (Art. 236 ZPO)	en état d'être jugé	ripe for judgment
Sprungrekurs	recours direct	leapfrog appeal
St. Gallen (SG)	Saint-Gall (SG)	St. Gallen (canton)
staatenloses Kind (Art. 38 BV)	enfant apatride	stateless child
Staatsangehörigkeit	nationalité	nationality
Staatsanleihe	emprunt d'État	government bond
Staatsanwaltschaft	ministère public	public prosecutor
Staatsbesuch	visite d'État	state visit
Staatschreiber	chancelier d'État	official recorder (publicly elected head of cantonal government chancery)
Staatsdienstbarkeit	servitude d'État	state easement
staatsgefährliche Propaganda (Art. 275bis StGB)	propagande subversive	subversive propaganda
Staatshaftung	responsabilité de l'État	liability of the State (The State is only liable for damage caused by government officials if liability is provided for by a special law. If there is no law, or liability is excluded, the State does not have to compensate for damages caused by government officials.)
Staatskanzlei	chancellerie d'Etat	cantonal government offices
Staatsoberhaupt	chef d'état	head of state

Staatsrecht	droit de l'État	constitutional and administrative law
staatsrechtliche Beschwerde (D: Verfassungsbeschwerde)	recours de droit public	public law appeal, constitutional complaint (a general remedy against constitutional rights, including those set forth in the ECHR)
Staatssekretär	secrétaire d'état	state secretary
Staatssekretariat für Bildung, Forschung und Innovation (SBFI)	Secrétariat d'État à la formation, à la recherche et à l'innovation (SEFRI)	State Secretariat for Education, Research and Innovation
Staatssekretariat für internationale Finanzfragen (SIF)	Secrétariat d'État aux questions financières internationales (SFI)	State Secretariat for International Financial Matters
Staatssekretariat für Migration (SEM)	Secrétariat d'État aux migrations (SEM)	State Secretariat for Migration
Staatssekretariat für Wirtschaft (SECO)	Secrétariat d'État à l'économie (SECO)	State Secretariat for Economic Affairs
Staatssteuer	impôt cantonal	cantonal tax
Staatsvertrag	traité international	international treaty
Stadtammann (D: Bürgermeister)	maire	mayor
Städtebau	urbanisme	urban development
Stadtpräsident (D: Oberbürgermeiester)	maire, syndic (Vaud et Fribourg)	mayor
Stammanteil	part sociale	share in a company or partnership
Stammeinlage	part sociale (société à responsabilité limitée)	share in a limited liability company
Stammgrundstück	immeuble de base	original parcel
Stand (1) (Kanton)	canton	canton
Stand (2)	état	last updated on
Stand der Technik	état de la technique	state of the art
Ständeinitiative	initiative déposée par un canton	cantonal initiative

Ständemehr	majorité des cantons	majority of the cantons
Ständerat	Conseil des Etats	Council of States (upper house of the Federal Assembly)
Ständeratswahl	élection du Conseil des Etats	election of the Council of States
Standesinitiative	initiative des cantons	cantonal initiative
Standesrecht	déontologie	code of ethics, professional ethics
ständige Wasserführung (Art. 4 GSchG)	débit permanent	permanent flow
Standort	emplacement	location
Statthalter	préfet	prefect (representative of the Cantonal Government responsible for the administration of the district)
Statthalteramt	préfecture	Chancellery of State
statutarisch (D: satzungsgemäß)	statutaire	pursuant to the bylaws
statutarischer Einzelabschluss mit zuverlässiger Darstellung	bouclement individuel statutaire avec présentation fiable	reliable assessment statutory single-entity financial statements
Statuten (D: Satzung)	statuts	bylaws
Statutenänderung (D: Satzungsänderung) (Art. 647 OR)	modification des statuts	amendment of the bylaws, bylaw amendment
Statutenbestimmung (D: Satzungsbestimmung)	disposition statutaire	provision of the bylaws, bylaw provision
Statutenwechsel	conflit mobile	mobile conflict of laws
Stauwehr	barrage	dam
Steigerungsbedingungen	conditions des enchères	auction terms and conditions
Steigerungsgegenstand	objet en vente	item for sale (at auction)
Steigerungsprotokoll	procès-verbal des enchères	auction record
Stellungnahme der Gegenpartei (Art. 330 ZPO)	avis de la partie adverse	response by the opposing party
Stellvertretung (Art. 32-40 OR)	représentation	agency
Stempel	tampon	stamp
Stempelabgaben	droits de timbre	stamp duties
Stempelabgabengesetz	Loi sur les droits de timbre	Stamp Duties Act
Stempelabgabenverordnung (StV)	Ordonnance sur les droits de timbre (OT)	Stamp Duties Ordinance

Steuer	impôt	tax
Steuer vom Einkommen	impôt sur le revenu	income tax
Steuer vom Vermögen	impôt sur la fortune	wealth tax
Steueramnestie	amnistie fiscale	tax amnesty
Steueramt	bureau des impôts	tax office
Steueraufschub	report de l'imposition	tax deferral
Steuerausfall	préjudice financier	loss of tax
Steuerausscheidung	répartition intercantonale	tax apportionment
Steuerausweis (Art. 27 MWSTG)	mention de l'impôt	VAT details
Steuerbefreiung	exonération d'impôt	tax exemption
Steuerbehörde	autorité fiscale	tax authority
Steuerbelastung	charge fiscale	tax burden
Steuerbetrug	escroquerie fiscale	tax fraud
Steuerbezug	perception de l'impôt	tax collection
Steuererklärung	déclaration d'impôt	tax return
Steuererlass	remise d'impôt	tax abatement, tax remission
Steuerexperte	expert fiscal	tax expert
steuerfreie Einkünfte	revenu exonéré d'impôt	tax-exempt income
Steuerharmonisierung	harmonisation fiscale	tax harmonization
Steuerhinterziehung	soustraction d'impôts (F : évasion fiscale)	tax evasion
Steuerhoheit	souveraineté fiscale	tax sovereignty
Steuerinventar	inventaire fiscal	tax inventory
Steuermass	calcul de l'impôt	calculation of the tax
Steuernachfolge (Art. 16 MWSTG)	succession fiscale	succession to tax liability
Steuerordnung	réglementation fiscale	tax regulation
Steuerpflicht	assujettissement	taxation
Steuerpflichtiger	contribuable	taxpayer
Steuerplanung	planification fiscale	tax planning

Steuerpolitik	politique fiscale	tax policy
Steuerrecht	droit fiscal	tax law
steuerrechtlicher Wohnsitz (Art. 3 DBG, Art. 3 StHG)	domicile fiscal	tax domicile
Steuerregister	registre de l'impôt	tax register
Steuerrückerstattung	restitution de l'impôt	tax refund
Steuerrückstellungen	provisions pour impôts	tax provisions
Steuersolidarität	solidarité fiscale	tax solidarity
Steuerstrafrecht	droit pénal fiscal	criminal tax law
Steuerstrafverfahren	procédure pénale fiscale	criminal tax procedure
Steuersubjekt	sujet de l'impôt	taxable person
Steuersubstitution (Art. 17 MWSTG)	substitution fiscale	tax substitution
Steuerüberwälzung (Art. 6 MWSTG)	transfert de l'impôt	passing on of the tax
Steuerumgehung	évasion fiscale	tax evasion
Stichentscheid	voix prépondérante	deciding vote, tie-breaking vote
Stiefkind	enfant du conjoint	stepchild
Stifter	fondateur	founder
Stiftung (Art. 80-89 ZGB)	fondation	foundation
stille Gesellschaft	société tacite	silent partnership
stille Reserve	réserve latente	hidden reserve
stille Wahl	élection tacite	silent election
Stillhalteroption	option couverte	covered option
stillschweigende Annahme (Art. 6 OR)	acceptation tacite	implied acceptance (of an offer)
Stimmabgabe	exercice du droit de vote	voting, casting of votes
Stimmberechtigter	électeur	eligible voter
Stimmbeteiligung (D: Wahlbeteiligung)	participation aux élections	voter turnout
Stimmbürger (D: Wahlberechtigter)	électeur	eligible voter
Stimmbüro	bureau électoral	polling station
stimmen gehen (D: wählen gehen)	voter	to vote
Stimmenfang (Art. 282bis StGB)	captation de suffrages	vote catching
Stimmengleichheit	égalité des voix	tied vote, tie
Stimmenmehr (D: Stimmenmehrheit)	majorité des voix	majority of votes
Stimmenzähler	scrutateur	teller (of elections)

Stimmgeheimnis	secret de vote	secrecy of voting
Stimmlokal (D: Wahllokal)	local de vote	voting location
Stimmrecht (D: Wahlrecht)	droit de vote	voting right, right to vote
Stimmrechtsaktie (Art. 693 OR)	action à droit de vote privilégié	preferred stock
Stimmrechtsausweis	carte civique	voter registration card
Stimmregister	registre des électeurs	list of registered voters
Stimmvolk	corps électoral	registered voters
Stimmzettel	bulletin de vote	ballot
Stimmzwang	vote obligatoire	mandatory voting
Stipendium	bourse d'études	scholarship
Stockwerkeigentum (StWE) (D: Eigentumswohnung) (Art. 712a ZGB)	propriété par étages (PPE)	condominium
Stockwerkeigentümer-gemeinschaft (Art. 712a ff ZGB)	communauté des copropriétaires d'étages	community of condominium owners
Stockwerkeigentümer-versammlung	assemblée des copropriétaires d'étages	meeting of condominium owners
Stockwerkeinheit	unité d'une propriété par étages	condominium unit
Störer	perturbateur	polluter
Störfallverordnung (StFV)	Ordonnance sur les accidents majeurs (OPAM)	Major Accidents Ordinance
Störung der Glaubens- und Kultusfreiheit (Art. 261 StGB)	atteinte à la liberté de croyance et des cultes	attack on the freedom of faith and the freedom to worship
Störung der militärischen Sicherheit (Art. 276 StGB)	atteinte à la sécurité militaire	disruption of military security
Störung des Eisenbahnverkehrs (Art. 238 StGB)	entrave au service des chemins de fer	disruption of rail traffic
Störung des Militärdienstes (Art. 278 StGB)	entraver le service militaire	disruption of military service
Störung des öffentlichen Verkehrs (Art. 237 StGB)	entrave à la circulation publique	disruption of public traffic
Störung des Totfriedens (Art. 262 StGB)	atteinte à la paix des morts	disturbing the peace of the dead
Störung und Hinderung von Wahlen und Abstimmungen (Art. 279 StGB)	violences	disruption and obstruction of elections and votes

Störung von Betrieben, die der Allgemeinheit dienen (Art. 239 StGB)	entrave aux services d'intérêt général	disruption of public services
stossen (D: drücken)	pousser	to push
Strafanstalt	établissement pénitentiaire	penal institution
Strafanstaltspersonal	gardien de prison	prison guard
Strafantrag (Art. 30-33 StGB)	plainte pénale	criminal complaint
Strafantragsteller	plaignant	criminal complainant
Strafanzeige (Art. 301 Abs. 1 StPO)	dénonciation à l'autorité	crime report
Strafaufschub	peine suspendue	postponed sentence
strafbare Handlung	infraction	offense
strafbare Handlungen gegen das Vermögen (Art. 137-172ter StGB)	infractions contre le patrimoine	offenses against property
strafbare Vorbereitungshandlung (Art. 260bis StBG)	acte préparatoire punissable	acts preparatory to the commission of an offense
strafbarer Schwangerschaftsabbruch (Art. 118 StGB)	interruption de grossesse punissable	illegal abortion
Strafbarkeit	punissabilité	criminal liability
Strafbefehl (Art. 352 StPO)	ordonnance pénale	summary penalty order
Strafbefreiung (Art. 52 StGB)	exemption de peine	exemption from punishment
Strafbehördenorganisationsgesetz (StBOG)	Loi sur l'organisation des autorités pénales (LOAP)	Criminal Justice Authorities Act
Strafbescheid (Art. 64 VStrR)	mandat de répression	sentence order
Strafe	peine	penalty, punishment
Strafen und Massnahmen	peines et mesures	penalties and measures
Strafenterbung (Art. 477 ZGB)	exhérédation punitive	punitive disinheritance
Straferhöhungsgrund	circonstance aggravante	aggravating circumstance (justifying the imposing of a harsher sentence)
Straferlass	remise de peine	remission of penalty (or sentence)
Straffälliger	délinquant	offender, perpetrator
Strafgericht	tribunal pénal	criminal court
Strafgesetzbuch (StGB)	Code pénal (CP)	Criminal Code

Strafkammer	Cour des affaires pénales	Criminal Chamber of the Federal Criminal Court
strafloser Schwangerschaftsabbruch (Art. 119 StGB)	interruption de grossesse non punissable	legal abortion
Strafmilderung (Art. 48, 308 StGB)	atténuation de la peine	mitigation of the sentence
Strafmilderungsgrund	circonstance atténuante	mitigating circumstance (justifying the imposing of a lesser sentence)
Strafmündigkeit	majorité pénale	age of criminal responsibility
Strafprozess	procédure pénale	criminal procedure
Strafrecht	droit pénal	criminal law
Strafregister (Art. 365-371a StPO)	casier judiciaire	criminal record
Strafregisterauszug	extrait du casier judiciaire	criminal record extract
Strafsache	affaire pénale	criminal case
Strafschadenersatz	dommages-intérêts punitifs	punitive damages
Strafschärfung	aggravation de la peine	aggravation of the sentence
Strafschärfungsgrund	circonstance aggravante	aggravating circumstance (justifying the imposing of a harsher sentence)
Straftaten gegen den öffentlichen Verkehr	infractions contre les communications publiques	violations against public traffic
Straftaten gegen den Volkswillen	infractions contre la volonté populaire	violations against the will of the people
Straftaten gegen die Amts- und Berufspflicht	infractions contre les devoirs de fonction	violations against official or professional duty
Straftaten gegen die Ehre	infractions contre l'honneur	violations against honor
Straftaten gegen die Familie	infractions contre la famille	violations against the family
Straftaten gegen die Freiheit	infractions contre la liberté	violations against liberty
Straftaten gegen die Landesverteidigung	infractions contre la défense nationale	violations against the national defense
Straftaten gegen die öffentliche Gesundheit	infractions contre la santé publique	violations against public health

Straftaten gegen die öffentliche Gewalt	infractions contre l'autorité publique	violations against public authority
Straftaten gegen die Rechtspflege	infractions contre l'administration de la justice	violations against the administration of justice
Straftaten gegen die sexuelle Integrität (Art. 187-212 StGB)	infractions contre l'intégrité sexuelle	violations against sexual integrity
Straftaten gegen die Sicherheit des Rechtsverkehrs	infractions contre la sécurité des rapports juridiques	violations against the security of legal relationships
Straftaten gegen Leib und Leben (Art. 111-136 StGB)	infractions contre la vie et l'intégrité corporelle	violations against life and limb
Strafuntersuchung	enquête pénale	criminal investigation
Strafverfahrensrecht	droit de procédure pénale	criminal procedure
Strafverfolgung (Art. 302 StGB)	poursuite pénale	prosecution
Strafverfolgungsbehörde	autorité de poursuite pénale	prosecuting authorities (includes the police, the investigator, the prosecutor, and the indicting authority)
Strafvollzugspolitik	politique pénitentiaire	prison policy
Strafzumessung (Art. 47 StGB)	fixation de la peine	sentencing
Strahlenschutzgesetz (StSG)	Loi sur la radioprotection (LRaP)	Radiological Protection Act
Strahlenschutzverordnung (StSV)	Ordonnance sur la radioprotection (ORaP)	Radiological Protection Ordinance
Strahlung (Art. 684 ZGB)	rayonnements	radiation
Strangulation	strangulation	strangulation
Strasse (D: Straße)	route	road, street
Strassenverkehr (D: Straßenverkehr)	circulation routière	road traffic
Strassenverkehrsgesetz (SVG)	Loi fédérale sur la circulation routière (LCR)	Road Traffic Act
Streichung (1)	radiation du rôle	striking from the docket

Streichung (2) (Wahlliste)	latoisage	voter's deletion of candidates from a list
Streik	grève	strike
Streitberufener	tiers appelé en cause	third-party defendant (the impleaded party)
Streitgegenstand	objet du litige	subject matter of the dispute
Streitgenosse	consort	colitigant
Streitgenossenschaft (Art. 70 ZPO)	consorité	joinder of parties
streitige Gerichtsbarkeit	procédure contentieuse	adversary proceedings
streitiges Urteil	jugement contradictoire	judgment in a defended action
Streitverkünder (Art. 78 ZPO)	dénonçant	third-party plaintiff
Streitverkündung (Art. 193 OR, Art. 78 ZPO)	dénonciation d'instance	impleader (notice of pending litigation and request for litigation support sent by defendant to a third party)
Streitverkündungsklage (Art. 81 ZPO)	appel en cause	third party action
Streitwert (Art. 91-94 ZPO)	valeur litigieuse	amount in controversy
Streitwertgrenze (Art. 74 BGG)	valeur litigieuse minimale	minimum amount in controversy
Streuung	diffusion	free float
Strombörse (Art. 47 FinfraG)	bourse de l'électricité	power exchange
Strukturpolitik (Art. 103 BV)	politique structurelle	structural policy
Stückkauf	vente d'un corps certain	sale of a specific thing (as opposed to sale of a type of thing)
Stückschuld	dette de corps certain	obligation to deliver a specific thing (as opposed to a type of thing)
Stundenlohn	salaire horaire	hourly wage
Stundung	sursis	moratorium, stay
Stundung von Zinsen	ajournement du paiement d'intérêts	moratorium on interest
Stundungsvergleich	concordat-sursis	remission debt restructuring agreement
Subakkordant (D: Subunternehmer)	sous-traitant	subcontractor
Subdelegation	subdélégation	subdelegation
subeventualiter (D: weiter hilfsweise)	plus subsidiairement encore	in the further alternative
Subfonds	compartiment	subfund, compartment

subjektiv	subjectif	subjective
subjektiver Tatbestand	éléments subjectifs (de la typicité)	mens rea (in the definition of a crime)
subjektives Recht	droit subjectif	right (as opposed to law, which is objektives Recht or droit objectif)
Submissionsabsprache	accord de soumission	collusive bidding
Submittent	soumissionnaire	bidder, tenderer
Subrogation	subrogation	subrogation
Subsumtion	application de la règle de droit	applying the law to the facts of the case
Subunternehmer	sous-traitant	subcontractor
Subunternehmervertrag	contrat de sous-traitance	subcontracting agreement
Subvention	subvention	subsidy
Subventionsgesetz (SuG)	Loi sur les subventions (LSu)	Subsidies Act
Sucharrest	séquestre investigatoire	fishing expedition, attachment to determine what assets the debtor has (this is not allowed in Swiss law)
Sucht	dépendance	addiction
Suchtbehandlung (Art. 60 StGB)	traitement des addictions	treatment of addiction
Sühnbeamter (Friedensrichter)	juge de paix	justice of the peace
Sühne	conciliation	conciliation
Sühnverfahren	procédure de conciliation	conciliation proceedings
Suizid	suicide	suicide
Suizidversuch	tentative de suicide	suicide attempt, attempted suicide
Sukzessivlieferungsvertrag	contrat de vente par livraisons successives	multiple delivery contract
summarisches Verfahren (Art. 248 ff ZPO, Art. 231 SchKG)	procédure sommaire	summary proceedings
Summenschuld	dette de somme	monetary obligation
supereventualiter (D: hoechstvorsorglich)	très subsidiairement	in the further alternative
superprovisorische Massnahmen (Art. 265 ZPO)	mesures superprovisionne lles	ex parte preliminary injunctive relief
Suppleant	suppléant	deputy

Suspensivbedingung (D: aufschiebende Bedingung)	condition suspensive	condition precedent
suspensives Rechtsmittel	appel suspensif	appeal with a stay of execution (of the lower court's judgment pending appeal)
Swapvertrag	contrat de swap	swap agreement
systematische Auslegung	interprétation systématique	systematic interpretation
Tagebuch	journal	journal (accounting)
Tagesgeschäft	day trading	day trading
Tageslohn	salaire journalier	daily wage
Tagessatz	jour-amende	daily penalty unit
Taggeld (D: Tagegeld)	indemnité journalière	daily sick pay
Talbetrieb	entreprise agricole de plaine	low land farm
Tantieme (Art. 627 OR)	tantième	director profit-sharing
Tarif	tarif	rate
Tarifeinheit	principe de la convention unique	principle of one collective bargaining agreement per business
Tarifstreit	litige en matière de tarif	wage dispute
Tatbestandsmässigkeit	typicité	fulfillment of the elements of the offense, meeting the statutory definition of a crime
Täter	auteur (droit pénal)	perpetrator
Tatfrage	question de fait	issue of fact
tätige Reue (Art. 23 StGB)	repentir actif	active repentance
Tätigkeit	activité	activity
Tätigkeitsdelikt	délit formel	offense that is a crime even without actual harm (such as perjury, or driving without a driver's license, or illegal possession of weapons, all of which are crimes whether they cause harm or not)
Tätigkeitsverbot (Art. 67 StGB)	interdiction d'exercer une activité	prohibition on engaging in an activity

tätliche Angriffe auf fremde Hoheitszeichen (Art. 298 StGB)	atteinte aux emblèmes nationaux étrangers	attacks on the national emblems of a foreign state
tätliche Angriffe auf Schweizerische Hoheitszeichen (Art. 270 StGB)	atteinte aux emblèmes suisses	attacks on Swiss national emblems
Tätlichkeiten (Art. 126 StGB)	voies de fait	acts of aggression
Tatsachen	faits	facts
Tatsachendarstellung	présentation de faits	presentation of the facts
tatsächlicher Konsens	accord de fait	actual consensus
tatsächliches Vorbringen	moyen de fait	factual argument, argument based on the facts
Tausch (Art. 184-238 OR)	échange	barter
Tauschender	copermutant	party to a barter agreement
Täuschung	tromperie	fraud
Tauschvertrag	contrat d'échange	barter agreement
Technische Verordnung über Abfälle (TVA)	Ordonnance sur le traitement des déchets (OTD)	Technical Ordinance on Waste
technischer Zins	taux technique	actuarial interest
Technologietransfer	transfert de technologie	technology transfer
Teilarbeitsfähigkeit	capacité de travail partielle	partial disability
Teilarbeitslosigkeit	chômage partiel	partial unemployment
teilbare Leistung	obligation divisible	divisible obligation
teilbare Sache	chose divisible	divisible thing
teilbedingte Strafe (Art. 43 StGB)	sursis partiel à l'exécution de la peine	partially suspended sentence
Teilbewilligung	autorisation partielle	partial authorization
Teilenteignung	expropriation partielle	partial expropriation
Teilentscheid (Art. 91 BGG)	décision partielle	partial decision
Teilerlass	remise partielle	forgiveness of part of the debt
Teilhaftung	responsabilité partielle	partial liability
Teilindossament	endossement partiel	partial indorsement
Teilinvalidität	invalidité partielle	partial disability

Teilklage (Art. 86 ZPO)	action partielle	partial action (action for part of a divisible claim)
Teilnahme an der Straftat	participation à l'infraction	participation in an offense (e.g. instigation and complicity)
Teilnahme an Unruhen	participation à des troubles	participation in civil unrest
Teilnahmebegehren	réquisition de participation	request to participate
Teilnichtigkeit	nullité partielle	severability
Teilungsklage	action en partage	action for distribution of an estate
Teilzahlung	paiement partiel	partial payment
Teilzahlungsgeschäft	vente à tempérament	installment sale, sale on the installment plan
Teilzeitarbeit	travail à temps partiel	part-time work, part-time employment
Telefonabhörung	surveillance téléphonique	phone tapping
Telefonlinie (D: Telefonleitung)	ligne téléphonique	telephone line
teleologische Auslegung	interprétation téléologique	teleological interpretation
Temporärarbeit	travail temporaire	temporary work, temporary employment
Temporärfirma	agence de travail temporaire	"temp agency"
Terminbörse	marché à terme	futures market
Termingeschäft	opération à terme	futures trading
Territorialitätsprinzip	principe de la territorialité	principle of territoriality (a person who commits a crime in Switzerland is subject to the jurisdiction of the Swiss courts)
Tessin (TI)	Tessin (TI)	Ticino (canton)
Testament (Art. 498-511 ZGB)	testament	last will and testament
Testamentseröffnung	ouverture du testament	probate of a will, probate proceedings
Testamentsvollstrecker (Art. 517 ZGB)	exécuteur testamentaire	executor (of the will)
Testat	livret d'étudiant	course attendance record
Testatbuch	livret de cours	course attendance booklet
testieren	tester	to make a will
Teuerung	renchérissement	inflation
Teuerungsausgleich	compensation du renchérissement	adjustment (of wages and pensions) for inflation

Thesaurierung	thésaurisation	capitalization
Thesaurierungsfonds	fonds de thésaurisation	capitalization fund, growth fund
Thurgau (TG)	Thurgovie (TG)	Thurgau (canton)
Tiefbauvertrag	contrat de génie civil	civil engineering agreement
Tiere des häuslichen Bereichs (Art. 651a ZGB)	animaux vivant en milieu domestique	animals kept as pets
Tierhalter	détenteur d'animal	keeper of an animal
Tierhalterhaftung (Art. 56-57 OR)	responsabilité du détenteur d'animal	liability of the keeper of an animal
Tierquälerei	cruauté envers les animaux	cruelty to animals
Tierseuchengesetz	Loi sur les épizooties	Animal Diseases Act
Titelankaufsspesen	frais d'achat de titres	securities purchase fee
Titelanmassung	usurpation de titre	abuse of title
Tochtergesellschaft	société fille	subsidiary
Tod	mort	death
Todesbescheinigung	certificat de décès	death certificate
Todeserklärung (Art. 21 ZPO)	déclaration de décès	declaration of death
Todesfall	cas de décès	event of death
Todesfallkapital	capital en cas de décès	capital sum payable upon death
Todesfallversicherung	assurance en cas de décès	death risk insurance
Todesregister	registre des décès	register of deaths
Todesstrafe (Art. 10 BV)	peine de mort	death penalty, capital punishment
Topographiengesetz (ToG)	Loi sur les topographies (LTo)	Topographies Act
Topographienverordnung (ToV)	Ordonnance sur les topographies (OTo)	Topographies Ordinance
Totalschaden	dommage total	total loss, total write-off
Totalunternehmer	entrepreneur total	turnkey contractor

Totalunternehmervertrag	contrat d'entreprise totale	turnkey contract
Totenfrieden (Art. 262 StGB)	paix des morts	the peace of the dead
Totschlag (Art. 113 StGB)	meurtre passionnel	manslaughter
Tötung	homicide	homicide
Tötung auf Verlangen (Art. 114 StGB)	meurtre sur la demande de la victime	homicide at the request of the victim
Tourismusbüro (D: Fremdenverkehrsamt)	Association des Intérêts (F : syndicat d'initiative)	tourist office
Trager nichtkaufmännischer Prokura (TnkProk)	porteur d'une procuration non-commerciale	holder of a noncommercial power of attorney
Traktanden (D: Tagesordnungspunkte)	points de l'ordre du jour	agenda items
Traktandenliste (D: Tagesordnung)	ordre du jour	agenda
Traktandierung	inscription à l'ordre du jour	inclusion on the agenda
Transaktion	transaction financière	transaction
Transaktion mit erhöhten Risiken	transaction à risques accrus	high-risk transaction
Transaktionsregister (Art. 74 FinfraG)	référentiel central	trade repository
Transferpreis (D: Verrechnungspreis)	prix de transfert	transfer pricing
transitorische Aktiven	actifs transitoires	accrued assets, prepaid expenses
transitorische Passiven	passifs transitoires	accrued liabilities
Transplantationsgesetz	Loi fédérale sur la transplantation	Transplantation Act
Transport der Güter	transport des marchandises	forwarding of the goods
Transportmittel	moyen de transport	means of transportation
Trauung (Art. 101 ZGB)	célébration du mariage	wedding ceremony
Trax (D: Bagger, Schaufellader)	bulldozer, excavatrice, pelle mécanique	bulldozer, excavator

Trennung statt Scheidung (Art. 117-118 ZGB)	séparation de corps	legal separation
Trennung von Staat und Kirche	séparation de l'état et de l'église	separation of church and state
Trennung von Verfahren	disjonction de causes	severance of proceedings
Trennungsklage	action en séparation de corps	action for legal separation (as opposed to divorce)
Tresor	coffre-fort	safe
Treuepflicht (OR 717)	devoir de fidélité	duty of loyalty
Treugeber	fiduciant (F : constituant)	trustor, settlor (of a trust)
Treuhänder	fiduciaire	trustee, fiduciary, escrow agent
Treuhandexperte	expert fiduciaire	certified fiduciary
Treuhandgesellschaft	société fiduciaire	accounting firm
Treuhandvertrag	contrat fiduciaire	fiduciary agreement, trust agreement, escrow agreement
Trödelvertrag	contrat estimatoire	agreement to sell on commission
Trödler	consignataire	consignee
trölerisches Verhalten	comportement dilatoire	dilatory conduct
Turnus	tournus	rotation
Überbau	empiètement	encroachment
Überbaurecht	servitude d'empiétement	encroachment easement
überbieten	surenchérir	to outbid
Überbrückungshilfe	aide transitoire	transitional assistance
Überbrückungsrente	rente-pont	interim pension
Übereinkommen gegen die grenzüberschreitende organisierte Kriminalität	Convention contre la criminalité transnationale organisée	UN Convention against Transnational Organized Crime
Übereinkommen über das öffentliche Beschaffungswesen (ÜoeB)	Accord sur les marchés publics (AMP)	Government Procurement Agreement
Übereinkommen über das Verbot der schlimmsten Formen der Kinderarbeit	Convention concernant l'interdiction des pires formes de travail des enfants	Worst Forms of Child Labor Convention

Übereinkommen über den bezahlten Urlaub in der Landwirtschaft	Convention concernant les congés payés dans l'agriculture	Holidays with Pay (Agriculture) Convention
Übereinkommen über die gerichtliche Zuständigkeit und die Anerkennung und Vollstreckung von Entscheidungen in Zivil- und Handelssachen (Lugano-Übereinkommen, LugÜ)	Convention concernant la compétence judiciaire, la reconnaissance et l'exécution des décisions en matière civile et commerciale (Convention de Lugano, CL)	Convention on jurisdiction and the recognition and enforcement of judgments in civil and commercial matters (Lugano Convention)
Übereinkommen über die Leichenbeförderung	Accord sur le transfert des corps des personnes décédées	Agreement on the Transfer of Corpses
Übereinkommen über die Rechtshilfe in Strafsachen	Convention d'entraide judiciaire en matière pénale	European Convention on Mutual Assistance in Criminal Matters
Übereinkommen über die Verbreitung der Programmtragenden	Convention concernant la distribution des signaux porteurs de programmes	Convention relating to the Distribution of Programme-Carrying Signals Transmitted by Satellite
Übergabe (Art. 188 OR)	délivrance	delivery of possession
Übergang der Deckung (Art. 1053 OR)	transfert de la provision	transfer of cover
Übergang einer Forderung	transfert d'une créance	transfer of a claim
Übergang kraft Gesetzes	cession légale	transfer by operation of law
Übergangsbestimmung (UeB; ÜbBest.)	disposition transitoire (disp. trans.)	transitional provision
Übergangsentschädigung	indemnité pour changement d'occupation	severance benefit
Übergangsrecht	droit transitoire	interim law
Übergangszeit	période transitoire	transitional period
überlebender Ehegatte	conjoint survivant	surviving spouse
übermässige Bindung (Art. 27 ZGB)	engagement excessif	excessive restriction

Übernahme eines Vermögens oder eines Geschäftes (Art. 181-183 OR)	cession d'un patrimoine ou d'une entreprise	assignment of assets or a business with assets and liabilities
Übernahmekommission (UEK)	Commission des OPA (COPA)	Swiss Takeover Board
überragende Bauten (Art. 674 ZGB)	constructions empiétant sur le fonds d'autrui	encroaching buildings, buildings that cross the property line
Überschuldung (Art. 725 Abs. 2 OR)	surendettement	overindebtedness
Überschuldungsanfechtung (Art. 287 SchKG)	révocation pour cause de surendettement	challenge of overindebtedness
Überschuss	excédent	surplus
Überschussbeteiligung	participations aux excédents	surplus sharing
Überstundenarbeit	heures de travail supplémentaires	overtime work
Übertrag auf Seite 10	repris à la page 10	continued on page 10
Übertrag von Seite 10	repris de page 10	continued from page 10
Übertragbarkeit	transmissibilité	transferability
Übertragung	transfert	transfer
Übertretung (Art. 103, 106 StGB)	contravention	infraction
Übertretungsstrafbehörden (Art. 12 StPO)	autorités pénales compétentes en matière de contraventions	authorities responsible for prosecuting infractions
Übervorteilung (Art. 21 OR)	lésion	unconscionable bargain
Überwachung	surveillance	monitoring
Überwälzbarkeit	transférabilité	transferability
Überweisung	virement	wire transfer
Überweisungsrichter	juge de renvoi	remand judge
überwiegende öffentliche Interessen	intérêts public prépondérants	compelling public interests
Überzeit	travail supplémentaire	overtime
üble Nachrede (Art. 173 StGB)	diffamation	defamation
übler Geruch (Art. 684 ZGB)	mauvaises odeurs	noxious vapors
Uhrenindustrie	industrie horlogère	watch- and clockmaking industry
Uhrmacher	horloger	watchmaker
Umbuchung	extourne	reversal (of an entry)
Umfang der Pfändung (Art. 97 SchKG)	étendue de la saisie	extent of the attachment
umfassende Beistandschaft (Art. 398 ZGB)	curatelle de portée générale	general curatorship

umhüllende Vorsorgeeinrichtung	institution de prévoyance enveloppante	comprehensive pension institution
Umkehr der Beweislast	renversement du fardeau de la preuve	reversal of the burden of proof
Umlageverfahren	système de la répartition	pay-as-you-go system (payment of benefits from the contributions collected in the same period)
Umlaufvermögen	actif circulant	current assets
Umrechnung	conversion (de devises)	translation of foreign currency
Umrechnungskurs	cours de conversion	translation rate
Umsatz	chiffre d'affaires	revenue, sales
Umsatzabgabe	droit de timbre de négociation	transfer stamp tax
Umschuldung	rééchelonne-ment de dettes	debt rescheduling
Umschulung	reconversion professionnelle	retraining
Umsetzung des Gemeinschaftsrechts	mise en œuvre du droit communautaire	transposition of EU law
Umstrukturierung	restructuration	restructuring
Umtausch	troc	barter, exchange
Umtriebe	inconvénients	trouble, time and expense (associated with something difficult)
Umtriebsentschädigung (Art. 95 ZPO)	indemnité pour les démarches effectuées	compensation for personal efforts when a party is not represented by a lawyer
Umwandlung der Gesellschaft	transformation de la société	transformation of the company (change of corporate form)
Umwandlung der Unternehmung	transformation de l'entreprise	transformation of the company (change of corporate form)
Umwandlungssatz	taux de conversion	conversion rate
Umwelt	environnement	environment
umweltgefährdende Stoffe	substances dangereuses pour l'environnement	substances hazardous to the environment

Umweltpolitik	politique environnementale	environmental policy
Umweltrisiko	risque écologique	environmental risk
Umweltschutzfachstelle	Service de la protection de l'environnement	environmental protection agency
Umweltschutzgesetz (USG)	Loi sur la protection de l'environnement (LPE)	Environmental Protection Act
Umweltsteuer	impôt écologique	environmental tax
Umweltverträglichkeit	impact sur l'environnement	impact on the environment
Umweltverträglichkeitsbericht	rapport d'impact sur l'environnement	environmental impact report
Umzonung	reclassement	rezoning
Unabänderlichkeit der Fristen (Art. 129 OR)	délais péremptoires	mandatory limitation periods
Unabhängige Beschwerdeinstanz für Radio und Television (UBI)	Autorité indépendante d'examen des plaintes en matière de radio-télévision (AIEP)	Independent Complaints Authority for Radio and Television
unbefristete Verbindlichkeit (Art. 75 OR)	obligation sans terme	open-ended obligation
unbefristeter Vertrag	contrat de durée indéterminée (F : contrat à durée indéterminée)	open-ended contract, permanent contract
unbefugte Datenbeschaffung	soustraction de données	obtaining data without authorization
unbefugtes Aufnehmen von Gesprächen (Art. 179ter StGB)	enregistrement non autorisé de conversations	unauthorized recording of conversations
unbefugtes Beschaffen von Personendaten (Art. 179novies StGB)	soustraction de données personnelles	obtaining personal data without authorization
unbefugtes Eindringen in ein Datenverarbeitungssystem (Art. 143bis StGB)	accès indu à un système informatique	unauthorized access to a data processing system
unbekannt	inconnu	unknown

unbeschränkt haftender Gesellschafter (UG)	associe indéfiniment responsable	unlimited partner
unbeschränkte Haftung	responsabilité illimitée	unlimited liability
unbestimmte Dauer	durée indéterminée	unlimited duration
unbestritten	incontesté	undisputed, uncontested
unbestrittene Forderung	créance incontestée	uncontested claim
unbewegliches Vermögen	fortune immobilière	real estate assets
unbewusste Fahrlässigkeit	négligence inconsciente	unconscious negligence
unbezahlter Urlaub	vacances non payées	unpaid vacation
unbezifferte Forderungsklage (Art. 85 ZPO)	action en paiement non chiffrée	action for an unquantified debt
unbezifferte Forderungsklage (Art. 85 ZPO)	action non chiffrée	action for an unquantified debt
unechte Noven (Art. 229 ZPO)	novas improprement dits	improper new facts and evidence (facts or evidence that existed before the close of the exchange of written submissions or before the last hearing but could have not been submitted despite reasonable diligence)
unechte Solidarität	solidarité imparfaite	"imperfect" joint and several liability (the tortfeasors do not act jointly but their negligence results in the same harm)
unechter Vertrag zugunsten Dritter	stipulation pour autrui imparfaite	contract in favor of an incidental beneficiary
uneinbringliche Prämie	prime irrécouvrable	irrecoverable premium
unentgeltliche Rechtspflege (Art. 29 Abs. 3 BV, Art. 117 ZPO)	assistance judiciaire gratuite	right to proceed in forma pauperis
unentgeltliche Verfügung (Art. 286 SchKG)	libéralité	gift
unentgeltlicher Rechtsbeistand (Art. 29 Abs. 3 BV)	assistance gratuite d'un défenseur	free legal representation in court
Unentgeltlichkeit	gratuité	non-commercialism

unerlaubte Entfernung	absence injustifiée	unjustified absence
unerlaubte Handlung	acte illicite (F : délit civil)	tort
unerlaubtes Wegbleiben	omission illicite de rejoindre	absence without leave (AWOL)
unerneuerbare Energie	énergie non renouvelable	nonrenewable energy
Unfall	accident	accident
unfallähnliche Körperschädigung	lésion corporelle assimilée à un accident	accident-like bodily harm
Unfallfolge	suite d'un accident	result of an accident
unfallfremder Faktor	facteur étranger à l'accident	factor unrelated to the accident
Unfallstandort	lieu d'accident	accident site
Unfallverhütung	prévention des accidents	accident prevention
Unfallversicherer	assureur-accidents	accident insurer (similar to workers' compensation insurer)
Unfallversicherung	assurance-accidents	accident insurance (similar to workers' compensation)
Unfallversicherungsgesetz (UVG)	Loi sur l'assurance-accidents	Swiss Federal Accident Insurance Act
Unfallversicherungsprämie	prime d'assurance-accidents	accident insurance premium (similar to workers' compensation premium)
ungebührliches Benehmen	comportement irrespectueux	disorderly conduct
Ungehorsam gegen amtliche Verfügungen (Art. 292 StGB)	insoumission à une décision de l'autorité	contempt of official orders
ungerechtfertigte Bereicherung (Art. 62-67 OR)	enrichissement illégitime	unjust enrichment
ungesättigte Zone	zone non saturée	unsaturated zone
ungetreue Amtsführung (Art. 314 StGB)	gestion déloyale des intérêts publics	misconduct in public office
ungetreue Geschäftsbesorgung (Art. 158 StGB)	gestion déloyale	criminal mismanagement

Ungewöhnlichkeitsregel	règle de l'insolite	rule regarding unusual clauses (A party cannot be expected to have agreed to a clause contained in a text to which the main contract or another document refers if the content of such clause is unusual, i.e., if it departs from a reasonable person would expect in the same circumstances.)
Ungültigkeitsklage	action en nullité	action for annulment
unheilbare Zerrüttung	rupture irrémédiable	irretrievable breakdown
Universalitätsprinzip	principe d'universalité	principle of universality (bankrupt estate includes all of debtor's assets, including those located abroad)
Universalsukzession	succession universelle	universal succession (all of the decedent's assets go to the heirs)
Universalversammlung (Art. 701 OR)	assemblée universelle	meeting of all shareholders
Universitätstitel	titre universitaire	university degree
Unkosten	frais généraux	overhead costs
Unkostenabzug	déduction des frais généraux	deduction of overhead costs
unkurant	non-courant	not easily marketable, illiquid (e.g., the shares of a family-owned business)
unlauterer Wettbewerb	concurrence déloyale	unfair competition
Unmittelbarkeitsprinzip	principe de l'immédiat	principle of immediacy
Unmöglichkeit	impossibilité	impossibility
unpfändbar	insaisissable	unseizable
Unpfändbarkeit	insaisissabilité	unseizability
unrechtmässige Aneignung (Art. 137 StGB)	appropriation illégitime	unlawful appropriation
unrechtmässige Bereicherung	enrichissement illégitime	unlawful gain
unrechtmässige Entziehung von Energie (Art. 142 StGB)	soustraction d'énergie	unlawful abstraction of energy
unrechtmässige Verwendung von Vermögenswerten (Art. 141bis StGB)	utilisation sans droit de valeurs patrimoniales	unlawful use of financial assets
Unrechtsbewusstsein	conscience de l'illicéité	awareness of wrongdoing

unrichtige Auskunft	renseignement erroné	erroneous information
unschädliche Offenbarungen (Art. 7b PatG)	divulgations non opposables	non-prejudicial disclosures
Unschuldsvermutung (Art. 10 StPO)	présomption d'innocence	presumption of innocence
unselbständige Verordnung	ordonnance dépendante	dependent ordinance
Untätigkeitsklage	recours en carence	action on grounds of administrative inaction
untauglicher Versuch (Art. 23 StGB)	délit impossible	impossible attempt
unteilbare Leistung (Art. 70 OR)	obligation indivisible	indivisible obligation
Unterbrechung der Verjährung (Art. 135-138 OR)	interruption de la prescription	interruption of the limitation period
Unterbruch (D: Unterbrechung)	interruption	interruption
Unterdrückung von Urkunden (Art. 254 StGB)	suppression de titres	suppression of documents
Unterführung	passage sous voie	underpass
Untergeschoss	sous-sol	basement
Untergrund	sous-sol	substratum, subsoil
Unterhaltsklage (Art. 26 ZPO)	action en entretien	action for maintenance
Unterhaltskosten	frais d'entretien	maintenance costs
Unterhaltspflicht (Art. 276-294 ZGB)	obligation d'entretien	maintenance obligation, duty of maintenance
unterirdisches Gewässer (Art. 4 GSchG)	eaux souterraines	underground water
Unterlassung	omission	omission, failure
Unterlassung der Buchführung (Art. 166 StGB)	violation de l'obligation de tenir une comptabilité	failure to keep proper accounts
Unterlassung der Nothilfe (Art. 128 StGB)	omission de prêter secours	failure to offer aid in an emergency
Unterlassungsdelikt (Art. 11 StGB)	délit d'omission	crime of omission
Unterlassungsklage	action en interdiction	action for an injunction
unterliegen	succomber	to lose
unterliegende Partei	partie qui succombe	losing party
Unterlizenz	sous-licence	sublicense
Untermiete (Art. 262 OR)	sous-location	sublease
Untermieter	sous-locataire	subtenant

Unternehmensgewinne	bénéfices des entreprises	business profits
Unternehmenszusammenschluss (Art. 4 KG)	concentration d'entreprises	combination of enterprises
Unternehmer	entrepreneur	business owner
Unterschrift	signature	signature
Unterschriftenbogen	feuille de signatures	petition form
Unterschriftensammlung	récolte de signatures	petition
Unterschriftsberechtigter	personne autorisée à signer	person authorized to sign, authorized signatory
Unterschriftsberechtigung	droit de signature	authority to sign
Unterstützungsklage (Art. 26 ZPO)	action en paiement	action for assistance
Untersuchung im Körperinnern (Art. 85 StGB)	examen de l'intérieur du corps	search of body cavities
Untersuchungen an Leichen (Art. 253 ff StPO)	examen du cadavre	examination of dead bodies
Untersuchungshaft (Art. 110 StGB)	détention avant jugement	pretrial detention
untertags (D: tagsüber)	pendant la journée	during the day
Unterversicherung	sous-assurance	underinsurance
Untervertrag	sous-contrat	subcontract
ununterbrochener Aufenthalt	résidence ininterrompue	uninterrupted residence
Unvereinbarkeit	incompatibilité	incompatibility
Unverjährbarkeit der Strafverfolgung	imprescriptibilité de l'action pénale	no time limit for criminal prosecution
Unverletzlichkeit der Wohnung	inviolabilité du domicile	inviolability of the home
Unvermögen der Partei (Art. 69 ZPO)	incapacité de procéder	inability to appear
unverzinsliche Forderung (Art. 208 Abs. 2 SchKG)	créance ne portant pas intérêt	non-interest-bearing claim
unvollendeter Versuch (Art. 21 StGB)	tentative simple	uncompleted attempt

unwahre Angaben gegenüber Handelsregisterbehörden (Art. 153 StGB)	fausses communications aux autorités chargées du registre du commerce	false statements to the commercial register authorities
unwahre Angaben über kaufmännische Gewerbe (Art. 152 StGB)	faux renseignements sur des entreprises commerciales	false statements about commercial business
unzulässige Ausübung der Prostitution (Art. 199 StGB)	exercice illicite de la prostitution	unauthorized practice of prostitution
unzulässige Wettbewerbsbeschränkungen (Art. 5 KG)	restrictions illicites à la concurrence	unlawful restraints of competition
Unzulässigkeit	irrecevabilité	inadmissibility
Unzurechnungsfähigkeit	irresponsabilité	insanity
Urheber	auteur	author
Urheberpersönlichkeitsrecht	droit moral	moral right
Urheberrecht und verwandte Schutzrechte	droit d'auteur et droits voisins	copyright and related rights
Urheberrechtsgesetz (URG)	Loi fédérale sur le droit d'auteur (LDA)	Copyright Act
Urheberrechtsverletzung	violation du droit d'auteur	copyright infringement
Urheberrechtsverordnung (URV)	Ordonnance sur le droit d'auteur (ODAu)	Copyright Ordinance
Urheberrechtsvertrag	contrat de droit d'auteur	copyright agreement
Uri (UR)	Uri (UR)	Uri (canton)
Urkundenfälschung (Art. 251 StGB)	faux matériel dans les titres	forgery of documents
Urkundenfälschung im Amt (Art. 317 StGB)	faux dans les titres commis dans l'exercice de fonctions publiques	forgery of documents by a public official
Urnengang	votation, aller aux urnes	going to the polls, voter turnout
ursprüngliche Unmöglichkeit	impossibilité initiale	initial impossibility
Urteil	jugement	judgment
Urteilsberatung	délibérations	court deliberations
Urteilsfähigkeit (Art. 16 ZGB)	capacité de discernement	discernment, capacity to make rational decisions

Urteilsspruch	sentence	judgment, verdict
Urteilsvorschlag (Art. 210 ZPO)	proposition de jugement	proposed judgment
Usanz (D: Usance)	usance du marché	market practice
Valorennummer (D: Wertpapierkennnummer)	numéro de valeur	security number
Valutaverhältnis	rapport de valeur	underlying debt relationship (relationship between the promisee and the beneficiary)
Vaterschaft	paternité	paternity
Vaterschaftsanerkennung	reconnaissance de paternité	acknowledgment of paternity
Vaterschaftsklage (Art. 261 ZGB)	action en paternité (F : action en recherche de paternité)	paternity suit
Vaterschaftsvermutung	présomption de paternité	presumption of paternity
Velo (D: Fahrrad)	vélo	bicycle, bike
Verabreichen gesundheitsgefährdender Stoffe an Kinder (StGB 136)	remise à des enfants de substances pouvant mettre en danger leur santé	administering substances capable of causing injury to children
Veränderung der Verhältnisse	faits nouveaux	change of circumstances
Veranlagung	taxation	assessment
veranschlagen	estimer	to estimate
Verantwortlichkeitsgesetz (VG)	Loi sur la responsabilité (LRCF)	Government Liability Act
Verantwortlichkeitsklage (Art. 325 SchKG)	action en responsabilité	liability action
verarrestieren	séquestrer	to attach
Veräusserer	aliénateur	seller
veräussern	aliéner	to sell
Veräusserung	aliénation	sale
Verbaloblation	offre verbale	oral offer
Verband (Art. 60 ZGB)	association	association
Verband der Schweizer Unternehmen	Fédération des entreprises suisses	Swiss Business Federation

Verbandsklage (Art. 89 ZPO)	action collective	group action (this is not the same thing as a "class action" in the USA)
Verbeiständung (Art. 29 Abs. 1 BV)	assistance d'un défenseur	legal representation in court
verbindlich	ayant force obligatoire	binding
Verbindlichkeit	force obligatoire	binding force, binding nature
Verbindlichkeit zu einem Tun oder Nichttun (Art. 98 OR)	obligation de faire ou de ne pas faire	obligation to act or refrain from action
Verbot	interdiction	prohibition
Verbot der Annahme von Geschenken	interdiction d'accepter des dons	prohibition on accepting gifts
Verbot der doppelten Strafverfolgung (Art. 11 StPO)	interdiction de la double poursuite (art. 11 CPP)	prohibition of double jeopardy
Verbot der Zwangsarbeit	interdiction du travail forcé	prohibition of forced labor
Verbot des Doppelschutzes (Art. 140 PatG)	interdiction de cumuler la protection	prohibition of double patenting
Verbot des Handels	interdiction du commerce	prohibition of trade
Verbot des Schuldverhafts	interdiction de la contrainte par corps	prohibition of debtor's prison
Verbot unmenschlicher Behandlung (Art. 10 Abs. 3 BV)	interdiction des traitements inhumains	prohibition of inhuman treatment
verbotene Beweiserhebungsmethoden (Art. 140 StPO)	méthodes d'administration des preuves interdites	prohibited methods of taking evidence
verbotene Handlungen für einen fremden Staat (Art. 271 StGB)	actes exécutés sans droit pour un état étranger	unlawful activities on behalf of a foreign state
verbotener Nachrichtendienst (Art. 272 StGB)	espionnage	espionage
verbrauchbare Sache	chose consomptible	consumables
verbrauchen	consommer	to consume
Verbraucher	consommateur	consumer
Verbraucherschutz	protection des consommateurs	consumer protection
Verbrauchssteuer	impôt de consommation	consumption tax

Verbrechen (Art. 10 Abs. 2 StGB)	crime	felony (Swiss law divides offenses into three groups: felonies [*Verbrechen*], misdemeanors [*Vergehen*] and infractions [*Übertretungen*]. The punishment for a felony is a *Freiheitsstrafe von mehr als 3 Jahren*).
Verbrechen gegen die Menschlichkeit (Art. 264a StGB)	crime contre l'humanité	crime against humanity
Verbrechen und Vergehen gegen den öffentlichen Frieden (Art. 260ter StGB)	crimes ou délits contre la paix publique	felonies and crimes against public order
Verbreiten menschlicher Krankheiten (Art. 231 StGB)	propagation d'une maladie de l'homme	transmission of human diseases
Verbreiten von Tierseuchen (Art. 232 StGB)	propagation d'une épizootie	transmission of epizootic diseases
Verbreitung	diffusion	distribution, circulation
Verbreitungsrecht	droit de mise en circulation	right of distribution
verbrieft	matérialisé	certificated
verbundenes Unternehmen	entreprise associée	associated enterprise
Vercharterer	fréteur	charterer
Verdacht	soupçon	suspicion
verdächtig	suspect	suspicious
Verdachtsperiode	période suspecte	reach-back period (in bankruptcy)
verdeckte Ermittlung (Art. 285a StPO)	investigation secrète	undercover investigation
verdeckte Gewinnausschüttung	distribution dissimulée de bénéfices	hidden profit distribution
Verdienstausfall	perte de gain	loss of earnings
vereidigen	assermenter	to swear someone in, to administer an oath to someone
Vereidigung	assermentation	swearing in
Verein (Art. 60-79 ZGB)	association	association
Vereinbarung	convention, accord	agreement
vereinfachtes Verfahren (Art. 243 ff ZPO)	procédure simplifiée	simplified procedure (applies in financial disputes where the amount in controversy does not exceed CHF 30,000)

Vereinigte Bundesversammlung	Assemblée fédérale (Chambres réunies)	United Federal Assembly
Vereinigung (Art. 118 OR)	confusion	merger (of obligations)
Vereinigung von Verfahren	jonction de causes	joinder of cases
Vereinigungsfreiheit (Art. 23 BV)	liberté d'association	freedom of association
Vererblichkeit	transmissibilité par succession	transferability by succession
Verfahren	procédure	procedure, proceedings
Verfahrensablauf	déroulement de la procédure	course of the proceedings
verfahrensabschliessender Entscheid	décision qui met fin à la procédure	final judgment
Verfahrenshandlung	acte de procédure	procedural act
Verfahrenskosten (Art. 262 SchKG)	frais de la procédure	cost of the proceedings
verfahrensleitende Anordnung	ordonnance rendue par le tribunal	procedural order
Verfahrensprotokoll (Art. 77 StPO)	procès-verbal de procédure	record of proceedings
Verfahrensrecht	droit de procédure	procedural law (as opposed to substantive law)
Verfall der Sicherheitsleistung (Art. 240 StPO)	dévolution des sûretés	forfeiture of the bail payment
Verfall von Teilzahlungen (Art. 162 OR)	droit du créancier aux versements partiels en cas de résiliation	forfeiture of partial payments
Verfallrendite	rendement à l'échéance	yield to maturity
Verfalltag (Art. 102 Abs. 2 OR)	terme comminatoire, jour de l'exécution	deadline for performance
Verfassung	constitution	constitution
Verfassungsbeschwerde	recours constitutionnel	constitutional appeal
Verfassungsentwurf	projet de constitution	draft constitution
Verfassungsgericht	tribunal constitutionnel	constitutional court

Verfassungsgerichtsbarkeit	juridiction constitutionnelle	constitutional jurisdiction
Verfassungsinitiative	initiative constitutionnelle	constitutional initiative
verfassungskonforme Auslegung	interprétation conforme à la constitution	constitutional interpretation
verfassungsmässiger Grundsatz	principe constitutionnel	constitutional principle
verfassungsmässiges Recht auf Treu-und -Glaubensschutz	droit constitutionnel à la protection de la bonne foi	constitutional right to the protection of good faith
Verfassungsmässigkeit	constitutionna-lité	constitutionality
Verfassungsrat	assemblée constituante	constitutional assembly
Verfassungsrecht	droit constitutionnel	constitutional law
Verfassungsrüge	grief constitutionnel	constitutional claim
Verfehlung	offense	offense
Verfolgung	persécution	persecution
verfügbarer Teil (Art. 470 ZGB)	quotité disponible	disposable portion (of an estate, i.e., the part that the testator may freely dispose of; it is subordinate to the amount of each heir's compulsory portion)
Verfügung (1)	acte administratif	administrative act
Verfügung (2)	disposition	disposition
Verfügung (3)	décision	ruling
Verfügung pendente lite	décision pendente lite	interlocutory decision
Verfügung über mit Beschlag belegte Vermögenswerte (Art. 169 StGB)	détournement de valeurs patrimoniales mises sous main de justice	disposal of seized assets
Verfügung von Todes wegen	disposition pour cause de mort	testamentary disposition
Verfügungsfähigkeit (Art. 457f ZGB)	capacité de disposer	testamentary capacity
Verfügungsfreiheit	liberté de disposer	freedom to dispose of assets
Verfügungsgeschäft	acte de disposition	act of disposal

Verfügungsmacht	pouvoir de disposer	power to dispose of assets
Verfügungsunfähigkeit des Schuldners (Art. 204 SchKG)	incapacité du failli de disposer	insolvent's lack of capacity to dispose of his assets
Vergehen (Art. 10 Abs. 3 StGB)	délit	misdemeanor
Vergeltungskündigung	congé de représailles	retaliatory termination (of a lease)
Vergewaltigung (Art. 190 StGB)	viol	rape
Vergiftung	intoxication	poisoning
Vergleich: einen Vergleich schliessen	transaction: transiger	settlement to settle
Vergleichsvorschlag	proposition d'arrangement	proposed settlement
Vergütungsausschuss	comité de rémunération	compensation committee
Vergütungszins (Art. 61 MWSTG)	intérêt rémunératoire	refund interest
Verhaltensregeln	règles de comportement	rules of conduct
Verhaltensstörer	perturbateur par comportement	polluter by virtue of misconduct
Verhältnismässigkeit	proportionnalité	proportionality
Verhandlung	audience	hearing
Verhandlung vor dem Nachlassgericht (Art. 304 SchKG)	audience d'homologation	ratification hearing
Verhandlungsfähigkeit (Art. 114 StPO)	capacité de prendre part aux débats	fitness to plead
Verhandlungsmaxime	maxime des débats	rule that the parties control the subject matter of the proceedings and may present the case as they see fit
Verhör	interrogatoire	examination, questioning
Verhörrichter	juge d'instruction	investigating magistrate (no longer exists in Swiss law – criminal investigations are now conducted by the prosecutor)
Verjährung (Art. 127-138 OR)	prescription	statute of limitations, limitation period (the basic one is 10 years)
Verkauf aus freier Hand	vente de gré à gré	private sale (as opposed to a public auction)
Verkäufer	vendeur	seller
Verkaufsautomat	distributeur automatique	vending machine

Verkaufsgeschäft (D: Verkaufsstelle)	magasin	retail store
Verkaufskommissionär (Art. 425 OR)	commissionnaire en matière de vente	selling commission agent
Verkehrsregel	règle de la circulation	traffic rule
Verkehrsregelnverordnung (VRV)	Ordonnance sur les règles de la circulation routière (OCR)	Traffic Regulations Ordinance
Verkehrssicherheit	sécurité de la circulation	traffic safety
Verkehrsunfall	accident de la circulation	traffic accident
Verkehrsversicherungsverordnung (VVV)	Ordonnance sur l'assurance des véhicules (OAV)	Vehicles Insurance Ordinance
Verkehrswert	valeur vénale	market value
Verkehrswert des enteigneten Rechts	valeur vénale du droit exproprié	market value of the expropriated right
verkürzte Fraktionsdebatte	débat de groupe réduit	time-limited group debate
Verlagsvertrag (Art. 380-393 OR)	contrat d'édition	publishing agreement
Verlängerung	prolongation	extension
Verleiher (Art. 305-311 OR)	prêteur (prêt à usage)	lender (loan for use)
Verleitung zum Selbstmord (Art. 115 StGB)	incitation au suicide	inciting suicide
Verletzung der Fürsorge- oder Erziehungspflicht (Art. 219 StGB)	violation du devoir d'assistance ou d'éducation	neglect of duties of care, supervision or education
Verletzung der Pflicht der militärischen Unterordnung (Art. 63-64 MStG)	insubordination	insubordination
Verletzung der Pflicht zur Dienstleistung (Art. 84 MStG)	infractions au devoir de servir	violation of the duty to serve
Verletzung der Verkehrsregeln	violation des règles de la circulation	traffic violation
Verletzung des Abstimmungs- und Wahlgeheimnisses (Art. 283 StGB)	violation du secret du vote	breach of voting secrecy
Verletzung des Amtsgeheimnisses (Art. 320 StGB)	violation du secret de fonction	breach of official secrecy

Verletzung des Berufsgeheimnisses (Art. 321 StGB)	violation du secret professionnel	breach of professional confidentiality
Verletzung des Fabrikations- oder Geschäftsgeheimnisses (Art. 162 StGB)	violation du secret de fabrication ou commercial	breach of manufacturing or trade secrecy
Verletzung des Geheim- oder Privatbereichs durch Aufnahmegeräte (Art. 179quater StGB)	violation du domaine secret ou du domaine privé au moyen d'un appareil de prise de vues	breach of secrecy or privacy through the use of an image-carrying device
Verletzung des Schriftgeheimnisses (Art. 179 StGB)	violation de secrets privés	breach of the privacy of a sealed document
Verletzung des Völkerrechts	infraction commise contre le droit des gens	violation of international law
Verletzung fremder Gebietshoheit (Art. 299 StGB)	violation de la souveraineté territoriale étrangère	violation of foreign territorial sovereignty
Verletzung kantonalen Rechts	violation du droit cantonal	violation of cantonal law
Verletzung kriegsrechtlicher Bestimmungen	violation des lois de la guerre	violations of the law of war
Verletzung militärischer Geheimnisse	violation de secrets militaires	violation of military secrets
Verletzung schweizerischer Gebietshoheit (Art. 269 StGB)	violation de la souveraineté territoriale de la Suisse	violation of Swiss territorial sovereignty
Verleumdung (Art. 174 StGB)	calomnie	intentional defamation
Verlöbnis (Art. 90-95 ZGB)	fiançailles	engagement to marry
verlorene Chance	perte d'une chance	loss of a chance
Verlust	perte	loss
Verlustanteil	participation aux pertes	participation in losses, share of the losses
Verlustschein (Art. 149 ff SchKG)	acte de défaut de biens	certificate of unpaid debt (if the liquidation proceeds do not cover the debts in question and the costs of the proceedings, the creditors will receive a certificate of unpaid debt allowing them to recommence debt collection proceedings later)

Verlustverrechnung	imputation des pertes	offsetting of losses
Vermächtnis (Art. 484 ZGB)	legs	legacy
Vermächtnis einer einzelnen Sache (Art. 526 ZGB)	legs d'une chose déterminée	specific legacy
Vermächtnisklage (Art. 601 ZGB)	action du légataire	action by a legatee
Vermächtnisnehmer	légataire	legatee
Vermeidung der Doppelbesteuerung	élimination des doubles impositions	relief from double taxation
Vermessungsplan	plan de mensuration	survey plan
Vermessungstechniker	technicien géomètre	surveying technician, topographer
Vermieter	bailleur	landlord, lessor
Vermieterverband	association de bailleurs	landlord association
verminderte Schuldfähigkeit	responsabilité restreinte	diminished responsibility
Vermittler	intermédiaire	justice of the peace
Vermittleramt (D: Friedensrichter)	juge de paix	justice of the peace court
Vermittlungsbereitschaft	disponibilité au placement	availability for hiring
Vermittlungsfähigkeit	aptitude au placement	ability to be placed (in a job)
Vermittlungsvorstand	audience de conciliation	mediation hearing
Vermögen	fortune	assets, wealth
Vermögensbildung	constitution d'un capital	wealth creation
Vermögensertrag	revenu de la fortune	investment income
Vermögenslage	état de la fortune	financial position, financial condition
Vermögensrechte	droits patrimoniaux	economic rights (embodied in a share, i.e., the right to receive dividends, the right to a portion of any liquidation proceeds, and subscription rights)
vermögensrechtliche Streitigkeit	litige patrimonial	financial dispute
Vermögensschaden	dommage patrimonial	pecuniary damage, economic loss
Vermögensstand	état de la fortune sociale	statement of assets

Vermögenssteuer	impôt sur la fortune	wealth tax
Vermögensübertragung	transfert de patrimoine	asset transfer, transfer of assets
Vermögensverheimlichung	célation de biens	concealment of assets
Vermögensversicherung	assurance du patrimoine	property insurance
Vermögensverwalter	gérant de fortune	asset manager
Vermögensverwaltung	gestion de fortune	asset management
Vermögensverwaltungsauftrag	mandat de gestion de fortune	asset management mandate
Vermögensverzicht	dessaisissement de fortune	renunciation of assets
Vermögenswerte	biens	assets
Vermutung	présomption	presumption
Vermutung der Schuldlosigkeit	présomption d'innocence	presumption of innocence
Vermutung der Vaterschaft des Ehemannes (Art. 255-258 ZGB)	présomption de la paternité du mari	presumption of the paternity of the husband
Vernachlässigung von Unterhaltspflichten (Art. 217 StGB)	violation d'une obligation d'entretien	neglect of duty to support the family
Vernehmlassung	procédure de consultation	consultation procedure
Vernehmlassungsgesetz (VlG)	Loi fédérale sur la procédure de consultation	Federal Act on the Consultation Procedure
Vernehmlassungsverfahren	procédure de consultation	consultation procedure (the phase in the preparation of legislation in which bills (draft laws) are verified by the cantons, parties, associations and sometimes other stakeholders throughout Switzerland, in order to determine the likelihood of their adoption)
Vernichtung	destruction	destruction
Veröffentlichung amtlicher geheimer Verhandlungen (Art. 293 StGB)	publication de débats officiels secrets	publication of secret official proceedings
Verordnung	ordonnance	ordinance
Verordnung (Gemeinschaftsrecht)	règlement (droit communautaire)	regulation

Verordnung betreffend die Oberaufsicht über Schuldbetreibung und Konkurs (OAV-SchKG)	Ordonnance relative à la haute surveillance en matière de poursuite et de faillite (OHS-LP)	Ordinance on the Oversight of Debt Collection and Bankruptcy Matters
Verordnung der Bundesversammlung über die Organisation der Armee (AO)	Ordonnance de l'Assemblée fédérale sur l'organisation de l'armée (OOrgA)	Ordinance of the Federal Assembly on the Organization of the Armed Forces
Verordnung des Bundesgerichts über den Genossenschaftskonkurs (VGeK)	Ordonnance du Tribunal fédéral sur la faillite de la société coopérative (OFCoop)	Ordinance of the Federal Supreme Court on the Bankruptcy of a Cooperative
Verordnung des Bundesgerichts über die Zwangsverwertung von Grundstücken (VZG)	Ordonnance du Tribunal fédéral sur la réalisation forcée des immeubles (ORFI)	Ordinance of the Federal Supreme Court on the Forced Sale of Real Estate
Verordnung über Belastungen des Bodens (VBBo)	Ordonnance sur les atteintes portées aux sols (OSol)	Soil Pollution Ordinance
Verordnung über den Schutz der Arbeitnehmerinnen und Arbeitnehmer vor Gefährdung durch Mikroorganismen (SAMV)	Ordonnance sur la protection des travailleurs contre les risques liés aux microorganismes (OPTM)	Ordinance on Protection of Employees from Dangerous Microorganisms
Verordnung über den Stab Bundesrat Nationale Alarmzentrale (V Stab BR NAZ)	Ordonnance relative à l'état-major Centrale nationale d'alarme du Conseil fédéral (O EM CF CENAL)	Ordinance on the Federal Council National Emergency Operations Centre Staff
Verordnung über den Verkehr mit Abfällen (VeVA)	Ordonnance sur les mouvements de déchets (OMD)	Waste Movements Ordinance

Verordnung über die Gebühren für den Tierverkehr (GebV-TVD)	Ordonnance relative aux émoluments liés au trafic des animaux (OEmol-TA)	Ordinance on Animal Movement Fees
Verordnung über die Geschäftsführung der Konkursämter (KOV)	Ordonnance sur l'administration des offices de faillite (OAOF)	Ordinance on Procedures for Bankruptcy Offices
Verordnung über die in die Schweiz entsandten Arbeitnehmerinnen und Arbeitnehmer (EntsV)	Ordonnance sur les travailleurs détachés en Suisse (Odét)	Ordinance on Workers posted to Switzerland
Verordnung über die kalte Progression (VKP)	Ordonnance sur la progression à froid (OPFr)	Bracket Creep Ordinance
Verordnung über die Personensicherheitsprüfungen (PSPV)	Ordonnance sur les contrôles de sécurité relatifs aux personnes (OCSP)	Ordinance on Personnel Security Screening
Verordnung über die Personensicherheitsprüfungen (PSPV)	Ordonnance sur les contrôles de sécurité relatifs aux personnes (OCSP)	Ordinance on Personnel Security Screening
Verordnung über die Umweltverträglichkeitsprüfung (UVPV)	Ordonnance relative à l'étude de l'impact sur l'environnement (OEIE)	Environmental Impact Assessment Ordinance
Verordnung über die Unfallversicherung (UVV)	Ordonnance sur l'assurance-accidents (OLAA)	Accident Insurance Ordinance
Verpächter	bailleur à ferme	usufructuary lessor
Verpfänder	metteur en gage	pledgor
Verpflichtung zu einer Arbeitsleistung	astreinte au travail	order to perform work
Verpflichtungskredit	crédit d'engagement	guarantee credit (the maximum financial commitment that the Federal Council can make for a specific project)
Verpfründungsvertrag (Art. 516-529 OR)	contrat d'entretien viager	lifelong support agreement

Verrechnung (D: Aufrechnung) (Art. 120-126 OR)	compensation de créances	offset
Verrechnungscheck (Art. 1123 OR)	chèque à porter en compte	account-payee-only check
Verrechnungsrecht	droit de compensation	right of offset
Verrechnungssteuer (VSt) (D: Quellensteuer)	impôt anticipé (IA) (F : retenue à la source)	withholding tax
Verrechnungssteuergesetz (VStG)	Loi sur l'impôt anticipé (LIA)	Withholding Tax Act
Verrechnungssteuerverordnung (VStV)	Ordonnance sur l'impôt anticipé (OIA)	Withholding Tax Ordinance
Versammlungsfreiheit (Art. 22 BV)	liberté de réunion	freedom of assembly
Versatzpfand (Art. 907 ff ZGB)	prêt sur gage	pawn, pawning
versäumte Klageantwort (Art. 223 ZPO)	défaut de réponse	failure to file an answer (to the complaint)
Verschiebung	report	postponement, deferral
verschmutztes Abwasser (Art. 4 GSchG)	eaux polluées	polluted waste water
Verschmutzungsfahne	panache de pollution	pollution plume
Verschollenerklärung (Art. 21 ZPO)	déclaration d'absence	declaration of presumed death
Verschrieb (D: Schreibfehler)	faute d'orthographe, faute de frappe	spelling mistake, typo
Verschulden	faute	fault (either negligence or intentional misconduct)
Verschuldenshaftung	responsabilité pour faute	liability based on fault, fault-based liability (as opposed to no-fault liability, known as "strict liability")
verschuldensunabhängige Haftung	responsabilité objective	strict liability, liability without fault, no-fault liability
Verschwendung	prodigalité	profligacy
Versicherer	assureur	insurer
versicherte Sache	chose assurée	insured item
Versicherter	assuré	the insured
versichertes Risiko	risque assuré	insured risk
Versicherung	assurance	insurance
Versicherungsaufsichtsgesetz (VAG)	Loi fédérale sur la surveillance des assurances (LSA)	Insurance Supervision Act

Versicherungsausweis	certificat d'assurance	certificate of insurance
Versicherungsfall	cas d'assurance	insured event
Versicherungsleistung	prestation d'assurance	insurance benefit
Versicherungsleistungsentzug	suppression de la prestation d'assurance	elimination of the insurance benefit
Versicherungsleistungskürzung	réduction de la prestation d'assurance	reduction of the insurance benefit
Versicherungsnehmer	preneur d'assurance	the insured
Versicherungspflicht	obligation d'assurance	insurance obligation
Versicherungspolice	police d'assurance	insurance policy
Versicherungspool	pool d'assurances	insurance pool
Versicherungsprämie	prime d'assurance	insurance premium
Versicherungsrecht	droit des assurances	insurance law
Versicherungsreglement	règlement d'assurance	insurance regulations
Versicherungsschein	certificat d'assurance	certificate of insurance
Versicherungsschutz	couverture d'assurance	insurance coverage
Versicherungssumme	somme assurée	sum insured, amount insured
Versicherungsverhältnis	rapport d'assurance	insurance relationship
Versicherungsvertrag	contrat d'assurance	insurance policy
Versicherungsvertragsgesetz (VVG)	Loi sur le contrat d'assurance (LCA)	Insurance Policies Act
Versicherungsvorbehalt	réserve d'assurance	insurance reserve
Versicherungswert	valeur d'assurance	insurance value
Versorgerschaden	perte de soutien	loss of upkeep
Versorgung	approvisionne-ment	supply, provision
Verspätung	retard	delay
Verspätungsschaden	dommage dû au retard	damage due to delay

Verstaatlichung	nationalisation	nationalization
Verständigungsverfahren	procédure amiable	mutual agreement procedure
versteigern	vendre aux enchères	to auction off
Versteigerung	vente aux enchères	auction
Verstossung	répudiation d'une personne	repudiation of a person
Verstümmelung weiblicher Genitalien (Art. 124 StGB)	mutilation d'organes génitaux féminins	female genital mutilation
Versuch (Art. 22 StGB)	tentative	attempt
Verteidigung (Art. 128 ff StPO)	défense, défenseur	defense, defense lawyer
Verteilerzentrum	centre de distribution	distribution center
Vertrag (1)	contrat	contract, agreement
Vertrag (2)	traité	treaty
Vertrag auf Hinterlegung Sicherheitshalber	contrat de consignation à titre de sûreté	escrow agreement
Vertrag mit Konsumenten	contrat conclu avec des consommateurs	consumer contract
Vertrag mit Schutzwirkung zugunsten Dritter	contrat avec effet de protection envers les tiers	third-party beneficiary contract
Vertrag zu Lasten eines Dritten (Art. 111 OR)	porte-fort, promesse de porte-fort	guarantee of performance by third party
Vertrag zugunsten eines Dritten (Art. 112 OR)	stipulation pour autrui	third party beneficiary contract (contract conferring rights on third parties)
Vertrag zwischen Kantonen (Art. 48 BV)	convention intercantonale	intercantonal agreement
vertraglich vorbehaltene Form (Art. 16 OR)	forme réservée dans le contrat	form stipulated by contract
Vertragsabschluss	conclusion du contrat	entry into the contract
Vertragsfreiheit (Art. 19 Abs. 1 OR)	liberté contractuelle, liberté du contrat	freedom of contract
Vertragshaftung	responsabilité contractuelle	contractual liability

Vertragsklausel	clause contractuelle	contract clause
Vertragslücke	lacune du contrat	matter as to which a contract is silent
Vertragspartei	partie au contrat	party to the contract
Vertragsrecht	droit des contrats	law of contracts
Vertragstreue	fidélité contractuelle	loyalty to the terms of the contract
Vertragsübernahme	cession de contrat	assignment of contract
Vertragsverhandlung	pourparlers	contract negotiations
Vertragsverletzung	inobservation du contrat	breach of contract
Vertragsverletzungsklage	recours en manquement	action for breach of contract
Vertrauensarzt	médecin conseil	independent medical examiner
Vertrauenshaftung	responsabilité fondée sur la confiance	liability based on creating trust
Vertrauensperson (Art. 432 ZGB)	personne de confiance	authorized representative
Vertrauensprinzip	principe de la confiance	principle of good faith
Vertrauensschaden	dommage né de la confiance déçue	negative interest, damage caused by breach of contract
vertretbare Behauptung	allégation défendable	defensible allegation
vertretbare Sache	chose fongible	fungible thing
vertreten	représenter	to represent
Vertretener (Art. 38 OR)	représenté	the principal
Vertreter	représentant	representative
Vertretung bei der Stimmabgabe	vote par procuration	proxy voting
Vertretung ohne Vollmacht	représentation sans pouvoirs	unauthorized agency
Vertretungsbeistandschaft (Art. 394 ZGB)	curatelle de représentation	representative curatorship
Vertretungsmacht	pouvoir de représentation	power of representation
Vertretungsverhältnisse (Art. 29 StGB)	rapport de représentation	agency relationships
Vertriebssystem	système de distribution	distribution system
Vertrödler	consignateur	consignor

Verübung einer Tat in selbstverschuldeter Unzurechnungsfähigkeit (Art. 263 StGB)	actes commis en état d'irresponsabilité fautive	committing an offense while in a state of voluntarily induced mental incapacity
verunfallen (D: verunglücken)	avoir un accident, être accidenté	to have an accident
Verunfallte (D: Unfallopfer)	victime d'un accident	accident victim
Verunreinigung (Art. 4 GSchG)	pollution	pollution
Verunreinigung von Trinkwasser (Art. 234 StGB)	contamination d'eau potable	contamination of drinking water
Veruntreuung (Art. 138 StGB)	abus de confiance	misappropriation
Veruntreuung und Entzug von Pfandsachen und Retentionsgegenständen (Art. 145 StGB)	détournement de choses frappées d'un droit de gage ou de rétention	misappropriation and removal of property subject to a pledge or lien
Verursacher	pollueur	polluter
Verursacherprinzip (Art. 3a GSchG)	principe de causalité	"polluter pays" principle
Verursachung einer Explosion (Art. 223 StGB)	explosion	causing an explosion
Verurteilter	condamné	convict
Verurteilung	condamnation	conviction
Verwahrer	dépositaire	custodian
Verwahrstelle	dépositaire	securities depository
Verwahrung (Art. 56 ff. StGB)	internement	incarceration, imprisonment
Verwahrung von Gewohnheitsverbrechern (Art. 42 StGB)	internement des délinquants d'habitude	incarceration of habitual offenders
verwaltete Vermögen	masse sous gestion	assets under management (AuM)
Verwaltung	administration	administration
Verwaltungs- und Verwaltungsgerichtsverfahren	procédure administrative	administrative procedure
Verwaltungsbehörde	autorité administrative	administrative authority
Verwaltungsbeistandschaft (Art. 394 ZGB)	curatelle de gestion	representative curatorship
Verwaltungsbeschwerde	recours administratif	administrative appeal
Verwaltungsbeschwerdeverfahren	procédure administrative de recours	administrative appeal procedure

Verwaltungsdelegation	délégation administrative	administrative delegation
Verwaltungsentscheide der Bundesbehörden (VEB)	Jurisprudence des autorités administratives de la Confédération (JAAC)	Decisions of the Administrative Authorities of the Confederation
Verwaltungsgebühr	émolument administratif	administrative fee
Verwaltungsgericht	tribunal administratif	administrative court
Verwaltungsgerichtsbeschwerde	recours de droit administratif	administrative court appeal
Verwaltungskommission	Commission administrative	Administrative Commission (of the Swiss Federal Supreme Court)
Verwaltungskosten	frais administratifs	administrative costs
Verwaltungsrat (Art. 707 OR)	conseil d'administration	board of directors
Verwaltungsrecht	droit administratif	administrative law
verwaltungsrechtliche Klage	action de droit administratif	administrative lawsuit
Verwaltungssachen	affaires administratives	administrative matters
Verwaltungsstrafrecht	droit pénal administratif	administrative criminal law
Verwaltungsstrafverfahren	procédure pénale administrative	administrative criminal proceedings
Verwaltungsvermögen	patrimoine administratif	administrative assets
Verwaltungsverordnung	ordonnance administrative	administrative ordinance
Verwandtschaft	parenté	relationship, kinship
Verwechslungsgefahr (Art. 3 MSchG)	risque de confusion	likelihood of confusion
Verweigerung von Geschäftsbeziehungen (Art. 7 KG)	refus d'entretenir des relations commerciales	refusal to do business
Verweigerungsrecht	droit de refus de collaborer	right to refuse to cooperate
Verweis	réprimande	reprimand
Verweisung (1)	renvoi (1)	reference

Verweisung (2)	renvoi (2)	renvoi (in private international law)
Verweisungsbruch (Art. 291 StGB)	rupture de ban	breach of an expulsion order
Verwerflichkeit	caractère odieux	reprehensibility
Verwertbarkeit rechtswidrig erlangter Beweise (Art. 141 StPO)	exploitation des moyens de preuves obtenus illégalement	admissibility of unlawfully obtained evidence
verwerten	réaliser	to sell
Verwertung	réalisation	sale
Verwertungsbegehren	réquisition de réaliser	request for a sale
Verwertungsfrist (Art. 154 SchKG)	délai de réalisation	deadline for a sale
Verwertungsgesellschaft	société de gestion des droits d'auteur	copyright collecting agency, copyright collective
Verwertungsmodus (Art. 256 SchKG)	mode de réalisation	means of selling the assets
Verwertungsverfahren (Art. 155 ff SchKG)	procédure de réalisation	sale procedure
Verwirklichung der Grundrechte (Art. 35 BF)	réalisation des droits fondamentaux	upholding of fundamental rights
Verwirkung	péremption, déchéance	forfeiture
Verzeihung	pardon	pardon
Verzicht	renonciation	waiver
Verzicht auf die gesetzlichen Gerichtsstände (Art. 35 ZPO)	renonciation aux fors légaux	waiver of statutory jurisdiction
Verzicht auf die Verwertung (Art. 127 und 142a SchKG)	renonciation à la réalisation	waiver of realization
verzögerte Heimschaffung von Kriegsgefangenen (Art. 264i StGB)	retardement du rapatriement de prisonniers de guerre	delayed repatriation of prisoners of war
Verzug (Art. 102-106 OR)	demeure	default
Verzug des Gläubigers (Art. 91 OR)	demeure du créancier	default by the obligee
Verzug des Schuldners (Art. 102 OR)	demeure du débiteur	default by the obligor
Verzugszins	intérêt moratoire	default interest
Vetorecht	droit de veto	veto right
Viehhandel (Art. 198 OR)	commerce du bétail	livestock trading
Viehverpfändung (Art. 885 ZGB)	engagement de bétail	pledge of livestock

vinkuliert	de transmissibilité restreinte	with restricted transferability
vinkulierte Aktien	actions liées (F : actions à cessibilité restreinte)	restricted shares, shares with restricted transferability
vinkulierte Namenaktie	action nominative liée	registered shares with restricted transferability
Vinkulierung	limitation de la transmissibilité	restricted transferability
visieren (D: beglaubigen)	authentifier, certifier conforme	to authenticate, certify
Visum (D: Namenszeichnen)	paraphe	initials
V-Mann	agent provocateur	informer
Völkergewohnheitsrecht	droit coutumier international	customary international law
Völkermord (Art. 264 StGB)	génocide	genocide
Völkerrecht	droit international public	public international law, the law of nations
völkerrechtlicher Vertrag	traité international	international treaty
Volksabstimmung	votation populaire	popular vote, popular ballot
Volksbegehren	requête populaire	popular request
Volksinitiative	initiative populaire	popular initiative
Volksmehr	majorité du peuple	popular majority, majority of those voting
Volkszählung	recensement	census
vollendeter Versuch (Art. 22 StGB)	délit manqué	completed attempt
Vollmacht	procuration	power of attorney
vollstreckbar	exécutoire, doté de la force exécutoire	enforceable
vollstreckbare Urteilsausfertigung	expédition exécutoire de jugement	enforceable copy of a judgment
vollstreckbarer Entscheid	décision exécutoire	enforceable decision
Vollstreckbarerklärung	déclaration d'exécution	declaration of enforceability
Vollstreckbarkeit	force exécutoire	enforceability

Vollstreckbarkeitserklärung	exequatur	declaration that a judgment is enforceable
Vollstreckung	exécution (procédure)	enforcement
Vollstreckungsverfahren	procédure d'exécution	enforcement
Vollstreckungsverfügung (Art. 41 Abs. 1 VwVG)	mesure en matière d'exécution	enforcement measure
Vollwaisenrente	rente d'orphelin double	orphan's pension
Vollzeitbeschäftigung	travail à plein temps	full-time work
Vollziehungsverordnung (VV)	règlement d'exécution	implementing order
von Amtes wegen	d'office	sua sponte, at the court's initiative ("ex officio" is a mistranslation)
von Amtes wegen aufgenommene Forderung (Art. 246 SchKG)	créance inscrite d'office	automatically registered claim
Vorabklärung (D: erstes informelles Sammeln von Information)	enquête préalable	preliminary investigation
Voranschlag	budget	budget
Voraussehbarkeit	prévisibilité	foreseeability
Voraussetzung	condition	prerequisite, condition
Vorausvermächtnis	legs préciputaire	advance legacy
Vorauszahlungsvertrag (Art. 227a OR)	vente avec paiements préalables	contract with payment in advance
Vorbehalt der kantonalen Gesetzgebung	réserve de la législation cantonale	reservation of cantonal law
vorbehalten – Völkerrechtliche Verträge sind vorbehalten.	réservé – Les traités internationaux sont réservés.	take precedence – International treaties take precedence.
Vorbenutzung	usage antérieur	prior use
Vorbereitungshaft (Art. 75 AuG)	détention préparatoire	preparatory custody (prior to repatriation)
vorbörslich	avant bourse	pre-market trading
Vorentscheid (Art. 92 BGG)	décision préjudicielle	interlocutory decision on a substantive matter
Vorerbe	héritier grevé	encumbered heir
Vorfahre	ascendant	ancestor, ascendant
Vorfrage	question préjudicielle	incidental question

Vorführungsbefehl (Art. 208 StPO)	mandat d'amener	warrant for an enforced appearance
Vorhersehbarkeit	prévisibilité	foreseeability
Vorinstanz	autorité précédente	the lower court, the court below
Vorkauf	préemption	right of first refusal
Vorkaufsberechtigter	titulaire du droit de préemption	holder of a right of first refusal
Vorkaufsfall (Art. 216c OR)	cas de préemption	right of first refusal event
Vorkaufsrecht	droit de préemption	right of first refusal
Vorkaufsvertrag (Art. 216 OR)	pacte de préemption	contract conferring a right of first refusal
Vorkumulieren	cumul officiel	pre-cumulation (entry in duplicate of a candidate's name on a pre-printed ballot paper on the instructions of the candidate's own party)
Vorladung (Art. 170 ZPO, Art. 201 StPO)	citation, mandat de comparution	summons
Vorlage der Beweismittel (Art. 73 SchKG)	présentation des moyens de preuve	presentation of evidence
Vorlagen zur Vorabentscheidung	renvoi préjudiciel	reference for a preliminary ruling
vorläufige Freilassung	mise en liberté provisoire	temporary release
Vorleben	antécédent	backstory
Vorlegung eines Wechsels (Art. 1011 OR)	présentation d'une lettre de change	presentment of a draft/bill of exchange
Vorlegung zur Sichtnahme (Art. 1099 OR)	présentation à vue	presentment at sight
Vorleistungspflicht	prise en charge préalable	advance performance obligation
Vormerkung im Grundbuch (Art. 101 SchKG)	annotation au registre foncier	priority notice in the land register
Vormietrecht	droit de prélocation	lease option
Vormund (Art. 358 ZGB)	tuteur	guardian
Vormundschaft (Art. 360-456 ZGB)	tutelle	guardianship
vormundschaftliche Behörde (D: Vormundschaftsgericht)	autorité de tutelle	guardianship authority
Vormundschaftsbehörde	autorité tutélaire	guardianship authority
Vorname	prénom	first name, given name

vorobligatorische Guthaben	avoir surobligatoire	pre-compulsory credit balance
Vorpachtrecht	droit de préaffermage	leaseholder's right to extend the lease
Vorrang des Bundesrechts (Art. 49 BV)	primauté du droit fédéral	supremacy of federal law
Vorrat	stock	inventory
Vorratsmarke	marque de réserve	reserve mark, reserve trademark
Vorrecht	privilège	preferential right
Vorsatz	intention	intent
Vorsatzdelikt	infraction intentionnelle, délit intentionnel	intentional offense, offense committed with intent
vorsätzliche Tötung (Art. 111 StGB)	meurtre	intentional homicide
Vorschlag (1)	proposition	proposal
Vorschlag (2) (Güterrecht) (Art. 210 ZGB)	bénéfice de l'union conjugale	net gain (assets acquired during marriage by one spouse after debts are paid)
Vorschussgewährung	avance de fonds	advance
Vorsitzender der Geschäftsleitung (D: ~Vorstandsvorsitzender)	président de la direction	chairman of the board of managers (CEO)
Vorsitzender des Anwaltsverbands	bâtonnier	president of the Bar Association
vorsitzender Richter	président du tribunal	presiding judge
Vorsorgeauftrag (Art. 360 ZGB)	mandat pour cause d'inaptitude	advance care directive
Vorsorgeausgleich	partage de la prévoyance professionnelle	pension splitting
Vorsorgeausweis	certificat de prévoyance	pension statement
Vorsorgeeinrichtung	institution de prévoyance	pension institution, pension fund
Vorsorgekommission	commission de prévoyance	pension committee
Vorsorgeleistung	prestation de prévoyance	pension benefit
Vorsorgesparen	épargne de prévoyance	saving up for pension provision
Vorsorgewerk	œuvre de prévoyance	pension organization
vorsorgliche Beweisführung (Art. 158 ZPO)	preuve à futur	precautionary taking of evidence, preservation of evidence

vorsorgliche Massnahme (Art. 261 ff ZPO) (D: einstweilige Verfügung)	mesure provisionnelle	preliminary injunctive relief
Vorspiegelung	affirmation fallacieuse	misrepresentation, false pretenses
Vorstand	direction	executive board
Vorstoss (D: Initiativantrag)	intervention parlementaire	parliamentary procedural request
Vortat (Art. 160 StGB)	infraction initiale	original offense
Vorteilsannahme (Art. 322sexties StGB)	acceptation d'un avantage	acceptance of an advantage
Vorteilsgewährung (Art. 322quinquies StGB)	octroi d'un avantage	granting an advantage
Vortritt (D: Vorfahrt)	priorité	right of way (in traffic)
vorübergehende Zuführung (Art. 58 IRSG)	remise temporaire	provisional surrender
Voruntersuchung	investigation préalable	preliminary investigation of a contaminated site
Vorverfahren (Art. 299 ff StPO)	procédure préliminaire	preliminary proceedings
Vorvertrag (Art. 22 OR)	promesse de contracter, précontrat	contract creating an obligation for one or both parties to enter into a contract in the future
Vorwirkung	effet anticipé	advance effect
vorzeitige Kündigung	résiliation anticipée	early termination
vorzeitige Pensionierung	retraite anticipée	early retirement
vorzeitige Rückgabe der Sache (Art. 264 OR)	restitution anticipée de la chose	early return of the premises
vorzeitige Rückzahlung	remboursement anticipé	early repayment
Vorzugsaktie	action privilégiée	preferred shares
Vorzugsrecht des Pfandgläubigers (Art. 198 SchKG)	droit de préférence	paramount right (of the pledgee)
Vorzustand	état antérieur	previous condition
Votant (D: Diskussionsredner im Parlament)	intervenant, orateur	speaker
votieren (D:Stellung nehmen)	intervenir	to speak
Votum(D: Diskussionsbeitrag)	intervention	speech
Waadt (VD)	Vaud (VD)	Vaud (canton)
Waffe	arme	weapon
Waffenbesitz	détention d'armes	possession of weapons
Waffengesetz (WG)	Loi sur les armes (LArm)	Weapons Act

Waffengleichheit	égalité des armes	equal fighting power, equal fighting chance
Waffenhandel	commerce d'armes	arms trade
Waffenstillstand	armistice	armistice
Waffentragschein	permis de port d'armes	weapons permit
Wagnis	entreprise téméraire	hazardous business, hazardous enterprise
Wahl	élection	election
Wahlanleitung	explications de vote	voting guide
Wählbarkeit	éligibilité	eligibility for election
Wahlbehörde	autorité électorale	election official
Wahlberechtigter	électeur	voter
Wahlbestechung (Art. 281 StGB)	corruption électorale	corrupt electoral practices
Wahlbeteiligung	taux de participation électorale	voter turnout
Wahlbezirk	circonscription électorale	voting district
Wahlfälschung (Art. 282 StGB)	fraude électorale	electoral fraud
Wahlkampf	campagne électorale	electoral campaign
Wahlkreis	circonscription électorale	voting district
Wahlobligation (Art. 72 OR)	obligation alternative	obligation involving choice of performance
Wahlprotokoll	protocole d'élection	election record
Wahlverteidigung (Art. 129 StPO)	défense de choix	right to choose a defense lawyer
Wahlvorschlag	proposition de candidat	candidate list
Wahlzettel	bulletin électoral	ballot
Wahndelikt	délit putatif	act wrongly assumed by perpetrator to be criminal
Wahrheitsbeweis	preuve de la vérité	proof of the truth
Währung	monnaie	currency
Waisenrente	rente d'orphelin	orphan's benefit, orphan's allowance
Wallis	Valais	Valais (canton)

Wandelanleihe	emprunt convertible	convertible bond
Wandelpön	peine résolutoire	penalty for termination
Wandelrecht	droit de conversion	conversion right (right to convert bonds into shares or participation certificates)
Wandelung bei Untergang der Sache (Art. 207 OR)	résiliation en cas de perte de la chose	rescission when the object is destroyed
Wandelungsklage (Art. 205 OR)	action rédhibitoire	action for rescission of a sale
Wandelungsrecht	droit à la résolution du contrat	right to rescind the contract
Warenfälschung (Art. 155 StGB)	falsification de marchandises	counterfeiting of goods
Warenpapier	titre représentatif de marchandises	title document (document of title to goods)
Warenprüfung	contrôle des marchandises	inspection of goods, inspection of merchandise
Warenterminkontrakt	contrat à terme de marchandises	commodity futures
Warnungsentzug	retrait d'admonestation	temporary suspension of a driver's license
Wartezeit	période d'attente	waiting period
Wartungsvertrag	contrat d'entretien	maintenance agreement
Wechsel (Art. 177-189 SchKG)	effet de change	bill of exchange
wechselähnliche Papiere (Art. 1147 OR)	titres analogues aux effets de change	bill-like securities
Wechselbetreibung (Art. 177 ff SchKG)	poursuite pour effets de change	enforcement of bills of exchange
Wechselbürge (Art. 1020 ff OR)	donneur d'aval	guarantor (on a bill)
Wechselbürgschaft	aval	guaranty (on a bill)
Wechselfähigkeit	capacité de s'obliger par effet de change	ability to draw or accept bills of exchange
Wechselkursrisiko	risque de change	exchange rate risk
Wechselregress	recours de change	recourse against guarantors of a bill of exchange
wegbedingen	exclure	to exclude
Wegbedingung (Art. 199 OR)	exclusion	exclusion
Wegbedingung der Haftung	clause exclusive de responsabilité	disclaimer of liability

Wegnahme der Leiche	levée du corps	removal of the body
Wegrecht	droit de passage	right of way
wegweisen	expulser	to expel, kick out
Wegweisung (Ausländerrecht)	renvoi (droit des étrangers)	expulsion
Wehrpflicht	obligation militaire	compulsory military service
Weibel (D: Gerichtsvollzieher)	huissier	bailiff, process server
Weisungen	règles de conduite	specific orders as to conduct
Weiterbildung	formation continue	continuing education
weiterer Schaden	dommage supplémentaire	additional damage
weiterziehen	recourir	to appeal
Weiterziehung (Art. 174 und 185 SchKG)	recours	appeal
Werbung	publicité	advertising
Werk (Urheberrecht)	œuvre (droit d'auteur)	work
Werk zweiter Hand	œuvre dérivée	derivative work
Werkeigentümer	propriétaire d'ouvrage	property owner
Werkeigentümerhaftung (Art. 58-59 OR)	responsabilité du propriétaire d'ouvrage	liability of the property owner
Werktag	jour ouvrable	working day
Werkvertrag (Art. 363-379 OR)	contrat d'entreprise	contract for work and services
Wert	valeur	value
Wertminderung	moins-value	reduction in value, loss of value
Wertpapier (Art. 965 OR)	papier-valeur	security
Wertpapierrecht	droit des papiers-valeurs	securities law
Wertrechte (Art. 973c OR)	droits-valeurs	uncertificated securities
Wertsache	objet de prix	object of value
Wertschriftendepot	dépôt de titres	securities account
Wettbewerb	concurrence	competition
Wettbewerbsabrede (Art. 4 KG)	accord en matière de concurrence	agreement affecting competition
Wettbewerbsbeschränkung	restriction à la concurrence	restraint of competition
Wettbewerbsfreiheit	liberté de la concurrence	freedom of competition

Wettbewerbskommission	Commission de la concurrence	Competition Commission
Wettbewerbsverzerrungen	distorsions de la concurrence	distortion of competition
Wette	pari	bet
wetterbedingter Arbeitsausfall	perte de travail due aux intempéries	loss of working hours due to bad weather
Wettschlagen der Parteikosten (D: Kostenaufhebung)	compensation des dépens	each party paying his own costs
wettschlagen: Die Parteikosten werden wettgeschlagen. (D: Die Parteikosten werden gegeneinander aufgerechnet).	compenser les dépens	Each party pays his own costs.
wichtiger Grund	juste motif	good cause
Widerbeklagte	défendeur reconventionnel	counterclaim defendant
Widerklage (Art. 224 ZPO)	demande reconven-tionnelle	counterclaim
Widerkläger	demandeur reconventionnel	counterclaim plaintiff
widerrechtlich	illicite	unlawful
Widerrechtlichkeit	illicéité	unlawfulness
Widerruf	révocation	revocation
Widerruf des Konkurses (Art. 195 ff SchKG)	révocation de la faillite	revocation of the insolvency proceedings
Widerruf des Nachlassvertrags (Art. 305 SchKG)	révocation du concordat	revocation of the debt restructuring agreement
Widerruf des Zuschlags (Art. 143 Abs. 1 SchKG)	révocation de l'adjudication	revocation of the auction sale
Widerspruch (Art. 31 MSchG)	opposition	opposition (to registration of a trademark)
Widerspruchsklage (Art. 106-109 SchKG)	action en revendication	third party objection action (action filed by a creditor against a third party when the item to be seized is not in the debtor's possession, but in the possession of the third party, who claims to own it or hold a lien on it)
Widerspruchsverfahren (1) (Art. 106-109 SchKG)	procédure de revendication	third party objection procedure
Widerspruchsverfahren (2) (Art. 31 MSchG)	procédure d'opposition	opposition proceedings (to registration of a trademark)
Wiederanlage	réinvestissement	reinvestment

Wiederanlagerabatt	rabais de réinvestissement	reinvestment discount
Wiederaufbaupflicht	obligation de reconstruire	obligation to rebuild
Wiederaufnahme (Art. 397 StGB)	révision	motion for a retrial
Wiedereintragung	réinscription	re-entry
Wiedererwägungsgesuch	demande de reconsidération	motion for reconsideration
Wiedergutmachung (Art. 53 StGB)	réparation	reparation
Wiederherstellung (Art. 148 ZPO)	restitution de délai	restitution of deadlines
Wiederherstellung des rechtmässigen Zustandes	rétablissement de la situation conforme au droit	remedy of any violations
Wiederholungsgefahr	risque de récidive	danger of recidivism
wiederverheiratete Person	personne remariée	remarried person
Wiederverkauf	revente	resale
Wiederwahl	réélection	reelection
Wille	volonté	will
Willensäusserung	manifestation de volonté	statement of intent
Willenserklärung	déclaration de volonté	declaration of intent
Willensmangel	vice du consentement	defect in consent
Willensvollstrecker	exécuteur testamentaire	executor of a will
wirksam gegenüber Dritten	opposable aux tiers	enforceable against third parties
Wirksamkeit	efficacité	effectiveness
Wirkung	effet	effect
Wirkungspfad	voie de contamination	pollution path
Wirtschaft	économie	economy
wirtschaftlich bedingte Entlassung	licenciement économique	layoff for economic reasons
wirtschaftlich Berechtigter	ayant droit économique	beneficial owner
wirtschaftliche Landesversorgung	approvisionnement économique du pays	economic supply
wirtschaftlicher Nachrichtendienst (Art. 273 StGB)	service de renseignements économiques	industrial espionage

wirtschaftliches Interesse	intérêt économique	economic interest
Wirtschaftlichkeit (1)	rentabilité	profitability
Wirtschaftlichkeit (2)	efficience économique	economic efficiency
Wirtschaftsdelikt	délit économique	economic offense, white-collar crime
Wirtschaftsfreiheit (Art. 27 BV)	liberté économique	economic freedom
Wirtschaftskriminalität	criminalité économique	white collar crime
Wirtschaftsprüfung	révision	audit
Wirtschaftswachstum	croissance économique	economic growth
Wirtschaftszweig	branche de l'économie	branch of the economy
wissenschaftliche Gegenstände (Art. 724 ZGB)	objets ayant une valeur scientifique	objects of scientific value
Wissenschaftsfreiheit (Art. 20 BV)	liberté de la science	academic freedom
Witwenrente	rente de veuve	widow's pension
Witwerrente	rente de veuf	widower's pension
Wochenaufenthalt	séjour hebdomadaire	weekly residence
Wochenaufenthalter	semainier	weekly resident
wohlerworbenes Recht	droit acquis	vested right
Wohlfahrtsfonds	fonds de bienfaisance	welfare fund
wohltätiger Zweck	but de bienfaisance	charitable purpose
Wohlverhalten	amendement (comportement)	good conduct, good behavior
Wohnanteilplan	plan de quote-part de logements	plan reserving a certain percentage for residences
Wohnbaugenossenschaft	société coopérative d'habitation	residential building cooperative
Wohnbewilligung	permis d'habiter	housing permit
Wohneigentumsförderung	encouragement à la propriété du logement (EPL)	promotion of home ownership
Wohnhaus	immeuble d'habitation	residential building
Wohnraum	logement	residence
Wohnräume (Art. 253a OR)	habitations	residential premises

Wohnrecht	droit d'habitation	right of residence
Wohnsitz (Art. 23 ZGB)	domicile	domicile (place where a person resides with the intention of settling)
Wohnsitz im Ausland	domicile à l'étranger	domicile abroad
Wohnsitzprinzip	droit du domicile	right of domicile
Wohnsitzwechsel	changement de domicile	change of domicile
Wohnung der Familie	logement de la famille	family home
Wohnungsbau	construction de logements	residential construction
Wohnungsmarkt	marché locatif	housing market
Wohnungsnot	pénurie de logements	housing shortage
Wohnzone	zone d'habitation	residential area
Wortmarke	marque verbale	word mark
Wucher (Art. 157 StGB)	usure	profiteering
Wucherer	usurier	profiteer, usurer
Wucherzins	taux usurier	usurious interest
zahlbar	payable	payable
Zahlstelle	agent payeur	paying agent
Zahlung	paiement	payment
Zahlung einer Nichtschuld (Art. 63 OR)	paiement de l'indu	payment of a non-existent debt
Zahlungsaufforderung	sommation de payer	request for payment
Zahlungsaufschub	sursis au paiement	extension of the time in which to pay a debt
Zahlungsauftrag	ordre de paiement	payment order (by check, wire transfer, etc.)
Zahlungsbedingungen	conditions de paiement	payment terms
Zahlungsbefehl (Art. 69 ff SchKG)	commandement de payer	order to pay (beginning of debt collection)
Zahlungsbilanz	balance des paiements	balance of payments
Zahlungseinstellung	cessation de paiements	insolvency
zahlungsfähig	solvable	solvent
Zahlungsfähigkeit	solvabilité	solvency
Zahlungsfrist (Art. 137 SchKG)	délai de paiement	payment deadline

Zahlungsmittel	moyen de paiement	means of payment
Zahlungssystem (Art. 81 FinfraG)	système de paiement	payment system
Zahlungsunfähigkeit	insolvabilité	insolvency
Zahlungsverbot	interdiction de payer	injunction against payment
Zahlungsverkehr	trafic des paiements	payment transactions
Zahlungsversprechen	promesse de payer	promise to pay
Zahlungsverweigerung	refus de payer	refusal to pay
Zahlungsverzug (Art. 143 SchKG)	demeure	default
Zahnpflegeversicherung	assurance pour soins dentaires	dental insurance
Zechprellerei (Art. 149 StGB)	filouterie d'auberge	leaving a hotel, restaurant or bar without paying
Zedent	cédant	transferor, assignor
Zeichnung	souscription	signature
Zeichnungsart	mode de signature	type of signature required (individual or joint)
Zeichnungsberechtigter (ZB)	personne ayant qualité pour signer	authorized signatory, person with power to sign
Zeichnungsschein (Art. 652 OR)	bulletin de souscription	subscription form
zeitgerecht	dans les délais	timely
Zeitlohn (Art. 319 OR)	salaire fixé d'après le temps	wage paid on the basis of time worked
Zeitwert	valeur résiduelle	current value
Zensur	censure	censorship
zentrale Anlaufstelle	point de contact central	single point of contact
zentrale Ausgleichsstelle	centrale de compensation	clearing house
zentrale Gegenpartei (Art. 48 FinfraG)	contrepartie centrale	central counterparty
Zentralverwahrer (Art. 61 FinfraG)	dépositaire central	central securities depository
Zerrüttung	désunion	irretrievable breakdown (of a marriage)
Zerrütungsprinzip	principe de désunion	principle of irretrievable breakdown
Zerstückelung (Art. 833 ZGB)	morcellement	parceling, division
Zession (Art. 164 ff OR)	cession	transfer, assignment
Zessionar	cessionnaire	transferee, assignee

Zessionskredit	crédit contre cession	assignment credit (book credit secured by the assignment of existing receivables)
Zessionsverbot	interdiction de la cession	prohibition of assignment
Zessus	débiteur cédé	assigned debtor
Zeuge	témoin	witness
Zeugenaussage	témoignage, déposition du témoin	witness testimony
Zeugenbestechung	instigation à un faux témoignage	bribing a witness
Zeugeneid	serment du témoin	witness oath
Zeugeneinvernahme (Art. 177 StPO)	audition des témoins	examination of witnesses
Zeugenentschädigung	indemnité au témoin	witness fee
Zeugenschutzstelle	service de protection des témoins	witness protection agency
Zeugenvernehmung	audition des témoins	examination of witness
Zeugnis (Art. 169 ff ZPO)	témoignage	testimony
Zeugnisfähigkeit (Art. 163 StPO)	capacité de témoigner	capacity to testify
Zeugnispflicht (Art. 163 StPO)	obligation de témoigner	duty to testify
Zeugnisverweigerungsrecht (Art. 168 StPO)	droit de refuser le témoignage	right to refuse to testify
Zins (1)	intérêt	interest
Zins (2) (D: Wohnungsmiete)	loyer	rent
Zinsenlauf (Art. 209 SchKG)	cours des intérêts	accrual of interest
Zinseszins	intérêts composés	compound interest
Zinsfuss	taux d'intérêt	interest rate
Zinssatz	taux d'intérêt	interest rate
Zinsswap	swap de taux d'intérêt	interest rate swap
Zinsterminkontrakt	contrat à terme sur taux d'intérêt	interest rate future
Zirkularbeschluss (Art. 255a Abs. 1 SchKG)	décision proposée par circulaire	decision by circular letter

Zirkulationsverfahren	procédure par voie de circulation	circulation procedure
zitieren	assigner	to summon
Zivildienst	service civil	civil service
Zivildienstgesetz (ZDG)	Loi fédérale sur le service civil (LSC)	Federal Civil Service Act
Zivildienstverordnung	Ordonnance sur le service civil	Civil Service Ordinance
zivile Frucht	fruit civil	civil fruit
Zivilgericht	tribunal civil	civil court
Zivilgesetzbuch (ZGB) (D: Bürgerliches Gesetzbuch)	Code civil	Civil Code
Zivilhaftung	responsabilité civile	civil liability
Ziviljury	jury civil	civil jury
Zivilklage (Art. 122 ff StPO)	action civile	civil action
Zivilprozess	procédure civile	civil procedure
Zivilprozessordnung (ZPO)	Code de procédure civile (CPC)	Code of Civil Procedure
Zivilrecht	droit civil	civil law
zivilrechtlicher Anspruch	droit de caractère civil	civil claim
Zivilrechtspflege	administration de justice civile	administration of civil justice
Zivilrechtsstreitigkeit	contestation civile (F : litige de droit commun)	civil dispute
Zivilsache	affaire civile	civil case
Zivilschutz (Art. 61 BV)	protection civile	civil defense
Zivilschutzangehöriger	personne servant dans la protection civile	person serving in the civil defense
Zivilschutzdienst	service dans la protection civile	civil defense service
Zivilstand (D: Personenstand)	état civil	marital status, civil status
Zivilstandsamt (D: Standesamt)	office d'état civil	civil registry, office of vital records
Zivilstandsbeamte (D: Standesbeamte)	officier de l'état civil	civil registrar, vital records official
Zivilstandsregister (D: Personenstandsregister)	registre de l'état civil	civil register, vital records register
Zivilstandsurkunde	acte de l'état civil	vital record

Zivilstandsverordnung (ZStV)	Ordonnance sur l'état civil (OEC)	Civil Status Ordinance
Zoll	douane	customs
Zollabfertigung	dédouanement	customs clearance
Zollabgabe	droits de douane	customs duties
Zollager	entrepôt douanier	inbond warehouse
Zollausweis	acquit de douane	customs clearance document
Zollbefreiung	franchise douanière	customs exemption
Zollbehörde	autorité douanière	customs official
Zollerhebung	perception des droits douaniers	collection of customs duties
Zollmeldepflicht	assujettissement au contrôle douanier	duty to declare to customs officials
Zollnachforderung	supplément de droits de douane	additional customs duty
Zollnachlass	remise des droits de douane	abatement of customs duty
zollpflichtig	passible de droits de douane	dutiable
Zollpolitik	politique douanière	customs policy
Zollrekurskommission (ZRK)	Commission de recours en matière de douane (CRD)	Customs Appeals Commission
Zollrückerstattung	remboursement des droits de douane	refund of customs duties
Zollunion	union douanière	customs union
Zollwiderhandlung	infraction douanière	customs violation
Zone	zone	area, zone
Zonenkonformität	conformité à la zone	compliance with zoning requirements
Zonenplan (D: Flächennutzungsplan)	plan de zones	zoning plan
Zubringerdienst gestattet	sauf riverains	access for residents only
Zuchthaus	pénitencier	penitentiary
Züchtigungsrecht	droit de correction	right to use corporal punishment
Zufahrt	accès à la route	access (road)
Zuführung (Art. 725 ZGB)	épaves	driftage
Zug (ZG)	Zoug (ZG)	Zug (canton and city)

Zugang zu einem Gericht	accès à un tribunal	access to a court
Zugehör (Art. 644 ZGB)	chose accessoire	accessory
zügeln (D: umziehen)	déménager	to move (house)
Zügerrecht (Art. 70 Abs. 4 KVG)	libre passage	right to transfer from a group health insurance policy to an individual policy upon termination of employment
Zug-um-Zug-Geschäft (Art. 75 OR)	donnant donnant, réciproque	reciprocal and simultaneous transaction
Zulässigkeit der Berufung	recevabilité du recours	admissibility of the appeal
Zulassung zum Handel	admission au négoce	admission to trading
Zumessung der Strafe	application de la peine	sentencing
zur Unzeit	temps inopportun	at an inopportune juncture
zurechenbar	imputable	imputable
Zurechenbarkeit	imputabilité	imputability
zurechnen	imputer	to impute
Zurechnungsfähigkeit	responsabilité (pénale)	soundness of mind (consists of the ability to understand one's acts and to govern one's conduct accordingly)
Zürich (ZH)	Zurich (ZH)	Zurich (canton and city)
zurückdatieren	antidater	to backdate
Zuruf-System	négociation à la criée	open outcry trading
Zusammenarbeit	collaboration	cooperation
Zusammenrottung	attroupement	mob
Zusammensetzung des Gerichts	composition du tribunal	composition of the court
Zuschlag (1)	supplément	surcharge, additional fee
Zuschlag (2)	adjudication	award
zuschlagen	adjuger	to award
Zusendung einer unbestellten Sache (Art. 6a OR)	envoi d'une chose non commandée	delivery of an unsolicited object
Zusicherung	assurance donnée	representation (and warranty)
Zuständigkeit	compétence	jurisdiction
Zuständigkeitsübertragung	délégation de compétence	delegation of jurisdiction
Zustandsstörer	perturbateur par situation	polluter by virtue of situation

zustellen	notifier	to serve, to notify
Zustellung durch den Weibel (D: Zustellung durch den Gerichtsvollzieher)	notification par huissier	service by a process server
Zustellungsdomizil (Art. 140 ZPO, art. 87 StPO)	domicile élu	address for service
Zustellungsempfänger	destinataire de l'acte	agent for receipt of process
Zutrittsrecht	droit d'accès	right of access
Zuwanderung	immigration	immigration
Zuweisung	attribution	allocation
Zuwendungen (Art. 286 SchKG)	libéralités	gifts
Zuwendungen auf Anrechnung an den Erbteil	libéralités entre vifs faites à titre d'avancement d'hoirie	advances against a person's share of an inheritance
Zuwendungen unter Lebenden (Art. 475 ZGB)	libéralités entre vifs	inter vivos gifts
Zuzüger (D: Zugezogene)	nouveaux arrivants	newcomers
zuzustellende Urkunden (Art. 136 ZPO)	actes à notifier	documents to be served
Zwängerei	coup de force, chantage	blackmail
Zwangsgeld	astreinte	fine, penalty
Zwangsheirat (Art. 181a StGB)	mariage forcé	forced marriage
Zwangsmassnahme (1) (Art. 343 ZPO)	mesure de contrainte	compulsory measure (such as taking away the chattel or vacating real property) in civil procedure
Zwangsmassnahme (2) (Art. 50 StPO)	mesure de contrainte	coercive measure (such as arrest or detention) in criminal procedure
Zwangsmassnahmengericht (Art. 13 StPO)	tribunal des mesures de contrainte	coercive measures court
Zwangsmitgliedschaft	participation obligatoire	mandatory participation
Zwangsmittel	moyen de contrainte	enforcement measure
Zwangsversteigerung (Art. 234 OR)	vente aux enchères forcées	mandatory auction sale
Zwangsverwaltung	mise sous régie	receivership
Zwangsverwertung	réalisation forcée	forced sale
Zwangsvollstreckung	exécution forcée	judicial execution, enforcement of a judgment

Zweck (D: Gegenstand)	but	purpose (of a company or partnership)
zweckgebundenes Vermögen	bien à affectation déterminée	earmarked asset
Zweckmässigkeit	opportunité	expediency
zweifelhafte Schuldfähigkeit (Art. 20 StGB)	doute sur la responsabilité de l'auteur	doubt as to legal responsibility
zweifelhafter Rechtsanspruch (Art. 269 Abs. 3 SchKG)	droit douteux	questionable right
Zweigniederlassung (Art. 641 OR)	succursale	branch
zweiseitiger Vertrag	contrat bilatéral	bilateral contract
zweiseitiges Rechtsgeschäft	acte juridique bilatéral	bilateral legal transaction
zweiter Schriftenwechsel	second échange d'écritures	second round of written submissions
Zweitwohnung	résidence secondaire	secondary residence
zwingende Zuständigkeit (Art. 9 ZPO)	compétence impérative	mandatory jurisdiction
zwingender Gerichtsstand (Art. 9 ZPO)	for impératif	mandatory place of jurisdiction
zwingendes Recht	droit impératif	mandatory legal rule (one that cannot be contracted out of)
Zwischenbilanz	bilan intermédiaire	interim balance sheet
Zwischenentscheid	décision incidente	interlocutory decision on a procedural issue (cf. Vorentscheid, an interlocutory decision on a substantive issue)
Zwischengesellschaft	filiale mère	intermediate company
Zwischenprodukt	produit intermédiaire	intermediate product
Zwischenveranlagung	taxation intermédiaire	interim assessment
Zwischenverdienst	gain intermédiaire	work while registered as unemployed
Zwischenverfügung (Art. 45 und 46 VwVG)	décision incidente	interim order

Deutsche Abkürzungen

A.	Auflage
a.A.	am Anfang
a.a.O.	am angeführten Ort
Abh.	Abhandlung
Abhndl.	Abhandlung
Abhn.	Abhandlungen
Abk.	Abkommen
Abs.	Absatz
Abt.	Abteilung
ABV	Aktionärbindungsvertrag
abw.	abweichend
a.E.	am Ende
a.F.	alte Folge
AGB	Allgemeine Geschäftsbedingungen
AGer	Arbeitsgericht
AK	Aktienkapital
allg.	allgemein
a.M.	anderer Meinung
AmtsB.	Amtsbericht
Anm.	Anmerkung
Ann.	Annalen
Arb.	Arbeiten
Arch.	Archiv
Art.	Artikel
AT	allgemeiner Teil
AusfV	Ausführungsverordnung
BB	beklagtische Beilage
BG	Bundesgesetz; Bezirksgericht
BK	Berner Kommentar
BKomm.	Berner Kommentar
BO	Beweisofferte
BRB	Bundesratbeschluss
BRV	Verordnung des Bundesrates
BT	besonderer Teil
BV	Bundesverfassung
BVers	Bundesversammlung
BzGr.	Bezirksgericht
c.i.c.	culpa in contrahendo
das.	daselbst
DBA	Doppelbesteuerungsabkommen
Dep.	Departement
dergl.	dergleichen
ders.	derselbe
dgl.	dergleichen
dies.	dieselbe(n)
E	Entwurf; Erwägung

EAK	Eidgenössische Arzneimittelkommission
EAV	Eidgenössische Alkoholverwaltung
EBBK	Eidgenössische Berufsbildungskommission
EBMK	Eidgenössische Berufsmaturitätskommission
ebd.	ebenda
EFD	Eidgenössisches Finanzdepartement
EFK	Eidgenössische Finanzkontrolle
EFV	Eidgenössische Finanzverwaltung
eG	einfache Gesellschaft
EJFD	Eidgenössisches Justiz- und Polizeidepartement
ESTV	Eidgenössische Steuerverwaltung
FER	Fachempfehlungen zur Rechnungslegung
Festg.	Festgabe
Festschr.	Festschrift
GB	Grundbuch
GD	Generaldirektion
gl.A.	gleicher Ansicht
gl.M.	gleicher Meinung
h.L.	herrschende Lehre
Hlbs.	Halbsatz
i.c.	in casu
i.e.S.	im engeren Sinne
i.f.	in fine
i.G.	im Gegensatz
IPR	internationales Privatrecht
i.S.v.	im Sinne von
i.V.	in Vertretung
i.V.m.	in Verbindung mit
i.w.S.	im weiteren Sinne
Jb.	Jahrbuch
Jhrb.	Jahrbuch
Jber.	Jahresbericht
K	Kreisschreiben
KG	Kollektivgesellschaft
KGer	Kantonsgericht
KGr.	Kantonsgericht
Kl.	Kläger
KmAG	Kommanditaktiengesellschaft
KmG	Kommanditgesellschaft
Komm.	Kommentar
Konk.	Konkordat
Konv.	Konvention
KR	Kotierungsreglement
Lfg.	Lieferung
LS	Loseblattsammlung
lt	laut
mat.	materiell
MStG	Militärstrafgesetz
m. Verw.	mit Verweis

m.w.H.	mit weiteren Hinweisen
m.w.Verw.	mit weiteren Verweisen
NAV	Normalarbeitsvertrag
o.a.	oben angeführt
o.ä.	oder ähnliches
o.D.	ohne Datum
o.J.	ohne Jahr
o.O.	ohne Ort
OR	Obligationenrecht
ppa.	per procura
PS	Partizipationsschein(e)
RandT	Randtitel
RechB.	Rechenschaftsbericht
Rechtsw.	Rechtswissenschaft
Ref.	Referat; Referent
RegR	Regierungsrat
Rek.	Rekurs
rev	revidiert
Richtl.	Richtlinien
RR	Regierungsrat
RS	Revisionsstelle
RSpr.	Rechtsprechung
Rz	Randziffer
S	Ständerat
SAV	Schweizer Anwaltsverband
SchKG	Bundesgesetz über Schuldbetreibung und Konkurs
SchlT	Schlusstitel
s.ed.	sine editore
Slg.	Sammlung
SNB	Schweizerische Nationalbank
SNV	Schweizerische Normen-Vereinigung
SR	Ständerat
StGB	Strafgesetzbuch
StPO	Strafprozessordnung
VR	Verwaltungsrat
Vschr.	Vorschrift
Vw.	Verwaltung
Z	Zeitschrift
Z.	Ziffer
ZB	Zeichnungsberechtigter
ZDG	Zivildienstgesetz
ZGB	Zivilgesetzbuch
ZK	Zürcher Kommentar
ZKomm.	Zürcher Kommentar
ZPO	Zivilprozessordnung
ZRK	Zollrekurskommission
zust.	zustimmend

ABOUT THE AUTHOR

Thomas L. West III received his B.A. degree in French and English from the University of Mississippi *summa cum laude* and his M.A. in German from Vanderbilt University, where he was a Harold Stirling Vanderbilt fellow. He earned his J.D. at the University of Virginia School of Law and was admitted to the State Bar of Georgia in 1990. After practicing law for five years, he started Intermark Language Services Corporation, a translation firm specializing in legal and financial translation. From 2001 to 2003, he served as President of the American Translators Association. Over the past 25 years, he has conducted seminars on legal translation throughout the United States, Europe, Latin America and South Africa. West is ATA certified for translation from French, Spanish, German and Dutch into English, also speaks Swedish, Afrikaans and Russian, and has studied Danish, Italian, Portuguese and Modern Greek. The second edition of his *Spanish-English Dictionary of Law and Business* was published to wide acclaim in June 2012.

www.ingramcontent.com/pod-product-compliance
Lightning Source LLC
LaVergne TN
LVHW052213200926
848481LV00001B/100